SEX EQUALITY LAW IN THE EUROPEAN UNION

Wiley Series in
EUROPEAN LAW

Burrows/European Social Law
0-471-96537-5 480 Pages

Emiliou/The European Union and World Trade Law
0-471-95552-3 390 Pages

Caiger/1996 Onwards: Lowering the Barriers Further
0-471-95768-2 300 Pages

Cross/Electric Utility Regulation in the European Union
0-471-95793-3 350 Pages

Hervey/Sex Equality Law in the European Union
0-471-96436-0 400 Pages

Forthcoming titles

Docking/EC Pensions Law, Second Edition
0-471-96615-0 384 Pages

Farr/Harmonisation of Technical Standards, Second Edition
0-471-95926-X 400 Pages

Goyder/EC Distribution Law, Second Edition
0-471-96122-1 350 Pages

Kaye/European Case Law on the Judgments Convention
0-471-94089-5 512 Pages

Yaqub/European Travel Law
0-471-94354-1 568 Pages

Barnard/EC Employment Law, Revised Edition
0-471-93917-X 500 Pages

Ehlermann/Proceedings of the European Competition Forum
0-471-96668-1 270 Pages

See page 429 for titles of related interest

CENTRE FOR THE LAW OF THE EUROPEAN UNION
UNIVERSITY COLLEGE LONDON
TRIER ACADEMY OF EUROPEAN LAW

SEX EQUALITY LAW IN THE EUROPEAN UNION

edited by

Tamara K. Hervey

Lecturer in Law, University of Manchester

David O'Keeffe

Professor of European Law, University College London

ERA
DIE EUROPÄISCHE RECHTSAKADEMIE
ACADEMY OF EUROPEAN LAW TRIER
ACADÉMIE DE DROIT EUROPÉEN DE TRÈVES

JOHN WILEY & SONS
Chichester • New York • Brisbane • Toronto • Singapore

Published in the United Kingdom by   John Wiley & Sons Ltd,
Baffins Lane, Chichester,
West Sussex PO19 1UD, England

National   01243 779777
International   (+44) 1243 779777
e-mail (for orders and customer service enquiries):
cs-books@wiley.co.uk
Visit our Home Page on http://www.wiley.co.uk
or
http://www.wiley.com

Other Wiley Editorial Offices

John Wiley & Sons Inc., 605 Third Avenue,
New York, NY 10158-0012, USA

Jacaranda Wiley Ltd, 33 Park Road, Milton,
Queensland 4064, Australia

John Wiley & Sons (Canada) Ltd, 22 Worcester Road,
Rexdale, Ontario M9W 1L1, Canada

John Wiley & Sons (Asia) Pte Ltd, 2 Clementi Loop #02-01,
Jin Xing Distripark, Singapore 0512

British Library Cataloguing Publication Data

A catalogue record for this book is available from the British Library

ISBN 0-471-96436-0

Typeset in 10/12pt Baskerville by Footnote Graphics, Warminster, Wilts
Printed and bound in Great Britain by Bookcraft (Bath) Ltd, Midsomer Norton

This book is printed on acid-free paper responsibly manufactured from sustainable forestation,
for which at least two trees are planted for each one used for paper production.

CONTENTS

CONTRIBUTORS

Judge David Edward	European Court of Justice
Evelyn Ellis	Reader in Public Law, University of Birmingham, UK
Elaine A. Whiteford	Lecturer in Law, University of Nottingham, UK
Richard Townshend-Smith	Senior Lecturer in Law, University of Wales Swansea, UK
Erika Szyszczak	Senior Lecturer in Law, London School of Economics and Political Science, UK
Helen Fenwick	Lecturer in Law, University of Durham, UK
Claire Kilpatrick	European University Institute, Florence, Italy and Lecturer in Law, University of Bristol, UK
Silvana Sciarra	Professor of European Labour Law and Social Law, European University Institute, University of Florence, Italy
Josephine Steiner	Professor (Associate) of Law, University of Sheffield, UK
Sarah Moore	Barrister, Legal Secretary at the Court of First Instance, Luxembourg
David O'Keeffe	Professor of European Law and Director of the Centre for the Law of the European Union, University College London, UK
Lorraine Fletcher	Head of Pensions, Benefits and Consumer Affairs, Equal Opportunities Commission (GB), UK
Brian Bercusson	Professor of European Law, University of Manchester, UK
Michelle Everson	Research Fellow, Centre for European Legal Policy, University of Bremen, Germany
Louise Ackers	Lecturer in Social Policy, University of Plymouth, UK
Clare McGlynn	Lecturer in Law, Newcastle Law School, University of Newcastle-upon-Tyne, UK

Siofra O'Leary	Assistant Director of the Centre for European Legal Studies, University of Cambridge, UK
Virginia Harrison	Lawyer with the Department of the Environment, UK
Jo Shaw	Professor of European Law, Centre for the Study of Law in Europe, University of Leeds, UK
Leo Flynn	Centre for European Law, Kings College London, UK
Catherine Barnard	Lecturer in Law, Trinity College, University of Cambridge, UK
Ronnie Eklund	Professor of Private Law, School of Law, Stockholm University, Sweden
Anne Lise Ryel	The Gender Equality Ombudsman in Norway
Ian Ward	Professor of Law, University of Dundee, UK
Fiona Beveridge	Lecturer in Law, Feminist Legal Research Unit, University of Liverpool, UK
Sue Nott	Senior Lecturer in Law, Feminist Legal Research Unit, University of Liverpool, UK
Tamara K. Hervey	Lecturer in Law, University of Manchester, UK

FOREWORD

The law on sex equality in the European Union is largely based on a few texts containing two key words, "equality" and "discrimination". The first is defined in terms of the second. Equality is taken to mean the absence of discrimination, and the principle of equality is given legal effect by prohibiting discrimination. The clarity and scope of Article 119 are obscured by the English text, but the words of the directives are unambiguous: "there shall be no discrimination whatsoever on grounds of sex either directly or indirectly".

The Court of Justice has been called upon to apply these texts to a wide variety of situations, and its decisions have given rise to a correspondingly wide range of reactions. Some critics find the results absurd, unexpected, meddlesome, financially burdensome or just politically inconvenient. At the opposite end of the spectrum, the Court's approach is criticised as excessively formalistic and male-orientated. Others, again, find ambiguities and inconsistencies. But there are many who praise the Court for insisting that the words of the texts mean just what they say: discrimination is illegal.

The principle of non-discrimination underlies many provisions of the Treaty and much of the case law of the Court. Its attraction for lawyers is that it can be used to apply familiar techniques of objective analysis to economic and social problems which do not otherwise fit comfortably into established legal categories. By contrast, as Isaiah Berlin said of freedom, equality is a "term so porous that there is little interpretation that it seems able to resist".

Non-discrimination also has the advantage of expressing an idea with which it is very difficult to disagree. Robert Marjolin, the French negotiator of the EEC Treaty, tells of the sensation he created, and the breakthrough he achieved, when he proposed that instead of talking preference, they should talk non-discrimination. "Preference is vice, non-discrimination virtue".

From a legal point of view, non-discrimination has been an invaluable starting-point. But this approach has given rise to two main problems. The first, raised by *Kalanke*, is whether removal of discrimination is really the path to equality. Is it any more than the necessary starting-point from which progress can be made in achieving substantive equality? That is, by now, a relatively familiar theme, the legal implications of which are extensively discussed in this book. The point focussed by the *Kalanke* case is whether, if non-discrimination is the necessary starting-point, it is permissible in any circumstances to derogate from the rule against it.

The second problem is less obvious, but perhaps more fundamental. It goes to the meaning, not of equality, but of discrimination as such, and therefore affects other areas of Community law as well.

Does a rule, which affects the individual members of two classes in the same way, "discriminate" in favour of one class and against the other simply because, statistically, there are more members of the latter class than of the former? If not, what more is required to constitute discrimination? Must the larger class suffer some disadvantage because of the rule? If so, must the disadvantage be weighed against any advantages that also flow from the rule? Can the disadvantage be justified by reference to other policy considerations? This is the problem underlying *Nolte, Megner & Scheffel* and, most recently, *Lewark* in the field of sex equality and *Keck & Mithouard* in that of free movement of goods.

Professor Ole Due, the former President of the Court, has said that discrimination is the most important legal concept to be developed in the last part of this century. Detailed exploration of its implications and nuances has only just begun. This book is to be welcomed as a thought-provoking contribution to the debate.

6 February 1996   DAVID EDWARD
Court of Justice of the European Communities
Luxembourg

TABLES

Cases

Table of Acts

Table of EC Decisions

Table of EC Recommendations

Table of EC Regulations

Table of EC Documents

EC Proposed Legislation

INTRODUCTION

"Sex Equality Law in the European Union" represents a new contribution to scholarship on the subject of the European Union's legal regulation of sex discrimination, and the contribution of the law of the European Community and Union to the position of women and men in the Member States.

The classic substantive provisions of EC sex equality law (Article 119 EC Treaty, the equality in employment and social security Directives) have now reached a relatively advanced stage in their interpretation by the European Court of Justice and their application in the Member States. However, in no sense have those provisions ossified into a fixed understanding of sex equality entitlements in Community law, as, for example, the ongoing litigation over equality in pensions schemes, and that over the scope of the equality in social security provisions, illustrates. The contributions of Evelyn Ellis, Elaine Whiteford, Richard Townshend-Smith and Josephine Steiner to this volume contain analytical and critical exposition of various unresolved areas of this body of legal norms.

Another area of sex equality law which continues to raise difficult issues of principle is that of special entitlements for women, in particular, though not exclusively, connected with pregnancy and childbirth. Erika Szyszczak, Helen Fenwick, and Claire Kilpatrick each offer analysis of women's different treatment according to EC law from a particular perspective. These chapters complement one another, giving the reader a broad perspective on the approach of the European Community legal order to the difficulties posed by women's special position in respect of pregnancy and maternity. Silvana Sciarra's contribution shows how legal regulation of a specific aspect of the special entitlement problem – that of night-work for women – can reveal the dynamic of the institutional process of integration in the EU context. This analysis serves to remind us that EC sex equality law has a distinct flavour of its own.

A third problematic area for substantive EC sex equality law is that of enforcement. Here the chapters of Sarah Moore and David O'Keeffe show how the EC

sex equality rules have been an important *locus* for the development of EC constitutional rules concerning effective protection for individuals with respect to
their Community rights. Broader perspectives are provided by Lorraine
Fletcher, and by Brian Bercusson, who reminds us that the collective aspect of
labour law will be crucial in the enforcement of sex equality for the greater
proportion of women workers.

The European Court of Justice itself reminds us that sex equality is a broader
concept than the substantive provisions of Community sex equality law imply:
sex equality is no less than a general principle of Community law. We feel that it
is time that the sex equality aspects of Community law in general are explored,
and have therefore adopted an innovative approach in determining the contents of this collection on sex equality in the European Union. In addition to
the coverage of the more "traditional" areas of employment and social security,
the book focuses in particular upon the exploration of the gendered perspectives of rights which inhere in individuals within the Union, such as free movement of persons (Louise Ackers) and citizenship of the European Union
(Michelle Everson). These contributions show that apparently gender-neutral
legal concepts are open to question when their specific application to women is
considered. They also show how the institutions and provisions of the legal
system of the European Union may make assumptions about the gender of
characters familiar to European legal scholars: characters such as the migrant
worker, "his" family, and the citizen of the European Union.

As the relationship between fundamental human rights and sex equality is as
yet unsettled in Community law – although the Community is fast developing a
jurisprudential position on the subject – there are also chapters exploring this
relationship. One important facet of this subject is the issue of abortion and
women's rights over their bodies. This is explored by Leo Flynn and by Siofra
O'Leary, who also explores the question of family rights. The assumption that
Community law has little to tell us about these issues is exploded, with careful
analysis of EC legislation, and in particular, the jurisprudence of the European
Court of Justice. Another issue is the concept of "women's rights" in a more
general sense, which is the subject of the contribution of Clare McGlynn, who
posits that the EU should now develop a specifically woman-centred human
rights law. Virginia Harrison, using a comparative methodology which draws on
jurisprudence from the United States and Canada, asks whether the right to sex
equality in EC law can be extended to protection of individuals from discrimination on grounds of sexual orientation.

Taking the picture wider still, a number of contributors have begun to question
the significance of reference to gender as a method of analysis of the legal
order of the market which characterises the whole of the Community endeavour.
These points are particularly raised by Jo Shaw, but also appear in the contributions of Louise Ackers, Catherine Barnard, Michelle Everson, Leo Flynn and
Tamara Hervey. This part of the book reflects an emergent dynamic critique of
the Community legal order, and of the European Union as a political entity
constituted in law, from various perspectives of gender.

The final section of the book is concerned with proposals for reform of sex equality law in the European Union. As comparative analysis can be a significant tool for reform, the book contains chapters by Anne Lise Ryel (the Norwegian Gender Equality Ombudsman) and by Ronnie Eklund on the Nordic model of sex equality law. Even the most cursory of comparisons with the current EC provisions shows how these might prove a valuable source of inspiration for future development of equality law in the European Union. The chapters by Ian Ward, and by Fiona Beveridge and Sue Nott (along with that of Everson) concern themselves with women's representation, and more crucially participation, in policy-making in the European Union institutions. The democratic legitimacy of the European Union has long been a subject of contention: this too has a particular dimension when viewed from women's perspectives. Fiona Beveridge and Sue Nott introduce the innovative and challenging concept of a "gender audit" for EC law, with a view to examining the specific impact on women of new Community or Union policies. Finally, Tamara Hervey argues for a differentiated approach to the concept of sex equality in EC law, as an alternative to the sameness/difference debate which has thus far tended to dominate thinking on sex equality in the European Union.

The book is the product of collaboration between judges, academics, and legal practitioners, from various Member States of the EU and EEA, and therefore represents different types of legal scholarship. We believe that it is these diverse understandings of the subject of sex equality in the European Union which add to the value of the collection. Inevitably, there are variations in terminology: terms such as sex, gender, equality and difference appear with (sometimes nuanced) divergent meanings within the book.

The predominant consideration, which appears explicitly in some contributions, and is, we believe, implicit in all the contributions to "Sex Equality Law in the European Union", is an understanding of the function of sex equality law (in the EU, as elsewhere) as protecting undervalued or excluded individuals. This understanding may aid the development of a general law of the European Union promoting equality for all, which we view as a crucial foundation for the future of the European Union.

This book has its origin in a conference which we organised for Trier Academy of European Law and the Centre for the Law of the European Union, at University College London. We have invited the speakers at that conference, together with other specialists in the area, to write the book, in order to have as wide a coverage as possible. We are most grateful to them for the quality of their contributions and for meeting our tight deadlines. Judge David Edward, Chairman of the Centre, has kindly written the Preface. Finally, we would like to thank our publisher, David Wilson, for his enthusiasm for the project and his co-operation.

TAMARA K. HERVEY
DAVID O'KEEFFE

Part I
EQUAL PAY

Chapter 1

EQUAL PAY FOR WORK OF EQUAL VALUE: THE UNITED KINGDOM'S LEGISLATION VIEWED IN THE LIGHT OF COMMUNITY LAW*

(i) Introduction

The United Kingdom's equal value legislation holds considerable interest for the student of Community law. It poses questions in at least three separate areas. The first concerns the technical requirements of Community law in the field of equal value: what precisely must a Member State do in order to comply with the requirements of Article 119 EC and the Directive on Equal Pay?[1] The second relates to the good faith, or otherwise, with which a Member State approaches its Community obligations. The third concerns the discretion enjoyed by the Commission to prosecute a Member State which it believes to be in breach of Community law; this last has, of course, a distinctly political flavour.

(ii) The factual background to the present situation

It is well known that the United Kingdom's present equal value laws were enacted as a consequence of the Court of Justice's ruling in 1982 that the Equal Pay Act 1970, as it originally operated, did not constitute compliance with Community obligations. This was because it provided no judicial remedy for those seeking equal pay whose work was not identical with that of a colleague of the opposite sex but was, nevertheless, alleged to be of equal value to that performed by a worker of the opposite sex.[2] The United Kingdom's grudging

---

* This chapter was written by Evelyn Ellis. The author is indebted to Professor Tony Arnull who read a draft of this chapter and made helpful comments on it.
[1] Directive 75/117/EEC (OJ 1990 L 45/19).
[2] Case 61/81 *Commission* v *United Kingdom* [1982] ECR 2601. When the Equal Pay Act was debated in Parliament in 1970, the Government expressly rejected the notion of equal value.

response has been well documented[3] and took the form of the Equal Value
(Amendment) Regulations 1983[4], which amended the Equal Pay Act, and the
Industrial Tribunal (Rules of Procedure) (Equal Value Amendment) Regulations 1983.[5] At the time of their enactment, there was widespread scepticism
about the adequacy of these Regulations to meet the demands of Community
law and the House of Lords took the unusual step of qualifying its approval of
the draft Equal Value (Amendment) Regulations with the rider that "The
House believes that the Regulations do not adequately reflect the 1982 decision
of the European Court of Justice and Article 1 of the Equal Pay Directive of
1975".[6]

Since then the Regulations have, nevertheless, provided the basis for equal
value claims in the United Kingdom.[7] Around 8,000 equal value applications
have been made to industrial tribunals and some 560 employers have been
involved in proceedings.[8] However, these raw statistics mask enormous shortcomings in the present system, the most glaring of which is delay. The average
time taken for a claim to complete the equal value procedure is now about 18
months, with the average time taken for completion of the independent
expert's report on equal value being 11 months. However, many cases take
much longer to resolve; in particular, several cases brought shortly after the
new legislation came into operation are still in progress; for example, *Enderby* v
Secretary of State for Health is only now embarking on its substantive phase nearly
nine years after the first lodging of the claim. Moreover, this is a test case whose
outcome affects some 1,500 other similar claims. In addition, cases are
extremely costly for employees to bring since the opportunities are rife for
employers to mount legal challenges; the EOC estimates that the average cost
of an equal value case which is not appealed is £6,670.25 and, where there is an
appeal, frequently exceeds £50,000. The lack of legal aid for industrial tribunals
compounds the employee's difficulties, since the complexity of the legislation
renders it impossible in practice to contemplate litigation without skilled legal
representation. The legislative scheme also rests upon the individual's action to
challenge pay discrimination, and does not address the wider issues of inequality in collective agreements[9] and pay structures.

The EOC has been vocal and active in its criticisms of the present legislation.
Stimulated in part by adverse judicial comments on the working of the legislation[10], it embarked on a programme of research into the operation of the

---

[3] See in particular the "Request of the Equal Opportunities Commission (EOC) to the Commission
of the European Communities in Relation to the Implementation of the Principle of Equal Pay",
EOC, (1993), at 25 *et seq.* See also Rubenstein, *Equal Pay for Work of Equal Value* (1984).
[4] SI 1983/1794.
[5] SI 1983/1807.
[6] Parliamentary Debates (Hansard) HL, 5 Dec 1983, vol 445, col 890.
[7] For discussion of the possibility of the direct effect of the relevant Community law on equal value,
see Ellis, *European Community Sex Equality Law* (1991) 90–91.
[8] Figures taken from "Equal Value Update", 58 EOR 11 (1994).
[9] See Bercusson, in this volume.
[10] In particular the comments of Wood J (President of the Employment Appeal Tribunal) in *Aldridge*
v *British Telecommunications plc* [1990] IRLR 10.

system in the late 1980s. In 1988 it published a report[11] which showed a disturbing slowing down in the rate of new cases; this tendency it attributed to delay and complexity in the legal process. Two more pieces of research published around the same time[12] indicated that the existing methods for review of discriminatory collective agreements were unsatisfactory and that those entrusted with the task of conducting voluntary reviews of collective agreements tended to focus on increases in pay, rather than on existing pay structures which were regarded as "fair" despite apparently discriminatory patterns of gender distribution within grades. A consultation paper was issued in 1989[13] which evoked a large number of responses from distinguished and informed quarters suggesting that there was very widespread dissatisfaction with the law. In 1990, the EOC published "Equal Pay for Men and Women: Strengthening the Acts"[14], a 27-page document analysing the equal value legislation and making a number of quite radical recommendations for its amendment regarding both law and procedure and also in relation to both individual claims and more generalised forms of pay inequality.

The chorus of criticism mounted further in the following years. In 1992, a Warwick University report described the process of arriving at equal value judgments as "a lottery rather than an objective assessment of worth[15]" and Government plans to abolish Wages Councils[16], which fixed minimum rates of pay and in practice regulated the pay of many women, provoked a general outcry. The patience of both the EOCs (that for Northern Ireland as well as that for Great Britain) and the Trade Union Congress (TUC) snapped in late 1993 and early 1994, when all three organisations lodged formal complaints with the European Commission that the United Kingdom's equal pay laws were in breach of Community obligations. This followed a letter to the EOC(GB) in July 1993 in which the Employment Minister at that time, David Hunt, rejected most of the EOC's proposals for change as articulated in its 1990 document.

The TUC's complaint primarily concerned the abolition of Wages Councils which, in accordance with the Government's plans, took place on 30 August 1993. The argument was that the inadequacies of United Kingdom equal pay law, especially its costliness and complexity, make it particularly inaccessible to women employed in Wages Council industries, who are unlikely to be either unionised or sufficiently wealthy to fund their own proceedings. The TUC argued that the former threat of criminal sanctions and wages inspections was much more likely to deter employers in Wages Council industries from cutting

---

[11] Bowey, "Evaluation of the Role of Independent Experts in Equal Value Cases in Britain 1984–88", EOC, (1988).

[12] Dickens, Townley and Winchester, *Tackling Sex Discrimination through Collective Bargaining* (1988); and Colling and Dickens, *Equality Bargaining: Why Not?* (1989).

[13] "Equal Pay . . . Making it Work", EOC, (1989).

[14] See also the comments on this document in "Equal Pay Law: Paradise for Lawyers—Hell for Women", 35 EOR 30, (1991).

[15] Plumer, "Equal Value Judgments: Objective Assessment or Lottery" 40 Warwick papers in industrial relations (1992).

[16] See Townshend-Smith in this volume.

women's pay than the remote possibility of an equal pay claim before an industrial tribunal.

(iii) The requirements of Community law in relation to equal value claims

The Court of Justice set out the essential requirements of Community law in relation to equal value claims in its 1982 judgment in *Commission* v *UK*.[17] In response to the United Kingdom Government's argument that the Equal Pay Directive[18] says nothing about the right of an employee to insist on having pay determined by a job classification system, the Court stated:

> The UK's interpretation amounts to a denial of the very existence of a right to equal pay for work of equal value where no classification has been made. Such a position is not consonant with the general scheme and provisions of Directive 75/117. The recitals in the preamble to that Directive indicate that its essential purpose is to implement the principle that men and women should receive equal pay contained in Article 119 of the Treaty and that it is primarily the responsibility of the Member States to ensure the application of this principle by means of appropriate laws, regulations and administrative provisions in such a way that all employees in the Community can be protected in these matters.
>
> To achieve that end the principle is defined in the first paragraph of Article 1 so as to include under the term "the same work", the case of "work to which equal value is attributed", and the second paragraph emphasises merely that where a job classification system is used for determining pay it is necessary to ensure that it is based on the same criteria for both men and women and so drawn up as to exclude any discrimination on grounds of sex.
>
> *It follows that where there is disagreement as to the application of that concept a worker must be entitled to claim before an appropriate authority that his work has the same value as other work and, if that is found to be the case, to have his rights under the Treaty and the Directive acknowledged by a binding decision. Any method which excludes that option prevents the aims of the Directive from being achieved.*
>
> This is borne out by the terms of Article 6 of the Directive which provides that Member States are, in accordance with their national circumstances and legal systems, to take the measures necessary to ensure that the principle of equal pay is applied. They are to see that effective means are available to take care that this principle is observed.[19]

The United Kingdom's view that the concept of equal value is too abstract to be applied by courts was given short shrift:

> The Court cannot endorse that view. The implementation of the Directive implies that the assessment of the "equal value" to be "attributed" to particular work, may be

---

[17] *Commission* v *UK, supra* n 2.
[18] Directive 75/117 EEC, *supra* n 1.
[19] [1982] ECR 2601 at 2615–6. Emphasis supplied.

effected notwithstanding the employer's wishes, if necessary in the context of adversary proceedings. The Member States must endow an authority with the requisite jurisdiction to decide whether work has the same value as other work, after obtaining such information as may be required.[20]

(iv) The case today against the United Kingdom

The gist of the EOC's complaint to the Commission is that the United Kingdom's present equal value legislation, whilst formally acknowledging the demands of Community law, fails to give practical recognition to the rights enshrined in that law, both in individual cases and at the collective level. More specifically, it believes that:

(i)   The United Kingdom has failed properly to implement Article 2 of the Equal Pay Directive in the following respects:
   (a) The complexity and lack of clarity of the equal pay legislation, and the equal value procedure, mean that the majority of complainants do not have practical and effective access to a judicial remedy (whether within a reasonable time or at all) to secure equal pay and deter employers from operating pay practices which are in breach of Community law.
   (b) Because legal aid is unavailable for equal pay claims, women who are unable to obtain support from a trade union (and no more than 39% of women are members of trade unions) or the EOC and do not have the resources to fund litigation are, in practice, denied effective access to judicial protection or remedies.
   (c) The complexity and obscurity of the equal pay legislation has resulted in inordinate and unreasonable delays in equal value claims, both because of the time taken to follow the various stages of the procedure, and because of the numerous appeals on complex and opaque legal issues which the legislation has generated. These delays result in serious financial detriment to the applicants for which they cannot be compensated, since industrial tribunals may not award interest on their back pay. The delays in themselves amount to a denial of the right of access to a court, which the Government is bound to provide under Article 2 of the Directive read together with Article 6 of the European Convention on Human Rights.
(ii) The United Kingdom has further failed properly to implement Article 6 of the Equal Pay Directive in the following respects:
   (a) The delays, complexity and expense of equal value claims have deterred individual applicants and their trade unions from bringing equal value claims. A very small number of claims have been brought, and even fewer have been won. The legislation has thus proved unworkable and ineffective in ensuring that the principle of equal pay is observed.
   (b) The gap between men's and women's pay has not been significantly affected by the operation of the amending legislation, and remains substantial, in

---

[20] *Ibid* 2617.

part because of continuing sex discrimination in employers' pay practices. This is a further indication that the Government has failed to ensure that effective means are available to ensure that the principle of equal pay is observed.

(c) The abolition of Wages Councils will remove an integral part of the statutory means by which the principle of equal pay is maintained in the United Kingdom. They have been the *only* means by which national law protects a relatively large number of women in sex-segregated industries from sex discrimination in pay. They have offered a form of collective protection to low-paid women, which did not oblige them to bring expensive and lengthy legal proceedings as individuals. The evidence suggests that the abolition of Wages Councils will have a disparate adverse impact upon the pay of women workers, particularly part-timers, and will widen the pay gap in the United Kingdom.

(iii) The EOC further considers that the United Kingdom has failed properly to implement Articles 5 and 119 of the Treaty in the following respect. The United Kingdom is obliged by Articles 5 and 119 to take no measures that would jeopardise the attainment of equal pay. In the absence of alternative national measures (including effective collective remedies for sex discrimination in pay structures and collective agreements) which effectively guarantee equal pay, the abolition of Wages Councils has jeopardised the attainment of the principle of equal pay.[21]

(a) The Government's response to the EOC

Some Government concessions followed quite swiftly from the EOC's more bullish stance. The procedure rules were amended from the end of 1993 so as to require independent experts to estimate how long their reports will take to finalise, to notify the tribunal of any "material delay" in submitting a report, and to empower the tribunal to revoke the expert's instructions and appoint a new expert.[22] At the same time, the Government announced that it was planning to abolish the industrial tribunal's power to dismiss an equal value claim as disclosing "no reasonable grounds", provided that hopeless cases could still be weeded out at an early stage. It also invited views on a variety of possible changes to the system of independent experts.

From April 1994, the tribunal rules were amended to provide that employers who raise the genuine material factor defence before the independent expert's report has been commissioned will not normally be allowed to reopen that defence after submission of the report. The Government justified its refusal to adopt the EOC's advice that the defence should be confined to the period after delivery of the expert's report on the basis of savings to the public purse.

The Government's most recent public pronouncements in this field came with the publication in December 1994 of the Green Paper "Resolving Employ-

---

[21] "Request to the Commission of the European Communities by the EOC for Great Britain in Relation to the Implementation of the Principle of Equal Pay", EOC, (1993), 71–4.
[22] The Industrial Tribunals (Constitution and Rules of Procedure) Regulations 1993 SI 2687 Sched 2.

ment Rights Disputes: Options for Reform".[23] It is perhaps significant that the Government's ideas on equal value are buried in the middle of this fairly substantial document, whose origins are to be found in a Department of Employment internal review of the operation in general of industrial tribunals "with a view to identifying any changes which would help them to cope with an increasing volume and complexity of cases with reduced delays, while containing demands on public expenditure". Most importantly, the Green Paper announces the Government's intention to change Section 2A(1)(b) of the Equal Pay Act so that it is at the tribunal's discretion whether or not to seek an independent expert's report on an equal value claim. The Government arrived at this conclusion on the basis of evidence it received from tribunal chairs, indicating that they believed that they were today better equipped through experience than they were in 1984 to identify the key considerations in equal value cases and to determine how such cases should be handled. The Government also comments that the proposals in the Green Paper for changing general tribunal procedures could help to simplify and speed up equal value cases, particularly through ensuring that parties are better prepared for hearings; by requiring written evidence in advance where appropriate; by using the chair's powers to issue directions and ask questions to clarify the issues before the hearing; and by setting time limits for the presentation of evidence.

It also moots two other possible procedural changes, the first being that tribunals could be given the power to set a timescale within which an expert's report should be completed; the idea underlying this suggestion is that it "would focus the minds of both experts and tribunals, and give them an added incentive to chase up submissions and comments from the parties".[24] Second, the Government suggests that claimants could be required to cite no more than one comparator, the rationale for this being that "some claimants in the past have cited several comparators, all of whose jobs are investigated at once, thus making the independent expert's, and tribunal's, tasks longer and more difficult".[25]

The Government insists that movement on these fronts has not been produced through the threat of Commission proceedings against the United Kingdom, but rather that it has itself been concerned for some while about delay in equal value cases and had proposed several amendments to the law *before* the formal complaints were made. It is true that David Hunt's letter to the EOC of July 1993 presages the changes in relation to the material factor defence, to the expert's time-frame for producing a report, and to the "no reasonable grounds" defence. It nevertheless seems something of a coincidence that no alterations to the equal value legislation of any substance had taken place before this date, notwithstanding mounting pressure from a number of quarters, and the

---

[23] Cmnd 2707.

[24] *Ibid* para 6.68.

[25] *Ibid* para 6.70. This is, of course, a worrying suggestion and could well present yet another hurdle to the would-be claimant, as well as magnifying the risks of delay and cost if the wrong comparator is chosen first and further proceedings have to be brought. However, shortly before going to press, the Government announced its intention to drop this proposal.

implication must be that the threat of formal proceedings has gone at least some of the way to forcing the Government's hand.

(b) Is there really a breach by the United Kingdom of its Community obligations?

It is submitted that there are essentially two parts to this question, one probably rather more straightforward than the other. The first, and simpler, – though admittedly much more limited – concerns the right of claimants to a proper judicial remedy. This is mandated by Article 2 of the Directive:

> Member States shall introduce into their national legal systems such measures as are necessary to enable all employees who consider themselves wronged by failure to apply the principle of equal pay to pursue their claims by judicial process after poss- ible recourse to other competent authorities.

This Article is in identical terms to Article 6 of the Equal Treatment Directive[26], as to which there is important authority from the Court of Justice in the *Johnston*[27], *Von Colson*[28], and *Marshall No 2*[29] decisions. These cases establish that the judicial remedies envisaged must be effective, must have a real deterrent effect on employers, must be appropriate in the circumstances and, where they take the form of compensation, must be adequate in the sense of enabling the loss actually sustained to be made good in full.[30] It is arguable that these decisions represent a change of direction on the part of the Court of Justice; it is well known that its strategy for enforcing the Member States' obligations in Com- munity law has involved the enforcement by individuals of their own directly effective Community rights in the national courts.[31] Whilst its early decisions in this area focused on the *cause of action* provided by Community law, leaving to the jurisdiction of the Member States the remedies and procedures necessary to give effect to those causes of action[32], in more recent times the Court seems to have become aware that *effective remedies and non-obstructive procedures* are essential if substantive rights are not to be undermined.[33] If this trend is main- tained, it seems strongly arguable that the United Kingdom's dilatory, unpractical and labyrinthine equal value procedures, together with the lack of legal aid in industrial tribunals and the limit on back-pay to two years[34], fall short of the requirements of Community law.

The second part to the question of whether the United Kingdom is in breach

---

[26] Directive 76/207/EEC (OJ 1976 L39/40).
[27] Case 222/84 *Johnston* v *Chief Constable of the RUC* [1986] ECR 1651.
[28] Case 14/83 *Von Colson and Kamann* v *Land Nordrhein-Westfalen* [1984] ECR 1891.
[29] Case C-271/91 *Marshall* v *Southampton and SW Hants Area Health Authority (No 2)* [1993] ECR I-4367.
[30] See Moore, in this volume.
[31] Case 26/62 *Van Gend en Loos* v *Nederlandsie Tariefcommissie* [1963] ECR 1.
[32] Case 33/76 *Rewe-Zentralfinanz eG* v *Landwirtschaftskammer fur das Saarland* [1976] ECR 1989.
[33] Case C-208/90 *Emmott* v *Minister for Social Welfare and Attorney General* [1991] ECR I-4269.
[34] Equal Pay Act 1970 s2(5).

of its obligations as regards equal value claims concerns the alleged failure over-all to ensure the principle of equal pay within this country. The EOC argues that the United Kingdom is in breach of Article 6 of the Equal Pay Directive, which provides:

> Member States shall, in accordance with their national circumstances and legal systems, take the measures necessary to ensure that the principle of equal pay is applied. They shall see that effective means are available to take care that this principle is observed.

This much more complex allegation involves saying that the Government has failed across the board to establish systems which ensure that there is no gender discrimination in relation to pay. It is very much more difficult to establish then that the practical obstacles facing an individual woman claimant are such as to make her "right" to equal pay a sham.

The causes of unequal pay are, of course, many and various; discrimination in the legal sense is only one. In addition, one must add, at the very least, cultural and educational factors, history and women's reproductive functions.

To require a State to put in place systems for ensuring equal pay is to require that state to identify all these causes of unequal pay and then to take effective action to counteract them. Desirable as this outcome seems, it is unreasonable to expect it to be achieved at a stroke.

A compromise position might be to argue that a State breaches Article 6 where it does not guarantee pay equality for all persons doing "the same work or work to which equal value is attributed", in situations where there is a comparator of the opposite sex. Again, however, this would seem to be a difficult argument to sustain, since there must be many reasons, apart from the inadequacies of the legal process, which account for a continuance of pay disparities even where the right could, technically, be vindicated.

(v) The legal consequences of any such breach

It has been argued above that there is a strong case for supposing the United Kingdom to be in breach of Article 2 of the Equal Pay Directive, but a much weaker case in relation to breach of Article 6 of that Directive. Proceeding on this basis, two important legal consequences would seem to follow.

First, there is the prospect of a would-be claimant of equal pay for work of equal value bringing a *Francovich*[35] claim. As the Court explained in that case, "the possibility of obtaining redress from the Member State is particularly indis-pensable where . . . the full effectiveness of Community rules is subject to prior action on the part of the State and where, consequently, in the absence of such action, individuals cannot enforce before the national courts the rights

---

[35] Cases C-6 and 9/90 *Francovich and Bonifaci* v *Italy* [1991] ECR I-5357. See Moore, in this volume.

conferred upon them by Community law".[36] The Court of Justice's judgment in *Commission* v *UK*[37] itself provides authority that the equal value situation is one dependent upon the State taking action to protect the individual's rights.

In *Francovich*, the Court went on to set out three conditions which must be fulfilled, in order for an individual to be entitled to damages from a Member State for the non-implementation of a Directive: the result required by the Directive must include the conferring of rights for the benefit of individuals; the content of those rights must be determinable by reference to the provisions of the Directive; and there must be a causal link between the breach of the State's obligations and the damage suffered by the claimant. These three conditions appear to be satisfied in the equal value context: the rights conferred by the Equal Pay Directive are, by their very nature, intended to benefit individuals; the content of those rights is, according to the Court of Justice in *Commission* v *UK*, determinable by reference to the provisions of the Directive, since the Court there rejected the United Kingdom's argument that the concept of equal value was too abstract to be applied by courts; and, in a case where the claimant argues that there is no practical possibility of her bringing proceedings for equal pay for work of equal value, because of the shortcomings of the legislation, then it would certainly appear that there is a causal connection between her loss and the State's breach of obligation.

It is sometimes maintained that there is a further element required in order to trigger *Francovich* liability and that is a degree of culpability on the part of the Member State.[38] In *Francovich* itself such culpability was clearly established since the Member State concerned had been held in infringement proceedings in 1989 to have been in breach of its obligations through non-implementation of the relevant Directive since 1983. It is, therefore, clear that breach of a ruling of the Court of Justice constitutes sufficient wrongdoing. However, the United Kingdom would presumably argue that, far from breaching the Court of Justice's 1982 ruling in relation to equal value claims, it took prompt action to ensure compliance. The reply might be that this action was in reality a cynical flouting of the substance of the Court's ruling and that all that the Government achieved in the Equal Pay Regulations of 1983 was the *appearance* of compliance; its real intention was to make the law and procedure surrounding equal value claims so byzantine as to be unworkable in practice. Such a reading would be consistent with the Prime Minister at that time, Margaret Thatcher's, dislike of employment regulation. It would also be consistent with the recorded fact that the Minister of State for Employment at the time, Alan Clark, was drunk when laying the draft regulations before the House of Commons.[39] If

---

[36] *Ibid* 5414.

[37] *Commission* v *UK, supra* n 2.

[38] See the discussion in Steiner, "From Direct Effects to *Francovich*: Shifting Means of Enforcement of Community Law" 18 ELRev (1993), 3–22. Further elucidation of this point may emerge with the Court of Justice's decisions in *Brasserie du Pêcheur* and *Factortame* Joined Cases C-46/93 and C-48/93.

[39] Alan Clark, *Diaries* (1993) 28–33. Clark, however, explains that his drunken state was purely fortuitous and that the text of the draft regulations had, apparently at a late stage, twice been amended by officials. He declares himself firmly in favour of the principle of equal pay: "As I started, the

ignoring a Court of Justice ruling amounts to sufficient culpability for *Francovich*, so surely must a deliberate attempt to pay no more than lip service to such a ruling – although it has to be admitted that this would be very hard to prove in practice.

A second, and nicely ironic, consequence would follow from a finding that the United Kingdom was in breach of Article 2 of the Equal Pay Directive; it would follow that the United Kingdom would still be failing to provide proper judicial redress to the victims of unequal pay for work of equal value. Since this is the very issue on which the Court of Justice delivered judgment in 1982, the United Kingdom would not merely be in breach of its Community obligations and thus liable to a Commission prosecution under Article 169, it would have failed "to take the necessary measures to comply with the judgment of the Court of Justice" and therefore be liable to a further Commission prosecution pursuant to the procedure laid down in Article 171. The irony lies in the fact that this is the situation in which, at the insistence of the United Kingdom itself, an amendment to the original Treaty which was agreed at the Maastricht Conference now provides for the imposition of financial penalties on the recalcitrant Member State.

(vi) The Commission's discretion in relation to prosecutions under Article 169

Where the Commission considers that a Member State is in breach of its Community obligations, both Article 169 and Article 171 confer a discretion on it as to whether to proceed to the Court of Justice.[40] Assuming that the Commission was convinced of the United Kingdom's breach of the equal value requirements of Community law, the question remains as to what factors might influence its decision about how to exercise this discretion. It should be added at this point that, as far as the present author is aware, no formal steps have been taken at the date of writing (June 1995). The United Kingdom Permanent Representative, whilst stressing the confidentiality which is habitually observed in pre-litigation exchanges in relation to Article 169, and also confirming that informal discussions on equal value have taken place with the Commission over the past year or so, states that no formal complaint has yet been received.

---

sheer odiousness of the text sank in. The purpose of the Order, to make it more likely (I would put it no stronger than that) that women should be paid the same rate for the same task, as men, was unchallengeable. In my view, in most instances, women deserve not less but *more* than the loutish, leering cigaretting males who control most organisations at most levels. But give a civil servant a good case and he'll wreck it with clichés, bad punctuation, double negatives and convoluted apology. Stir into this a directive from the European Community, some contrived legal precedent and a few caveats from the European Court of Justice and you have a text which is impossible to read . . . I found myself dwelling on, implicitly, it could be said, sneering at, the more cumbrous and unintelligible passages". (At 29–30).
[40] See further Wyatt and Dashwood, *European Community Law* (1993), 3rd ed, 109–120.

On the one hand, there are reasons for thinking that the Commission might take an extremely dim view of the United Kingdom's actions. An indication of the seriousness with which it regards equal pay was provided by its issue in June 1994 of a Memorandum on Equal Pay for Work of Equal Value.[41] This was precipitated by recent Eurostat figures showing that the pay differential between men and women remains high throughout the Community and is even widening in some areas, despite the existence of equality legislation. Although acknowledging that further data is needed, the Commission's Memorandum contains a Table showing that the United Kingdom is at the bottom of the league in this respect: women in the United Kingdom are paid 54.2% of the average male non-manual rate and 68.25% of the average male manual rate; only in Luxembourg and Ireland are the figures worse and there only in relation to manual rates (68.1% in Ireland and 65.1% in Luxembourg).

The Commission pledges itself in its Memorandum to the achievement of equal pay in practice, saying: "It is imperative that the fundamental right to equal pay under Article 119 of the European Community Treaty as amplified by Directive 75/117/EEC is fully implemented at Community level. This is especially important in view of the fact that the Maastricht Treaty has reiterated the Community's commitment to this principle".[42] Later, it adds: "The Commission will continue to have recourse to proceedings under Article 169 of the Treaty where this is considered appropriate".[43]

In addition, as has already been discussed, this may in truth be an Article 171 proceeding, rather than an Article 169 action. This can surely only increase the pressure on the Commission to take judicial proceedings, since it evinces an unacceptable degree of flagrancy in the breach of Community law.

On the other hand, whilst the political complexion of the new Commission and, especially, its sensitivity to questions of sex equality has yet to emerge fully, there are a number of factors which militate against proceedings being brought against the United Kingdom. The Commission's Memorandum, although acknowledging the seriousness of the situation in the United Kingdom, hints that at least the United Kingdom has made some effort to ensure equal pay for work of equal value; by contrast, it points out that there has been no litigation at all on this matter in France, Luxembourg, Greece and Italy, and very little litigation in a number of other Member States. Although it is not a defence to Article 169 proceedings to show that other Member States are also in breach of the same provision[44], it seems likely that the Commission would take into account basic notions of equity in such a case and refrain from bringing proceedings. Such a position might be supported by reference to the recent minor changes to the equal value procedures announced by the Government. Of a

---

[41] COM (94) 6 final.

[42] *Ibid* 38.

[43] *Ibid* 40. See also the emphasis placed by the Commission on pursuing Member States which are slow in implementing social policy directives contained in "European Social Policy – the Way Forward" (White Paper – Social Europe, DGV).

[44] Case 232/78 *Commission* v *France* [1979] ECR 2729.

similarly political nature is the possibility of public outrage being generated in the United Kingdom if this country were to be sued over a matter which may – sadly – not lie close to the heart of the "Sun's" readership; with the looming possibility of a referendum on closer integration within the European Union, it would be naive to suppose that the Commission would not be swayed by the effects of its action on public opinion. It may also apprehend that, if a Labour government were to be returned at the next General Election, there would be a strong possibility of amending legislation being passed voluntarily and without the need for enforcement proceedings.

A final factor which may weigh with the Commission is that it need not become involved in this delicate area, since there are alternative routes by which a judgment of the Court of Justice against the United Kingdom might be obtained. In addition to claims by individuals seeking the enforcement of their individual rights to equal pay, it is established as a matter of United Kingdom law that the EOC has *locus standi* to challenge domestic legislation by way of judicial review proceedings on the basis that that legislation breaches the United Kingdom's Community obligations in relation to sex equality.[45] The EOC could, therefore, bring judicial review proceedings in which it alleged that the equal value legislation obstructs claims under Article 119 and the Equal Pay Directive, and a preliminary ruling under Article 177 could then be sought from the Court of Justice in the course of those proceedings.

(vii) Conclusions

There can be little doubt that, in making complaints to the Commission over equal value, the two EOCs and the TUC have opened a Pandora's Box. The "bona fides" of the United Kingdom Government in relation to compliance with its Community obligations have been exposed to public scrutiny; the "goody-goody" image which it is fond of projecting in this respect could well be seriously tarnished and the Government may even be exposed to claims for damages made by individuals who have been denied a remedy under the equal value legislation.

Formal enforcement proceedings brought by the Commission against the United Kingdom could clearly precipitate root and branch reform of this most complex area of law. However, even if such proceedings are not taken by the Commission, the pressure on the Government to reform the equal value legislation has palpably been stepped up, the consciousness of the informed public has been raised in relation to the issue of sex-based pay inequality and the prospect has emerged of a broadly-based debate on the underlying causes of sex discrimination and the practical forms which an equal value law might take.

EVELYN ELLIS
Reader in Public Law,
University of Birmingham, UK

---

[45] *R* v *Secretary of State for Employment, ex parte the EOC* [1994] 2 WLR 409.

Chapter 2

OCCUPATIONAL PENSIONS AND EUROPEAN LAW: CLARITY AT LAST?*

The subject of the applicability of Article 119 EC to occupational pension schemes has confronted the European Court of Justice with a number of difficult problems over the last few years. In a number of recent judgments, however, the Court has managed to clarify its case law laying out the scope of the requirements of European law in this field. In the discussion which follows, attention will first focus on the requirements of European Union law *vis-à-vis* the individual elements of occupational schemes – access, contributions and benefits – before moving on to analyse the difficult issue of the temporal effects of Article 119 in this sphere. In the second main section of this chapter, an attempt will be made to outline the extent to which occupational schemes may legitimately take account of differences in the statutory pension schemes upon which they commonly build.

(i) Occupational pensions

When considering sex equality in occupational pensions, it is normal to focus first on the benefit which it is the function of the scheme to provide. However understandable this may be, it is not particularly helpful. The final benefits paid out by a scheme reflect the rights accrued by individuals over time: they are offered membership, they (and their employers) pay contributions, and many years later benefits are paid out. Consequently, in this description of European pension law attention will first focus on access to the scheme. A brief discussion of contributions will follow; thereafter benefits will be considered.

* This chapter was written by Elaine A. Whiteford, who is particularly grateful to Erik Berk for his willingness to discuss some of the matters touched upon in this chapter.

(a) Access

It is common for employers to offer occupational pensions to only some of their employees; before an individual can begin to accrue pension benefits, (s)he must be entitled to join the scheme. The most common conditions set for obtaining access to a pension scheme concern years of service with the employer, hours of work or seniority.[1]

The Court first addressed the question of access to occupational pension schemes in *Bilka*.[2] *Bilka* concerned the non-contributory occupational pension scheme which a German department store offered to its employees. To qualify for payment of the benefit, a part-time employee had to have been employed full-time for at least 15 years over a 20-year period. Ms Weber argued that the imposition of a minimum requirement of full-time employment worked to the disadvantage of women and formed a discrimination prohibited by Article 119. The United Kingdom government had argued that the conditions placed by an employer on the admission of employees to an occupational scheme did not fall within the scope of Article 119. In finding that the scheme offered by *Bilka* discriminated between women and men, the Court not only confirmed[3] that the benefits paid out by occupational schemes are "pay" within the meaning of Article 119,[4] but also that the conditions of access to such schemes fall within its scope.[5] This case law was recently confirmed in *Vroege*[6] and *Fisscher*[7] where the Court held that individuals can claim equal treatment in relation to the right to join an occupational pension scheme for employment after 8 April 1976.

(b) Contributions

Another condition which is commonly set before an individual can obtain entitlement to a benefit under a scheme is the payment of a contribution. The Court has recently stated very clearly that employee contributions to occupational

---

[1] Government Actuary, *Occupational Pension Schemes 1991 Ninth Survey by the Government Actuary* (London, 1994).

[2] Case 170/84 *Bilka-Kaufhaus GmbH* v *von Hartz* [1986] ECR 1607.

[3] It can be considered to have confirmed what many had read in its judgment in Case 80/70 *Defrenne* v *Belgium* [1971] ECR 445. See, for example, Curtin, "Occupational pension schemes and article 119: Beyond the fringe?" 24 CML Rev (1987), 215–257.

[4] Case 170/84 *Bilka, supra* n 2 at para 22 ("Benefits paid to employees under the scheme therefore constitute consideration received by the worker from the employer in respect of his employment").

[5] This emerges not only from the express terms of the judgment but also from the comparison which the Court made. In concluding that the scheme in *Bilka* discriminated against part-timers, it compared the treatment of full-time and part-time workers (at para. 27 it considered that "Since . . . a pension falls within the concept of pay for the purposes of . . . Article 119 it follows that, hour for hour, the total remuneration paid by *Bilka* to full-time workers is higher than that paid to part-time workers"). Had the conditions of access to the scheme not fallen within the scope of Article 119, the appropriate comparison would have been between full-timers who were entitled to benefits under the scheme and part-timers who enjoyed similar entitlement.

[6] Case C-57/93 *Vroege* v *NCIV Instituut voor Volkshuisvesting BV and Stichting Pensioenfonds NCIV* [1994] ECR I-4541.

[7] Case C-128/93 *Fisscher* v *Voorhuis Hengelo BV and Stichting Bedrijfspensioenfonds voor de Detailhandel* [1994] ECR I-4583.

pension schemes constitute "pay" within the meaning of Article 119.[8] The general rule in relation to employer contributions appears to be that they also fall within the concept of "pay"[9] but that where they reflect the use of actuarial tables[10] which differentiate between women and men, they need not be equal.[11]

(c) Benefits

The benefits paid to members by occupational pension schemes constitute "pay" within the context of Article 119.[12] As such, where individuals are engaged in the same employment, they must receive the same pension benefit. As the Court stressed in Barber, "the principle of equal pay applies to each element of the remuneration granted to men or women".[13] Consequently, the periodic pension payments made to men and women must be equal.[14]

The various requirements of European law in relation to occupational pension schemes will be summarised with the aid of an example. An employer offers a final salary scheme providing members with benefits of 70% of their final salary. This scheme must be open to male and female members on the same conditions, which includes the requirement that in a contributory scheme, equal contributions be levied from women and men. Where the scheme uses actuarial tables which differentiate on grounds of sex to calculate its future liabilities, the employer is released from the obligation to pay equal contributions in respect of male and female employees to enable any funding shortfall which would otherwise arise as a consequence of the use of such tables to be made good.

For money purchase schemes, the position is slightly more complex. There, as with final salary schemes, the employer must open the scheme to male and female employees on the same conditions, including the condition that their contributions be equal. In money purchase schemes, it is submitted that equality requires either that the employer contributions be equal,[15] or that the obligation to pay equal contributions in respect of male and female employees is

---

[8] Case C-200/91 Coloroll Pension Trustees Ltd v Russell and others [1994] ECR I-4389 at para 80.

[9] See Case 192/85 Newstead v Department of Transport [1987] ECR 4753 at para 14. See also Curtin, "Scalping the Community legislator: Occupational pensions and Barber" 27 CML Rev (1990), 475–506 at 481.

[10] For the general arguments against the use of different actuarial tables for women and men see the two articles by Curtin cited supra nn 3 and 9 at 225–229 and 492–498; and Hervey, "Case note on Case C-152/91, Neath" 31 CML Rev (1994), 1387–1397 at 1394–1396. See also the observations of Advocate General Van Gerven in his opinion in Cases C-109/91, C-110/91, C-152/91 and C-200/91 at paras 27–43.

[11] Case C-152/91 Neath v Hugh Steepner Ltd [1993] ECR I-6935 at para 32; Case C-200/91 Coloroll, supra n 8 at para 81.

[12] Case 170/84 Bilka, supra n 2 at para 22; confirmed in inter alia, Case C-262/88 Barber v Guardian Royal Exchange [1990] ECR I-1889 at para 30.

[13] Case C-262/88, supra n 12 at para 34.

[14] This was clearly the consideration which prompted the statement of the Court in Barber cited above. See also Prechal, "Bommen ruimen in Maastricht. Wijziging van Artikel 119 EEG" 67 Nederlands Juristenblad (1992), 349–354 at 352. See also the discussion in the next section.

[15] Which, where the insurance company uses actuarial tables, will result in female employees being offered a lower level of benefit.

suspended where the inequality in contributions is designed to make the levels of benefit received by the sexes equal.

(d) Temporal effects revisited

Many of the controversies which have dogged this subject recently can be traced back to the divergent approaches taken by the European legislator and the European judge. Some two months after the Court's unambiguous confirmation in *Bilka* that occupational pension schemes fell within the scope of Article 119, the Council adopted Directive 86/378/EEC[16] which purported to permit pension schemes to continue to differentiate between women and men in respect of particular aspects of pension provision. The uncertainty engendered by these two apparently contradictory lines of authority was resolved by the judgment in *Barber* where the Court confirmed[17] that the scope of Article 119 could not be limited by provisions of secondary legislation.[18]

Nevertheless, the Court recognised that the exceptions which the Directive contained had created legitimate expectations on the part of the pension schemes that the conduct in question continued to be legal, as a result of which it decided to impose a temporal limitation on the effects of its judgment in time. In taking this course, the Court expressly referred to legal certainty as a consideration which had prompted it to act as it had.[19]

Unfortunately, in formulating this temporal limitation, the Court's choice of language resulted in a passage which was capable of a wide variety of interpretations, most of which were canvassed in the academic press.[20] In essence, the debate centred on two separate questions. First, did the Court have the future benefits[21] or the future service[22] interpretation in mind? Second, was the temporal limitation confined to the contracted-out occupational schemes at issue

---

[16] Directive 86/378/EEC on the implementation of the principle of equal treatment for men and women in occupational social security schemes (OJ 1986 L 225/40). See the discussion in Prechal and Burrows, *Gender Discrimination Law of the European Community* (Aldershot, 1990) 276–290.

[17] Case 96/80 *Jenkins* v *Kingsgate (Clothing Productions) Ltd* [1981] ECR 911.

[18] Case C-262/88 *Barber*, *supra* n 12 at para 32.

[19] Case C-262/88 *Barber*, *supra* n 12 at para 44.

[20] Compare Curtin (1990), *supra* n 9; Dallett, "Sex discrimination in pensions and non-retroactivity of relief" British Business Law (1992), 91–98; Dierx, "Barberisme" *Nemesis* nr. 4 (1991), 1–4; Hanau and Preis, "Beschränkung der Rückwirkung neuer Rechtsprechung zur Gleichberechtigung im Recht der betrieblichen Altersversorgung" *Der Betrieb* 1991, 1276–1284; Honeyball and Shaw, "Sex, law and the retiring man" 16 EL Rev (1991), 47–58; Hoving, "Gelijke behandeling mannen en vrouwen in pensioenregelingen. Commentaar op Hof van Justitie EG 17 mei 1990 (Zaak *Barber*)" *Tijdschrift voor Pensioenvraagstukken* (1990), 50–55; Hudson, "Some reflections on the implications of the *Barber* decision" 17 EL Rev (1992), 163–171; Mortelmans, "Zaak C-262/88, Douglas Harvey Barber vs. Guardian Royal Exchange Assurance Group" 39 *Sociaal-Economische Wetgeving* (1991), 143–153; Prechal (1990), *supra* n 16; Sjerps, "Van Doornroosje en haar hardnekkige prins, oftwel: hoe het EG-Hof de pensioenwereld probeert te wekken" *Sociaal Recht* (1990), 212–217; and Steyger, "Hof van Justitie EG, 17 mei 1990" *Actualiteiten nr. 116, Nemesis* (1990), 210–215.

[21] The future benefits interpretation of the temporal limitation held that the Court required that all benefits paid out by occupational schemes after 17 May 1990 should be equal, irrespective of the contributions which the individuals and their employers had paid in the past.

[22] The future service interpretation required that individuals accrue rights to equal benefits for service falling after 17 May 1990.

in *Barber*[23], or did it extend to all the forms which occupational pension schemes take in the Union?

The politicians made their position known on this debate by appending a Protocol[24] to the Treaty on European Union agreed at Maastricht in December 1991. This stated that the future service interpretation was to prevail, that is, that benefits need only be equal in relation to periods of employment falling after 17 May 1990. In addition, it extended the temporal limitation to all kinds of occupational pension schemes, not just to British contracted-out schemes. Prior to the entry into force of the Treaty of European Union (TEU) on 1 November 1993, the Court indicated that it shared this view.[25]

However, the approach which the Court and the politicians had appeared to take was not without its problems. In appearing to require equality in pension accrual only in relation to periods of employment subsequent to 17 May 1990, it seemed that *Bilka* had been overruled, albeit *sotto voce*.[26] In that judgment, the Court had held that Article 119 required that men and women be granted equal access to and benefits from occupational pension schemes, a judgment which was not subject to a temporal limitation with the result that individuals had been entitled to claim these rights in relation to all periods of service lying after 8 April 1976. The breadth of the temporal limitation (and Protocol) appeared – retroactively – to strip individuals of the rights which had been recognised in *Bilka*.[27]

In *Vroege* and *Fisscher* the Court revealed that this interpretation of the temporal limitation was much too broad. It confirmed the logic which had moved it in *Barber*, holding that the temporal limitation applied only in respect of:

> those kinds of discrimination which employers and pension schemes could reasonably have considered to be permissible owing to *the transitional derogations for which Community law provided* and which were capable of being applied to occupational pensions. (emphasis added)[28]

---

[23] See in this vein, Curtin (1990), *supra* n 9 at 486–7.

[24] According to Art 239 EC, Protocols form an integral part of the Treaty. Confirmed by the Court in Case C-57/93 *Vroege*, *supra* n 6 at para 35. See Prechal (1992), *supra* n 14; Hervey, "Legal Issues concerning the *Barber* Protocol" in O'Keeffe and Twomey, *Legal Issues of the Maastricht Treaty* (1994) at 329–337; Curtin, "The constitutional structure of the union: A Europe of bits and pieces" 30 CML Rev (1993), 17–69.

[25] Case C-109/91 *Ten Oever* v *Stichting Bedrijfspensioenfonds voor het Glazenwassers-en Schoonmaakbedrijf* [1993] ECR I-4879.

[26] See comments to this effect in Whiteford, "Collectief Geheugenverlies? Het EG-recht en de aanvullende pensioenen" 18 NJCM-Bulletin (1993), 998–1004.

[27] Extending the temporal limitation in this way also robs the Court's reasoning in imposing the temporal limitation in the first place of all its logic. It will be recalled that it was prompted to act in this as it did because the pension funds had been led to believe that certain derogations from the equality principle were permissible in the field of occupational pensions by the exceptions contained in Directive 86/378. Extending the temporal limitation to all benefits, irrespective of whether the Directive contained an exception, does not square with this approach.

[28] Case C-57/93 *Vroege*, *supra* n 6 at para 27; Case C-128/93 *Fisscher*, *supra* n 7 at para 24. See in general, Whiteford, "Lost in the Mists of Time: The ECJ and Occupational Pensions" 32 CML Rev (1995), 801–840.

The temporary derogations for which European law had made provision were in relation to pensionable age and survivor's benefits.[29] As the Court stressed, there was no justification for extending this to cover access to occupational schemes, which therefore continues to be governed by *Bilka*. This requires equality in access to and benefits from occupational schemes.

These considerations indicate that the temporal limitation applies as follows. Women and men have to be granted equal access to occupational schemes for post-8 April 1976 employment, and the resulting benefits must also be equal, unless the schemes had previously differentiated in respect of pensionable age and/or survivors' benefits, in which case benefits need only be equal for employment subsequent to 17 May 1990. In other words, where an employer requires that men have been employed for two years before they qualify for scheme membership, the employer may not set a different threshold for female members. In addition, where it offers men benefits of, say, 70% of their final salary on retirement, it may not offer women benefits of a mere 50%. The only differentiation which is permissible is where in the past schemes had differentiated in relation to pensionable age or survivor's pensions.[30]

Having established the scope of the temporal limitation which the Court imposed on the effects of Article 119 on occupational pension schemes, the final matter which has to be addressed is whether this conclusion has to be adjusted because of the Protocol. The Court observed that:

> while extending it to all benefits payable under occupational social security schemes and incorporating it in the Treaty, Protocol No 2 essentially adopted the same interpretation of the *Barber* judgment as did the *Ten Oever* judgment.[31]

It is suggested that this indicates that the temporal limitation[32] and the Protocol are to be read as synonymous. The Protocol merely confirmed the future service interpretation and that it was available to all kinds of occupational pension schemes operating in Europe, not just the contracted-out schemes at issue in *Barber*.

The alternative interpretation would be that the Protocol extends the temporal limitation of *Barber*[33] to all benefits provided for post-8 April 1976 service.[34] On

---

[29] Art 9(a) and (b) of Directive 86/378/EEC. See in greater detail, Whiteford (1995), *supra* n 28 at 832–839.

[30] The logic of this interpretation is demonstrated by an example of what any other interpretation would mean. If equal access does not have to lead to equal benefits, it would mean that the employer would be free to offer men benefits of 70% of their final salary but restrict the benefits accrued for the same contributions by female employees to a mere, say, 50%. This hardly seems consistent with the principle of equal pay.

[31] Case C-57/93 *Vroege*, *supra* n 6 at para 41.

[32] As clarified in the case law. See Whiteford (1995), *supra* n 28.

[33] Only those schemes which had differentiated in relation to pensionable age or survivor's pensions are exempted from the obligation to provide for the accrual of equal benefits for service lying after 8 April 1976, and only to that extent. These schemes must provide for the accrual of equal benefits for service falling after 17 May 1990.

[34] Tether, "Sex Equality and Occupational Pension Schemes" 24 ILJ (1995), 194–203 at 196–198; Wouters, "Gelijke Behandeling van mannen en vrouwen inzake bedrijfspensioenen: de "post-*Barber*"-arresten van het Hof van Justitie" 20 NJCM Bulletin (1995), 274–302 at 280–287; Hoving, "Gelijke

this interpretation, the Protocol differs significantly from the case law,[35] making it difficult to state that the Protocol contains an interpretation of the temporal limitation which is "essentially the same" as that in the case law. Consequently, it is suggested that this interpretation ought to be rejected.

To conclude, it is the submission of this contribution that it is only schemes which had differentiated in relation to pensionable age and or survivors' pensions which enjoy an exemption from the obligation to provide equal benefits for service accruing after 8 April 1976.[36] This result is entirely in line with the Court's previous case law and respects the expectations of individuals based on its earlier pronouncements. By limiting the temporal limitation to two specific situations, the Court not only ensures that Article 119 enjoys far-reaching effects in relation to occupational pension schemes, but remains true to its general position that exceptions to the equality principle must be extremely narrowly construed.[37]

(ii) Links with statutory schemes

Despite the fact that they generally pre-date state involvement in old age income provision, occupational pension schemes traditionally link their conditions of entitlement to benefit and/or benefit levels to payments made from the state scheme. This explains why it has been common for schemes to provide that occupational benefits become payable at the same age as the state pension becomes payable. Similarly, occupational schemes often deduct statutory entitlement from the levels of benefit which they pay to beneficiaries, to mention only two of the most common of the ways in which occupational schemes build upon the pension provision made by the state.

Given the close links which exist between occupational and statutory schemes, any difference in the applicable legal regimes will cause considerable difficulty. As a matter of European law, statutory schemes are subject to the provisions of Directive 79/7/EEC,[38] whereas occupational schemes fall under Article 119. Unfortunately, the obligations imposed on the state on the one hand and on the employer on the other differ significantly, posing schemes with a number of difficult dilemmas with which the Court has been confronted on a number of occasions. The aim of this section is to explain how the Court appears to consider that employers may bridge the gap between the law on statutory and the law on occupational pension schemes. In the discussion which

---

behandeling en de gevolgen voor de pensioenaanspraken" *Tijdschrift voor Pensioenvraagstukken* (1995), 26–29 at 27.

[35] In practice, this interpretation would mean that an employer *could* offer male employees benefits of 70% of their final salary and female employees 50%.

[36] Subject, of course, to having paid the requisite contributions and to the operation of the relevant national procedural rules. For detailed consideration of these issues, see Whiteford, *supra* n 28 at 812–817; Moore, "'Justice Doesn't Mean a Free Lunch': The Application of the Principle of Equal Pay to Occupational Pension Schemes" 20 EL Rev (1995), 159–177 at 166–169.

[37] Case 222/84 *Johnston* v *Chief Constable of the RUC* [1986] ECR 1651.

[38] See Steiner, in this volume.

follows, first the problematic aspects of Directive 79/7/EEC will be highlighted, together with the older body of case law. Next three relatively recent cases will be discussed which may signal a refining of the Court's approach to this area.

As has been described elsewhere in this volume,[39] Directive 79/7/EEC aims progressively to implement the principle of equal treatment for men and women in matters of social security. Entirely in conformity with the progressive nature of the Directive, it contains a number of exceptions[40], the most controversial of which has been Article 7(1)(a) which permits the Member States to postpone the implementation of equality in relation to "the determination of pensionable age for the purposes of granting old-age and retirement pensions and the possible consequences thereof for other benefits".[41] The "possible consequences thereof for other benefits" are limited to consequences for statutory[42] social security benefits which are "objectively necessary in order to avoid disrupting the complex financial equilibrium of the social security system or to ensure consistency between retirement pension schemes and other benefit schemes".[43]

As was mentioned in the previous section, the Directive on occupational pension schemes, Directive 86/378/EEC, originally contained a provision mirroring for occupational schemes, the temporary derogation contained in Article 7(1)(a) of Directive 79/7/EEC for statutory schemes.[44] This suggested that the practice which occupational schemes had developed of linking entitlement and the amount of benefits they paid to those paid under the statutory scheme, would be found compatible with European law. However, in a series of judgments in relation to another Directive,[45] doubt was cast about the accuracy of this conclusion.

The Court was first asked to consider linkage between statutory pensionable age and other employment conditions in *Burton*.[46] Here the employer offered women voluntary redundancy from a lower age than men, the difference in ages reflecting the differences in statutory pensionable age. The Court held that the employer's practice was in conformity with European law, suggesting that different age conditions linked to differences in the statutory scheme were legitimate. However, by 1986 the Court's position on this matter appeared to have changed. In *Marshall*,[47] *Roberts*[48] and *Beets-Proper*[49] the Court concluded that employers could not set different age conditions for terminating employment even where they reflected different normal statutory pensionable age. In the

---

[39] See Steiner, in this volume.

[40] Article 7 of Directive 79/7/EEC.

[41] Case C-9/91 *R* v *Secretary of State for Social Security, ex parte the EOC* [1992] ECR I-4297; Case C-154/92 *Van Cant* v *Rijksdienst voor Pensioenen* [1993] ECR I-3811.

[42] *Cf.* for an early smokescreen on this point, the judgment in Case 19/81 *Burton* v *British Railways Board* [1982] ECR 554.

[43] Case C-328/91 *Secretary of State for Social Security* v *Thomas and others* [1993] ECR I-1247.

[44] Art 9(a) of Directive 86/378/EEC.

[45] Directive 76/207/EEC on the implementation of the principle of equal treatment for men and women as regards access to employment, vocational training and promotion and working conditions (OJ 1976 L39/40).

[46] Case 19/81 *Burton*, *supra* n 42.

[47] Case 152/84 *Marshall* v *Southampton and South West Hampshire Area Health Authority* [1986] ECR 723.

[48] Case 151/84 *Roberts* v *Tate and Lyle Industries Ltd.* [1986] ECR 703.

[49] Case 262/84 *Beets-Proper* v *Van Lanschot Bankiers NV* [1986] ECR 773.

context of Article 119, in *Barber*[50] and *Moroni*[51] the Court refused to countenance occupational pension schemes offering male and female employees their benefits at different ages, even where these differences merely replicated the differences in the national statutory schemes.

With the exception of *Burton*, all these cases suggested that no reliance could be had on differentiation in the statutory scheme for matters falling outside the ambit of the national social security scheme itself. They also raised serious doubts as to the compatibility with European law of the widespread practice of linking occupational schemes to their statutory counterparts. However, three recent judgments, although at first glance contradictory, suggest that established practice is compatible with European law, at least where it satisfies the requirements of the overall objectives of European equality law. These cases provide elucidation about both the extent to which links may be maintained for the purposes of setting conditions of entitlement to occupational benefits and also the extent to which schemes may take account of the benefits received from the statutory scheme in calculating the amount of occupational entitlement.

In *Commission* v *Belgium*[52] the Commission had raised an Article 169 infringement action in respect of a collective agreement which had been declared compulsory in Belgium. According to the collective agreement, all those made redundant over the age of 60 qualified for a supplementary payment financed by their last employer, where they also qualified for unemployment benefit. However, individuals ceased to qualify for unemployment benefit when they passed state pensionable age, which at that time was 60 for women and 65 for men. The effect of the provision was to exclude women from entitlement to the supplementary payment.

The Court appeared to have no difficulty in concluding that the supplementary payment in question constituted "pay" within the meaning of Article 119, and that to provide that only men between the ages of 60 and 65 who have been made redundant qualify for it while women in the same situation do not, violated Article 119. This suggests, in line with *Marshall, Roberts, Beets-Proper, Barber* and *Moroni*, that links between entitlement to benefits under the statutory scheme and those under occupational schemes may not be maintained where this imports into the occupational scheme differentiation in the statutory scheme.

In *Birds Eye Walls* v *Roberts*[53] however, the Court reached an apparently different conclusion. Ms Roberts had complained about the method of calculating bridging pensions[54] under the scheme operated by her employers, whereby

---

[50] Case C-262/88 *Barber, supra* n 12.
[51] Case C-110/91 *Moroni* v *Collo GmbH* [1993] ECR I-6591.
[52] Case C-173/91 [1993] ECR I-673.
[53] Case C-132/92 [1993] ECR I-5579.
[54] A bridging pension is a pension, usually, but as the facts of *Birds Eye Walls* demonstrate not exclusively, paid to men between the ages of 60 and 65 to compensate them for the unavailability of their statutory pension. The scheme pays to the men a sum of money representing the statutory benefit payable to women from the age of 60 resulting in the total amounts received by women and men being equal. This subject has not received much attention in the academic press. For an exception, (pre-*Barber*) see Luckhaus, "Bridging pensions: a question of difference?" 19 ILJ (1990), 48–54.

account was taken of the amount of pension payable under the statutory scheme. Where an employee had ceased paid employment due to ill health prior to the age of 60, the scheme paid equal amounts to women and men. However, on reaching the age of 60, women saw their payments under the occupational scheme reduced by the amount of statutory pension to which they were deemed entitled,[55] a reduction which took place in relation to men only from the age of 65. According to Ms Roberts, the reduction in the amount paid to her under her employer's scheme resulted in her receiving less pay than her male colleague.

The Court's apparently uncategorical rejection of links between statutory and occupational schemes in its previous case law seemed clearly to suggest that the scheme operated by *Birds Eye Walls* would be found to conflict with Article 119. However, the Court in fact held that the payment of the statutory pension to men and women at different ages constituted an:

> objective premise, which necessarily entails that the *amount* of the bridging pension is not the same for men and women and cannot be considered discriminatory. (emphasis added)[56]

In this case, in other words, links between the statutory scheme and the occupational scheme were found compatible with European law.

Despite their apparent contradiction, these judgments can in fact be reconciled. It has already been mentioned that after a false start in *Burton*, the Court had consistently held that differences in statutory pensionable age could not be replicated in matters falling outside the scope of the statutory social security system. This would suggest that *Commission* v *Belgium* was consistent with this line of case law and *Birds Eye Walls* represented a break with the past. However, if we turn again to the previous cases, they share one feature which is not to be found in *Birds Eye Walls*. In all the previous cases, the age condition which the occupational schemes proposed to import from the statutory scheme resulted in women and men being granted different access to benefits under the occupational scheme. In other words, it meant that women and men could claim their benefits at different ages. Seen from this perspective, *Birds Eye Walls* can be seen to raise a different issue. In *Birds Eye Walls* there was no differentiation in relation to the age at which individuals were granted access to the benefits under the scheme; instead the differentiation concerned the level of benefits. Women and men qualified for payment of the bridging pension at the same age but women saw the amount of their entitlement to the employer-funded part reduced five years earlier than men. If this analysis is correct, it suggests that although differentiating conditions of access may not be replicated in occupational schemes, occupational pension schemes may continue to take account of

---

[55] In the past, married women in the UK could choose to pay reduced social security contributions in return for obtaining lower social security benefits. The scheme operated by *Birds Eye Walls* subtracted a standard sum representing statutory entitlement without enquiring into the actual entitlement of individual members.

[56] Case C-132/92, *supra* n 53 at para 20.

benefits received from statutory schemes in calculating the levels of benefits which they will pay.

Tentative support for this conclusion is to be found in the third of the recent cases on links between occupational and statutory schemes; the *ABP* case.[57] It also indicates the circumstances in which schemes will be allowed to link the amount of benefit which they offer to entitlement to a statutory pension.

The *ABP* case concerned the system of taking account of the Dutch social security pension in the pensions paid to Dutch civil servants. The ABP promised its members pensions of 70% of final salary over a 40-year career, with the 70% being defined as including the benefit paid by the State. Prior to 1985, the Dutch statutory old age pension scheme, the AOW, paid single individuals benefits at 70% of the minimum wage. Married men received an AOW amounting to 100% of the minimum wage, to reflect the extra expenses involved in providing for a household of two individuals. Married women accrued no independent entitlement to an AOW pension. In taking account of the AOW in calculating benefits payable by the ABP, 100% minimum wage was deducted from married male civil servants, whereas merely 70% AOW was subtracted from the ABP entitlement of married women. This resulted in married male civil servants receiving lower payments from the ABP than their married female colleagues.

At first glance, the analysis of *Birds Eye Walls* outlined above would suggest that the rules of the ABP should have been found to be compatible with European law because the link with the statutory scheme did not affect access to benefits but their amount. Instead, the Court found that the scheme operated by the ABP conflicted with Article 119.

The key to reconciling these apparently diverse judgments is to be found in the opinion of the Advocate General in *Birds Eye Walls*. He cited with apparent approval the observations of the Commission in which it was pointed out that the linking rules of the schemes which had previously fallen foul of the Court in *Marshall, Roberts, Beets-Proper,* and indeed *Barber,* perpetuated the differentiation in the statutory schemes which European law currently, but temporarily[58], tolerates. By contrast, in *Birds Eye Walls*, reducing the levels of bridging pensions paid to women after the age of 60 to take account of the amounts they received under the statutory scheme resulted in male and female ex-employees receiving the same total pension. In this sense, the linkage in *Birds Eye Walls* was considered not to perpetuate, but rather to reduce, the differentiation currently countenanced by European law in relation to statutory pensionable age.

That this was not the situation in the *ABP* case is clarified by an example: 100% of the minimum wage is set at, say, ƒ100; 70% of the minimum wage is ƒ70. A married man and woman who are each promised a total pension of ƒ200 receive the following amounts from the ABP having taken account of the AOW. The man receives ƒ100 and the woman receives ƒ130. However, unlike the rule

---

[57] Case C-7/93 *ABP* v *Beune* [1994] ECR I-4471.
[58] Arts 7 and 8 of Directive 79/7/EEC demonstrate clearly that further legislative action is intended to remove these forms of discrimination. See the Draft Directive COM(87) 494 final.

in *Birds Eye Walls*, this does not eradicate the discrimination in the statutory scheme. Rather, because the woman receives no AOW at all, it perpetuates the discrimination and the Court consequently rejects it.

In this way it is possible to reconcile the Court's three apparently contradictory judgments.[59] To recapitulate, they suggest that occupational schemes may not use age conditions operated in the statutory scheme to determine entitlement to payment of benefits under the occupational scheme, at least where the age conditions used in the statutory scheme differ between women and men. On the other hand, even where the statutory scheme pays pensions to women and men at different ages, occupational schemes can take account of payment of statutory benefits to their members in calculating the levels of benefits to which members gain entitlement where as a result of this calculation the benefits to which male and female members are entitled become more equal.[60]

Reaching the conclusion that the linkage with the statutory scheme in *Birds Eye Walls* resulted in a reduction in discrimination relied upon examination of the "total" pension income received by an individual from the statutory scheme and the occupational scheme. Great store was set by the Court in *Birds Eye Walls* on the fact that the result of the rules in question was equality of total pension income (thus defined). However, in *Barber* the Court had apparently eschewed an interpretation of equality which focused on the total income received by an individual, holding instead that "the principle of equal pay applies to each of the elements of remuneration granted to men or women".[61] This would have suggested that no account should have been taken of the amounts received under the state scheme and required that the occupational scheme pay identical amounts to its male and female members. In taking the view that the scheme in *Birds Eye Walls* reduced discrimination, the Court not only appeared to abandon this approach, but to acquiesce in account being taken of sources of income (the statutory pension) falling outside the scope of Article 119.[62] The total income received from both sources may well have been equal as a result of the

---

[59] It is true that in *Birds Eye Walls* the Court did not focus on the precise amount obtained by Ms Roberts. However, that concerned a situation in which she had chosen to contribute lower amounts to the UK statutory scheme in return for which she accrued entitlement to a lower level of benefit. To have required that her employer compensate her for the results of her choice, can be seen to amount to unjust enrichment, *pace* the Advocate General. The difference between this and the *ABP* case, is that there the deduction made for female employees was for an amount to which they were not entitled under the law; choice had nothing to do with it, nor was there any question of unjust enrichment.

[60] Still in the field of pensions, other evidence for such an approach can be gleaned. It will be recalled that the Court was willing to countenance employers paying different levels of contribution to final salary schemes in respect of their male and female employees, where the funding of the scheme required this as a consequence of the use of different actuarial tables for women and men. There, the objective served was to equalise benefits. It was suggested that the Court would also accept an employer contributing higher amounts in respect of female employees to money purchase schemes where this resulted in more equal benefits being paid. This possible equality of result orientation on the part of the Court can be seen as a new development. For a critique of the Court's previous position, see Fenwick and Hervey, "Sex Equality in the Single Market: New Directions for the European Court of Justice" 32 CML Rev (1995), 443–470.

[61] Case C-262/88, *supra* n 12 at para 34.

[62] See Case 80/70 *Defrenne* v *Belgian State* [1971] ECR 445.

scheme operated by Birds Eye Walls, but the "pay" (the amounts paid by the occupational scheme) of male and female employees between the ages of 60 and 65 was different.[63] A discrimination in the statutory scheme which is generally seen to favour women was used in this case to justify a discrimination in the occupational scheme which favours men, because the outcome was seen to be neutral. Two wrongs do apparently make a right.

Commission v *Belgium*, *Birds Eye Walls* and *ABP* suggest that links can indeed be maintained between statutory and occupational schemes. However, this is only permissible where it results in the total benefits received by male and female employees being equal. Links may not be maintained when setting conditions of access to benefits under the scheme. It should be noted in passing that this conclusion is not inconsistent with that drawn in the first part of this paper. There it was observed that schemes have been obliged to grant men and women equal access to and benefits from occupational schemes for all employment after 8 April 1976. Only where the scheme previously differentiated in relation to pensionable age or survivor's benefits are they released from this obligation which then applies merely in respect of post-17 May 1990 service. If the line traced in this second part of the paper is correct, it merely refines slightly the concept of benefits and the matters which are to be taken into consideration in evaluating equality in the pension sphere.

(iii) Conclusion

Although at first glance, the paths which this contribution argues have been followed by the Court may seem unduly circuitous, it is suggested that on reflection they emerge as appropriate to reach the ends pursued. In relation to the temporal limitation, the Court's analysis has allowed the scope of Article 119 to be maximised, while taking account of the legitimate difficulties which pension schemes may face in introducing equality into a sphere long characterised by differentiation.

Similarly, in relation to linkage with statutory schemes, the Court has taken an approach which reflects reality and maximises individual benefit. Occupational pension schemes are offered by employers to their employees to supplement the benefits paid by the state. With this objective in mind, they have often mirrored the terms and conditions of the statutory schemes which they are designed to supplement, with the objective of creating a coherent system of benefits for beneficiaries. The differences between the legal regimes to which

---

[63] The Advocate General appeared to recognise that this was a weak point in his reasoning. He attempted to bolster his submissions by focusing on the fact that were no deduction to be made for the statutory pension payable to the woman, the employer would for that period be paying her twice: once in the form of her pension and a second time in the form of his contribution to the statutory scheme. The weakness of this argument is that, as the same Advocate General recognised in *Barber*, employer contributions to the statutory scheme do not constitute "pay" in the hands of the employee. Accordingly, his subsidiary argument is flawed by the same features as the principal argument.

statutory and occupational schemes are subject mean that the latter are often forced to build on an uneven foundation. It confronts them with the dilemma of pursuing formal or substantive pension equality: of providing equal benefits themselves or ensuring that their members receive the same levels of retirement income.

The recent case law of the Court demonstrates its sensitivity to this dilemma. It is suggested that the solution which the Court has found is the best possible one in the circumstances. Although it does mean that the Court has taken a step backwards from its bald statement that equality must be ensured in relation to each element of the remuneration paid to employees, the result of its case law is that inequalities in statutory entitlement can be rectified within occupational schemes. Once equality has been introduced into statutory schemes, occupational schemes will have equal foundations upon which to build, removing the necessity for the mechanisms discussed in the second section of this contribution. Until then, it is suggested that the Court's approach is to be applauded, since it seems more likely than any other to result in equality between women and men in terms of their retirement income.

ELAINE A. WHITEFORD
Lecturer in Law,
University of Nottingham, UK

Chapter 3

ECONOMIC DEFENCES TO EQUAL PAY CLAIMS*

(i) Introduction

If the European Union stands for one idea above all, it is that it is both possible and desirable to create one market covering all Member States. This is clearest when considering the supply of goods and more of an ideal than a reality when considering the supply of services. So far as the supply of – and the demand for – labour is concerned, it seems to be assumed that it is appropriate to treat the market for labour in the same way as the market for goods and services, but that the unfettered *freedom* of that market needs to be tempered for two reasons. First, significantly lower wages and conditions in one Member State may act as an economic magnet and thus distort the Europe-wide market.[1] Secondly, market freedom may need to be limited in the interests of other social policy considerations, such as gender equality and the need to prevent or alleviate poverty or unacceptable working conditions. The requirement of equal pay contained in Article 119 of the Treaty of Rome is justifiable and explicable under both approaches.[2]

The fact that equal pay legislation pre-dates the Social Chapter and the Maastricht Treaty means that these developments have no *direct* relevance to this chapter, although it is strongly arguable that the most useful development for women employees generally would be the implementation of the right to an equitable wage[3] contained in Article 5 of the Community Charter of Fundamental Social Rights.[4] While such aspirational declarations may cause problems for

---

* This chapter was written by Richard Townshend-Smith.
[1] See Barnard, in this volume.
[2] See Deakin and Wilkinson, "Rights vs Efficiency? The Economic case for Transnational Labour Standards" 23 ILJ (1994), 289–310, in particular 306–7.
[3] See Ellis, in this volume.
[4] See Rubery and Fagan, *Wage Determination and Sex Segregation in Employment in the European Community* (1993), Network of Experts on the Situation of Women in the Labour Market, Report for DGYV, European Commission, 229–232.

lawyers because of the lack of specificity and enforcement mechanisms, there is potential significance at the political level, despite the inevitable resistance for its supposed threat to international competitiveness. In addition, the more the concept of subsidiarity – itself partly led by a belief in the efficacy of market solutions – gains a political hold, the more deferential national courts may be to employer defences to equal pay claims.

Turning to economic defences to equal pay claims, the potential clash between the market approach and the Social Europe approach is self-evident. The Union is committed both to the freedom of the market[5], including the labour market, and to the removal of gender discrimination in pay, which is by definition an interference with the market. The extent to which the former is permitted to override the latter is crucial both politically and legally.

This chapter will first examine the aims of pay equality legislation in the European and the British domestic context, focusing on the defence of genuine material factor[6], especially the so-called market forces defence. It will be shown how neither European nor domestic case law has done more than scratch the surface of the issue. It will be contended that proper resolution of the conflict requires appreciation of the aims and methods involved in fixing pay levels.

Whether these issues are suitable for resolution by judges is another matter. I am here arguing for a particular approach to a narrow legal issue; I am not arguing that were that to happen, the prospects for women's pay and women's equality would be transformed. The weaknesses of a litigation strategy, especially one based on individual employee complainants, do not need repeating. In addition, the complexities and variations in the determination of pay levels and the causes of pay inequalities seriously hamper *any* legal regime in dealing rigorously with practical day-to-day pay issues.

(ii) The aims of legislation

The objectives of anti-discrimination legislation do not command universal agreement. There is general support for what might be termed the process approach, which concentrates on equality of opportunity and the procedures by which employment decisions are taken. In the context of equal pay this manifests itself in the requirement of equal pay for like work.[7] Here, nothing prevents an employer re-organising work so that men and women are not in fact

---

[5] See Hervey, in this volume.
[6] As Article 119 contains no specific reference to indirect pay discrimination, it took the decision of the European Court in Case 96/80 *Jenkins* v *Kingsgate (Clothing Productions) Ltd* [1981] ECR 911, [1981] 2 CMLR 24 to hold that such discrimination was nevertheless contrary to European Law, unless the factor giving rise to unequal pay "had a manifest relationship to the services involved". This last principle, modified in subsequent cases, is functionally equivalent to, in UK law, the defence of justification to a claim of indirect sex discrimination under s1(1)(b) of the Sex Discrimination Act 1975, and to the defence of genuine material factor in s1(3) of the 1970 Equal Pay Act.
[7] Article 119 as interpreted by Case 43/75 *Defrenne* v *Sabena* [1976] ECR 455, [1976] 2 CMLR 98; Equal Pay Act 1970 s1(4).

engaged on like work.[8] The more radical approach seeks in some form for equality of outcome. In British anti-discrimination law this dichotomy is somewhat concealed in that at first sight indirect discrimination appears to be concerned with outcomes. Deeper analysis suggests, however, that it may be no more than a rather sophisticated challenge to traditional procedural arrangements.[9]

The caution about a results approach to job allocation is because it seems necessarily to lead to a quota system. A parallel conceptual problem arises in relation to equal pay for work of equal value[10] – are we concerned with equality at the micro level of the individual employer or at the macro level of society? Should all those doing the same jobs, whether male or female, be paid the same? While it is clear that on average women in all Member States earn very substantially less than men[11], it does not follow that the reason for such inequality is *necessarily* discrimination – in any of its many different possible meanings. Very many women work in low-paying all female firms, but it is difficult to attribute such pay levels to discrimination by their particular employer. Even if such pay levels are the result of discrimination in society generally, it is not self-evident that individual employers should bear the brunt of tackling such discrimination. In addition, utilising the conceptual tool of discrimination may be far more complex and inefficient than tackling the problem more directly by such means as a national minimum wage[12], which falls equally on all employers rather than being left to the vagaries of litigation, and where the alleged undue cost burden on employers can be resolved at the appropriate macro economic and political level.

Current equal pay law only permits an argument that there should be equality between employees employed by the same employer.[13] This may do little to reduce the overall *inequality* in pay between men and women. For example, despite the apparently impressive gains won by British female local authority manual workers through job evaluation[14], their overall position in the national pay hierarchy deteriorated.[15] For this reason many argue that a means should be found to enable cross-establishment comparisons to be made, though no one underestimates the practical problems involved in so doing, and there must be doubts whether such an approach is compatible with the conventional framework of individual litigation.

---

[8] See Snell, Glucklich, Povall, *Equal Pay and Opportunities: A Study of the implementation and effects of the Equal Pay Act and the Sex Discrimination Act in 26 organisations* (1981).
[9] See, for example, Lacey, "Legislation against Sex Discrimination: Questions from a Feminist Perspective" 14 JLS (1987), 411–421; Gardner, "Liberals and Unlawful Discrimination" 9 OJLS (1989), 1–22; Morris, "On the Normative Foundations of Indirect Discrimination Law: Understanding the Competing Models of Discrimination Law as Aristotelian Forms of Justice" 15 OJLS (1995), 199–228.
[10] See Ellis, in this volume.
[11] Rubery and Fagan, *supra* n 4 at 154–161.
[12] See Wilkinson, *Why Britain needs a Minimum Wage* (1992); Rubery, *The Economics of Equal Value* (1992) 25–7.
[13] Equal Pay Act 1970 s1(6). See *Leverton v Clwyd County Council* [1989] 1 CMLR 574 (HL); Case 129/79 *Macarthys Ltd v Smith* [1980] ECR 1275, [1980] 2 CMLR 205 (ECJ).
[14] See Bercusson, in this volume.
[15] Rubery, *supra* n 12 at 30.

It is contended that it remains important to root equal pay law – as opposed to other measures designed to reduce pay inequality and low pay – in a theory of discrimination rather than one of inequality. Nevertheless, it is entirely rational to conclude that the failure to grant equal pay for work of equal value is presumptively discriminatory in the same way as a practice with adverse impact. Furthermore, the difficulty and complexity involved in establishing a link between a particular factor, such as experience or qualifications, and actual pay levels, means that a significant difference in average pay should be sufficient to raise a prima facie case.[16] However, just as an employer may justify prima facie indirect discrimination, so may an employer show that the unequal pay is explained by a genuine material factor which is not the difference in sex. This requires the employer to show not just that there was no discriminatory intent but also that the adverse impact of its payment system on women was not justified.

(iii) The legal principles

The leading case on the defence is the decision of the European Court in *Bilka-Kaufhaus GmbH* v *Weber von Hartz*.[17] The ruling applies to the objective justification of any pay practice for economic reasons. The key holding was that such a practice must "meet a genuine need of the enterprise", must be "necessary for that purpose", and must "be suitable for attaining the objective pursued". Thus, the employer must establish that the practice under scrutiny was introduced for a good reason (the "ends" test), that the practice will in fact achieve such purpose (the "means" test), and that, even if the above two are satisfied, that the means chosen are appropriate and suitable for attaining the end (the "proportionality" test). This test has been followed in subsequent decisions, none of which cases has challenged the basic correctness of the requirement for objective justification.[18] One problem is that each of the three elements gives great scope for impressionistic decision-making which may depend on the Court's overall sympathy with the employer defendant.

At a British domestic level, on the other hand, this objective "close-fit" approach has competed with a less onerous "rational relationship" approach, exemplified by cases such as *Boozer*[19], *Calder*[20], the Employment Appeal Tribunal in *Enderby*[21] and the Court of Appeal in *Ratcliffe*.[22] I am taking for granted

---

[16] Case C-127/92 *Enderby* v *Frenchay Health Authority* [1993] ECR I-5535. It was not for the applicant to explain the reason for the disparity. How far this would also be true where the applicant's statistics were less clear-cut remains to be seen. But the Court took a different, more restrictive approach, in Case C-400/93 *Royal Copenhagen*, Judgment of 31 May 1995. See Hervey, forthcoming *JSWFL*.

[17] Case 170/84 [1986] ECR 1607, [1986] 2 CMLR 701.

[18] Apart from cases cited below, see, for example, Case C-360/90 *Arbeiterwohlfahrt der Stadt Berlin* v *Bötel* [1992] 3 CMLR 446; Case C-57/93 *Vroege* v *NCIV Instituut Voor Volkshuisvesting BV* [1994] ECR I-4541, Case C-128/93 *Fisscher* v *Voorhuis Hengelo* [1995] 1 CMLR 881.

[19] *Reed Packaging Ltd* v *Boozer* [1988] ICR 391, [1988] IRLR 333 (EAT).

[20] *Calder* v *Rowntree Mackintosh Confectionery Ltd* [1993] ICR 811 (CA).

[21] [1991] ICR 382.

[22] [1994] ICR 810, reversed by the House of Lords, [1995] 3 All ER 597.

that this latter approach is both wrong in principle and contrary to European Law.[23]

The main thrust of this chapter is thus to discuss precisely what the *Bilka* defence requires where it is claimed that some aspect of the labour market necessitated the payment structure under attack. In order to do this, consideration must be given to the way in which wages are fixed and the purpose of particular payment arrangements. Neither the European Court nor British courts have so far given more than very general guidance as to the proper approach, especially as the European Court has made it clear that the actual resolution of this factual question is for national courts. It will be contended that it is necessary to give the strictest scrutiny to a claim of labour market necessity – in particular where the employer is seeking to justify a long-established practice. But it will also be contended that there is no point in erecting a test which can in practice never or virtually never be satisfied. There is little merit in pushing employers towards avoidance mechanisms. Making it practically impossible ever to defend such claims may not advance the cause of women's overall pay equality.

There are two broad categories of case. The first concerns the operation of the employer's internal labour market and covers issues such as seniority, merit payments and productivity bonuses. Proof of justification here is by no means straightforward, but at least the scope of the enquiry is limited to the employer's operations. If we turn to external labour market considerations, even this relative advantage is missing. The argument is that unequal pay is necessary either to prevent the employer suffering economically because of a cost overrun or to enable the most productive employees to be hired. The stringency of the proof required is problematic: on the one hand reference to the external market cannot be permitted to re-incorporate factors which have led to the systematic under-payment of women; on the other hand there is no gain – at least in the short-term – in requiring the payment of wages beyond the employer's economic capacity.

(iv) The operation of the labour market

It is contended that, at least so far as litigation is concerned, there is no such thing as "the market". For economists, the market is an aggregation of the behaviours of actors who are presumed to be free to choose how to act. Thus, the market is an essentially descriptive concept. It pays no regard to the reason choices are made, and, *a fortiori*, is not concerned with their rights or wrongs.

---

[23] See Kilpatrick, "Deciding when Jobs of Equal Value can be Paid Unequally: an Examination of s1(3) of the Equal Pay Act 1970" 23 ILJ (1994), 311–325. She concludes at 319, that "the predominant tendency in British case law . . . is . . . to accept a factor which plausibly explains some of the difference in pay as accounting for all of it and discouraging both tribunals and applicants from trying to pin down the relationship between the particular factor and the amount of the variation in pay".

There is no logical reason why the operation of a particular market may not reinforce women's inequality. As any anti-discrimination legislation aims to change the behaviour of market actors, reference to market activity without more is clearly no defence.

Furthermore, because it is an aggregate of behaviours, market theory cannot by itself explain the behaviour of an individual actor. Rubery argues that:

> economic theory . . . suggests that there is a considerable area of indeterminacy surrounding pay determination and that many different payment structures and payment systems can be designed within the overall constraints of ensuring a reasonable return on investments and training.[24]

In addition, Clegg found that "while there was usually little difficulty in forming an impression as to whether a given type of labour is tight or plentiful, measurement is another matter".[25] Moreover,

> the decline of some industries and the expansion of others . . . normally occurs . . . without any large inducements in the form of exceptionally higher earnings in the expanding industries. The main mechanism is simply that the expanding industries offer more vacancies than the declining industries at the going rate of pay.[26]

Rubery concludes that "the differential between men's and women's wages has been too constant over long periods of varying demand for it to be explained by the interaction of supply and demand curves".[27] These approaches seek to demonstrate that pay is regulated more by institutional factors than by the classical economic model of supply and demand, that these very factors may incorporate discrimination, and that therefore such factors require to be justified as any other indirectly discriminatory factor.

The concept of the market is fundamentally ambiguous. At one level it refers to those factors regarded by employers as worthy of reward, such as seniority, qualifications and individual performance. In a sense there is a "market" in these qualities, yet the second meaning relates to the supply of, and the demand for, workers irrespective of their personal qualities. A third meaning, hardly discussed in litigation but significant in Governmental thinking, relates pay to the employer's ability to pay, which may be affected by profitability or by cash limits. Each argument may become the defence to an equal pay claim, and each must be tested by the objective standard outlined above. Labelling a defence based on "market forces" does not change the applicable legal rules, both because the very concept is ambiguous and because in policy terms the defence should be tested by the same standard.

---

[24] Rubery (1992), *supra* n 12 at 23.

[25] "Standing Commission on Pay Comparability, Report No.1", Cmnd 7641 (1979), para 25. This was written at a time of full employment, when collective bargaining was more prevalent and when there was less variety in payment methods. If anything, the point is surely even stronger in the 1990s.

[26] Sapsford and Tzannatos, *The Economics of the Labour Market* (1993), 204.

[27] Rubery, (1992), *supra* n 12 at 7.

There is a common link, however, in that the concept of equal pay for work of equal value is concerned with assessing the job not the worker, and does so by reference to the depersonalised qualities required for that job. The notions of the market, whatever their differences, all seek to fix pay by reference to criteria apart from input to the job, whether that be qualities of the workers concerned, particular objectives of management, such as flexibility or individual pay determination, the availability or non-availability of suitable workers, or the overall profitability of the enterprise.

The use, or desired use, of the notion of market forces also has a political meaning. British opposition to labour market regulation relies on a *faith* that such regulation is harmful to job creation, though it has been frequently argued that this view has little or no empirical foundation.[28] While this view is strongest in the United Kingdom, the remainder of the EU is not immune to its influence. This chapter concerns judicial decisions which have the potential for wide impact at the level of the political economy; it is not surprising that that political context may sometimes appear to influence judicial reasoning and outcomes.[29] Again, the focus of this chapter is on those very judicial decisions, always while querying the appropriateness of such a forum to make them.

The unspoken assumption appears to be that there is a uniformity in the way wages are fixed based on the universal, immutable economic laws of supply and demand. In reality systems vary at three levels at least; between Member States; within Member States; and within individual enterprises.

First, payment strategies tend to differ between Member States. For example, Germany tends to value qualifications while France places greater weight on seniority.[30] The concept of the single market in goods and services entails that the market should operate in the same way, valuing the same features, in each Member State. Even if that could be attained for the labour market, it is not self-evident that such an objective is desirable for payment structures, given the variation in the social meaning of wage structures between different countries. Equal value law needs to work within such social expectations and not against them.

Not only are there differences between countries[31], there are also significant differences within countries, even between similar employers. One employer might operate an internal labour market characterised by high investment and training and a well-established career structure; another might invest less in training and prefer to "buy in" already trained employees.[32] At a level of individual

---

[28] See, for example, Deakin, "Labour Law and Industrial Relations" in Mickie, *The Economic Legacy 1979–1992* (1992), 19; see also *R v Secretary of State for Employment, ex parte Equal Opportunities Commission* [1992] ICR 301 (DC); [1995] 1 CMLR 391, [1994] ICR 317 (HL).

[29] For a decision of the European Court which appears to accept a lower standard of justification because of the supposed particular economic constraints on small businesses, see Case C-189/91 *Kirshammer-Hack v Sidal* [1994] IRLR 185, noted by Hervey at 23 ILJ 267 (1994). See also Case C-399/92 *Stadt Lengerich v Helmig* [1994] ECR I-5727.

[30] Rubery and Fagan (1993), *supra* n 4 at 111–113; Rubery (1992), *supra* n 12 at 68.

[31] See Barnard, in this volume.

[32] Rubery (1992), *supra* n 12 at 41.

litigation it would be inappropriate to describe one policy as better than the other.

Thirdly, employers frequently have different approaches to pay covering different areas of the workforce: "Most organisations have several different pay structures and each pay structure tends to be dominated by either male or female dominated jobs".[33] Again it is contended that it is both undesirably interventionist and beyond the objective of equal value legislation to require uniformity of approach. For this reason, enterprise-wide job evaluation schemes, even gender sensitive ones, are not a universal panacea. However, employers should be required to justify different approaches, a task very many will fail if the structures have developed without proper planning and the exercise of deliberate choices.

Payment systems are enormously variable in their aims, their methods, and in the degree to which they have been thought through and planned. It is contended that equal value law must accept this reality and not attempt to force employers into a pay straightjacket by seeking a universal, cross-establishment or cross-border system of comparison. Even if this could be achieved via litigation, it would be undesirably interventionist at the social and economic level. Employers should nevertheless be required to justify the systems they do utilise; the precise nature of that burden is the subject of the last section of this chapter.

(v) The Bilka Test in action

(a) The employer's objective

It is a major contention of this chapter that the law should exercise reasonable deference to the payment *choices* made by employers, even those which have an adverse impact on women, though the *degree* of adverse impact will be significant. A key caveat to this point is that they should indeed be choices. The labour market is characterised by ill-thought out and ill-planned behaviour, where payment strategies may simply reflect long-standing tradition or what other similarly-situated employers habitually do. It is central to the operation of an appropriately balanced equal value law that employers are not permitted to engage in *ex post facto* rationalisations or justifications for their payment strategies.[34] Deference should be paid to choices, but the employer should face the burden of showing that such a choice was indeed made. This approach prevents women from continuing to be victims of historically discriminatory structures reproduced without thought, while at the same time permitting innovative approaches to pay.

Employers should therefore be required to produce evidence of how such decisions were taken and why. That this may require them to disclose the

---

[33] Rubery (1992), *supra* n 12, 104.
[34] This is a major reason why the decisions in *Boozer, supra* n 19, and *Calder, supra* n 20, are ill thought-out.

internal workings of the firm, internal memoranda, etc is inevitable. This goes beyond the requirement of transparency laid down in *Danfoss*,[35] which concerned openness in the implementation of decisions rather than in the prior decision to utilise particular criteria.[36] Indeed, greater openness in pay is essential to enable courts to make, and to be seen to make, a fair assessment of an equal value claim, given that in the end such decisions are impressionistic rather than scientific or purely logical.[37] The detailed facts on pay are necessary for a strict scrutiny, in the literal sense, to occur.

The requirement to demonstrate a specific choice may be particularly problematic in two situations: where there is collective bargaining over pay and where seniority systems have become an entrenched part of the social structure. Collective bargaining implies joint decision-making and compromise, so it may not be possible for employers to reveal their own internal mechanism by which a decision was taken. In fact, though, bargaining is more likely to be over the means of implementing a strategy than its very existence. If the union does persuade an employer to introduce, for example, a bonus scheme with adverse impact, the employer must fail as the reason for the implementation will not relate closely enough to the needs of the enterprise. It should be a basic aim of the law to force employers to consider *in advance* the equality consequences of their payment strategies; concessions to a union for the sake of compromise cannot provide a defence.

Again, it should not be a defence that seniority has traditionally been rewarded or that the unions have insisted upon it. It should be a potential defence that the reward of seniority was, for example, designed to reduce labour turnover or to reduce initial training costs. Where seniority systems are widely used in a Member State and have thereby come to reflect a social consensus, the reason for their use is likely to be a belief that older workers should be paid more. In such circumstances part-time workers should be equally covered; failure here will contravene Article 119. Apart from this situation, it is inappropriate to use equal pay law to challenge one of the essences of a national payment system, one which may have a declining adverse impact on women. Here, as opposed to its use to reward increased productivity, the use of seniority is insufficiently within the control of an individual employer to be appropriate for challenge at that level. This view is, of course, highly problematic, as it depends on the acceptance of a social consensus on pay which may be changing and may be unmeasurable. It is nevertheless contended that, at a time when women are acquiring greater seniority, it would be perverse and over-interventionist to hold that rewarding seniority was normally impermissible.[38] This is in line with

---

[35] Case 109/88 *Handels-og Kontorfunktionaerernes Forbund i Danmark v Dansk Arbejdsgiverforening (acting for Danfoss)* [1989] ECR 3199, [1991] 1 CMLR 8.
[36] On this approach the decision in *Byrne v The Financial Times Ltd* [1991] IRLR 417 (EAT), where disclosure was refused to an applicant seeking information on the way in which the pay of comparators was made-up, must be regarded as wrongly decided.
[37] Rubery and Fagan (1993), *supra* n 4 at 238, argue that rights to information may be as important as any policy measures in stimulating action on equal value.
[38] Rubery and Fagan (1993), *supra* n 4 at 127–9, 203.

Nimz[39], where the European Court simply said that the objective justifiability of length-of-service based criteria is a matter for national courts and depends on the circumstances of each individual case. These must be proved and may not simply be assumed, though again little guidance is given as to the precise mechanics and burden thereby placed on employers.

In all situations, the employer should be required to spell out the objective of the challenged pay practice. It should not be enough to allege "increased productivity" or "lower costs"; to prove the objective the employer should have to show how the decision was taken and why it was thought that the supposed benefit would result. That this must be quite specific is shown by the ruling in *Rinner-Kühn*[40] where it was held that average pay differentials could not be based on "generalisations about certain categories of worker" – the criteria were neither objective nor specifically related to the individual complainants.

(b) The means used to reach the objective

If there is no question of *ex post facto* rationalisations, the court should normally be unwilling to strike down the very objective of the employer. More problematic for the court is the question of whether the means chosen will indeed achieve the objective. Does a bonus scheme lead to greater productivity? Does a seniority system reduce turnover? Is it necessary (or was it when the decision was made) to offer higher pay to attract suitable workers?

I take it for granted that, in all the above cases, proof will not and probably cannot be forthcoming which would satisfy any kind of scientific burden of proof. In these circumstances, the question of what level of proof should be regarded as sufficient is central to the operation of the justification defence.[41]

Both the European and British courts now claim to apply reasonably stringent standards. In the former case that has in fact never been in doubt since *Bilka-Kaufhaus*. The British courts have manifested numerous examples of an all-too-easy assumption that the employer's – or the Government's – aims will be attained by the means employed.[42] That period has surely been terminated by the House of Lords in the *Equal Opportunities Commission* case[43] and by *Ratcliffe*.[44] There are many situations where proof of the requisite causal connection is clearly inadequate. It is much harder to define the minimum level to establish adequacy. The task is not made easier by the principle of the European Court that, while an objective standard must be used, applying that standard to the facts is always a matter for the national court.

---

[39] Case C-184/89 *Nimz* v *Freie und Hansestadt Hamburg* [1991] ECR I-297, [1992] 3 CMLR 699.

[40] Case 171/88 *Rinner-Kühn* v *FWW Spezial Gebäudereinigung GmbH* [1989] ECR 2743.

[41] In relation to indirect discrimination as opposed to equal pay, see Townshend-Smith, "Justifying Indirect Discrimination in English and American Law: How Stringent should the Test Be?" *1 International Journal of Discrimination and the Law* [1995] 103–129.

[42] See, for example, *Reed Packaging Ltd* v *Boozer, supra* n 19, the EAT in *Enderby, supra* n 16, and especially the Divisional Court in the *EOC* case, *infra* n 43.

[43] [1995] 1 CMLR 391, [1994] ICR 317.

[44] *Ratcliffe* v *North Yorkshire District Council* [1995] 3 All ER 597 (HL).

Transparency is clearly required, as held in *Danfoss*.[45] The court stated that the employer could "justify the remuneration of adaptability by showing it is of importance to specific tasks . . .". For the same reason, an employer may pay more to employees who have undergone a course of vocational training.[46] It follows that the employer must show that employees knew the applicable criteria in advance in order to establish a correlation with increased performance. Beyond that, there must be a system for measuring performance which is both objectively and consistently applied, which may cause problems especially in relation to higher level jobs where accurate measurement of performance is often not possible. Employers should be required to produce statistics where these are logically relevant. If it is claimed that productivity would be improved, the methods used for its assessment must be demonstrated. Similarly, the employer should be required to show how, for example, qualifications and work performance, or bonus payments and absenteeism are linked. To re-iterate, this cannot be done at a scientifically satisfactory level of proof, but, where appropriate, reasonable effort must be made. It is especially important in relation to performance-related pay, which carries an obvious risk that subjectivity may perpetuate gender pay inequalities.

However, if this approach were applied literally, employers would be unable to introduce changes to their payment systems which had an adverse impact until those changes had been shown to be effective in attaining the required purpose. This is to impose an unrealistic, often impossible, standard. Reference to the experience of other employers is neither necessary nor sufficient proof of the causal connection. Employers must be permitted to innovate, without proof of effectiveness, if the possible adverse impact is considered and if it can be shown that the attainment of the objective is a reasonably plausible consequence.

There is a further reason for stressing the procedures by which pay changes are introduced. Most strategies do not necessarily operate to the average disadvantage of women in all circumstances.[47] If a policy is carefully developed and the consequences for women are specifically articulated, it will probably transpire that there is, at least at the level of the individual employer no, or no significant, adverse impact.

Turning to external labour market arguments, objective proof may be even more problematic, and the possible adverse impact far more serious. That is why such arguments must receive the strictest scrutiny. It is here that the historic labour market discrimination against women is thrown into sharpest relief. Those presently on higher wages whom the defendant employer might wish to attract are more likely to be male; those on lower wages with whom such employer may need to compete are more likely to be female. The European

---

[45] Case 109/88, *supra* n 35.

[46] On re-hearing by the Danish arbitration court, the seniority defence failed as, over a five-year period, average differences between men and women had increased whereas seniority differences had decreased. See Precht, 21 ILJ (1992), 323–325.

[47] See Rubery and Fagan (1993), *supra* n 4 at 126–153, for a helpful discussion of different payment strategies and systems and their potential benefits and disadvantages for women.

Court in *Enderby* held that market forces *may* be a defence, that there should be apportionment should the defence prove a partial explanation of the pay disparity, but that, once more, these were fundamentally matters for national courts to decide.

In *Rainey* v *Greater Glasgow Health Board*[48] the desire to persuade private sector prosthetists to transfer to the new state scheme was to ensure the latter was as efficient, attractive and reliable as possible. It would be impossible to establish the truth of this assertion; it is nevertheless contended that it is sufficiently self-evident that a new service would benefit by employing those with prior experience that it is right to conclude that the causal connection is made out. However, the court also accepted the need to maintain the inequality into the future. It may very well be that this pay protection was needed to secure the transfer, but the issue received inadequate consideration. In addition, no specific consideration was given to the issue of proportionality.

Similar reasoning can be applied to *Ratcliffe* v *North Yorkshire County Council*.[49] Noone seems to have questioned the defendant's assertion that failure to reduce the wages of the school dinner ladies would eventually have resulted in loss of the contract from the council Direct Labour Organisation to a private contractor with consequent job losses.[50] The real question is whether that is an appropriate and permissible response to the social problem of low female pay in heavily segregated areas of employment. Both these cases will therefore be re-examined below.

In these two cases the cause and effect is as clear as it is ever likely to be; they are of little assistance for more problematic cases. *Rainey* establishes that it is permissible to pay more than the properly evaluated rate to attract the desired employees. The link between pay and recruitment is insufficiently clear to be an automatic defence. The employer would need to prove that the target employees were the best available, an easy task in *Rainey* where there was only one available source for the defendants to tap. Where the choice is more individuated, the employer claiming to have identified the best potential employee, it is unlikely that proof of a real need to hire *that* employee, at a consequential higher salary, would be forthcoming. On the other hand, the more individuated the decision, the less the cause of the disparity is likely to be rooted in structural discrimination, and thus the less likely the employer's decision will be disproportionate.

---

[48] [1987] AC 224; [1987] 2 CMLR 11 (HL); see Schofield, "Equal Pay – What's the Difference?" 50 MLR (1987), 379–383; Townshend-Smith, "Equal pay and the material factor/difference defence" 16 ILJ (1987), 114–118.

[49] [1995] 3 All ER 597 (HL).

[50] The applicants were made redundant and subsequently re-employed by the council's Direct Labour Organisation at wages sufficiently low to enable the contracts in four of the six areas to be obtained. It was at this point that the claims were made. As the contract had to be fulfilled, it appears that the applicants and their colleagues were in no danger of losing their jobs and the contract going elsewhere, at least for the duration of the current contract.

(c) Proportionality – the degree of adverse impact involved

This is not, and cannot be, an issue of proof. It is a matter of the judgment of the court whether, if the employer succeeds in proving ends and means, the adverse impact on women is nevertheless so great – so disproportionate – that the employer's practice should be struck down. The degree of adverse impact is crucial here, both the degree of the disparity within the defendant's enterprise and the numerical impact of the practice on women's employment as a whole. While the proportionality principle is well known as a basic principle of European law, the details have not yet been fleshed out in equal pay cases. For reasons of space, discussion will be confined to *Rainey* and *Ratcliffe*.

The most significant factor in support of the applicants' claim in *Rainey* was that all those transferring from the private sector were male. However, to grant the applicants' claim would surely have led to consequential claims by other employees whose pay was settled in the same way – disruption to existing machinery is relevant when assessing proportionality. It is thus contended that the granting of higher pay to the new entrants was not disproportionate.

Ratcliffe is disappointing in that the House of Lords failed to give general guidance, confining the decision to the particular facts.[51] The House of Lords seemed to say that this kind of discrimination is prevalent, that it is the kind of behaviour the Act was designed to counter, and that therefore the employer's response was disproportionate even if understandable. The great significance is that the perpetuation of pay inequality in the most segregated and perhaps lowest-paid sector of the economy, the part-time service sector exemplified by work in cleaning and catering, is held judicially to be undesirable at a macro socio-economic level.[52] Certainly, this is not a case where low pay is due to concern for international competitiveness; rather, it reflects the demand for *any* job at a time of high unemployment.

Because *Rainey* and *Ratcliffe* are cases in the public sector, their impact will be wider and a conclusion on disproportionality easier to reach. This is also likely to be true whenever the claim is of adverse impact on part-time workers. Where the challenge is to the payment structure adopted by a single employer, as in *Danfoss*, a finding of disproportionality will be rarer. No such structure has an overwhelming adverse impact, at least at the macro level, and, if the employer proves ends and means, that should normally be sufficient.

Where reliance is placed on external market considerations, the employer's task is harder, for those considerations are more likely to reflect women's general employment inequality. In other words, the greater the degree of occupational segregation in the two jobs under comparison, looked at both in percentage

---

[51] It was held that the pay of school dinner ladies was reduced because they were women. But the key causal factor was surely not their gender but their job and thus, rather than the House of Lords' apparent use of direct discrimination analysis, the adverse impact approach seems more appropriate.

[52] For a wider discussion, see Collins' case-note on the Court of Appeal decision, "CCT, equal pay and market forces" 23 ILJ (1994), 341, 345.

terms and in the absolute number of employees concerned, the harder the employer's task. Where the comparison is between two employees and there is little or no element of structural discrimination, it is less likely that a tribunal would find lack of proportionality.

There is, however, a second aspect of proportionality: is the pay gap too wide based on an admittedly permissible and proved factor? *Enderby* holds that the fact-finder may conclude that the pay gap is disproportionate and reduce the disparity in consequence. This will occur rarely: if the pay gap is too large, it will be hard for the employer to establish that the procedures were adequate to satisfy the ends and means tests, especially the latter.

(vi) Conclusion

I am arguing for two basic propositions. First, it is incumbent on the employer to establish how pay decisions were taken, what the objectives were and why it was considered that the objectives would be met. Second, if the employer satisfies this admittedly rather stringent test, the defence should not fail because the employer cannot prove the case scientifically or statistically. In this way, the policies of equal pay legislation can be advanced whilst at the same time the employer is not faced with a burden of proof which is logically and scientifically virtually impossible to satisfy.

RICHARD TOWNSHEND-SMITH
Senior Lecturer in Law,
University of Wales,
Swansea, UK

Part II
EQUAL TREATMENT

Chapter 4

COMMUNITY LAW ON PREGNANCY AND MATERNITY*

(i) Introduction

Lucinda Findlay has argued that

> The fact that women bear children and men do not has been the major impediment to women becoming fully integrated into the public world of the workplace.[1]

The problems of handling this fact have focused sharply on the limitations of the equality model prescribed by equal treatment law, divided feminist jurisprudence and set an unenviable task for the courts in attempting to hold a balance between the needs of a responsible employer and the needs, not only of women, but of society as a whole.[2]

The European Union inherited a haphazard history on pregnancy and maternity protection. There was some disappointment with the Court of Justice's early response to requests to allow fathers a greater role in child care. In cases such as *Commission* v *Italy*[3], the Court accepted the Italian government's explanation for failing to grant parental leave to adoptive fathers on the same terms as the leave granted to adoptive mothers on the ground that there was:

> . . . a legitimate concern to assimilate as far as possible the conditions of entry of the child into the adoptive family to those of the arrival of a new-born baby in the family during the very delicate initial period.[4]

Similarly in *Hofmann* v *Barmer Ersatzkasse*[5] the Court was unresponsive to a request for paternity leave, arguing that the Equal Treatment Directive 76/207/

---

* This chapter was written by Erika Szyszczak.

[1] Findlay, "Transcending equality theory: a way out of the maternity and workplace debate" 86 *Columbia Law Review* (1986), 1118–1182 at 1119.
[2] A fact recognised in the House of Commons Health Committee Second Report *Maternity Services* Session 1991–92 (HMSO, 1992). *Cf.* the Government's response in the Employment Committee's Second Special Report (House of Commons Paper No 458 (1994–95)). See Fenwick, in this volume.
[3] Case 163/82 [1983] ECR 3273.
[4] *Ibid* para 16.
[5] Case 184/83 [1984] ECR 3047. See Curtin, *Irish Employment Equality Law* (1989) 80.

EEC[6] was not intended to deal with matters of family organisation or to "alter the division of responsibility between parents". However, as Docksey[7] points out, such litigation was instrumental in bringing about the revision of the national measures under scrutiny.

Initiatives proposed by the EC Commission on such issues as parental and family leave met with opposition in the Council of Ministers. It was not until 1991, when qualified majority voting could be used on matters relating to health and safety issues, that a common position was reached on Council Directive 92/85/EEC[8] giving some protection to women who are pregnant or have recently given birth. That Directive was a diluted version of the EC Commission's initial proposal.[9] The original minimum 16-week period of paid maternity leave became a 14-week period, not necessarily paid in full but merely at an adequate level defined as at least equal to the value of sick pay in the Member State concerned.[10] The Member State could make the right to sick pay conditional on a service qualification of up to 12 months. An obligation to assess whether working conditions represented a health and safety risk was transferred from the Member States onto employers and the provisions relating to night work were watered down.

The Court of Justice had already spelt out in *Dekker*[11] and *Hertz*[12] that because pregnancy is something which uniquely affects women, a dismissal or refusal to hire a woman because she is pregnant amounts to direct discrimination contrary to the Equal Treatment Directive, without the need to draw comparisons with how a man would be treated. This case law was codified in Article 10 of Council Directive 92/85/EEC. In arriving at this conclusion, however, the Court created a number of ambiguities which may cause further litigation on the interpretation of Article 10 of Council Directive 92/85/EEC and continue to question the commitment of the EC to protecting women at a time when they are most vulnerable.

Firstly, the Court of Justice has implied that the crucial issue in pregnancy discrimination is the employer's motive for his/her actions. This has already led to an Article 177 EC reference in *Webb* v *EMO Cargo (UK) Ltd*[13] when the House of Lords referred the issue of whether an employer could dismiss a woman employed on an indefinite contract but whose more immediate task was to provide cover for another women due to take maternity leave. Relying upon the

---

[6] OJ 1976 L 39/76.

[7] Docksey, "The Principle of Equality between Women and Men as a Fundamental Right under Community Law" 20 *Industrial Law Journal* (1991), 258–280 at 272.

[8] OJ 1992 L 348/1.

[9] See Burrows, "Maternity Rights in Europe – An Embryonic Legal Regime" 11 *Yearbook of European Law* (1991), 273–293; Cromack, "The E.C. Pregnancy Directive – Principle or Pragmatism?" 2 *Journal of Social Welfare and Family Law* (1993), 261–272. See also Kilpatrick, in this volume.

[10] *Supra* n 8 Article 11.

[11] Case C-177/88 *Dekker* v *Stichting Vormingscentrum voor Jong Volwassenen Plus* [1990] ECR I-3941.

[12] Case C-179/88 *Hertz* v *Dansk Arbejdsgiverforening (acting for Aldi Marked KS)* [1990] ECR I-3979. See More, "Reflections on Pregnancy Discrimination Under EC Law" 1 *Journal of Social Welfare and Family Law* (1992), 48–56.

[13] Case C-32/93 [1994] ECR I-3567.

interpretation of the Sex Discrimination Act 1975 under national law, the House of Lords was able to find that such action would amount to direct discrimination.[14] However, when examining the motive for the dismissal – in this case the motive given was that at the crucial time the applicant would be unavailable for work – the House of Lords reverted to making a comparison with the treatment given, or likely to be given, to a man in a comparable situation. Ostensibly to seek guidance from the Court of Justice on the implications of *Dekker* (and perhaps to invite the Court to reconsider the ambit of its ruling), the matter was referred under Article 177 EC. The Court ruled that the protection afforded to a woman during pregnancy and after childbirth cannot be dependent upon whether her presence was essential to the proper functioning of the employer's business. To adopt any other approach would render the Equal Treatment Directive ineffective. Equally the Court of Justice held that a comparison could not be made between the treatment of an actual or hypothetical man who was unable to carry out the work at the crucial time because of illness or some other reason otherwise the distinction drawn between illness and pregnancy in *Hertz* would be blurred.[15]

The result in *Webb* is not surprising and perhaps of transient importance in the employment field.[16] Had Council Directive 92/85/EEC been in existence at the material time, the national courts would have found Ms Webb's dismissal to be illegal. Given that the implementation period for the Directive expired on 19 October 1994, it was unlikely that the Court would give a ruling out of step with the principles relating to pregnancy and maternity protection contained in that Directive. The principle of *Webb* retains an importance for acts of discrimination outside the area of dismissal, such as discrimination in relation to terms and conditions of employment (for example, promotion, training, job flexibility opportunities); dress codes; occupational pay and benefits; and state social security. This is where pregnancy-related discrimination has been the focus of litigation in the United States[17], before the European Court of Human Rights[18] and even in the European Union post-*Dekker*.[19]

---

[14] See Bamforth, "The Changing Concept of Sex Discrimination" 56 MLR (1993), 872–880.

[15] The United Kingdom Government's submissions in *Webb* relied upon *Hertz* as showing that not every link between pregnancy and dismissal constituted direct sex discrimination. *Hertz* was handled by the Court, however, as an instance of dismissal on the grounds of *illness* not pregnancy. Such arguments are continuing to be pursued at the domestic level see *Brown* v *Rentokil Ltd* [1992] IRLR 302 EAT, currently on appeal to the House of Lords.

[16] One advantage of bringing a sex discrimination claim is that since the ruling in Case C-271/91 *Marshall (No 2)* [1993] ECR I-4367, the statutory limit on the amount of compensation for sex discrimination claims has been removed, allowing for higher awards of compensation, with interest for a successful claim. See Moore, and O'Keeffe, in this volume.

[17] See *Geduldig* v *Aiello* 417 US 484 (1974); *General Electric* v *Gilbert* 429 US 125 (1976).

[18] A/263 *Schuler-Zgraggen* v *Switzerland* [1993] 16 ECHR 405.

[19] Case C-342/93 *Gillespie* pending; Case General Roll No 15.527/88 Cour du travail, Liege. This was a dispute between an unemployed woman and the National Employment Office, where the latter had suspended the former's rights to unemployment benefit as a sanction when the woman had refused a suitable job and had restricted her availability for employment. At the interview the prospective employer had questioned the woman about her intentions relating to family life and the woman had answered that she hoped to have a second child. Although the Court found that the

Secondly, in *Hertz* the Court of Justice has drawn an arbitrary distinction between action relating to a woman's pregnancy and action taken after the pregnancy which may be equated with the treatment of an illness. In relation to the latter, Member States are given discretion to determine how long post-confinement protection should last[20] and, once this has elapsed, the traditional comparison with the treatment of a male employee may play a part in deciding if sex discrimination has occurred. *Hertz* is a difficult case to explain. Like the *Webb* litigation it is the classic trouble case of testing the parameters of law and politics. In *Hertz*, as in *Dekker*, the employer did not want to bear the economic consequences (in this case what was seen as excessive sick leave) of employing a mother. The case gives us a non-medical, male view of what represents normal pregnancy, childbirth and post-confinement recovery. For a woman who does not fit this normal model (she and/or her baby may have post-confinement problems) the protection of the law is partially removed. If we are beginning to recognise the special nature of pregnancy and motherhood, what justification is there for protecting a mother only before childbirth and not afterwards when she and her new born baby are equally as vulnerable?[21] Other than the fact that the former is of a finite period, the rationale for distinguishing between the two can only be on policy, that is, economic grounds – precisely those grounds rejected in *Dekker*. Another explanation of *Hertz* is that it introduces a justification or defence to what has already been accepted as *direct* discrimination by shifting the discrimination model's focus of inquiry back to the question of whether the alleged discriminatory treatment was based on sex discrimination. The issue of justifying direct discrimination will be suspended for discussion later.

(ii) Diluting the discrimination concept

(a) Temporary/fixed term appointments

One question which remains unanswered is the question of temporary, fixed term or specific task employees. Under Council Directive 92/85/EEC there is no qualifying period and the only derogation from the employment protection rights granted to pregnant women is to be found in Article 10(1):

> Member States shall take the necessary measures to prohibit the dismissal of workers, within the meaning of Article 2, during the period from the beginning of their pregnancy to the end of the maternity leave referred to in Article 8(1), save in

---

sanction was not justified it did state that "an employer remains free not to hire a person in consideration of family intentions". *Cf.* Case T-45/90 *Speybrouck v European Parliament* [1990] ECR II-705. Further examples are recorded in Senden, *Monitoring Implementation and Application of Community Equality Law 1993–94* (EC Commission, V/5728/95-EN, Brussels, March 1995).

[20] See Kilpatrick, in this volume.
[21] See Fenwick, and Kilpatrick, in this volume.

exceptional cases not connected with their condition which are permitted under national legislation and/or practice and, where applicable, provided that the competent authority has given its consent.

The employer must cite the grounds for such a dismissal in writing.

It was accepted that Ms Webb had been engaged on a permanent basis even though one of her functions was to replace an employee due to take maternity leave in the future. The *amicus curiae*, David Pannick QC, the EC Commission and the United Kingdom Government spent time in their submissions drawing what must be inherently wrong comparisons and analogies to spell out the perceived unfairness and inconvenience to employers taking on temporary staff for particular periods (Christmas, the Wimbledon fortnight) or choosing "employees" for crucial events such as playing cricket for England. Such comparisons were dealt with tersely by Advocate General Tesauro:

> Nor does it seem to me to be possible *a fortiori* to draw comparisons, although these were referred to in the course of the proceedings, between a woman on maternity leave and a man unable to work because, for example, he has to take part in a sporting event, even if it were the Olympic Games. Other considerations apart, a sportsman, even a champion (whether a man or a woman) is confronted with a normal choice reflecting his needs and priorities in life; the same cannot be reasonably said of a pregnant woman, unless the view is taken – but it would be absurd – that a woman who wishes to keep her job always has the option of not having children.[22]

In at least two Member States (France and Germany) a distinction is drawn between the rights of permanent staff and the rights of temporary staff taken on for a specific period or task. In another pregnancy dismissal case, heard shortly before *Webb*, *Habermann-Beltermann*[23], the Court of Justice underlines the fact that sex discrimination could be found because the employee was a permanent employee and that a different result might occur if there was only a temporary contract. Here the applicant had been engaged under a contract to work only at night in a home for the elderly. Soon after starting work she became ill and was found to be pregnant, the pregnancy having commenced before her employment. Under paragraph 8(1) *Mutterschutzgesetz* pregnant women were not allowed to carry out night work, thus making the contract void (for contravening the German statute) or voidable by the employer due to mistake. The Court of Justice reiterated the points made in *Dekker* and *Hertz* that the termination of the contract because of the applicant's pregnancy amounted to sex discrimination since it applied to female employees only. The Court then went on to draw a distinction between fixed term contracts and those of indefinite duration:

> In this case, the questions submitted for a ruling relate to a contract for an indefinite period and the prohibition on night-time work by pregnant women therefore takes effect only for a limited period in relation to the total length of the contract.

---

[22] Case C-32/93 *Webb*, *supra* n 13 para 14, 3576.
[23] Case C-421/92 [1994] ECR I-1657.

In the circumstances, to acknowledge that the contract may be held to be invalid or be avoided because of the temporary inability of the pregnant employee to perform the night-time work for which she was engaged would be contrary to the objective of protecting such persons pursued by Article 2(3) of the Directive, and would deprive that provision of its effectiveness. Accordingly, the termination of a contract for an indefinite period on grounds of the woman's pregnancy, whether by annulment or avoidance, cannot be justified by the fact that she is temporarily prevented, by a statutory prohibition imposed because of pregnancy, from performing night-time work.[24]

While the Member States were given a wide discretion to lay down provisions for the protection of pregnant women[25] the prohibition against night work in German law took effect for only a limited period in relation to the total length of the contract. Thus to allow the contract to be avoided or found invalid due to a temporary inability to perform the work would undermine the effectiveness of the Equal Treatment Directive and would be contrary to its objective of protecting pregnant women.

In *Webb* the Court also underscores the fact that the contract was of indefinite duration[26]:

In circumstances such as those of Ms Webb, termination of a contract for an indefinite period on grounds of the woman's pregnancy cannot be justified by the fact that she is prevented, on a purely temporary basis, from performing the work for which she has been engaged . . .[27]

This was an important factor in the ruling given by the House of Lords in October 1995, applying the Court of Justice ruling. Lord Keith argued that:

It is apparent from the ruling of the Court and also from the opinion of the Advocate General, that it was considered to be a relevant circumstance that the appellant had been engaged for an indefinite period. . . . The emphasis placed by the Court upon the indefinite duration of the appellant's contract of employment suggests the possibility of a distinction between such a case and the case where a woman's absence due to pregnancy would have the consequence of her being unavailable for the whole of the work for which she had been engaged.[28]

From this, can we infer, that at least for the purposes of a sex discrimination claim, temporary staff may be treated in a different manner from permanent staff? In applying the ruling in *Webb*, the House of Lords has held that sex discrimination may not occur where a woman is not engaged or dismissed in the situation where her pregnancy makes her unavailable for work for the whole of

---

[24] Case C-32/93 *Webb, supra* n 13 at paras 23–25.
[25] Under Article 2(3) of Dir 92/85/EEC Member States may prohibit women from engaging in night-work.
[26] Compare the situation in the Nordic countries; see Ryel, in this volume.
[27] Case C-32/92 *Webb, supra* n 13 para 27.
[28] [1995] IRLR 245; [1995] 4 All ER 577, 581 (HL).

the contract period. Arguably this is rather a narrow factual situation. It is submitted that the Court should not undermine the general principle that pregnancy discrimination is *per se* sex discrimination but it may be that in future litigation the Court may allow discrimination of temporary employees to be justified. This would be contrary to the more general policy employed by the European Union of seeking to improve the position of "atypical" workers.[29] One consequence of the ruling, however, is to provide an incentive for employers to take on employees on temporary rather than permanent contracts.

(b) Justification/defence of direct discrimination

The question of whether direct discrimination can be justified has been floating around a number of cases appearing before the Court of Justice. To date, however, the Court has not tackled the issue head on. The EC Commission in *Birds Eye Walls Ltd* v *Roberts*[30] argued that a bridging pension was directly discriminatory but the direct discrimination could be justified on the basis that the employer was attempting to achieve overall equality between the sexes by compensating for an inequality. Advocate General Van Gerven endorsed the EC Commission's submissions arguing that, since direct and indirect discrimination cannot always be distinguished from one another, it was not reasonable to argue that a justification for discriminatory behaviour may be restricted to cases of indirect discrimination only.[31] Ominously the Advocate General invited the Court to apply the idea of a justification to cases of pregnancy discrimination:

> . . . although dismissal on account of pregnancy indisputably constitutes direct discrimination the possibility must not be ruled out that such discrimination in a case such as *Webb* might nevertheless be justified having regard to the specific circumstances of the case.[32]

In *Birds Eye Walls Ltd* the Court ruled that there was no infringement of Article 119 EC thus avoiding addressing the question of a justification defence to direct discrimination.[33] Again, in *Webb*, the EC Commission put forward the submission that in some situations direct discrimination could be justified despite the fact that in *Dekker* the Court was adamant that direct discrimination can never be

---

[29] Council Directive 91/383/EEC (OJ 1991 L 206/19). Two further proposals have not been adopted but may be transferred to the Social Policy Agreement structure. At the Labour and Social Affairs Council Meeting of 6 December 1994, the Council adopted a Resolution on Equal Participation By Women in an Employment-Intensive Economic Growth Strategy Within the European Union. The Member States are invited to "develop policies for reconciling the obligations of family and work, including measures to encourage and facilitate greater involvement by men in domestic life".

[30] Case C-132/92 [1993] ECR I-5579. See also Case C-152/91 *Neath* v *Hugh Steeper Ltd* [1994] ECR I-6935.

[31] The United Kingdom Government, while arguing for the employer's case, objected to the idea that direct discrimination can be justified, fearing that the discrepancy between UK and EC law would cause uncertainty and increase the amount of litigation in this area.

[32] Case C-132/92 [1993] ECR I-5579.

[33] See Whiteford, in this volume.

justified. In *Webb* the Court hints at the possibility of acts of direct discrimination being justified in its comments in paragraph 27:

> In circumstances such as those of Ms Webb, termination of a contract for an indefinite period on grounds of the woman's pregnancy cannot be justified by the fact that she is prevented, on a purely temporary basis, from performing the work for which she had been engaged . . .

The use of the term "justification" is confusing in the context of direct discrimination. The idea of defending or justifying discrimination claims in EC law has arisen in the context of indirect discrimination (where justification is permitted also at the national level). The effect of "justification" in this context, however, is to establish that a difference in treatment which impacts more heavily on one sex is not in fact based upon sex but some other factor.[34] Thus, as a matter of principle, it is not possible to justify direct discrimination on the grounds of sex: such discrimination is, by definition, based upon sex and therefore prohibited. The fact that the discrimination is based upon sex makes it impossible to show that it is based upon some other factor. The Court of Justice has stated unequivocally that where the alleged discriminatory action is based upon a woman's pregnancy, this amounts to sex discrimination because of women's unique biological role. Where EC law allows forms of discrimination to continue, these are treated as *derogations* from the fundamental principle of equal treatment[35], and, as such, must be construed strictly and are subject to the principle of proportionality.[36]

(iii) Future litigation

It is unlikely that we have seen the end of litigation on pregnancy and maternity discrimination. The ambiguities which exist as a result of the case law to date have already been discussed. In applying the ruling in *Webb*, the House of Lords was able to construe Sections 1(1)(a) and 5(3) of the Sex Discrimination Act 1975 in a way so as to accord with the rulings of the Court of Justice. This was achieved by ruling that the pregnancy is not a circumstance relevant to the case within the meaning of Section 5(3). The House of Lords, however, entered a caveat that this may not be the case where a woman is engaged upon a fixed-term contract and her pregnancy prevents her from being available for work for the whole period of the contract. Whether this will take the action outside the ambit of Section 1(1)(a), or whether the courts will entertain the idea of a

---

[34] See Case 170/84 *Bilka v Weber von Hartz* [1986] ECR 1607; Case 171/88 *Rinner-Kühn* [1989] ECR 2743, where the Court held that the measures under challenge would be contrary to Article 119 EC unless they could be "justified by objective factors *unrelated to any discrimination on grounds of sex*" (my emphasis).

[35] See, for example, Article 2(2) of Council Directive 76/207/EEC. See also Hervey, *Justifications for Sex Discrimination in Employment* (1993).

[36] Case 222/84 *Johnston v Chief Constable of the RUC* [1986] ECR 1651.

defence to direct discrimination, remains to be seen. This uncertainty will most likely lead to further litigation on the status and interpretation of fixed-term contracts, as well as the scope of equal treatment law.

In the near future the Court of Justice will address the reference from the Northern Ireland Court of Appeal in *Gillespie and others* v *Various Health Boards and the Department of Health and Social Services.*[37] Here nurses have complained that sex discrimination in breach of Article 119 EC occurred because their pay was reduced and they did not receive the benefit of an increase in pay because of the way in which maternity pay was calculated. The applicants have argued that the purpose of a period of maternity leave, with security of employment, is to protect the mental and physical health of pregnant women or women who have just given birth. Such protection is inadequate and lacking in substance unless it is accompanied by the payment of full remuneration. If employers are free to make no payment at all to women who are absent from work during maternity leave or to make progressive reductions in payments or to exclude them from the benefit of pay increases, the protection afforded by maternity leave is eroded significantly. Pressures therefore increase, particularly upon the poorer members of the workforce to return to employment before the expiry of the maternity leave to which they are entitled.

The respondents have argued for a comparative approach claiming that *Dekker* turns very much on its own facts. The respondents maintain that the women received a package of benefits to which male employees were not and could never be entitled:

> They were paid at a substantial rate while they were performing no work for their employer. They retained security of employment . . .
>
> Prima facie women are receiving preferential treatment. Such treatment is a protected right under Article 2(3) of the Equal Treatment Directive and cannot at the same time be alleged to be discriminatory against women.

Advocate General Leger delivered an Opinion on 6 June 1995, concluding that neither Article 119 EC, Council Directive 75/117/EEC nor Council Directive 76/207/EEC require the Member States to pay a woman on maternity leave the full salary to which she would be entitled if she had been working normally.

It may be that some references under Article 177 EC emerge from the Ministry of Defence pregnancy dismissal litigation – on limitation periods, discovery and remedies[38], for example, the issue of exemplary and aggravated damages when

---

[37] Case C-342/93, nyr.

[38] See the comment by Nielsen, (29 CMLRev (1992), 160–169 at 169) that in *Dekker* the ECJ goes one step further in the established case law of the Court on the duty to interpret national law in conformity with EC law: "It would appear that *Dekker* implies that when sanctions (as opposed to the substantive content of the Directive) are concerned, there is a duty to set aside national provisions incompatible with the Directive also in litigations against a private employer and irrespective of whether the national court is given a discretion to do so under national law. In that respect the Court in *Dekker* goes further than in *Colson*".

the State acts as employer.[39] The human rights element of pregnancy discrimination[40] which was raised by the Counsel in *Webb* before the Court of Justice has also been under-explored.

An indirect attack may be made on the Sex Discrimination Act 1975 (Application to Armed Forces etc) Regulations 1994.[41] These Regulations are designed to amend section 85(4) of the Sex Discrimination Act 1975 and also to impose a limitation period upon any future claims of sex discrimination. The Regulations came into force on 1 February 1995.[42] However, a proviso is added in Regulation 2(a) that:

> Nothing in this Act shall render unlawful an act done for the purpose of ensuring the combat effectiveness of the naval, military or air forces of the Crown.

This is justified by reference to Article 2(2) of the Equal Treatment Directive[43] and Article 224 EC.

An argument runs[44] that the Regulations are contrary to the ruling in *Johnston* v *RUC*[45] in that applying the principle of proportionality the Member States must take measures which are appropriate and necessary for achieving a desired goal. Since Article 2(2) is a derogation from an individual right, it must be interpreted strictly. In *Commission* v *France*[46] the Court held that the exceptions contained in Article 2(2) may relate only to specific activities and they must be sufficiently transparent.

Article 224 EC may only be used to deal with exceptional and clearly defined cases.[47] In *Johnston* v *RUC*, for example, not even the conditions of emergency and terrorism which existed in Northern Ireland justified the use of Article 224. The Maternity Alliance invited the Equal Opportunities Commission to seek judicial review of the legality of the Regulations but, after taking legal advice, the EOC declined to do so. An indirect challenge could emerge, however, in the course of individual litigation.

---

[39] See Case C-48/93 *Factortame III* (OJ 1993 C 94/13) and Case C-46/93 *Brasserie du Pecheur* (OJ 1993 C 92/44) pending.

[40] See O'Leary, in this volume.

[41] *R* v *Secretary of State for Employment ex parte EOC* [1994] 2 WLR 409.

[42] See Case C-208/90 *Emmott* v *Minister for Social Welfare* [1991] ECR I-4269.

[43] Article 2(2) contains the following derogation: "This Directive shall be without prejudice to the rights of Member States to exclude from its field of application those occupational activities and, where appropriate the training thereto, for which, by reason of their nature or the context in which they are carried out, the sex of the worker constitutes a determining factor".

[44] See *Joint Committee on Statutory Instruments Extract from the Eighth Report Session 1994–95* HL Paper 27; HC 8 – viii. The Committee concludes that there appears to be a doubt as to whether the Regulations are *intra vires* and that they are so significant in embodying a policy choice in the formulation of the new exception to the Sex Discrimination Act 1975 that it would have been more appropriate to have made the Regulations subject to the draft affirmative procedure. See also the speech by Lord Lester of Herne Hill, HL Deb, col 852, 16 February 1995.

[45] Case 222/84 [1986] ECR 1651.

[46] Case 312/86 [1988] ECR 6315.

[47] Article 224 EC states: "Member States shall consult each other with a view to taking together the steps needed to prevent the functioning of the common market being affected by measures which a Member State may be called upon to take in the event of serious internal disturbances affecting the maintenance of law and order; in the event of war; serious international tension constituting a threat to war; or in order to carry out obligations it has accepted for the purpose of maintaining peace and international security". See Case 13/68 *Salgoil* [1968] ECR 453.

(iv) Final comments

EC law has addressed the issue of pregnancy and maternity protection from two directions – as a discrimination issue and as a health and safety issue. Both recognise the specific needs of women but arguably neither goes far enough. The *Dekker*, *Hertz* and *Webb* rulings are important in breaking the symmetry and comparative approach to equal treatment law and may be useful in reconceptu-alising discrimination law methodology.[48] David Pannick QC[49] asks why then are men not protected against sex specific discrimination – hernia operations, discrimination as a result of dress codes, for example, growing a beard. The short answer is that, at least for the present, growing beards is not seen as important as producing babies.

Several lawyers have criticised the *Webb* litigation for taking the issue of maternity protection to extremes. It is so rare, however, to find a situation where the employer is willing to state specifically that the reason for the dismissal of a pregnant woman is unequivocally on the grounds of pregnancy[50] that *Webb* provides an important precedent to test the parameters of law. Equally it serves to question whether discrimination law is the most appropriate medium for providing European society with a responsible approach to maternity provision and parenting.[51] Formulating the legal duty in a negative way provides no positive guidelines as to how employers should handle *maternity* and parental rights in a positive way[52]; for example, reproductive hazards for men, the length of maternity (and paternity) leave; the level and length of maternity pay; the conditions on return to work, and so on.[53] These are the really difficult *policy* decisions which are only partially addressed in Council Directive 92/85/EEC. The political complexity of negotiations at the European level will inevitably

---

[48] See Hervey, in this volume.

[49] "Sex Discrimination Law" 1994 Bar Conference, 1 October 1994.

[50] In the situation where the woman has been employed for a longer period of time, closer to the two year qualifying period for employment protection rights, employers will usually settle out of court if there is any possibility of the case being appealed on the issue of unlawful sex discrimination. Part-time workers now have greater protection in this area as a result of the House of Lords' ruling in *R v Secretary of State for Employment ex parte EOC* [1993] 2 WLR 409; The Employment Protection (Part-time Employees) Regulations 1995 SI 1995/31.

[51] *Cf.* the arguments of Mackinnon in relation to the role of sex discrimination law in factors biologically unique to women, *Feminism Unmodified* (1987) chs 2, 3.

[52] Arguably the limited protective nature of Council Directive 92/85/EEC and the tenor of the *Webb* and *Habermann* rulings, while recognising the unique biological role of women, continue to reserve the domestic role of parenting to women which leads to problems in labour market participation. See Fenwick and Hervey, "Sex Equality in the Single Market: New Directions for the European Court of Justice" 32 CMLRev (1995), 443–470; EC Commission's White Paper *European Social Policy – A Way Forward For The Union* COM(94) 333 V.B. "Reconciling Employment and Household/Family Life". See also the report of the Employment Committee, *Mothers in Employment*, First Report 1994–95 HC227.

[53] See Morris and Nott, "The Legal Response to Pregnancy Under EC Law" 12 *The Journal of Social Welfare and Family Law* (1992), 54–73; Conaghan, "Pregnancy and the Workplace: A Question of Strategy?" 20 *Journal of Law and Society* (1993), 71–92; Fredman, "A Difference With Distinction: Pregnancy and Parenthood Reassessed" 110 LQR (1994), 106–123.

continue in a piecemeal, haphazard way which, intertwined with the use of the Social Policy Agreement, greater use of soft law and the effects of subsidiarity, will not consolidate into a coherent form of maternity and parental provision in the European society of the future.

ERICA SZYSZCZAK
Senior Lecturer in Law,
London School of Economics and Political Science,
UK

Chapter 5

SPECIAL PROTECTIONS FOR WOMEN IN EUROPEAN UNION LAW*

(i) Introduction

The relationship between protective provisions and equality tends to elicit a complex and ambiguous response from feminists and from policy-makers, especially as such provisions may tend to raise questions as to the relationship between foetal rights and equal treatment for women.[1] On the one hand, forms of special treatment for one sex seem to sit uneasily with the principle of equality[2]; on the other, women's difference of situation may be seen as something to be emphasised in an effort to escape from enforced adherence to the male norm in the name of equal treatment.[3] The political context within which special protections operate adds complexity to the issue. Should they be viewed as an essential safeguard, a necessary regulatory mechanism in a free market economy affording recognition to women's particular situation, or should they be viewed as a matter of individual choice? Should it be assumed that a woman worker in the market-place acts as an autonomous individual able to make free choices as to acceptance of risk for herself and her unborn child?[4]

This chapter sets out to examine the relationship between the equality principle

---

* This chapter was written by Helen Fenwick.

[1] See Szyszczak, in this volume.

[2] See in particular, the Preamble to 1987 Communication on Protective Legislation for Women COM(87) 105 final of 20 March 1987 which suggests a recognition of the evils of forcing women to accept protections carrying with them the risk of a negative impact on employment.

[3] See Gilligan, *In a Different Voice* (1982); Mason, "Equal Rights Fails American Mothers: the limitations of an equal rights strategy in family law and the workplace", 5 Int J Law & Fam (1991), 211–240.

[4] See, for example, the decision of the American Supreme Court in *Johnson Controls* [1991] 111 S Ct 1196. There it was found that a policy of excluding women from posts involving a high risk of exposure to lead had a disparate impact on women (was indirectly discriminatory) and was unjustifiable on the basis that: "it is no more appropriate for the courts than it is for individual employers to decide whether a women's reproductive role is more important to herself or her family than her economic role. Congress has left this choice to the woman as hers to make".

and special protective provisions within the context of EC law. It will be suggested that the difficulties inherent in such a relationship are peculiarly apparent within that context, since the Community is committed to a social purpose which involves acceptance of the principles both of equal treatment and of special protection for women and for the unborn child.[5] The social purpose thus encapsulates arguably contradictory aims which must be realised within the context of the creation of the single internal market, by means of market forces.[6] Thus, social benefits are conceived of as a by-product of economic integration[7] and therefore contradictions inherent in the social purpose must be resolved within a context which may itself be out of harmony with it. The tension thus created is exacerbated, it is suggested, since the conflict between such contradictions has been rendered obscure by the uncertain conceptual framework created by Community law within which to view special protections. It is unclear whether they should be viewed as forming part of a set of essential maternity rights, or as derogations from the equal treatment principle which may, or may not, be susceptible to justification.[8]

In order to clarify the issues at stake this chapter will begin by outlining possible theoretical perspectives from which special protections may be evaluated, with a view to contending that they are reconcilable with the aim of safeguarding women's employment position in the market. The two main forms of protective provisions recognised under EC law (those applicable to women in general[9] and those relevant only to their reproductive role) will then be considered from the standpoints of the different models of equality put forward. The chapter will end by evaluating the part played by Community law, not only in rejecting and curtailing special protection in the name of progressive furtherance of sexual equality, but also, it will be argued, in obscuring the parameters of the conflict between the two principles.

---

[5] See Case 43/75 *Defrenne* v *Sabena No 2* [1976] ECR 455, paras 8–10. Commitment to special protection is explicit in the case of women, implicit in the case of the foetus and child in the Pregnancy and Maternity Directive (see *infra*), due to the parameters of Article 118A on which the Directive was based.

[6] See Treaty of Rome, Preamble and Articles 1–3. For debate as to the promotion of workers' rights within the context of general regulation of the European labour market see Henley and Tsakalotus, "Corporatism and the European Labour Market after 1992" 30 BJIR (1992), 567–586; Deakin and Wilkinson, "Rights vs Efficiency? The Economic Case for Transnational Labour Standards" 23 ILJ (1994), 289–310.

[7] This is exemplified in the case of harmonisation of a minimal level of employment protection provisions in order to create a "level playing field" of competition for employers in the Single Market. See, for example, Nielsen and Szyszczak, *The Social Dimension of the European Community* (1993) 2nd ed 15–18; Hoskyns, "Women, European Law and Transnational Politics" 14 *International Journal of the Sociology of Law* (1986), 299–315; Szyszczak, "Future Directions in European Union Social Policy Law" 24 ILJ (1995), 19–32. See also Hervey, in this volume.

[8] It appears that the court has taken the latter approach. See Kilpatrick, in this volume.

[9] The Equal Treatment Directive Article 2(3), which expressly governs protective provisions, has been interpreted in such a way as to recognise only protections relating to pregnancy and maternity (see *Johnston* v *Chief Constable of the RUC*, *infra* n 30), but they may also fall within Article 2(2), as *Johnston* makes clear. See also Kilpatrick, in this volume.

(ii) Special protections and models of equality

Some feminists have considered that women cannot expect special entitlements without risking the imposition of special protections. Williams argues that special treatment has great costs for women, since it permits unfavourable, as well as favourable, treatment of women where differences between women and men can be perceived.[10] Furtherance of equality, on this view, means treating like as like – formal equality. Under a formal equality model[11] a woman can expect equal treatment so long as she adheres to the male norm. However, in so far as she fails to adhere to that norm the employer may justifiably treat her differently.

Under the formal equality model all broad-based special protections, such as excluding women in general from dangerous or burdensome work, would be suspect as leading to treating two likes unalike, and as detracting from the autonomy of the individual in the market place. The point at which the limitations of the formal equality model are revealed is reached in relation to women's reproductive role. It might appear that pregnancy would require no special response in the workplace so long as the pregnant woman adhered to "normal" (male) working patterns. If she failed to do so she would be asserting her unlikeness (her difference of situation) and might be ill-placed to resist the imposition of coercive protections creating detriment to employment opportunities on the basis that no male equivalent was available (therefore an unlike could be treated unlike), or on the basis that a near-equivalence in male terms would also invite detrimental treatment.

However, the position within the formal equality model is more complex than this. Equivalence or sameness necessarily using the male as a referent can hardly be asserted in relation to the physical interests of the unborn child or in relation to the congruence between such interests and those of the mother. Therefore protections aimed at such interests would be accepted under this model. This may also be said in relation to protections aimed at the woman with a view to benefiting the unborn or newly-born child. At this point, formal equal ity confronts the conflict between appearance and reality which, it is suggested, it is unable to resolve. A pregnant woman may adhere (to outward appearance) to a male norm but the reality is that she carries a child whose interests may, again,

---

[10] Williams, "The Equality Crisis: Some Reflections on Culture, Courts and Feminism" in Bartlett and Kennedy, *Feminist Legal Theory*, (1991), 15–34. She is associated with a body of thought which views formal equality as a safeguard against coercive special protections. On this view, special entitlements are "traded in" in order to keep protective provisions at bay. As Williams puts it: "If we can't have it both ways we ought to think carefully about which way we want it" (*ibid* 26). In contrast, Morris and Nott consider that the danger of accepting coercive protective provisions might be fended off within a formal equality model, even while accepting some special entitlements, so long as the latter were viewed as methods of allowing women to overcome their "handicaps" (i.e. their ability to bear children). Such "handicaps" presumably encapsulate the biological difference between women and men: women are "handicapped" in so far as they differ from the male norm. Morris and Nott, "The Legal Response to Pregnancy", 12 *Legal Studies* (1992), 54–73 at 55.
[11] Under classic liberalism as expressed by Mill in *On the Subjection of Women* (1929).

apparently or in reality[12], be bound up with hers. Thus, in relation to pregnancy, formal equality provides a limited, narrow and, it is suggested, flawed means of evaluating the relationship between equality and special protections.

In contrast to the formal equality approach, some feminists have advocated different, "special", treatment on the basis that biological and social differences between men and women may therefore be recognised (the double standard argument).[13] This approach focuses on women's special nurturing role and insists that equality means equal valuing of "feminine" values and culture.[14] Advocates of this approach, while needing no urging to accept special entitlements, might be unable, due to their emphasis on the caring and non-aggressive role of women, to resist the policy-makers' broadly-based special protective approach reflected in many of the laws discussed below.

As MacKinnon has argued, it may be possible to escape from the unfruitful difference/equality dichotomy[15] by adopting a substantive, as opposed to a formal, equality model as a means of evaluating special protections.[16] Substantive equality rejects reliance on the male as the norm and therefore refuses to justify detrimental treatment of women arising from biologically or socially determined differences between women and men, particularly from women's role as child bearers. Superficially, such an approach appears to focus upon women's difference from men, and to call for special treatment for women arising from such difference since it does not assume that a woman's situation will be the same as that of a man. However, it recognises that focusing on a perceived vulnerability of women, particularly that arising from pregnancy, may be merely another route to a categorisation of women entailing disadvantage. Thus, substantive equality recognises difference of situation but demands that no adverse consequences should flow from such recognition; it recognises but does not perpetuate difference and therefore it will not condone taking choices from women and thereby restricting their access to employment.

Taking into account the drawbacks of special protection, it is submitted that a substantive equality approach is one which first redefines "special" treatment, and second seeks to extend both family-related entitlements and undeniably

---

[12] The child born, or unborn, has certain biologically determined interests but may also be perceived to have interests, such as an interest in a special relationship with the mother after birth, which are arguably wholly or partly socially determined.

[13] See MacKinnon, "Difference and Dominance: On Sex Discrimination" in Bartlett and Kennedy, *supra* n 10, 81–94 at 82.

[14] See, *supra* n 3.

[15] The opposing positions indicated owe something to the sameness/difference debate conducted by feminists in the 1980s which has been stringently criticised by MacKinnon as failing to escape from a male viewpoint (MacKinnon, "Reflections on Sex Equality under Law" 100 *Yale Law Journal* (1991), 1281–1328). However, as More observes, the legal discussion of equality, in relation particularly to pregnancy, is still ongoing: More, "Reflections on Pregnancy Discrimination under European Community Law" 1 JSFWL (1992), 48–56.

[16] MacKinnon argues that "the goal is not to make legal categories that trace and trap the *status quo* but to confront by law the inequalities in women's condition in order to change them". In other words, substantive equality may be achieved if courts are prepared to ask whether a particular categorisation creates disadvantage for women as a group. See MacKinnon, *Towards a Feminist Theory of the State* (1989).

beneficial protective provisions to men[17], while confining the latter to as narrow a scope as possible in so far as it is necessary for them to remain gender-specific. Under this approach protective measures genuinely needed to safeguard the foetus would be acceptable so long as they were framed in such a way as to be costless in terms of women's employment opportunities: the principle should be that the risk, rather than the woman, should be removed from the work-place.

(iii) Special protections as derogations from the Equal Treatment Directive

The latter half of the twentieth century has seen a narrowing down of the scope of the special protective provisions for women which largely emerged and developed in Western Europe in the early part of that century and the latter part of the nineteenth[18], partly as a result of International Labour Organization agreements. In its 1987 Communication on Protective Legislation for Women[19] the Commission examined a large number of such national and international protective provisions for compatibility with the Equal Treatment Directive[20], and found that they could be divided into those which were "anomalous"[21], those which were "humanitarian"[22] (work perceived as burdensome for women, such as night-work[23]) and those which were concerned with "health and safety"[24], including provisions control-ling exposure to certain substances. The lists compiled for the Commission[25]

---

[17] This model of equality would accept special entitlements as temporary measures, necessary until a legal regime fully internalising equal treatment is established. Under such a regime the word "special" would disappear from all but the few gender-specific entitlements based on clear biological impera-tives, such as leave for ante-natal care.

[18] See Creighton, *Working Women and the Law* (1979), 19–37 for an account of the development of protective legislation in the UK. For discussion of gender-specific protective labour legislation see Banks, *Faces of Feminism: A Study of Feminism as a Social Movement* (1981), chapters 7 and 9. It would be impossible here to provide a survey of the removal of protective restrictions in the Member States, but examples include the denunciation by Ireland, Luxembourg and the Netherlands of Convention No 89 of the ILO of 9 July 1948 in 1981, 1982 and 1972 respectively (see further Sciarra, in this volume).

[19] COM (87) 105 final, of 20 March 1987, 23.

[20] Directive 76/207/EEC (OJ 1976 L39/40).

[21] COM (87) 105 final, *supra* n 19 at 9: anomalous provisions included the measures on hygiene at the place of work requiring the provision of separate sanitary facilities.

[22] *Ibid* 10–15. These provisions included limitations on women's working hours by providing for a maximum daily or weekly working time, and on forms of strenuous work such as working in high temperatures.

[23] France, Belgium, Greece, Italy, Ireland, Luxembourg and the Netherlands ratified Convention No 89 of the ILO of 9 July 1948 which prohibits night-work by women. See further Sciarra, in this volume.

[24] COM (87) 105 final, *supra* n 19 at 15–18. These concerned exposure to harmful substances associ-ated with reproductive risks. It was found that they had been applied only to women, although some of the risks also affected male reproductive capacity and health.

[25] Lists of the protective legislation in the individual Member States (apart from Spain and Portu-gal) together with sections dealing with changes, prospective changes and information on ratifica-tion and denunciations of ILO Conventions are set out in the Annex to the Communication.

reveal the possibility of tracing a development from the broadly-based "humanitarian" protections which largely emerged in the early part of the twentieth
century to those adopted in the Member States in its latter half which tended to
be of a "health and safety" nature and to concern specific risks to reproductive
capacity and health.

All the protective provisions considered had certain characteristics which
brought them to a greater or lesser extent into conflict with women's employment opportunities. The "anomalous" and "humanitarian" provisions particularly tended to apply to unacceptably broad categories of women workers and to
operate coercively, leading directly or indirectly[26] to the exclusion of women
from particular areas of employment. They meant that women were excluded
from certain occupational areas or could not obtain access to certain types of
experience or training, and therefore tended to contribute to the grouping of
women in lower status areas of work. The Commission found that such measures
"may contribute to a marginalisation of women into 'atypical' forms of employment".[27]

It is suggested that, within the EU Member States, the process of reducing the
scope of such provisions owed something to internal increased demands for
equality of employment opportunities in those countries,[28] but that the impact
of the Equal Treatment Directive made a contribution to the pace of such
change. The Member States were enjoined under Article 5 to abolish measures
contrary to the principle of equal treatment and, under Article 5(2)(c), to consider whether protective measures in particular could still be viewed as being
well founded. This was echoed under Article 3 in relation to the conditions for
access to all posts at all levels of the occupational hierarchy.

Thus it appeared that such protective measures as remained unrevised or un-
repealed must be justified under Article 2(2) and 2(3) of the Directive. These
allow Member States to derogate from the Directive in relation to "occupational
activities . . . for which, by reason of their nature or the context in which they
are carried out, the sex of the worker constitutes a determining factor"; or in
relation to "provisions concerning the protection of women, particularly as
regards pregnancy and maternity".[29] The decision in *Johnston* v *Chief Constable of
the RUC*[30] went some way towards confirming this. The Court found, in that

---

[26] The Commission found (COM (87) 105 final, *supra* n 19 at 5) that the distinction between bans
on employment and protective working conditions was not as great in practice as would have been
expected. Both had negative effects on women's work.
[27] *Ibid* at 5.
[28] For example, in 1972 the Netherlands denounced ILO Convention No 89, banning women in
industry from night-work specifically on the grounds of its negative impact on women's employment opportunities.
[29] In full, Article 2(2) provides: "This Directive shall be without prejudice to the right of Member
States to exclude from its field of application those occupational activities, and where appropriate,
the training leading thereto, for which, by reason of their nature or the context in which they are
carried out, the sex of the worker constitutes a determining factor". Article 2(3) provides: "This
Directive shall be without prejudice to provisions concerning the protection of women, particularly
as regards pregnancy and maternity".
[30] Case 222/84 [1986] ECR 1651.

case, that the provisions in question must fall within Article 2(2) or 2(3) if they were to be justified; general justifications on grounds of public safety arising from the Treaty could not be permitted.[31] However, the Court confined its judgment to matters of public safety, appearing to leave open the possibility, which was pursued in *Commission* v *France*,[32] that implicit justifications other than those falling within the derogations could be permitted in relation to different interests.

The decision in *Commission* v *France* concerned, *inter alia*, direct discrimination in recruitment to the prison corps. It was found that recruitment to the lower grades of the corps fell within Article 2(2), since the specific nature of the post of warder and the duties to be carried out provided justification for reserving posts in male prisons to men and in female prisons to women.[33] However, head warders did not have to carry out such duties and therefore in relation to such posts the sex of the worker could not constitute a determining factor. The Court found that "having regard to the need to provide opportunities for promotion within the corps of warders"[34] justification for the discrimination could be found, thereby departing from the principle that only factors falling within Article 2(2) or 2(3) could provide such justification. That principle was, however, affirmed in *Dekker* v *Stichting Vormingscentrum Voor Jonge Volwassenen (VJV-Centrum) Plus*[35] but, as will be argued below, it has since been undermined.

The decisions in *Johnston* and *Commission* v *France* are also of interest since they indicate the stance taken by the Court in relation to transparency in justifications for direct discrimination. They thereby make some contribution to the transition in the Member States from broad-based special protections ("humanitarian" measures) to those based, in the view of the Commission, on "health and safety".

Johnston arose from the decision of the Chief Constable of the Royal Ulster Constabulary (RUC) that male officers, but not women officers, should carry firearms as part of their regular duties. This decision was taken on the basis that women would be more at risk of assassination than men and that women would be less effective in dealing with families and children if they were armed. Since armed officers were needed for security duties, the Chief Constable decided not to renew the contracts of women members of the RUC, including that of Ms Johnston. The Court found that Article 2(2) might in principle allow a wide derogation from the principle of equal treatment since "in a situation characterised by serious internal disturbances the carrying of firearms by policewomen

---

[31] Express or implied escape clauses could not be found in the EEC Treaty (paras 26–28, 60–61).

[32] Case 318/86 [1988] ECR 3559, [1989] 3 CMLR 663.

[33] The Commission did not consider the question whether this restriction on employment was itself non-transparent.

[34] Case 318/86, *supra* n 32 at 3580 para 17.

[35] Case C-177/88 [1990] ECR I-3941. For discussion of the scope of justification for direct discrimination see Ellis, "The Definition of Discrimination in European Community Sex Equality Law" 19 EL Rev (1994), 563–580 at 567–568; Hepple, "Can Direct Discrimination be Justified?" 55 EOR (1994), 48. See also Szyszczak, in this volume.

might create additional risks of their being assassinated and might therefore be contrary to the requirements of public safety".[36] It was permissible to take account of the context within which the activity in question took place in arriving at this conclusion. Thus the sex of the worker could be a "determining factor". However, the national court might only rely on this derogation if it ensured compliance with the proportionality rule. It was for the national court to determine whether proportionality had been observed and therefore the Court did not give an opinion on the matter.[37]

It is suggested that the special protective rules under scrutiny in this instance would be unjustifiable as a derogation from the equal treatment principle under a substantive, or probably, a formal equality model. They led directly to the exclusion of women from certain areas of employment and did not answer to a clear biological imperative. This seems to have been recognised in relation to Article 2(3) and so far the decision is compatible with a formal equality view. This decision also appears to favour formal equality arguments in its determination to confine Article 2(3) to a narrow scope, relating only to pregnancy and maternity. It turns its back, however, on such arguments in focusing on special female vulnerability in relation to Article 2(2). Its ready acceptance of the assumption that women were more at risk than men and that they should be confined to a narrow, family-oriented role epitomises the dangers of emphasising differences between the sexes. The Court did not appear to recognise that there was a contradiction in rejecting a potential basis for derogation on the ground that it was founded on socio-cultural considerations but opening the way to acceptance of another which appeared to be equally open to such criticism.

Thus, the justification used here in a case of *direct* discrimination, is open to the charge of non-transparency. The approach of the Court may be contrasted with that taken in relation to indirect discrimination. It has insisted on a rigorous scrutiny of the factors put forward to justify unequal pay and has rejected not only those which appear to be based on generalised assumptions about groups of (predominantly female) workers[38], but also those which resist scrutiny due to their lack of transparency.[39] The Court did not state explicitly in *Johnston* that justifications for direct discrimination must be transparent, but this was made clear in *Commission v France*[40] in relation to one of the exceptions to the non-discrimination principle put forward under Article 2(2).[41] This aspect of the

---

[36] Case 222/84, *supra* n 30 para 16.

[37] It implied that it had doubts as to whether the policy was proportionate in suggesting that Ms Johnston might be offered a full-time contract but assigned to other duties which did not involve her in carrying firearms (*ibid* para 9).

[38] See Case C-33/89 *Kowalska* v *Freie und Hansestadt Hamburg* [1990] ECR I-2591, [1990] IRLR 447. In Case 171/88 *Rinner-Kühn* [1989] ECR 2743, the Court found that national legislation based on general assumptions concerning part-time workers (who were predominantly women) which excluded such workers from sick pay was not in accord with the objectives pursued by Article 119.

[39] See the ruling in Case C-109/88 *Handels-og Kontorfunktionaerernes Forbund i Danmark* v *Dansk Arbejdsgiverforening (acting for Danfoss)* [1989] ECR 3199.

[40] Case 318/86, *supra* n 32.

[41] *Ibid* 3581 para 25.

decision concerned the quota method of recruitment to certain posts in the French national police and prison service which allotted only 10–30% of the posts to women.

The Court found that although certain activities within the police could properly be performed by men this fact could not provide justification for a system of recruitment which left it unclear whether the quotas operating for each sex actually corresponded to the specific activities for which the sex of the person in question constituted a determining factor. The lack of transparency (the fact that no objective criteria determining the quotas laid down were available) made it impossible to verify such correspondence. This part of the decision therefore left open the possibility of allocating men and women to different specific activities and thereby excluding women from certain areas of employment on grounds which, like those accepted in *Johnston*, were in themselves non-transparent, since the assumption that women police officers would be unable to carry out effectively activities intended to maintain public order was in itself untested. In effect, one non-transparent factor (the system of recruitment) cloaked another; as in *Johnston* the first such factor was rejected but the second accepted.

Although both these decisions contain elements which are consistent with a formal or substantive equality stance, both ultimately focus on notions of women's weakness and special vulnerability in accepting broadly-based justifications for direct discrimination. In this respect, they differ from decisions concerning the special protection of excluding women from night-work[42] which were, it is suggested, more fully influenced by formal equality arguments.[43] The general principle enshrined in these night-work decisions appears to be that, aside from the operation of Article 234 of the Treaty, a like must be treated alike. They leave open the way to different treatment for an unlike which was taken in *Habermann-Beltermann* v *Arbeiterwohlfahrt, Bezirksverband Ndb./Opf. eV.*[44] The decision concerned the consistency with Community law of the German *Mutterschutzgesetz* (MSchG)[45], paragraph 8(1) of which prohibits the employment of pregnant or breast-feeding women on night-work. When the employer was notified of the applicant's pregnancy, it relied upon the MSchG to dismiss

---

[42] See Sciarra, in this volume.

[43] See Case C-345/89 *Ministère Public* v *Stoeckel* [1991] ECR I-4047, which concerned a general ban on night-work for women, subject to exceptions which had originally been founded on notions of the physical and mental vulnerability of women to the consequences of night-work and on the need to encourage women to remain in the home in order to fulfil their social role (para 5). It was found that although a ban on night-work might be justified in the case of pregnancy or maternity, it could not be justified under Article 2(3) in order to protect women, since the risks run by women undertaking night-work were not inherently greater than those run by men. However, in Case C-158/91 *Ministère Public* v *Levy* [1993] ECR I-4287, and Case C-13/93 *Office Nationale de l'Emploi* v *Minne* [1994] ECR I-371, the Court found that although general restrictions on night-work for women would not be susceptible to justification within Article 2(3), the relevant national provisions could be maintained pursuant to Article 234 EC if they were necessary in order to ensure observance of international obligations incurred as part of an agreement with non-Member States concluded before the entry into force of the EC Treaty (ILO Convention No 89 of 9 July 1948).

[44] Case C-421/92 [1994] ECR I-1657.

[45] Law on the Protection of Mothers; 1969, BGBl, 315.

her by rendering the employment contract void. The Court confirmed that the termination of an employment contract on account of pregnancy constitutes direct discrimination on grounds of sex contrary to the Equal Treatment Directive[46], but it distinguished *Dekker*[47] by holding that the unequal treatment of Habermann-Beltermann was *not* based directly upon her pregnancy, finding that the termination of the employment contract resulted from the provisions of the MSchG.[48] Although the Court held that the MSchG itself was compatible with Community law, it concluded that the termination of Habermann-Beltermann's contract was not compatible with the Equal Treatment Directive[49] since the contract in question was not for a fixed term; the MSchG would therefore only apply for a limited period in relation its total length.

The Court assumed that the MSchG itself was consistent with the Community concept of non-discrimination on grounds of sex, as propounded by the Equal Treatment Directive, due to the derogations in respect of women's pregnancy and maternity under Article 2(3). This decision seems to have been based on the formal equality argument that two unlikes may be treated unalike: Habermann-Beltermann was pregnant; since there is no male equivalent, she could be treated adversely. It therefore reveals, as arguably the decision in *Johnston* does not, the limitations of the formal equality approach. What the Court failed to consider was whether the provisions of the MSchG themselves stand up to scrutiny. In the night-work decisions considered above, the Court rejected the argument that the exclusion of all women from night-work could be justifiable. The biological reasons for exclusion of pregnant women from night as opposed to day-work are unclear and, in so far as they exist[50], could be weighed up, it is suggested, against the stresses caused to a worker by dismissal and unemployment. Thus, the Court should have attempted to look behind the apparent justification underlying the MSchG. It is submitted that the Court's approach in *Habermann-Beltermann* is based upon a model of sex discrimination law which focuses upon women's difference from men and which is ultimately unsupportive of substantive equality. This is an approach which is seen as particularly appropriate in the case of pregnancy discrimination and which cannot readily be combatted by means of formal equality arguments.

The ruling in *Habermann-Beltermann* encapsulates, it is suggested, a view of equality which was to an extent foreshadowed in the conclusions of the Commission's 1987 Communication.[51] The Communication indicated the progress

---

[46] Case C-421/91, *supra* n 44, para 15.

[47] Case C-177/88 *Dekker* v *Stichting Vormingscentrum Voor Jong Volwassenen Plus*, *supra* n 35.

[48] Case C- 421/92, *supra* n 44, para 16.

[49] *Ibid* paras 24 and 25. This aspect of the decision is criticised by Fenwick and Hervey, "Sex Equality in the Single Market: New Directions for the European Court of Justice" 32 CMLRev (1995), 443–470 at 450–457.

[50] See "World Labour Report" (Vol 2, Labour Relations, International Labour standards, training, conditions of work, women at work, ILO, Geneva 1985 229) for the argument that lack of sleep and disturbance of biological rhythm may be more harmful for pregnant women than for other adults. It might be argued, on the other hand, that there is no standard pregnant woman who may be compared, in her reaction to night-work, to a standard adult.

[51] *Supra* n 19.

made in repealing or revising protective legislation which was no longer justified, pursuant to the duty imposed on Member States under Articles 3(2)(c) and 5(2)(c) of the Equal Treatment Directive. The Commission examined a large number of remaining national and international protective provisions in order to consider whether they fell within the scope of Article 2(3), and concluded that many of them were no longer justified. It endorsed the view that "this legislation protects women less than it maintains their difference",[52] and therefore found that the majority of the protections should be extended to both sexes or repealed: "Protective legislation should in principle be consistent across sexes and across occupational areas".[53] In other words, women and men are alike in their reaction to burdensome or hazardous work and therefore should be treated alike. Thus, in relation to women in general the Communication took a stance consistent with formal equality arguments and strongly rejected a "different treatment" stance. It could equally be said that the Commission rejected categorisations of women which led to a negative impact on their employment. However, although the Commission indicated that derogation from the principle of equal treatment required clear justification and appraisal in a restrictive manner, it did not, it is suggested, clearly indicate that this rigorous approach should be applied to protections relating to pregnancy and maternity. Thus it gave an unqualified endorsement to the finding in *Johnston*[54] that "the Directive is intended to protect . . . the special relationship which exists between a woman and her child"[55] and assumed that justification existed for maintenance of bans on night-work for pregnant and nursing women.[56] Thus, it failed to demonstrate a clear commitment to a substantive equality position in relation to the stance indicated regarding pregnancy and maternity.

Broadly speaking, although the stance taken by the Commission and the Court in relation to the special protections under consideration diverge to an extent (that taken by the Commission being the more radical), both institutions indicate a rejection of the notion of protection for women in general but an acceptance of a protective stance towards maternity: the construct – protection for womankind–becomes protection for motherhood. It is suggested that perhaps the explanation for this stance, which was eventually reflected in the Pregnancy and Maternity Directive, lies, at least in part, in perceptions of "propriety" and women's vulnerability associated with their role as child bearers. The special protection of excluding pregnant women from various arenas of work may

---

[52] *Ibid* at 23.

[53] Thus, for example, the UK responded to the Communication in the Employment Act 1989 which removed restrictions on the work women could undertake and the hours they might work. For example, s 9 of the 1989 Act provided that women were no longer prevented from working underground in mines.

[54] Case 222/84, *supra* n 30.

[55] *Supra* n 19 at 2.

[56] *Ibid* at 12. Article 7 of the Pregnancy Directive provides that workers who are pregnant or have recently given birth must not be obliged to undertake night-work. This implies that workers who wish to undertake such work will not be prevented from doing so, but it may open the door to national legislation such as that at issue in Case C-42/92 *Habermann-Bellermann*, *supra* n 44, possibly leading to detriment in employment terms for the women affected.

mask a desire to remove such employees from the public and dangerous work-place wherever possible. Thus, the special protection model harmonises with liberal notions of equality in the public sphere and implies that the mother's place lies in the private sphere, thereby revealing its divergence from substantive equality.

(iv) Special protections under the Pregnancy and Maternity Directive[57]

A Directive on the protection of pregnant women at work was proposed in the Action programme[58] produced by the Commission in response to the Social Charter agreed by 11 of the Member States. The draft of the Directive was based on Article 118A which authorises Directives on the health and safety of workers, thereby avoiding the requirement of unanimity.[59] This procedural manoeuvre was highly significant, since it led to characterisation of the Directive as one concerned with the health and safety rights of pregnant women and new mothers[60], although it also supported the equal treatment principle. The Direct-ive includes the right to maternity leave (Article 8) and to time off for ante-natal examinations (Article 9), but makes no attempt to distinguish between these special entitlements and its protective protections, characterising them all as employment rights. Thus, the rights-based approach to equal treatment maintained under the Equal Treatment Directive is not sustained under the Pregnancy and Maternity Directive, which chooses instead to characterise special protections as employment rights as opposed to derogations from the equal treatment principle.[61] This might have been unobjectionable had the pro-visions ensured that no detriment to employment opportunities could arise as a consequence of the operation of the protective provisions. Put another way, had the provisions operated neutrally in terms of such opportunities the case for characterising them as rights would have been stronger.[62]

---

[57] Council Directive 92/85/EEC (OJ 1992 L348/1).

[58] COM (89) 568 final.

[59] The use of a Health and Safety Directive to enshrine maternity rights may have been a strategy adopted to allow the Directive to proceed on the basis of Art 118A, thus allowing for qualified majority voting. For commentary on the legislative history of the Directive see Ellis, 22 ILJ (1993) 63–67.

[60] See Kilpatrick, and Szyszczak, in this volume.

[61] Moreover, as Conaghan points out, the use of Health and Safety legislation as a vehicle for the delivery of maternity rights may provide the wrong signals: the suggestion that pregnancy should be associated with ill-health (a tendency which is already apparent) is reinforced (Conaghan, "Preg-nancy and the Workplace: A Question of Strategy" 20 JLS (1992), 71–92 at 82).

[62] In its departure from the principles underlying the Equal Treatment Directive, it could be sug-gested that the Pregnancy Directive goes further. It implies that the principle of equal treatment requires justification in stating in the Preamble: "the risk of dismissal for reason associated with their state may have harmful effects on the physical and mental condition of [the relevant groups of workers]; whereas provision should be made for such dismissal to be prohibited". Although this goes some way to recognising (albeit in the context of dismissal only) the detrimental consequences of forcing women to choose pregnancy or employment disadvantage, it also implies that prohibition

It will be suggested below that the Directive fails to maintain a principle of protection from employment disadvantage, although it holds out the promise of reconciling protections with equal treatment. The Directive seeks to encapsulate the principle that certain groups of women should be protected: "pregnant workers, workers who have recently given birth, or who are breast-feeding must be considered a special risk group in many respects",[63] but at the same time that the principle of equal treatment should be maintained, that is "the protection of the health and safety of [such workers] should not treat women in the labour market unfavourably nor work to the derogation of directives concerning equal treatment for men and women". However, as Jacqmain observes,[64] the Directive only envisages the relationship between equality and maternity protection in a negative form: the former "does not prejudice the latter".[65]

It is contended that treating protective provisions as entitlements is invidious if they carry with them the possibility of creating a negative impact on women's employment. In contrast, maternity entitlements are desirable as avoiding the need to rely on the notion of non-discrimination (at least during a period of non-provision of parental leave), which may include problematic comparisons with men. It follows, it is suggested, that special protections, such as exclusion of pregnant women from underground work, can and should be distinguished from special entitlements, such as the right to maternity leave. This is because part of the rationale of special entitlements is to further, or at least safeguard, equality of employment opportunities, whereas the rationale of special protections (whether or not expressed as rights) is to protect women due to their perceived vulnerability, or to safeguard the welfare of the foetus. Special entitlements may act as a vehicle for the effective operation of equal treatment. Special protective provisions may act as a means of allowing escape from the equal treatment principle.

It should, however, be pointed out that viewed from a substantive equality standpoint the postulated distinction between special entitlements and special protections may break down to some extent if employers and others react to them in a manner which leads to detriment to women in employment; for example, because women are perceived as more costly employees. Moreover, the existence of socially, as opposed to biologically, determined special entitlements means that some provisions which appear on the face of it to have the character of special entitlements are revealed on closer scrutiny to operate in practice more like special protections. An example is provided by the entitlement to maternity leave under Article 8 of the Directive which is only available

---

of dismissal of a woman for a pregnancy-related cause (direct discrimination: Case C-177/88, *Dekker*, *supra* n 35) may be said to rest not on any fundamental right to equal treatment but on the instrumental reason that otherwise the woman may suffer harm. In a sense, this turns the Equal Treatment Directive on its head: the "derogations" from the principle of equal treatment are presented as rights, while the principle itself requires justification.
[63] *Ibid* Article 2.
[64] Jacqmain, "Pregnancy as grounds for dismissal" 23 ILJ (1994), 357–359.
[65] See the Preamble to the Directive.

for women: no provision is made for family leave.[66] In practice, if such leave is not available for men, it operates as a near-mandatory requirement and it may lead indirectly to the exclusion of women from employment. In relation to this point it may be noted that Article 8 provides that pregnant women are entitled to 14 weeks' continuous maternity leave and are obliged to take two weeks of such leave either before or after the expected date of confinement. Thus it is made clear that the special entitlement of maternity leave must contain a coercive protective element. The choice as to allocation of the maternity leave, or of the proportion of it actually taken, is not left up to the individual woman, depending on her own circumstances.[67]

On the other hand, it should be pointed out that the present dual effect of parental rights, both detrimental and beneficial in terms of women's employment, is not intrinsic to them since it is a product only of a particular and gendered view of the division of family responsibilities. It is suggested that the postulated distinction between special entitlements and special protections still holds good, partly on the basis that the maternity rights under the Directive still leave leeway for the woman to exercise choice and are referable only to women who have need of them. In contrast, the special protections it provides may operate coercively in terms of excluding women from employment and may extend to those who do not want or need them.

The most significant special protections under the Directive concern the protection of the specified groups of women from certain agents, processes or working conditions, and a non-exhaustive list of these, which includes underground mining work[68], is contained in Annex One to the Directive. Article 5 encapsulates the principle that once an assessment of risk is made in relation to the relevant group of workers, which reveals that a member of the group is exposed to a certain risk, attention should focus on action taken in respect of the worker rather than in respect of the risk. Under Article 5(1) the employer "shall take the necessary measures to ensure that by temporarily adjusting the working conditions and/or hours of the worker, the exposure of the worker to such risks is avoided". It is notable that this provision does not state unambiguously that the first concern should be to prevent the risk without materially affecting the hours or conditions of the worker, by, for example, providing pro-

---

[66] It is suggested that the most satisfactory form of family leave would allow either partner to opt for either a short or a long period of leave, the longer period to be at least equivalent to the maternity leave provision under the Directive. The original draft of the Directive included an entitlement to paternity leave, although it was not equivalent to the maternity leave. The European Draft Directive on Parental Leave (OJ C 315/84) would allow men to take paternity leave but the UK Conservative Government opposes it and therefore, since unanimity in the Council of Ministers is required, it has little hope of being enacted during the lifetime of that government. See also, Kilpatrick, and Ryel (concerning the Nordic model of family leave), in this volume.

[67] Given that the expected date of confinement may be up to 14 days before the actual birth, this means that women may be forced to take one month off work before the birth. Some women, especially in sedentary occupations, might consider that that month of leave, or most of it, would be more valuable to them after the birth.

[68] This protection may be open to the charge of non-transparency particularly as it operates as a blanket ban, regardless of the circumstances of individual women.

tective clothing. The provision allows the workers' hours to be changed as an *alternative* to changing the conditions, which may include the use of protective clothing. Under Article 5(2) if changes in hours or conditions are not objectively feasible, the worker should be moved to another job and, finally, under Article 5(3), if this is not feasible or cannot reasonably be required, the worker shall be granted leave. Under Article 6 there are certain cases as set out in Annex II in which exposure of the relevant group of workers to such risks is prohibited.

If a worker falls within Article 6 or Article 5(2) or (3) she has no guarantee that she will suffer no loss of pay or of employment rights although this was originally envisaged[69]; she will be granted leave "in accordance with national legislation and/or national practice" and under Article 11(1), which provides for protection of employment rights in accordance with national practice, must receive payment or an allowance in accordance with national practice. The Directive itself does not provide for full protection of employment rights; it provides only under Article 10 that workers in this situation must not be dismissed during the beginning of their pregnancy to the end of the maternity leave (the protected period). This does not confront fully the various forms of negative impact on women's employment which might arise from the provisions of Articles 5 and 6. For example, an employer might refuse to make an offer of employment to a pregnant woman on the ground that she would be exposed to a risk referred to in Articles 4 or 6. Moving a worker from one job to another might mean a demotion or loss of the opportunity of promotion or of access to training. At this point the relationship between the Pregnancy Directive and the Equal Treatment Directive is called into question, presenting the national courts with a difficult task in fulfilling their duty to interpret provisions of national law in accordance with Community law. If the Court accepted that the examples given of negative impact on women's employment could be considered within the Equal Treatment Directive the protection thereby offered to women might be flawed due to the rulings as to causation in direct discrimination and as to its relationship with justification[70] in *Hertz*[71], *Webb* v *EMO Air Cargo (UK) Ltd*[72] and in *Habermann-Beltermann.*

In *Hertz* the Court found that dismissal due to absences caused by illness, where those absences arise outside the protected period of maternity leave, is permissible, even where the illness is pregnancy-related. Similarly, the Court's conclusion that the termination of Habermann-Beltermann's contract was not "on the ground of pregnancy", but by reason of the statutory provision in the MSchG, opened the door to a narrow interpretation of the *Dekker* ruling[73] that

---

[69] See the 1990 Proposal of the Commission (COM(90) 406 final). As Ellis notes ("Protection of Pregnancy and Maternity" 22 ILJ (1993), 63–67 at 65) the arguments of the UK Government in relation to the Pregnancy Directive had a measure of success in creating an attenuated set of maternity rights.

[70] See Szyszczak, and Hervey, in this volume.

[71] Case C-179/88 [1990] ECR I-3979.

[72] Case C-32/93 [1994] ECR I-3567.

[73] Case C-177/88, *supra* n 35.

adverse treatment on grounds of pregnancy is direct discrimination.[74] The Court's more restrictive interpretation in *Habermann-Beltermann* of "on the ground of pregnancy" could permit many reasons for potentially adverse treatment of pregnant workers which are not directly related to the pregnancy. It would be consistent with this line of argument for an employer to contend that unavailability of a pregnant woman during the protected period due to the operation of Articles 6 or 5(3) of the Pregnancy Directive could be seen as the "cause" of the adverse treatment (for instance demotion or failure to appoint). This argument might be accepted if the employment contract was of a fixed term nature due to the finding in *Webb* and in *Habermann-Beltermann* that unavailability of a pregnant employee for work cannot justify the termination of the contract if the unavailability arising from the pregnancy relates to a period of time which is only a small proportion of the total period of the contract. In both judgments, the crucial fact upon which the Court relied was that the employment contracts in question were of a permanent and not fixed term nature.

Moreover, the judgments in both *Webb* and *Habermann-Beltermann* impliedly accept that adverse treatment flowing from pregnancy is susceptible to justification. Therefore an employer may be able to contend successfully that not only costs associated with unavailability, but also *other* costs arising from pregnancy and creating detriment to the position of the undertaking in the market, not the pregnancy itself, were the "cause" of the refusal to appoint or the demotion of a pregnant woman. This might include adjustment of working conditions or removal of hazardous substances from the working environment, or other measures of special protection for pregnant workers required by the Pregnancy and Maternity Directive. Thus, these decisions open the way to obscuring the distinction between causation and justification which had previously been established in relation to direct discrimination.[75] Following *Dekker* the question to be asked in relation to direct discrimination was simply: did the adverse treatment arise from the sex of the worker? If so, justification had to be found within Article 2(2) or 2(3) if it was to be found at all. The question now becomes, it seems: did the *cost* of the pregnancy cause the adverse treatment, thus undermining the express derogations from the equal treatment principle and introducing other justifications into direct discrimination under the cloak of causation?

These findings invite the conclusion that the scope left by the rulings in *Hertz*, *Webb* and *Habermann-Beltermann* for arguing that adverse treatment of a pregnant woman is not causally related to the pregnancy, coupled with the lack of full protection of employment rights under the Pregnancy Directive, create a situation in which reconciliation of special protections and equality cannot readily be achieved under Community law. Thus the apparently benevolent provisions of the Directive appear on close examination to conceal lacunae which

---

[74] See further Shaw, "Pregnancy Discrimination in Sex Discrimination" 16 EL Rev (1991), 313–320.
[75] In Case C-177/88 *Dekker, supra* n 35. For argument on this point see Ellis, "The Definition of Discrimination in European Community Sex Equality Law" 19 ELRev (1994), 563–580 at 567–568. See also Szyszczak, in this volume.

open the way to direct discrimination but leave the remedial treatment for it unclear.[76] It may therefore be concluded that the promise of a commitment to substantive equality which the Directive appears to hold out remains unfulfilled.

(v) Conclusions

Under a substantive equality model it is suggested that the overriding concern should be to confine "special" protections to those which are genuinely necessary due to biological factors, and to outlaw those which have no clear biological basis but appear to be founded on socio-cultural perceptions of women's weakness and vulnerability. Thus, it is as necessary to question such perceptions in relation to pregnancy and maternity as it is in relation to women generally. The principle encapsulated in protective provisions should be that women should not suffer or be disadvantaged due to their child-bearing function. Protective provisions should not force women to choose between pregnancy and employment advantage. The divide between the public arena of the market and the private sphere of the home must not obscure, it is suggested, a recognition that the possibility of disadvantage at work and even dismissal may lead women to undergo abortions, sterilisation or to forego the possibility of child-bearing.[77] If women accept the risk of such disadvantage and the risk materialises, they may suffer stress, poverty and other detrimental consequences, all of which may also affect their other children and indeed the child sought to be protected itself.[78]

To put forward this argument is not, however, to recommend de-regulation of the European labour market in the sphere of protection as a means of safeguarding women's employment opportunities. It is not to suggest that the position of women in that market, which may often be weak, is such that all protections can be viewed as a matter of individual choice[79]; rather, it is to suggest that the creation of beneficial protections presently confined to women

---

[76] On this point see Jacqmain, 23 ILJ (1994), at 357–359.

[77] See *Oil, Chemical and Atomic Workers International Union v American Cyanamid Co.* 741 F 2d Series 444 (1984) 444–50. The case concerned women subject to a foetal protection policy who had to be sterilised in order to keep their jobs. For an account of the case and its background see Faludi, *Backlash: The Undeclared War Against Women* (1991) 477–491. See also, in the UK context, *Page v Freight Hire (Tank Haulage) Ltd* [1981] 1 All ER 394.

[78] In relation to the ruling in *Habermann-Beltermann*, for example, it might be borne in mind that it was made clear (para 3) that Habermann-Beltermann could *only* undertake night-work, and not day time work, due to her family responsibilities. In refusing to scrutinise the protective legislation at issue, the Court removed from many women the possibility of choosing to undertake night-work on a fixed term basis, during pregnancy.

[79] Care must be taken, it is suggested, in using arguments such as those put forward in *Johnson Controls, supra* n 4, which support individual choice, if they are not to lead to the stance of the UK Government as regards de-regulation of the European labour market reflected in its refusal to ratify the Social Charter and in its challenge to Council Directive 93/104 OJ L 307/93: Case C-84 *UK v Council.*

[80] This view was clearly adopted by the Commission in its Communication and has been prevalent for some time. Creighton argues that the Short Time Committees of the North of England who argued for the passing of Althorp's Act in 1833 (often seen as a forerunner of modern health and safety legislation) wished to restrict the hours of labour of all adult workers but considered that this objective might be achieved by arguing firstly for restriction on the hours worked by women (Creighton (1979), *supra* n 18 at 20).

should as far as possible occur as the forerunner of their extension to men.[80]

Under this analysis it is contended that the reconciliation between protection and equality sought to be achieved under the EU scheme, and held out as a promise in the Pregnancy Directive[81], remains unrealised. Further, conceptualisation of special protections as entitlements in the Pregnancy Directive has obscured their potential to lead to negative effects on women's employment. The inherent contradictions revealed within the EU's social purpose and the part played in creating them by the different Community institutions indicate, it is suggested, certain of the limitations affecting the EU in its role as a mechanism able to bring about beneficial social change.

HELEN FENWICK
Lecturer in Law,
University of Durham, UK

---

[81] See in particular the Preamble which suggests a recognition of the evils of forcing women to accept protections carrying with them the risk of a negative impact on employment.

Chapter 6

HOW LONG IS A PIECE OF STRING? EUROPEAN REGULATION OF THE POST-BIRTH PERIOD*

(i) Introduction

The post-birth period exists in a twilight zone between pregnancy provision, maternity provision and young child-care provision. This chapter wishes to analyse the regulation of this period by different provisions of EC law. The EC provisions currently regulating this area are the Equal Treatment Directive (ETD) as interpreted by the European Court of Justice (ECJ), and the Pregnancy Directive.

I wish to argue that focusing explicitly on this period challenges current doctrinal interpretations of ECJ equality jurisprudence. It suggests that, while the Court's jurisprudence is inadequate in its conceptualisation of the post-birth period, this inadequacy is not due to incoherence and is a deliberate and coherent strain in its jurisprudential approach. This has been somewhat neglected in the stampede to define the ECJ's jurisprudence as formal or substantive, and in the division maintained between the "pregnancy" cases and cases dealing with Article 2(3) and 2(4). The other prong of post-birth regulation, the Pregnancy Directive, is incapable of remedying this inadequacy, as it is based on a health and safety rationale. The inadequacy consists in the failure of Court, European legislator or doctrine to enter the magic circle of maternity leave. Examining the reasons for this more carefully reveals a black hole at the centre of the ECJ's equality jurisprudence and in current EC regulation. This black hole is created by the determination not to consider the equality implications of leave and other legislative provisions on the allocation, regulation and remuneration of time spent on market and care work by women and men.

---

* This chapter was written by Claire Kilpatrick.

(ii) Regulation of the post-birth period: the pregnancy perspective

The pregnant working woman has constituted, and continues to constitute, a hard case for legislatures, courts, equal treatment laws and feminist jurisprudence. In particular, in jurisdictions where low or no legislative protection has been afforded to pregnant employees, attempts have been made by these pregnant employees to use equal treatment provisions to challenge decisions taken by actual or potential employers based on pregnancy. This often provides the only possible avenue of legal redress open to them. These challenges have produced a series of court (and legislative) responses conceptualising the relationship between sex discrimination and pregnancy. These responses can be classified as adopting four different approaches.

The first notorious (and now discredited) approach adopted in English-speaking jurisdictions was the "no comparison possible" approach. This reasoned that like had to be compared with like to sustain a sex discrimination claim. As men could not get pregnant, there was no masculine equivalent to a pregnant woman and consequently pregnancy discrimination could never equal sex discrimination.[1]

The second approach, often developed as a reflex to the door-closing exercise the first approach adopted *vis-à-vis* pregnancy and sex discrimination[2], involves comparing a woman with a man in a similar condition. In this analysis, a woman is, because of her pregnancy, to be treated no less favourably than a man with a similar inability to work. This approach has often been dubbed the "sick man" approach as the courts tried to find which sort of sick man the pregnant woman (or a particular pregnant woman) was most like: a man with a hernia, a man undergoing a hip replacement or prostate operation. This approach has been tenaciously adhered to by the British courts[3] and is the approach adopted in the US Pregnancy Discrimination Act 1978.

In the third "no comparison necessary" approach the focus is on the inextricable link between pregnancy and sex. Hence, there is no need for a male comparator as pregnancy discrimination *per se* constitutes direct discrimination on grounds of sex. This approach has been adopted by the ECJ in a series of decisions beginning with *Dekker*[4] where the Court decided that refusal to employ a pregnant woman was direct discrimination. This approach, which Rubenstein has accurately characterised as placing a "badge of protection"[5] on the pregnant woman, is the equivalent, in terms of the protection it provides, to

---

[1] In the UK, see *Turley* v *Allders Department Stores* [1980] IRLR 4 (EAT); in the US, see *General Electric Company* v *Gilbert* 429 US 125 (1976); in Canada, see *Attorney-General of Canada* v *Bliss* 92 DLR (3d) 317 (1978).
[2] See in the UK, *Hayes* v *Malleable Working Men's Club* [1985] ICR 703 (EAT).
[3] But now see *Webb* v *EMO Air Cargo UK Ltd* [1995] IRLR 245.
[4] Case 177/88 *Dekker* v *Stichting Vormingscentrum voor Jonge Volwassenen Plus* [1990] ECR I-3941.
[5] Rubenstein, "Understanding pregnancy discrimination: a framework for analysis" 42 *Equal Opportunities Review* (1992) 22 at 25. See also Fenwick, in this volume.

national legislation which protects pregnancy from a wide range of undesirable employment consequences but which regulates it separately from provisions dealing with sex equality. Not all legislative provisions reflect this "badge of protection" model. The badge of protection model implies the unconditional protection of pregnancy from undesirable employment consequences during the period in which the badge is deemed to apply.

There are two main components to this model. The first is the right not to be refused a job because of pregnancy, the corollary of this being the right not to be dismissed when pregnant.[6] Thus legislative models containing length of service requirements to avail of these rights do not conform to a badge of protection model. The second is the right not to suffer undesirable employment consequences because of other legislative requirements dealing with pregnancy. Thus, if a woman who becomes pregnant works at night in an area where pregnant women are not permitted to work at night or works with a substance which legislation deems pregnant women should not work with, she must not be dismissed because she cannot carry out her job for the duration of the pregnancy. A similar logic applies to periods of leave the legislature may lay down as necessary for the pregnant woman to take off work before and after the birth (usually called maternity leave).[7] Here again, if the legislator makes these rights conditional on, for example, the size of the enterprise, availability of other suitable employment, whether the woman in question has fulfilled certain service requirements, it does not conform to the badge of protection model.[8]

Therefore, the badge of protection model implies (1) a set of basic uniform rights for all those who are pregnant; and (2) that these rights ensure that a pregnant woman's status in employment (or her capacity to have employment status) cannot be altered because of her pregnancy. It is unclear whether reduction of a woman's income during periods of leave (whether compulsory or optional) taken during and following pregnancy contravenes a badge of protection norm. On one reading, it clearly does as any reduction in income is inextricably linked to pregnancy and childbirth and therefore constitutes direct discrimination on grounds of sex. On another, employment status and benefits flowing from that status can be distinguished. This means that the badge of protection applies only to access to and maintenance of a job position while the badge is worn.[9]

---

[6] The very fine line between discrimination in hiring and discrimination in dismissal in pregnancy cases is perfectly illustrated by the facts in *Dekker* (*supra* n 4), Case 32/93 *Webb* v *EMO Cargo (UK) Ltd* [1994] ECR I-3567 (ECJ) and, most particularly, by Case 421/92 *Habermann-Beltermann* v *Arbeiterwohlfahrt, Bezirksverband Ndb/Opf eV* [1994] ECR I-1657 (ECJ). This is recognised by A.G. Tesauro who states at para 11 of his Opinion in this case that this formal legal distinction would lead in either case to the woman losing her job.

[7] Discriminating against pregnant employees on these grounds has been specifically outlawed by the ECJ in *Dekker, supra* n 4, *Webb, supra* n 6, and *Habermann-Beltermann, supra* n 6.

[8] The main question mark remaining over whether ECJ jurisprudence constitutes a "badge of protection" model is the distinction drawn by the Court in *Webb* and *Habermann-Beltermann* (*supra* n 6) between pregnant employees on indefinite contracts (badge applies) and pregnant employees on definite or fixed-term contracts (badge may not apply).

[9] This issue will shortly be decided by the Court when it rules on the preliminary reference made by the Northern Ireland Court of Appeal in Case C-342/93 *Gillespie* v *Northern Health and Social Services Board*. The ECJ has been asked whether any of the EC's equality provisions "require that, while a

The fourth approach is not strictly speaking an approach but is a convenient way of characterising two very different methods of combining the second and third approaches. These are best understood by examining, respectively, EC and United Kingdom jurisprudence.

At EC level, the *Hertz*[10] decision came hot on the heels of *Dekker*. This case concerned the dismissal of a woman repeatedly absent for pregnancy-related illnesses which continued well beyond childbirth. The Court, examining Article 2(3) ETD which permits measures for "the protection of women, in particular those which concern pregnancy or maternity", designated two periods. During the first "protected period" equivalent to the duration of pregnancy plus maternity leave in each Member State, it is direct discrimination to dismiss a pregnant woman. However, at this point the "badge of protection" is removed; the only protection to be had is of a comparative nature; thus in Ms Hertz's case, if a man who had been absent from work as often as her would have been dismissed, it would not be discriminatory to dismiss her. Thus, this combination of the non-comparative and comparative discrimination approaches draws a temporal distinction between the two approaches.[11]

The second combination, adopted by the British courts in the wake of these developments in ECJ jurisprudence is best described as a false combination which illustrates the dogged reluctance of the United Kingdom courts to adopt the "no comparison necessary" approach. It is exemplified by the first House of Lords' decision in *Webb* v *EMO*[12] and the recent decision in *Brown* v *Rentokil Ltd*.[13] The House of Lords in *Webb* state (following *Dekker*) that to dismiss a woman because she is pregnant is unlawful direct discrimination. Since childbearing and the capacity to bear children are characteristics of the female sex, to apply these characteristics is to apply a gender-based criterion. Where, however, the employer has a gender-neutral explanation which is put forward and accepted by the court as genuine, the question then becomes whether a man would have been dismissed in comparable circumstances. It is not difficult to envisage how few employers would put forward pregnancy as the real reason for the dismissal and how easy it would be to find a "gender-neutral" reason for dismissal of the pregnant employee.

In the second case, Mrs Brown was absent almost from the beginning of her pregnancy in August 1990 and was dismissed in 1991. The Court of Session, applying the United Kingdom *Webb* formula, stated that it is clear that at EC level, a clear distinction was drawn by the ECJ between dismissal due to illness

---

woman is absent from work on the maternity leave provided for by the national legislation or by her contract of service she be paid the full pay to which she would have been entitled if at the time she had been working normally by her employer". A.G. Léger gave a negative response to this question on 6 June 1995.

[10] Case 179/88, *Handels-OG Kontorfunktionaerernes Forbund Danmark (acting for Hertz)* v *Dansk Arbejdsgiverforening (acting for Aldi Marked KS)* [1990] ECR I-3979.

[11] See Szyszczak, in this volume.

[12] *Webb* v *EMO Air Cargo (UK) Ltd* [1993] IRLR 27 (HL); for commentary on this decision see Szyszczak, "Sex Discrimination and Pregnant Women" 22 ILJ (1993), 133–136.

[13] [1995] IRLR 211 (Court of Session).

caused by pregnancy and dismissal due to the mere fact of being pregnant. In their view, the *Hertz* decision makes it clear that the ETD does not apply in the case of an employee whose illness was attributable to pregnancy, unless a provision giving protection applies under the employee's own national law. *Hertz* could not be distinguished on the grounds that it dealt with an illness sometime after pregnancy, whereas the present case dealt with an illness during pregnancy. This combination approach is a barely veiled attempt to introduce the comparative approach during the "protected period" through the back door.

The ECJ's pregnancy jurisprudence has been subjected to considerable critical analysis in the United Kingdom. Critique has mainly clustered around the combined effect of the sister-cases *Dekker* and *Hertz.* For some, *Dekker* obscures the fact that the real issue in pregnancy cases is not the fact of being pregnant but the financial consequences.[14] For others, the Court followed basically the same approach in both cases.[15] Positive comment on *Hertz* focuses largely on pragmatic considerations; on the fact that it provides women with protection during pregnancy *and* throughout statutory or maternity leave[16] and that, in order to provide certainty for employers and employees alike, the establishment of a "protected period" is appropriate.[17]

However, most comment on these cases has drawn a sharp normative line between the approach followed in *Dekker* and that followed in *Hertz.* Thus, *Dekker* represents the "greatest strides towards transcending a purely male norm"[18] taken by the European Court; an "essentially feminist"[19] approach amounting to a "reconceptualisation" of EC discrimination law[20] giving reason to believe that the Court "was moving towards a new approach to gender discrimination".[21] Unfortunately (for these authors), *Dekker* was not unaccompanied: it came in a package with *Hertz.* For Sandra Fredman, *Hertz* represents the reassertion of the equivocal nature of equality. She argues, "if pregnancy is unique to women, so are its longer term consequences: it is difficult to see why a rigid dividing line should be drawn at the moment maternity leave ends, however short the leave may be".[22] More argues that *Hertz* demonstrates that the Court "remains caught in the sameness/difference trap"; while for Shaw, *Hertz* suggests that hopes of a reconceptualisation of EC equality law are premature.[23]

Although the *Hertz* decision is heavily criticised, it is less clear what the Court

---

[14] Hare, "Commentary: Pregnancy and Sex Discrimination" 20 ILJ (1991), 124–130.
[15] Cromack, "EC Pregnancy Directive: Principle or Pragmatism" *Journal of Social Welfare and Family Law* (1993), 262; Rubenstein, "Highlights: January 1991" IRLR [1991], 1.
[16] Ellis, "Discrimination on the grounds of pregnancy in EEC law" *Public Law* (1991), 159–163 at 162–3.
[17] Hervey, *Justifications for Sex Discrimination in Employment* (Butterworths, 1993) 165.
[18] Fredman, "European Community Discrimination Law: A Critique" 21 ILJ (1992), 119–134 at 122.
[19] Ellis, *supra* n 16 at 160.
[20] Shaw, "Pregnancy discrimination in sex discrimination", 16 EL Rev (1991), 313–326 at 320.
[21] More, "Reflections on pregnancy discrimination under European Community Law" 1 *Journal of Social Welfare and Family Law* (1992), 48–56 at 52.
[22] Fredman, *supra* n 18 at 122.
[23] More, *supra* n 21 at 53; Shaw, *supra* n 20 at 320.

should have done. Does it mean that the length of the "protected period" should have been extended by the Court to cover Ms Hertz or that open-ended protection should be provided for pregnant employees? Prescriptions focusing on the pregnancy period tend to argue for the improvement of pregnancy and maternity rights either within equal treatment laws, or preferably in the improvement and expansion of free-standing maternity rights. This path is preferred for a number of reasons, both theoretical and practical. Improved and simplified maternity rights are seen as providing greater clarity and consistency for pregnant employees. Equal treatment laws, by comparison, are seen as an "unreliable legal tool"[24] where solid legal precedents can quickly dissolve into myriad distinguishings. On the theoretical level, many feel that the anchoring of maternity rights in discrimination law weds it to the sameness/difference debate in a way that involves the use of artificial comparisons and makes pregnancy rights a derogation from equality, a special right or preferential treatment. Given that the Court's equality "attitude" is suspect so far as pregnancy is concerned, Fredman suggests the jettisoning of equality and its replacement by "directives containing specific rights . . . thus pregnancy attracts rights for its own sake rather than on the basis of artificial comparisons".[25]

For our purposes, what is important to note is that the critiques of *Hertz* are directed against not protecting the pregnant woman *enough* by not recognising the realities of pregnancy complications, which can continue long after the birth of the child and by providing a cut-off point for protection after which she is thrown back into the comparative approach.

(iii) Regulation of the post-birth period: delineating the exceptions in the ETD

Here again some clear lines can be drawn. The Court of Justice, almost without exception, has condemned as breaching the principle of equality all female-specific protective measures which do not relate to pregnancy, maternity and the post-birth period.[26] How has it done this? The ETD sets out a number of

---

[24] Lacey, "Dismissal by Reason of Pregnancy" 15 ILJ (1986), 43–46 at 45.

[25] Fredman, *supra* n 18 at 134; Fredman, "A Difference with Distinction: Pregnancy and Parenthood Reassessed" 110 *Law Quarterly Review* (1994), 106–123 in particular at 121–122.

[26] If we take as the conceptual distinction between genuine occupational qualifications (covered by Article 2(2)) and protective measures the fact that the former are concerned with the impact of "sex" on persons other than the job-holder, while the latter concern the impact of a particular employment activity on the job-holder. The only real case where a protective measure not falling within Article 2(3) has been upheld by the ECJ is *Johnston* where the Court (wrongly) allowed an exclusion from an employment activity impacting on the job-holder (female police-officers) to fall under Article 2(2): Case 222/84 *Johnston* v *Chief Constable of the RUC* [1986] ECR 1651. See Fenwick, in this volume.

exceptions. Article 2(2) is the genuine occupational qualification exception. Article 2(3), as we saw above, provides that the Directive is to be without prejudice to provisions concerning the protection of women, particularly as regards pregnancy and maternity. Article 2(4) provides that the Directive shall be without prejudice to measures to promote equal opportunities for men and women, in particular by removing existing inequalities which affect women's opportunities. Article 3(2)(c) requires Member States to revise female-specific protective provisions "when the concern for protection which originally inspired them is no longer well founded".

In *Johnston* v *RUC*[27] the Court held that a refusal to allow women police-officers to carry firearms could not fall within Article 2(3) as it did not allow women to be excluded from a certain type of employment where the risks involved affected men and women in the same way and which are distinct from women's specific needs for protection. Furthermore, it held that Article 2(3) determines the scope of Article 3(2)(c). The upshot of this reasoning is that protective measures not falling within Article 2(3) cannot fall within the terms of the Directive. Moreover, until the Court has considered more specifically what falls within Article 2(4), the only safe bet for a female-specific provision which does not wish to fall foul of the ETD is to be a measure falling within Article 2(3).[28] Hence, the Court has rejected a general clause maintaining female-specific rights in French collective agreements[29], the maintenance of a prohibition on female night-work (again in France)[30] and of a differential system of night-work derogations for men and women in Belgium.[31] As the female-specific rights in these cases did not fall within Article 2(3) they contravened the principle of equal treatment and had to be removed. Arguments by national governments that the wording of Article 2(3), which does not confine itself to protecting pregnancy and maternity (by focusing on the word "particularly"), permitted the maintenance of these measures or that these measures were directed chiefly at the recognition that women bore a heavier burden of domestic and childcare responsibilities (thus making it much more difficult for them to rest during the day) met with an unsympathetic response from the Court.[32] These decisions have been largely applauded in the United Kingdom.

The Court has therefore clearly defined what falls outside Article 2(3). But what falls inside? This has been considered by the Court in a number of cases which have been subsequently examined through the perspective of childcare.

---

[27] *Ibid.*

[28] The Court gave its first ruling specifically on the scope of Article 2(4) in Case 450/93 *Eckhard Kalanke* v *Freie Hansestadt Bremen,* judgment of 1995, nyr.

[29] Case 312/86 *EC Commission* v *France (Re Protection of Women)* [1988] ECR 6315.

[30] Case 345/89 *Criminal Proceedings against Alfred Stoeckel* [1991] ECR I-4047. See Sciarra, in this volume.

[31] Case 13/93 *Office National de l'Emploi* v *Madeleine Minne* [1994] ECR I-371. See Sciarra, in this volume.

[32] See Fenwick, in this volume.

(iv) Regulation of the post-birth period: the childcare perspective[33]

In *Commission* v *Italy*[34], the Court was asked whether the grant of a paid women-only three month leave on the adoption of a child under six years of age contravened the Equal Treatment Directive. The Italian Government argued that as this provision was a simple extension of the rights given in the event of maternity to the case of adoption, it could not be considered as a working condition in the sense of Article 5 of the Directive but rather fell under Article 2(3). The Commission argued that Article 2(3), being an exception, must be interpreted strictly to cover only measures relating to pregnancy and maternity. From this perspective, rights to leave or other benefits granted for the purpose of bringing up children are to be regarded in the same way as other types of leave, such as annual leave. Thus, they clearly constitute working conditions and as such, must be available to both fathers and mothers. Advocate General Rozès, considering that the leave was for the benefit of the child rather than for the mother (who had not given birth), felt that maternity leave and adoptive leave were not of the same nature. While leave following childbirth was to allow the mother to rest and could rightly be regarded as a provision to protect women in relation to maternity, adoption leave was predominantly for the benefit of the child. Therefore, mother-specific adoption leave constituted a breach of the Directive which could not be saved by Article 2(3) and adoptive fathers should be entitled to it on the same basis as their working wives. The Court disagreed with the Advocate General and the Commission and agreed with the Italian Government, stating that the distinction was justified by the need to assimilate as much as possible the entry of the child into the family to those of the arrival of a new-born child during the initial delicate period.

In *Hofmann*[35], a German father challenged the conformity of a mother-specific leave with the Equal Treatment Directive. The German legislation provided for two different periods of leave. The first period was compulsory post-natal leave and covered a period of eight weeks from childbirth. The second period was also mother-specific but optional and covered the period between the end of the compulsory leave and the day on which the child reaches six months. During this period, the mother received a state allowance and was guaranteed the right to return to her employment on the same conditions. Ulrich Hofmann took leave during this second optional period but was refused the daily allowance on the grounds that he was not the mother of the child.

Hofmann argued before the Court that Article 2(3) which protects women particularly as regards pregnancy and maternity did not apply to such leave when it extends beyond the 12 weeks following the birth of the child. He argued that the optional nature of the leave, the fact that it is withdrawn in the event of

---

[33] See also the discussion by Fenwick, in this volume.
[34] Case 163/82 [1983] ECR 3273.
[35] Case 184/83 *Hofmann* v *Barmer Ersatzkasse* [1984] ECR 3047.

the child's death and that it was only available to women who had fulfilled service requirements prior to the birth, clearly demonstrated that the leave is not intended to meet the biological or medical needs of the mother but rather to meet the interests of the child. The protection of the mother from the multiplicity of burdens imposed by motherhood and employment could best be achieved by non-discriminatory measures, such as a period of parental leave, thus giving the father the option of caring for the child and the mother the option of resuming employment when the compulsory maternity leave came to an end.

The Barmer Ersatzkasse and the German Government argued that evidence exists that the mother has not recovered from the physical and psychological changes which she has undergone by the end of the post-natal leave of eight weeks, but only some months thereafter. As the effects of pregnancy and childbirth become increasingly diverse as time goes by and the duties involved in caring for a child vary widely from case to case, the legislature, in providing optional leave, deliberately left the choice up to the individual mother. The Commission argues that, while Article 2(3) is clearly designed to allow Member States to maintain or introduce provisions protecting women in relation to the period encompassing pregnancy and childbirth, a national rule which is described as a provision for the protection of the mother may not *ipso facto* fall within the scope of that derogation which covers only those provisions which serve objectively to protect the mother and in which the reference to sex is a necessary condition for ensuring the desired protection. A sex-based distinction designed to allow only the mother to care for the child is not permissible within Article 2(3). Advocate General Darmon rejects the Commission's contention that the difference in treatment should be necessary for the protection of women. Rather, it is sufficient that the measure seeks to protect them for an objective reason. It is the relationship between that aim (protection) and the objective reason determining that aim (pregnancy and maternity) which justifies the measure, not the absence of alternatives. The extra condition imposed by the Commission is tantamount to requiring Member States to choose which-ever measure is most appropriate for the protection of women. However the choice of measures suitable for justifying a difference in treatment is a matter for the Member State alone. The national measure cannot be appraised by reference to a criterion (parental equality) which is wholly outside the scope of the Directive.

The Court accepted the argument that the granting of this period of leave to mothers only fell within Article 2(3) and this did not contravene the Equal Treatment Directive. Its reasons for this decision were three-fold.

First, Article 2(3) envisaged not just the protection of the mother's biological condition during or after pregnancy until such time as her physiological and mental functions have returned to normal but also of the special relationship between a woman and her child which may be disturbed by the multiple burdens which would ensue from simultaneous pursuit of employment.

Second, the Equal Treatment Directive was not designed to settle questions concerned with the organisation of the family or to alter the division of responsibility between parents.

Third, the Directive leaves Member States with a discretion as to the social measures which they adopt to guarantee the protection of women in connection with pregnancy and maternity and to offset the disadvantages which women, by comparison with men, suffer with regard to the retention of employment. The Member States enjoy a reasonable margin of discretion as regards both the nature of the protective measures and the detailed arrangements for their implementation.

The Court's interpretation of what falls inside Article 2(3) meets with the same response from all commentators: universal condemnation. The decisions in *Hofmann* and *Commission* v *Italy* have been criticised as "disappointing", as encouraging naturalistic ideas of women's role in an "unfortunate" line of jurisprudence which cannot be described as "sensible".[36] This condemnation is based on the fact that there is a clear distinction to be drawn between perpetuating women's disadvantage by refusing to recognise their difference and perpetuating ideologies of the "natural" role of women as the primary childcarer and homemaker. The practical illustration of this is in the distinction between "mother-only" leave and parental leave. As Hervey states, "after a certain point ... maternity rights should give way to equal rights for both parents".[37] While the former is a legal strategy perpetuating stereotypes, the latter is a strategy designed to "challenge the ideology of motherhood and create a climate of shared parental responsibility".[38] Therefore, while *Hertz* is criticised for not protecting the woman in the post-birth period *enough*, this line of decisions is criticised for protecting the woman in the post-birth period *too much*.

Commission v *France*[39] may seem to represent some movement by the Court towards a stricter interpretation of Article 2(3); that is, one which confines itself to the stricter biological consequences of pregnancy and does not attempt to encompass the dangerous and hazy area of special mother-child relationships and ideals of motherhood. This case concerned the maintenance in the French equal treatment law of a provision permitting collective or contractual female-specific rights in force before the law to continue their existence with an exhortation to the social partners to revise these clauses. The rights in question ranged from extended maternity leave, to childcare allowances, to early retirement for mothers and days off on Mothers' Day. It is true that this decision represents a development in the Court's reasoning in so far as in their judgment they exclude from the scope of Article 2(3) special rights relating to "the protection of women in their capacity as older workers or parents – categories to which both men and women may belong". This would seem to indicate that at some point in the child's development Article 2(3) ceases to apply. However, both A G Slynn and the Court make it clear that the demarcation of Article 2(3) in *Hofmann* still stands; therefore provisions protecting the mother's bio-

---

[36] Ellis, *European Community Sex Equality Law* (1991) 171: Prechal and Burrows, *Gender Discrimination Law of the European Community* (Dartmouth, 1990) 128: Fredman, *supra* n 18 at 127.

[37] Hervey, *supra* n 17 at 169.

[38] Conaghan and Chudleigh, "Women in Confinement: can labour law deliver the goods?" 14 *Journal of Social and Welfare Law* (1987), 133–147, at 144.

[39] Case 312/86 *Commission* v *France* [1988] ECR 6315.

logical condition and her "special relationship" with the child are not affected by the ruling.

(v) Regulation of the post-birth period: protection or positive action?

These cases also raise the issue of the relationship between the post-birth period, Article 2(3) and Article 2(4), widely known as the positive action exception. The clean separation of these issues in the Directive is belied in particular factual constellations and by the difficulties of classification faced by those attempting to resolve these issues. For the Advocates General in *Hofmann* and in *Hertz* and *Dekker*, Article 2(3) should be conceptualised as an illustration selected by the Community legislature of the general derogation contained in Article 2(4).[40] Article 2(3) involves what American law knows as affirmative action.[41] The Court in *Commission* v *France* does little to clarify this distinction. It states that Article 2(4) is specifically and exclusively designed to allow measures which, although discriminatory in appearance, are in fact intended to eliminate or reduce actual instances of inequality which may exist in the reality of social life. It is the generality of the "save-all" clause in the French law which prohibits it falling under Article 2(4); the issue of which of the rights, taken individually, might correspond to Article 2(4) is not addressed. This is not merely a theoretical issue. In the United Kingdom, extended periods of maternity leave in both public and private sector form a central plank of equal opportunity programmes.

(vi) Regulation of the post-birth period: the health and safety perspective

What does the Pregnancy Directive[42] say about the post-birth period? The Pregnancy Directive is the tenth directive in a series of 17 directives envisaged under Directive 89/391/EEC, a framework health and safety directive, which in turn derives its legitimacy from Article 118A EEC, added to the Treaty in the Single European Act. Article 118A provides that the Council shall adopt, by means of directives, minimum requirements for encouraging improvements, especially in the working environment, to protect the health and safety of workers. The original proposal required *inter alia* a minimum of *16 weeks* fully paid maternity leave and a ban on dismissal and non-selection for a job on account of pregnancy. The final version of the Directive lost the right to full pay during maternity leave, this now being pegged to sick pay. A joint statement by Commission and

---

[40] A G Darmon, in *Hofmann* at 3086.
[41] Para 26 of the A G opinion in *Hertz* and *Dekker*.
[42] The Directive's full title is Council Directive 92/85/EEC of 19 October 1992 on the introduction of measures to encourage improvements in the safety and health at work of pregnant workers and workers who have recently given birth or are breastfeeding (OJ 1992 L 348/1).

Council appended to the Directive, however, declares that this is for purely technical reasons and that "such a reference is not intended in any way to imply that pregnancy and childbirth be equated with illness". The ban on non-selection for a job was also dropped although the *Dekker* line of jurisprudence in fact enacts this right at European level.[43]

Article 8 of the Directive deals with maternity leave. Workers are to be entitled to "a continuous period of maternity leave of at least *14 weeks* allocated before and/or after confinement in accordance with national law and/or practice . . . [this] must include compulsory maternity leave of at least two weeks allocated before and/or after confinement in accordance with national legislation and/or practice". Thus maternity leave has been reduced by two weeks during the passage of the Directive.

I wish solely to point out here potential problems revealed through examination of the principal axes on which all the Community health and safety legislation, stemming from Article 118A, is oriented. Emphasised in Article 118A itself and consistently reiterated and underlined in Directive 89/391/EEC and the Pregnancy Directive itself are three themes. The first is that the measures are designed to establish "minimum requirements". The second is that the measures are taken with a view to harmonising conditions while maintaining any improvements made. Thirdly, it is stressed that these Directives do "not justify any reduction in levels of protection already achieved in Member States". The contradiction contained therein between minimum standards, harmonisation and improvements seems to reflect a compromise model of upward harmonisation. While the aim is to reach the level of the Member State with most protection, Community legislation will settle for a standard generally slightly higher than the lowest standards found in the Member States to prevent harmonisation downwards and in the hope that the conditions will be created to harmonise upwards. If these conditions are not created, at least this model ensures that the level of protection will not decrease. To some extent, therefore, this model privileges the *status quo* (which inevitably entails differing levels of protection) over harmonisation. This in turn reflects a basic maxim of health and safety regulation, that is, that more protection is always better. While in many health and safety areas it may be a good policy strategy to forbid regression towards the minimum standards laid down by a directive, in the case of pregnancy, childbirth and breastfeeding it is not at all evident that this clear equation holds.[44]

(vii) Equality and the post-birth period: a question of time?

It is evident that the post-birth period has proved difficult to analyse in terms of equality. While during pregnancy, some kind of consensus exists that this is a

---

[43] Except perhaps where fixed-term contracts are concerned. See *Webb* and *Habermann-Bellermann*, *supra* n 6. See also Szyszczak, in this volume.
[44] See Fenwick, in this volume.

unique period, whether this be expressed as seeing pregnancy provisions as a legitimate derogation from equality, as necessary to realise equality or as necessary to prevent disadvantage[45]; when the child is born, the clear waters of this analysis quickly become muddied. Taking the different perspectives outlined above, we obtain an apparently contradictory set of responses to the regulation of the post-birth period. Going from pregnancy and women like Ms Hertz, who are subjected to a pregnancy complications lottery, the outcome of which depends on which Member State they reside in and who their employer happens to be, one natural response is to demand that all women should be adequately protected or should not be placed at a disadvantage for an unlimited period in time during which pregnancy-related illnesses may arise. Looked at from a childcare perspective, and the fate of the Hofmann couple, we see that a long period of mother-only leave following the birth may be positively detrimental to women's chances on the labour market, in particular women who wish to return quickly to their employment. It furthermore has negative effects on male parents who wish to care for their young child and more generally on the facilitation or promotion of a repartition of caring responsibilities between parents. This would suggest that maternity leave should not be extended beyond the period necessary for the physical recovery of the mother and all care-periods thereafter should be packaged as parental leave periods.[46] If maternity leave is seen as a positive action measure, the longer it is, and the more women benefit, the better. Similarly, from a health and safety perspective, the longer the female-specific post-birth period, the better.

I feel that the Court's rulings on the post-birth period, doctrinal critiques of various facets of these rulings and the Pregnancy Directive are all inadequate for the same reason. Comparing the unfavourable comments on the Court's decisions to maintain mother-specific rights with the unfavourable comments on the Court's refusal to extend the period of protection in *Hertz* clarifies a central point which may be overlooked in broad discussions of equality and difference. Those who disagree with *Hertz* generally also disagree with *Hofmann*. While this is not contradictory, the central question is often not confronted. It is insufficient to present a Janus-faced image of the Court of Justice: showing its feminist friendly face in *Dekker* and its privileging of patriarchy in *Hofmann* and *Hertz*. It is inadequate to state that motherhood is protected *too much* or to critique the *Hertz* decision for not protecting *enough* without confronting the issue of how much is too much and how much is enough; without delineating more precisely what conditions or periods should be protected, for how long and for what reasons. Vague appeals to motherhood, parenthood or the continuing effects of pregnancy do little to resolve or clarify these difficult decisions.

Herein lies the common problem with the Court's approach to not only the "pregnancy" decisions and the "childcare" decisions but also the "protective legislation" and "part-time work" decisions. The Court refuses to explore the

---

[45] See Szyszczak, in this volume.
[46] See Fenwick, in this volume.

content and implications of "maternity leave", "protected periods" and other legislation affecting the division of mothers' and fathers' time between care work and market work. Thus in *Hertz*, the Court states, "it is a matter for each Member State to fix the period of maternity leave in such a way as to allow female workers to be absent during the period during which problems due to pregnancy and confinement may arise".

In *Hofmann*, as we saw above, this discretion argument was combined with the statement that the ETD was not designed to settle questions concerned with the organisation of the family or to alter the division of responsibility between parents. This means that the Court is, in effect, doubly "blind". First, if a Member State decides to call or not call something maternity leave, the Court will not scrutinise the content or length of the leave. Secondly, if the Court has to make a decision on a particular rule, it will not examine the implications of the maintenance, modification or removal of this rule for the organisation of the family or the division of responsibility between parents. Whatever else we can say about this approach, the consistency of its application cannot be denied. It has been applied not just in the cases so far examined but in the part-time work cases and in the female night-work cases.

In *Bilka*[47], the ECJ was asked whether an undertaking was under a duty to structure its pension scheme in such a way that appropriate account is taken of the special difficulties experienced by employees with family commitments in fulfilling the requirements for an occupational pension. Mrs Weber von Hartz argued in particular that the employer should have to regard periods during which women workers have had to meet family responsibilities as periods of full-time work.[48] The Court replied that the imposition of an obligation such as that envisaged by the national court in its question goes beyond the scope of Article 119 and has no other basis in European Community law as it now stands. Therefore, it ruled that Article 119 does not have the effect of requiring an employer to organise its occupational pension scheme in such a manner as to take into account the particular difficulties faced by persons with family responsibilities in meeting the conditions for entitlement to such a pension.[49] In *Stoeckel*, the French night-work case, it restated that part of its *Hofmann* decision which stated that "as far as family responsibilities are concerned, the Court has already held that the Directive is not designed to settle questions concerned with the organisation of the family or to alter the division of responsibilities between parents".[50]

What are the problems associated with the Court's refusal to investigate how long the protected period should be and to investigate the consequences for organisation of the family of particular measures?

First, no investigation can be made of whether different types of protected periods are needed for different types of pregnancy. Ms Hertz needed protection for 104 weeks (two years) after the birth of her child. If Member States gave

---

[47] Case 170/84 *Bilka-Kaufhaus GmbH* v *Weber von Hartz* [1986] ECR 1607.
[48] *Ibid* para 39 of the judgment.
[49] *Ibid* paras 42 and 43 of the judgment.
[50] *Supra* n 30 at para 17 of the judgment.

each woman two years post-birth or maternity leave, would this be an adequate response? Surely, this is an over-inclusive measure while current maternity leave in all Member States is under-inclusive for the *Hertz* situation. All types of leave in the post-birth period do not have to be labelled as either maternity leave or parental leave. For example, under Italian law, while maternity leave lasts 12 weeks after the birth, dismissal of a woman on grounds related to pregnancy is outlawed for 12 months after the birth. While this would not have captured Ms Hertz's situation, it is this type of provision which is most promising. If there are a range of known post-confinement complications which last beyond the maximum female-specific post-birth leaves in all Member States (and the longest is 29 weeks) these can be regulated either on a health and safety basis or on an equality basis by saying that it is forbidden to dismiss a woman suffering from these symptoms. To mask these in sick leave or parental leave provisions misses the point.

   The second problem with failing to look inside maternity leave is that no maxima can be placed on its length. This is less easily resolved on a health and safety basis, as the Pregnancy Directive aptly illustrates. That this is an equality issue can be demonstrated by imagining that the Hofmann couple are United Kingdom citizens. Mr Hofmann wanted to have paid leave in the 12–24 week period after the birth of his child. In the United Kingdom, which, at 29 weeks, has by far the longest period of mother-only leave in the EC, all of this period is swallowed up by maternity leave. Furthermore, if Mr Hofmann's partner was employed by certain public or private sector companies in the United Kingdom, she could have the right to up to 63 weeks' maternity leave. Periods of extended maternity leave are often presented as a type of positive action. The EOC has rightly questioned whether leave of this length can be considered as maternity leave.[51] Looking at post-birth maternity leave in most countries, particularly following the implementation of the Pregnancy Directive, the failure by the Court to consider how long maternity leave should be is also blind to legislative provision in almost all Member States. In four countries of the EC, the maximum post-birth maternity leave[52] ranges from six to eight weeks[53]; in eight countries it lies between 10–14 weeks[54]; in two countries between 16 and 18 weeks and in the United Kingdom 29 weeks. Furthermore, in Spain, as the maximum maternity leave is also 16 weeks, the post-birth leave is likely to be less than 16 weeks and in Ireland, 14 weeks' maternity leave (pre- and post-) is the norm with four extra weeks being granted on the mother's request. Bar the United Kingdom, the maximum length of post-birth mother-only leave in the EC hovers around 14 weeks.[55] Recognition of this by the Court would clarify considerably regula-

---

[51] For details of extended maternity leave in the UK see Cohen, *Caring for Children: Services and Policies for Childcare and Equal Opportunities in the United Kingdom* (1988), Commission of the European Communities, at 88 and 136. See also *Industrial Relations Review and Report* 567 September 1994, 16 reporting extension of maternity leave to 52 weeks by some UK food industry companies as part of a growing commitment to equal opportunities.

[52] Excluding extra weeks for multiple births, premature births or pathological pregnancies which are allocated extra weeks of leave in some countries.

[53] Sweden, Austria, Luxembourg and Germany.

[54] France, The Netherlands, Belgium, Denmark, Greece, Portugal, Italy and Finland.

tion of the post-birth period, allow situations such as that in *Hertz* to be regulated adequately but separately and give the Court a clearly defined operating space for the second area it has so far steadfastly refused to confront: the effects of leave packages and other legislative provisions on the division of responsibilities between parents.

Third, re-examining the application of the *Hofmann* dictum in *Stoeckel* demonstrates both the untenability and the seriousness of the Court's refusal to examine the effects of leave packages and other legislative provisions on the division of responsibilities between parents. One of the central arguments in *Stoeckel* was that a flexible night-work ban on female industrial employment took into account the greater workload women bear as a result of family responsibilities. It is one thing for the Court to require a Member State to remove a rule which at best is imperfectly and overinclusively aimed at removing the double burden. It is quite another for it simultaneously to refuse to accept that while the ETD will remove such a rule, it will not acknowledge that this burden exists and should be removed, albeit using different means. Yet, this is precisely what the Court does in *Stoeckel.*

This is not to argue that equality laws or judicial rulings can (or should) be employed to *create* periods of maternity or parental leave or oblige employers or legislatures to build crèches. It does mean, however, that equal treatment laws, as interpreted by courts including the European Court of Justice, could, and should, play a central role in *evaluating* the equality effects of the particular packages adopted by Member States. This is of increasing importance given the fact that most Member States now have both maternity and parental leave provisions and that a European level collective agreement under the Maastricht social policy Protocol and Agreement procedures (excluding the United Kingdom) on the reconciliation of professional and family life has recently been ratified.[56] The terms "maternity leave" and "parental leave" can cover a wide range of very different provisions. Thus, a fully remunerated or non-transferable period of parental leave is a completely different right from a lowly-remunerated right to be absent from the labour market. The textual instruments to scrutinise more closely the length and content of post-birth leave provisions exist. The ETD outlaws discrimination on grounds of family status and discrimination on grounds of sex. While the Court continues to abstain from using these provisions to regulate post-birth leave, a black hole exists at the centre of European equality law and critical assessment of the equality implications of current provisions or suggestions for future reform are less likely to take place.

CLAIRE KILPATRICK
European University Institute, Florence, Italy
and Lecturer in Law, University of Bristol, UK

---

[55] Information on length of maternity leave is taken from European Commission Network on Childcare and other Measures to Reconcile Employment and Family Responsibilities, *Leave Arrangements for Workers with Children: A review of leave arrangements in the Member States of the European Union and Austria, Finland, Norway and Sweden*, V/773/94-EN (accurate as of November 1994).

[56] For the progress of this initiative, see 263 *European Industrial Relations Review* (1995), 3.

Chapter 7

DYNAMIC INTEGRATION OF NATIONAL AND COMMUNITY SOURCES: THE CASE OF NIGHT-WORK FOR WOMEN*

(i) A few introductory remarks: the limits of European social policies

Labour lawyers who view Community sources as an instrument by which to understand domestic law better find that their greatest challenge lies in having to deal with a system (the Community system) which is hindered by two limits. The first of these concerns the way in which decisions are adopted within the European Community. Until the entry into force of the Single European Act in 1987, the prevailing rule for the adoption of legislative measures by the Council was through the process of unanimity, which basically meant that a lack of activity and the maintenance of the *status quo* was guaranteed, rather than a focus being brought on the promotion of innovation and change.

With the Single European Act, this decision-making system was partially modified, through the introduction of a qualified majority voting rule, which is limited to the fields of the health and safety of workers in their working environment (Article 118A).[1]

Up to the point at which the Protocol on social policy was attached to the Maastricht Treaty, European labour law existed in this contradictory state. Everything that could not reasonably enter under the notion of health and safety (which is to say, could not be based on Article 118A of the Treaty modified by the Single European Act) was placed under the decisions to be adopted unanimously. This meant effectively that it fell into the meshes of opposing governmental vetoes and, above all, into the sights of the strongly oppositional United Kingdom.

---

*This chapter was written by Silvana Sciarra.
[1] Lord Wedderburn, "European Community Law and Workers' Rights after 1992: Fact or Fake?" in *Labour Law and Freedom* (1995) 247 ff; Sciarra, "Social Values and the Multiple Sources of European Social Law", *European Law Journal* (1995), 60 ff.

The reference to the legal basis in the Treaty, which I have labelled as a limit, is relevant to the arguments developed in this chapter. The fact that social rights are weak and somewhat marginal adds to the uncertainty and the interpretative difficulties which national judges have had when dealing with the case law of the Court of Justice on night-work, as we shall see.

The second limit has to do with the fundamental principles of Community labour law. In the Agreement on social policy attached to the Maastricht Treaty (Article 2.6), the exclusion of several areas of competence from the Treaty is made explicit, that is pay, the right to strike and impose lock-outs, and the right of association.[2] The latter point needs to be treated in detail, although this is not meant to undermine the importance of the other two points.

This topic is of exceptional importance in connection with the relations between the Community system and national systems. Right of association is a principle which has in many Member States marked the evolution of the rights of individual employees in a significant way. It cannot be denied that its absence in Community sources weakens the whole framework of social rights in concrete terms.[3]

Having pointed out these two limits, which sometimes make the use of the term "Community labour law" daring and perhaps too adventurous, it should be added immediately that in the search for "strong" basic principles, Article 119 of the Rome Treaty represents an essential point of reference. Conceived with the very precise and narrow intention of avoiding distortions in competition (where different remunerative conditions for male and female labour were in force in the Member States), this law has produced effects which are very much more significant than was originally intended.[4] In proposing a principle of equal treatment, the aim was, above all, to regulate the market; instead, principles of constitutional relevance have been generated, capable of giving rise to important changes in the domestic systems. All this can be explained by the fact that, unlike the other laws regarding social matters, Article 119 places a direct obligation on Member States and consequently allows workers to claim new rights from the direct application of Community law in their domestic systems. The doctrine of direct effect has proved in this field strong enough to counterbalance the inherent feebleness of the Treaty provisions; this in itself is a lesson to be learnt by the short and yet intense story of European social policies.

---

[2] The exclusion of the right to strike and lock-out has provoked a strong reaction among French labour lawyers. See Verdier and Lyon-Caen, "Sur le lock-out et l'accord européen relatif à la politique sociale du 7 février 1992" 1995 Droit Social 49 ff, criticising Teyssié, "Le droit de lock-out" 1994 Droit Social 795 ff, who draws from Art. 2.6 a right to impose lock-outs equal to the right to strike, thus confusing the limit on Community competences put by the same article.

[3] Sciarra, European Social Policy and Labour Law: Challenges and Perspectives, Collected Courses of the Academy of European Law, vol IV.1 Kluwer (1995) 301 ff.

[4] Davies, "The Emergence of European Labour Law", in McCarthy, Legal Intervention in Individual Relation Gains and Losses (1992) 344 ff; Hepple, "Social Values in European Law", 1995 Current Legal Problems, 39 ff. See Barnard, in this volume.

(ii) Negative integration and its effects

These premises are aimed at providing a general frame of reference for the analysis of the sources with which I shall be directly concerned. Another aspect can be underlined: when discussing the adjustment of national systems to the Community system, integration of a positive type (for example, when the state intervenes with a legislative measure to adjust to Community law) can be distinguished from integration of a negative type. This latter consists in the dis-application of domestic law as the expression of adjustment to supranational law.[5]

Such a procedure may seem like an attack on the sovereignty of the states. It is not so, if one considers that Community law is not hierarchically overordered, but functions in parallel, using its power to infiltrate into domestic systems and to become part of these. This is why negative integration, which can cause surprise on account of the consequences to which it gives rise, is an important aspect of European integration. This last is achieved not only through formal acts, including policies by which the fiscal, monetary and economic policies of the states move closer, but also by following the decision of a judge not to apply a norm of domestic law in order to comply with Community law.

Negative integration should not be viewed as a pathological feature of the moving of domestic and Community systems closer towards each other, but as a physiological one; always given that in negative integration national courts can function as the driving force so as to spur intervention on the part of the legislator at the national level.[6] The interpretative problems which form the basis of the preliminary ruling procedures to the Court of Justice, making reference to Article 177 of the Treaty, show the uneasiness with which national judges evaluate the domestic law sources in the light of Community sources, or with which they interpret the Community source directly. It is rarely a question of uneasiness alone; it should rather be understood as a need for clarification, which can in turn have significant institutional effects. The activity of national courts can be seen as a sign of the end of the lethargy of the domestic system, and of its attempt to move closer towards the Community system. This is also due to the fact that judges act more rapidly than the state legislators.

Because of references made on the basis of Article 177, even before the related Court of Justice's decision, national legislators, not yet in a position to legislate, feel almost hunted by the awaited judgment and politically obliged to intervene with greater rapidity. This expected reaction might be one of the

---

[5] Among the authors adopting this terminology, see Curtin and Mortelmans, "Application and Enforcement of Community Law by the Member States: Actors in Search of a Third Generation Script" in Curtin and Heukels, *Institutional Dynamics of European Integration* (vol II, Liber amicorum H G Schermers, 1994). See also Scharpf, *Negative and Positive Integration in the Political Economy of European Welfare States* (manuscript), who measures the limits of negative integration against the background of competitiveness to be gained by the European market in the global economy.
[6] Weiler, "Journey to an Unknown Destination: a Retrospective of the European Court of Justice" 1993 *Journal of Common Market Studies*, 417 ff.

reasons behind strategic choices in litigation[7]: positive integration is demanded indirectly, under the threat of the unpredictable results provoked by negative integration, especially when coherent legislative policies have been neglected for too long. The rejection of an external interference, which is exactly what a judgment from the Court of Justice can appear to be to national parliaments, gives rise to an adjustment of the domestic system towards that of the Community, in an attempt to give a new equilibrium to the internal and external powers within national states. This issue is interesting from the point of view of the relations to be established among legal sources; among all of these, case law is capable (as mentioned before) of making its moves prior to those of governments and thereby to bring into discussion the complex equilibrium of the institutions.

National courts seem to promote such a dynamism among institutions and be at the same time the leading actors of integration, also by means of the doctrine of direct effect of Community sources in the domestic order. Judgments of the Court of Justice, whether they are or are not expressly included by national law among the sources to which the state must adjust[8], bring about an element of visibility in Community law, which is symbolically important apart from being practically relevant in granting rights to individuals.

The case of night-work for women can be presented as exemplary of the current process of exchange between national judges and the Court of Justice, and can be used to understand the chain reaction to which it gives rise. This is precisely the aspect that I would like to highlight, pointing out that there are even more complex cases[9], in which other actors are involved in a dynamic enactment of Community law. The chain reaction, set into motion by a judgment given by the

---

[7] An Article 177 reference brought by *Tribunale di Milano* (31 March 1994, reported in Riv Italiana di Diritto del Lavoro 1994, II, 273 ff) has to do with the ban (under Italian law) on hiring temporary employees through intermediaries and on its compatibility with Arts 86 and 90, EC Treaty. Strategic litigation in this case is the outcome of long awaited legislation (still to be agreed upon) aiming at the reform of the hiring system and the introduction of new forms of temporary employment. The Court decided in C-111/94 *Job Centre* (not yet reported) that there was not jurisdiction to rule on the question, since it had been raised by a court performing a non-judicial function, namely the confirmation of a company's articles of association, which should have performed the role of intermediary in employment. Apart from the technical mistake in proposing the Article 177 procedure, this case can be quoted as an example of an unrealistic call on the ECJ to solve a domestic problem, the solution of which can only remain in the hands of the legislator.

[8] In Italy the law dealing with the enforcement of Community sources (9 March 1989, n 86, GU 10 March 1989, n 58) includes the Court of Justice's decisions among the sources creating an obligation on the state to intervene. In Germany, the Constitutional Court made a direct reference to the ECJ's case law, when deciding on night-work for women, as a way to fulfil integration and consequently to enforce Treaty obligations. See the case of 28 January 1992, Case Nos 1 BvR 1025/82, 1 BvL 16/83 and 10/91. The reference to the Constitutional Court on the constitutionality of the German law provision prohibiting night-work for women was no longer admissable since it had already been established by the ECJ that such provision was in conflict with European Community law and therefore inapplicable (Int Law Rep, vol 98, 190 ff).

[9] Although in a different field, Case C-179/90 *Merci convenzionali Porto di Genova* [1991] ECR I-5889, can be quoted as an example in which Italian administrative courts at a regional level, as well as the national anti-trust authority, the port authorities, and, last but by no means least, the port workers' associations were alerted by the ECJ's decision and indeed included in a slow and often painful process of integration.

Court of Justice, underlines the dimensions of the phenomenon to be regulated and the existing difficulties when trying to coordinate domestic law coherently with Community law.

As regards the point of integration which I have defined as negative, namely, on the disapplication of domestic law in view of the accurate application of Community law, a judgment of the Italian Constitutional Court may be mentioned as a further example of the multiplicity of outcomes arising from case law.[10] The Court argues that the State can go as far as interrupting the law-making process at a regional level, if it is found that this contrasts with Community law; this is asserted not because of a formal respect for the hierarchy of sources (which is not justifiable in view of the direct application of Community law in the domestic order), but in view of an even wider guarantee for the certainty and clarity of law. Since the State is responsible for the violations of Community laws, States are required not to introduce regulations which will contrast with such laws. The Constitutional Court, being guarantor, under these circumstances, of the correct application of Community law as well as of the enforcement of constitutional principles, must stop a legislative process in progress at the regional level, not in order to pay formal homage to the hierarchy of sources, but in order to avoid objective contradictions between domestic and Community sources. This is a good example of integration, although it is difficult to say whether it is positive or negative, due to the initiative of a national court.

(iii) *Stoeckel* and its impact on national law

Having dealt with the premises, I shall now focus on the specific area of night-work. The *Stoeckel*[11] judgment would seem to all intents and purposes to be very straightforward.

Given the grave financial situation in which the firm run by Mr Stoeckel had found itself, and which necessitated reorganisational measures, management had begun negotiations for a plant agreement which, by means of shift-work, including night shifts, had as its objective the maintenance of all the work-force. This agreement, signed by the unions and meant as enforceable for all male and female employees, foresaw as its main condition for coming into effect that the support for it would be voluntary, and that this would be expressed collectively by a majority vote on the part of the female workers. The agreement would be understood as having been legitimately stipulated and therefore effective, if the applicability of a *branch* agreement to that particular firm could be shown.

---

[10] Corte Cost 10 November 1994, n 384, GU 16 November 1994, serie speciale n 47. In another case the Constitutional Court vindicates its leading role in adjudicating the contrast between national and Community norms and specifies that the mere non-enforcement of the domestic rule is often an inadequate measure, as for Article 5 EC and Article 11 of the Italian Constitution, both establishing obligations to comply with Community law.

[11] Case C-345/89 *Ministère Public* v *Stoeckel* [1991] ECR I-4047.

According to the provisions of a 1987 order, derogations from the general ban on night-work for women had to be specified in a collective agreement wider in its scope than the plant one.

The firm had checked that this condition applied, and had initiated night-work. The agreement had been signed in June, but applied only in October 1988. During the delay the *Tribunal de grande instance* had delivered a judgment, after an appeal by one of the signatory unions, and confirmed the full legitimacy of the agreement. However, the labour inspectors were not of the same opinion; as a result, Mr Stoeckel had to defend himself in a penal court and this he did by invoking the conflict between domestic and Community law (Directive 76/207/EEC of 9 February 1976).

The Article 177 reference was thus centred on the interpretation of Article 5 of the Council Directive 76/207/EEC with regard to the equality of treatment between men and women in a penal judgment for the violation of Article 213-1 of the French labour code. This norm places a wide-ranging ban on night-work for women, since the derogations admitted allow only the specific characteristics of a few types of jobs, such as those which involve managerial positions, with heavy responsibilities; or else in the field of health; or, finally, when particularly serious circumstances of a national relevance arise.

The Court held that the Directive was precise enough to be invoked by national judges, so as to disapply those laws in contrast with Article 5. What was not taken into account was that the ban on night-work for women had been inspired by other criteria of a "social order", as both France and Italy attempted to show during the hearing of the case. Both countries were linked by a more protective attitude on the part of the legislator towards the female worker, since she has been viewed more subject to risk and bearing greater family commitments.

On this point the Court maintained that it no longer recognised the legitimacy of the ban. From this derives the obligation of the States to remove it, according to Article 5.2 of the Directive which was invoked, and to conform to the principle of equal treatment in access to work, in professional training and promotion, and in the conditions of work of both sexes. This meant that no ban could be placed on women's working at night, if there was not also an analogous ban for men.

There is no lack of institutional references in regard to this decision: the Commission had already expressed its point of view in a Communication[12]; that is to say, in a source which by its nature is not binding. It did, importantly however, highlight the directions that were to be imposed on legislative policies. The Member States were therefore put on the alert on a formal level. With the entry into force of all the directives treating equality, all the domestic norms in contrast with these were to be removed – even those which protected women, and which were inspired by a previous model of tutelage.

The call by the Commission for a coherence of sources (which in this case

---

[12] COM (87) 105 final, 13 March 1987, dealing with protective legislation for women in Member States. See Fenwick, in this volume.

also implies a coherence of values) underlines the fact that the need for harmonisation between national juridical systems is essential for the fulfilment of Community aims. The principle of equality was brought down from its pedestal as a basic value towards which all national legal systems aspire by means of different solutions, and became a legally binding rule, the result of market functioning as well as of the internal coherence of national systems.

This need for coherence is complicated by the comparison carried out with another system of rules, namely those of the ILO Convention No 89 of 1948 prohibits the assignation of night-work to women. The Protocol attached to this, which was approved in 1990, authorises derogations of the ban by means of collective bargaining on the part of sectors or firms, subject to consultation with the work representatives and after verification by a competent authority. Before the ratification of this Protocol, the Commission had invited Member States who adhered to Convention No 89 to denounce it, in line with the principle of equality expressed in *Stoeckel*. In a Resolution[13] the European Parliament criticised the activity of the Commission, in particular because these reports had been presented before the States which had ratified Convention No 171 of 1990. This latter source was in reality much more significant because it was oriented towards limiting and regulating night-work for both sexes.

This acceleration in events goes to show that the theme of night-work, which is seemingly marginal in the framework of national and international labour law, becomes much more controversial when it is at the centre of comparisons about levels of protection. The action taken by the Commission towards Member States (felt by some to be excessively intrusive[14]) can be interpreted as an attempt to favour negative integration, leading to choices which do not, strictly speaking, capture the "Community" spirit.

The possibility that the judges of the Court of Justice decided on the removal of the prohibition of night-work in order to facilitate the chances of women's finding a job on the market should not be excluded. Neither should one exclude the possibility that the judges gave priority to protecting the market as such, providing it with a chance to be more flexible and to lighten its burden of over-stringent laws, unable as they were to judge upon the role of collective agreements in regulating this matter.

The fact that the laws protecting women frequently belong to a major (as well as intimate) sphere of national social law, in as much as they are the expression of consolidated traditions, places national judges in a dilemma, i.e. that of having to compare two worlds which are the result of two different systems of law and values. Thus, the market value is better protected if the ban on night-work is

---

[13] Adopted on 9 April 1992. The European Parliament also indicated that the best way to bring together opposite needs was to ban night-work for male and female employees, allowing derogations through collective bargaining at all levels. See, for a similar opinion referred mainly to the French system, Junter-Loiseau, "Le travail de nuit de femmes" *Liaisons Sociales Mensuel*, January 1992, n 65. Up to September 1995 only three governments seem to have ratified Convention 171, namely Cyprus, Dominican Republic and Lithuania.

[14] Marchand, "Rivalité entre normes européennes et normes internationales du travail" 1993 *Droit Social* 702 ff.

eliminated. On the other hand, the social value of protection, which carries with it a series of traditional arguments, such as the family and caretaking functions of women, the greater risks that a woman runs of being attacked, and so on, can be better preserved if national legislators can be left some room for manoeuvre, particularly in the relations between legal and voluntary sources. The Court of Justice chose to clarify social values in a way that is traumatic, if realistic. The risks of the world today bring men and women closer together, and therefore also the night-workers of both sexes.

Behind this lesson in realism conflicting forces can be seen: market versus social values; the needs of firms to restructure and to gain greater flexibility versus equality between employees, regardless of their sex; and collective agreements versus direct state intervention.

A year after *Stoeckel*, the Tribunal of Catania[15] decided to disapply national law, in particular Article 5 of law 903/1977 which, in maintaining the ban on night-work for women, foresees the derogation of this prohibition via collective bargaining, also at plant level. This decision, well-grounded in its justifications, is based on the application of *Stoeckel* and Directive 76/207 (Article 5). What is less clear, is the question on which the lower court judge had based its previous decision, namely the interpretation of the derogatory plant agreement and of its enforceability for all employees.[16]

The question at stake is the direct effect which national judges (in this case the Tribunal of Catania) carry out as a consequence of the Court of Justice's judgments. In deciding on this same matter the *Corte di Cassazione*[17] has argued that such judgments play the same role as regulations: they put the national judge in the position to decide as if the internal norm was abrogated, although a removal from the legal system did not formally occur.

In the same decision it is underlined that there is a substantial similarity between the French and Italian legal systems and that the coincidence in legal solutions adopted on night-work was brought about by the preliminary ruling procedure in *Stoeckel*. This passage in the reasoning of the *Cassazione* must be emphasised: a comparative evaluation of legal systems is presented as a parallel justification to the central argument, based on the supremacy of Community sources, including the Court's case law. A possible "misuse" of comparative law

---

[15] 8 July 1992, Foro Italiano 1993, I, 2970. A similar case was decided by Pretura di Matera, 14 luglio 1994, annotated by Cavalli, "Esenzione delle donne dal lavoro notturno", 1994 *Dir Comm Scambi Int* 745, in which the direct effect of ECJ's judgments is presented acritically in its consequences, that is to say in the non-enforcement of domestic law.

[16] This aspect of the problem is taken into account by Cass 24 April 1993, n 4802, Mass Giur Lav 1993, 353, in which a previous decision of the Tribunal of Matera is overruled. Cassazione held that dissenting votes expressed by female employees, when approving a plant agreement on the introduction of night-work do not as such impede the enforcement of the same agreement. Its legitimacy must be measured in relation to the protection of health and safety at the place of work. The latter constitutes the essential "condition and limit" for engaging in collective bargaining. This confrontation among judges shows that an unsolved problem in Italian Labour Law remains central, namely the enforceability of collective agreement, based on *de facto* rather that *de jure* principles, due to the lack of legislation on this point.

[17] Corte di Cass 3 February 1995, n 1271, Dir Lav 1995, II, 8.

could be envisaged, if one saw the reflection in the Italian system of what was decided with reference to the French system, unless one had to argue that the Italian judges bring to the extreme limit the argument on supremacy, incorporating in it a value judgment on the comparability of two legal systems. Certainly, it cannot be denied that in this particular decision, the Court of Justice's judgment is truly treated as if it was an internal source, so much part of the judges' tools, to allow for a breakthrough in a very sensitive area of the law.

Negative integration, through direct reference to the Community source, gives rise to the disapplication of domestic law, before the legislator has had an opportunity to intervene. It is not surprising that in a law under discussion in Parliament, aimed at fulfilling Community obligations, abrogation of the banning on night-work for women had been introduced. Nor is it surprising that the legislator has since decided to remove this subject from the same law, proposing to regulate *funditus* the whole comprehensive field of working time.[18]

Dynamic integration foresees this too: a process of reciprocal highlighting, as well as solicitation and reflection, on the part of the various powers of the State, giving rise to an anything but acritical acceptance of the supranational source.

What *Stoeckel* and *Tribunale di Catania* fail to take into consideration is the role that collective agreements play in systems such as those of Italy and France.[19] It might be maintained that it was not possible to raise an issue of this kind before the Community judges. It should, however, be taken into account that a system allowing collective agreements to lift the ban on night-work, is a system which has reflected on this possibility, and which has chosen a way of rendering compatible the requirements of the employer with those of the employees.

In no company organization is it easy to establish night shifts without ever having to face a series of derogations. For this reason even if a law abolishes the ban on female employees and leaves in force only that on pregnant women, the role which collective agreements play in the practical handling of this issue is not likely to stop, since it is important for employers, just as it is for employees of both sexes.

Reconciliation between these different interests, while respecting entrepreneurial prerogatives, should be treated within a coherent regulation of working time. Among Community sources, there is only the (very controversial) Directive 93/104, which does not treat night-work for women in any particular detail. The fact that this Directive is based on Article 118A and is therefore inspired by the protection of employees' health and safety, enables us to hope that the area of night-work will also receive more attention, independent of which sex needs to benefit from it.

---

[18] On 4 April 1995, at the *Camera dei deputati* government withdrew the amendments presented, in order to modify Art 5, L903/1977, in compliance with *Stoeckel* and asked to be empowered to propose legislation on working time, in the framework of Directive 93/104. This is another example of wide-ranging legislation being officially announced under the threat of minor changes imposed by a decision of the Court.

[19] See Bercusson, in this volume.

(iv) The relevance of ILO sources

The reference that can be made to the International Labour Office sources mentioned above, and in particular Convention No 171 of 1990 is useful in this regard. In this Convention the starting point is that night-work be allowed only in exceptional circumstances, in which entrepreneurial motivations must give ample demonstration of the reasons lying behind organizational choices of this kind. The issue is very heavily regulated by means of recourse to rest periods and periodic checkups. Indeed, the safety of the employees is the most important feature of this activity, which attempts to coordinate opposite needs.

It is therefore surprising that Member States, constrained by the Community system to make choices leading to greater internal coherence, are not now being encouraged to include in their systems this important ILO source. Other examples can also be quoted: as well as a Belgian proposal for law which would make night-work possible only under exceptional circumstances, a Spanish law of 1994 already exists.[20]

In this very conflicting picture of the relations between sources, there is another judgment of the Court of Justice, *Levy*[21] of 1993, which should be discussed. This judgment deals with the interpretation of international sources (such as ILO Convention of 1948 which precedes the Rome Treaty) and restates their binding force (Article 234-1) relative to one or more Member States.

Since the denunciation of Convention No 89 was in the meantime made on the part of all the Member States, *Levy* was important for the affirmation of a general principle, as well as to give indications of a direction to be taken in relations with international organizations. Following this decision, and strengthened by an important Opinion from the Court of Justice[22] (given about a year before, having to do with health and safety), the Commission presented the Council with a proposal concerning relations among Member States, the Community and the ILO.[23]

This is a very interesting document, because it reminds all the Community institutions of their obligation to respect the Member States as subjects which comply autonomously with ILO sources. Even if the European Community sits in its own right, together with the Member States in the negotiations for the

---

[20] The proposed Belgian law goes into the direction of banning night-work and allowing deroga-tions for both male and female employees. Art 36 of the Spanish Workers' Statute has been modi-fied (as for L 19 May 1994, n 11, para 6 B) in order to take into account Directive 93/104. See Murcia Claveria, "Trabajo nocturno, trabajo a turnos y ritmo de trabajo" in F. Valdes Dal Re (ed.), *La reforma del mercado laboral* (Valladolid 1994) 293 ff.

[21] Case C-158/91 *Ministère public et Direction du Travail et de l'emploi* v *Levy* [1993] ECR I-4287. See Wuiame, "Night Work for women- Stoeckel revisited", 23 ILJ (1994), 95–100.

[22] Opinion 2/91, 19 March 1993, OJ 1993 C109/1 as for Art 228.1.2 of the EEC Treaty, on the matter of ILO Convention 170 when the use of chemical materials occurs at work.

[23] COM(94) 2, 12 January 1994, Proposal for a Council Decision on the exercise of the Commu-nity's external competence at international labour conferences in cases falling within the joint com-petence of the Community and its Member States.

stipulation of new conventions, it cannot act independently of the governments, and it must make sure that the consultation procedure of the social partners, which always precedes the formation and the ratification of these sources, takes place.

This proposal constitutes an example of proceduralisation of the complex relations occurring among international organizations. The Commission reminds the Member States to respect this trilaterality, which is the guiding principle in ILO conventions, and it commits itself to reproducing at Community level the consultation procedure of the social partners. If the decision is adopted by the Council, the *iter* sparked off by a decision from the Court of Justice can be said to be closed, with a revisitation of the general principles regulating the external relations of the Community. Such a result, which has seen judges as some of its principal protagonists in this process of transformation, should be considered as important for the expected results it provokes at the level of Community institutions.

A last judgment should be discussed to complete the picture of Community case law on night-work. In *Minne*[24], the female worker in question was unemployed. First she had been resident in Luxembourg, where she had worked in a hotel, accepting to be on night-shifts. She then transferred to Belgium, where she applied for unemployment benefit. The state office concerned rejected her application because Mrs Minne declared that she would be unable to work at night on account of her family commitments. The interesting point in this case is that in Belgium there is legislation banning night-work for men and women, which includes a detailed list of derogations in relation to various activities and to the duties carried out therein.

The derogations, it is claimed in this decision, should not be decided differently for men and women, given the principle of equality sanctified by Article 5 of Directive 76/207/EEC, with the exception of cases in which a different treatment can be justified, as indicated in *Johnston*.[25]

If we put to one side the adjacent problem that Italy and France are facing today, that is, in their attempts to comply with Community obligations, then legal regulation of night-work cannot be treated in a much wider set of terms. A judgment from the Court of Justice has led to differing reactions among the governments of the Member States, but also among judges and, in all likelihood, also among the negotiators of collective agreements. Negative integration could prove not to be the best path to take, since the need to arrive at protection for the health and safety of night-workers, and also a detailed regulation of the derogations for employees of both sexes is of paramount importance. To reach this last objective, coordination between legal and voluntary sources seems to be necessary. This goes together with the adoption, on the part of national legislators, of flexible legislative measures regarding working hours, capable of reconciling specific individual demands with work organization.

---

[24] Case C-13/93 *Office national de l'emploi (ONEM)* v *Madeleine Minne* [1994] ECR I-371.

[25] Case 222/84 *Johnston* v *Chief Constable of the Royal Ulster Constabulary* [1986] ECR 1651. See Fenwick, and O'Leary, in this volume.

(v) Conclusions

Night-work for women has been used in this chapter as an example of dynamic integration, with a particular emphasis on the role of lower courts when they make use of Community sources. The outcome is a legal system in constant transformation, driven by a multiplicity of actors both internal and external to the Community. It is a procedure permanently open, to be perfected and completed through existing tools and through new ones. In particular, it has been shown that international standards, wider in their scope than the Community's, can represent an authoritative parameter when combining the rules of the market with social policies.

An attempt has also been made to point out that integration moves in various directions (from the centre to the periphery and vice versa) and that it manifests itself in different shapes and forms. In the absence of fundamental principles capable of becoming visible to the individuals (as it happened for Article 119) and of representing the spine of social policies, national legal systems may be tempted to pursue deregulatory policies, in line with the weak legislative choices made by the central institutions. The greatest danger lies in the fact that such policies may hide themselves behind negative integration and be presented as the ultimate result of a necessary approximation to Community law.

The issue of equality, when referred to night-work, acquires different and more complex connotations[26], often reflecting very specific choices made by national legislators, themselves influenced by the attitude of the social partners and by the more or less central role played by collective bargaining. Such peculiarities should not be lost in the dynamics of integration, neither should they be swept away by the loss of initiative which is often the outcome of negative integration.

SILVANA SCIARRA
Professor of European Labour Law and Social Law,
European University Institute,
University of Florence,
Italy

---

[26] As outlined by Supiot, "Principi di eguaglianza e limiti della razionalità giuridica", 1992 *Lavoro e diritto*, 218.

Part III

SOCIAL SECURITY

Chapter 8

THE PRINCIPLE OF EQUAL TREATMENT FOR MEN AND WOMEN IN SOCIAL SECURITY*

(i) Introduction

The principle of equal treatment for men and women in social security is enacted in two Directives; Directive 79/7/EEC[1], which applies to statutory social security schemes, and Directive 86/378/EEC[2], which applies to occupational social security schemes. Their enactment was envisaged in Article 1(2) of the general Equal Treatment Directive 76/207/EEC[3], which provided for the adoption of "further measures defining the substance, scope and arrangements for the application" of the principle of equal treatment in the field of social security. The two Directives were based on the general enabling provisions of Article 235 of the EC Treaty[4], there being no specific treaty provision for equal treatment for men and women parallel to Article 119 EC in respect of pay.

Directives 79/7/EEC and 86/378/EEC are enacted in near-identical terms as regards the persons and the benefits covered. Both provide for certain exclusions from the equal treatment principle.[5] In the case of Directive 86/378/EEC, however, these exceptions have been largely circumvented as regards employed persons by decisions of the Court of Justice in *Barber*[6] and subsequent cases[7] based on Article 119 of the EC Treaty.[8] Directive 86/378/EEC alone allows for exceptions to be made on the basis of actuarial calculation factors.[9] Since the principal issues relat-

---

*This chapter was written by Josephine Steiner.
[1] OJ 1979 L6/24.
[2] OJ 1986 L225/40.
[3] OJ 1976 L39/40.
[4] Directive 86/378/EEC was also based on Article 100 EC.
[5] Article 7(1) of Directive 79/7/EEC: Article 6(1) (d)(h)(i)(j), Article 9 of Directive 86/378/EEC.
[6] Case C-262/88 [1990] ECR I-1889.
[7] Case C-152/91 *Neath* v *Hugh Steeper Ltd* [1993] ECR I-6935; Case C-110/91 *Moroni* v *Firma Collo GmbH* [1993] ECR; Case C-200/91 *Coloroll Pensions Trustees Ltd* v *Russell, Mangham & Others* [1994] ECR J-4389.
[8] See Whiteford, in this volume.
[9] Article 6(1) (d)(h)(i), Article 9(c).

ing to Directive 86/378/EEC are discussed elsewhere in this book[10] the focus of this chapter will be on statutory social security schemes and Directive 79/7/EEC.

As a measure concerned with social security Directive 79/7/EEC may be seen as supplementary to the principal EC social security Regulation (EEC) 1408/71.[11] Both provisions operate to modify national social security rules, which otherwise remain governed by national law. However, the scope of Directive 79/7/EEC, in terms of the persons and the benefits covered, is considerably narrower than Regulation (EEC) 1408/71. Regulation (EEC) 1408/71, which was based on Article 51 EC[12], was designed to remove the barriers to the free movement of EC workers and their families throughout the Community by eliminating all discrimination based on nationality and by providing for the aggregation of social security entitlements acquired in different Member States and the payment of benefits wherever the claimant might be resident. Rights under the Regulation apply to all social security benefits and to any person who is (or has been) insured, "compulsorily, or on an optional continued basis, for one or more of the contingencies covered by the branches of a social security scheme for employed or self-employed persons".[13] The purpose of Directive 79/7/EEC was to ensure equality of treatment for male and female workers, both employed and self-employed, in the provision of social security benefits. It provides for the introduction of the equal treatment principle "in the first place"[14] only in respect of some statutory social security schemes, and is subject to express exclusions. These limitations reflect Member States' qualified acceptance of the equal treatment principle in this area, derived from a concern to avoid disrupting the financial equilibrium of national social security schemes, in which benefits are calculated on the basis of contributions made over a working lifetime, by too radical a change. These factors have no doubt tempered the Court's approach to interpretation of the Directive, which has been less bold than in other areas involving the free movement of workers, particularly in its more cautious post-Maastricht phase. Here, as elsewhere however, its jurisprudence during this period has not been consistent.

(ii) Direct effects: the scope of Directive 79/7/EEC for individual and representative action

The principal provisions of Directive 79/7/EEC have been held by the Court of Justice on many occasions to be sufficiently clear and precise to be directly

---

[10] See Whiteford, in this volume.
[11] OJ sp Ed 1971 (II), 416. As amended and updated by Reg 2001/83 (OJ 1983 L 230/6), as finally amended by Reg 1249/92 (OJ 1992 L 136/28).
[12] Contained in Title III Chapter I Free Movement of Workers.
[13] Article 1(a)(i) as amended by Regulation (EEC) 1390/81, Article 1(2)(a); see also Case 75/63 *Hoekstra (née Unger)* [1964] ECR 347.
[14] Preamble, recital 2.

effective. They became directly effective[15] on the expiry of the time limit for implementation, 23 December 1984. After that date Member States were no longer free to enact or maintain in force any provisions, transitional or otherwise, breaching the principle of equal treatment as laid down in the Directive. Where national law, following amendment to comply with the equal treatment principle, preserves the effects of past discrimination (that is discrimination permitted prior to 23 December 1984), by maintaining an advantage enjoyed by one sex during a transitional period (for example by linking eligibility to past discriminatory criteria) it will breach Directive 79/7/EEC. This has been found to occur in a number of cases.[16] Provided the claimant falls within the scope of the Directive and the benefit in respect of which equality is claimed is covered by the Directive, the Directive may be invoked directly to demand a particular benefit, or level of benefit, or to challenge an award or refusal of benefit as discriminatory on the grounds of sex. As long as the provision in question is sufficiently clear and precise there will be no problem concerning its direct effects, since it will always be invoked vertically, against the state, or an agency of the state.[17] The Court has held that, even where an individual has not relied on the Directive before a national court, that court may take the Directive into account, and may, of its own motion, refer questions of interpretation of the Directive to the Court of Justice under Article 177 EC where they are relevant and an interpretation from that Court is necessary to enable the judge to decide the case.[18]

Where discrimination contrary to Directive 79/7/EEC is found to occur "the class of persons placed at a disadvantage is entitled to be treated in the same way, and according to the same rules, as other recipients of the allowance, such rules remaining the only valid point of reference so long as the Directive has not been implemented correctly".[19] The national court or tribunal deciding the case is thus obliged, as a matter of Community law, to supply the appropriate remedy. Any inconsistent provisions of internal law are automatically inapplicable.[20]

As well as providing a direct source of rights for individuals, directly effective provisions of Directive 79/7/EEC may also be invoked by a representative body such as the Equal Opportunities Commission in order to challenge national measures, including legislative measures, for their compatibility with the Directive. This is so provided that it can demonstrate a "sufficient interest in the matter to which the application relates".[21] Such was the case in *R* v *Secretary of State ex parte*

---

[15] Except in the case of new Member States still within the transitional period of adjustment to membership.

[16] Case 384/85 *Clarke* v *Chief Adjudication Officer* [1987] ECR 2865; Cases C-87–89/90 *Verholen, van Wetten-van Uden & Heiderijk* v *Sociale Verzekeringsbank* [1991] ECR I-3757; Case C-31/90 *Johnson* v *Chief Adjudication Officer* [1991] ECR I-3723; Case C-343/92 *Roks & Others* v *Bestuur van Bedrijfsvereniging* [1994] ECR I-571; Case C-154/92 *Remi van Cant* v *Rijksdienst voor Pensioenen* [1993] ECR I-3811.

[17] Distinction between vertical and horizontal direct effects established in Case 152/84 *Marshall* v *South West Hants AHA* [1986] ECR 723. "State" agency is defined in Case C-188/89 *Foster* v *British Gas* [1990] ECR I-3313.

[18] Case C-88/90 *Verholen* [1991] ECR I-3757.

[19] Case 71/85 *Nederlands* v *Federatie Nederlandsee Vakbeweging* [1986] ECR 3855.

[20] Principle established in Case 106/77 *Simmenthal SpA (No 2)* [1978] ECR 629.

[21] RSC Order 53 rule 7.

EOC.[22] Although the claim was unsuccessful on the merits, the EOC's standing to sue was accepted by the High Court. Likewise the House of Lords accepted the EOC's standing to sue in *EOC* v *Secretary of State for Employment.*[23] Here the EOC succeeded in obtaining a declaration from the House of Lords that certain provisions of the Employment Protection (Consolidation) Act 1988, which discriminated against part-time workers, were incompatible with Equal Treatment Directive 76/207/EEC.[24]

(iii) Relationship between Directive 79/7/EEC and Article 119

Where a particular benefit, prima facie a social security benefit, is financed by an employer, either as a substitute for or a supplement to a statutory social security scheme, it may be possible to claim equal treatment in respect of that benefit under Article 119 EC as discriminatory pay. Article 119 is wider in scope than the social security Directives, since it is not subject to exceptions. Moreover, the Court has held that the Directives may not in any way restrict or alter the meaning and scope of Article 119. They may only operate to supplement or extend its effects.[25]

Although Article 119 has been invoked principally in the context of challenge to employers' contributions to occupational schemes (as in *Barber*[26], *Moroni*[27] and *Coloroll*[28]) it has on occasions been applied to statutory schemes. The line between pay, in respect of which action may be brought under Article 119, and social security, falling within Directive 79/7/EEC, is still not wholly clear.[29] In *Defrenne* v *Belgian State (No 1)*[30] the Court held that:

> Although consideration in the nature of social security benefits is not . . . in principle alien to the concept of pay, there cannot be brought within this concept, as defined in Article 119, social security schemes or benefits, in particular retirement pensions, directly governed by legislation without any element of agreement within the undertaking or the occupational branch concerned, which are obligatorily applicable to general categories of workers.
>
> These schemes assure for the workers the benefit of a legal scheme, (to) the financing of which workers, employers and possibly the public authorities contribute in a measure determined less by the employment relationship between the employer and the worker than by considerations of social policy.[31]

---

[22] Case C-9/91 [1992] ECR I-4297.
[23] [1994] 1 All ER 910.
[24] OJ 1976 L39/40.
[25] *Moroni, supra* n 7.
[26] *Barber, supra* n 6.
[27] *Supra* n 7
[28] *Supra* n 7
[29] But for some clarification see Whiteford, in this volume.
[30] Case 80/70 [1971] ECR 445.
[31] At paras 7, 8.

However, not all statutory schemes in the nature of social security schemes determined by considerations of social policy rather than by the "employment relationship" have been excluded from the concept of pay. The scope of the Court's ruling in *Defrenne* v *Belgian State (No 1)*[32], although consistently cited, has been whittled down over the years. In *Liefting*[33] a contribution by employers to a statutory pension scheme for civil servants (including provision for widows and orphans, supplementing and replacing the general statutory social security scheme, calculated by reference to the employed person's salary, and paid by the employer directly into the revenue) was held to be included in the concept of pay:

> Sums which public authorities are required to pay as social security payable by persons working for the authority, when such sums are included in calculating the gross salary payable to civil servants, should be considered as pay within the meaning of Article 119 in so far as they determine the calculation of other salary-related benefits (such as compensation for dismissal, unemployment benefits, family allowances and credit facilities).[34]

In *Rinner-Kühn*[35] a part-time office cleaner working ten hours a week was permitted to challenge as indirectly discriminatory German legislation requiring payment by employers of six weeks' sick pay only to employees working more than ten hours a week or 45 hours per month, in a claim against her employer based on Article 119. This was so even though the employer's contribution was required under German law and was subject to reimbursement. Advocate-General Darmon reasoned that since the payment "had its genesis in the employment relationship" it was "determined more by the employment relationship than by considerations of social policy". The Court, ruling under Article 177[36] was content simply to point out that "as the national court observes, the continued payment of wages to an employee in the event of an illness falls within the concept of pay within the meaning of Article 119".

The Court was required to clarify the relationship between Article 119 and Directive 79/7/EEC in the recent case of *Beune*.[37] The claim here, as in *Liefting*[38], concerned provisions of a statutory retirement pension scheme for civil servants, allegedly discriminatory against men. It was challenged on the basis of Article 119 and Directive 79/7/EEC. The Court held that the fact that a benefit is governed by statute provides strong evidence that it constitutes social security within Directive 79/7/EEC. But this does not prevent it from falling under

---

[32] *Supra* n 30.
[33] Case 23/83 [1984] ECR 3225.
[34] At paras 13, 12.
[35] Case C-171/88 [1989] ECR 2743.
[36] This procedure, in which rulings are given by the ECJ in response to questions referred by the national court, enables the former court to sidestep wider issues not raised by the national court.
[37] Case C-7/93 *Bestuur van het Algemeen Burgerlijk Pensionfonds* v *G A Beune* [1994] ECR I-4771. See Whiteford, in this volume.
[38] *Supra* n 33.

Article 119. Schemes replacing or supplementing statutory social security schemes which result from an agreement between employer and employee and which are not financed by the public purse may constitute pay, even, as was the case in *Beune*[39], if the scheme is compulsory for the entire industry concerned. Similarly, employers' contributions to schemes which concern particular categories of worker, such as civil servants, as opposed to schemes for workers in general, may also fall within the concept of pay. "The only decisive criterion", the Court suggested, is "whether they are paid by reason of the employment relationship".

This test of payment "by reason of the employment relationship" has been invoked in a number of different situations, albeit not involving Directive 79/7/EEC, in order to include a particular benefit provided, directly or indirectly, by the employer, within the concept of pay. It was applied, resulting in successful claims under Article 119, to employers' contributions to occupational pension schemes in *Worringham & Humphries* v *Lloyds Bank Ltd*[40] and in slightly different circumstances in *Barber* v *Guardian Royal Exchange Assurance Co Ltd*.[41] It was also applied to employers' compulsory contributions to statutory redundancy and unfair dismissal schemes in *Barber*, even though these schemes were applicable to the general working population and were undoubtedly determined by considerations of social policy. In *Barber* the Court suggested at paragraph 28 that the only benefits paid by the employer by reason of the employment relationship which lie outside Article 119 are "benefits awarded by national statutory social security schemes". Thus, whilst extending the ambit of Article 119 in *Barber* to include employers' contributions to occupational schemes and employment protection benefits, the Court clearly felt unable wholly to deny the basic exemption for national statutory social schemes established in *Defrenne* v *Belgian State (No 1)*[42] by suggesting that employers' contributions to these schemes might also constitute pay. However, its broad dictum in paragraph 28 of *Barber* is not consistent with *Rinner-Kühn*.[43] Nor is it desirable or consistent with the general principle of equality[44] that an individual's right to equal treatment in respect of social security benefits should depend on whether the benefit is provided under a statutory or an occupational scheme; *a fortiori* when the relationship between, and relative responsibilities of, state and employer in the provision of such benefits varies from State to State.

This possibility of a claim under Article 119, alternative to or concurrent with a claim under Directive 79/7/EEC, is important since, as will be seen, the categories of persons entitled to claim and of social security benefits covered by

---

[39] See, *supra* n 37.
[40] Case 69/80 [1981] ECR 767.
[41] See *Barber*, supra n 6. *Barber* concerned the *payment* of retirement pensions at different ages for men and women; *Worringham & Humphries* concerned employers' *contributions* to such pensions at different ages.
[42] *Defrenne* v *Belgian State*, *supra* n 32.
[43] *Rinner-Kühn supra* n 35.
[44] Respected by the Court as part of EC law, see Cases 103, 145/77 *Royal Scholten Honig* v *Intervention Board for Agricultural Produce* [1978] ECR 2037.

the Directive are strictly limited. Certain social security benefits are still expressly excluded from its scope. The Court's approach to interpretation of its provisions has tended to be strict.[45] Unlike a claim under Directive 79/7/EEC, a claim under Article 119 against an employer in respect of the employer's contribution to a statutory social security scheme poses no threat to public expenditure or the financial balance of social security funds. To allow such a claim could, and no doubt would, cause disruption in national social security *schemes*, but no more than was caused in the field of occupational schemes by the line of cases beginning with *Barber*. The Court's attitude to this latter disruption has been cavalier.[46] If it were thought desirable to achieve greater consistency between occupational and statutory social security schemes by extending the ambit of Article 119[47], the impact of such a decision could be controlled by imposing a limit on its retroactivity, as it was in *Barber*.

(iv) Personal scope of Directive 79/7/EEC

Directive 79/7/EEC is expressed to apply to

> The working population – including self-employed persons, workers and self-employed persons whose activities have been interrupted through illness, accident or involuntary unemployment and persons seeking employment and to retired and invalided workers and self-employed persons.[48]

The Court has not been ungenerous in its approach to these provisions. In *Drake* v *Chief Adjudication Officer*[49] it held that the Directive could be invoked to claim an invalid care allowance by a daughter who had given up her work to look after her disabled mother even though the "risk" which had interrupted her work had occurred not to her but to her mother, the person for whom she gave up work to care. This interpretation was based on the purpose of the Directive, to ensure equal treatment of men and women as regards social security; it was clearly influenced by the Commission's argument that the effect of the

---

[45] Although two decisions of 1995, Case C-137/94 *R* v *Secretary of State for Health ex parte Richardson* Judgment of 19 October 1995, nyr, and Case C-116/94 *Meyers* v *Chief Adjudication Officer* Judgment of 13 July 1995, nyr, indicate a shift towards a more generous approach. *Cf.* Case C-92/94 *Secretary of State for Social Security* v *Graham*, Judgment of 11 August 1995, nyr ; see postscript.

[46] In Case C-408/92 *Smith & Others* v *Avdel Systems Ltd* [1994] ECR 1–4435, the Court held in a challenge to an occupational pension scheme based on Article 119 that "any financial difficulties affecting the pension scheme or the undertaking concerned could not be relied on as justification for a difference in treatment between men and women". The Court was similarly dismissive in Case C-137/94 *R* v *Secretary of State ex parte Richardson*, *supra* n 45, that extending the right to exemption from prescriptions charges to men at the age of 60 would increase the burden borne by the State in the funding of the National Health Service.

[47] There is a case for saying that it is not, and that, given the confusion that has ensued, the Court went too far in respect of occupational pension schemes in *Barber*. See Whiteford, "Lost in the Mists of Time; the ECJ and Occupational Pensions" 32 CML Rev (1995), 801–840.

[48] Dir 79/7/EEC Article 2.

[49] Case 150/85 [1986] ECR 1995.

Directive would be "seriously compromised if it were to be held that the way in which the benefit was paid could determine whether or not the benefit was covered by the Directive". As the Court pointed out, the payment of the benefit to the person who provides care still depends on the existence of a situation of invalidity. There is a "clear economic link between the benefit and the disabled person as the disabled person derives an advantage from the fact that an allowance is paid to the person caring for him".[50]

The Court was more literal in its approach to Article 2 in *Achterberg Te Riele*.[51] Here it held that the claimants, three female old-age pensioners who had been refused an old-age pension on the basis of criteria (wife not insured unless husband insured; not vice versa) which were undoubtedly discriminatory, were outside the scope of Directive 79/7/EEC. One of the claimants had given up her job voluntarily; one had lost her job but did not subsequently look for work; and the third had never worked. The Court pointed out that the principle of non-discrimination of Directive 79/7/EEC did not apply generally, but only to men and women in their capacity as workers. It did not apply to persons who had never worked or were not seeking work or to persons who have had an occupation which was not interrupted by one of the risks laid down in Article 3(1)(a); that is, the risks falling within the material scope of the Directive.

The effects of *Achterberg Te Riele* were mitigated in *Verholen and Others*.[52] In Case 89/90, Mr Heiderijk, who was claiming an old-age pension in respect of his dependent wife, which had been reduced on account of past rules which discriminated against his wife, was held entitled to rely on Directive 79/7/EEC in order to challenge those rules. Citing its ruling in *Achterberg Te Riele* that "where the provision of a Directive like Article 2 of Directive 79/7 determines precisely the person to whom the Directive is to apply, a national court cannot extend the scope *ratione personae* of the Directive on the grounds that the persons concerned are covered by national rules . . .". However, "an individual who bears the effect of a discriminatory national provision may be allowed to rely on the Directive if his wife, who is the victim of the discrimination, herself comes within the scope of the Directive" (para 25). This applies even if she is not a party to the proceedings. This ruling was based on a line of case law, beginning with *Johnston* v *RUC*[53], establishing national authorities' obligation (under Article 6 of Directive 76/207/EEC and Articles 6 and 13 ECHR[54]) to ensure effective judicial protection for individuals' Community rights. "The application of national legislation must not render virtually impossible the exercise of rights conferred by Community law."

The scope for claims under Directive 79/7/EEC by persons seeking work was considered in *Johnson* v *Chief Adjudication Officer*.[55] Here the Court

---

[50] *Ibid* para 24.
[51] Cases 48, 106, 107/88 [1989] ECR 1963.
[52] Cases C-87–89/90 [1991] ECR I-3757.
[53] Case 222/84 [1986] ECR 1651.
[54] European Convention on Human Rights and Fundamental Freedoms 1950.
[55] Case C-31/90 [1991] ECR I-3723.

established that a person who gives up work voluntarily to look after children is not within the scope of the Directive. She will only be within the scope of the Directive if she is seeking work at the time when the risk outlined in Article 2 materialises. This must be proved. It is for the national court to establish whether the claimant was in fact seeking work at the relevant time either by evidence of the claimant having registered with the appropriate employment organization, or sent off job applications, or attended job interviews.

It may be presumed that a person who gives up work voluntarily may still rely on the Directive in circumstances such as obtained in *Drake*.[56]

(a) Part-time workers

As noted above, *Rinner-Kühn*[57] established that a part-time worker was entitled to challenge German social security legislation concerning sick pay under Article 119, as being indirectly discriminatory against women. To what extent may Directive 79/7/EEC be invoked by part-time workers in order to claim equality of treatment with full-time workers as regards access to or conditions of social security schemes?

The matter was considered in *Ruzius Wilbrink*.[58] The case concerned a claim by a part-time worker seeking to challenge a Dutch statute governing disability allowance, which she claimed was indirectly discriminatory against women. The Court's ruling, delivered in Article 177 proceedings, was in her favour. The rules, which denied the allowance to employees whose income was 15% below the minimum wage, but which did not apply to certain comparable low income groups, such as the self-employed, was found to be indirectly discriminatory against women, and not objectively justified. Both the referring Dutch Court and the Court of Justice assumed that the claimant was entitled to rely on Directive 79/7/EEC.

It is submitted that this view is correct. Any social security benefit covered by Directive 79/7/EEC should in principle be capable of being claimed by part-time workers on a basis of equality with full-time workers. Equal access, and equal rights, may only be refused where this is objectively justified. The question of objective justification will be considered further below.

(v) Material scope of Directive 79/7/EEC

Article 3(1) provides that this Directive shall apply to:

(a) statutory schemes which provide protection against the following risks: sickness, invalidity, old age, accidents at work and occupational diseases, and unemployment;
(b) social assistance, in so far as it is intended to supplement or replace the schemes referred to in (a).

---

[56] *Drake, supra* n 49.
[57] *Rinner-Kühn, supra* n 35.
[58] Case 102/88 [1989] ECR 4311.

Survivors' benefits and family benefits, except in the case of family benefits granted by way of increases of benefits due under Article 3(1), both of which are covered by Regulation 1408/71 (Article 4), are excluded (Article 3(2)). Further exclusions are provided in Article 7 (see below).

In *Drake* v *Chief Adjudication Officer*[59] the Court held that in order to constitute a social security benefit within Directive 79/7/EEC a benefit "must constitute the whole or part of a statutory scheme providing protection against one of the specified risks or a form of social assistance having the same objective". The Court suggested that:

> In order to ensure that the progressive implementation of the principle of equal treatment . . . is carried out in a harmonious manner throughout the Community, Article 3(1) must be interpreted as including any benefit which in a broad sense forms part of one of the statutory schemes referred to or a social assistance provision intended to supplement or replace such a scheme.

Despite this promising start, recent interpretations of Article 3 have been, for the Court, unusually strict. Even when it might justifiably have adopted the purposive approach, as it did in *Drake* and *Verholen*[60], it has declined to do so. In *R* v *Secretary of State for Social Security ex parte Smithson*[61] it refused to admit a challenge to a "higher pension premium". The premium was linked to, and dependent on, receipt of invalidity pension, the conditions for the granting of which were seemingly discriminatory, being calculated by reference to retirement age. Its refusal was based on the fact that the challenge arose in the context of a claim for housing benefit, the rate of which was linked to the higher pension premium. Advocate-General Tesauro had "no doubt" that a challenge concerning the higher pension premium "rightly belonged" within the scope of Directive 79/7/EEC. In view of the individual's "fundamental right" to protection against sex discrimination:

> Article 3(1) must be interpreted as including any benefit which in a broad sense forms part of one of the statutory schemes referred to or a social assistance provision intended to supplement or replace such a scheme.

Invoking *Drake*, he suggested that:

> Any other approach would enable Member States to escape their obligations under the Directive with ease. They would only need to include in a scheme of general scope, or at least one not specifically intended to provide protection against one of the risks set out in Article 3 of the Directive, a benefit which was, taken in isolation, designed precisely to provide protection against those risks.

Without addressing these compelling arguments the Court simply found that, unlike the invalidity care allowance in *Drake*, the benefit in question, a housing

---

[59] *Drake, supra* n 49.
[60] *Drake, supra* n 49; *Verholen, supra* n 16.
[61] Case C-243/90 [1992] ECR I-467.

benefit, was "not directly and effectively linked to the protection provided against one of the risks specified in Article 3(1)". Age and invalidity were only two of the criteria applied to determine the extent of the claimant's need. The fact that these criteria were decisive as regards eligibility for a higher pension premium, and that the rate of housing benefit was tied to the higher pension premium, was not sufficient to bring that benefit within the scope of Directive 79/7/EEC.

A similarly restrictive approach was adopted in *Jackson & Cresswell* v *Chief Adjudication Officer*.[62] Both cases involved claims by single mothers. The claims arose as a result of a change of circumstances (and benefits) resulting in a loss of deductions for child-minding expenses.

Ms Jackson had been in receipt of supplementary benefit. This benefit was withdrawn when she began a course of vocational training, at which point she received a weekly allowance from the Manpower Services Commission. Child-minding expenses were not deducted from the latter benefit whereas they had been from the former. Child-minding expenses were also deductible from unemployment benefit.

Ms Cresswell had been in receipt of income support. This was not payable to persons working more than 24 hours per week, who were regarded as "engaged in remunerative work". Ms Cresswell embarked on part-time work involving less than 24 hours per week. Such work was treated under United Kingdom regulations as not constituting "remunerative work". Child-minding expenses were not deductible from those in part-time work. They had been deducted when she was in receipt of full income support.

Both claims, alleging indirect discrimination[63], were brought under Directive 79/7/EEC and Equal Treatment Directive 76/207/EEC. Both involved a challenge to the adjudication officer's refusal to deduct child-minding expenses when calculating supplementary allowances and income support. In both cases the benefit in question had the same purpose – to provide financial support to persons whose means are insufficient to meet their needs. The Court's judgment was harsh and extremely brief. As regards the claim under Directive 79/7/EEC, it held simply that the Directive "did not refer to a statutory scheme which provided persons with means below a legally defined limit with a special benefit designed to enable them to meet their needs. "That finding was not affected by the fact that the recipient was in one of the situations covered by Article 3 (i.e. unemployment)." Since the benefits in question exempted claimants from the obligation to be available for work these benefits were not "directly and effectively linked with protection against the risks of unemployment".

The claims under Directive 76/207/EEC also failed. Such a claim would only be admissible, the Court held, if it concerned access to employment, which included access to vocational training. Benefits such as the ones in question were intended not to provide access to employment but to provide income

---

[62] Cases C-63, 64/91 [1992] ECR I-4737.
[63] The principle will be discussed *infra.*

support. These decisions[64], particularly that of *Jackson*[65], stand in stark contrast to earlier cases involving the interpretation of similar provisions of Regulation (EEC) 1612/68[66] concerning the free movement of workers. There, access to grants to enable workers and their families to pursue educational courses have been freely admitted under provisions allowing for equality of access to vocational and educational courses.[67]

(vi) The principle of equal treatment

The principle of equal treatment as defined in Article 4(1) requires that:

> There shall be no discrimination whatsoever on the grounds of sex either directly or indirectly by reference in particular to marital or family status, in particular as concerns:
> - the scope of the schemes and the conditions of access thereto;
> - the obligation to contribute and the calculation of contributions; and
> - the calculation of benefits including increases due in respect of a spouse and for dependants and the conditions governing the duration and retention of entitlement to benefits.

Thus the principle of equal treatment is broadly defined and includes a prohibition on direct and indirect discrimination. Its application is not confined to the examples given in Article 4(1). Article 4(2) allows for positive discrimination for the protection of women on the grounds of maternity.

Direct discrimination as defined in Article 4(1) is not difficult to identify; such discrimination has now largely been eliminated in the United Kingdom, except in the areas in which it is expressly permitted, in Article 4(2) and Article 7(1).

(a) Indirect discrimination

Indirect discrimination is not confined to discrimination on the grounds of marital or family status. It occurs whenever a rule, prima facie neutral, can be proved to affect one sex, the disadvantaged sex, to a disproportionate extent.[68] For example, in the social security context a rule which grants a certain benefit to those with dependants, or which ties benefit or access to benefit to a certain level of income will benefit men disproportionately, since the majority of families still conform to the traditional pattern in which the man is the principal bread-winner and the woman assumes (unpaid) responsibility for the family, more often than not working part-time.

---

[64] But see, *Meyers* v *Chief Adjudication Officer, supra* n 45.
[65] See, *supra* n 52.
[66] OJ (Special ed) 1968 (II), 475. As amended Reg (EEC) 312/76 (OJ 1976 L 39/2).
[67] See Regulation (EEC) 1612/68, Article 10 and Case 9/74 *Casagrande* v *Landeshauptstadt Munchen* [1974] ECR 773.
[68] Principles of indirect discrimination laid down in Case 170/84 *Bilka-Kaufhaus GmbH* v *Weber von Harz* [1986] ECR 1607, decided under Article 119.

Where a particular rule is found to work disproportionately[69] to the disadvantage of one sex, the Court has held that this will give rise to a presumption that the discrimination is based on sex. The burden is then on the party responsible for the difference in treatment to prove that the rule, and the difference in treatment, is "objectively justified". It will be objectively justified if it can be proved to be necessary and appropriate to achieve a particular legitimate end. The term "objective" probably means no more than that the need for such a measure is not based on subjective assessments but on verifiable objective criteria. In deciding whether a particular rule or condition is necessary or appropriate, the Court applies a proportionality test: the rule or condition applied must be no more than is appropriate and necessary to achieve its particular ends. It is for the national court to test this question of justification, although it may seek help on this matter from the European Court.

The Court of Justice has considered a number of grounds for justification.

(1) Social justification

In *Rinner-Kühn*[70] the German authorities had sought to justify their rules on sick pay, which discriminated against employees working less than ten hours per week or 45 hours per month, on the grounds that part-time workers were not fully integrated into the work force. The Court rejected that argument, pointing out that "such considerations only represent generalised statements concerning certain categories of workers and do not admit the conclusion of objective justification unrelated to any discrimination on the grounds of sex". However, it conceded that a State might succeed in justifying a measure if it could prove that the means selected "corresponded to an objective necessary to its social policy" and were "appropriate and necessary to the attainment of that purpose".

A social policy justification was argued, again unsuccessfully, in *Ruzius-Wilbrink*.[71] Here the Dutch authorities sought to justify a system of invalidity benefit designed to guarantee a minimum subsistence income in which payment was linked, in the case of part-time workers, to the claimant's previous income. Full-time workers, and other groups such as students and the self-employed, were entitled to claim the minimum income regardless of previous earnings. The system was thus clearly discriminatory against part-time workers such as the claimant whose earnings were insufficient to entitle her to the full minimum income. In justification it was argued that it would be unfair to those working full-time to grant part-time workers an allowance higher than the wages they had received in employment. The Court refused to accept that argument. It

---

[69] The Court has not yet clarified the threshold at which an effect will be deemed disproportionate, although a substantial disparity appears to be required. There is also a problem in defining which categories are to be compared for the purpose of assessing disproportionality: see Herbert, "Social Security and Indirect Discrimination" in McCrudden, *Equality of Treatment between Women and Men in Social Security* (1994).

[70] *Rinner-Kühn, supra* n 35.

[71] *Ruzius-Wilbrink, supra* n 58.

found the system, designed to provide a benefit for those in need of support, had the effect of depriving of assistance those who were most in need of support. Moreover, the system was "unjust", since many claimants in comparable groups such as students and full-time workers on low incomes received a subsistence income substantially above their previous income.

In *Rinner-Kühn*[72] and *Ruzius-Wilbrink* the discrimination was expressly against part-time workers as a class. It is submitted that a social justification will be hard to establish when it operates to the detriment of an already disadvantaged group, such as part-time workers. On the other hand, where the criteria for benefit are linked to objective factors such as responsibility for dependants, or partner's income, the Court has been prepared to accept a social policy justification. It did so in a challenge to a system of invalidity benefit based on these criteria in the case of *Teuling*[73], on the grounds that the benefit was designed to compensate for the greater burden borne by persons in these categories. Similarly in *Commission* v *Belgium*[74] rules designed to provide a guaranteed minimum income for persons with family responsibilities, although benefiting men disproportionately, were found to constitute a legitimate objective of social policy. It could be argued that since the rules were expressed in neutral terms, and benefit was tied to a legitimate social objective, no discrimination had occurred.[75] The situation of those who fulfilled the criteria and those who did not was not comparable.

(2) Economic justification

Whilst the Court of Justice is alert and not unsympathetic to Member States' concern to control public expenditure and maintain budgetary stability[76], attempts to justify discriminatory rules on purely economic grounds are unlikely to be successful. The Court's position on this matter was set out succinctly in the recent case of *Roks*.[77] Whilst affirming that

> Directive 79/7 leaves intact the powers reserved to Member States to define their social policy within the framework of close cooperation by the Commission, and consequently the nature and extent of measures of social protection, including those relating to social security, and the ways in which they are implemented; and The Community does not prevent Member States from taking measures in order to control their social expenditure which have the effect of withdrawing social security benefits from certain categories of persons . . .,

---

[72] *Rinner-Kühn*, *supra* n 35.
[73] Case 30/85 [1987] ECR 2497.
[74] Case C-229/89 [1991] ECR I-2205: see also Case C-226/91 *Molenbroek* [1992] ECR I-5943.
[75] A point not so far explored by the Court; see further comment by Herbert, *supra* n 69.
[76] See Case C-343/92 *Roks* v *Bestuur van de Bedrijfvereniging voor de Gezondheid, Geestelijke en Maatschappelijke Belangen* [1994] ECR I-571; Case C-9/91 *R* v *Secretary of State for Social Security ex parte EOC* [1992] ECR I-4297; Case C-328/91 *Secretary of State for Social Security* v *Thomas* [1993] ECR I-1247; *cf.* the Court's approach to the problems of occupational pension funds, e.g. in Case C-408/92 *Smith* v *Avdel, supra* n 46.
[77] Case C-343/92, *supra* n 76.

such measures must be compatible with the principle of equal treatment between men and women.[78] Budgetary considerations must not be allowed to justify a difference in treatment between men and women. To do so would be:

> to accept that the application of as fundamental a rule of Community law as that of equal treatment for men and women might vary over time and place "according to the state of public finances of the Member States".[79]

This ruling, in line with the Court's decision in *Smith* v *Advel Systems Ltd*[80], that Community law does not prevent the "levelling down" of benefits by raising the pensionable age for women from 60 to 65 in order to achieve equality with men, provides a necessary reminder that the application of EC sex discrimination rules does not necessarily result in benefit to women.

(3) Administrative efficiency justification

A justification for indirect discrimination based on administrative efficiency might succeed where the cost of providing equal treatment is out of all proportion to its purpose, as could be argued in the case of casual or marginal employees. In *Kirshammer-Hack*[81] the Court accepted that the exclusion of part-time workers from German employment protection legislation for firms comprising five or less employees could be objectively justified in order to lighten the legal, administrative and financial burden on small enterprises.

Although the decision was based on the need to alleviate the constraints on small businesses a similar administrative/financial justification might be admitted in a claim for equal treatment under Directive 79/7/EEC by employees working minimal hours.

The Commission's proposed Directives on part-time and temporary workers[82] would have permitted exemption from the equal treatment principle for employees working less than eight hours per week. Similarly, where benefits are contributory, a lower rate of benefit, tied to a lower contribution rate, both proportionate to the number of hours worked, might be regarded as justified.

A system under which benefits were proportionate to the number of hours worked was approved in principle by the ECJ in *Kowalska*[83], in the context of a claim against an employer, based on Article 119, for a severance grant payable under a civil service collective agreement on termination of employment only to full-time workers.

On the other hand in *Ruzius-Wilbrink*[84] the Court refused to contemplate, albeit on social grounds, a lower rate of benefit for part-time workers where that benefit represented a minimum subsistence income.

---

[78] *Ibid* paras 28, 29.
[79] *Ibid* paras 35, 36.
[80] *Smith* v *Avdel Systems Ltd, supra* n 46.
[81] Case C-189/91 [1993] ECR I-6185.
[82] OJ 1990 C 224/4, 224/6.
[83] Case C-33/89 [1990] ECR I-2591.
[84] *Ruzius-Wilbrink, supra* n 58.

Although the Court has not so far expressly distinguished between contributory and non-contributory benefits, or between different categories of benefit, it would be more likely to approve a contributory system in which benefits were proportionate to contributions, than a non-contributory scheme in which benefit was related to hours of work, a *fortiori* when the latter benefit was designed to meet a particular social need. On the other hand to distinguish between contributory and non-contributory benefits would lead to inequality in the application of EC sex discrimination rules, given the variations in the mode of financing and delivery of social security benefits in different Member States. The problem admits of no easy or clear-cut solutions.

(vii) Excluded areas: Article 7(1)

Express exclusions from the equal treatment principle are provided in Article 7(1)(a) to (e). Article 7(1) provides that:

This Directive shall be without prejudice to the right of Member States to exclude from its scope:
(a) the determination of pensionable age for the purposes of granting old-age and retirement pensions and the possible consequences thereof for other benefits;
(b) advantages in respect of old-age pension schemes granted to persons who have brought up children, the acquisition of benefit entitlements following periods of interruption of employment due to the bringing up of children;
(c) the granting of old age or invalidity benefit entitlements by virtue of the derived entitlements of a wife;
(d) the granting of increases of long-term invalidity, old-age, accidents at work and occupational disease benefits for a dependant wife; and
(e) the consequence of the exercise, before the adoption of this Directive, of a right of option not to acquire rights or incur obligations under a statutory scheme.

Member States are required periodically to examine matters excluded under Article 7(1) in order to ascertain, in the light of social developments, whether there is justification for maintaining the exclusions concerned.[85]

Consistently with its approach to all exceptions to fundamental EC rules, the Court has interpreted Article 7(1) restrictively. In *Marshall* v *Southampton AHA*[86] in the context of a challenge by Mrs Marshall[87] to different ages of retirement for men and women, defended on the basis of Article 7(1)(a) of Directive 79/7/EEC[88], it held that the exclusion in respect of pensionable age only applied "for the purposes of granting old age and retirement pensions and the possible consequences thereof for other benefits". It did not allow Member

---

[85] Article 7(2).
[86] Case 152/84 [1986] ECR 723.
[87] Under Equal Treatment Directive 76/207/EEC.
[88] Invoked by reason of Article 1(2) of Directive 76/207/EEC.

States to maintain different ages of retirement.[89] In *Van Cant*[90] it held that once a State has abolished a difference in pensionable age, as Belgium had done in 1990, it cannot maintain a discrimination in the method of calculating the amount of men's and women's pension.

However, in *R* v *Secretary of State for Social Security ex parte EOC*[91] the Court, in more cautious mood, held that a different period of *contribution* towards statutory social security benefits by men and women (44 years for men, 39 years for women) to qualify for the same full basic retirement pension was permitted under Article 7(1)(a), since the difference in treatment was "necessarily linked" to the different statutory pensionable age. Such a scheme reflected the purpose of Article 7(1), which was to:

> allow Member States to maintain temporarily the advantages accorded to women with respect to retirement in order to enable them progressively to adapt their pension systems without disrupting the complex financial equilibrium of those systems, the importance of which could not be ignored.

In *Secretary of State for Social Security* v *Thomas*[92] the Court considered the scope of Article 7(1)(a) with regard to the "possible consequences" of a difference in pensionable age for "other benefits". The case concerned the United Kingdom system governing eligibility for severe disablement and invalid care allowances, whereby benefits were not payable to those who were not in receipt of such benefits on reaching retirement age, whether or not they received an old-age pension. The Court found, it is submitted correctly, that the difference in treatment regarding these benefits was not "necessarily and objectively linked" to the difference in retirement age. Discrimination in respect of "other benefits" under Article 7(1)(a) would only be necessary "to avoid disrupting the complex financial equilibrium of the social security system or to ensure consistency between retirement schemes and other benefit schemes". Since the benefits in question were non-contributory there was no question of disruption of the financial equilibrium of the United Kingdom social security scheme. Nor was discrimination necessary to avoid inconsistency between different benefit schemes. Since, as the United Kingdom had argued, benefits were intended to replace income in the event of materialisation of a risk, the principle of consistency required that they should be available in cases such as the applicants', where claimants were unable to work and were not in receipt of an old-age pension.

The United Kingdom, and allegedly over 40,000 potential claimants, are now awaiting (but see now Postscript) another ruling from the Court of Justice in the case of *Secretary of State for Social Security* v *Graham*[93], referred to the Court of

---

[89] In *Barber* (Case C-262/88, *supra* n 6), a similarly worded exclusion in Article 9 of Directive 86/378/EEC, governing occupational schemes, was circumvented by the Court's finding that different periods of contribution by an employer in respect of male and female employees, arising from the difference in pensionable age, constituted, discriminatory pay prohibited under Article 119.

[90] Case C-154/92 [1993] ECR I-3811.

[91] Case C-9/91 [1992] ECR I-4297.

[92] Case C-328/91 [1993] ECR I-1247.

[93] Case C-92/94 referred to ECJ on 2 March 1994: joined by claims by Mrs Connell and Mrs Nicholas.

Justice by the Court of Appeal, concerning the compatibility of United Kingdom rules governing invalidity pensions and invalidity allowances with Directive 79/7/EEC, in particular Article 7(1)(a). Both benefits are long-term benefits which follow on from sickness benefit, which is a short-term benefit. The benefits, unlike those in *Thomas*[94], are contributory, and are payable only to those who have made the relevant contributions.

Under the United Kingdom Social Security (Contributory Benefits) Act 1992:

– *Invalidity pension* is payable to men and women:
(a) who are under pensionable age; and
(b) who are not more than five years above pensionable age and have deferred their state pension or elected not to receive it.

For those who opt for invalidity pension under (b), in lieu of retirement pension, the rate of benefit is limited to the actual rate of the claimant's retirement pension. Invalidity pension, however, unlike retirement pension, is not taxable.

– *Invalidity allowance* is payable to men and women who are more than five years below pensionable age (60 for women, 65 for men) when the period of incapacity began.

Thus as regards *invalidity pension* both men and women are treated alike in that they enjoy a five-year tax advantage beginning at the age of retirement. But men may claim it up until the age of 70; whereas for women it ceases at 65. Also women who opt to receive invalidity benefit on reaching 60 may suffer a reduction in benefit as a result of having failed to pay sufficient contribution for entitlement to a full retirement pension. Such was the case with all three claimants in *Graham*.[95] The reduction in Mrs Graham's case was over £33 per week. This was the principal issue considered by the Court.

As regards *invalidity allowance* men and women are treated equally in that they both suffer a five-year period immediately prior to pensionable age when they are barred from benefit. However women, unlike men, cannot claim benefit between the age of 55 and 60. Such was the case of Mrs Thomas. This was the second issue considered by the Court.

Thus both schemes operate to the disadvantage of women as a result of their benefits being tied to pensionable age. The question is whether the difference in treatment as between men and women is "necessarily and objectively" linked to the difference in pensionable age for men and women. Is it necessary to ensure consistency between retirement and other benefit schemes or to avoid disrupting the complex financial equilibrium of the social security scheme?

To ascertain the former it is necessary to consider the purpose of these provisions. The purpose of granting invalidity pension, with its tax advantages, in lieu of retirement pension, for the five years subsequent to reaching pensionable age, could be construed as providing some additional income to assist claimants in coping with disability during the early years of retirement. On this

---

[94] See, *supra* n 92.
[95] See, *supra* n 93. See also Postscript at the end of this chapter.

construction, arguably it is neither necessarily and objectively linked to pensionable age nor necessary to ensure consistency between retirement and other benefit schemes. Moreover, to peg the rate of benefit to that of retirement pension on claimants' reaching pensionable age is to impose a double disadvantage on women, since they are less likely than men to have made sufficient contribution to gain entitlement to a full retirement pension.

The purpose of invalidity allowance appears to be to boost the income of those whose disability is long term, beginning more than five years before the claimant's anticipated age of retirement. It appears to presume that such a benefit is dispensable when disability arises in the five years immediately prior to, and in the run down to, retirement. But the allowance is clearly not intended as a substitute pension. A woman who suffers disability between the age of 55 and 60 is as much in need of assistance as a man. Thus the difference in treatment does not appear to be necessarily and objectively linked to retirement age; nor is it consistent with the overall scheme of benefits.

The question remains as to whether these benefits might nonetheless be permitted as necessary to avoid disrupting the "complex financial equilibrium of social security schemes"? Invalidity benefits and allowances are contributory benefits. It could be argued that a change of rules in respect of a contributory, as opposed to a non-contributory benefit as in *Thomas*[96], could disrupt the equilibrium of the social security scheme, especially in a case such as *Graham*[97], involving a large number of pending and potential claims. But is there such a difference in impact as between contributory and non-contributory schemes? Might it not be said, as was claimed by the United Kingdom authorities in *Johnson* v *Chief Adjudication Officer*[98], that any change which would place an increased burden on the social security budget would disturb its financial equilibrium? Should an individual's entitlement to equal treatment depend on whether a benefit is contributory or non-contributory, or simply on the number of potential claims?

Whilst logic and existing authority might point to a decision in favour of the claimants[99], fear of financial disruption and political backlash (on the eve of the inter-governmental conference) may well sway the Court against them. Such an outcome, if regrettable, would be legitimate, given the uncertain ambit of Article 7(1)(a). If real equality for men and women is to be achieved in this difficult and complex area it may be that it can only be effectively achieved by legislation. For the Court's decision in *Graham* see the postscript at the end of this chapter.

(viii) Remedies

In actions based on Community law national courts and tribunals are required to provide the same remedies and procedures as are available in respect of

---

[96] See, *supra* n 92.
[97] See, *supra* n 93.
[98] Case C-410/92 *Johnson No 2* [1994] ECR I-5483.
[99] See, *Supra* n 76.

equivalent claims based on national law, provided that the remedies are applied in a non-discriminatory manner and are effective both to protect individuals' Community rights and to deter breaches of Community law (the "effectiveness" principle).[100] National rules and procedures must not render the exercise of Community rights "virtually impossible" or "impossible in practice" or "excessively difficult".[101] The effectiveness principle has had a significant impact on domestic law, not least in the area of sex discrimination.

Pursuant to this principle the Court decided in *Emmott v Minister for Social Welfare*[102], in a claim based on Directive 79/7/EEC, that where an individual is seeking to invoke directly effective provisions of a Directive, time will not begin to run for limitation purposes until the Directive has been fully and correctly implemented in national law. The ruling was based on the fact that until a Directive has been fully implemented, the individual is in a state of uncertainty and she will be unaware of the full extent of her rights. This decision clearly carried serious implications for Member States (and for the public bodies of Member States), since many years may elapse following the date for implementation before a Directive is properly implemented. This may result not from wilful or deliberate or even knowing non-implementation, but simply because the precise meaning and scope of a particular provision may not be clear until it has been interpreted by the Court.

However, the scope of *Emmott* has now been restricted in two recent rulings of the Court (also in social security claims based on Directive 79/7/EEC), in *Steenhorst-Neerings*[103] and *Johnson v Chief Adjudication Officer*.[104] Both cases involved challenges to British social security rules which deny entitlement to social security benefit in respect of any period more than 12 months before the date on which the claim is made (the "12 month" rule). In both cases the claimants were seeking to invoke the Directive to claim benefit for a period outside the 12 month limit, relying on *Emmott*. In both cases the rule was found compatible with EC law.

In *Steenhorst-Neerings* the Court drew a distinction between the time limit for bringing an action, in issue in *Emmott*, and a rule simply restricting the retroactive effect of a claim for benefits. The latter served to ensure sound administration, particularly by enabling the authorities to ascertain (in the case of invalidity benefit, which was claimed in the case) the degree of disability, and whether the conditions for eligibility were satisfied. It also reflected the need to preserve the financial balance in a scheme in which claims submitted in the course of a year must be covered by contributions collected during that same year.

The claim in *Johnson* was for a severe disablement allowance. Mrs Johnson sought to distinguish *Steenhorst-Neerings*. She pointed out that there was no diffi-

---

[100] Case 14/83 *Von Colson v Land Nordrhein Westfalen* [1984] ECR 1891. See Moore, in this volume.
[101] Case 130/79 *Express Dairy Foods v Intervention Board for Agricultural Products* [1980] ECR 1887.
[102] Case C-208/90 [1991] ECR I-4269.
[103] Case C-338/91 [1993] ECR I-5475.
[104] Case C-410/92, *supra* n 98.

culty in her case in proving degrees of disability; all she need prove was that she was unfit to work, which she was able to do. She urged the Court to reconsider its position in *Steenhorst-Neerings*, arguing that there was no real difference between her case and *Emmott*. As Advocate-General Gulmann acknowledged, both cases concerned national time limits the effect of which was to preclude claims for arrears of social security payments; in both cases the claimants had a substantive claim to the benefits in question under Community law. Nevertheless the Court (as did the Advocate-General) endorsed the distinction introduced in *Steenhorst-Neerings* between a "time bar which had the result of depriving the applicant of any opportunity whatever to rely on her right to equal treatment under the Directive", as in *Emmott*, and a rule which "merely limited to one year the retroactive effect of claims for benefits for incapacity for work". The fact that the effect of both rules was the same, namely to deprive the applicant of a remedy which was effective to protect the applicant's Community rights, appeared to be irrelevant. The 12 month rule "(did) not make it impossible to exercise the rights based on the Directive".[105]

Following these rulings, Member States will be able to avoid the ill effects of *Emmott* by limiting claimants' opportunity for retroactive claims, at least in the context of social security claims. It remains to be seen whether the Court will accept any further erosion of *Emmott* outside the sphere of social security. But *Steenhorst-Neerings* and *Johnson* have undoubtedly undermined the effective protection of individuals' rights under Directive 79/7/EEC. Whilst a limit on retroactivity may be acceptable where a State's non-compliance with the Directive has been inadvertent and non-culpable, these rulings appear to provide States with an opportunity knowingly to evade their obligations under Directive 79/7/EEC with relative impunity. It is here that an alternative remedy may need to be considered in the form of a claim for damages against the state based on *Francovich* v *Italian State*.[106]

(a) Remedy under *Francovich*[107]

In *Francovich* v *Italian State*, in a claim based on the Italian Government's failure to implement Employment Protection Directive 80/987/EEC, the Court ruled that where the plaintiff can prove that the State has failed to take all necessary steps to achieve the results required by a Directive, and

- the result required by the Directive includes the conferring of rights for the benefit of individuals;
- the content of these rights may be determined by reference to the provisions of the Directive; and
- there is a causal link between the breach of the obligation imposed on the State and the damage suffered by the person affected;

---

[105] Case C-410/92 *Johnson*, at para 35.
[106] Cases C-6, 9/90 [1991] ECR I-5357.
[107] See also the discussion by Moore, in this volume.

the State will be liable to compensate for damage resulting from that failure.[108] To what extent then may individuals claim damages under *Francovich* for losses arising from the state's failure to protect their rights under Directive 79/7/EEC?

In enunciating the principle of state liability in *Francovich*, and the conditions under which it might arise, the Court suggested that liability was to be determined "within the context of national law on liability". National law in the United Kingdom, as elsewhere, however, may not as it stands be effective to protect individuals' Community rights under *Francovich, a fortiori* since it does not admit liability in respect of legislative failures. Nor is this problem confined to the United Kingdom. Even in States such as France in which damages may be obtained in respect of unlawful legislative acts or omissions, damages are only awarded under very limited circumstances. Thus national law on State liability in the United Kingdom as in most Member States will have to be modified to meet the demands of Community law. Unless the matter is settled by legislation by the Community, the nature of these modifications will fall to be determined on a case-by-case basis by the Court of Justice, in rulings on the interpretation of Community law under Article 177, on questions referred by national courts.

A number of questions, including the important question of whether, or to what extent, fault is a prerequisite of liability, and questions concerning damages, have been referred to the Court of Justice in *Factortame (No 3)*[109] and *Brasserie du Pêcheur*.[110] Whatever the Court's answer to these questions it is likely that liability will have to be admitted in respect of legislative failures, and that it will arise at the least where the State was aware that it had failed, or failed adequately, to implement an EC Directive. Thus, even if the scope of the right claimed under a Directive was not originally clear (in which case the content of the right, (condition (b) in *Francovich*) would neither be clear), it would become clear once the Court had interpreted the provision in question. Thus, the State should be liable to pay compensation for damage occurring after that date. However, until the Court of Justice provides clear guidance on these issues, the extent to which individuals may obtain protection under *Francovich* for their rights under EC sex discrimination (or any other EC) rules remains uncertain.[111] It would be optimistic to suggest that *Factortame (No 3)* and *Brasserie du Pêcheur* will provide

---

[108] In addition to this specific ruling on the particular facts referred the Court appeared to lay down a wider ruling that a state might be liable for any breach of Community law "for which it (was) responsible".

[109] Case C-48/93 (OJ 1993 C94/13).

[110] Case C-46/93 (OJ 1993 C92/4).

[111] There is already an extensive literature on this subject: for a non-exhaustive list see commentary by Bebr, 29 CMLRev (1992), 557–584; Duffy, "Damages against the State; a new remedy for failure to implement Community obligations" 17 ELRev (1992) 133–138; Greenwood, "Effect of EC Directives in National Law" 51 CLJ (1992), 3–6; Caranta, "Governmental Liability after *Francovich*" 52 CLJ (1993), 272–297; Parker, "State Liability in Damages for Breach of Community Law" 108 LQR (1992), 181–186; Craig, "*Francovich*, Remedies and the Scope of Damages Liability" 109 LQR (1993), 592–621; Steiner, "From direct effects to *Francovich*: shifting means of enforcement of Community Law" 18 ELRev (1993), 3–22; Lewis and Moore, "Duties, Directives and Damages in European Community Law" PL (1993), 151–170; Van Gerven, "Non-contractual Liability of Member States, Community institutions and Individuals for breaches of Community Law with a View to a Common Law for Europe" 1 *Maastricht Journal of European and Comparative Law* (1994), 6–40.

all the answers. Given the difficulty of achieving a satisfactory judicial solution, particularly in the context, and subject to the limits, of the Article 177 procedure, perhaps Member States may be persuaded to address these questions at the 1996 Inter-governmental Conference with a view to devising a clear and comprehensive framework of Community rules governing state liability.

(ix) Postscript

The Court of Justice's judgment in *Secretary of State for Social Security* v *Graham*[112] was delivered on 11 August 1995. The Court found the United Kingdom provisions governing both invalidity pension and invalidity allowance to be permissible under Article 7(1)(a) of Directive 79/7/EEC. Applying the test introduced in *Secretary of State for Social Security* v *Thomas*[113], the Court found that the rule limiting invalidity pension on claimants' reaching pensionable age (60 for women, 65 for men) to the rate of the claimant's actual retirement pension was "objectively and necessarily" linked to the permitted difference in pensionable age. It was objectively linked in that the difference in treatment "flowed directly from" the difference in pensionable age. It was also necessarily linked to that difference. To prohibit a Member State from limiting the rate of invalidity pension to the actual rate of the retirement pension to which a claimant was entitled would be to restrict the very right which a Member State had under Article 7 (1)(a) to set different pensionable ages for men and women. Furthermore, it would undermine consistency between social security schemes to give women whose incapacity began before the age of 60 an advantage in the form of an enhanced rate of benefit between the age of 60 and 65, which was not available to able-bodied women who had simply retired from employment at the age of 60. Since invalidity allowance was paid as a supplement to, and only to persons entitled to, invalidity pension, that too must be regarded as "objectively and necessarily linked" to the difference in pensionable age, for the same reasons as applied to invalidity pensions.

The judgment, if not surprising in its outcome, is thinly reasoned and not without logical flaws. Although purportedly based on the "necessary and objective link" between the benefits in question and the permitted difference in pensionable age, and the principle of consistency, there is little doubt that the decision was in part policy-based, designed to allay Member States' concerns over the erosion of Article 7(1)(a). The question of whether a particular provision is "objectively and necessarily" linked to difference in pensionable age is largely subjective, and depends on the Court's view as to its purpose.

It is therefore surprising that the Court, having legitimately construed the purpose of invalidity pension as to replace income from employment, found that its discriminatory elements "flowed directly" from the difference in pen-

---

[112] Case C-92/94, Judgment of 11 August 1995, nyr.
[113] Case C- 328/91 [1993] ECR I-1247.

sionable age, and were consistent with the overall scheme of benefits. If such was its purpose, the Court might have concluded on grounds of consistency that since women were entitled, following *Marshall No 1*[114], to remain in employment until the age of 65 (where men are so entitled), they should be entitled to a replacement income should they seek but be deprived by illness of the opportunity to do so.[115] Similar arguments apply *a fortiori* to invalidity allowance, which was not designed as a pension but to provide additional replacement income during the claimant's normal working life.

Even more surprising is the fact that the Court did not seek to justify its decision on the grounds of the need to preserve the financial equilibrium of social security schemes, as Advocate General Lenz had suggested. Given the number of potential claimants, and that the benefits in question were contributory, such an approach would have been justified, and consistent with established policy and principle. It thus remains unclear whether *Graham* is a case decided solely and unsatisfactorily on the objective and necessary link between the rules in question and pensionable age, or signals a move towards a more cautious (if covert) "hands off" approach on the part of the Court to Article 7(1)(a).

If *Graham* represents the Court in conservative mood, demonstrating (albeit not overtly) respect for Member States' reserved powers under Article 7(1)(a), *R* v *Secretary of State for Health ex parte Richardson*[116] and *Meyers* v *Adjudication Officer*[117], decided in October and July 1995 respectively, show the Court extending the reach of EC sex equality law beyond the confines of social security *strictu sensu* by means of a welcome and unexpectedly generous interpretation of Directive 79/7/EEC and Equal Treatment Directive 76/207/EEC. In *Richardson* the Court found that United Kingdom regulations granting exemption from prescription charges for women over 60 and men over 65 fell within Article 3(1) of Directive 79/7/EEC and were not permitted under Article 7(1)(a). Since the rules formed part of a statutory scheme providing direct and effective protection against one of the risks covered by the Directive, namely sickness, and since benefit depended on materialisation of that risk, the scheme could not be excluded from the scope of the Directive. In view of the fundamental importance of the principle of equal treatment and the aim of the Directive, a system of benefits such as that provided under the United Kingdom regulations could not be excluded from the scope of the Directive simply because it did not strictly speaking form part of national social security rules.[118] Nor was the difference in treatment between men and women objectively, and necessarily, linked

---

[114] Case 152/84 [1986] ECR 723.

[115] Surprisingly, not dissimilar arguments were invoked in Case C-137/94 *Richardson*, Judgment of 19 October 1995, nyr, to justify its finding that the UK rules setting different ages for exemption for prescription charges were *not* necessarily linked to differences in pensionable age.

[116] *Supra* n 45.

[117] Case C-116/94, Judgment of 13 July 1995, nyr.

[118] The Court here appears to be reverting to its original position on the scope of Article 3(1) in Case 150/85 *Drake* v *Chief Adjudication Officer* [1986] ECR 1995, and Advocate General Tesauro's view in Case C-243/90 *R* v *Secretary of State for Social Security ex parte Smithson* [1992] ECR 1, which the Court declined to follow.

with a difference in pensionable age for the purposes of Article 7(1)(a). It was not objectively necessary to ensure coherence between the retirement pension scheme and the free prescription scheme. Just as a woman who had reached statutory pensionable age was entitled to continue in employment beyond that age and thus find herself in the same position as a man, so a man might draw a retirement pension before he reached statutory pensionable age and find himself in the same position as a woman of the same age. Since the benefit in question was non-contributory, a decision as to its illegality would have no direct influence on the financial equilibrium of contributory pension schemes. The Court's conclusion was "not affected by the mere fact that extending entitlements to exemption from prescription charges would increase the burden borne by the State in the funding of the NHS".

Meyers concerned a situation similar to that in *Jackson & Cresswell*[119], involving the non-deductibility of child-minding expenses in a claim for family credit. Family credit is available in the United Kingdom as a "top up" benefit for low income workers with responsibility for children. Ms Meyer's claim for family credit was rejected because her income exceeded the permitted minimum. She claimed that the rules which did not permit the deduction of child-minding expenses, which were fatal to her claim, were indirectly discriminatory, having a disproportionate adverse effect on single mothers such as herself. A question was referred to the Court as to the legality of the family credit rules under Equal Treatment Directive 76/207/EEC. It may be presumed that Directive 79/7/EEC was not invoked because of the Court's ruling on the inapplicability of the Directive in *Jackson & Cresswell.* The Court's suggestion in that case that measures concerning access to employment might fall within Directive 76/207/EEC offered at least some chance of success. Contrary to its findings in respect of supplementary allowances and income support in *Jackson & Cresswell* the Court found that family credit, by providing assistance and an incentive to work to low-income workers, concerned both "access to employment" within Article 3, and "conditions of employment" within Article 5 of Directive 76/207/EEC, and thus must be provided on the basis of equality.

Accordingly, recent case law shows the Court blowing hot and cold. Clearly the Court is torn between its commitment to the "fundamental importance" of the principle of equal treatment and the need, at this delicate time in the Union's history, to be seen to respect the legitimate concerns of Member States. If equality between men and women is to be achieved, it is no doubt right to adopt a generous purposive approach to the interpretation of the substantive rights contained in the Directives, a position to which the Court has reverted in *Richardson* and *Meyers*. But it is probably also correct at this time to be cautious, as it was in *Graham*, in construing derogations from EC obligations contained in EC secondary legislation such as Article 7(1)(a) of Directive 79/7/EEC, when the meaning and scope of these provisions may be far from clear and the consequences of finding incompatibility between national and Community law far-reaching.

---

[119] Cases C-63 and 64/91 [1992] ECR I-4737.

If the Court finds it necessary, in the absence of political will on the part of the Member States, to resolve genuine ambiguities and advance the cause of sex equality in unexpected ways, causing serious financial and administrative disruption, it would be better to acknowledge that fact, and limit the temporal effect of its rulings under Article 177.

JOSEPHINE STEINER
Professor (Associate) of Law
University of Sheffield, UK

Part IV

ENFORCEMENT OF SEX EQUALITY IN EMPLOYMENT

Chapter 9

ENFORCEMENT OF PRIVATE LAW CLAIMS OF SEX DISCRIMINATION IN THE FIELD OF EMPLOYMENT*

(i) Introduction

Over the last decade the practice of sex discrimination law before the United Kingdom courts has become increasingly complex. This is partly due to the fact that a claim of discrimination may be based upon a variety of Community and national provisions. These are Article 119 of the Treaty of Rome, the Equal Treatment Directive (ETD)[1] and Equal Pay Directive (EPD)[2], and finally domestic legislation in the form of the Sex Discrimination Act 1975 (SDA) and the Equal Pay Act 1970 (EPA). Unfortunately, because of decisions of the Court of Justice which have interpreted the Community measures more broadly than anticipated by the United Kingdom legislation, the latter imperfectly reflect the provisions of the former. As a result of this legislative tangle, questions have arisen about the operation of Community law in the national courts and its inter-relationship with national legislation. It is specifically this aspect, that is, the enforcement of sex discrimination law in the United Kingdom courts, which this chapter seeks to outline.

(ii) Jurisdiction of the industrial tribunals

In the United Kingdom most disputes which concern the enforcement of private law rights in the field of employment protection are brought before industrial tribunals pursuant to the Employment Protection (Consolidation) Act 1978 (EPCA)[3] and

---

* This chapter was written by Sarah Moore.

[1] Directive 76/207/EEC (OJ 1976 L 39/40).

[2] Directive 75/117/EEC (OJ 1975 L 45/19).

[3] See s 128(1) of the EPCA 1978, which provides that the Secretary of State may, by regulation, make provision for the establishment of tribunals to be known as industrial tribunals, to exercise the jurisdiction conferred on them by or under the EPCA 1978, or any other Act, whether passed before or after that Act.

this includes claims of sex discrimination.[4] Although industrial tribunals were established to exercise jurisdiction given by statute only, it has been accepted that they also have power to hear claims based directly upon Community law, even where the applicant's case is based only on Community law, with no corresponding claim under domestic law. In *Albion Shipping Agency* v *Arnold*[5], Browne-Wilkinson J said that the conclusion that the industrial tribunals could apply relevant provisions of Community law was one:

> which we reach with relief since to hold otherwise would produce a chaotic result in which cases under the [Equal Pay] Act of 1970 where Article 119 might be in point would have to be conducted partly before the Industrial Tribunal (which has exclusive jurisdiction under the Act of 1970) and partly in the ordinary courts.

(iii) The legal framework

(a) Community Law

(1) Direct effect of Article 119

In *Defrenne No 2*[6], the Court held that Article 119 is directly effective where there exists "direct and overt discrimination which may be identified solely with the aid of the criteria based on equal work and equal pay". It drew a distinction, however, between this and "indirect and disguised discrimination which can only be identified by reference to the more explicit implementing provisions of a Community or national character".[7]

It was subsequently clarified, however, that Article 119 applies directly to "all forms of discrimination which may be identified solely with the aid of the criteria of equal work and equal pay"[8] – including claims based on indirect discrimination. This has now been confirmed by the Court on a number of occasions.[9]

It is now likely that Article 119 may fail to have direct effect only in equal value cases; that is where the discrimination alleged arises in respect of two jobs which are not identical but are said to be of equal value. Nevertheless, the Court seems to have accepted the possibility that Article 119 may be directly effective even in these circumstances.[10]

---

[4] Jurisdiction is conferred on the industrial tribunals by s 63 of the SDA 1975 and s 2 of the EPA 1970.
[5] [1981] IRLR 525. See also *Combes* v *Shields* [1978] IRLR 263; Case 129/79 *Macarthys* v *Smith* [1979] 3 All ER 325, [1981] 1 All ER 111 (CA); *SOS Scotland and Greater Glasgow Health Board* v *Wright and Hannah* [1991] ICR 187; *McKechnie* v *UBM Building Supplies* [1991] ICR 710; *Biggs* v *Somerset CC* [1995] IRLR 452.
[6] Case 43/75 *Defrenne* v *Sabena* [1976] ECR 455.
[7] *Ibid* at para 18. See also Case 129/79 *Macarthys* v *Smith*, *supra* n 5.
[8] Case 69/80 *Worringham and Humphreys* v *Lloyds Bank* [1981] ECR 767 at para 23. See also the opinion of A G Warner at 802–803.
[9] For example Case 96/80 *Jenkins* v *Kingsgate* [1981] ECR 911; Case 170/84, *Bilka-Kaufhaus* v *Weber von Hartz* [1986] ECR 1607; Case C-33/89 *Kowalska* [1990] ECR I-2591; Case C-184/89 *Nimz* [1991] ECR I-297.
[10] Case 157/86 *Murphy* v *Bord Telecom Éirann* [1988] ECR 673 at para 12; and see Case 69/80 *Worringham* v *Lloyds Bank Ltd* [1981] ECR 767 at para 23. See, however, *Pickstone* v *Freemans plc* [1988] 2 All ER 803.

Directly effective Treaty articles have horizontal, and not just vertical direct effect.[11] This means that where Article 119 has direct effect, it can be pleaded before the domestic courts and tribunals of the United Kingdom in the same way as a piece of domestic legislation.[12]

(2) Direct effect of the ETD

The direct effect of the ETD was first considered in *Marshall No 1*.[13] Ms Marshall was dismissed at the age of 62 from her position of senior dietician, because her employer, a local authority, had a policy that employees were to retire at the age at which they became entitled to a state pension. According to that policy, had Ms Marshall been a man she would have been entitled to work until the age of 65. The Court held that this was contrary to Article 5(1) of the ETD, which applies the principle of equal treatment to working conditions, including conditions covering dismissal, and that these provisions were unconditional and sufficiently precise to be directly effective in the national courts.

Subsequently in *Johnston* v *Chief Constable of the RUC*[14], the Court held that both Article 3(1) of the ETD, which prohibits discrimination in the conditions, including selection criteria, for access to all jobs or posts, and Article 4(1), which prohibits discrimination in respect of access to all types and all levels of vocational guidance and training, are also directly effective.[15] Similarly it has been suggested that Article 7 of the ETD which deals with victimisation is also capable of having direct effect. This question, however, has not been the subject of a specific ruling of the Court of Justice.[16]

Article 6 of the ETD has proved more complicated. This provision deals with remedies, rather than substance, and requires the Member States to introduce into national law "such measures as are necessary to enable all persons who consider themselves wronged by failure to apply to them the principle of equal treatment within the meaning of Articles 3, 4 and 5 to pursue their claims by judicial process after possible recourse to other competent authorities". The Court held in *Von Colson*[17] that Article 6 confers no directly effective right to a particular sanction because in this respect it leaves the Member States free to choose which sanction to enact. The applicants, who had suffered discrimination when they applied for posts at a German prison, could not therefore rely upon Article 6 in order to demand appointment to the posts, since the remedy prescribed in German law was one of compensation. Nonetheless, the Court did hold that if a remedy of compensation is chosen then it "must be adequate in relation to the damage sustained". If, as it seemed, German law only entitled

---

[11] For example Case 36/74 *Walrave and Koch* v *Association Union Cycliste Internationale* [1974] ECR 1405.
[12] *Ibid* paras 39–40.
[13] Case 152/84 *Marshall* v *Southampton and South West Hampshire AHA* [1986] ECR 723.
[14] Case 222/84 [1986] ECR 1651.
[15] Art 3(1) has been applied to prevent discrimination against job applicants on grounds of pregnancy, see Case C-177/88 *Dekker* [1990] ECR I-3941.
[16] Ellis, *European Sex Equality Law* (1991) 161.
[17] Case 14/83 [1984] ECR 1891.

the applicants to reimbursement for their expenses incurred in the application process, that was plainly inadequate.

Article 6 was considered again in *Johnston*.[18] Following her dismissal from the Royal Ulster full-time reserve because, as a woman, she was considered unsuitable for firearms training, Mrs Johnston brought a claim for sex discrimination against the Chief Constable of the Royal Ulster Constabulary. He sought to rely upon a statutory provision which provided that a certificate signed by the Secretary of State certifying that an act was done for the purpose of safeguarding national security, or protecting public safety or public order, was conclusive evidence of that fact. The Court found that this was contrary to Article 6, since it denied Mrs Johnston access to any judicial remedy at all. Furthermore, in this respect, Article 6 was unconditional, and sufficiently precise to be relied upon in the national courts.

Following *Von Colson* and *Johnston*, it seemed that Article 6 conferred a directly effective right of access to the courts, but not to a specific judicial remedy. In *Marshall No 2*[19] the Court found that Article 6 also confers a directly effective right to contest the *effectiveness* of the remedy provided by the Member State. This meant that the statutory limits on compensation payable by an industrial tribunal under the SDA 1975 had to be set aside because they prevented Miss Marshall from recovering her full quantum of damages, as assessed by the industrial tribunal.[20]

Unlike Article 119, an applicant can only rely upon the direct effect of ETD as against the State or an emanation of the State, that is vertically.[21] In *Foster* v *British Gas*[22] the Court formulated a very broad test which suggested that any organization or body which is "subject to the authority or control of the State" *or* has "special powers beyond those which result from the normal rules applicable to relations between individuals" falls within the definition of an emanation of the State.[23] It then held (confusing matters) that the ETD could be relied upon as against a body which fulfils *both* these conditions.[24] Clearly in this case it had in mind British Gas[25] which did satisfy both requirements, and subsequently the English courts have appeared to apply this stricter conjunctive test.[26]

The kinds of categories which the Court has held constitute a State body have included tax authorities[27], local and regional authorities[28], constitutionally independent authorities responsible for the maintenance of public order and safety[29], and public authorities providing public health services.[30] It is irrelevant,

---

[18] Case 222/84, *supra* n 14.
[19] Case C-271/91 *Marshall* v *Southampton and South West Hampshire AHA* [1993] ECR I-4367.
[20] See *infra*, and s 65(2) of the SDA 1975. See also O'Keeffe, in this volume.
[21] Case 152/84 *Marshall* v *Southampton and South West Hampshire AHA* [1986] ECR 723.
[22] Case C-188/90 [1990] ECR I-3313.
[23] *Ibid* para 18.
[24] *Ibid* para 20.
[25] Before privatisation.
[26] E.g. *Rolls-Royce plc* v *Doughty* [1992] ICR 538.
[27] Case 8/81 *Becker* [1982] ECR 53; Case C-221/88 *ECSC* v *Acciaierie e Ferriere Busseni* [1990] ECR I-495.
[28] Case 103/88 *Fratelli Constanzo* v *Commune di Milano* [1989] ECR 1839.
[29] Case 222/84 *Johnston* v *Chief Constable of the RUC*, *supra* n 14.
[30] Case 152/84 *Marshall* v *Southampton and South West Hampshire AHA*, *supra* n 21.

for these purposes, whether the State body is acting in a public or private capacity. Miss Marshall, for example, was able to enforce the ETD against a local authority acting in a private capacity as her employer.

Notably, three Advocates-General have recommended in relatively recent jurisprudence that Directives may also have horizontal direct effect, a development which would abolish the need to determine whether or not a body is an emanation of the State.[31] However the Court has so far resisted this development.[32]

(3) The Equal Pay Directive

The EPD was originally intended to oblige the Member States to implement the concept of equal pay contained in Article 119. However, soon after its enactment, the Court held that Article 119 had direct effect and hence deprived the EPD of much purpose. It may still be used to "facilitate the practical application of the principle of equal pay outlined in Article 119"[33] although, as a piece of secondary legislation it cannot modify the scope, or temporal effect, of Article 119.

(4) Further Directives

The ETD has been supplemented by Council Directive 86/613/EEC[34] which extends the principle of equal treatment to the self-employed (notably those engaged in business, farming and the professions[35] and Council Directive 92/85/EEC[36] which aims to protect the health and safety at work of pregnant workers and workers who have recently given birth or are breast-feeding. With the exception of *Webb* v *EMO Air Cargo*[37], in which the Court referred to Directive 92/85/EEC in support of the prohibition on the dismissal of pregnant women, these Directives have not yet been considered by the Court.

(5) Temporal effect of Community law

A directly effective Treaty article has direct effect from the moment the Treaty becomes operative in national law. However, in *Defrenne No 2*, the Court held

---

[31] Advocates General Van Gerven in Case C-271/91 *Marshall* v *Southampton and South West Hampshire AHA, supra* n 19; Jacobs in Case C-316/93 *Vaneetveld* v *Le Foyer SA* [1994] ECR I-763; and Lenz in Case C-91/92 *Faccini Dori* [1994] ECR I-3325.

[32] Case C-91/92 *Faccini Dori, supra* n 31.

[33] Case 96/80 *Jenkins* v *Kingsgate* [1981] ECR 911 at para 22. See also Case 61/81 *Commission* v *United Kingdom and Northern Ireland* [1982] ECR 2601; Case 143/83 *Commission* v *Denmark* [1985] ECR 427; Case 237/85 *Rummler* [1986] ECR 2101; Case 109/88 *Danfoss* [1989] ECR 3199; Case C-360/90 *Bötel* [1992] I-3589; Joined Cases C-399/92, C-402/92, C-425/92, C-34/93, C-50/93 and C-78/93 *Helmig et al* [1994] ECR I-5727; Case C-297/93 *Grau-Hupka* [1994] ECR I-5535; Case C-400/93 *Dansk Industri* (judgment of 31 May 1995).

[34] OJ 1986 L359/56. This Directive came into force on 30 June 1989; or 30 June 1991 in the case of Member States which had to amend their legislation on matrimonial rights and obligations.

[35] Therefore women partners in, for example, a law firm, accountancy firm or medical practice are guaranteed equal treatment.

[36] OJ 1992 L 348/1. This Directive came into force on 19 October 1994.

[37] Case C-32/93 [1994] ECR I-3567.

that the direct effect of Article 119 could not be relied upon in order to support claims concerning pay periods prior to the date of the judgment, that is 8 April 1976, except as regards those workers who had by then already started an action.

This temporal limitation continues to be of some relevance. For example, in *Vroege*[38] and *Fisscher*[39] the Court confirmed[40] that the exclusion of employees from an occupational pension scheme on grounds of sex was a breach of Article 119. Employees in the same position as Ms Vroege and Ms Fisscher are now theoretically entitled to claim membership of the scheme from which they were excluded with effect from the date of *Defrenne No 2*. In practice the actual numbers of years which may be claimed will depend, *inter alia*, upon the operation of time-limits in the various Member States; assuming these time-limits are compatible with Community law. It seems that applicants in the United Kingdom will only be able to obtain access to a scheme in respect of periods within two years of the date of the claim.[41]

A Directive can only have direct effect after the expiry of the time-limit within which it was supposed to be implemented by the Member States.[42] In the case of the ETD this was 9 August 1978. This date is still of crucial significance because in *Emmott*[43] the Court held that where a litigant relies upon a Directive, a Member State cannot rely upon national time-limits if the Directive has not been correctly implemented into domestic law when the claim is presented. Where, therefore, a litigant brings a claim under the ETD (which cannot be brought under the SDA, because the latter does not properly implement the former) the breach of the Directive which is the substance of the claim may have taken place as long ago as August 1978.

One recent example of these rules in operation has been the introduction of hundreds of cases against the Ministry of Defence (MoD) following their policy of dismissing service women who became pregnant. Section 85(4) of the Sex Discrimination Act 1975, as it then stood, excluded from the scope of the Act "service in . . . the naval, military or air forces of the Crown"; an exception which is not reflected in the ETD. Following *Hertz*[44] and *Dekker*[45], in which the Court held that the dismissal of female workers on account of pregnancy constitutes direct discrimination on grounds of sex, it became apparent that the policy pursued by the MoD was unlawful, and claims were subsequently made by ex-service women who had been dismissed many years previously. Moreover, following the judgment in *Marshall No 2* the applicants were able to claim an unlimited amount of compensation. In certain cases awards in excess of £100,000 were made.

---

[38] Case C-57/93 *Vroege* v *NCIV Instituut voor Volkshuisvesting BV* [1994] ECR I-4541.
[39] Case C-128/93 *Fisscher* v *Voorhuis Hengelo BV* [1994] ECR I-4583.
[40] See Case 170/84 *Bilka-Kaufhaus, supra* n 9.
[41] See *infra*.
[42] Case 148/78 *Pubblico Ministero* v *Tullio Ratti* [1979] ECR 1629.
[43] Case C-208/90 [1991] ECR I-4269.
[44] Case C-179/88 [1990] ECR I-3979.
[45] Case C-177/88 [1990], *supra*, n 15.

(b) National law

The EPA 1970 and Part II of the SDA 1975 essentially reflect the obligations of the EPD and the ETD.[46] Obviously an applicant can rely on this legislation as against both State and private bodies in the same way as any other piece of national legislation.

In interpreting national legislation which reflects Community obligations the courts are required to take a teleological approach in order to give effect to Community law and, if necessary, the underlying Community objective.[47] The great advantage of this approach is that it side-steps the problems attached to direct effect. If national law is construed in a manner compatible with a Directive, then an individual can rely upon the national law and has no need to invoke the provisions of the Directive themselves (other than as an aid to construction).

However, the extent to which methods of interpretation can be used to overcome failings in national legislation is limited since, as the Court seems to have accepted, national courts are not obliged to distort national legislation in order to give effect to Community law.[48] Moreover, although English courts have been prepared to read words into the relevant national legislation in order to achieve a result compatible with Community law[49], they have also been ready to conclude that national legislation is not capable, without distortion, of being interpreted in a manner consistent with Community law.[50] In any event, the effective implementation of Community law now depends less on teleological interpretation of national legislation. This is because of the judgment of the Court of Justice in *Francovich*.[51]

(c) A *Francovich* claim

(1) The *Francovich* judgment

Francovich concerned a Directive which had neither been implemented by the Italian government nor was directly effective. The Court held that the Directive was not directly effective because, although it clearly intended to give rights to employees in the event of the insolvency of their employer, it did not specify the bodies against whom those rights could be exercised but instead left that to the discretion of the Member States. In a fundamentally important judgment, the Court held that the applicants were nevertheless entitled to bring a claim in damages against the Italian State because three conditions were met:

---

[46] A substantive comparative analysis is not possible within the confines of this chapter.
[47] Case 14/83 *Von Colson, supra* n 17; Case C-106/89 *Marleasing* [1990] ECR I-4135.
[48] Opinions of Advocate General Van Gerven in Case C-106/89 *Marleasing, supra* n 47 at para 8; and Case C-271/91 *Marshall* v *Southampton and South West Hampshire AHA, supra* n 19 at para 10.
[49] *Pickstone* v *Freemans* [1989] AC 66; *Litster* v *Forth Dry Dock and Engineering Co* [1990] AC 546; *Garland* v *BRE* [1983] 2 AC 751; *Macmillan* v *Edinburgh Voluntary Organisations Council* EAT/9/95.
[50] See *Webb* v *EMO Cargo (UK) Ltd* [1992] 1 CMLR 793 (CA), [1993] 1 WLR 49 (HL); Case C-32/93 *Webb* v *EMO Air Cargo (UK) Ltd* [1994] ECR I-3567.
[51] Joined Cases C-6/90 and C-9/90 [1991] ECR I-5357.

The first of those conditions is that the result prescribed by the Directive should entail the grant of rights to individuals. The second condition is that it should be possible to identify the content of those rights on the basis of the provisions of the Directive. Finally, the third condition is the existence of a causal link between the breach of the State's obligations and the harm suffered by the injured parties.[52]

In addition to liability in respect of Directives, it also seems probable that *Francovich* was intended to establish, as a general principle, that Member States are liable in damages to individuals for loss caused to them by a breach of Community law for which the Member States can be held responsible. The scope of this obligation and the conditions on which it becomes operative are not apparent from *Francovich* itself. From the point of view of English law, the crucial question is whether, and in what circumstances, the State can be held liable in damages for legislative or administrative action; that is action taken in its public capacity, which constitutes a breach of Community law (or, indeed, failure to take action in breach of Community law). The most important English authority on this point[53], decided before *Francovich*, holds that liability in damages only arises where the tort of misfeasance in public office is made out. However, it is now doubtful that this is still correct.[54]

(2) Application of *Francovich* to claims of sex discrimination

For the purposes of claims of sex discrimination, a *Francovich* claim will arise most often where it is alleged that the United Kingdom government has failed to implement the ETD correctly. This may take one of two forms; first, where the party allegedly in breach of the ETD is a private body, and hence no claim can be made under the ETD; and secondly, where an applicant believes that a greater measure of damages is available by relying upon *Francovich* rather than upon the vertical direct effect of the ETD. One example of the latter situation is the pregnancy cases brought against the MoD, since it seems that exemplary damages may be awarded on a *Francovich* claim but not on a claim based on the ETD.[55]

Where the applicant can rely upon the vertical direct effect of a Directive, and the potential damages available under the ETD are the same as under *Francovich*, it is questionable whether a claim under *Francovich* can be made, since the applicant will have suffered no loss as a result of the State's inadequate implementation. If an applicant does try to bring a claim against both the State under *Francovich*[56]and a State body under the Directive it is, in any event, doubtful whether the former

---

[52] *Ibid* para 40.
[53] *Bourgoin SA* v *MAFF* [1986] 1 QB 716.
[54] See *Kirklees MBC* v *Wickes Building Supplies* [1993] AC 227; Opinion of Advocate General Léger of 20 June 1995 in Case C-5/94 *R* v *MAFF ex parte Hedley Lomas*. Opinion of Advocate General Tesauro of 28 November 1995 in Joined Cases C-46/93 and C-48/93 *Brasserie du Pêcheur* v *Germany* and *R* v *SOS Transport ex parte Factortame* [1990] ECR I-2433.
[55] See (iv) (d).
[56] One further question is whether a *Francovich* action must be brought against the State itself or whether the definition of the State is as wide for the purposes of a *Francovich* action as it is for the purposes of vertical direct effect. It is suggested that the former view is correct.

claim can be brought in the industrial tribunal together with the substantive claim under the ETD. Although it is established that the industrial tribunals have jurisdiction to deal with claims based upon Article 119, the EDT and the EPD, the reason for this, it is suggested, is because these claims are analogous to claims of sex discrimination brought under domestic provisions for which the industrial tribunals are the chosen forum. However, a *Francovich* claim is clearly not analogous to a claim of sex discrimination, but instead a remedy for a very different kind of wrong; namely the violation of Community law by the State in its public capacity.[57]

It is suggested that breach of Article 119 will rarely give rise to a claim under *Francovich* because, in the majority of cases, applicants will be able to rely upon their directly effective private law rights under Article 119 as against both State and private bodies. Therefore they will rarely be able to show that they have suffered loss as a result of the State's violation in the public law domain. In any event, applicants will have little incentive for trying to bring such an action unless either the potential quantum of damages available is greater, or the body against whom they would have asserted their rights under Article 119 is financially unable to meet the claim.

(iv) Effective judicial protection[58]

(a) The general principles

Although the Treaty of Rome is silent as to the question of remedies, it is well established that Article 5 of the Treaty requires the national courts to protect rights conferred on individuals under Community law.[59] The manner in which these rights are protected has been held by the Court to be a matter for national, and not Community, law since:

> in the absence of Community rules on this subject, it is for the domestic legal system of each Member State to designate the courts having jurisdiction and to determine the procedural conditions governing actions at law intended to ensure the protection of rights which citizens have from the direct effect of Community law. . .[60]

However, this general principle is subject to two provisos. The first is the requirement of non-discrimination. This means, essentially, that the procedural conditions in which a Community right is exercised and the substantive remedies

---

[57] Now see the decision of the EAT in *Secretary of State for Employment* v *Mann and others* EAT/930/94 and EAT 54/95 at 8–9 of the transcript, in which the EAT overturned the IT's decision that it had jurisdiction to hear *Francovich* claims.
[58] See also the discussion by O'Keeffe, in this volume.
[59] Joined Cases C-6/90 and C-9/90 *Francovich, supra* n 51.
[60] Case 33/76 *Rewe* [1976] ECR 1989 at para 5; see also Case 45/76 *Comet* [1976] ECR 2043 at paras 12–13, and Joined Cases C-6/90 and C-9/90 *Francovich, supra* n 51.

which may be obtained in the event of breach, must not be less favourable than the procedural conditions and substantive remedies which apply to an equivalent claim under national law.

The second proviso is that the national procedures must give effective protection to Community rights. The most fundamental aspect of this requirement is that the national courts must set aside any rule of domestic law which conflicts with Community law.[61] In addition, the need for effective judicial protection may affect the national rules which govern procedure and remedies. With respect to the former, the Court has held that national rules of procedure must not make the exercise of the Community right "impossible in practice"[62] or "excessively difficult".[63] Effective protection of Community rights also requires that the substantive remedy available in the national courts is adequate to redress the harm that has been done by violation of the Community right; and this must be assessed by reference to the objective of the legislation which was the source of the right infringed.[64]

(b) Equal pay

(1) Modification of contract terms/damages

Although the EPD and Article 119 do not specify the remedies which must be available in the national courts, it is well established that an applicant is entitled to claim a pay rate which is non-discriminatory. In the United Kingdom this result is achieved under the EPA by virtue of an equality clause, implied into the contract of employment[65], which operates to vary the terms of the contract in order to satisfy the requirements of equal treatment.[66] This means that, in the event of breach, the standard contractual remedies, including, of course, damages, are available. Since discrimination in respect of pay is established by reference to a comparator, assessment of the damages payable is relatively easy to quantify. This does not necessarily mean, however, that damages will be paid in order to reflect *identical* terms of employment for both sexes. Suppose, for example, a woman earns a rate of pay for day-work of £12 per hour and her male comparator, on a night shift, earns £24 per hour, and suppose further that night-work is paid at time-and-a-half. The man's notional rate for day work is consequently £16 per

---

[61] For example, Case 106/77 *Simmenthal* [1978] ECR 629; Case C-213/89 *Factortame* [1990] ECR I-2433.

[62] Case 45/76 *Comet, supra* n 60. Case 33/76, *Rewe, supra* n 60.

[63] Case 199/82 *San Georgio* [1983] ECR 3595. For an application of this principle see Case 45/76 *Comet, supra* n 60; Case 386/87 *Bessin and Salson* [1989] ECR 3551; Case 130/79 *Express Dairy Foods* [1980] ECR 1887; Joined Cases 331, 376 and 378/85 *Bianco* [1988] ECR 1099; Case C-312/93 *Peterbrueck* v *Belgium*, judgment of 14 December 1995. See also the Opinion of Advocate General Van Gerven in Case C-128/92 *HJ Banks* v *British Coal Corporation* [1994] ECR I-1209.

[64] See Case C-271/91 *Marshall* v *Southampton and South West Hampshire AHA, supra* n 19.

[65] See s 1 of the EPA 1970.

[66] See s 1(2) of the EPA 1970.

hour and the tribunal will therefore calculate the damages payable by reference to an hourly rate of £16, rather than £24, per hour.[67]

In practice Article 119 operates to modify the terms of an employment contract in much the same way as the EPA, as it also requires that incompatible provisions of national law be set aside and disadvantaged employees given benefits equal to their comparators.[68]

(2) Other remedies

Under the EPA other contractual remedies, including declarations and injunctions, are also available.

(c) Equal treatment

(1) Damages

The principal remedy chosen by the United Kingdom for breach of equal treatment is, again, damages.[69] In *Marshall No 2*, the Court of Justice was asked whether this remedy was effective in the light of the fact that the SDA limited the amount of compensation payable by an industrial tribunal[70] and made no provision for the award of interest. As a result, although the industrial tribunal had assessed the damage suffered by Miss Marshall at £19,405 (including interest) it was only able to award her £6,250. The Court spelt out that since the purpose of discrimination laws is to achieve "real equality of treatment", the quantum of damages payable must be sufficient to redress fully the discrimination suffered. Moreover, interest must also be available, since if the award of damages made no provision for the effluxion of time, it would not fully compensate the discrimination suffered. Article 6 of the ETD could therefore be relied upon (against a State body) to set aside national rules imposing a limit on the amount of compensation recoverable.

The national legislation has now been amended in order to comply with the ruling in *Marshall No 2* so that there is now no limit on the compensation which may be awarded for breach of the equal treatment and equal pay provisions.[71] This means that, although a claim for unfair dismissal on grounds, for example, of pregnancy, may be brought under the EPCA 1978[72], it is better, where damages are sought, to base the claim on the ETD or SDA[73] in order to avoid the statutory limitation still applicable to the former kind of claims. On the

---

[67] For example, *Electrolux Ltd* v *Hutchinson* [1977] ICR 252 at 255: cf. *Kerr* v *Lister & Co Ltd* [1977] IRLR 259.
[68] Case C-184/89 *Nimz*, *supra* n 9, at paras 16–21; Case C-200/91 *Coloroll Pension Trustees* [1994] ECR I-4389 at paras 31 and 32; Case C-408/92 *Smith* v *Advel Systems* [1994] ECR I-4435 at paras 16 and 17.
[69] See s 65(1)(b) of the SDA 1975.
[70] See s 65(2) of the SDA 1975.
[71] The Sex Discrimination and Equal Pay (Remedies) Regulations 1993, SI 1993 2798, made by the SOS for Employment under s 2(2) of the European Communities Act 1972.
[72] As amended by the Trade Union Reform and Employment Rights Act 1993 (TURERA) to comply with Directive 92/85/EEC. See s 60 of the EPCA (commenced 10 June 1994).
[73] Depending on the decision of the House of Lords in *Webb* v *EMO Air Cargo (UK) Ltd*, *supra* n 50.

other hand, however, the remedies available under the EPCA are wider than those available under the SDA and include the power to order reinstatement or re-engagement.[74]

In some cases it will be more difficult to assess the level of compensation needed to arrive at "real equality" than in others, and the Court of Justice has specifically recognised that "such requirements necessarily entail that the particular circumstances of each breach of the principle of equal treatment be taken into account".[75] For example, where an individual is refused access to a job on the grounds of sex it will be difficult to quantify the appropriate compensation. *Von Colson* was an example of that situation and may explain why the Court was only able to specify that the "compensation must be adequate in relation to the damage sustained" and that a "purely nominal amount did not satisfy that criterion".[76]

Strangely the SDA specifically provides that no damages are payable at all in the event of *indirect* discrimination, unless it is shown that the respondent intended to discriminate on grounds of sex.[77] The stark distinction between the remedies available for direct and indirect discrimination is unsatisfactory and, it is suggested, not compatible with Community law. First, discrimination on grounds of sex is not fault based.[78] In *Dekker* the Court specifically stated that "where a Member State opts for a sanction forming part of the rules on civil liability, *any infringement* of the prohibition of discrimination suffices in itself to make the person guilty of it fully liable, and no regard may be had to the grounds of exemption envisaged by national law".[79] Secondly, the distinction is illogical and, moreover, incompatible with the obligation on the Member States to provide an effective remedy as explained by the Court in *Von Colson*, and *Marshall No 2.*

Under the SDA, the tribunal is entitled to make an award for injury to feelings.[80] However, this head of damages is not available under the EPA, since breach of contract rarely includes a right to damages for injury to feelings.[81]

---

[74] See s 69 EPCA 1978. Note also that in *R v SOS for Employment, ex parte Equal Opportunities Commission and Another* [1994] 2 WLR 409, the House of Lords held that provisions of the EPCA which required an employee to work a specified number of hours per week during a specified period of employment, in order to have the right to compensation for unfair dismissal and the right to statutory redundancy pay, constituted indirect discrimination which was not objectively justified. In the light of this, the minimum hour requirements were removed by the Employment Protection (Part-time Employees) Regulations 1995 SI 1995/31 as from 6 February 1995. Moreover in *R v SOS for Employment, ex parte Seymour-Smith & Perez* [1995] IRLR 464, the Court of Appeal held that further provisions of the EPCA which required an employee to have two years' continuous service in order to bring a claim for unfair dismissal were indirectly discriminatory because they had a disproportionate impact on women which was not justified.
[75] Case C-271/91 *Marshall v Southampton and South West Hampshire AHA*, *supra* n 19 at para 25.
[76] *Ibid* para 28.
[77] See s 66(3) SDA 1975. See also *Turton v McGregor Wallcoverings Ltd* [1977] IRLR 249; See now the decision of the EAT in *Macmillan v Edinburgh Voluntary Organisations Council* EAT/9/95 in which the EAT held that the IT had not erred in law in holding that it was precluded from awarding compensation for indirect discrimination under the SDA.
[78] See Ellis, "The Definition of Discrimination in European Community Sex Equality Law" 19 EL Rev (1994), 563–580.
[79] Case C-177/88, *supra* n 15 at para 26.
[80] See ss 65(1)(b) and 66(4) SDA 1975.
[81] *Addis v Gramophone Co Ltd* [1909] AC 488; *O'Laoire v Jackel International Ltd (No 2)* [1991] ICR 718: *cf. Jarvis v Swan Tours Ltd* [1973] QB 233.

(2) Other remedies

In addition to damages, declarations are available under the SDA.[82] Furthermore, the tribunal has express power to recommend that the respondent take "practicable" action "for the purpose of obviating or reducing the adverse effect on the complainant of any act of discrimination to which the complaint relates".[83] If the respondent then fails to comply with this recommendation without "reasonable justification for doing so", the tribunal may increase the amount of compensation payable.[84]

(d) Exemplary damages

It is unlikely that exemplary damages can be awarded for breach of the equal treatment or equal pay provisions because this head of damages can only be awarded in respect of a limited group of actions.[85] Nevertheless, although it is doubtful that Community law requires, as a matter of general principle, that exemplary damages be made available (since damages which fully compensate the applicant for the discrimination suffered should in most cases constitute an effective remedy), it is arguable that exemplary damages must be available where they are necessary to have "a real deterrent effect on the employer".[86] This is a question of fact for the national court to decide.

Moreover, some claims based upon *Francovich* may be accommodated within one of the categories of cases for which exemplary damages are available; that is actions which include a "gross misuse of power, involving tortious conduct by agents of the government".[87] Therefore, where on a *Francovich* claim, a deliberate or intentional unlawful act on the part of a servant of government can be proved[88], there is no reason why exemplary damages should not, in principle, be payable. They are, in fact, being sought by some of the ex-service women dismissed by the Armed Forces on the grounds of pregnancy.[89]

(v) Time limits

(a) The SDA

Under the SDA an application by an individual must be lodged within three months of the act complained of[90], although industrial tribunals have jurisdic-

---

[82] See s 65(1)(a) of the SDA 1975.
[83] See s 65 (1)(c) of the SDA 1975.
[84] See s 1(3) of the SDA 1975.
[85] *Rookes v Barnard* [1964] AC 1129; *Cassell & Co v Broome* [1972] AC 1027; *AB v South West Water Services Ltd* [1993] 1 All ER 609. See, in particular, *Deane v London Borough of Ealing* [1993] IRLR 209.
[86] Case 14/83, *Von Colson, supra* n 17 at para 28.
[87] *AB v South West Water Services, supra* n 84 at 626.
[88] Proof of this is not a prerequisite for a claim based on the failure to implement a Directive and is unlikely to be a prerequisite for other types of *Francovich* claims; see the Opinion of Advocate General Léger of 20 June 1995 in Case C-5/94 *R v MAFF ex parte Hedley Lomas*.
[89] See *supra.*
[90] See s 76(1) of the SDA 1975.

tion to consider a complaint made out of time if "in all the circumstances of the case . . . [it] considers it just and equitable to do so".[91] A time-limit of three months is not incompatible with Community law since it does not make the right "virtually impossible" or "excessively difficult" to exercise. By comparison the Court, in *Comet*,[92] accepted the validity of a time-limit of just 30 days.

The Employment Appeal Tribunal (EAT) held in *Foster* v *South Glamorgan HA* that it *may* be "just and equitable" to extend the limitation period where the law is changed shortly after the time period has expired and under the new law the applicant has a good claim.[93] This may happen, for example, if the Court of Justice rules that the United Kingdom has not properly implemented the ETD and, in the light of this, the SDA is subsequently amended. According to the EAT, where the line is to be drawn is a question of fact to be decided according to the circumstances of each individual case. This judgment was given before that of the Court of Justice in *Emmott*,[94] but if still applicable would mean that an applicant claiming, out of time, against a private body under the amended SDA would be in a weaker position than an applicant who brought a claim, out of time, under the ETD before the SDA was amended. According to *Emmott*, the latter applicant had, at that time, an unqualified right to invoke the ETD without regard to national time-limits, even though (s)he was able to bring that claim under the ETD before those time-limits expired.[95]

Where the discrimination arises because of a term in the employment contract, then the discriminatory act is treated as extending throughout the duration of the contract and, similarly, a discriminatory act extending over a period is considered as done at the end of that period.[96] A deliberate omission is treated as having been done when the person in question decided upon it.[97]

(b) The EPA

The time-limit for claims brought under the EPA is effectively six months but is expressed differently from that in the SDA since it provides that the applicant must have been employed (by the relevant employer) within six months preceding the date on which the claim is brought.[98] This reflects the fact that an equal pay claim is based on an unlawful contractual term with the result that any discrimination in respect of pay continues until the last day of employment.

In addition, the EPA also restricts the number of past years of service for which equal pay may be claimed ("arrears limit"). It provides that an applicant

---

[91] See s 76(5) of the SDA 1975.
[92] Case 45/76, *supra* n 60.
[93] [1988] IRLR 277.
[94] See Case C-208/90 *Emmott* v *Minister for Social Welfare and the Attorney General* [1991] ECR I-4269.
[95] Case C-208/90, *ibid.*
[96] See s 76(6)(a) and 76(6)(b) of the SDA 1975; also *Amies* v *Inner London Education Authority* [1977] ICR 308; *Calder* v *James Finlay Corp Ltd* [1989] ICR 157.
[97] *Swithland Motors plc* v *Clarke* [1994] ICR 231.
[98] See s 2(4) of the EPA 1970 as interpreted in *Etherson* v *Strathclyde Regional Council* [1992] IRLR 392.

cannot claim damages or arrears of remuneration in respect of periods of employment earlier than two years upon which the proceedings were instituted.[99]

Unlike the SDA, the EPA does not make provision for these limits to be
extended if it "would be just and equitable to do so". Moreover, it currently seems
likely that claims based upon Article 119 are subject to a time-limit similar to that
of six months and further that the arrears limit of two years may also be applied,
by analogy with the EPA, to such claims.[100] Indeed, recent legislation[101]expressly
applies the same arrears limit to claims made by part-time workers to join occupational pension schemes, even though many part-time workers did not realise that
Article 119 gave them these rights before the *Vroege*[102] and *Fisscher*[103] judgments.

It is arguable that the inflexible application of such arrears limits is not compatible with the right of the applicant to an effective remedy and, in particular,
the judgment in *Marshall No 2*. However, in *Steenhorst-Neerings*,[104] the Court, in
the context of a claim under the Directive on equal treatment in matters of
social security[105] (SSD), did not cast any doubt on the validity of a Dutch provision which only allowed arrears of *one* year to be claimed, even though the
applicant presented her claim shortly after the Dutch courts had clarified her
rights (and, in fact, at the time when the claim was presented the Netherlands
had not correctly implemented the SSD).[106]

(c) Community law

(1) Applicable time-limits

As discussed above, the Court has held that it is for the Member States to determine the procedural conditions governing actions based upon direct effect,[107]
subject to the general principles of non-discrimination and effectiveness.
Although there is no provision of national law laying down a time-limit for
claims under Community law, the EAT has stated that:

> . . . it does not follow from that that any claim under European law can be made at
> any point of time, however remote. That would be a truly intolerable situation. In
> principle, English law is perfectly capable of evolving, if necessary by analogy to statu-
> tory or common law periods which are clearly laid down in terms of months and
> years, a time-limit for the bringing of similar but sufficiently different claims for them
> not to fall within the strict letter of the statutory or common law limitation period.[108]

---

[99] See s 2(5) of the EPA 1970.
[100] See s 2(5) of the EPA 1978 as amended by regs 11 & 12 of the Occupational Pension Schemes
(Equal Access to Membership) Amendment Regulations 1995 (SI 1995/1215). See now the decision of the IT in *Preston* v *Wolverhampton Healthcare NHS Trust and SOS Health* IT/so7497/95.
[101] *Ibid.*
[102] Case C-57/93, *supra* n 37.
[103] Case C-128/93, *supra* n 38.
[104] Case C-338/91 *Steenhorst-Neerings* [1993] ECR I-5475.
[105] Directive 79/7 (OJ 1979 L 6/24).
[106] See *infra* (v) (c) (3).
[107] Case 33/76 *Rewe, supra* n 60; Case C-128/93 *Fisscher, supra* n 39.
[108] *Cannon* v *Barnsley Metropolitan Borough Council* [1992] IRLR 474 at 477.

According to this approach, time-limits of between three and six months would apply to claims brought under Article 119, the ETD and the EPD by analogy with the time-limits laid down in the SDA, the EPA and the EPCA[109], and this is, in fact, the approach which the English courts have recently adopted. However, since some claims may be categorised as both equal treatment and equal pay claims (for example reduced redundancy payments), for which the respective analogous time-limits differ, it may be difficult to determine which time-limit is appropriate. In order to side-step this problem, the English courts have generally adopted a pragmatic approach to reach a fair result on the facts of the particular case.[110]

(2) Commencement of time-limits

The point at which the applicable time-limit starts to run is, at the time of writing, wholly unclear and badly needs resolution by the Court of Appeal. The root of the problem is the decision of the Court of Justice in *Emmott*.[111] Here the Court held that where a claim is made under a Directive which is directly effective and which has not been correctly implemented by the Member State – in that case the SSD – the applicable time-limit will only run from the day when the State's failure to comply with its obligations has been rectified.[112]

The judgment in *Emmott* is explicable on its own facts. The administrative authorities had first refused to adjudicate on Ms Emmott's claim, while awaiting a decision of the Court of Justice, and had then tried to argue that her claim was out of time, even though the SSD had not then been correctly transposed into national law. Nonetheless, the Court's judgment pronounced a general principle according to which the State is unable to invoke national time-limits to defeat a claim based on a Directive which it has failed to implement. This principle is directly applicable to claims brought under the ETD in which it is claimed that the United Kingdom government is guilty of non-implementation. However, since a claim based upon a directly effective Directive may be made independently of implementing national legislation, the ruling in *Emmott* and its application to the ETD, is open to criticism.

Subsequently the question arose whether *Emmott* is also applicable to claims for equal pay brought under Article 119, with the result that the relevant time-limits do not start to run unless, and until, this provision is correctly reflected in domestic law.[113] The recent decision in *Biggs* v *Somerset County Council*[114], in which the EAT held that the claim of a part-time worker who had been dismissed 18 years previously was out of time, answers this question in the negative. Ms Biggs sought to claim that until the decision of the House of Lords in *R* v

---

[109] See s 101 of the EPCA 1978.
[110] *Livingstone* v *Hepworth* [1992] IRLR 63; *Cannon* v *Barnsley MCB, supra* n 9; *Rankin* v *British Coal Corporation* [1993] IRLR 69.
[111] Case C-208/90, *supra* n 94.
[112] *Ibid.*
[113] See *Cannon* v *Barnsley, supra* n 19; ss 16(2) and 30(3) of the Employment Act 1989.
[114] [1995] IRLR 459.

Secretary of State for Employment, ex parte EOC[115] it was not clear that the provisions of the EPCA which prevented her from claiming unfair dismissal, because she worked too few hours each week, were contrary to Article 119. Hence, she argued that the normal three month time period did not start to run until either the date on which the relevant amendments were made to the EPCA or the date of the judgment. Rejecting this argument, the EAT stated that it had not been impossible for Ms Biggs to invoke her directly effective rights under Article 119 within three months of being dismissed and "to argue then that the qualifying conditions in United Kingdom domestic law in force at that time were ineffective barriers to her claim by reason of their incompatibility with Article 119".[116]

It is suggested that the distinction made in this respect between Treaty articles and Directives is justifiable. Member States have a particular duty to transpose Directives into national law in a sufficiently clear and precise manner and, until they do so, the rights which are thereby conferred on individuals may only be ascertained and enforced to a limited extent. By comparison, Treaty articles which are directly effective, such as Article 119, confer a free-standing right which is directly applicable before the national courts without the need for further implementing measures.[117] As a result there is less justification for depriving, as a matter of principle, the Member State of its rights to rely upon an individual's delay in initiating proceedings. Moreover, were *Emmott* to apply to claims based on Article 119, private litigants as well as State bodies would be prevented from invoking national time-limits.

Notably, the EAT in *Biggs* also rejected the approach taken by the EAT in the earlier case of *Rankin* v *British Coal.*[118] Here the EAT held that if, at the time of the discriminatory conduct, an applicant did not have a claim under domestic law and nor was it obvious that a claim under Article 119 existed, the time period should be calculated from the date on which it could reasonably be said to be clear that a claim under Article 119 could be made.[119] In *Rankin*[120] this was held to be the date of the amending legislation.

A further complication arises where a claim is based, or could be based, on both the ETD and Article 119. It appears from the judgment of the EAT in *Cannon* v *Barnesley*[121] that the State, or an emanation of the State, is prevented by *Emmott* from relying upon national time-limits in respect of any claim brought under the ETD (or any other Directive); even one falling within the scope of Article 119. However, in *Biggs*, the EAT proposed that *Emmott* is not applicable if the applicant has a directly enforceable right under Article 119. It is suggested that this latter view is correct.

---

[115] *R* v *Secretary of State for Employment, ex parte EOC, supra* n 74.
[116] *Ibid* para 68.
[117] See *Rankin* v *British Coal Corporation, supra* n 10 at 76.
[118] See *Rankin* v *British Coal Corporation, supra* n 10.
[119] *Ibid.*
[120] Here the United Kingdom legislation was amended in January 1990 and in May 1990 the *Barber* judgment finally clarified that statutory redundancy payments fell within the scope of Article 119. Mrs Rankin's claim was presented before *Barber* and within three months of the amendment.
[121] *Cannon* v *Barnsley, supra* n 9. Now see the decision of the IT in *Preston* v *Wolverhampton Healthcare NHS Trust and SOS Health* IT/so7497/95.

(3) Arrears limits

The Court of Justice has made a clear, if not convincing, distinction between time-limits *per se* and arrears limits. It has held in both *Steenhorst-Neerings*[122] and *Johnson No 2*[123], that *Emmott* has no application to situations where these kinds of retrospective limitations are imposed, by analogy with the relevant national law, on claims made under a Directive which the State has failed to implement correctly. The Court held that arrears limits are different from time-limits because they do not prevent the action from being brought, but merely restrict the number of years in respect of which benefits can be claimed. They do not, thus, make it impossible to exercise the rights conferred by the Directive. By contrast:

> the solution adopted in *Emmott* was justified by the particular circumstances of that case, in which a time-bar had the result of depriving the applicant of any opportunity whatever to rely on her right to equal treatment under the [ETD].[124]

This ruling will be of particular importance in claims made under directly effective Community law where the retrospective limitations under the EPA[125] are held to apply by analogy. This is most likely to happen in claims brought under Article 119 (and the EPD).

It is difficult to see any basis for the black and white distinction made between national rules which prevent a right from being exercised at all and rules which severely restrict the exercise of that right.[126] A second possible justification for the Court's acceptance of the arrears limit in *Steenhorst-Neerings* was the fact that in that case large claims for arrears of incapacity benefit might have upset the financial balance of the relevant system and the validity of such claims would, in addition, have been difficult to verify. However, in *Johnson No 2*, the Court refused to distinguish *Steenhorst-Neerings* on this basis. It therefore seems that the *Emmott* principle will not be applied to national rules which lay down arrears limits.

(vi) Burden of proof

(a) Community law

It is the task of the person alleging facts in support of a claim to adduce proof of such facts and therefore, in claims of sex discrimination, the applicant must prove that his or her sex was the cause of the detriment suffered.[127] However,

---

[122] Case C-338/91 [1993] ECR I-5475.
[123] Case C-410/92 [1994] ECR I-5483.
[124] *Ibid* para 26.
[125] See s 2(5) of the EPA 1970.
[126] See O'Keeffe, in this volume.
[127] Case C-127/92 *Enderby* v *Frenchay HA* [1993] ECR I-5535 at para 13. See also *Robins* v *National Trust Co* [1927] AC 515 *Constantine Line* v *Imperial Smelting Corporation* [1942] AC 154 *Oxford* v *DHSS* [1977] ICR 884.

the burden of proof may shift when a claim of indirect discrimination is made. This arises when distinct groups of workers are treated differently because of differences which do not appear to be based upon sex but the treatment *in fact* operates to the disadvantage of one sex when there are no objective grounds for doing so. In order to avoid depriving employees of any effective means of enforcing such a claim, the Court stated in *Bilka-Kaufhaus* that in these circumstances it is for the employer to show that the different treatment is "based on objectively justified factors unrelated to any discrimination on grounds of sex".[128] Similarly, in the context of equal value claims, the Court held in *Enderby* that:

> where significant statistics disclose an appreciable difference in pay between two jobs of equal value, one of which is carried out almost exclusively by women and the other predominantly by men, Article 119 of the Treaty requires the employer to show that that difference is based on objectively justified factors unrelated to any discrimination on grounds of sex.[129]

The Court has subsequently repeated this formula several times, indicating that potential grounds of justification may include the employees' flexibility or adaptability to hours and places of work, their training and their length of service, and the state of the employment market.[130] However, although the Court may give guidelines, the question of objective justification is ultimately a question of fact for the national court to determine. In the case of an equal value claim, for example, it is open to the national court to decide to what extent, if any, the differences in pay are attributable to the sex of the worker and to what extent they have been objectively justified by the employer.[131] It has recently been suggested that the Court will be able to give more detailed guidance to the national court where it is sought to justify the measure on grounds of social policy rather than economic grounds. This is because the latter explanation, unlike the former, requires an evaluation of the specific circumstances of the relevant market and circumstances of the employer.[132]

In *Danfoss*[133], the Court extended the above line of reasoning to deal with pay systems that lack transparency. Here it held that where a female employee could only establish that the average pay for women was less than the average pay for men but was not able to understand, and hence compare, the criteria used to determine that pay, it was for the employer to prove that the system did not systematically work to the disadvantage of women. It has recently reiterated the same principle in *Dansk Industri*.[134]

---

[128] Case 170/84 *Bilka-Kaufhaus, supra* n 9 at para 31.
[129] Case C-127/92, *supra* n 28, at para 19.
[130] Case 171/88 *Rinner-Kühn* [1989] ECR 2743. See also Case 109/88 *Danfoss, supra* n 33; Case C-33/89 *Kowalska, supra* n 9; Case C-184/89 *Nimz, supra* n 9; Case C-360/90 *Bötel, supra* n 33.
[131] Case C-127/92 *Enderby, supra* n 28, at para 29.
[132] Case C-457/93 *Lewark*, Opinion of Advocate General Jacobs of 29 June 1995, at para 38; judgment of 6 February 1996, at paras 32-38.
[133] Case 109/88, *supra* n 33.
[134] Case C-400/93, *supra* n 33.

(b) National law

The concept of "objective justification" is reflected in the SDA and EPA. Both relevant statutory provisions must be interpreted in the light of Community law.

Indirect discrimination is defined in the SDA in terms of a requirement or condition which causes a detriment to women and cannot be justified on factors unrelated to sex.[135] Although the SDA is generally silent as to the burden of proof, the approach of the English courts seems to be compatible with Community law. They have readily accepted that a victim of sex discrimination often faces great difficulty in proving her case and have held that:

> If the discrimination takes place in circumstances which are consistent with the treatment being based on grounds of sex or race, the industrial tribunal should be prepared to draw the inference that the discrimination was on such grounds unless the alleged discriminator can satisfy the tribunal that there was some other innocent explanation.[136]

This means that the employer must *prove* that "some other innocent explanation" was the cause of the behaviour; it is not enough merely to advance a credible alternative basis for the conduct in issue.[137]

Moreover, where an employer relies upon a statutory provision in response to a claim of indirect discrimination, the SDA explicitly provides that it is for the employer to prove that the "requirement or condition" which it imposes is justifiable within the meaning of the SDA.[138] In *Rinner-Kühn*, the Court of Justice stated that a Member State which alleges that a statutory provision said to be indirectly discriminatory is in fact objectively justified, must show "that the means chosen meet a necessary aim of its social policy and that they are suitable and requisite for attaining that aim".[139]

Although the EPA makes no distinction between direct and indirect discrimination, an employer has a defence to a claim in respect of "like work" and "work of equal value" on the grounds, respectively, that the difference is due to a "genuine material difference"[140] or a "genuine material difference . . . or any other material factor apart from sex".[141] It is for the employer who seeks to establish such a defence to prove it.[142]

The domestic law makes no provision for the requirement of "transparency"

---

[135] See s 1(1)(b) of the SDA 1975.
[136] *Baker* v *Cornwall CC* [1990] IRLR 194 at 198.
[137] *Dornan* v *Belfast CC* [1990] IRLR 179. See also *King* v *Great Britain China Centre* [1992] ICR 516 as applied in *Leeds Private Hospital Ltd* v *Parkin* [1992] ICR 571. *Cf. Corning Glass Works* v *Brennan* 417 US 188, 94 S Ct 2223, 41 LEd2d 1 (1974).
[138] See s 1(3) of the Employment Act 1989.
[139] Case 171/88, *supra* n 31 at para 14.
[140] See s 1(3)(a) EPA 1970.
[141] See s 1(3)(b) EPA 1970.
[142] See s 1(3) of the EPA: *National Vulcan Engineering Insurance Co* v *Wade* [1977] ICR 455, [1988] ICR 800; *R* v *SOS for Employment, ex parte EOC, supra* n 74; *British Coal Corporation* v *Smith* [1994] IRLR 342; *Ratcliffe* v *North Yorkshire CC* [1995] IRLR 439.

as required by *Danfoss*, the burden of proof as to the existence of a discriminatory pay structure falling on the applicant at all times. However, in *Danfoss* the
Court stated:

> ... it should be noted that under Article 6 of the Equal Pay Directive Member States
> must, in accordance with their national circumstances and legal systems, take the
> measures necessary to ensure that the principle of equal pay is applied and that
> effective means are available to ensure that it is observed. The concern for effectiveness
> which thus underlies the Directive means that it must be interpreted as implying
> adjustments to national rules on the burden of proof in special cases where such ad-
> justments are necessary for the effective implementation of the principle of equality.[143]

Although Article 6 of the EPD may only be invoked in claims brought against
an emanation of the State, it is probable that a similar requirement would be
read into Article 119 in order to ensure that an applicant who brings a claim
with respect to a non-transparent pay system has an effective remedy.

(vii) Conclusion

In the field of sex discrimination careful thought is required to determine
which types of claim are available and appropriate for the wrong suffered.
Moreover, it has become increasingly apparent that Community law not only
dictates and inspires the scope of the rights available, but also influences, to an
increasing extent, the procedural conditions in which these rights may be
invoked. In this latter respect, the principles of non-discrimination and effectiveness are, in practice, surprisingly complex, and, since the procedural rules
in each Member State comprise intricate networks, specifically adapted to the
domestic forum, the prospect of harmonisation in this area is remote and probably not desirable. Sex discrimination cases will therefore continue to stimulate
difficult questions about the impact of Community law on the procedural
framework of the United Kingdom and, ironically, will be raised in industrial
tribunals, originally designed to give swift and pragmatic answers to disputes of
fact.

SARAH MOORE
Barrister,
Legal Secretary at The
Court of the First Instance,
Luxembourg

---

[143] Case 109/88, *supra* n 32 at para 14.

Chapter 10

THIRD GENERATION REMEDIES AND SEX EQUALITY LAW*

The Court of Justice has developed a remarkable case law concerning the judicial protection of the individual, initially based on direct effect, but which subsequently developed into a rights and remedy based case law.[1] The first generation case law concerns issues such as direct effect, primacy of Community law and the autonomy of the Community legal order, too well known to require discussion here.[2]

The second generation case law deals with the relationship of national law and Community law as regards enforcement of Community law rights. This case law is built on the assumption that national rules will apply in the resolution of disputes founded in Community law, in areas such as unjust enrichment and remedies. Clearly this may lead to lack of uniformity as the effective enforcement of Community law rights may differ from one Member State to another, depending on the national provisions for enforcement.[3]

The third generation case law, brilliantly identified by Curtin and Mortelmans[4], is based on the wish to achieve genuine solutions for the lack of *effet utile* of direct effect, in the absence of adequate or effective national enforcement measures of Community law rights.[5] In such circumstances, the Court has recently fashioned[6] a third generation case law which, while co-existing with the

---

* This chapter was written by David O'Keeffe, who would like to thank Tamara Hervey for her helpful comments on an earlier draft.
[1] See Prechal, *Directives in European Community Law. A study on EC Directives and their enforcement by national courts* (1995). See also the discussion by Moore, in this volume.
[2] Case 26/62 *Van Gend en Loos* [1963] ECR 3; Case 6/64 *Costa v ENEL* [1964] ECR 1141.
[3] The Court's case law concerning unjust enrichment in the case of recovery of taxes imposed by the Member States in violation of Community law is the classic example. See Case 33/76 *Rewe v Landwirtschaftskammer für das Saarland* [1976] ECR 1989; and Case 68/79 *Just* [1980] ECR 501.
[4] Curtin and Mortelmans, "Application and enforcement of Community law by the Member States: actors in search of a third generation script", in *Institutional dynamics of European integration. Essays in honour of Henry G Schermers*, vol II (1994), 423–466.
[5] *Ibid* 433–434.
[6] Not necessarily chronologically.

first and second generations, attempts to answer these problems by providing for effective remedies in the national legal order as a matter of Community law. The Court has thus developed a new cause of action in Community law, and altered the national rules as regards interim relief and procedure. The third generation case law penetrates not only into the procedural laws of the Member States, but also has effects on private law, as well as other fields such as constitutional law.[7] The development of the third generation case law is not in a linear progression. As this chapter will make clear, the Court currently relies on both second and third generation case law when dealing with sex equality issues. Thus, a third generation remedy applied by the Court in the area of equal treatment may be followed by cases where the Court applies second generation remedies; for example, in the fields of equal pay or social security.

(i) Direct effect of Directives

The Court's acceptance of the doctrine of the direct effect of Directives goes far beyond the wording of Article 189 of the Treaty. Clearly, the Court was concerned to ensure the *effet utile* of Community law, but this appeared to be linked to the notion of the judicial protection of the individual. Very often, the two principles appear together in the case law.[8]

Subsequently, the Court allowed individuals to rely on Directives where they have not been implemented by Member States in time, holding that a Member State in such a situation may not plead, as against individuals, its failure to perform the obligations which the Directive entails.[9] This was later extended to other authorities of the State such as regional or civic authorities.[10] The Court has also held that provisions of national law must be interpreted in conformity with Community law, even before the time-limit for implementing a Directive has expired[11], although recent case law appears to throw doubt upon this proposition.[12]

In *Marshall I*, the Court excluded the possibility that Directives might have horizontal direct effect. This would have allowed individuals to rely on the provisions of a Directive which met the conditions of the direct effect test in cases involving only individuals, rather than the State.[13] Following the *Marshall I* judgment, individuals were left in an absurd situation concerning access to legal

---

[7] Case C-213/89 *Factortame I* [1990] ECR I-2433.
[8] See Caranta, "Judicial protection against Member States: a new *jus commune* takes shape" 32 CML Rev (1995), 703–726, who remarks that it is not always easy to distinguish the two principles which are deeply connected in the case law. Thus, in Case 41/74 *Van Duyn* v *Home Office* [1974] ECR 1337, Rec 12, the Court held that "the useful effect [of a directive] would be weakened if individuals were prevented from relying on it before their national courts".
[9] Case 8/81 *Becker* v *Finanzamt Münster-Innenstadt* [1982] ECR 53.
[10] Case 103/88 *Fratelli Costanzo* v *Comune di Milano* [1989] ECR 1839.
[11] Case 80/86 *Kolpinghuis Nijmegen* [1987] ECR 3969.
[12] Case C-156/91 *Mundt* v *Landrat des Kreises Schleswig-Flensburg* [1992] ECR I-5567.
[13] Case 152/84 *Marshall* v *Southampton and South West Hampshire Area Health Authority* [1986] ECR 723 (*Marshall I*).

remedies, in that they could rely on a Directive if suing the State or an emanation thereof but not if they were suing an individual, even though the underlying problem may be identical in both cases.[14] It appears to be no coincidence
that following *Marshall I*, and in the light of the controversy generated by it, the
Court altered course, creating a remedies based case law which does not rely on
direct effect. The new case law does not replace direct effect, but is complementary to it.

(ii) Alternatives to direct effect

The Court had already given an intimation of another approach to the protection of individual rights in *Von Colson*[15], in which it relied on an extensive interpretation of Article 5 of the Treaty to impose an obligation on national courts to
interpret national law specifically introduced in order to implement a Directive
in the light of the wording and the purpose of the Directive, even where no
directly effective provision is available to provide an adequate remedy. Subsequently, in *Marleasing*[16], the Court extended this obligation even to national
legislation adopted before the Directive, adding that national courts were
required to so interpret "as far as possible".

In *Faccini Dori*[17], the Court consolidated these developments, adding that if
the result prescribed by a Directive cannot be achieved by way of interpretation,
Community law requires the Member States to make good damage caused to
individuals through failure to transpose a Directive, provided that the conditions
for State liability set out in *Francovich*[18] are met.

The requirement of interpretation of national laws in conformity with a
Directive and the principle of State liability in *Francovich* is complementary, or
alternative, to the doctrine of direct effect of Directives.[19] All three doctrines
have been developed by the Court in order to provide effective judicial protection for the individual. However, the first two doctrines are built on the assumption that direct effect is not necessary, and that remedies may be available even
where a Directive has no direct effect. They have the result that individuals may
claim remedies based on a Directive even in a horizontal situation, such as that
in *Marleasing*. They thus avoid the denial of remedy established by *Marshall I*.
Pending and subsequent case law will establish the limits of State liability and
the issue of liability of individuals for breach of Community law in horizontal
situations.[20]

---

[14] See Opinion of Advocate General Van Gerven in Case C-271/91 *Marshall II* [1993] ECR I-4367, at
para 12.
[15] Case 14/83 *Von Colson* v *Land Nordrhein-Westfalen* [1984] ECR 1891.
[16] Case C-106/89 *Marleasing* v *La Comercial Internacional de Alimentación* [1990] ECR I-4135.
[17] Case C-91/92 *Faccini Dori* v *Recreb Srl* [1994] ECR I-3325.
[18] Joined Cases C-6/90 and C-9/90 *Francovich and others* v *Italian Republic* [1991] ECR I-5357.
[19] Van Gerven, "Bridging the gap between Community and national laws: towards a principle of
homogeneity in the field of legal remedies" 32 CML Rev (1995), 679–702 at 682.
[20] Case C-46/93 *Brasserie du Pêcheur*, Case C-48/93 *Factortame III* and Case C-187/94 *Dillenkofer*.

(iii) Uniform remedies to protect Community law rights

Another development, that of the so-called third generation case law of the Court, is equally arresting. In its earlier case law, the Court had been reluctant to interfere in national procedural issues.[21] Thus in cases such as *Rewe*[22], the Court held that it was for each national legal system to determine the procedural aspects of actions relating to the protection of individual rights protected by Community law, provided that domestic remedies were effective, and no less favourable than those for the enforcement of comparable national rights (the "safeguard" clause). In terms of remedies, the national court must apply directly effective Community law either under the existing provisions of national law, or of its own motion, as in *Simmenthal*.[23] However, although this initial reluctance disappeared, in particular following *Simmenthal*, and the Court insisted on the obligation of national courts to make effective judicial remedies available, if necessary not applying relevant national procedural rules[24], the most decisive developments have occurred only recently.

Thus, in *Factortame I*[25], concerning national rules for interim relief, the Court held that:

> the full effectiveness of Community law would be just as much impaired if a rule of national law could prevent a court seised of a dispute governed by Community law from granting interim relief in order to ensure the full effectiveness of the judgment to be given on the rights claimed under Community law. It follows that a court which in those circumstances would grant interim relief, if it were not for a rule of national law, is obliged to set aside that rule.[26]

The national court was therefore obliged to set aside the rule of national law which prevented it from granting interim relief.

In *Zuckerfabrik*[27], the Court was confronted with a case which combined elements of *Factortame* and *Foto-Frost*.[28] In the latter case, it had held that only the Court itself may decide on the invalidity of Community legislation. In *Zuckerfabrik*, the issue was whether, in proceedings for interim relief, a national court could suspend the operation of a national measure adopted on the basis of a Community regulation and which was challenged on the ground that the regulation itself violated Community law. The difficulty was that, according to *Foto-Frost*,

---

[21] Caranta, *supra* n 8 at 705.
[22] See, *supra* n 3.
[23] Case 106/77 *Simmenthal* v *Amministrazione delle Finanze dello Stato* [1978] ECR 629.
[24] See for example Case 199/82 *San Giorgio* [1983] ECR 3595 and Case 222/84 *Johnston* v *Chief Constable of the Royal Ulster Constabulary* [1986] ECR 1651.
[25] *Supra* n 7.
[26] *Ibid* Rec 21 of the judgment.
[27] Cases C-143/88 and C-92/89 *Zuckerfabrik Süderdithmarschen AG* v *Hauptzollamt Itzehoe* [1991] ECR I-415.
[28] Case 314/85 *Foto-Frost* v *Hauptzollamt Lübeck-Ost* [1987] ECR 4199.

the national court could not rule on the invalidity of the Community regulation, but *Factortame* required effective judicial protection in interim proceedings. Applying the two cases, the Court held that national courts could suspend the enforcement of a national administrative measure adopted on the basis of a Community regulation (even though they could not rule on the invalidity of the Community measure), provided that serious doubts existed as to the validity of that measure which was an issue which could be decided by the Court. However, what is completely new in this case are the Court's observations on the national rules of procedure governing interim relief.

The Court noted that these national rules differ from one Member State to another, which may jeopardise the uniform application of Community law. Since the Court considered that uniform application of Community law was a fundamental requirement of the Community legal order, it held that:

> the suspension of enforcement of administrative measures based on a Community regulation, whilst it is governed by national procedural law, in particular as regards the making and examination of the application, must in all the Member States be subject, at the very least, to conditions which are uniform so far as the granting of such relief is concerned.[29]

The result of *Zuckerfabrik* is therefore to establish a minimum set of requirements for the granting of interim relief, these requirements being set out by the Court and including such considerations as urgency. The implications of the judgment are enormous, for they challenge the view, repeated by the Court in the very same case, that "the rules of the procedure of the courts are a matter of national law".[30] In short, *Zuckerfabrik* establishes standards of Community procedural law, which take priority over national rules of procedure. The Court's approach has been characterised as going from a merely negative application of the principle of effective judicial protection to a positive one.[31]

The *Francovich* case is another example of this trend. There the establishment of State liability was deduced from the principles of effective judicial protection of the individual and *effet utile*, and stated to be "inherent in the system of the Treaty".[32] The right is founded directly on Community law.[33] This new rule in the Community legal order has consequences for the legal orders of the Member States. Since the principle of State liability derives from the Treaty, it must clearly apply in a uniform manner throughout the Community. The Court held that the national rules on liability will apply. In the absence of Community legislation, it is for the internal legal order of each Member State to designate the competent courts and lay down the detailed procedural rules for actions intended to safeguard the rights which individuals derive from Community law.[34]

---

[29] *Ibid* Rec 26 of the judgment.
[30] *Ibid* Rec 25 of the judgment.
[31] Caranta, *supra* n 8 at 714.
[32] *Francovich, supra* n 18 at Rec 35 of the judgment.
[33] *Francovich, ibid* Rec 41 of the judgment.
[34] *Francovich, ibid* Recs 41–2 of the judgment.

As a result, the Court has introduced a new form of action into the legal order of every Member State, an action for damages against the State, at the suit of individuals, for damage caused by breach of Community law for which they can be held responsible. This introduces as much change into the procedural laws of the Member States as *Factortame* and *Zuckerfabrik*. All three cases demonstrate the introduction of common remedies to enforce Community law rights by the setting aside of national law, the granting of new procedural rights for interim relief, and the introduction of a new cause of action. It is clear that the effect on the national procedural rules will be enormous.

In *Marshall II*[35], the Court held that where a Member State has chosen financial compensation in order to compensate for discriminatory dismissal, then it must be "adequate" and offer full compensation. National rules on compensation which would offer a lesser remedy may not be applied. Clearly, this promotes the concept of a uniform rule of compensation, cutting across different national rules regarding damages. It is interesting to compare *Francovich* and *Marshall II* in this respect. In the first case, the amount of compensation would be a pre-determined amount, whereas in the second, the fixing of damages is inevitably discretionary. According to *Marshall II*, the damages must be adequate in that they must make reparation for the loss and damage sustained. Clearly, national courts' appreciation may vary from one Member State to another, and internally within a Member State.

The underlying theme of *Marshall II* is also interesting, as it is predicated upon the explicit premise that the Member States may choose how to achieve the aim of the Community Directive in question, provided that these measures will achieve the aims of the Directive. In *Marshall II*, the Court accepted that there were in fact only two choices; reinstatement of the plaintiff or damages. Although the Court accepted that "adequate" damages may be an effective remedy, the point remains that the remedy for discriminatory dismissal will differ from one Member State to another. It is not a matter of little account: dismissal in the current employment market can effectively mean the termination of a career, not simply of a given employment.

If the consequences of dismissal are indeed that a victim of a breach of sex equality law effectively cannot find another employment, then it must be questioned whether compensation is an adequate or sufficient remedy in such circumstances. There would appear to be a compelling argument that reinstatement would be the only sufficient remedy. This would be an example of a third generation remedy which would take account of the realities of market forces in the employment market for dismissed women. Admittedly it will not always be possible to predict that this may be the case, but as in the nature of judicial process, some time will have elapsed before the dismissed applicant's claim is ruled upon, the subsequent search for employment could be taken into account by courts, together with the likelihood of gaining alternative employment in the future. Circumstances may vary from one applicant to another, depending on

---

[35] Case C-271/91 *Marshall II* [1993] ECR I-4367.

subjective factors such as skills and age, but also on objective factors such as ease of re-employment in a particular industry for which the applicant may have trained, or on the conditions of the local or national employment markets. This writer recognises that this is a difficult point, but it is submitted that the current case law is predicated upon a concept of ease of access to labour markets and employment which simply does not reflect current conditions.

In establishing that adequate damages must be awarded, despite national limitations on the amount to be awarded, the Court has imposed a new duty on national courts, the application of which is difficult in the extreme. It is not clear to what extent national courts may take account of national law on assessing damages in order to arrive at an award. This is presumably the next step and, if pursued by the Court, will require some rather far-reaching guidance from the Court on basic principles of compensation, which quite inevitably will result in some form of harmonisation.[36]

The highlight of this case law is to be found in *Faccini Dori* where the Court held that where damage has been suffered as a result of the State's obligation, the national court must "uphold the right of aggrieved consumers to obtain reparation in accordance with the national law on liability".[37] Quite how this is actually to work in practice is not specified[38] although serious procedural difficulties will arise in some Member States.[39] What is clear, however, is that the Court, although referring to national laws on liability, in fact is harmonising national legal remedies.

(iv) Inconsistencies in the application of the remedies based case law to sex equality

There is a clear progression in the case law, although it cannot be characterised as linear or chronological. Disapplication of a national rule which conflicts with a Community rule, as required in *Simmenthal* and *Factortame*, is a largely negative process. On the other hand, as *Zuckerfabrik* demonstrates, disapplication of national rules leads to the introduction of new, harmonised, Community based procedural rules, which is a positive process. *Francovich* shows the next step: an entirely new cause of action based only on Community law, but enforceable in all

---

[36] Curtin and Mortelmans, *supra* n 4 at 452–3; Van Gerven, *supra* n 19 at 694–5 and 699.
[37] Case C-91/92, *supra* n 17 at Rec 29 of the judgment.
[38] There seem to be several possibilities: (i) may the State be "drawn in" to an action by way of joinder, by procedural means unknown in some Member States; or (ii) is the State to be sued directly as a co-respondent; or (iii) may the State be sued alone; or (iv) may damages be awarded against the State even if it is not a party to the action; or (v) must the action against the State be taken subsequent to the action between individuals?
[39] Robinson, Annotation of Case C-91/92 *Faccini Dori* 32 CML Rev (1995), 629–639, observes that national judges will either have to interpret national laws so far as to be *contra legem* or to find a suitable national law on liability upon which to found *Francovich*-based reparation.

Member States on the basis of national procedural law. The goals to be achieved are the uniform application of Community law and the effective judicial protection of the individual by the provision of adequate sanctions and remedies.[40]

The progression presented until now has been perhaps too linear. It also has elided the difference between some cases which cannot easily be characterised as second or third generation but may fall in between.[41] In recent cases, the Court has retreated to national standards and procedures in the area of sex equality as regards retroactivity of claims in the areas of social security[42] and equal pay.[43] In the area of employment law on the other hand, the Court granted a "third generation" remedy in *Marshall II*.[44]

In *Johnson II*[45], the Court ruled that a national rule which limited the period prior to the bringing of a claim based on Directive 79/7/EEC in respect of which arrears of benefit are payable was not incompatible with Community law. In that case, the national rule in question limited claims for arrears to 12 months before the claim was made.

The Court in *Johnson II* distinguished the case from its earlier judgment in *Emmott*[46], and confirmed its judgment in *Steenhorst-Neerings*.[47] The Court noted that the national rule does not make it virtually impossible for an action to be brought by an individual relying on Community law, but rather merely limits the time in respect of which a claim for arrears may be made. The Court distinguished this situation from that in *Emmott* where it maintained that the time-bar had the result of depriving the applicant of any opportunity whatsoever to rely on her right to equal treatment under the Directive. In *Johnson II* and *Steenhorst-Neerings*, on the other hand, a time-bar was acceptable. This is clearly a second generation case law approach to remedies in that reference to national law is permissible to determine the compensation which shall lie for breach of a right under Community law. The result, however, is to limit the relief actually granted to the applicant, by permitting reference to be made to rules of national law which restrict that relief. This approach was specifically approved by Advocate General Gulmann in *Johnson II*.[48]

---

[40] Van Gerven, *supra* n 19 at 690 considers that "the need for harmonised legal remedies . . . is . . . inherent in the concept of uniformity; in the absence of (sufficiently) harmonised legal remedies, uniform rights cannot be adequately secured throughout the Community".

[41] Thus Curtin and Mortelmans, *supra* n 4 at 438, consider *Factortame I, supra* n 7 as "hovering around the threshold of the third generation arch-way"; the result in *Fratelli Costanzo, supra* n 10 is described as being third generation in that it opts for a uniform Community-wide solution (at 443) and Case 222/86 *UNECTEF* v *Heylens* [1987] ECR 4097 and Case 178/84 *Commission* v *Germany* [1987] ECR 1227 ("Reinheitsgebot") as being "early birds" of the third generation (at 433), although examples of negative integration (at 448).

[42] Case C-338/91 *Steenhorst-Neerings* [1993] ECR I-5475; Case C-410/92 *Johnson II* [1994] ECR I-5483.

[43] Case C-57/93 *Vroege* v *NCIV Instituut voor Volkshuisvesting BV & Stichting Pensioenfonds NCIV* [1994] ECR I-4541; and Case C-128/93 *Fisscher* v *Voorhuis Hengelo BV & Stichting Bedrijfspensionenfonds voor de Detailhandel* [1994] ECR I-4583.

[44] *Marshall II, supra* n 35.

[45] *Supra* n 42. See Steiner, in this volume.

[46] Case C-208/90 *Emmott* v *Minister for Social Welfare* [1991] ECR I-4269.

[47] *Supra* n 42.

[48] *Supra* n 42 at 5499.

In *Fisscher*[49], Advocate General Van Gerven took the view that allowing the rights of persons who have suffered discrimination to be restored by granting them full entitlement to pension benefits without their having to pay the corresponding contributions would create new discrimination incompatible with the principle of equal pay for men and women. He therefore believed that this solution would result in unjust enrichment for the employee, which could be prevented by national courts compatibly with Community law, referring to the Court's standard second generation case law on unjust enrichment.[50]

As regards the question of the applicability of national limitation periods, Advocate General Van Gerven took the view in *Fisscher* that *Emmott* did not apply, as the principle that limitation periods laid down by national law could not be relied upon against individuals who invoke Community law applies only in "vertical" situations and may not be relied upon by individuals in "horizontal" situations. The horizontal disputes would, therefore, in his view be governed by second generation case law according to which national procedural rules may apply subject only to the conditions that the national rules must not be less favourable for actions based on Community law as compared to those based on national law, and they must not make the exercise of rights conferred by Community law practically impossible. The Court followed his Opinion.

One could distinguish between these judgments on the basis that where the Court allowed the application of national standards or procedures, a remedy was available, although not a "perfect" one, as in *Johnson II*, *Steenhorst-Neerings* and *Fisscher*, whereas in *Marshall II*, only full compensation, rather than that provided for under national law, would provide an adequate remedy. This is consonant with Van Gerven's distinction between essential or constitutive rules and rules laying down non-essential or "non-constitutive" conditions.[51] Where an "imperfect" remedy is available, this could be considered to be a rule laying down a non-essential condition, and may thus be left to the national level, provided that the national rule does not make enforcement impossible; where only a perfect remedy will suffice, this clearly meets the requirement of being essential or constitutive.

However, although this analysis is attractive in that it explains the recent "national standards" case law in a way which shows a continuity and coherence with the third generation cases discussed above, it begs the question as to what is to be considered as essential or constitutive, or when only the "perfect" remedy suffices. Impossibility of enforcing rights is not an adequate criterion as the "imperfect" remedies will generally, though not always, be available under national law, and where they are not available, a *Von Colson* remedy could be relied upon.

The third generation case law is ideally suited to promote the principle of equal treatment whereas the second generation jurisprudence, because of the

---

[49] *Supra* n 43.
[50] *Supra* n 3.
[51] Van Gerven, *supra* n 19 at 694.

effect of national rules of procedure and limitation periods, may fail to give an adequate remedy. Although some (rather than the "perfect") remedy will be available under the second generation case law, it must be seriously questioned whether this is appropriate in the case of a right as fundamental to the Community legal order as that of sex equality. Is it really acceptable that an applicant should have to enforce the Community law right under the generally restrictive conditions of national law? Whereas, in the current state of development of Community law, one could perhaps justify this in more technical areas, it is very difficult to defend the lack of uniformity and absence of *full* redress in sex equality cases which may occur as a result of resort to rules of national law for remedies.

The distinctions made by the Court in *Johnson II*, attempting to distinguish *Steenhorst-Neerings* and that case from *Emmott*, are based on impossibility of remedy on the one hand, and an imperfect remedy on the other. One cannot but suspect, however, that the real reason is another. The Court appears in these cases to be retreating on the principle of equality of treatment as regards remedies, giving priority to the economic balance of the system[52], and allowing a third generation remedy only where no remedy would be available at all. If that is so, then the principle of equality is being relegated in importance, partly as a result of the Court's fear of the economic implications of its judgments and its unwillingness to create large-scale costs for Member States with the attendant political implications. *Emmott* was admirable precisely because the Court gave such a high priority to the remedy necessary to guarantee the application of the equality principle, whereas the later case law appears to depart from that stance. *Marshall II* appears rather isolated in this perspective, but is a telling example of the potential of the third generation case law in ensuring equality.

(v) Conclusion

Thus far, the case law has developed common rules on State liability, judicial review and interim remedies. Commentators discern the emergence of a common law for Europe in that uniform cause of action and uniform remedies have been created, as a result of Community law. In these areas alone, there are a number of issues which remain to be resolved, such as State liability for breaches of the Treaty, or failure correctly (or partially) to implement Directives or the liability of individuals for breach of Community law. Another issue is the apparent dichotomy between the rules on State liability and those relating to the non-contractual liability of the Community. The impact on national law is already striking, and the creation of new remedies in these areas would accentuate this process. A *de facto* harmonisation of national rules in certain areas becomes inevitable.

---

[52] See the brilliantly perceptive note on the case by Sohrab, 31 CML Rev (1994), 875–887.

The Court's role in this process is crucial. By discerning rights and remedies which are "inherent in the system of the Treaty", the Court is engaging in classic judicial activism. The third generation case law is the indispensable development to ensure the enforcement of individuals' Community law rights. Nevertheless, this case law dictates a fundamental reassessment of national procedural rules and causes of action, within the context of Community minimum standards which will have to be provided by the Court. It is doubtful that the Community legislator will intervene, although such intervention would be welcome if the *acquis communautaire* were respected. Substantive conditions for the grant of third generation case law remedies must be specified. Issues such as compensation and the component rules governing the award of damages must be delineated.

The relationship of the Court with national courts will be decisive in this development, as the reception by the national courts of the third generation remedies will be crucial for their uniform application. So too will be the willingness of national courts to refer cases to the Court.[53] One positive signal is that the House of Lords[54], and apparently the Spanish Courts[55], have adopted the Court's case law as regards interim relief even in areas which are not governed by Community law, thus tending to show a receptive approach to a harmonisation of remedies.

The early case law of the Court, as expressed in *Van Gend en Loos, Costa* v *ENEL*[56] and *Simmenthal,* can be viewed as the logical articulation of the requirements of the Community legal order, and was largely a negative application of the principle of effective judicial protection. The third generation case law, on the other hand, by its imposition of judge-made remedies on national law, is a positive exercise requiring the grant of remedies on the basis of Community law alone in order to enforce Community law rights. The enforcement of Community law as a matter of Community law is now the focus, whereas previously, the Court's case law had concentrated largely on substantive law, leaving enforcement to national law rules subject to the "safeguard" clause. The new approach impinges on national law in a way that could scarcely have been foreseen. Future developments will depend upon three factors: the reception by the national courts of the third generation case law and their willingness to refer new cases; the forbearance of the Member States in the face of judicial activism with such wide-sweeping results; and the Court's own willingness to extend the case law. This propensity cannot always be assumed in the light of the recent

---

[53] As The Hon Mr Justice Donal Barrington, writing in a non-judicial capacity, points out, "the judicial branch reacts to external stimuli. What it decides depends upon the cases which come before it, but it cannot control the cases which come before it": Barrington, "The emergence of a constitutional court" in O'Reilly, *Human Rights and Constitutional Law. Essays in Honour of Brian Walsh* (1992), 251–261 at 253.

[54] M v *Home Office* [1993] 3 WLR 433; [1993] 3 All ER 537.

[55] Caranta, *supra* n 8 at 718.

[56] *Supra* n 2.

case law on equality of treatment, discussed above, which referred to second generation remedies. Nevertheless, it is a necessary step in ensuring full and uniform protection of Community law rights in the field of sex equality.

DAVID O'KEEFFE
Professor of European Law and
Director of the Centre for the Law
of the European Union,
University College London,
UK

Chapter 11

ENFORCEMENT OF COMMUNITY SEX EQUALITY LAW*

Progress on achieving equal treatment for men and women would have been much slower in the United Kingdom without the rights afforded by European Community (EC) law. The fact that EC provisions may in certain circumstances override national legislation has two major advantages; individual citizens of the European Union have a direct right of challenge in the domestic courts on some issues; and legislative change can be speeded up in those Member States where sex equality has not been a high priority. But are we getting the best from this legislative framework? How have cases reached the European Court of Justice? To what extent do individuals have genuine access to justice under EC law?

Detailed examination of the cases brought to the attention of the Equal Opportunities Commission confirms the stress on individuals who contemplate challenges under sex discrimination and equal pay legislation. Most people will not have a detailed knowledge of the national legislation on sex equality; certainly very few will understand even the basic provisions of EC law and will know little, or nothing, of the relevant case law of the Court of Justice. Essentially, when making a claim under domestic legislation, claimants may find themselves in a hostile environment; they can face opposition from employers, sometimes fellow workers, and occasionally trade unions. In addition, where they wish to invoke rights under the Treaty of Rome they must, under the formal procedures of the Court, be prepared to respond to the representations of their own government, the European Commission, and the governments of other Member States of the European Union. A daunting task, to say the least, and not a choice which many people would relish if they had to deal with it (and pay for it) alone.

It is at this point that the existence of a national body specialising in equality issues (like the Equal Opportunities Commission) must be one of the most

---

*This chapter was written by Lorraine Fletcher.

effective ways of ensuring that European Union equality standards are implemented in each Member State. This article examines the role of the Equal Opportunities Commission (EOC) for Great Britain in clarifying the rights of individuals under EC law on equal treatment of men and women. Some suggestions are also made about ways in which the enforcement of EC law could be improved across the European Union.

The Equal Opportunities Commission was set up in 1975 under the provisions of the Sex Discrimination Act (SDA). Its duties are:

- *To enforce the law* – now including EC law because national law must be read consistently with EC law;
- *To promote equal opportunities between men and women* – apart from research and educational projects, the EOC can contribute to (and use) EC Recommendations and EC-wide campaigns. This can also involve helping other organizations so that they are better able to give advice on issues of sex equality and equal pay; and
- *To review legislation* – it is fair to say that EC law has in the past proved to be a very much faster route to change than merely trying to persuade the government to amend national law.

The Equal Opportunities Commission's legal powers are as follows:

- To assist individuals taking claims under the Sex Discrimination and Equal Pay Acts, including payment of legal costs where appropriate. The EOC dealt with over 13,000 enquiries in 1989, rising to almost 23,000 in 1993 and the number continues to rise;
- To conduct Formal Investigations, for example, into the treatment of those seeking midwifery training with the South Derbyshire Health Authority[1]; and
- To take judicial review proceedings on issues of sex discrimination.

One very important aspect of the EOC's powers is the ability to take judicial review proceedings and to challenge the continuation of discriminatory national arrangements under EC law. In the case of National Insurance contribution arrangements for men aged 60 to 64, the EOC did not convince the EC that equal treatment should be the paramount consideration.[2] On employment protection for part-time workers, however, the House of Lords[3] accepted the EOC's arguments that there was indirect sex discrimination contrary to the requirements laid down in the 1976 EC Directive on equal treatment. This will have an impact on the lives of five million part-time workers in this country and could not have been successful without the existence of EC law on sex equality.

Another significant advantage of a national organization dealing with sex dis-

---

[1] Formal Investigation Report: South Derbyshire Health Authority, EOC, March 1990.
[2] Case C-9/91 *R* v *Secretary of State for Social Security ex parte the Equal Opportunities Commission* [1992] ECR I-4927.
[3] *R* v *Secretary of State for Employment ex parte the Equal Opportunities Commission and another* [1994] 1 All ER 910; [1994] IRLR 176.

crimination issues is that a body of expertise can be built up on the relationship between national and EC legislation. For example, an equality issue not covered by domestic law may nevertheless be within EC provisions and individuals may, therefore, have a freestanding right under EC law to bring a claim before the courts. Such a situation might not be identified by other organizations who provide advice services on a whole range of employment rights.

Simply taking an *ad hoc* approach to equality issues may not, however, bring about the desired result(s). It took some considerable time to clarify EC law on pensions and retirement. For some time retirement and pension ages were viewed as the same thing. The EOC had supported some cases on pensions without a great deal of success. *Worringham* v *Lloyds Bank*[4] was successful but was a fairly unusual situation; whereas the Court of Justice rejected the applicant's claim in *Burton* v *British Railways Board*[5] and *Newstead* v *(1) Department of Transport, (2) Her Majesty's Treasury*.[6] It was only after the two decisions in 1986 in *Marshall* v *Southampton and South West Hampshire Area Health Authority*[7] and *Bilka-Kaufhaus* v *Weber von Hertz*[8] that pensions and retirement began to be perceived more widely as separate issues.

At this point a clear strategy emerged around the application of EC law to occupational pension schemes and the link with the discriminatory State pension ages. Out of this process emerged the *Barber* case,[9] viewed as a final opportunity to persuade the Court that United Kingdom occupational pension schemes are required to give equal treatment. Sitting behind the *Barber* case, the EOC had a group of other pensions cases, mainly involving discrimination against women, which it planned to use to try to extend the principle of equal treatment if *Barber* were partially or wholly successful. As things turned out, these claims were settled in the wake of the *Barber* decision. The applicants had submitted claims prior to the Court's judgment in *Barber* and thus had no difficulty with retrospective rights to equal treatment.

What was important was the identification of the key cases which would test the law. In a wider context, it is interesting to explore what existing arrangements assist, or hamper, the enforcement of EC law.

(i) Reliance on individual cases[10]

Individuals cannot face litigation without support. The complexity of the task, and the costs, present insuperable obstacles. Any person contemplating a challenge under national and EC law on sex equality needs the assistance of an equality

---

[4] Case C-60/80 [1981] ECR 1329.
[5] Case C-19/81 [1982] ECR 554.
[6] Case C-192/85 [1987] ECR 4753.
[7] Case C-152/84 [1986] ECR 723.
[8] Case C-170/84 [1986] ECR 1607.
[9] Case C-262/88 *Barber* v *Guardian Royal Exchange Assurance Group* [1990] ECR I-1889.
[10] See the contribution of Bercusson, in this volume, on the importance of collective labour law on sex equality.

body like the EOC or a trade union. Reliance on the willingness of an individual to pursue legal action may not provide the best foundation for the clarification of EC law. The facts of a particular case may be weak and/or may not address all the important questions so that the final judgment of the Court of Justice fails to be comprehensive. A better alternative is to adopt a test case strategy with selective support of complaints. To present a case where the issue is based on a simple set of facts with the widest possible application provides the Court with the opportunity to isolate the legal principles involved and provide clear guidance to the domestic courts in Member States. A statutory independent equality body is in a very good position to analyse issues of equality and identify the main types of claim which should be considered by the national courts. This allows individuals in similar circumstances to register a claim and then await the outcome of the test case(s), thus removing the concerns about litigation and easing the pressure on national courts.

In certain circumstances judicial review proceedings may also be a strategic option where they are based on the role of the European Commission. The Commission may be crucial in ensuring that Member States have consistent and "workable" legislation on equal treatment. Infringement proceedings brought by the European Commission against the United Kingdom Government in 1984 resulted in the introduction in national legislation of the concept of equal value.[11] Prior to this, domestic law had been built around the principle of the same or similar work. Equal value is a fundamental concept without which the pay gap cannot be narrowed in a labour market where extreme job segregation still persists. More recently, formal complaints have been made to the European Commission about the abolition of Wages Councils and the expected negative impact predominantly on the pay rates of women.[12]

Although the European Court of Justice did not agree with the conclusions of the European Commission, the proceedings brought by the Commission against Belgium in respect of benefit payments for family members clarified an important issue. This was a matter relevant to all, or most, Member States. The Commission's action and the subsequent decision of the Court may have saved a great deal of complex and time-consuming individual litigation on the subject before legal clarity was achieved.

The Commission may also wield great influence with the Court. Certainly its written observations in the *Barber* case were a fascinating and absorbing analysis of the logic of EC law on equality. On the other hand, the submission in *Avdel Systems Ltd*[13] was very disappointing to the EOC since it failed to acknowledge that achieving equality by levelling down devalues the principle of equal treatment and may discourage people from embarking on legal challenges. It was nevertheless influential in terms of the *Avdel* judgment.

Much useful information may also be gained from the requirement of Member States to report to the Commission on the implementation of Directives and on

---

[11] See Ellis, in this volume.
[12] See Townshend-Smith, in this volume.
[13] Case C-408/92 [1994] ECR I-4435.

the continuance of exclusions set down in Directives. The details provided on the exclusion of State pension ages and related benefits in Directive 79/7/EEC were, for example, quoted in the arguments put before the Court of Justice in the EOC's judicial review proceedings on National Insurance contributions.

Could the European Commission, given adequate resources, take a more proactive role in enforcing EU law? Infringement proceedings would result in decisions of the Court which would provide legal certainty across the Member States and would not be complicated or clouded by the facts of an individual case, or differences in the practices of Member States. Proceedings could be considered in a programme of work which scrutinised specific provisions according to an agreed timetable. This would also give Member State governments the motivation and the opportunity to review their own domestic legal provisions.

(ii) Procedures

The main concern here is the length of time taken before a final decision is reached. An untypical example is *Barber*. For a number of reasons, some specific to the particular case, Mr Barber's case took ten years before the issue was resolved and by that time, sadly, he had died and his widow received the settlement. The initial problems lie with the domestic courts. With some notable exceptions, industrial tribunals are reluctant to refer questions directly to the Court of Justice. When questions have been referred by tribunals[14] this does not seem to have created problems. Where this does not happen, however, there are delays to await hearings in the higher courts. Once questions have been referred to the Court of Justice, there is then a further time lapse before a judgment is given.

All this potential for long delays may then be made worse if the decision of the Court is not sufficiently clear in its application to the circumstances in a particular Member State. Again, *Barber* is an obvious example. Faced with uncertainty about the retrospective limitation in the judgment, the only option available was to look for further test cases which would obtain the required clarification. The situation was considered sufficiently serious for the United Kingdom Government to agree to pay the costs of a reference in *Coloroll*[15] since it involved a wide range of questions on pensions and equal treatment. The EOC had also agreed to support a clutch of test cases, including *Neath*. In the meantime, of course, a Protocol was agreed to the Maastricht Treaty which, at least initially, raised more questions than it answered. Even so, it was not until October 1993 that the Court provided guidance on retrospection in its judgment in *Ten Oever*.[16]

---

[14] For example, Case 222/84 *Johnston v Chief Constable of the Royal Ulster Constabulary* [1986] ECR 1651 and, more recently, Case C-152/91 *Neath v Hugh Steeper Ltd* [1993] ECR I-6935.

[15] Case C-200/91 *Coloroll Pension Trustees Ltd v Russell and others* [1994] ECR I-4389. See Whiteford, in this volume.

[16] Case C-109/91 *Ten Oever v Stichting Bedrijfspensioenfonds voor het Glazenwassers en Schoonmaakbedrijf* [1993] ECR I-4879.

In conclusion, there should be a review of the procedures of the Court of Justice to find ways of speeding up the process. The Court would not seem to be such a distant institution to the population of the EU Member States if the procedures were faster and more "user-friendly". Secondly, would it be feasible to construct an arrangement for clarification of decisions from the Court, to avoid the expensive and time-consuming process of starting new test cases on the path to Luxembourg? This could be considered as enlightened self interest since it would ultimately create a lighter caseload for the Court.

(iii) Conclusion

There is no doubt that EC law as interpreted by the Court has extended the boundaries of equal treatment and given individuals new rights to challenge discrimination in the domestic courts. Better enforcement could, however, be achieved and would bring people closer to the deliberations of the Court of Justice. National equality bodies are likely to continue to play a significant role in helping individuals to bring complex claims before the national courts prior to a reference being made to the Court of Justice. This process should also result in the "best" test cases coming before the Court and will provide the means of informing individual citizens of the Court's important role within the EU.

Cases need to be dealt with more quickly and judgments need to be sufficiently clear to create legal certainty.

A final thought for future consideration: United Kingdom law provides, however inadequately, for victimisation claims where those alleging acts of discrimination have pressure put on them in various ways. Should EU law also provide a means of redress for those who are victimised merely because they have decided to use the rights to equal treatment granted to them in EU law?

LORRAINE FLETCHER
Head of Pensions, Benefits and Consumer Affairs,
Equal Opportunities Commission (GB),
UK

Chapter 12

EC EQUALITY LAW IN CONTEXT: COLLECTIVE BARGAINING*

(i) Introduction

The inspiration of EU equality law was Article 119 of the Treaty of Rome requiring equal pay for equal work.[1] Article 119 was held to have direct effect by the decision of the European Court in *Defrenne*.[2] As such it became the basis for numerous claims before national courts and references to the European Court. The development and analysis of the law on equal pay and equal treatment in employment, not surprisingly, has been focused on legislation and case law.

It is acknowledged, however, that, in most Member States of the EU, pay and conditions of employment of men and women workers are largely determined by collective agreements. It is through collective bargaining, conducted by trade unions and employers and their associations, that the payment systems and structures, and other terms and conditions of employment, are fixed. Litigation through national courts, basing claims on EU legislation and decisions of the Court of Justice, directly affects only a tiny number of litigants. Any legal rules so established have to be mediated through the collective bargaining system.

It is that system which interprets and applies, for better or worse, the legal rules in the actual determination of pay and conditions of employment of men and women workers. If most workers in the EU experience the EU law on sex equality only through the collective bargaining activity of employers and trade unions, it is that context which really determines the application of EU law. An understanding of that context becomes essential to an understanding of the legal rules on equality.

* This chapter was written by Brian Bercusson. He is indebted to the members, in particular Professor Linda Dickens, of the International Research Group on Equal Opportunities and Collective Bargaining, supported by the European Foundation for the Improvement of Living and Working Conditions.
[1] A slightly different formulation was substituted by the Maastricht Treaty.
[2] Case 43/75 *Defrenne* v *SABENA* [1976] ECR 455.

This chapter focuses on the relatively underdeveloped area of EU equality law as it interacts with collective bargaining. It is, arguably as, if not more, important to analyse the legal rules as they relate to the reality of collective determination of pay and employment conditions, than to apply them to the circumstances of an individual case of sex discrimination. To that end, it is an essential skill for the EU labour lawyer to comprehend the collective dimension of the law on equality.

National systems of collective bargaining are embedded in industrial relations systems of great variety. The *actors* involved, trade unions and employers' organizations, the *processes* of collective bargaining and social dialogue at different levels (national, sectoral, enterprise, workplace), and the *outcomes* in the form of collective agreements differ widely from country to country. The EU law on equal pay and equal treatment in employment interacts with these national industrial relations contexts to produce an outcome which belies any pretence to a uniform EU law. To understand the significance of the EU labour law on equality, it has to be considered in the industrial relations and collective bargaining context in which it operates.

This chapter begins with a general account of the interaction of collective bargaining and equal opportunities. There follows outlines of five different national contexts (France, Italy, Germany, Denmark and the United Kingdom) which illustrate the variety of this interaction in the EU.

(ii) Collective bargaining and equality

The legal implementation of equal opportunities policy has frequently encountered collective bargaining.[3] Collective bargaining as a concept, however, is not particularly focused on equal opportunities.[4] Hence, mutual understanding has not been easy to achieve. There is a well developed literature on equal opportunities and on collective bargaining in Europe, but relatively little which aims to link the two.

It has already been pointed out that there are many differences between countries as regards the composition and structure of the social partners, the nature of the negotiation processes between them, and the character of the various outcomes which emerge in the form of collective agreements. For example, collective agreements, including those on equal opportunities, possess very dif-

---

[3] Case 143/83 *Commission v Denmark* [1985] ECR 427; Case 165/82 *Commission v UK* [1983] ECR 3431; Case 235/84 *Commission v Italy* [1986] ECR 2291; Case 237/85 *Rummler v Dato Druck Gmbh* [1986] ECR 2101; Case 109/88 *Handels-og Kontorfunktionaerernes Forbund i Danmark v Dansk Arbejdsgiverforening (Danfoss)* [1989] ECR 3199; Case 33/89 *Kowalska v Freie und Hansestadt Hamburg* [1990] ECR 2591; Case C-127/92 *Enderby v Frenchay Health Authority* [1993] ECR I-5535.

[4] There is a parallel with law: law also is not particularly focused on equal opportunities, and it also is the subject of analysis as to its utility in achieving equal opportunities objectives. A major focus of research has been on the issue of the limitations of legal processes. See the Report on the 1992 Louvain-la-Neuve Conference on procedures and remedies: access to equality between women and men in the EC, McCrudden 22 ILJ (1993), 77–83.

ferent characteristics: different formats; different legal effects; different nature of the entitlements (specific and general) described in agreements and whether agreements are "representative" or constitute "good practice". Agreements may articulate among themselves at different levels: national, sectoral, regional, enterprise, workplace, and also with legislation and management practices. Collective agreements on equal opportunities have to be analysed in their specific national context in order to make sense of collective bargaining on equal opportunities in each country.

The two concepts of collective bargaining and equality combine at the *national* level due to the growth in women's labour force participation and their presence within the trade unions. The sophisticated concepts of equal opportunities policy contrast with the relatively restricted agendas of trade unions' bargaining platforms and employers' personnel practices. This has already led to legal clashes before the European Court of Justice.

The two concepts combine at EC level due to the development of social policy regulation towards European social dialogue.[5] Equal opportunities policy at EC level has to adjust to the new form of regulation. Furthermore, the new form of social regulation at EC level (the European social dialogue articulated with different national industrial relations systems) has to accommodate the sophistication of EC equal opportunities policy as it has developed.

(a) Dimensions of equal opportunities and collective bargaining

The *combination* of equal opportunities and collective bargaining has several dimensions: scope/content; regulatory form; coverage/diffusion; actors/motives; and process/result.[6]

(1) Scope/content

The wide range of *potential* topics for collective bargaining on equal opportunities policy highlights the relatively impoverished content of most collective agreements, when compared to the scope and content of equal opportunities policy as it has been developed at EC and national levels. If the regulation of equal opportunities in the EC is to depend more on social dialogue and collective bargaining at EC and national levels, this gap assumes great importance. For the purpose of achieving a uniform implementation of equal opportunities, it becomes all the more important to spread knowledge of collective agreements which have sought to encompass less common areas of equal opportunities policy.

---

[5] Bercusson, *European Labour Law*, (1996 forthcoming), chapters 6, 9 and 35–36.
[6] These dimensions were sketched in a memorandum by Dr Hubert Krieger of the European Foundation for the Improvement of Living and Working Conditions, Dublin, and were developed in a Background Report by Bercusson for the International Research Group on Equal Opportunities and Collective Bargaining in Europe, 1994.

(2) Regulatory form

EC equal opportunities law and policy have repeatedly clashed with the regulatory form of *collective bargaining*. The contradiction has affected the actors, processes and outcomes of collective bargaining.

Actors	The separation of bargaining units into categories producing agreements more favourable to men has been declared discriminatory (*Enderby*[7]);
Processes	Pay bargaining processes which lack transparency as regards lower paid women (*Danfoss*[8]) or include criteria which discriminate against women (*Rummler*[9]) are declared unlawful; and
Outcomes	Collective agreements which contain clauses which directly or indirectly discriminate against women are unlawful (*Kowalska*[10]) or must be capable of being so declared (*Commission of the EC* v *UK*[11]).

On the other hand, the regulatory *legal* strategies of implementation of equal opportunities policy have been criticised, and collective bargaining has been proposed as a possibly more effective strategy.[12] The emergence of the European social dialogue as a primary form of EC regulation highlights the potential of collective bargaining as a regulatory strategy for equal opportunities policy.

(3) Coverage/diffusion

At the level of legislation, the coverage of equal opportunities policy is EC-wide and national. At the level of collective bargaining, the coverage is patchy. It varies among countries and sectors and by topic. Coverage and diffusion of equal opportunities in collective agreements are not necessarily the same as that of collective bargaining in general.

For example, collective bargaining might be expected to be more developed as regards equal opportunities policy in those sectors where there is high female employment. However, an ILO study demonstrates that in countries where a sector is highly feminised, union density for women may be low or high.[13] It is argued that there is no correlation between female predominance and union density. Equal opportunities collective bargaining may be focused not only on sectors which are highly feminised, but on those which have high union density.[14]

---

[7] Case C-127/92 *Enderby*, *supra* n 3.

[8] Case 109/88 *Danfoss*, *supra* n 3.

[9] Case 235/85 *Rummler*, *supra* n 3.

[10] Case 33/89 *Kowalska* [1990] ECR I-2591.

[11] Case 165/82 [1983] ECR 3431.

[12] McCrudden, *supra* n 4.

[13] Hastings and Coleman, *Women Workers and Unions in Europe: An Analysis by Industrial Sector*, ILO, Geneva, IDP Women/WP-4, 22.

[14] However, where a sector is highly feminised in two countries but with different union density in each, it may still be that the country with low density still has *relatively* high density in that sector compared to other sectors in that country. So the criterion is not absolute density, but relative union density of a sector in the country. *Ibid* Tables 17–20, 22–25 show this for different sectors.

(4) Actors/motives

Employers may be involved in equal opportunities policy where there are women workers even in the absence of collective bargaining. Equal opportunities policy cannot ignore employers' unilateral policies, and how this affects equal opportunities and collective bargaining. The emphasis, however, on collective bargaining means special regard must be had to trade unions. It is their role in pushing on women's issues that is crucial. Employers may take initiatives but they are unlikely to push for them against union opposition.

It is clear that the social partners may play a positive role in the pursuit of equality through collective bargaining. It should be noted, however, also that collective bargaining may pose problems for achieving that objective. Collective bargaining is itself a gendered process and collective agreements may reflect, embody or perpetuate discriminatory practices:[15]

> Most unions, whatever their egalitarian pretensions, have typically been biased in the composition of their officials and activists towards relatively high status, male, native born, full-time employees. Intentionally or otherwise, the programmes developed in collective bargaining, and even more crucially, those issues assigned real priority, reflect the dominant concerns of these hegemonic groups.

That collective agreements may be discriminatory was acknowledged in, for example, the Equal Treatment Directive. Measures which the Member States are required to take under that Directive include those necessary to ensure that:[16]

> any provisions contrary to the principle of equal treatment which are included in collective agreements, individual contracts of employment, internal rules of undertakings . . . shall be, or may be declared, null and void or may be amended.

The precise ways in which discrimination may be embodied in collective bargaining and collective agreements has been revealed by research in different Member States,[17] while in a number of legal cases the development of the European concept of discrimination and equal opportunities has contrasted with the relatively restricted agendas of trade unions' bargaining platforms and employers' personnel practices.

The ILO study noted that growth of employment in a sector, combined with a rising proportion of women workers in the sector and a low and falling general level of union density, created the conditions for a potentially important area of union membership recruitment. This factor is indicative of potential union interest in equal opportunities policy in order to attract new members. This is so especially because the ILO study argues that union density is not lower for

---

[15] Hyman, "Changing Trade Union Identities and Strategies" in Hyman and Ferner, *New Frontiers in European Industrial Relations* (1994).
[16] Council Directive 76/207/EEC of 9 February 1976 (OJ 1976 L 39/40) Article 4(b).
[17] In the UK, Dickens et al., *Tackling Sex Discrimination Through Collective Bargaining* (1988).

women because of feminised sectors, but because these sectors have general low union density and many women work in them.[18]

(5) Process/result

Collective bargaining on equal opportunities in Member States (the collective agreements) provides a starting point for developing the process of the *European social dialogue*. This does not mean that national processes of negotiating equal opportunities agreements will be replicated at European level. The question is, what lessons may be learned from national experience? The European social dialogue may produce agreements which have to be articulated with national systems of collective bargaining.[19] The importance of collective bargaining on equal opportunities lies in its significance at:

- the pre-EC social dialogue phase: by drawing on experience of collective bargaining over equal opportunities policy within the Member States, ideas and inspiration may be obtained, and valuable lessons about what not to do may be learned; and
- the post-EC social dialogue phase: as national collective bargaining systems may well become the means of implementing EC-level agreements on equal opportunities, it is essential to understand the present practice of collective bargaining on equal opportunities.

(b) Feminisation of the labour force and scope of collective bargaining

The interaction of collective bargaining and equal opportunities has additional importance given the increased feminisation of the European labour market and the need for employment policies and trade union strategies to respond to such change. Women's activity rates have consistently increased over the last 20–30 years. Between 1960 and 1990 the recorded labour force in the EC increased by just under 29 million, of which over 20 million were women.[20]

The increasing number of economically active women is reflected in female trade union membership. Surveys show that women's share of union membership is steady or rising, though there is great variation among countries in Western Europe with respect to overall union density, female union density, and ratio of female to male union density.[21] Issues of internal equity (the position of women within trade unions) are connected to issues of external equity (including

---

[18] Hastings and Coleman, *supra* n 13 at 25–26.

[19] See generally, Cockburn, *Women and the European Social Dialogue: Strategies for Gender Democracy*, Doc V/5465/95–EN, European Commission (1995); Cockburn, Alemany Gomez, Bergamaschi, Nickel and Rogerat, *Women in the Europeanising of Industrial Relations: A Study in Five Member States*, Doc. V/664/94–EN, European Commission (December 1993).

[20] Commission of the EC, *Employment in Europe*, 1992, COM(91) 354.

[21] Hastings and Coleman, *supra* n 13 at 10–12 and Table 16 at 21. For recent data on UK unions, "Women in the unions", *Equal Opportunities Review* No 59, January/February 1995, 38.

collective bargaining for equality). This has been recognised in initiatives taken by a number of organizations to facilitate the articulation and representation of women's particular interests and to increase the number of women in leadership positions in the trade unions.[22] It is, however, still the case that women are under-represented on decision-making structures and in leadership positions.[23]

The focus on collective bargaining recognises the importance of joint regulation in the determination of terms and conditions of work for large numbers of citizens in Europe. The degree of union density (proportion of eligible workforce in membership of unions) and coverage of collective bargaining (the number of workers covered by collective agreements as a percentage of those wage and salary earners) varies as between Member States.

Great Britain has a collective bargaining coverage of 39% of the workforce; figures for other countries in Europe are in excess of 60%; in many the proportion of workers covered is over 80% (for example, Austria, Belgium, France, Finland, Germany, Sweden).[24] It should be noted that the coverage of collective bargaining may be considerably greater than union density in countries (for example, France and Spain) where there is provision for the extension of collectively agreed terms to those who are not members of the contracting organizations.

Any consideration of the potential role for collective bargaining in promoting women's equality inevitably raises questions about the health and future of collective bargaining in general. The 1980s were marked by union decline in Europe, particularly in the private sector, often reversing membership gains made in the 1970s. One among many facets of this concerns the actual and potential female membership of trade unions and the extent to which union interest representation "can genuinely include constituencies formerly marginalised as a result of such factors as gender, ethnicity and employment status".[25] This raises questions to do not only with women's representation among the membership of trade unions, and mechanisms of interest representation and how they connect with collective bargaining mechanisms, but also questions concerning women's representation in leadership and decision-making positions, including among negotiators. Research within some national contexts indicates a positive link between women's presence in leadership positions and in collective bargaining arenas and the development and prioritising of equality agendas.[26]

---

[22] Trebilcock, "Strategies for strengthening women's participation in trade union leadership", 130 *International Labour Review* (1991), 407–426.

[23] See, e.g., Braithwaite and Byrne, *Women in decision-making in trade unions*, ETUC and European Commission (1994). Concerning representation of women on decision-making bodies in general, see Flynn, and Beveridge and Nott, in this volume.

[24] Figures from OECD, *Employment Outlook*, July 1994, and Hyman and Ferner, *supra* n 15. The collective bargaining coverage figures are adjusted to take account only of those employees who are not excluded from bargaining rights.

[25] Hyman, *supra* n 15.

[26] Heery and Kelly, "Do female representatives make a difference", *Work, Employment and Society* (1988) (December); Colling and Dickens, *Equality bargaining: why not?* (1989); Kumar, "Collective bargaining and workplace concerns" in Briskin and McDermott, *Women – Challenging Unions* (1993).

In discussing the potential for collective bargaining as a mechanism for promoting gender equality it is necessary to observe that, even where collective bargaining is securely established and extensive, there will be areas outside the scope of joint regulation and within employer prerogative which are crucial for equal opportunities. Employers' opportunities to tackle discrimination and promote gender equality in the workplace are, therefore, potentially greater than those open to trade unions, since employers can act not only through collective bargaining but also by unilateral action in their employment strategies and human resource policies.[27]

(c) Collective agreements on equality

How does the EU law on sex equality manifest itself in collective agreements? These may take a variety of forms. One type of equal opportunities agreement seems easy to identify. Its contents declare it to be a good practice agreement, or an innovative agreement. It is the result of a successful process of collective bargaining on equal opportunities. Illustrations include self-declared "equal opportunities agreements", which may be procedural (for example, setting up structures; monitoring arrangements) and/or substantive[28]; positive action for women agreements (for example, as in Germany in respect of access to particular forms of vocational training; or specific jobs[29]); single issue agreements on areas with a stated or assumed relevance to gender equality (for example, sexual harassment procedures); or provisions within more general collective agreements which are intended to contribute to equal opportunities. These cover a range of topics, for instance sexual harassment, family leave, equal pay, atypical working and access to training.

Collective bargaining is often active in the equal opportunities area by way of specific reference to legal rules on equal opportunities. Examples include agreements picking up on legal requirements, such as the case law on the need for transparency in pay systems (*Danfoss*[30]); particular approaches to pay determination/job evaluation (*Nimz*[31], *Rummler*[32]); treatment of part-time workers (*Nimz, Rinner-Kühn*[33], *Kowalska*[34]); filling gaps where there is no legal regulation (as in the case of paternity leave in the United Kingdom); or going beyond legal provision (that is using legal provision as a floor on which to build through collective bargaining).

---

[27] Scope for *unilateral* union action to determine terms and conditions within the workplace may exist but to a lesser extent. An example might be where the union controls entry to a particular trade or job. Unions have greater scope for unilateral action in respect of their own internal structures.

[28] For examples, see Appendices to Dickens, *Collective Bargaining and the Promotion of Equality: The Case of the United Kingdom* (ILO, 1993).

[29] But see now Case C-450/93 *Kalanke* v *Freie und Hansestadt Bremen*, Judgment of 17 October 1995, nyr.

[30] Case 109/88, *supra* n 3.

[31] Case C-184/89 *Nimz* v *Freie und Hansestadt Hamburg* [1991] ECR I-297.

[32] Case 237/85 *Rummler*, *supra* n 3.

[33] Case 171/88 *Rinner-Kühn* v *FWW Spezialgebäudereinigung GmbH* [1989] ECR 2743.

[34] Case C-33/89 *Kowalska* v *Freie und Hansestadt Hamburg* [1990] ECR I-2591.

There is a more complex category of collective agreements which *appear* to be equal opportunities agreements, in that they ostensibly favour women workers, but, in light of critiques of the equality concept, are arguably negative in their consequences for women.[35] The case law of the European Court has encountered and challenged such agreements.[36] Illustrations include collective agreements and provisions within agreements which appear not to be of any direct relevance to equal opportunities. These provisions (for example, on pay and pay opportunities, working time, access to benefits, job security) appear neutral, but may in effect (intentionally or not) serve to underpin or perpetuate gender inequalities in the workplace. Here the discriminatory dimension is *invisible* in the agreement and only made visible when the agreement or provision is seen in the context of sex segregation in the workplace where it has effect.[37] It is also necessary to consider the *relationship* between separate collective agreements, especially where bargaining units are sex segregated (as in *Enderby*[38]).

Perhaps the most interesting category of collective bargaining bearing on equal opportunities comprises those agreements which do not appear to be equal opportunities agreements at all. There is nothing about them which appears to be specifically relevant to women. Yet their effects, or the way they are applied, are discriminatory.

It is the "equality dimension" of collective agreements in general (for example, indirect discrimination in payment systems, seniority systems, dismissals procedures) which is the real problem. The most difficult issue is to discern the discriminatory effect of apparently neutral agreements, such as wage scales and pay structures. Such agreements are *not* obviously equal opportunities agreements. Yet they present the law on equality with perhaps its greatest challenge. The problem for the law is to identify those agreements and expose their discriminatory effects. In a sense, the task of the law is to make the invisible visible. The invisible is not easy to locate. The problem lies in the process of application of the agreement, which renders the agreement discriminatory. The objective is to make the application process visible.

Some agreements themselves seek to avoid discrimination in the application of their apparently neutral provisions. Innovative agreements attempt explicitly to address the invisibility of the process which leads to discrimination. Illustrations of "innovative" agreements, those making visible hidden discrimination, include:

(a) agreements which explicitly attempt to address discrimination identified in previous processes, which attempt to inject an equality dimension into general provisions on pay, terms and conditions;

---

[35] Bercusson, *European Labour Law, supra* n 5, chapter 13.

[36] For example, Case 312/86 *Commission* v *French Republic* [1988] ECR 6315, which concerned collective agreements providing leave for mothers in connection with childcare; or agreements prohibiting women from working certain hours, see, for example, Case C-345/89 *Stoeckel* [1991] ECR I-4047; Case C-13/93 *Minne* [1994] ECR I-371.

[37] A range of examples of this can be found in Dickens et al., *Tackling Sex Discrimination Through Collective Bargaining* (1988).

[38] Case 127/92 *Enderby* v *Frenchay Area Health Authority* [1993] ECR I-5535.

(b) agreements seeking to remove present discrimination by, for example, identifying and eliminating provisions which resulted in inequitable terms as between men and women;

(c) agreements redressing past discrimination (for example, providing for positive action);

(d) agreements which have been "equality-proofed"; guarding against discriminatory outcomes by assessing outcomes from a gender perspective; injecting an "equality dimension"; and

(e) agreements providing for implementation (monitoring/enforcement provisions).

Such agreements address *formerly* hidden discrimination, and attempt to bring the issue into the open. This is done by making it the subject of explicit provision in the agreement, explaining how earlier processes discriminated, and hence how the agreement (often in the form of a procedure) aims to remedy this.

They have the advantage of having a strong and sophisticated reinforcement in the EU law on sex discrimination, manifested in various ways:

(i) the requirement of *transparency* articulated in the *Danfoss* case is precisely aimed at making the invisible visible.[39] Employers using apparently neutral criteria for pay systems are required explicitly to articulate the process of application of these criteria;

(ii) the concept of equal pay for work of equal value creates a pressure in favour of *job evaluation* procedures, which can reveal the discrimination inherent in traditional payment systems. Job evaluation systems themselves can be scrutinised;[40] and

(iii) the concept of *indirect discrimination* is based precisely on the discriminatory application or effects of ostensibly neutral criteria. It incorporates the requirement that employers articulate *justifications*[41] for such discriminatory effects and prescribes strict conditions over what justifications are acceptable in EC law.[42]

In conclusion, collective agreements best reflecting the EU law on equality are those which are most explicit, elaborate, detailed and persuasive about how to overcome the invisible discrimination which occurs in the application of the agreement.

---

[39]Case 109/88 [1989] ECR 3199.

[40] As in the *Rummler* case, which held that if ostensibly neutral factors in job evaluation discriminate against women, they must be compensated for by other factors which favour women (Case 237/85 [1986] ECR 2101).

[41] See Townshend-Smith, in this volume.

[42] Illustrations can be found in specific areas; for example, pay. Pay agreements may incorporate mechanisms to achieve equal opportunities. Examples would be agreements reviewing pay structures, remarking on discriminatory effects, and proposing measures to combat them: e.g. abolishing the bottom grades of a structure, comprising mainly women; reducing percentage wage increases in favour of flat rate increases favouring low-paid women; higher increases for the lowest paid categories (often women).

(iii) National contexts of collective bargaining on equality

It must always be borne in mind, however, that collective agreements within each Member State have to be considered in their particular national context, without pre-judging the nature of any provisions. The ways in which pay discrimination is tackled and pay equity is sought can be expected to differ, and, similarly, the nature of provisions dealing with employment conditions other than pay. In this section, a number of different national contexts are briefly explored to demonstrate the complexities confronting equality law in the EU in the national context of collective bargaining.

(a) France

In France, collective bargaining takes place at both industry-wide and enterprise levels. There is a legal duty to bargain, although there is no obligation to reach an agreement. Bargaining at industry level is obligatory and must cover minimum wages (annual negotiations) and job classifications (every five years). Bargaining at enterprise level is obligatory on, among other subjects, wage bargaining by categories of employees and working time. It is possible to extend the legal effect of a collective agreement by an administrative procedure to all employers and employees in a sector ("*erga omnes*").

A law of 13 July 1983 made it obligatory for those collective agreements capable of extension to include new provisions concerning equal treatment in employment and for pregnant and nursing mothers. These were to be added to those clauses already required regarding the application of the principle of equal pay for equal work.

The *Commission Nationale de la Negotiation Collective* has the duty to secure the elimination of all elements in collective agreements that are discriminatory and to check that all new national agreements take into account, and include, provisions on the issues of promotion, hiring and compensatory measures for indirect discrimination. An annual report has been published from 1984.[43]

Soon after the law of 1983, the report published in 1985 described the state of collective agreements on the principles of equal pay and equal treatment between women and men, as well as women and work generally. The conclusion was that the texts of agreements in force at the end of 1983 were virtually silent as regards equal pay, and, above all, as regards equal treatment. There were relatively frequently clauses concerned with consequences of pregnancy and maternity on the working lives of women, but even these clauses needed to be updated and generalised. A review of developments over the four years following the law demonstrates the relatively modest contextual impact of the law.

---

[43] *Bilan Annuelle sur l'Egalité Professionnelle entre les Femmes et les Hommes.*

During 1984, compared to the previous year, the situation had developed very little. Of 927 agreements in force in 1984, less than 4% (32) involved one or more of the three topics (equal pay, equal treatment, maternity); 16 agreements included a clause concerning equal treatment between men and women; the principle of "equal pay for equal work", even though enacted by the legislature in 1973, appeared in only 12 agreements.

The content of these clauses on equal treatment or equal pay was always very brief: a simple statement of the principle prohibiting all discrimination on grounds of sex and specifying some areas of application of the principle: hiring; promotion; dismissal and training. There was also a tendency to abolish discriminatory clauses which reserved certain more favourable rights to women: leave to care for a sick child; leave to raise children after maternity; or adoption.

The report made two general observations. First, the law of 13 July 1983 on equality in employment had not given rise to a significant development of collective bargaining at industry level on this issue. Secondly, the contents of the negotiations that did take place were modest. On the other hand, two positive points can be highlighted. Clauses on equal treatment were introduced in most of the new or replaced agreements, and discriminatory provisions were being eliminated.

Subsequent years have not revealed great changes. The slow pace of change was the reason why, in *Commission of the European Communities* v *French Republic*,[44] the Commission challenged the French government's delegation to the social partners of the task of amending agreements violating the provisions of Directive 76/207/EEC on equal treatment. Advocate General Sir Gordon Slynn argued that "it was not sufficient to leave it to labour and management without specific requirements as to the time or methods of enforcement".[45] He pointed out that: "There is no State guarantee of effective enforcement of the principle of equality should the negotiation process between the two sides of industry fail".[46] To support this he added:[47]

> The results of the legislation in practice demonstrate the absence of any effective State guarantee of compliance, notwithstanding the existence of a procedure for government approval of collective agreements. It appears that in 1983 in France 1,050 collective agreements were concluded in branches of working activity and 2,400 in individual undertakings. In 1984 the figures were 927 and 6,000, respectively. By contrast, only 16 collective agreements were renegotiated on a non-discriminatory basis.

Citing these figures, the Court concluded:[48]

> Such figures are extremely modest when compared with the number of collective agreements entered into each year in France . . . The requirement that collective

---

[44] Case 312/86 [1988] ECR 6315.
[45] *Ibid* 6329.
[46] *Ibid.*
[47] *Ibid.*
[48] *Ibid* 6637–8 paras 20–23.

agreements must be approved, and the possibility that they may be extended, by the public authorities have therefore not led to a rapid process of renegotiation.

It follows from those considerations that the French government's argument that the task of removing special rights for women should be left to the two sides of industry working through collective negotiation cannot be accepted.

However, this case also illustrates the limitations of the litigation procedure. The figures cited do not indicate what proportion of agreements contained discriminatory clauses. The figure of 16 agreements amended has to be assessed *not* against the total number of agreements, but against those containing clauses requiring amendment. The reports by the *Commission Nationale de la Negociation Collective* on the number of agreements containing such clauses indicate that relatively few contain clauses pertaining to equality.[49] This puts the evaluation by the Court and the Advocate General in a different light.

The review of sectoral level agreements does not touch upon enterprise agreements. It is the sectoral level, however, which has tended to be more important in collective bargaining in France. Albeit their coverage of a sector is extensive, the issue of equality does not appear to have made great inroads immediately following the enactment of legislation intended to achieve that effect.

(b) Italy

Collective bargaining in Italy also takes place at different levels. Collective bargaining at plant level is informal, often limited to specific issues, and there is relatively little organised documentation. However, national or regional sectoral bargaining and agreements appear to be particularly rich in provisions on equality, and are relatively well documented.

One publication prepared by the trade unions was dedicated to provisions in collective agreements on equal opportunity.[50] It included provisions of agreements re-negotiated in 1986–87 in ten industries: food, agriculture, chemicals, commerce, media, metalworking, civil service, research, textiles and road transport; also agreements still in the stage of re-negotiation in the air and rail transport and construction industries; together with contracts re-negotiated in 1984–86: banking and telecommunications. Significantly, the volume concludes with the text of the Council Recommendation on positive action.[51]

Another volume presented the negotiating demands adopted by the three trade union confederations (CGIL, CISL and UIL) and the national collective agreements concluded in six industries (metalworking, chemicals, textiles, food, printing and agriculture).[52] The contents of these demands and agree-

---

[49] *Commission Nationale de la Negociation Collective, Bilan Annuel de la Negociation Collective 1984, L'Egalité professionnelle entre les femmes et les hommes, Ministère des Affaires Sociales et de l'Emploi,* June 1985, mimeograph, and similar reports published in following years.

[50] Gilardi, *Le pari opportunità nei contratti* (1987).

[51] *Ibid* 143–145. Recommendation No 84/635 of 12 December 1984 (OJ 1984 331/84).

[52] Sabbatucci, *Contratti a confronto* (1988).

ments were classified under various headings, and included headings which had significant impact on women.

For example, a section on occupational training included an extract from the national collective agreement in agriculture which explicitly covered training for women.[53] Another section contained extracts from collective agreements under the heading "positive action for equal opportunity", with extracts from the national agreements in private and public sector metalworking, public sector chemicals, textiles and agriculture. Each of these agreements included, *inter alia*, an explicit reference to the Council's 1984 Recommendation on Positive Action.[54]

The complexity of collective bargaining on issues of equality in Italy can be illustrated by the case of equal pay. In the perspective of Italian trade unions, the labour law on equal pay is influenced by the changing pattern of collective bargaining. The inter-confederal (all sector) agreement of 1960 reduced the existing wage differential between men and women workers for the same jobs, but maintained an explicit wage gap of about 10%. This was subsequently annulled by the courts on the basis of the principle of equal pay for equal work in Article 37 of the Constitution. The result was a progressive upward adjustment of women's pay in industry-wide agreements.

Direct discrimination does not appear in agreements, but indirect discrimination persists. Women remain concentrated at the lowest wage levels and classification systems operate so that female-dominated jobs are undervalued. The egalitarian wage policies of Italian unions have aimed less at realising equal pay, than at eliminating low pay, and thus aim to reduce the impact of this indirect discrimination.

On the other hand, although the concept of "pay" has been generally construed to include all types of benefits, some agreements have excluded certain items (for example, special bonuses linked to individuals' or groups' seniority or responsibility or qualifications). The indirectly discriminatory effects of this are still not widely appreciated. The growth of productivity-linked bargaining in certain sectors threatens a policy of equal pay for work of equal value. As it allows for variations in pay among individuals according to productivity, it becomes more difficult to compare men and women when the productivity bonus is linked to groups or individuals. As with other premium payments, the application of the bonus system can become discriminatory, as in the food processing industry productivity agreement of 1987.

Following judicial interpretations, different sectoral agreements, negotiated by different unions and resulting in different wage structures, cannot be compared. This allows for a classification of jobs having similar characteristics, even within a sector (let alone in different sectors) and even when signed by the same unions and employers' associations, which allocates lower grades to jobs in women dominated sub-sectors. An example is in textiles: male dyeing versus female hosiery.

---

[53] Sabbatucci, *Contratti a confronto* (1988) 228–229.
[54] *Ibid* 231–236.

Job evaluation is largely unknown. Attempts during the 1960s failed because the mobility entailed in their application (re-classification of jobs as re-evaluated, including downwards where male jobs are re-evaluated) encountered legally guaranteed protections against such downward mobility. There have been calls for re-thinking of job evaluation factors, but implementation is not considered likely through judicial processes. Rather, progress will likely come through collective bargaining, stimulated by legal pressures. Though not systematically addressed by Italian unions, some developments may be found.[55]

(c) Federal Republic of Germany

There are two different kinds of agreements between collectivities of workers and employers. The first are collective agreements between unions and employers or an organization of employers; the second are agreements between works councils and an employer: works council agreements, which are not regarded as "collective agreements" in German law. Collective agreements proper are usually based on regional bargaining: an organization of employers on one side and a union, normally affiliated to the central union confederation (DGB), on the other. Sometimes the collective agreement, regional or national, is only a framework agreement, filled in by enterprise level bargaining.

Many important cases decided by courts in the area of equal pay have involved collective agreements.[56] In the 1950s, most cases resulted from collective agreements on pay, according to which women doing the same work as men received only 70–80% of the male wage. The Federal Labour Court declared such provisions void. In spite of the number of judgments against these *Frauenabschlagsklauseln* they continued to exist until 1972, when they were replaced by the so-called *Leichtlohngruppen* (light wage group) (a group of usually female workers paid less than male workers in comparable jobs because the work of the men was physically heavier). One of the last cases dealing with a directly discriminatory provision in a collective agreement was decided by the Federal Labour Court as recently as 1985.[57] The Berlin Metalworkers' wage agreement provided that only married men could receive a monthly married person's wage supplement (10 DM). The Federal Labour Court declared this provision void.

A number of agreements can illustrate the advantages and disadvantages of collective agreements for women. An agreement in the paper-producing industry includes wage groups I and II, which cover "easy or light work"; only from

---

[55] Borgogelli and Treu, "Parità e pari opportunità nella contrattazione collettiva", in *Donne e Lavoro: Analisi e Proposte*, Ministero del Lavoro e della Previdenza Sociale, Comitato Nazionale per la Parità, 2nd ed, 1986, 159–174. Borgogelli, *Il Lavoro Femminile tra Legge e Contrattazione: Una Ricerca sulla Contrattazione Collettiva in Tema di Lavoro Femminile*, Franco Angeli (1987). For a recent review, Bergamaschi, "Valutazione del lavoro femminile e contrattazione", in *Pari e dispari*, Annuario, 5, Franco Angeli, 1995, 105–119.

[56] Discriminatory provisions in the normative part of a collective agreement can be attacked relying on Article 3 II of the Basic Law. Norms of the agreement have the same legal effect as other legal norms. When an employer applies a discriminatory provision contained in a collective agreement, the worker can bring a claim based on section 611 ff. Bürgerlicher Gesetzbuch (BGB) against the employer.

[57] 13 November 1985. DB 86, 542.

group III onwards does the agreement speak of "employees of full worth". In practice, male jobs start with group III. In chemicals, the agreement unified conditions for blue and white collar workers and formed 13 new wage groups. The division between technical and commercial white collar workers, however, continued to favour technical workers despite unified wording. In practice, the male-female gap increases because of higher evaluation of "typically male jobs". Six years' seniority is necessary to reach the top wage. Additional pay is only for "nasty" work – typically male work.

In the agreement in MTV clothing there is to be found discriminatory treatment of part-time workers, seniority rules, exemption of mothers from excess hours, leave for the care of sick children, but also counting of former periods of employment for mothers interrupting work to care for children. In metal-working, the agreement does not discriminate on its face: it applies to part-time workers, and there are no light-wage groups. Section 5 requires gender-neutral job evaluation and uses analytical job evaluation with the following criteria (in diminishing importance): knowledge, dexterity, additional thought process, responsibility for work, strain on senses and nerves, strain on muscles, and environmental influences.

(d) Denmark

There are special features of the Danish welfare state and industrial relations system which characterise the relationship between collective bargaining and sex equality.

Within the largest umbrella organization, the Confederation of Danish Trade Unions (LO), there are some 31 unions, three to five of which cover the majority of the female work-force. Whereas in Germany, organisation is by industry; in Denmark it is by qualification, in principle, and, to some degree, by sex. Unskilled workers organise by sex: men are members of one union, women of another. More than half of working women are employed in the public sector.

The social security system includes legislation protecting women during pregnancy and after childbirth, including provisions for parental leave. Collective agreements provide additional benefits. These benefits are not necessarily better in the agreements negotiated by the unskilled women's union. The best maternity provisions are found in the male-dominated sectors. These have very progressive provisions on parental leave and childcare. Childcare provisions are usually sex-neutral in their formulation, and are available to men also.[58] Otherwise they would be unlawful as discriminatory. Collective agreements may also provide benefits not allowed under legislation: there are no statutory provisions for leave to care for sick children, but clauses providing for this are found in collective agreements.

Prior to 1973 there were different rates for men and women in collective agreements. Since 1973, specific provisions have abolished the differences.

---

[58] See also Ryel, in this volume, concerning the Nordic model.

Agreements do not explicitly provide for equal pay; it is implicit. Hence, there are no equal pay clauses. Unions are opposed to job evaluation and it is practically never used. Instead, unions in Denmark favour low wage policy in order to raise the level of the low paid. Flat rate increases or the abolition of the lowest rates in an agreement or wage structure would usually be called a low pay policy, even though it benefitted women disproportionately.

This does not mean that unequal pay does not exist in collective agreements in Denmark. The issue manifests itself in two forms. First, different collective agreements; differentials in an enterprise's wage structure are not determined by job evaluation between grades in one collective agreement. Different jobs come under different agreements. Unions negotiate wage rates for their members based on their qualifications. Each union has its own collective agreement. The differentials arise from different collective agreements.

Secondly, it is possible to have differentiation among workers covered by one collective agreement, though the differential is not fixed in the agreement. This results from what is called the "minimum wage system". The agreement only lays down a minimum (usually exceeded in practice). Every employee has an individual wage, which in principle is negotiated on an individual basis. Collective agreements are not usually negotiated at workplace level in Denmark, but by the national or regional union. On the basis of these agreements, the individual employee negotiates individual supplements.

The unions and employers saw it as important to deal with equal pay without State intervention. They opposed the Equal Pay Directive's provisions on enforcement. The unions retain control by taking what they see as breaches of the Directive to arbitration. The machinery to ensure compliance with the EU Directive is that if a woman or a union feels there has been discrimination, they can take the case, not to the civil courts, but to arbitration, claiming that it is a violation of the Danish implementing legislation. Only very few individuals outside the collective industrial relations system go to the civil courts.

The proliferation of collective agreements within one establishment, each negotiated by a different union representing an occupational grouping, means that it can happen that exactly the same job is done by women paid under one agreement and men paid under another agreement. An unskilled woman member of the women's union may be under one collective agreement; an unskilled male worker doing the same or approximately the same work may be under another. Since equal value is accepted as binding in Denmark, if the same job or jobs of equal value are covered by two separate agreements, and the male workers' union has been able to negotiate better rates than the women workers' union, the women workers' union has, on occasion, gone to arbitration claiming that their own agreement is not valid because it violates the Equal Pay Act and the employer must now give what it could not achieve at the negotiating table. The first such case was won in 1977[59] and another succeeded in 1987.[60]

---

[59] Arbitral award of 8 December 1977; the "FDB" case.
[60] Arbitral award of 19 April 1987; the "Premier-IS" case.

After these cases, the existing practice was changed and there were many voluntary settlements out of court by individual companies. After the 1987 case the biggest employers' organization circulated its members with a letter telling them to correct such arrangements. If not, the letter informed the members that they would receive no support in the event of a court case.

The employers had to raise the wage level for women workers. The difference usually consisted of some kind of basic rate, typically the same for men and women, but with some increments in the male collective agreement. These now had to be added to the female collective agreement. There was some activity regarding merit increments, described in the male agreement, but not found in the female agreement (for instance, lifting). After the case, if there were provisions in the male agreement which were not in the female agreement, employers had to include the same kind of provision (the "lifting" clause, for example).

(e) United Kingdom

Collective agreements in the United Kingdom are negotiated at national, enterprise and workplace levels, by full-time national and regional officials of trade unions with senior management, and by local shop stewards representing the employees in a workplace with local management. Although the decline of multi-employer, industry-wide agreements had already begun in the 1950s, a survey by the Confederation of British Industry found that during the period 1979–86 here was a "marked diminution" in the influence of such agreements, matched by a pronounced growth in single-employer bargaining at company or establishment level. By 1986, 87% of employees in plants with collective bargaining had their basic rates of pay negotiated at establishment or company level.

This had implications for collective bargaining and equal pay. Following condemnation by the European Court,[61] British law was changed so as to allow for claims that women's work was of equal value to that of men only with effect from 1 January 1984, when the Equal Pay (Amendment) Regulations 1983 came into force.[62] The law became a potential basis for negotiations between unions and management with the objective of equal pay agreements.

In the first three years, over 2,000 formal claims were made to industrial tribunals. Over the first ten years, almost 8,000 equal value applications were made to industrial tribunals. This impressive quantitative impact is belied by putting it in context. Only just over 560 employers are, or have been, involved in equal value proceedings over this ten-year period, with just over a quarter in the health sector alone. The large total of claims included large numbers of multiple claims from women working for the same employer. In 1986, of 1,481 applications, 1,115 were against British Coal; in 1987, of 1,738 applications, 1,395 were from speech therapists.[63] This large number of multiple claims

---

[61] Case 61/81 *Commission of the European Communities* v *United Kingdom of Great Britain and Northern Ireland* [1982] ECR 2601 para 14.

[62] See Ellis, in this volume.

[63] "Equal value update", *Equal Opportunities Review*, No 58, November/December 1994, 11.

against single employers demonstrates the vital role of trade unions and collective bargaining as a factor in equal value claims, whether as a support or a target
for litigation.

In a context of extreme de-centralisation of pay bargaining, co-ordination
among unions in pursuing equal pay strategies was both important and
extremely difficult. A review of the equal pay strategies pursued by 16 unions
revealed a wide variation.[64] A few unions provided for centralised direction of
equal pay claims; others preferred to allow local officials to take the initiative,
with varying attempts at co-ordinating these local efforts. Some unions did not
attempt any centralised co-ordination, or have any specific strategy on equal
pay.

Negotiations on equal pay were related to the law on equal value in different
ways. The legal claim might be launched as a prelude to negotiations; or negotiations and litigation might be linked in a deliberate strategy; or might be perceived as separate but parallel strategies, as when test case litigation strategies
were used. In some cases, litigation was discouraged by unions, with the emphasis
placed solely on negotiating equal pay agreements. However, as one observer
commented:[65]

> Reliable and detailed information concerning out-of-court equal value settlements is
> difficult to obtain. Having elected to resolve a particular claim internally, both man-
> agement and trade union are likely to adopt and maintain a low profile approach,
> at the very minimum, until an agreement is reached. Thereafter, information might
> be more forthcoming, but this will often be superficial and might be misinterpreted
> by those unfamiliar with the structure, practices and procedures of the specific
> organization.

One major undertaking, however, received a great deal of deserved attention: a
job evaluation exercise for local authority manual workers agreed in 1986.[66]
The agreement affected about one million workers, three-quarters of whom
were women. Basic wage rates were negotiated nationally in the National Joint
Council comprising the organisation of local authority employers and the three
major trade unions.

The previous grading structure was the result of a job evaluation exercise
carried out at the end of the 1960s. The result was that the majority of the
women, working part-time, were in the lower grade jobs with lower basic rates,
whereas workers in the higher grades with higher basic rates were mainly men,
who also had greater opportunities to increase their basic rate through overtime payments and various bonuses.

By 1985 the scheme was criticised as discriminatory and the new Equal Value

---

[64] *Equal Opportunities Review*, No 11, January/February 1987, 10–18.
[65] Collinson, describing an equal value agreement in the UK financial sector (Eagle Star Insurance
Group and the Banking, Insurance and Finance Union); *Equal Opportunities Review*, No 11, January/
February 1987, 18.
[66] A detailed account, from which the following is derived, is in *Equal Opportunities Review* No 13,
May/June 1987, 21–24.

Regulations allowed for individual complaints, the results of which were un-predictable, and could undermine the collective bargaining machinery. Rather than support individual claims by dissatisfied members, therefore, the unions undertook to achieve equal pay for work of equal value through the negotiating machinery. The job evaluation scheme was agreed at the beginning of 1986.

A team was engaged and drew up 540 job descriptions based on a breakdown into six factors: skill, responsibility, initiative, mental and physical effort, and working conditions. Care was taken to ensure that these factors were not skewed so as to reflect considerations which favoured one sex. For example, the factor of skill took account not only of traditional formal training and qualifications but also informal training, acquired experience, caring as well as communica-tive skills and literacy and numeracy. The factor of responsibility took account of women's jobs having more responsibility for people and men's having more responsibility for resources; so this factor was divided into three sub-factors: responsibility for people, for resources and for supervision. Physical effort was not limited to heavy lifting, which unduly favours men's jobs, but also included bending and kneeling and continuity of effort, which ensured that jobs frequently undertaken by women were not undervalued. Similarly, working con-ditions were defined so that they included not only traditionally considered unfavourable working conditions, such as noise and dirt, but also noise and people, and that working conditions inside could be as unpleasant as working outside.

The analytical breakdown of different jobs having been completed, the task of evaluating the jobs involved allocating values to them. This was undertaken by panels equally representing employers and unions, and with equal numbers of men and women. The panels evaluated 40 major occupations, covering approximately 90% of the labour force. Each was analysed in terms of the factor headings, with each factor having four or five possible levels. For example, a job might be allocated to level three for skill; level two for responsibility and level four for working conditions, and so on.

A co-ordinating panel, comprising seven employer and six union representa-tives, and including five women, then applied weights to the different factor levels, so as to reach a potential overall total of 1,000 points. The co-ordinating panel decided that the major factors in local government manual jobs were skill and responsibility, and awarded each a factor weighting of 36%. Responsibility was sub-divided into responsibility for people, resources and supervision, with 12% each. Initiative, considered to overlap with responsibility, was allocated 6%, as were working conditions. To balance out, mental and physical effort were each allocated 8%. The outcome of the exercise could be represented in the follow-ing table.[67]

Each job was allocated its quota of points according to the factors it was deemed to comprise and their weighting. This produced a rank order of jobs for local authority manual workers.

_____
[67] See p 201.

Weighting by level and factor

Factor	Evaluation level					Factor weighting
	1	2	3	4	5	
Skill	26	72	108	306	360	36%
Responsibility:						
for people	12	30	90	120		
for resources	12	30	90	120		36%
for supervision	6	12	54	108		
Initiative	6	18	36	60		6%
Mental effort	8	24	48	80		8%
Physical effort	8	24	48	80		8%
Working conditions	6	18	36	60		6%

Source: 13 *Equal Opportunities Review*, May/June 1987, 21–4 at 23. Reproduced by permission of IRS/Eclipse Group Ltd.

Of the outcome it was stated that some "caring" jobs, such as home helps, predominantly female, had been evaluated more highly than was the case in the previous job evaluation, whereas other jobs, such as refuse collectors, predominantly male, had moved down. But there remained difficult negotiating tasks involving the drawing up of pay grade boundaries and consequent allocation of jobs to different grades, and, not least, the negotiating of pay rates for each new grade. A major problem regarded the bonus earning schemes so important to the predominantly male jobs.

Apart from such major co-ordinated collective endeavours, individual unions undertook initiatives. The second largest trade union in Britain at that time: the General, Municipal and Boilermakers' Union, as of 1987 developed a new head of claim: "eliminating sex bias". This was presented to all employers on the occasion of the review of a collective agreement. The new head of claim encompassed 13 items and stated that its aim was to achieve, among other things: overtime payments for part-time workers, unsocial hours payments for twilight shift workers, equal access to bonus schemes, an end to job segregation which places women in low paid, low status jobs, and paid leave for family circumstances. Progress on the elimination of sex bias was monitored by the union's National Industry Conferences and its National Equal Rights Advisory Committee. Agreements were to be collected and made accessible through a computerised database.

On the negative side, the United Kingdom had been condemned again by the European Court,[68] so that section 6 of the Sex Discrimination Act 1986 rendered void discriminatory provisions in collective agreements. Under section 3 of the Equal Pay 1970, a collective agreement containing a term which applied specifically to men only or to women only could be referred to the Central Arbitration Committee for amendment or to remove the discrimination. This provision appeared to hold great potential following the award of the Committee in *ASTMS and the Norwich Union Insurance Group*.[69] In this decision,

---

[68] Case 165/82 *Commission of the European Communities* v *United Kingdom of Great Britain and Northern Ireland* [1983] ECR 3431.
[69] Award 87/2, 30 January 1987.

the Committee relied on Article 119 to extend its jurisdiction under section 3 to amending indirectly discriminatory (as well as directly discriminatory) provisions in collective agreements.

Unfortunately, this was the Committee's last award before the repeal of this jurisdiction by the 1986 Act. In the event, the decision was later overruled by the High Court in *R* v *Central Arbitration Committee, ex parte Norwich Union*.[70] There remains no specific mechanism whereby allegedly discriminatory collective agreements can be challenged.

(iv) Conclusion

The significance of this exercise in sketching national contexts is to demonstrate how much the European law on equal pay for work of equal value was integrated into the national context of collective bargaining, and its associated qualities of multiple actors on both employer and trade union sides, complex negotiating procedures and outcomes. The collective bargaining context could not afford to ignore the EU law on equality, but that law had to accommodate the national context, which allowed for a distinctive shaping of the law in its application.

BRIAN BERCUSSON
Professor of European Law,
University of Manchester,
UK

---

[70] 22 EOR (1988), 41. See Davies, "The Central Arbitration Committee and Equal Pay" 33 *Current Legal Problems* (1980), 165–190; Davies, "European Equality Legislation, UK Legislative Policy and Industrial Relations" in McCrudden (ed.), *Women, Employment and European Equality Law* (1987) 23–51.

Part V
CITIZENSHIP AND HUMAN RIGHTS

Chapter 13

WOMEN AND CITIZENSHIP OF THE EUROPEAN UNION*

(i) Introduction

Within the context of the liberal constitution, the concept of citizenship is laden not only with historical significance, but also with contemporary political and social relevance. To T H Marshall,[1] the father of modern citizenship, it was the successive endowment of all individuals with civil, political and social rights which constituted the institution of the citizen. As a result, this formal institution is said to embody the historical progression whereby feudalism was overcome, the inequalities of the capitalist market were compensated for, and all persons were made equal heirs to the government of their community: a community to which they might only now, on the basis of their sovereign status, be said truly to belong.[2] Modern liberal constitutionalism has accordingly placed the normative institution of the citizen at the very core of contemporary constitution-making: the furnishing of individuals with civil, social and political rights being designed both to include them within modern society, and to constitute them as a very particular sovereign polity; one capable of fulfilling the task of self-limiting democratic governance which the liberal constitution requires of it.[3]

Consequently, whilst the drafters of Article 8(1) of the Treaty on European Union might not share the eloquence of the framers of the United States Constitution, their sanguine assertion that "citizenship of the Union is hereby established", would at first glance appear to embody an equally "self-evident truth": not only are the benefits of the European Union supposedly to be shared amongst all individual Europeans, but those same impliedly sovereign Europeans are to

---

*This chapter was written by Michelle Everson.
[1] Marshall, *Citizenship and Social Class and Other Essays* (1950).
[2] Van Gunsteren, "Four Conceptions of Citizenship" in van Steenberg, *The Condition of Citizenship* (1994) 36–48.
[3] Murphy, "Constitutions, Constitutionalism, and Democracy" in Greenberg, Katz, Oliveiro and Wheatley, *Constitutionalism and Democracy: Transitions in the Contemporary World* (1993), 3–25.

play an equal part in governing this new international community. Seen in this light, the question of women and citizenship of the European Union initially seems to be a simple one of whether the new Union citizenship is constructed to ensure that women, as well as men, will be fully included within Europe, and that they too will have their say in the democratic governance of the Union.

Such simplicity notwithstanding, two immediate and complementary problems nevertheless arise. First, even the most vociferous supporters of contemporary liberalism have come to accept that their traditional version of constitutional citizenship has failed to fully include women within modern society.[4] This may be due to the rigid insistence on a strict distinction between public and private spheres which leaves women trapped in a private and male-dominated family structure.[5] Alternatively, it may be due to the liberal emphasis on the morality of universal justice rather than that of particular care which overlooks the over-whelmingly female task of caring and condemns the majority of women to social and political anonymity.[6] The result is the same: private power structures and obligations deny women the *autonomous* exercise of their rights of citizenship and prevent them from becoming sovereign members of their communities.

Second, the merest glance at the limited catalogue of individual rights found in the Treaties of Rome and European Union, reveals that Union citizenship is not the fully-fledged civil, social and political citizenship historically associated with the constitutions of Nation States. The weak political status of the Union citizen alone, confirms that this particular citizen is not a conventionally sovereign member of a conventional Union community.[7]

Such difficulties raise the worrying spectre that despite their new status as Union citizens, women in Europe will be nothing more than "doubly un-sovereign" Europeans. The following analysis, however, in investigating the pos-sibility that Union citizenship is designed to achieve the altogether more modest aim of establishing a European civil society, uncovers positive elements within European law which may in the future be built upon to help ensure that individual European women might attain a more prominent position in the life of the Union.

More specifically, however, this study also pursues a particular thesis. It is readily apparent that modern feminist critiques do not apply to the traditional institution of citizenship in isolation. Rather, such criticism focuses on the shortcomings of the entire liberal constitutionalist structure in which the tradi-tional citizen is embedded; its public/private distinction and its irrevocable commitment to an objective universalist justice. Accordingly, given that certain commentators have come to regard the Treaties establishing the European Communities and Union as a unique form of supranational "constitutionalist

---

[4] Kymlicka, *Contemporary Political Philosophy: An Introduction* (1990).
[5] Pateman, *The Sexual Contract* (1988).
[6] Bubeck, "A Feminist Approach to Citizenship", European University Institute Working Paper, EUF No 95/1 (1995).
[7] D'Oliveira, "Citizenship: Its Meaning, Its Potential", in Dehousse, *Europe After Maastricht: An Ever Closer Union?* (1994) 126–148.

experiment",[8] it is possible to speculate whether a "new constitutionalism" may not be developed at the European level: a constitutionalism generally more favourable to the autonomy of women.

(ii) The autonomous exercise of rights of Union citizenship by women

No individual is ever "completely autonomous". This fact arises as "freedom and the desire to act upon it" always exists within "a social framework".[9] Such social structures inevitably dictate that an individual can only choose how to exercise his or her rights following due consultation with other closely-related individuals whose personal interests may be affected by such actions. Consequently, it might be suggested that the use of the term "autonomous" is generally a touch redundant.

Nevertheless, if defined in accordance with recent feminist discussion, the notion of autonomy takes on a distinct meaning, summarised in the statement that "comparable capacities" between men and women "to behave autonomously, sometimes require" that they be treated the same, and sometimes require that they be treated differently.[10] In this way the futile, and often "exasperating," debate[11] which accompanies the notion of formal equality between the sexes, and which is distinguished only by its inability to settle the question of whether women demand identical or distinct treatment to men, is thankfully circum-navigated. The point is simple and is as follows: the very particular biological or social conditions which apply to women alone, should not lessen their capacity to act equally autonomously to men when exercising their constitutionally-secured rights. Women should have comparable freedom of choice. On occasions, this goal may require that they receive distinctive consideration. This, however, will not always be the case.

Therefore, rather than merely ask whether women Union citizens receive formal equal treatment under the law of the European Communities and the European Union, the analysis now moves on to ascertain whether women might auton-omously exercise their rights of Union citizenship.[12] Do European women possess a comparable freedom of choice to that of European men? This enquiry never-theless requires two stages; the somewhat nebulous status of Union citizenship necessitating an analysis of how the limited rights which it entails appear to have as their goal the institutionalisation of a nascent form of European civil society.

---

[8] Bellamy and Castilgione, "The Reconfiguration of Politics in the New Europe: Constitutionalism, Democracy and Identity", Paper Presented to the 17th IVR World Congress – Challenges to law at the End of the 20th Century, Bologna June 16–21 (1995).

[9] Meehan and Sevenhuijsen, "Problems in Principles and Policies" in Meehan and Sevenhuijsen, *Equality, Politics and Gender* (1991) 1–16 at 7.

[10] *Ibid.*

[11] Bacchi, "Pregnancy, the Law and the Meaning of Equality" in Meehan and Sevenhuijsen, *Equality, Politics and Gender* (1991) 71–87.

[12] See Shaw, in this volume.

(a) Rights of Union citizenship and the European civil society

In purely legal terms, the establishment of rights, enforceable between the Union and individual Europeans, is a highly significant development. As one author has suggested, it is the character of the Union as a supranational "cohesive legal unit which confers rights on individuals" which in turn constitutes its "unique *sui generis* . . . its true-world historical significance".[13] The rights of the Union citizen, however, are undeniably limited.[14] Rights of political participation are weak, whilst social rights are non-existent. At the level of philosophical analysis it is this flimsy status which creates difficulty.

As intimated, the philosophical import of the conventional national notion of citizenship lies *not* in its being an umbrella term for a collection of loosely-related individual rights. On the contrary, individual rights of citizenship are seen as being *cumulative* in effect and, when gathered together as an institution, as serving a specific and fundamental purpose vital to the well-being of the national community. The very distinct series of civil, political and social rights of citizenship, are fashioned to include individuals within a community, simultaneously making them governors of that community.

On this score, the notion of Union citizenship, significant as it may be, appears to have little in common with its traditional counterparts; the clearest disparity arising in relation to the Union citizen's poor political standing: the Union citizen is not a governor of the Union.[15] This deviation of Union citizenship from the conventional norm, however, might not *per se* be taken as a confirmation that this new institution does not possess a normative significance to match its legal one. Indeed, if the exact nature of the rights of the Union citizen are examined in closer detail, it transpires that they too represent something slightly more than a loose collection of individual rights. Instead, they appear to serve a distinct, if still somewhat evolutionary, aim of establishing a right of individual participation in a European civil society.

It has thus been convincingly asserted that Union citizenship contributes significantly to new and revolutionary structures of supranational political and social organization.[16] In that it equips individuals with rights enforceable outside the borders of the National State, this supranational form of citizenship is argued to embody a vital functional evolution: one whereby individual citizens might be encouraged to develop a differentiated set of loyalties to those various levels of government which are necessarily emerging in response to the difficulties of effective administration in an increasingly complex and interrelated

---

[13] Curtin, "The Constitutional Structure of the Union: A Europe of Bits and Pieces", 30 CMLRev (1993), 17–96 at 67.

[14] D'Oliveira, *supra* n 7.

[15] Granted, the extension of personal voting rights in relation to the make-up of a supranational European Parliament may represent a giant leap forward in general political theory (Article 8b 1. Treaty on European Union). The powers of that body, however, remain heavily circumscribed (Articles 137–144 EC).

[16] Meehan, *Citizenship and the European Community* (1993).

international environment.[17] Seen in this light, it then becomes appropriate to ask whether those particular individual rights which constitute Union citizenship in fact seek to foster an increased degree of loyalty between the individual European and the European Union.

Strikingly, the most immediately resonant of the rights of the Union citizen, are those of unconditional free movement and of the freedom to participate in the newly integrated European market.[18] Being universal in nature and guaranteed by the European Court of Justice, such rights are endowed upon all. They likewise determine that each and every European may move freely throughout the continent, conversing on cultural or economic terms with each and every national culture and economy thereby encountered. On the purely practical level, the importance of such rights to individual Europeans is immediately apparent; gone are the days when Europeans were confined to their own national settings. Translating this phenomenon into the language of the political and constitutionalist theorist, however, the significance of such an evolution might importantly be said to lie in its attempt to institutionalise a newly emerging "European civil society".

Rights of economic and cultural interaction have thus traditionally been regarded as belonging within that civil sphere of society not generally subject to direct political intervention.[19] Being the engine of creative societal interaction, however, such a sphere of civil society, was nevertheless to be safeguarded by the national constitution via the means of specific civil rights, such as those of civic association or professional freedom.

Whilst in this regard the rights of the Union citizen do not cloyingly reproduce those of the traditional national citizen, they might nevertheless be argued to be securing this more conventional civil society in a distinctly new European manner. Although there is no catalogue of civil rights detailing such items as the Union citizen's freedom of speech, the unconditional right of free movement though Europe should nevertheless ensure free association between all Europeans. Likewise, although there is no explicit right of professional freedom, the four economic freedoms have already been shown to secure the right of Europeans to engage in full commercial activity, regardless both of their nationality and where in Europe they might find themselves.

In ensuring such rights, the Union can be said to be creating a potential sphere of creative cultural and economic interaction *common* to all Europeans.[20] When regarded cumulatively, the goal of the various rights of Union citizenship might in turn be argued to be a universal right of participation in this nascent European civil society. This furthermore may be said to comprise the major carrot whereby the loyalty of the individual Union citizen is today to be won. Whilst an

---

[17] *Ibid.*

[18] Articles 8a, 48, 52, 58, 67 EC Treaty.

[19] Cohen and Arato, *Civil Society and Political Theory* (1991).

[20] Support for such an argument coming from the rather unexpected quarter of international relations theory. See Stone, "What is a Supranational Constitution?: An Essay in International Relations Theory" 56 *Review of Politics* (1994), 441–474.

extended civil society may not add to the individual's right to control his or her own destiny, the right to participate within it does, at the very least, increase the available options.[21] Although slight when compared with the dense web of sovereignty bestowing rights present in the Nation State, such a mechanism might nevertheless be tentatively welcomed in relation to a supranational organization, the exact governmental structures of which have yet to be fully evolved.[22]

(b) Universal rights of union citizenship and the autonomous participation of women in a European civil society

Ultimately a universal right of participation in a European civil society may not be a sufficient basis for supranational government, and, as a consequence, the quest for a European polity goes on. Given the present status of the Union citizen, however, the specific question of whether women might today autonomously exercise their rights of citizenship, is best formulated in the following limited terms: do European women have a comparable capacity to European men to exercise their right of participation in the emergent European civil society?

Boiling this query further down into its essential ingredients, the question is simply one of how easy is it for women themselves to choose to move around Europe and to engage in cultural and economic interaction. To return briefly to the two major strands current in recent feminist thought, however, a common sense response is immediately forthcoming: women Union citizens have little freedom of choice with regard to relocation.[23] On the one hand, many European women remain irrevocably locked into private family structures. If such women themselves have little control over these units, the choice to move is simply not theirs to make. Equally, if women continue to constitute the major caring force within modern society, then the restrictive practical demands which this private obligation entails will continue to dictate that men and not women will choose whether, and how, to move around Europe. European men, rather than European women, will determine the composition of the emerging European civil society.

Translating such common sense into philosophical terms, however, it is equally apparent that the universal nature of the rights of Union citizenship is incompatible with the demands of women that they be granted a measure of autonomy or freedom of choice in relation to the exercise of those rights. By their very definition, universal rights are to be applied "impersonally".[24] Consequently, there is no room within the legal analysis accompanying their

---

[21] To pervert somewhat the point of Dahrendorf's distinction between rights and entitlements. See Dahrendorf, *Der Moderne Soziale Konflikt* (1992).
[22] Weiler, "Fin-de-Siècle Europe" in Dehousse, *Europe After Maastricht: An Ever Closer Union?* (1994) 203–216.
[23] But see Ackers, in this volume.
[24] Meehan, *supra* n 16 at 121.

application, to make special allowance for the peculiarities of the social framework within which women operate. Where the structures of private power and
obligations prevailing throughout Europe continue to dictate that women are
practically less able than men to choose to engage in European economic or
social interaction, Union citizenship cannot in itself compensate for this lack of
comparable choice.

In this regard, the historical example of the European right of sexual equality
proves particularly illuminating. Thus whilst it is now beyond doubt that the
extensive interpretation given to Article 119 EC by the European Court of
Justice has had a revolutionary affect, bettering the working conditions of
"working" European women in a manner seemingly unimaginable within the
Nation State.[25] It is similarly accepted that the necessarily impersonal application
of this universal right by the Court has done little to enhance the position of
European women in general.[26] In short, formal equality for those women who
do work, holds but little interest for those women who desire to work but are
prevented from so doing by their subordinate position in relation to the needs
of the family and those who demand their care. Alternatively, it is the inability
of this (significant) European right either to reach into the private sphere or to
take caring obligations care into account, which has failed European women as
a whole.

In this regard the more extensive rights of Union citizenship found in Article 8
EC as amended by the Union Treaty differ little from Article 119 EC. Participation in a European civil society is to be secured. This, however, is to be achieved
through the medium of universal rights; rights which are ill-suited to the particular demands of European women.[27]

If such an analysis is accepted, it must be conceded that Union citizenship is
less favourable to women than to men. However, it should at the same time be
noted that certain women in Europe will be better placed to exercise their
rights of Union citizenship than others. Such a differentiated position arises by
virtue of divergences within the various concepts of citizenship found in the
Member States. Union citizenship has not replaced its national counterparts,
but instead operates in a manner subsidiary to them. Amongst these traditional
concepts, it is noteworthy that some do more than others to correct the general
lack of women's autonomy. On a practical level this fact determines that some
European women might already possess a generally greater degree of freedom
of choice and might thus have a greater capacity than others to migrate
throughout Europe. At the level of this study, however, it also provides the next
line of inquiry: might not certain of the solutions already mooted in relation to
the problem of women and conventional citizenship, be transferable to the
European Union?

---

[25] Ellis, "The Definition of Discrimination in European Community Sex Equality Law" 19 ELRev
(1994), 563–580.
[26] Meehan, *supra* n 16.
[27] But see McGlynn, in this volume, who calls for "women's rights" to be adopted in the law of the
European Union.

(iii) The institution of citizenship and women

As a precursor to the examination of whether citizenship of the European Union might not be made somewhat more "woman-friendly", the analysis now moves on to consider various feminist critiques of traditional citizenship, together with certain of the existing proposed solutions to the puzzle of how to reshape the institution of the citizen so that it includes women, as well as men, within society.

Importantly, however, an initial distinction is drawn between the historical failure of citizenship fully to integrate and empower women within their communities and more contemporary evaluations of the institution's deficiencies. Such an approach proves illuminating, underlining the claim that whilst in the past women were simply disadvantaged as they were denied full access to the benefits of citizenship, today their grievances are of a more intricate and fundamental nature. In short: it is no longer the isolated notion of citizenship which fails women. Instead, modern feminist thought argues that it is the liberal constitutionalist philosophy upon which that institution is based which lies at the heart of its inability fully to include women within contemporary society.

(a) The historical failure of citizenship

Citizenship finds its most powerful expression as a liberal constitutional concept with the rights of the citizen generally secured in higher legal texts. As such, it is naturally inextricably entwined with and reflective of the values of the liberal constitution within which it is embedded. The arming of the citizen with universal rights is a mere reflection of constitutionalism's general commitment to the recognition that all persons be equal and equally worthy of determining their own destinies. Only such persons might join together to create the sovereign liberal constitution. Equally, the dichotomy between the private individual and the public citizen mirrors the general constitutional distinction made between public and private spheres. Public life and democracy should be self-limiting.[28] The community should never be intrusive, but should leave the private individual sufficient private space to develop an individual persona.

Historically, the institution of the public and universal citizen, or rather the view held of it by men, was one which might indeed be criticised in isolation from the constitutional values from which it was derived. This arose quite simply, as paradoxically those values were not fully reflected by the institution of the citizen as it then applied to society.

The nineteenth Century refusal to extend the franchise to women was based on the argument that women were better suited to the private role of care rather than the public task of policy-making, as their inherently "irrational" nature

---

[28] Soltan, "What Is the New Constitutionalism?" in Elkin and Soltan, *A New Constitutionalism* (1993).

automatically disqualified them from participating in such a necessarily object-ive political debate.[29] Alternatively, the historical institution of the citizen did not extend supposedly "universal" political rights to women. Similarly in the case of contractual notions which claimed marriage to be a contract between equal contracting parties, under which women might nevertheless contract away their personal freedom to their husbands. Here the unbounded universalism of constitutional civil rights was again restricted: in an illogical construction it was deemed that women might simply sign away their inherent (and thus irrevocable) capacity to control their own destinies.[30]

In the contemporary world, however, such isolated deficiencies no longer obtain. Universalism is universal and has been extended to women as to men. Instead, as will be argued below, the problem now lies within that universalist constitutionalism itself: on the one hand, its neglect of, and inability to value, the particular demands made upon women in relation to their caring role; and on the other, its continued dedication to the public/private distinction and its abdication of any responsibility for the need to compensate for the imprison-ment of women within the family.

(b) The feminist critique and the institution of citizenship

The leading feminist critiques as they apply to the institution of citizenship have already been highlighted. In brief, their unifying theme is the simple conclusion that citizenship does not fully include women within society since private power structures and obligations deny such women the autonomous exercise of their rights of citizenship.

Beyond this, however, such critiques follow two major lines of attack. The first, represented in its most extreme form by Carol Pateman, argues that in confining itself to the creation of a public citizen, this institution effectively betrays women leaving them trapped in private male-dominated family struc-tures. In Pateman's analysis,[31] this failure is inevitable since the social contract establishing the structures of modern governance was itself built upon an earlier "sexual contract", under which women were subordinated to men. More moder-ate arguments, however, also accept the consequences of Pateman's thesis, if not her reasoning; recognising that the historical division of labour between men and women has left men with, at the very least, the financial power of decision within what is seen to remain an essentially natural social unit, that of the fam-ily.[32] In that institutions of citizenship do not intervene into what are deemed to be private marital and family structures, they have generally failed to redress this imbalance.

The second line of feminist reasoning concentrates its efforts upon the

---

[29] Vogel, "Is Citizenship Gender Specific" in Vogel and Moran, *The Frontiers of Citizenship* (1991) 58–85.
[30] *Ibid.*
[31] Pateman, *supra* n 5.
[32] Summaries of such positions most readably reported in Kymlicka (1990), *supra* n 4.

inadequacies of a public morality based upon justice, and a parallel attempt to infuse public debate with a morality of care. Such discussions can, and do, reach dizzying heights of complexity.[33] For the limited purposes of this study, however, they will be condensed into their simplest form as follows. Universal legal rights of citizenship find their most poignant philosophical reflection in the Rawlsian notion of "justice". This is an impersonal recognition of each and every person's equal moral capacity to choose between what is right and what is wrong, requiring that an objective framework of rules be established and applied in equal measure to all beings, regardless of their particular character-istics or social circumstances. This justice of morality perforce holds sway in a public sphere bounded by just rules.

This objective normative view of humanity, however, might nevertheless be fairly contrasted with a subjective reality, which sees individuals dependent for most of their lives upon the care of others. "All of us inevitably spend our lives evolving from an initial to a final stage of dependence. If we are fortunate enough to achieve power and relative independence along the way it is a tran-sient and passing glory."[34] In our dependence, we are of necessity selfish and amoral. The child demanding food from a parent cannot determine whether it is just to make such a demand. Similarly, and crucially, neither would the par-ent responding to such a demand *expect* it to be phrased in a moral or just man-ner: the personal or subjective characteristics of the child are taken into account, and a response is forthcoming regardless. Outside the public sphere of objective moral justice, a parallel subjective morality would appear to be in operation. A morality which dictates that individuals interact with one another, not on the basis of their being equally moral beings, but in the light of the simple fact that dependents may on occasions make selfish claims which must nevertheless be satisfied. Simplifying somewhat, this duty to fulfil subjective demands which is necessarily imposed upon the carer (in this case the parent), forms the core of what is then termed the "morality of care".

Given the vast numbers of dependents within society, and therefore the general preponderance of quite possibly selfish individual claims upon others, an imme-diate question thus arises as to why citizenship, via the universality of the rights it entails, is so obsessed with the morality of justice, and so wholly disregarding of that of care. If viewed from the perspective of women, who remain the primary carers in society, this failure to place an adequate value upon an alternate form of morality, becomes yet another cause for their exclusion from the universal community which citizenship claims to constitute. Simply stated, those who are primarily engaged in the "indulgence" of "amoral" demands have but little time or opportunity to take part in the supremely objective and just sphere of public interaction.

In conclusion, it is evident that the modern feminist critique as it applies to citizenship is censorious not merely of the isolated institution of citizenship, but

---

[33] Bubeck, *supra* n 6.
[34] Willard Gaynor, quoted in Kymlicka (1990), *supra* n 4 at 284.

also of the values of liberal constitutionalism which it embodies. Clearly, at the heart of the private/public critique of citizenship, lies a deep disillusionment with an institution which does not override the demand for self-limiting democracy and has failed to extend its levelling influence into a private sphere where women remain subordinate. Equally, the avowed disapproval of universal, rather than subjective, morality strikes at the very core of the liberal constitution.

The feminist critique has not, however, confined itself to identifying the inadequacies of the liberal citizen. Instead, much effort has also been invested in the attempt to create forms of citizenship better adapted to the distinct position of women.

(c) Feminist solutions to the problem of female inclusion

Within traditional national debates, possible blue-prints for a women-friendly citizenship, one designed to ensure that women might autonomously exercise their citizenship rights, run a full gambit from attempts to create a fully new citizen based upon the distinct personal characteristics of women, to more vague expressions of hope that the high profile of women within new social movements may herald the development of a novel and powerful form of political expression for women.[35]

This inquiry, however, will initially restrict itself to a brief presentation of two particular approaches to the problem of women, the family, caring and citizenship. The first, that of the Scandinavian model of the woman-friendly state, is chosen by virtue of its generally accepted status as the most successful European attempt fully to include women citizens in a national society.[36] Although it varies in detail from State to State,[37] this Scandinavian model generally seeks to create a "moral" form of citizenship, which pays a far greater degree of regard to the need of society as a whole to attend to the subjective requirements of its members.[38] The task of caring undertaken within the family, is accordingly designated a collective social responsibility, and thus one to be fostered by the State. On the one hand, this leads to an intervention of the public into the private sphere with the State seeking to encourage all members of society, male and female, to concern themselves with the development of caring policies. On the other hand, social rights of citizenship are extended to ensure that those engaged in the task of caring are supported financially, in much the same manner as are other economically disadvantaged classes.

Generally effective as such an approach may be, it is nevertheless the subject of a certain degree of criticism. The most readily grasped and predictable of such critiques is the argument that State formulation of policies for the daily course of family life is an unwelcome intrusion into one of the few private areas

---

[35] Vogel, *supra* n 29.
[36] Meehan and Sevenhuijsen, *supra* n 9.
[37] See Ryel, in this volume.
[38] Siim, "Welfare State, Gender Politics and Equality Policies" in Meehan and Sevenhuijsen, *Equality, Politics and Gender* (1991) 175–192.

remaining within a complex modern society. Added to this, however, is a partic-ular feminist critique which states that such intervention has done little to change the fact that women remain the primary care-givers within society, and that their dependency upon their partners is merely replaced with a depend-ency on the State.[39] Equally, in paying women for their role as carers the state has merely created a new role of "citizen-mother",[40] bearing a strange re-semblance to the "citizen-soldier" of traditional republican thought. In effect, women perform a public duty to gain inclusion within society: a sexual division of labour nevertheless continues to pertain; whilst men are soldiers, women are mothers.

It is perhaps in response to these difficulties that more recent inquiries into the dilemma of caring and citizenship have sought further modes of incorporating the morality of care into what remains essentially a universal institution. The second feminist-solution highlighted here is thus distinguished by its reference to new models of the active citizen,[41] or more particularly, the return to the notion that citizens are required to perform positive acts to foster and sustain the society in which they live.

Under this approach the focus is shifted away from rights of citizenship to the duties of the citizen. As a result, the problem of caring may be inverted: rather than concentrate on dependents' subjective rights to receive care, society might take a closer look at exactly who is providing care. Alternatively, this moral necessity to provide care might be translated into a "duty", imposed on each and every citizen, male and female, to undertake to care for those within the community who require it.[42]

(iv) A woman-friendly version of Union citizenship?

In the national setting, the recognition that women have yet to be fully included within society, and have failed to become sovereign members of their communities, has been accompanied by extensive and specific research into why the benefits of the institution of citizenship have not been fully registered by women. This brief resumé of solutions to this conundrum, likewise demon-strates that such efforts have furnished significant results. Accordingly, the ques-tion for this analysis now becomes one of whether the European Union may gain from such experience, include certain aspects of this debate within its own process of constitution-building, and thus seek itself to reconstruct the notion of Union citizenship in a woman-friendly form.

---

[39] *Ibid.*
[40] Meehan and Sevenhuijsen, *supra* n 9.
[41] Kymlicka and Norman, "Return of the Citizen: A Survey of Recent Work on Citizenship Theory" 104 *Ethics* (1994), 352–381.
[42] Bubeck, *supra* n 6.

As a note of caution, however, the analysis returns to the earlier assertion that Union citizenship at is present best thought of as being limited to the establishment of a right of participation in an emergent European civil society. The difficulties which the Union is now facing with regard to the construction of a revolutionary form of supranational government, are mirrored by the weak nature of Union citizenship. Just as it is unclear whether the true centre of governance within the Union lies in Brussels or the capitals of the Member States, it is uncertain just how a true form of sovereignty might be secured for the individual European. Union citizenship is not the comprehensive civil, social and political citizenship found at the Member State level.

The weakness of Union citizenship might then in turn be shown to dictate that neither the Scandinavian model of the woman-friendly state, nor the concept of a duty of care may at present be transferred to the Union level. Both these notions were developed with reference to national settings, where the existing framework of citizenship is strong. Accordingly, both are based upon the assumption that all the conventional rights of citizenship (civil, political and social) are available. Consequently, when an attempt is made to translate these solutions to a forum where there is no full citizenship package, it transpires that they be may less than optimal.

To begin first with the notion of the woman-friendly State; the distinguishing characteristic of the Scandinavian model of citizenship is its elevation of the need to care for dependents to a "moral" task to be borne by society as a whole. Consequently, the entire community is included within the process of determining how caring policies should be shaped, whilst the "State" undertakes to put those policies into action. Alternately, this model contains a vital political element: the community formulates caring policies for society in its guise as the polity. At the Union level, there is no polity. Those political rights of Union citizenship which do exist, are heavily circumscribed. In short, there is no effective European political forum in which individual Europeans might meet to debate policies of care for a caring European society.

Equally, the notion of a duty of care would appear inappropriate in the light of prevailing European conditions. Whilst Article 8(2) EC, as amended by the Treaty on European Union provides that Union citizens shall be subject to the "duties" imposed by that Treaty, significant doubts must nevertheless be raised as to the willingness of Europeans to accept the imposition of any European duties which might be regarded as onerous. In the national setting, the imposition of burdensome duties upon the individual is balanced by the benefits inherent to full civil, social and political citizenship. At the Union level no such package exists. Consequently, in the light of the weak nature of the benefits provided by Union citizenship, there remains a danger that individual Europeans will simply refuse to fulfil such European duties.

In brief conclusion: whilst on the national level much work has been undertaken to develop appropriate solutions to the perennial problem of women, caring, the family and citizenship, such blue-prints might not simply be transferred to the European Union. The frailty of Union citizenship today dictates that new methods needs be found to ensure that women, as well as men, might effectively exercise their rights of participation in a European civil society.

(v) A "new constitutionalism" and the enabling of the woman Union citizen

At the normative level, liberal constitutionalism claims to be a progressive force for good within society. Its just and inclusive structures are said to constitute ethical, democratic and self-perpetuating communities. Seen in this light, the failure of the liberal constitution fully to empower women in relation to contemporary life presents what must be seen as a moral challenge. If the structures of the liberal constitution itself are failing women, then it might be argued that modern constitutionalists are faced with nothing short of a moral imperative at last to design constitutional mechanisms which might aid in overcoming the problem of women and citizenship.

The difficulties facing constitutionalists are, however, readily apparent. As has been shown, contemporary feminist thought reserves its most stinging critiques for the two pivotal constitutional values of universalism and the strict distinction between private and public spheres. Equally, however, it is very hard to see how constitutionalism might ever withdraw from its support for such core principles.[43]

Accordingly, the challenge of integrating women into universal constitutional structures must be approached in an innovative spirit. New mechanisms must be found which do justice both to the specific demands of women and to the objective principles upon which the liberal constitution is based. In this regard, however, the study returns to the assertion that the Treaties of the European Communities and Union are a "constitution in the making" which furnishes a ready forum for constitutionalist experiments. Might not then the Treaties already contain structures which may be built upon in the spirit of a "new constitutionalism"? Are there mechanisms already available which might be developed to ensure that European women have full autonomous recourse to their right to participate in a European civil society?

This author would argue that the self-governing women's networks established under the European structural funds represent just such structures. To reach this conclusion, however, the analysis draws upon two separate strands in recent academic research: the first, the normative development of the concept of the "new" constitutionalism; the second, the empirical observation that women have played a conspicuous role in new "social movements", themselves identified as novel and revolutionary modes of political participation.[44]

The first theoretical body of thought itself draws on the growing discussion

---

[43] Thus, for example, if the purpose of universal rights is to recognise the ability of equal beings to determine their own destinies and so to join together to create a Constitution, then a withdrawal from universalism would be tantamount to destroying the founding act from which the liberal constitution draws its constituent power.

[44] Vogel, *supra* n 29.

centred on the concept of the "active" citizen.[45] In other words, a basic recognition that the functioning of a good society is as much dependent upon the personal quality of its citizens as the perfection of its institutions, has led to a refocussing of debate upon the need to support and *enable* the activities of such "good" citizens.[46] Consequently, in a movement which has been christened the "new constitutionalism",[47] theorists have begun to develop and design institutional structures which might help this active citizen to play a fuller part in the society in which he or she lives.

As intimated, the second such strand derives from the empirical observation that women appear to have found a powerful political voice within the new, and much vaunted, social movements.[48] In other words, it seems that women themselves possess a capacity for self-mobilisation, not previously taken into account within the discussion on women's citizenship.

Bringing these two very different debates together it might then be stated that women, in that they have already demonstrated their capacities for self-mobilisation, have similarly proven their ability to be "active" citizens. They are consequently fitting candidates for just that form of institutional support advocated by the new constitutionalism. More specifically, it might be suggested that given a suitable institutional framework, women may be capable of finding their own solutions to the dilemma of their subordinate position in society. If correctly harnessed, the collective creative energy of women may itself hold the key to the solution of the conundrum of women, the family, caring and citizenship.

Such a thesis may seem a little obscure in the abstract. With the aid of concrete examples it can nevertheless be shown to represent a tenable strategy by which the autonomy of women can be enhanced. Here, the connection to the problem of women and Union citizenship becomes apparent. Thus, as has been suggested, such new mechanisms may in fact already exist in an embryonic form at the European level.

Arguably, the attempts made under the umbrella of the European structural funds to improve the quality of European women's lives, embody just such "enabling institutions". Granted, such efforts have to date drawn more scorn than praise from European women. Criticism, however, has focused more upon the limited funds available than the structures established,[49] and has as a consequence somewhat underestimated the normative potential of such a framework.

To begin first with the fundamental purpose underlying the structural funds, in seeking to compensate for *existing* inequalities throughout Europe, the Funds undertake to engage in exactly that form of practical corrective action which traditional constitutionalism has declined to contemplate. If the Treaties of the European Community and the European Union, may be taken to be a "constitution in the making", then the structural funds may similarly be deemed to

---

[45] Kymlicka and Norman, *supra* n 41.
[46] Soltan, *supra* n 28.
[47] Elkin and Soltan, *supra* n 28.
[48] Siim, *supra* n 38.
[49] Meehan, *supra* n 16.

incorporate a constitutional commitment to the correction of "structural" inequalities. Just as social rights are employed to equalise the inequalities which perforce arise out of the structures of a market economy, so structural funds for women might similarly be argued to compensate for those inequalities which of necessity arise out of the framework of the family and of society's duty to care for its members. If identified as a "new" constitutionalist principle, such an approach would consequently herald a radical departure from conventional constitutionalism's abdication of any responsibility to correct the subordinate position of women.

More importantly, however, the specific nature of certain of the programmes funded under the European structural funds may similarly be argued to represent a radically new constitutionalist approach. This approach which through its attempts to *enable* rather than normatively constitute women, might be claimed to overcome the traditional problem of the constitution's refusal to enter into the private sphere, and its imperative commitment to universal rather than particular rights of citizenship.

Central to the funds' attempt to better the general conditions of women in Europe is the mechanism of "women's networks".[50] Financial support is accordingly forthcoming for associations of European women who join together across national frontiers to organise various initiatives such as woman-friendly economic enterprises and child-caring arrangements. At the practical level of the question of whether women might autonomously avail themselves of their rights of Union citizenship, the import of such programmes is at once apparent. Once again, economic activity and cultural interaction form the subject with which Europe is engaged. Financial incentives are offered to women to take part in the common sphere of a European civil society. More importantly, however, women themselves are left to determine just how they engage in this cultural and social interaction. Based on their own experience, they might create new economic and social structures which better reflect their family and caring obligations. Women are not simply financially compensated for their subordinate position within the family and thus made dependent upon governmental bodies rather than their partners. Instead, they are furnished with the means to reorganize their lifestyles so that they too might play a role in the nascent European civil society: they are thus "enabled".

Returning once again to the notion of new constitutionalism, it might accordingly be argued that were the support of such networks to be institutionalised, possibly by means of a "right" to support,[51] this would represent the creation of a new enabling institution of citizenship. The possible advantages of such a constitutional step are manifold. On the one hand, the concept of the active citizen underlying such an institution would overcome the problem of traditional constitutionalism's aversion to entering the private sphere. The public need not enter into the private to recreate family and caring relations. Instead, the active

---

[50] Ranzio-Plath, *Frauenförderung und die EU-Strukturfonds* (1994) 265–271.
[51] Though finance would be a problem.

women citizen might be drawn out of the private, and be left to determine her own preferred mode of interaction with society and the economy. On the other hand, only a very limited element of subjectivity need be infused into the universal institution of citizenship. Granted the right of women to institutional support would be a particular one, available only to women; the basic universality of the core social and political rights of citizenship need not, however, be altered.

(vi) Conclusion

The claim that a constitutionalisation of those women's networks established under the Structural Funds of the European Communities and the European Union might not only enable European women to exercise their rights of participation autonomously in a European civil society, but in addition might form the basis for a general liberal and "constitutionalist" solution to the conundrum of women, the family caring, and citizenship, is clearly an ambitious one. As such it will require a great deal of further consideration. It is neverthe-less asserted that should such a suggestion prove itself tenable, the benefits will have been worth the wait.

In the European setting, it is clear that the nascent European civil society will at some point be complemented by a "new" European polity. If, in the mean-time, women have been enabled to become full members of this European civil society, then they too will have a chance to determine the characteristics of that polity through European-wide discussion. Similarly, the experience gained from experiments with the new notion of the institutionalisation of the active European "civil" citizen may prove invaluable when the question of the constituting of the "active" European political citizen is eventually tackled.

At a general level, however, the inability of conventional liberal constitution-alism to address the specific situation of women must be seen to be a moral failure. To constitutionalists, inextricably committed to the creation of "good" societies, the task of developing a constitutionalist solution to the exclusion of women from society is quite simply an imperative.

MICHELLE EVERSON
Research Fellow,
Centre for European Legal Policy,
University of Bremen,
Germany

Chapter 14

CITIZENSHIP, GENDER AND DEPENDENCY IN THE EUROPEAN UNION: WOMEN AND INTERNAL MIGRATION*

(i) Introduction

This chapter considers the impact of the EU on the citizenship experience of European migrant women (that is, EU nationals moving within the Community), both because they constitute an important group in their own right and also because they provide a litmus test for the future development of citizenship in social Europe. It is in its capacity as guardian of the rights of internal migrants that the EU behaves most like a modern welfare state. Once a national of an EU Member State leaves his or her country of nationality to reside in another Member State, the European Union assumes important social responsibilities shaping their experience of citizenship. This chapter focuses on the development of social rights under the free movement provisions drawing on the case law of the European Court of Justice to demonstrate how the male breadwinner model of "normal" family relations permeates the Court's understanding of internal migration, thus reproducing and reinforcing gendered patterns of dependency. It presents evidence from the most recent Community Labour Force Survey[1] which demonstrates the presence of women in migration flows and calls into question assumptions about the characteristics of women migrants. These findings represent part of a larger comparative research project involving qualitative interviews with EU migrant women in five Member States funded jointly by the European Commission and the University of Plymouth.

(ii) Citizenship and welfare

For many the concept of citizenship is essentially concerned with formal political rights. The exercise of such rights does not operate in a vacuum, however,

* This chapter was written by Louise Ackers. It is a modified version of a paper published in *Social Politics: International Studies in Gender, State and Society* (1996).
[1] Community Labour Force Survey, Eurostat, 1992.

and is clearly linked to broader aspects of social and economic inequality which may render formal political equality meaningless. As Meehan states, "social, civil and political rights must form an indivisible triad for universal citizenship to be a reality".[2]

The discussion here is concerned primarily with the evolution of what Marshall[3] termed "social citizenship"[4] which developed as an alternative system of social distribution to that based on social class. This development of social citizenship rights was to Marshall a mark of civilised society, cushioning citizens from the vagaries of the market. Access to key resources such as education, health and basic social protection should no longer be dependent solely on income and wealth but accrue, equally, to all members of society. The problem of defining membership (who has citizenship status?) has dominated discussion about citizenship and free movement at EU level fuelled by concerns about social dumping, welfare tourism and xenophobia. Preoccupation with the nationality issue has, however, tended to reinforce the presumption of a duality of entitlement based on ownership of EU nationality creating the impression of a broad equality amongst those defined as EU citizens. In practice, however, social entitlement does not derive from simple membership of the Union but from more complex notions of social contribution. In this sense, as we shall see, all citizens are not equal.

A number of attempts have been made in recent years to develop an appropriate methodology for the comparative analysis of welfare systems.[5] Most notably the work of Esping-Anderson sought to identify a typology of welfare regimes according to the impact of systems of social entitlement on labour market dependency. This process of insulation from labour market dependency he termed "decommodification" and occurs "when a service is rendered as a matter of right, and when a person can maintain a livelihood without reliance on the market".[6] Despite acknowledgment of the usefulness of the welfare regime approach in highlighting some important issues about the position of women in the labour market, it has been widely criticised on the grounds that it fails adequately to account for the role of the family and the position of women in relation to social welfare.[7] The question of key concern here is whether this method of categorisation, and particularly its focus on only one aspect of public dependency, adequately reflects the gendered nature of welfare regimes. As Pascall notes: "While Marshall asserts the rights of citizenship, nowhere does he

---

[2] Meehan, *Citizenship and the European Community* (1993) 101.
[3] Marshall, *Class, Citizenship and Social Development* (1973 reprint [original 1964]).
[4] See Everson, in this volume.
[5] Esping-Anderson, *The Three Worlds of Welfare Capitalism* (1990); Cochrane and Clarke, *Comparing Welfare States* (1993); Dominelli, *Women Across Continents: feminist comparative social policy* (1991); Lewis, "Gender and the Development of Welfare Regimes" 2 *Journal of European Social Policy* (1992), 159–173; Taylor-Gooby, "Welfare State Regimes and Citizenship" 1 *Journal of European Social Policy* (1991); Langan and Ostner, "Gender and Welfare. Towards a Comparative Perspective" in Room, *Towards a European Welfare State* (1991).
[6] See Esping-Anderson, *supra* n 5 at 22.
[7] See Everson, in this volume.

analyse the problematic relationship between citizenship and dependency in the family as he does between citizenship and social class".[8]

It is important to remember here that many women gain social entitlement not via their labour market status but by virtue of their relationship with a male breadwinner partner. O'Connor is also critical of the concept of decommodification as a measure of dependency and proposes instead the comparison of welfare regimes according to their impact on personal autonomy, which she defines as "insulation from involuntary personal and/or public dependence (by the family and the state)".[9] This does not imply the absence of interdependence where this is based on choice, equality and reciprocity. Involuntary interdependence, on the other hand, implies unequal power relations and the absence of choice: "full interdependence is possible only when involuntary economic dependence is absent".[10] This broader concept of personal autonomy thus enables us to assess the impact of welfare systems on three inter-related aspects of dependency; on the labour market, on male breadwinners and on the State. A reduction in levels of dependency in any one of these areas may not imply increased personal autonomy but simply a "transfer" of dependency from "public" labour market dependency to "personal" dependency on a male breadwinner.

In a similar vein, Lewis argues that recent comparative work, "misses one of the central issues in the structuring of welfare regimes: the problem of valuing the unpaid work that is done primarily by women in providing welfare, mainly within the family, and in securing those providers social entitlements".[11] On the basis of this analysis she develops an alternative framework stressing the broad commonality of women's experience and the dominance of the male breadwinner family model which cuts across established typologies of welfare regimes. Although the strength of this model varies depending upon the extent and nature of social entitlement, Lewis emphasises its persistence and universal impact:

> Modern welfare regimes have all subscribed to some degree to the idea of a male breadwinner model – the strength or weakness of [that] model serves as an indicator of the way in which women have been treated in social security systems, of the level of social service provision particularly in regard to childcare; and of the nature of married women's position in the labour market.[12]

The work on welfare regimes and citizenship has sought to determine how national welfare systems shape the citizenship experience. Whilst much of this work takes a European focus, it has often failed to consider the role of the EU both as a source of citizenship entitlement in its own right and also in terms of

---

[8] Pascall, *Social Policy: A Feminist Analysis* (1986) 6.

[9] O'Connor, "Gender Class and Citizenship in the comparative Analysis of Welfare States: Theoretical and Methodological Issues" 44 *The British Journal of Sociology* (1993), 501–519 at 511.

[10] Lister, "Women, Economic Dependency and Citizenship" 19 *Journal of Social Policy* (1990), 445–469 at 446.

[11] Lewis, "Gender and the Development of Welfare Regimes", 2 *Journal of European Social Policy* (1992), 159–173 at 161.

[12] Lewis, *supra* n 11 at 162.

its wider impact on domestic welfare systems.[13] The purpose of this chapter is to test the relevance of the male breadwinning family model to an understanding of the development and impact of EU citizenship.

(iii) Citizenship of the Union

It might be argued that limited legal competency in the social field has largely restricted the role of the EU to one of safeguarding the interests of paid workers.[14] This is certainly true of most areas of EU social policy. Whilst the European Commission has long recognised the impossibility of achieving genuine progress in the equal opportunities field in the absence of measures to reconcile family and working life, its activities have been largely restricted to persuasive soft law measures aimed at encouraging policy convergence in areas like childcare and parental leave. Issues of family policy, it seems, fall within the exclusive preserve of Member States[15] and equal opportunities becomes little more than a form of labour market regulation aimed primarily at the pursuit of procedural equality in the workplace. This approach is best exemplified by the judgment of the ECJ in a case[16] involving a father's claim for maternity leave under the Equal Treatment Directive.[17] The Court found that it was not in contravention of the Directive to restrict such leave to women on the grounds that "the Directive is not designed to settle questions concerned with the organisation of the family, or to alter the division of responsibility between parents".[18] As far as the equal opportunities laws are concerned, it seems that the impact of the EU is largely restricted to the regulation of public dependency and the protection of paid workers.[19]

Whilst feminist concern has focused on developments in social rights arising from the equal opportunities legislation, developments have been taking place in other areas of EU law, with more profound implications for citizenship and social rights. The ECJ has interpreted the free movement provisions broadly, thus elevating the principle of free movement of persons into one of the fundamental rights of Community law.[20] Indeed, the extension of a framework of social rights under these provisions has been said to mark a trend towards the

---

[13] With the notable exception of Leibfried's work on poverty regimes; Leibfried, "Towards an European Welfare State? On integrating poverty regimes into the European Community" in Ferge and Eivind Kolberg, *Social Policy in a Changing Europe* (1992) 245–279.

[14] See McGlynn, in this volume.

[15] See O'Leary, in this volume.

[16] Case 184/83 *Hofmann* v *Barmer Ersatzkasse* [1984] ECR 3047.

[17] Council Directive 76/207 (OJ 1976 L39/40).

[18] See *Hofmann* v *Barmer Ersatzkasse, supra* n 16 para 25.

[19] See McGlynn, and Hervey, in this volume.

[20] Nielsen and Szyszczak, *The Social Dimension of the European Community* (1994); Ackers, "Women, Citizenship and European Community Law: The Gender Implications of the Free Movement Provisions 4 *Journal of Social Welfare and Family Law* (1994), 391–406; Scheiwe, "EC Law's Unequal Treatment of the Family: The Case Law of the European Court of Justice on Rules Prohibiting Discrimination on Grounds of Sex and Nationality" 3 *Social and Legal Studies* (1994), 243–265.

realisation of an overall European citizenship.[21] Here the principles of subsidiarity restricting EU incursion into areas of social assistance and family policy have been waived as a more holistic approach to citizenship developed. The evolution of citizenship rights under the free movement provisions thus provides a basis for comparing EU citizenship with that in Member States. In this sense it serves as an indicator of how "Social Europe" might develop in the future. The remainder of this chapter considers the nature of social entitlement which has evolved under these provisions and the extent to which they both presume and reinforce traditional models of family structure and migration behaviour. It then seeks to test these models against recent empirical evidence on internal migration.

The first point to make is that the status of "Citizenship of the Union" does not imply uniform access to social rights. Wilkinson reminds us that the original purpose of the free movement provisions, "was not to establish free movement and residence rights for all citizens of the Community, rather it was to establish free movement for workers as one of the factors of production. Consequently, from the outset any incipient form of European citizenship was only to be enjoyed by those who would contribute economically through their labour in the economy of the host Member State".[22]

In practice, a hierarchy of citizenship rights has developed based on notions of social contribution and family relationships resulting in a tiered system of entitlement. At the apex of the hierarchy are those citizens with full and independent entitlement (paid workers), followed by those citizens with derived entitlement via marriage,[23] and finally by those with effectively no social rights. Whilst the general right of residence applies to all EU nationals, this does not give rise to any other social rights and is circumscribed by the requirement that the persons concerned have "sufficient resources to avoid becoming a burden on the social assistance system of the host Member State".[24] The EU migrant worker, in contrast, "stands in a uniquely favourable position in claiming a wide panoply of social rights available under national law".[25] These rights for migrant workers derive largely from Regulation (EEC) 1612/68[26] and include the right to equal treatment in matters of employment, vocational training and conditions of work. Article 7(2) entitles the Community migrant worker and "his" family to the same "social and tax advantages as national workers", including forms of social assistance.[27] Community competence in relation to migrant workers thus extends beyond the rights associated with employment contracts to encapsulate all aspects of social entitlement from social security to educational grants, public housing and discretionary bus passes. Furthermore, entitlement

[21] Nielsen and Szyszczak, *supra* n 20 at 55.
[22] Wilkinson, "Towards European Citizenship? Nationality, Discrimination and Free Movement of Workers in the European Union" *European Public Law* (1995), at 2.
[23] See O'Leary, in this volume.
[24] Council Directive 90/364/EEC (OJ 1990 L 180/26).
[25] Weatherill and Beaumont, *EC Law* (1993) 484.
[26] Council Regulation 1612/68/EEC (OJ 1968 L 257/2).
[27] Ackers (1994), *supra* n 20.

to such social rights extends to both the worker and "his" family. Indeed, the concept of family is broad enough here to include family members from outside the EU.

Of particular concern here is the interpretation by the ECJ of the concept of family and worker under Community law (neither of which are adequately defined in the Treaty). The Court has held that the concept of "worker" must have a Community meaning in order to ensure even application and to protect this fundamental freedom. It has therefore interpreted the provisions broadly to include part-time workers and those on very low incomes (below subsistence level).

It has, however, held that the work performed must fulfil or derive from some economic purpose. Thus, paid activity as part of a drug rehabilitation scheme under Dutch social employment law did not represent "real and genuine economic activity".[28] The Court's ruling in this case suggests that areas of voluntary work and informal care would not be construed as having any economic purpose and would not therefore give rise to entitlement under these provisions.

The concept of worker has been extended by the Court to include the right to enter in search of work but this group of citizens are not entitled to full residency and social rights.

Article 7(1) of Directive 68/360/EEC[29] also restricts the entitlement of those citizens who are construed as being "voluntarily" unemployed.[30] It may not be unlawful, for example, for a Member State to deport people who have not found work after a six month period. One of the migrant women interviewed in Ireland during the pilot phase of the research informed us that she had been told by the Irish police to leave the country because she had no job: "I was told that if I didn't have a job within two weeks I was out as my three months were already over. It was not that I had to stop signing, it was that I had to go". Other interviews suggest considerable variation in the interpretation of these rules both within Member States and between them.

This restriction on entitlement raises two important concerns for migrant women; first, because the rights of non-working spouses are derived, where a male breadwinner loses his access to social rights as a result of "voluntary" unemployment, his spouse and family also lose theirs. The second concern is whether interruptions in a woman's employment, as a result of family responsibilities (or migration), may be interpreted as "voluntary" unemployment resulting in reduced social entitlement. Women who thus fail any "availability for work" test on the grounds of caring responsibilities may be denied access to important social rights. In the United Kingdom and Ireland at least, unemployed mothers may be refused unemployment benefit if they "look after children and are not available to start work or attend an interview at a moment's notice".[31]

---

[28] Case 344/87 *Bettray* v *Staatsecretaris van Justitie* [1989] ECR 1621.
[29] Council Directive 68/360/EEC (OJ 1968 L 257/13).
[30] Case 2826 *Giangregorio* v *Secretary of State for the Home Department* [1983] 3 CMLR 472 (Immigration Appeals Tribunal).
[31] Poynter and Martin, "Rights Guide to non-means tested benefits", Child Poverty Action Group, 18th edition (1995), 17.

It will be recalled that members of a worker's family are also entitled to derived social rights. Of particular concern here has been the Court's interpretation of "spouse" and the position of co-habitants and divorcees. The Court has ruled that the term "spouse" in Article 10, Regulation (EEC) 1612/68[32] refers to legally married partners only.[33] Cohabiting partners are thereby excluded. The impact of separation was referred to the Court of Justice in *Diatta* v *Land Berlin*.[34] The Court held that there was no requirement to cohabit and that marriage subsisted until divorce so Ms Diatta retained her family rights. The effect of divorce on spousal rights was left open in this case and has not been subject to an ECJ ruling. However, the issue of divorce was raised in the English High Court in a case involving a non-Community spouse.[35] The judge in this case described the issues as follows:

Can an EEC national admitted to this country as such together with her non-EEC husband deprive him of EEC protection by, for example, deserting him, separating from him, by going to live elsewhere in this country, by going back to her native State or by going somewhere else abroad? If she can automatically and over any interval of time do that, it would . . . add a new terror to marriage.

The Court of Appeal, however, took a different view on the grounds that the worker's right to be joined by his family did not imply, "the family's right to join the worker".[36] Family rights were coterminous with the residency of the worker and subsist only as long as the working spouse is themselves exercising them.

The problem in relation to spousal rights is clearly most acute where the spouse is a non-Community national as in *Sandhu* and *Diatta*. A spouse who is a "Citizen of the Union" may derive an independent right of residence under Directive 90/364/EEC.[37] Whilst protecting such a spouse from the risk of expulsion, however, this new Directive does not provide for access to the panoply of social rights available to migrant workers and their spouses. More recently the question of entitlement of homosexual couples has been raised, throwing traditional concepts of the family into further disarray.[38]

This expansion of the rights of migrant workers beyond strictly economic activities, and to some "non-working" citizens has been explained by the ECJ's "generous and teleological mode of interpreting law"[39] and the Court's assumption of a close relationship between labour mobility and the family as a potential obstacle to free movement. The rationale behind this incursion of Community competence into the "social field" stems from its perceived relationship with economic policy. Whilst the recognition that the extension of family rights is a

---

[32] Council Regulation 1612/68/EEC (OJ 1968 L 257/2).
[33] Case 59/85 *Netherlands State* v *Reed* [1986] ECR 1283. See O'Leary, in this volume.
[34] Case 267/83 [1985] ECR 567.
[35] *R* v *Secretary of State for the Home Department (ex parte Amarjit Singh Sandhu)* [1982] 2 CMLR 553.
[36] [1983] Imm AR 61.
[37] Council Directive 90/364/EEC (OJ 1990 L 180/26).
[38] Waaldijk and Clapham, *Homosexuality: A European Community Issue* (1993).
[39] Scheiwe (1994), *supra* n 20 at 252.

necessary pre-condition for the completion of the Internal Market is to be welcomed, the concept of family underpinning this aspect of Community law is,
however, open to question.

The legislation refers to the migrant worker and "his" family suggesting a
male breadwinning model and the ECJ has made it clear that these measures
are less concerned with the rights of family members *per se* but exist to "assist his
[the worker's] integration in the host State and thus to contribute to the
achievement of the freedom of movement of workers".[40] Based upon a narrow
conception of the family, the free movement provisions presume traditional
patterns of gender relations and inter-dependency and fail to recognise the
structural barriers facing women both as independent migrants and as the partners of migrant men. Scheiwe sets out the gender implications as follows:

> Provisions on the free movement of workers allow interventions into the family
> sphere and related areas of law, despite their market connections being rather indi-
> rect, in order to guarantee the stabilising function of the existing gendered division
> of labour and to augment the male migrant's mobility. In this model, a (male)
> worker's family is clearly a market-related issue that matters. The woman is dealt
> with only as a subordinated part of the family unit not as a "head of household" or
> an individual of equal importance. This is also shown by the wide lack of special pro-
> visions or structural policies that could augment female workers' mobility through
> the improvement of childcare facilities or other infrastructures which would reduce
> obstacles to the free movement of the female workforce.[41]

The male breadwinning family model has thus permeated not only the domestic
social policy of Member States but is also enshrined in analyses of migration.
Notions of family structure and the apportionment of roles within families
translate into a convenient model of migration behaviour. Thus, the male
breadwinner family model takes on a spatial and temporal dimension. Such
models of migration typically interpret migration as the exercise of economic-
maximising behaviour with an initial phase of male "pioneer" migration followed by a phase of family reunion. Women are either rendered invisible by this
analysis or subsumed within the broader migrant family. The extension of social
rights under the free movement provisions, generous as they are, is founded
upon an ideologically-loaded conceptualisation of the family, and of migration
behaviour which both presumes and reinforces high levels of dependency
within families and ignores the barriers to labour mobility facing women
migrants. It is for this reason that Steiner refers to spousal rights as "parasitic".[42]

(iv) Women in internal migration

There is little evidence to assess the impact of this area of Community law on
migrant women. Scheiwe argues that the concern of Community law is essentially with members of male workers' families, "since migrant workers are pre-

---

[40] Case 59/85 *Netherlands State* v *Reed* [1986] ECR 1283.
[41] Scheiwe (1994), *supra* n 20 at 251.
[42] Steiner, *Textbook on EC Law* (1994).

dominantly male".[43] This view of migration is certainly echoed in the migration literature. Castles and Miller, for example, have recently identified the "feminisation of migration" as an important new feature in international population movement; "in the past most labour migrations were male-dominated, and women were often dealt with under the category of family reunion".[44] It is not the absence of women, however, but their invisibility in the research that is at issue here; and the increased awareness brought about by feminist researchers in this field. As Silvia Pedraza notes in her study of the role of women in Dominican settlement in the United States:

> Despite the overwhelming presence of women in migration flows (internationally), until recently the role of women in migration has been totally neglected . . . we have yet to develop a truly gendered understanding of the causes, processes, and consequences of migration. Paying attention to the relationship between women's social position and migration will help to fill the void regarding our knowledge of women as immigrants and contribute to a greater understanding of the lives of women.[45]

The tendency to obscure the gender dimension of migration flows has dominated migration research both internationally and at European level. Paula Jackson's study of Irish migrant women notes the manner in which the position of women in migration is concealed within this dominant paradigm: "The volume of literature on Irish migration or emigration is prolific, yet with rare exceptions, one is left with the overwhelming impression that Irish emigration has been a purely male phenomenon".[46]

The following section assesses the validity of the male breadwinning model of migration behaviour in the context of internal migration.

The most recent Eurostat data explode the myth that migration is exclusively male and that, where females do migrate, their primary purpose is to join male breadwinning partners. Whilst just below 50% of all EU migrants are women (48%) this figure masks considerable variation between Member States (see Figure 1).

In terms of the "export" of migrants, five countries export a greater proportion of females than males whilst five countries import a greater proportion of women. This comparison is interesting and raises important questions; of particular interest is the situation in the three Mediterranean countries and the United Kingdom, all of which export more males but import a greater proportion of women. Belgium, Denmark, France and Germany, on the other hand, export a greater proportion of women and receive a higher proportion of men. Closer analysis of the nationality of female migrants in particular countries shows even greater differences. EU migration into the United Kingdom, for example, is dominated by females (see Figure 2). Similar patterns can be seen in Italy, where 57% of EU migrants are female (see Figure 3). In many Member States women also dominate emigration. This is particularly the case in Ireland and Denmark (see Figure 4).

---

[43] Scheiwe (1994), *supra* n 20 at 249.
[44] Castles and Miller, *The Age of Migration* (1993) 8.
[45] Pedraza, "Women and migration: The Social Consequences of Gender" 17 *Annual Review of Sociology* (1991), 303–25 at 303.
[46] Jackson, *Migrant Women: The Republic of Ireland, Commission of Europe*, DGV, V/139/89 (1987), 5.

Figure 1. Women as a proportion of out-going and in-coming EU migrants, by nationality, 1992

	Out-Going	In-Coming
DK	58	41
F	54	47
D	53	44
B	52	46
IRL	52	52
E	48	53
UK	47	52
P	47	47
NL	47	44
GR	44	56
L	43	49
I	41	55

Source: Community Labour Force Survey, 1992

Figure 2. The proportion of female EU migrants in the UK by nationality, 1992

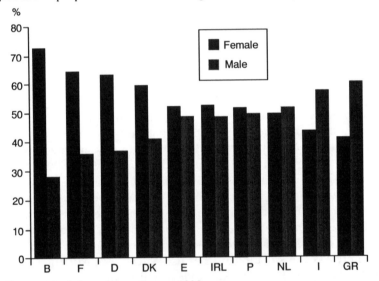

Source: Community Labour Force Survey, 1992

(v) The characteristics of European Union migrants

Data from the Community Labour Force Survey 1992 show no substantial differences between male and female migrants giving no indication that female
migration is a more recent phenomenon reflecting subsequent family reunion.
In terms of marital status, less than half of EU migrant women are married and
over a third are single, although in some countries the proportion of single
women reaches 52% (Portugal). Whilst overall, some 4% of EU migrant women

Figure 3. The proportion of female EU migrants in italy by nationality, 1992

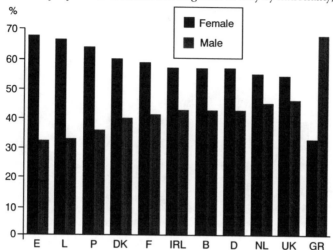

Source: Community Labour Force Survey, 1992

Figure 4. Females as a proportion of Danish citizens residing in another EU country, 1992.

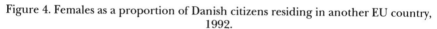

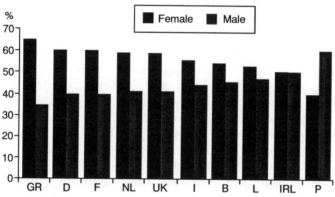

Source: Community Labour Force Survey, 1992

are legally separated/divorced (an equivalent figure to that for national women), this average masks a high of 9% for migrant women in the Netherlands and 7% in Denmark. Indeed, migrant women in the Netherlands experience twice the level of legal separation to that of Dutch nationals. The divorce/separation rate in the United Kingdom is also increased from 5% for nationals to 7% for migrants. Analyses of European migration based upon traditional family models are thus likely to be increasingly out of step with contemporary reality (as Ms Reed argued in *Netherlands State* v *Reed*).[47]

---

[47] Case 59/85 *Netherlands State* v *Reed* [1986] ECR 1283.

Figure 5. The activity rates of national and migrant women with children under 5 years of age, by nationality.

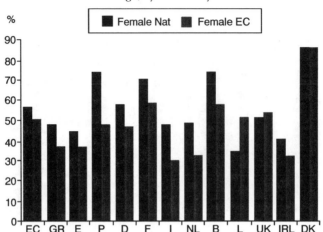

Source: Community Labour Force Survey, 1992

Labour market activity rates for migrants are generally higher than those for nationals for both sexes although female activity rates are considerably lower than those for men. Over 50% of migrant women are economically active, compared to 44% of female nationals. Whilst male activity rates remain at around 95% for all males aged 25–49, irrespective of the presence or number of children, female activity rates diminish in inverse relation to the number of children. This pattern is similar to that found in a recent Eurostat Report on women in the European Community.[48]

Both the number and presence of young children affects women's relationship with paid work. The presence of young children under the age of five has the most marked impact on the labour market activity of migrant women. This is felt particularly in the population of migrant women where, in all countries apart from Luxembourg and the United Kingdom, migrant women with children under five are less active than their national counterparts.

The relationship of mothers with very young children to paid work is not simple and reflects variations in cultural attitudes, occupational status, the existence of parental and maternity leave provisions, the availability and cost of childcare and the availability of part-time work. Migrant women are less likely to be able to depend upon unpaid informal or family care for their children due to dislocation of extended family structures and may therefore rely more heavily upon statutory provision and the private sector. As a result, in some countries almost 70% of EU migrant women with young children are not engaged in paid work.

The presence and number of children also has considerable impact on the

---

[48] Eurostat, *Women in the European Community* (1992).

Figure 6. The impact of children on female working hours, by broad nationality.

	No Child		1 Child		2 Children		3 or more children	
	National	EU	National	EU	National	EU	National	EU
1hr–15	8%	11%	9%	12%	14%	18%	21%	29%
16–25	14%	13%	19%	24%	23%	24%	24%	22%
26–35	12%	10%	13%	11%	14%	11%	14%	14%
36–45	56%	57%	52%	46%	43%	40%	33%	26%
46+	9%	9%	7%	7%	6%	8%	8%	9%

Source: Community Labour Force Survey, 1992

number of hours worked by women. Women with children are much more likely than men to be involved in part-time work, affecting women's financial autonomy and entitlement to contributory benefits. The pattern for female EU migrants replicates that of female nationals but is more marked with a greater proportion of migrant women engaged in "short" part-time work.

The higher activity rates of EU nationals exist alongside higher unemployment rates for this group. Female migrants were considerably more likely to have experienced problems in finding work (some 15% of those working part-time said they were doing so because they could not find full-time work). This is supported by other studies suggesting that female EU migrants suffer the highest rates of unemployment. This is particularly true in Belgium, Ireland and The Netherlands.[49]

(vi) Conclusion

Contrary to popular belief, and academic literature, women make up around half of all EU migrants. In many cases women actually dominate European migration flows. Of particular interest here is the destination of many migrant women. Women dominate both out-migration from countries typically regarded as "woman-friendly" with more progressive family policies and migration into the most woman-hostile countries.[50] The data do not support the theory that female migration is characterised by subsequent family reunion; the length of residence of male and female migrants being broadly coterminous. The data on marital status furthermore suggest that the majority of migrant women are not married; over a third are single, although the figure is much greater in some Member States. Research by Pauline Jackson in Ireland found that, in the 1961–71 period, 87% of Irish women emigrants were unmarried and a further 8% were widows: "Thus a full 95% of women emigrants left Ireland

[49] Guarini, Di Palma and Pennisi, "The Role of Non-Nationals on the EC Labour Market" (1994), Unpublished Report, Eurostat, 53.
[50] Cochrane and Clarke (1993), *supra* n 5; Lewis (1992), *supra* n 5; Langan and Ostner (1991), *supra* n 5.

without male protection".[51] Divorce is also increasingly significant, affecting some 4% of all migrant women and up to 9% in some Member States. Lichter's study of socio-economic returns to migration among married women found that, whilst "most married women do not receive positive returns to migration . . . migration-induced dependency may have serious adverse effects on the socio-economic well-being of women should they become separated or divorced".[52]

Migrant women experience generally lower levels of fertility (unlike third country migrants) despite their demographic structure. They are more actively involved in the labour market but when they do have children, this activity is considerably depressed resulting in reduced overall activity and higher levels of part-time and "short" part-time working. High levels of labour market activity exist alongside the highest levels of unemployment and job search.

These figures paint a very different picture of migration and suggest that while migrant women display a generally positive disposition towards the labour market, many of them are at risk from high levels of personal dependency. Their relationship with the labour market, like many national women, is fragile and the impact of caring responsibilities, particularly for mothers of young children, poses a particular threat to their autonomy. This is less the case in Denmark and France where state-provided child care is more readily available but very pronounced in the United Kingdom and Ireland, where it is not. Migrant women are less able to rely upon informal sources of support (particularly their own mothers) and are thus more likely to experience interrupted working patterns. The interviews have also shown that many women have (or expect to have) caring responsibilities for elderly dependents in their country of origin which, once again, condition their relationship with paid work. Higher levels of unemployment and short part-time working leave women with male breadwinning partners in a highly dependent position. This is of particular concern when their unemployment is construed as "voluntary" by the competent employment office. Unemployed single women, on the other hand, are at risk of losing their EU rights altogether if they have been unemployed for over six months.

Recent work by Bonney and Love on the impact of migration on wives "confirms one of [Janet Finch's] basic ideas – that marriage transforms women from independent persons to secondary or ancillary supporters of male partners in their primary occupational roles". This research was concerned primarily with inter-regional mobility (within the United Kingdom) and focused on the process of household decision-making in relation to migration and its impact on the autonomy of migrant wives.[53] If these conclusions hold for inter-regional migration, then married women moving between Member States are likely to be particularly disadvantaged as systems of social entitlement at EU level are

---

[51] Jackson, *supra* n 46 at 8.
[52] Lichter, "Socioeconomic Returns to Migration among Married Women" 62 *Social Forces* (1983), 487–503 at 500.
[53] Bonney and Love, "Gender and Migration: Geographical Mobility and the Wife's Sacrifice" 39 *Sociological Review* (1991), 335–348; Finch, *Married to the Job* (1983).

so tightly linked to employment status and marriage and informal support networks are fractured by the migration process.

Bonney and Love further speculate that the impact of inter-regional migration on women may be less serious than expected as wives often play a "secondary labour market role" (prior to migration) and some occupations (such as teaching), "positively facilitate discontinuous careers".[54] In a European context, however, this argument does not hold as these careers, particularly teaching, may prove especially difficult for migrant women to enter. Indeed the case law of the ECJ has held that the requirement of specific linguistic competencies may not contravene the non-discrimination principle.[55] The problem of recognition of teaching qualifications has arisen in many of the interviews conducted, preventing women from resuming teaching careers in the country of immigration and also, in some cases where the woman has trained in the host country, from returning to their home State.

What becomes clear from the above is that both EC law and academic migration studies are out of step with the contemporary reality of internal migration. Models of migration based upon male breadwinner, utility-maximising behaviour render migrant women invisible. Even those studies which attempt to examine the "problematic connection" between individual action and the household, subsume women within the broader family, failing to see them as individual actors in their own right.[56]

Thus, concludes Lichter, "migration would appear to be rational from the standpoint of the family as a whole . . . [furthermore] . . . many married women may willingly sacrifice their careers provided that migration improves the economic well-being of the family".[57] On the face of it, writes Lister, "the language of citizenship appears to be gender neutral"[58] – and so too is the language of migration.

Taylor-Gooby exposes the gendered nature of this apparent rationality in his work on welfare regimes and citizenship arguing that it is "inequalities in wages and in employment prospects [that] make it a rational household strategy for men to devote more energy to waged work".[59] The decision of a household to migrate may appear to be "rational" in any narrow cost-benefit analysis of aggregate family income, but at the cost of increased levels of dependency and loss of personal autonomy for female partners. Indicative findings from my own South West sample of interviews suggest that, ironically, the superior language skills of the female partner (I have found very few male migrants married to British women in this sample) appear to underline the justification of the male breadwinning strategy. In other words, it makes rational sense to locate in the country of his nationality as his lack of linguistic competency would adversely affect his career in another Member State.

---

[54] Bonney and Love, *supra* n 53 at 339.
[55] Case 379/87 *Groener v Minister for Education* [1989] ECR 3967.
[56] Bonney and Love, *supra* n 53.
[57] Lichter, *supra* n 52 at 600.
[58] Lister, *supra* n 10 at 446.
[59] Taylor-Gooby, *supra* n 5 at 101.

What this data also tell us is that many women do not migrate as partners but do so of their own volition as single women. Even here, however, the utility-maximising models of migration which apparently explain male migration so effectively, are inappropriate for examining the migration motivations of women. Pauline Jackson's study of Irish migrant women found "sex differences" in the reasons given for migration with 65% of young women giving non-economic reasons ("depressed with Ireland" or "family and personal problems – including pregnancy"). Sixty per cent of males, on the other hand cited financial and employment-related reasons.[60] This issue has also been raised in interviews with migrant women in the United Kingdom. An Italian woman, for example, said that she left Italy, "to escape from an oppressive and sexist society". Pre-liminary results from the interviews, however, suggest that, although single women form an important component of migration (over 90% of the South West sample migrated as single women), their subsequent marriage and associ-ated inter-regional migration also has a major impact on the careers of these women.

Any understanding of the citizenship experience of women in Europe re-quires an analysis of the impact of a complex web of inter-related dependencies. Women under different social systems effectively "spread" their dependency between male partners, the welfare state, female members of the wider family and the labour market (depending on the welfare system and cultural and eco-nomic climate). For migrant women the "choices" are more stark: reliance on informal support by other women (particularly mothers and sisters) is reduced through the dislocation of extended family networks. The achievement of financial independence (and independent entitlement to many occupational-based welfare benefits) is also threatened by the fragility of migrant women's relationship with the labour market, particularly during child-rearing years. Dis-continuous employment and higher levels of short part-time work, coupled with problems of unemployment, seriously undermine the value of occupational-based benefits shifting dependency very much into the private sphere and onto male partners (where they exist).

As to the extent to which the evolution of citizenship rights under the free movement provisions form the basis of an incipient European Union citizen-ship, the evidence presented here suggests a hierarchy of entitlement based on gendered assumptions about the labour market, the family and migration behaviour. At the top of the hierarchy those in paid employment (and their children) have full independent entitlement to equal treatment in the social advantages of the host Member State. A second tier provides derived entitle-ment for the legally married spouses of migrant workers for as long as their marriage and their spouse's status as a "worker" persists (that is, the "worker" is not voluntarily unemployed or deported for any reason). Finally, a third category of citizenship exists which gives rise to very minimal social entitlement, requiring those who claim a right to free movement to demonstrate financial autonomy.

---

[60] Jackson, *supra* n 46 at 14.

This group includes all non-working, non-married partners of migrant workers, for instance, job seekers, pensioners and students. For this group the right to free movement itself is circumscribed by the requirement that they, "avoid becoming a burden on the social security system of the host Member State".[61] In other words, they have no right to welfare in the host Member State.

LOUISE ACKERS
Lecturer in Social Policy,
University of Plymouth,
UK

---

[61] Council Directive 90/365/EEC (OJ 1990 L 180/28).

Chapter 15

EC SEX EQUALITY LAW: TOWARDS A HUMAN RIGHTS FOUNDATION*

(i) Introduction

The European Community has long recognised that women are systematically disadvantaged as a result of discrimination on the grounds of their sex. This awareness has resulted in the Community being instrumental in attempts to eliminate the discrimination suffered by women, both by means of legislation and non-binding codes or recommendations, but also via its relationships with other international organizations, and the Member States.

However, notwithstanding Community action thus far, which has, undoubtedly, made significant inroads into the discrimination suffered by women, and the continuing determination of the Community to eradicate sex discrimination, it is endemic. Thus, in the Community, women are far more likely to be unemployed than men, and the majority of the long-term unemployed are women.[1] The labour market of the EU continues to be rigidly sex segregated,[2] with the work of women being undervalued and consequently less well paid: 80% of part-time workers are women, and 50% of temporary workers are women.[3] There is a consistently high gender gap in the rates of pay, with women receiving, on average, only two thirds of the average pay for

---

*This chapter was written by Clare McGlynn.

[1] *Agence Europe*, 19 July 1995. In addition, the UN's Fifth Annual Human Development Report confirms that two thirds of women's work is unpaid; on average women work 13% longer than men; only 5% of credit world-wide goes to women; and, of the Gender Empowerment Measure (designed to establish women's participation in economic, political and professional activities), only the Nordic countries pass the acceptable 30% threshold, and Britain, France and Spain are among the poorest performers of the richer countries.

[2] See, *inter alia*, Mazey, "European Community Action on Behalf of Women: The Limits of Legislation" 27 Journal of Common Market Studies (1988), 63–84, who, at 82, states that "Community action on behalf of women has to date had no discernible impact on the problem of sex segregation in the labour market . . . . [n]or has it, in general terms, produced any significant reduction in the pay differential between men and women".

[3] *Agence Europe, supra* n 1.

men.[4] In the 1992 elections for the European Parliament, only 25.7% of MEPs elected were women.[5] Only 2% of the higher posts in the Commission are occupied by women.[6] In the Community as a whole, only 5% of mayors are women, only 7% of government advisors are women, and only 9% of governmental ministerial posts are held by women.[7]

In addition, women in the Community continue to be subjected to systematic violence and abuse as a result of their sex, including, in particular, domestic violence and sexual harassment, but also, genital mutilation, rape, and gender-based violence against women refugees or asylum seekers.[8] Although the Community and its Member States are bound by *jus cogens*, which prohibits torture,[9] this has had little impact on violence against women.[10] Indeed, it was only in 1993 that the United Nations, with the support of the Community, first recognised gender-based violence as a human rights concern, and specifically recognised that the human rights of women are an "inalienable, integral and indivisible part of universal human rights".[11]

Although as a result of the Vienna Declaration, the abuse of the human rights of women has, at last, been formally recognised, the abuse of women continues, not least because the human rights of women are rarely recognised as

---

[4] Women and men in the European Union: A statistical portrait, Eurostat (OPEC 1995). See Barnard, in this volume.

[5] Although this is a significant increase from the 1991 figure of 19.5%. The representation of women in the parliaments of the Member States varies: only in Sweden, Denmark and Holland does the percentage representation of women exceed 30%; in the UK, only 9.2% of MPs are women, and there has only ever been 167 women MPs.

[6] *Agence Europe*, 10 May 1995. See Flynn, and Beveridge and Nott, in this volume.

[7] *Ibid.*

[8] For example, it is estimated that four to five million girls are the victims of genital mutilation in many States, including Europe: see *Agence Europe*, 10 May 1995. The rape of women as a weapon of war is well documented and is particularly close to home in Europe because of the systematic rape of women in Bosnia: see Meron, "Rape as a Crime under International Humanitarian Law" 87 *The American Journal of International Law* (1993), 424–428; MacKinnon, "Crimes of War, Crimes of Peace" in Shute and Hurley, *On Human Rights* (1993). In relation to gender-based violence in other situations, see generally, Cook, "Women's International Human Rights Law: The Way Forward" 15 *Human Rights Quarterly* (1993), 230–261; and Mertus and Goldberg, "A Perspective on Women and International Human Rights after the Vienna Declaration: the Inside/Outside Construct" 26 *International Law and Politics* (1994), 201–234. It is welcomed that the European Parliament has called for gender-based violence to be recognised as a legitimate reason for granting asylum, see *Agence Europe*, 21 June 1995.

[9] Customary international law (*jus cogens*) is an unwritten code of legal norms which, through generally accepted practice, are accepted as fundamental human rights which cannot be subject to exceptions or derogations. The prohibition on torture is one such right. See further, Cunningham, "The European Convention on Human Rights, Customary International Law and the Constitution" 43 ICLQ (1994), 537–567; Elias, "The Nature of the Subjective Element in Customary International Law" 44 ICLQ (1995), 501–539.

[10] The prohibition of torture, as a norm of customary international law, but also as protected by the United Nations Convention Against Torture and Other Cruel, Inhuman or Degrading Treatment or Punishment, GA Res 39/46, 10 Dec 1984, offers little redress to women who are subject to pervasive, structural and systematic violence in the domestic environment. For a consideration of the arguments that such violence should constitute torture as presently interpreted in international law, see Charlesworth, Chinkin and Wright, "Feminist Approaches to International Law" 85 *The American Journal of International Law* (1991), 613–645 at 627–629, and Cook, *supra* n 8 at 248–250.

[11] World Conference on Human Rights, *The Vienna Declaration*, June 1993, United Nations Department of Public Information, DPI/1394-39399-August 1993 20M, para 18.

being mainstream or legitimate human rights concerns, and because women are generally invisible on the world stage.[12]

The Community has often expressed its deep commitment to the protection of the human rights of women, most recently in connection with the Fourth UN World Conference on Women.[13] In advance of the Conference, the Commission issued a communiqué noting that:

> Significant differentials between women and men persist in many countries in basic areas such as education, literacy, health and nutrition. Women are more likely not to be given proper financial recognition for the work they do, to have sole responsibility for childcare, to be subjected to violence, to be sexually exploited, to be refugees. The heavy burden of poverty falls disproportionately on women. Throughout the world there remains a significant lack of equality between women and men in access to rights and fundamental freedoms, whether civil, political, economic, social or cultural.[14]

It is clear that in the Community, as elsewhere in the world, the rights of women are marginalised, overlooked, or of only a limited nature. Sex discrimination and the abuse of women continues and is only beginning to receive the attention it deserves. The Community, in putting itself forward as progressive and determined to fight for the elimination of discrimination against women and to proclaim the necessity of human rights on the international stage, has taken on a considerable task, and one which is monitored closely and has a fundamental affect on the lives of many people. In doing so, it should, at least, be applauded.

However, in this chapter, the action taken thus far by the Community will be analysed in order to highlight the limitations of the Community's strategy to date, which has predominantly concentrated on the position of women in the employment market, and offers only warm words to women suffering discrimination and abuse in other areas of activity.

I will suggest that a more progressive and empowering strategy may be found in an evolution of the concept of Union citizenship;[15] a citizenship with a human rights foundation, but a foundation which respects the human rights of women. In such a development, the Community would find a strategy on which to base its activities, both on the international stage, and within the Community.

(ii) EC sex equality law

Community action to promote sex equality has been predominantly concerned with the position of women (and men) in the employment market. Within this

---

[12] See further: Mertus and Goldberg, *supra* n 8; Cook, *supra* n 8; Bunting, "Theorizing Women's Cultural Diversity in Feminist International Human Rights Strategies" 20 *Journal of Law and Society* (1993), 6–22; Charlesworth, Chinkin and Wright, *supra* n 10.

[13] See IP/95/537, 1 June 1995, and MEMO/95/121, 15 Sept 1995, both of which detail the EU's commitment to ensuring that the human rights of women are recognised and protected.

[14] IP/95/537, 1 June 1995.

[15] See also Everson, in this volume, who advocates a different approach based on citizenship.

limited ambit, legislation and action has been principally in the fields of equal pay, equal treatment and social security. Each of these areas of Community activity have been subject to sustained critique, with a growing consensus that the Community closely pursues its market (economic) concerns whilst promoting sex equality, with the result that effect is given to formal equality, at the expense of real substantive improvements in the position of women.[16] In addition, it is clear that Community action, by favouring the working population, is inherently limited in scope, and excludes substantial numbers of women and men from its emancipatory project.[17]

Thus, the Social Security Directive on the progressive implementation of the principle of equal treatment for men and women in matters of social security, adopted in 1979,[18] is concerned with "changing only certain forms of disadvantage that women suffer in relation to social security: that is, forms of discrimination against working women in relation to employment-related benefits".[19] In order to come within the protection of the Directive, a link with the world of work must be established; where a woman has left employment in order to care full-time for an invalid, she will come within the terms of the Directive;[20] however, the Directive has no application to women who may wish to enter the labour market having been primarily responsible for the care of children.[21] Further, unpaid work does not come within the scope of the Directive: the care and household work which many women undertake is not considered "real" work in the market world of the Community.[22]

The criticism which is directed at Community action in the field of social security can be similarly directed at legislation in the areas of equal pay and equal treatment. Article 119 EC provides that "men and women should receive equal pay for equal work", and Directive 75/117/EEC[23] extended the scope of Article 119 to provide for equal pay for work of equal value. Similarly, Directive 76/207/EEC[24]

---

[16] See Fenwick and Hervey, "Sex Equality in the Single Market: New Directions for the European Court of Justice" 32 CML Rev (1995), 443–470; Fredman, "European Community Discrimination Law: A Critique" 21 ILJ (1992), 119–134; Ackers, "Women, Citizenship and European Community Law: The Gender Implications of the Free Movement Provisions" *Journal of Social Welfare and Family Law* (1994) 391–406; Sohrab, "Women and Social Security: the Limits of EEC Equality Law" *Journal of Social Welfare and Family Law* (1994) 5–17.

[17] For example, the approximately 16 million unemployed, nearly 12% of the Community's population, are all but excluded from Community action on sex equality, and, moreover, such figures do not include those people who choose not to work. See further, Close, *Citizenship, Europe and Change* (1995) 34–35.

[18] Council Directive 79/7/EEC (OJ 1979 L 6/24). See Steiner, in this volume.

[19] Sohrab, *supra* n 16 at 6.

[20] See Case 150/85 *Drake* v *Chief Adjudication Officer* [1986] ECR 1995.

[21] See joined cases C-63/91 and C-64/91 *Jackson and Cresswell* v *Chief Adjudication Officer* [1992] ECR 4737. See Steiner, in this volume.

[22] Although reform is anticipated by the Commission's Fourth Action Programme on Equal Opportunities between Women and Men, IP/95/788, 19 July 1995, to promote the individualisation of rights, this will continue to be concerned only with the employment-related aspects of social security, and will not address issues such as the poverty of women, nor their subjection to the stereotyped and gendered structures of social assistance and welfare.

[23] OJ 1975 L 45/19.

[24] OJ 1976 L 39/40.

aims to secure equal treatment between women and men in three main areas, all of which are employment-related; namely access to employment and promotion, vocational training, and working conditions. Directive 86/613/EEC[25] deals with equal treatment between women and men in relation to self-employment, and provides for equality of treatment in a number of areas similar to those in the Equal Treatment Directive.[26] It also requires action, however, to eliminate sex discrimination in areas such as establishing a business, and forming a company. Where the Directives and Article 119 do not directly involve the employer-employee relationship, they are of little effect.

The emphasis on employment status can most clearly be seen in the decision of *Hofmann* v *Barmer Ersatzkasse*.[27] This case concerned an application for maternity pay by a father who was caring for his child during the period in which his wife would have been entitled to receive maternity pay. The Court of Justice rejected the claim that limiting maternity pay to women was contrary to the Equal Treatment Directive, stating that the law was specifically and deliberately designed for women only. In a now infamous ruling, the Court held that: "the Directive is not designed to settle questions concerned with the organization of the family, or to alter the division of responsibility between parents".[28] Thus, even though the Community is predominantly concerned with the employment market, the Court was not concerned with the very factors which may inhibit women from exercising their rights to sex equality in that market.

The limitation of the EC sex equality laws therefore lies in their dominant concern with the employment market, resulting from the essential economic basis and objectives of the Community.[29] As Fredman notes, the impact of anti-discrimination legislation will vary depending on whether the aim of the legislation is functional to the market, that is, it redresses under-utilisation of women's skills, or whether the legislation is designed to redress the imbalances of an inherently unequal market.[30] The concern of the Community with the economics of discrimination has meant that the sex equality laws have been aimed at, and interpreted to ensure only that, women are treated the same as men, like as like. This has had the effect of substantially limiting the impact of the legislation on those who are "differently situated", that is, women.[31] Accordingly, it has been concluded by Fenwick and Hervey that "the assumption that EC law is particularly beneficial to women should be viewed with caution".[32]

In addition to the scope of the legislation being limited, the use of the concept of equality has been severely criticised. Equality implies a comparison between those who are discriminated against, the disadvantaged, and those who

---

[25] OJ 1986 L 35.
[26] Council Directive 76/207/EEC, *supra* n 24.
[27] Case 184/83 [1984] ECR 3047.
[28] *Ibid* para 24. See O'Leary, in this volume.
[29] See Fredman, *supra* n 16 who at 130 states that: "Gender based inequality became a prime target, not because of social ideals, but economic imperatives".
[30] *Ibid.*
[31] Fenwick and Hervey, *supra* n 16 at 444.
[32] Fenwick and Hervey, *supra* n 16 at 469.

are not, the norm (men). The position of women is thereby compared to that of men, which takes no account of "women's different position resulting from prior discrimination and disadvantage".[33] Indeed, it is argued that the concept of equality itself "serves to disguise the fact that in order to improve their position, women have to become like men".[34] Fredman states that, in fact:

> it is the male norm itself which functions as an obstacle to the progress of women. Legislation framed in terms of equality based on the male norm is therefore fundamentally limited: it can assist the minority who are able to conform, but it cannot reach or correct the underlying structural impediments.[35]

The Community's preoccupation with the employment market is severely restrictive in that it expresses concern only with the "public" aspects of the position of women, the public being the realm of the workplace, regarded as the natural province of men, at the expense of the "private" or "domestic" arena, the world of the home and the family, where decisions regarding reproduction, childcare and morality are taken, often considered to be the traditional realm of women. The principal objective of the Community's sex equality programme is to redress only the inequality in the public sphere; allowing women to participate equally in the workplace.[36] Such a concentration of effort ignores the difficulties women tend to face in moving from the private to public areas of activity[37], in addition to the abuse and violence women suffer in private.

These factors have led many to decry the use of anti-discrimination laws aimed at the workplace. Lacey states that "anti-discrimination law should be seen as simply one symbolic and moderately functional thread in a web of measures aimed at securing more power for women", and that law reform should be seen as only a "minor" part of a feminist political strategy.[38] Mazey states that "the roots of sex discrimination lie in sexist public attitudes, education and employment practices which reinforce sexual stereotypes, and childcare responsibilities which are typically borne by women and which limit their employment options".[39] The answer appears to lie in "a much more radical focus on structural disadvantage and the causes thereof",[40] and on the need for primacy of action at a policy level.[41]

---

[33] Lacey, "Legislation Against Sex Discrimination: Questions from a Feminist Perspective", 14 JLS (1987), 411–421 at 413. See Hervey, in this volume.

[34] Cousins, "Equal Treatment and Social Security" 19 EL Rev (1994), 123–145 at 144.

[35] Fredman, *supra* n 16 at 121. On the value of equality as a reforming principle generally, see: MacKinnon, *Feminism Unmodified* (1987); Lacey, *supra* n 33; Ward in this volume. The inherent limitations of comparing women with men can easily be seen in relation to pregnancy. See Fredman, "A Difference with Distinction: Pregnancy and Parenthood Reassessed" 110 LQR (1994), 106–123, and McGlynn, "*Webb* v *EMO*: A Hope for the Future?" 46 NILQ (1995), 50–62.

[36] Although the Community does express concern with the equal participation of women and men in the home, such concern generally takes the form of soft words rather than legislative action. See, the Fourth Equal Opportunities Action Programme, *supra* n 22 and Mazey, *supra* n 2.

[37] This is most clearly seen in the decision in *Hofmann, supra* n 27.

[38] Lacey, *supra* n 33 at 420–421.

[39] Mazey, *supra* n 2 at 82.

[40] Fredman, *supra* n 16 at 134.

[41] Lacey, *supra* n 33 at 418.

(iii) New directions

New strategies and directions are required if the Community is to engage successfully with its aims and objectives regarding sex equality. Some commentators have argued that a reformulation and redefinition of the workplace and employment market are necessary. Thus, Fredman has argued for a "far less rigid divide between work in the market and work in the home".[42] Sohrab considers that men should be encouraged "to participate to a greater extent in caring",[43] and Fenwick and Hervey suggest the possibility of a "reconsideration of the concept of an 'employee' as an individual who is committed full-time, for a lifetime, to the job and only the job".[44]

The Commission is, apparently, alive to these issues and has presented further strategies for action. Its Fourth Action Programme on Equal Opportunities between Women and Men[45] proposes, inter alia, action on childcare, with a framework Directive being mooted. In addition, Community action on parental leave is being considered by the social partners under the Agreement on Social Policy annexed to the Treaty on European Union,[46] and further options are forthcoming on the rights of part-time workers.[47] However, although such proposals are indeed welcome, and are likely to encourage the development of an employment market and workplace more likely to favour equality of opportunity for women and men, it is unlikely that such limited options will revolutionise the workplace and employment market, as is advocated above.[48]

It is suggested that action is required at a more fundamental level. Strategies to improve the position of women need to be broadened beyond the marketplace and workplace; they need to encompass the community and the home, as well as all areas of public office and authority.[49] Although improvements in the provision and availability of childcare, and the introduction and enhancement of parental leave, will affect the sexual division of responsibility in the home and in the workplace, ultimately, such strategies are still employment-dominated. The means by which greater effect may be given to improving the position of women both in the public and private domains, is via the evolution of Union citizenship. This evolution will demand acceptance of human rights as the founding basis of Union citizenship, and, in particular, will mandate the recognition and protection of women's human rights.

---

[42] Fredman, "A Difference with Distinction", *supra* n 35 at 123.
[43] Sohrab, *supra* n 16 at 16.
[44] Fenwick and Hervey, *supra* n 16 at 470.
[45] IP/95/788, *supra* n 22.
[46] IP/95/745, 13 July 1995.
[47] See *The Guardian*, 28 Sept 1995.
[48] For example, although it is to be hoped that action on parental leave will have the effect of ensuring a greater division of family responsibility, sexual divisions will remain, and stereotypes entrenched, so long as the Community maintains its position in cases such as *Hofmann, supra* n 27.
[49] See Beveridge and Nott, Everson, Flynn, Shaw, and Ward, in this volume.

(a) Union citizenship[50]

The concept of Union citizenship, although having a substantial historical pedigree[51], came to fruition in the Treaty on European Union (TEU). The TEU grandly declares that it aims to "strengthen the protection of the rights and interests of the nationals of its Member States through the introduction of a citizenship of the Union".[52] The rights which are conferred on the citizens of the Union are limited in scope.[53] Nationality of a Member State is a prerequisite to the exercise of the majority of the rights on offer.[54] It is argued that the principal right on offer, that of free movement of workers, is highly gendered and thus restrictive, and in need of reform if citizenship is to mean anything to women.[55] Moreover, there is no catalogue of fundamental rights and freedoms, nor even a codification of the existing Community rights of nationals of Member States.

Nonetheless, it has been argued that the notion of Union citizenship is a "dynamic" concept, as provision is made in the TEU for the enumeration of further rights, and for the existing rights to be strengthened.[56] As long as citizenship is based on the limited economic[57] and democratic rights[58] which characterise the present determination of citizenship, little will be done to redress the inequality of women. Thus, it is the potential dynamism of Union citizenship which offers the most for women.

Union citizenship could evolve towards a form of "social citizenship", based on "membership of the Community with a uniform floor of social rights".[59] Close also considers that this development would be most suitable for the Union.[60] He argues that such a citizenship would not be reliant on establishing nationality, but would be "pluralist" in nature, giving rights to group and community interests, encouraging a participatory democracy, as well as establishing rights to welfare provision. Such a development could be to the advantage of women: greater interest in group rights, together with an increased participa-

---

[50] Compare the discussion by Everson, in this volume.
[51] See O'Keeffe, "Union Citizenship" in O'Keeffe and Twomey, *Legal Issues of the Maastricht Treaty* (1994) 87–107 at 87–89.
[52] TEU Art B.
[53] See O'Keeffe, *supra* n 51 and O'Leary, "Nationality Law and Community Citizenship: A Tale of Two Uneasy Bedfellows" 12 YEL (1992), 353–384.
[54] It is estimated that there are at least 8–9 million third country nationals in the EU, if not 13 million, who are not able to avail themselves of the majority of rights conferred by Union citizenship. See, O'Keeffe, *supra* n 51 at 104.
[55] *Supra* n 15. See Ackers, and Shaw, in this volume.
[56] O'Keeffe, *supra* n 51 at 102.
[57] That is, the concentration on free movement which is dependent on the status of worker, albeit that this is a term which is widely interpreted.
[58] For a consideration of the limitations of the rights to participate in a representative democracy which Union citizenship is offering, see Ward, "(Pre)conceptions in European Law" *Journal of Law and Society*, forthcoming.
[59] Ackers (1994), *supra* n 16 at 403. Compare Everson's concept of a "European civil society", in this volume.
[60] Close, *Citizenship* (1995). See also Ward, *supra* n 58.

tory democracy, could improve the position of women.[61] However, it is argued that it is citizenship with a human rights foundation that could significantly empower women and liberate them from discrimination. It could do so by establishing and defining fundamental values which are a priority for Union action, and which would have the benefit of the widely accepted political pedigree of the human rights discourse.

(b) Citizenship with a human rights foundation

The concept of human rights is a rare example of a moral code ascribed to internationally.[62] Although interpretations of human rights differ, and it can often seem that all States protect human rights,[63] it is generally accepted that the promotion of human rights is an acceptable goal, and, indeed, a political imperative. That this is the case is evidenced by the internationally recognised declarations of the United Nations regarding human rights.[64] Further endorsement comes closer to home in the form of the Council of Europe's Convention for the Protection of Human Rights and Fundamental Freedoms (ECHR).

Although not specifically bound by the above obligations, the EU subscribes to their basic intentions and beliefs, and its rhetoric continually engages their value systems as a means of international acceptability and supposed political maturity. Thus, the TEU declared that the EU shall "respect fundamental rights, as guaranteed by the European Convention for the Protection of Human Rights and Fundamental Freedoms . . . and as they result from the constitutional traditions common to the Member States".[65] In addition, the human rights discourse has been integrated into the language and practice of EC law by means of the development of human rights protection as a general principle of EC law,[66] albeit that human rights will only be protected within the "framework

---

[61] The empowerment of groups, for example, women, could do much to alleviate one of the limitations on sex equality laws which is its concern with the individual, as opposed to the general status of women. See Fredman, *supra* n 16 at 132–133.

[62] See Bunting, *supra* n 12.

[63] Witness the Chinese and Iranian delegations at the Fourth UN World Conference on Women held in Beijing in September 1995 proclaiming their adherence to human rights, and, in particular, the human rights of women. See, the report of the Xinhau News Agency, 19 Sept 1995, and the text of the report by the Iranian News Agency, IRNA, 15 Sept 1995, as reported by the BBC Summary of World Broadcasts, 18 Sept 1995.

[64] For example, the UN's International Covenant on Civil and Political Rights, the International Covenant on Economic, Social and Cultural Rights, and the Convention on the Elimination of All Forms of Discrimination Against Women (CEDAW).

[65] *Ibid* art F.2.

[66] The Court of Justice first asserted this in Case 29/69 *Stauder* v *City of Ulm* [1969] ECR 419, by stating simply that the provision in question did not prejudice "the fundamental human rights enshrined in the general principles of Community law protected by the Court". This jurisprudence was subsequently developed, and in Case 11/70 *Internationale Handelsgesellschaft* [1970] ECR 1125, the Court announced that the general principles of law which protect human rights are drawn from the constitutional traditions of the Member States. In Case 4/73 *Nold* [1974] ECR 491, reference was made to the fact that the general principles of law derive not only from the constitutional traditions of the Member States but also from "international treaties for the protection of human rights on which the Member States have collaborated or of which they are signatories".

of the Community's structure and objectives",[67] and are largely unspecified.[68] As a result of this narrow construction of human rights, and their effective subjugation to the economic norms of the Community, there have been calls for a more codified and effective human rights strategy. Thus, accession to the ECHR has been mooted[69], and others have advocated a catalogue of fundamental rights, a "Bill of Rights", for the Union.[70]

Although the present commitment of the Union to human rights is specifically isolated from the concept of citizenship[71], an evolution of Union citizenship offers the means by which human rights norms could be fully and effectively integrated into the legal, political and social discourse of the Union, and would help create an "integrationist *culture* of rights currently lacking at Community level".[72] In addition, the introduction of human rights into the concept of citizenship would represent a welcome and overdue move away from promotion of human rights as a means of preserving the supremacy of EC law, towards the objective of greater protection for the individual.[73] Indeed, the Commission, in its Report on the Functioning of the Maastricht Treaty, recommends that citizenship should be "developed to the full", and that the lack of a summary of fundamental rights and duties of the Union citizen is a "gap [which] should be filled".[74]

(c) Citizenship and women's human rights

A new concept of citizenship with a human rights foundation is welcome, and is only tempered by the caveat that such a development must be cognisant of the human rights of women. The creation of a "culture of rights" is only welcome if it includes the human rights of women, rather than continuing to condone (implicitly or not) their marginalisation, nor condemning them to the mores of the market. Such rights require specific protection as the history of women's human rights on the international stage tells us that the human rights of women are consistently programmatically isolated, forgotten, and treated with

---

[67] *Internationale Handelsgesellschaft, ibid* at 1134.
[68] See Clapham, "A Human Rights Policy for the European Community", 10 YEL (1990), 309–366, who at 331, having considered which human rights the Court actually protects, states that "the Court's case law leaves no clues as to which rights would be protected . . . . [r]eferences to common Constitutional principles, traditions, practices, precepts and ideas are unhelpful".
[69] See Clapham, *ibid* at 361–363; Twomey, "The European Union: Three Pillars without a Human Rights Foundation" in O'Keeffe and Twomey, *supra* n 51, 121–132 at 125–128; Weiler, "Eurocracy and Distrust: Some Questions Concerning the Role of the European Court of Justice in the Protection of Fundamental Human Rights within the Legal Order of the European Community", 61 *Washington Law Review* (1986), 1103–1142 at 1134–1136.
[70] See Twomey, *supra* n 69 at 128–131.
[71] See O'Leary, "The Relationship Between Community Citizenship and the Protection of Fundamental Rights in Community Law" 32 CML Rev (1995), 519–554 at 520.
[72] Twomey, *supra* n 69 at 129.
[73] See Coppel and O'Neill, "The European Court of Justice: taking rights seriously?" 12 *Legal Studies* (1992), 227–245, who argue that the Court's exposition of human rights norms owes more to its integrationist and jurisdictional claims, than to a fundamental belief in the sanctity of human rights.
[74] IP/95/465, 10 May 1995.

disdain.[75] Thus, where Community sex equality laws at present are predominantly concerned with the employment market, which itself is subject to the economic norms of the Community, the advantage of a rights culture which respects the human rights of women is that such rights could not easily be changed, and would not be subject to the influence or the vicissitudes of the market. They would be relatively fixed against the social and political forces which might seek to override them.[76] By so confirming and entrenching the rights of women, a signal would be sent to the Union, the Member States and all peoples in the EU, that certain values should be prioritised, despite immediate economic and political pressures. In addition, the adumbration of the rights of women, would represent the highest legal expression of the Union's fundamental aspirations and values, thus encouraging a high public and political profile.

At present, in addition to its promotion of sex equality, the EU attempts to use its influence on the international stage to ensure the protection and guarantee of human rights. Community policy in the spheres of development co-operation and common foreign and security policy aims to secure respect for human rights and fundamental freedoms;[77] and numerous references can be found in EU communiqués that respect for human rights, civic rights, and equality of opportunity are the bedrock of the policy and practice of the Union.[78] In its negotiation and conclusion of co-operation and trade agreements, the Community insists on the inclusion of a specific clause on human rights. Such a clause is said to be "guided by the principle that the human rights of women and the girl-child are an inalienable, integral and indivisible part of universal human rights".[79]

However, as well as continuing and developing such action on the international stage, attention must be diverted inwards towards the activities of the Member States of the Community: only when the human rights of women are effectively protected within the Union, should it participate on the international stage and advocate certain action by other States and international organizations. In addition, attention must be focused on more than just the public acts of States; protection of the human rights of women demands action in the private world of the peoples of the Union. Where abuse of women continues in private, it should be recognised that States and international organizations

---

[75] See MacKinnon, *supra* n 8; Cook, *supra* n 8; and Mertus and Goldberg, *supra* n 8.

[76] See further, Adjei, "Human Rights Theory and the Bill of Rights Debate" 58 MLR (1995), 17–36.

[77] TEU Arts 130u(2) and 130u(2).

[78] See, *inter alia*, Commission Press Release, IP/95/465, "Commission Adopts Report on the Functioning of the Maastricht Treaty", at 4, which states that: "The European model forges a link between the social dimension, human rights and civic rights"; Resolution of the European Parliament (OJ 1995 C 125), 22 May 1995, which states that the EU's foreign policy must be based on "respect for human rights and the promotion of democracy"; and, Commission Press Release, IP/95/537, 1 June 1995, "The Fourth UN World Conference on Women, Beijing, 4–15 September 1995", which states that the Community's objective for the conference is to achieve a "new partnership between women and men", which entails "the acknowledgement of women's fundamental rights".

[79] IP/95/941.

are complicit in that they are not likely (certainly at present) to have taken sufficient action to ameliorate the inherent risks in being a woman. A citizenship founded on human rights would constitute a basis for action, as well as constituting an expression of future intent. Clapham states that if the Community is to "take women seriously" it should "investigate initiatives relating to domestic violence, rape crisis centres, childcare facilities, contraception, and medical experimentation on women".[80]

In addition to specific policies, a human rights foundation would also aid the interpretation and development of Community law in general. Where the Court of Justice encounters a moral and political dilemma such as the one it confronted in *S.P.U.C.* v *Grogan*,[81] it would have a human rights foundation on which to base its judgment, rather than resorting to the determination of moral issues on the basis of economic norms.[82] When the Commission is considering Europe-wide proposals on child sex abuse and pornography, it may be guided by the principles and values underscored by the (women's) human rights foundation to citizenship.[83] In circumstances where the Commission is developing and reforming legislation which will free transnational media communications, and is faced with concerns regarding freedom of expression versus claims of the exploitation of women and children, it would have more than free market considerations to negotiate.[84] Where the Community is faced with action being taken by a Member State in the name of protecting the moral fabric of its society, potentially in breach of EC law, it may consider such questions in the framework of fundamental values and beliefs expressed and adopted by the Union.[85] A straightforward starting point would be the incorporation of the UN Convention on the Elimination of Discrimination Against Women (CEDAW) into the general principles of EC law. CEDAW is a comprehensive statement of women's rights which particularises the human rights of women and the actions which States committed to such rights should take. It touches every aspect of life, in the political, social, economic, legal, health, education and family spheres.[86] In addition, where there is debate regarding the accession of the

---

[80] Clapham *supra* n 68, 317.

[81] Case C-159/90 [1991] ECR I-4685; [1991] 3 CMLR 849.

[82] See further, Phelan, "Right to Life of the Unborn v Promotion of Trade in Services: the European Court of Justice and the Normative Foundations of the European Union" 55 MLR (1992), 670–689; and de Búrca, "Fundamental Human Rights and the Reach of European Law" 13 OLJS (1993), 283–319. See also Flynn, and O'Leary, in this volume.

[83] For a consideration of the proposals for action in relation to pornography and child abuse, see *European Report* 17 June 1995, and *Agence Europe*, 8 June 1995.

[84] On the potential human rights abuses resulting from the liberalisation of telecommunications and cable television networks, see the comments on the Commission's Green Paper on this subject, see *Agence Europe*, 24 May 1995, *The Reuter EC Report*, 16 June 1995.

[85] See the furore surrounding the UK Government's ban of the satellite channel Red Hot Dutch, because of its content of hardcore pornography, potentially in breach EC law. See *The Reuter EC Report*, 19 March 1995, and 2 April 1995.

[86] See further, Clark, "The Vienna Convention Reservations Regime and the Convention on Discrimination Against Women" 85 *The American Journal of International Law* (1991), 281–321; Tinker, "Human Rights for Women: The UN Convention on the Elimination of All Forms of Discrimination Against Women" 3 *Human Rights Quarterly* (1981), 32–43.

Community to the ECHR, reference should also be made to a consideration of accession to CEDAW.

(iv) Conclusion

The EU has proclaimed its commitment to ensuring and protecting the human rights of women, stating recently that it has "considerable and well-established experience in relation to the advancement of women".[87] Moreover, the Court of Justice considers that it also is a great respector of women's human rights: "respect for fundamental personal human rights is one of the general principles of Community law . . . [and that] [t]here can be no doubt that the elimination of discrimination based on sex forms part of those fundamental rights".[88] However, it can be seen from the discussion above that the Community strategy to eradicate discrimination and other human rights abuses thus far, particularly that of the Court of Justice, is limited in scope and does little to impact on the real inequalities facing women in Europe today. Notwithstanding this, note should be taken of the Commission's attempts to move beyond the workplace. It presently advocates the "mainstreaming" of equality issues, seeking to ensure that equality, and equal opportunities, are taken into account at all levels and in all policy areas.[89] In addition, it is proposed that there will be a Commission Communication on equal opportunities in relation to the structural funds, the objective of which is to ensure that programme documents used to guide the procedures for payments from the structural funds, refer specifically to equal opportunities as a matter of course.[90]

However, it is suggested that more effective "mainstreaming" of equality would come in the form of the development of Union citizenship with a (women's) human rights foundation. Citizenship offers the symbolism necessary to engage the minds of the peoples and institutions of the Union; it would be the means to "demonstrate some sort of social and political consensus among [the Union's] members and a reaffirmation of fundamental rights",[91] together with the offer of greater legitimacy for the European project as it continues to grow. De Búrca confirms that the time is ripe for action on human rights, stating that it is imperative that the Community develops "a consistent and principled justification for both the development and limitation of its 'human rights role'".[92] A (women's) human rights foundation to citizenship would enable the development of sex equality and women's human rights policies,

---

[87] IP/95/437, 1 June 1995. Indeed, considerable sums of money must have been spent by the Community in its attendance and preparation for the Fourth World Conference, as the delegation from the EU consisted of 30 people (MEMO/95/113, 30 Aug 1995).
[88] Case 149/77 *Defrenne* v *Sabena* [1978] ECR 1365 at 1378.
[89] See the Commission's Fourth Equal Opportunities Action Programme, IP/95/788, 19 July 1995. For a more ambitious proposal see Beveridge and Nott, in this volume.
[90] *Ibid.*
[91] O'Leary, *supra* n 71 at 551–552.
[92] *Supra* n 89 at 304.

to reach beyond the workplace, into all areas of activity. If the Community is to take the rights of women seriously, and that if the view that women are "more reluctant than men to support the construction of Europe"[93] is to be changed, positive and specific action must be taken, and a (women's) human rights citizenship is the suggested way forward.

CLAIRE McGLYNN
Lecturer in Law,
Newcastle Law School,
University of Newcastle-upon-Tyne,
UK

---

[93] IP/95/788, 19 July 1995.

Chapter 16

RESOLUTION BY THE COURT OF JUSTICE OF DISPUTES AFFECTING FAMILY LIFE*

(i) Introduction

Issues relating to childcare, domestic responsibilities and family life are regarded as some of the central causative features of sex discrimination.[1] These issues clearly do not fall neatly within the scope of application of Community law. Nevertheless, as effect is given to other areas of Community competence such as the equal treatment of men and women, the free movement of persons and the free provision of services, Community law has inevitably become entangled in issues which are not directly linked to the process of economic integration.[2]

The object of this chapter is to address how the Court of Justice has resolved some of the cases touching on family life which have come before it in recent years. It is suggested that the division of competence between the Community and the Member States, the Community's preoccupation with economic integration objectives and, possibly, the Court of Justice's lack of expertise with respect to family law issues, have led to a number of uncomfortable rulings with respect to family life, the rights of family members and women, in particular, in their traditional capacity as child-bearers and home-carers.

The Court of Justice should not base its decisions on the implicit assumption of "the old-fashioned view of family relations" with women working in the home.[3] Nevertheless, the majority of migrant workers are still male[4] and, as

---

*This chapter was written by Siofra O'Leary.

[1] See Fredman and Szyszczak, "Interaction of Race and Gender" in Hepple and Szyszczak, *Discrimination: The Limits of Law* (1992) 214–226 at 218.

[2] See, for example, Case 9/74 *Casagrande* v *Landeshauptstadt München* (education policy) [1974] ECR 773; and Case 65/81 *Reina* v *Landeskreditbank Baden Württemburg* (demographic policy) [1982] ECR 33.

[3] See Weiler, "Thou Shalt Not Oppress a Stranger: On the Judicial Protection of the Human Rights of Non-EC Nationals – A Critique" 3 *European Journal of International Law* (1992), 65–91 at 89.

[4] But see Ackers, in this volume.

Ackers points out, "where the female partner is also a migrant worker the male is less likely to be dependent upon her and/or assuming a caring role".[5]

The decision of the Court of Justice in *Society for the Protection of the Unborn Child (S.P.U.C.)* v *Grogan*[6] has been widely discussed and documentated.[7] This chapter compares the celebrated failure of the Court of Justice to address the substantive issues raised in *Grogan* with the Opinion of the Advocate General in the same case and with the decision of the European Court of Human Rights in *Open Door Counselling and Dublin Well Woman* v *Ireland*[8] (Section (ii)). The latter also concerned an Irish prohibition on abortion information, this time in the form of counselling by welfare clinics. The chapter then examines other decisions where the Court of Justice has been confronted with issues which concern family life (Section (iii)). The Court has been particularly unadventurous as regards family reunion, where it has failed to offer adequate protection to the family members of Community and third country workers.

It is arguable, as a result, that Community law has left the spouses and family members of migrant workers in a particularly vulnerable position. They are not victims of sex discrimination as such. Indeed, the possibility of identifying sex discrimination in the decisions discussed herein is obscured by the fact that the spouses attempting to rely on Community law are not always women, by the fact that the treatment of third country nationals relates to other factors such as their nationality and race and by the fact that, in the abortion context at least, there is no opposing male norm.

Nevertheless, it is argued that the Court's decisions have endorsed a dependent condition for the spouses of Community workers. By failing to address whether they may rely on fundamental human rights to support their residence in a Member State and not simply their derivative and highly circumscribed Community rights, the Court has not offered the legal protection which it could, and should, have done.

It has also demonstrated that family members enjoy rights as an instrumental means to enhance the Community's economic objectives, rather than in their capacity as human beings.

In the light of the case law, the chapter questions whether families, in general, and women, in particular, can be expected to welcome the case law of the Court of Justice in this field. On the one hand, the Court of Justice appears to have championed the social integration of workers and, to a certain extent, their families; while on the other, when delicate national moral and social issues have arisen, or when its judgments might impinge on an area of traditional national sovereignty such as immigration, it has failed to offer an adequate level

---

[5] See Ackers, "Women, Citizenship and European Community Law: The Gender Implications of the Free Movement Provisions" 4 *Journal of Social Welfare and Family Law* (1994), 391–406 at 396.
[6] Case C-159/90 [1991] ECR I-4685.
[7] See variously, Curtin, 29 CMLRev (1992), 585–603; De Búrca, "Fundamental Human Rights and the Reach of EC Law" 13 OJLS (1993), 283–319; O'Leary, 17 ELRev (1992), 138–157; and Phelan, "Right to Life of the Unborn v Promotion of Trade in Services: The European Court of Justice and the Normative Shaping of the European Union" 55 MLR (1992), 670–689.
[8] [1992] 15 European Human Rights Reports 244.

of
protection, even though the logic of its previous decisions, its adherence to
fundamental rights principles and even the spirit of the Treaty, did not preclude such protection.

(ii) Abortion information and Community law

(a) The Irish constitutional guarantee of the right to life[9]

Article 40.3.3. of the Irish Constitution guarantees the right to life of the
unborn child.[10] This provision has given rise to a number of disputes concerning the extent to which the Constitution requires the restriction or prohibition
of other activities such as welfare counselling or the publication of information
concerning abortion services in other States. In *Attorney General (S.P.U.C.) v Open
Door Counselling and Dublin Well Woman*[11], injunctions were sought in the Irish
High Court against welfare clinics which provided non-directive counselling to
pregnant women. These clinics set out the options, amongst them abortion,
which were available to women in the case of unwanted pregnancy.

The Irish High Court held that abortion was contrary to national policy and
public morality and granted an injunction preventing the clinics from persist-
ing in the proscribed activity which it held to be contrary to Article 40.3.3. The
Supreme Court, on appeal, identified the central question as whether the conduct of the defendants was "assisting in the destruction of the life of the
unborn"[12] and upheld the decision of the High Court.

Various Irish university students' associations also issued welfare guides to
their members which included information as to the identity, location of and
method of communication with abortion clinics in the United Kingdom.

In *S.P.U.C. v Grogan*[13] a declaration was once again sought in the High Court,
this time to the effect that any publication of information on abortion was also
contrary to Article 40.3.3. The High Court judge in *Grogan*, however, did not
grant the interlocutory relief sought by the plaintiffs and referred a number of
questions to the Court of Justice, requesting a preliminary ruling on the interpretation of Community law pursuant to Article 177 EC. The national court
wished to establish whether the activities of the abortion clinics constituted
"services" within the meaning of Article 60 EC and, if so, whether the Treaty
provisions on the freedom to supply services precluded a national rule prohibiting

---

[9] For further details see the annotation by the author, *supra*.
[10] Article 40.3.3 provides that "The State acknowledges the right to life of the unborn and, with due
regard to the equal right to life of the mother, guarantees in its laws to respect, and, as far as practicable, by its laws to defend and vindicate that right".
[11] [1987] ILRM (Irish Law Reports Monthly) 477 and, on appeal [1988] ILRM 19.
[12] Per Chief Justice Finlay [1988] ILRM 19 at 26.
[13] [1989] Irish Reports 753.

the provision of information concerning abortion services legally performed in another Member State. In the High Court's view the issue which arose in Grogan was the right to impart and receive information and a preliminary ruling on the matter was necessary for the Court to give a final judgment.[14]

(b) Abortion information and the Court of Justice

Both the Court of Justice and the Advocate General, in answer to the reference in *Grogan*, held that the medical termination of pregnancy covers a number of services which are normally provided for remuneration and which thus fall within the scope of Article 60 EC.[15] The Court of Justice, in particular, refused to be drawn into the moral aspects of the abortion issue on which SPUC sought to rely, simply stating that, "[I]t is not for the Court to substitute its assessment for that of the legislature in those Member States where the activities in question are practised legally".[16]

The Court and Advocate General diverged, however, in their treatment of the second and third questions posed by the national court. The Court simply held that the link between the students' associations and the clinics operating in another Member State was too tenuous for the prohibition on the distribution of information to be regarded as a "restriction" within the meaning of Article 59 EC.[17] The economic operators at issue were the medical clinics operating in the United Kingdom. The information distributed by the Irish students' associations was not distributed on their behalf and was independent of the economic activity which the clinics legally performed in the United Kingdom. In such circumstances the prohibition could not be regarded as a restriction falling within the provisions of Article 59 EC. It fell outside the scope of Community law and, as such, the Court did not have to assess whether it was compatible with the general principles of Community law with respect to fundamental rights and freedoms.[18]

In contrast, Advocate General Van Gerven did regard restrictions on informa-

---

[14] Note that the High Court and Supreme Court had denied the relevance of Community law in *Open Door*. The Supreme Court, for example, considered that the assistance offered by the clinics did not amount to a corollary right to whatever rights Irish women could claim under the EC Treaty. On appeal in *Grogan*, the Supreme Court did not interfere with the Article 177 EC reference made by the High Court, but it was clear from its judgment that it would have challenged the supremacy of Community law if unsatisfied with the outcome of the preliminary ruling. Walsh J argued that if, and when, a decision of the European Court of Justice ruled that some aspect of European Community law affected the activities of the students, the consequence of such a decision on constitutionally guaranteed rights and their protection by the Courts would fall to be considered by the Irish Courts in the light of the Irish Constitution.

[15] Article 60 para 1 EC provides that "services" within the meaning of the Treaty are activities which are normally provided for remuneration and which are not governed by the provisions relating to the freedom of movement for goods, capital or persons. In Joined Cases 286/82 and 26/83 *Luisi and Carbone* [1984] ECR 377, the Court of Justice had previously included "persons receiving medical treatment" as recipients of services.

[16] Case C-159/90, at para 20.

[17] *Ibid* at para 24.

[18] *Ibid* at para 31.

tion as capable of compromising the freedom of a recipient of services to go to another Member State to receive that service. The freedom to supply services in the Community could be promoted, in his opinion, "by means of the provision of information, whether or not for consideration, concerning services which the provider of information supplies himself or which are supplied by another person".[19] The national prohibition in *Grogan* was not discriminatory, but it was capable of overtly or covertly, actually or potentially, impeding intra-Community trade in services and as such it fell within the scope of Articles 59 and 60 EC.[20] However, he justified the prohibition on information as an imperative requirement of public interest.[21] In his Opinion, the protection of the unborn is a justifiable objective in the context of Community law which relates to a moral and philosophical policy choice which Member States are entitled to make and which they are entitled to defend and promote in the Community by invoking the public policy exception referred to in Articles 56 and 66 EC.[22]

It remained to be seen whether the prohibition was objectively necessary and indispensable, in the sense that it could not be replaced by an alternative equally effective rule less restrictive of the freedom to supply services and whether it was proportionate to the aim sought to be achieved. The objective of the Irish prohibition on information was the protection of unborn life. The actual effect of the prohibition on the number of women availing of services offered outside Ireland was more difficult to quantify. One national judge had been far from satisfied that granting an injunction to restrain the defendants from publishing the impugned material would save the life of a single unborn child. The Advocate General, however, carried out a very limited assessment of the proportionality of the measure. He stated that Ireland was "entitled, within its area of discretion" to regard this measure, which was intended to effect a value-judgment enshrined in the Constitution, as proportionate. Rather than examining whether the operation of the prohibition was useful, indispensable and proportionate to the aim sought to be achieved, he pointed to two different types of activity which would have been disproportionate; namely, restricting women's right to travel, or subjecting pregnant women to unsolicited examinations. He did refer to the possibility that the prohibition was not entirely effective in

---

[19] See the Opinion of the Advocate General, at 4713, and the reference to Case C-362/88 *GB-Inno-BM* [1990] ECR 667.

[20] The decision of the Court in Case C-76/90 *Säger* v *Dennemeyer and Co. Ltd* [1991] ECR I-4221, where it first explicitly held that Article 59 EC covers indistinctly applicable national measures, was handed down after the Opinion of the Advocate General in *Grogan*.

[21] See the summary of the imperative requirements of public interest which have been recognised by Community law in Case C-353/89 *Commission* v *Netherlands (Mediawet)* [1991] ECR I-4069: and a statement of the law as it stands in Fernandez-Martin and O'Leary, "Judicial Exceptions to the Free Provision of Services", 1 *European Law Journal* (1995), 308–329.

[22] See the Opinion of the Advocate General, at *ibid* 4719. The reference to both imperative requirements of public interest and the public policy exception in Article 56 EC is somewhat misleading. Although the two categories express different aspects of the same concept, a margin of discretion for the State, discriminatory measures can only be justified with reference to Article 56 EC. Imperative requirements of public interest, on the other hand, refer to indistinctly applicable national measures which, in addition, are generally assessed, as in the Advocate General's Opinion in *Grogan*, for compatibility with the principle of proportionality.

protecting unborn life, but dismissed this objection on the grounds that the national authorities were simply keeping their actions within the realms of what was proportionate and therefore permissible.[23]

However, the Advocate General's inquiry did not end there. He also recalled that fundamental rights form an integral part of the general principles of law which the Court is obliged to observe. In his view, the prohibition was one which restricted Article 59 EC and which, in order to be compatible with Community law, had to be justified with reference to imperative requirements of public interest. As a result, it fell outside the exclusive jurisdiction of the national legislature and was open to review with reference to the Community's fundamental rights principles.[24] Unlike the Court of Justice, the Advocate General was prepared to balance the two fundamental rights in question; the right to life of the unborn as guaranteed by a particular Member State and freedom of expression on the basis of the constitutional traditions of the Member States and Article 10 of the European Convention on Human Rights.[25] The prohibition clearly infringed the freedom of expression, but was it "necessary in a democratic society" and therefore permissible pursuant to Article 10(2)?

In his inquiry as to the compatibility of the prohibition with fundamental rights it is arguable that the Advocate General, once again, failed to subject the prohibition to a sufficiently rigorous examination. He stressed the ethical value-judgment aspect of the prohibition again and said that the national authorities were entitled to consider that the prohibition was necessary and proportionate given its limited nature, the fact that it was based on a national constitutional provision and the fact that only information by way of assistance was prohibited and that women were not actually prevented from travelling.[26]

By referring to these disproportionate measures the Advocate General may have been trying to show that the national authorities had kept the restrictions within certain limits. However, that is no answer to the charge that the limits which they actually did choose for the prohibition were disproportionate and contrary to fundamental rights. At least one national judge had doubted whether the objective in question could be fulfilled, since information was still available elsewhere. In addition, if information was available elsewhere in Ireland, it was surely difficult to establish a causal link between the distribution of this information by the students and the destruction of unborn life. The continued availability of information added to the possible negative consequences for the health and welfare of Irish women would seem to suggest that the prohibition

---

[23] *Ibid* at 4720–4721.

[24] *Ibid* at 4723. His reasoning in *Grogan* was subsequently confirmed by the Court of Justice in Case C-260/89 *Elliniki Radiophonia Tileorassi AE* v *Dimotiki Etairia Pliroforissis and Sotirios Kouvelas* [1991] ECR I-2925.

[25] Article 10 of the European Convention of Human Rights provides that "1. Everyone has the right to freedom of expression . . . . 2. The exercise of these freedoms, since it carries with it duties and responsibilities, may be subject to such formalities, conditions, restrictions or penalties as are prescribed by law and are necessary in a democratic society, in the interests of national security, territorial integrity or public safety, for the prevention of disorder or crime, for the protection of health or morals etc".

[26] *Ibid* 4729–4730.

was unacceptable as an ineffective and disproportionate means of implementing an otherwise legitimate national policy.

(c) Abortion counselling and the European Court of Human Rights

These facts were not lost on the European Court of Human Rights when the Open Door Counselling and Dublin Well Woman clinics claimed that the aforementioned Supreme Court injunction[27], restraining them from imparting information concerning abortion clinics outside Ireland, violated Articles 8, 10 and 14 of the European Convention on Human Rights.

Like Advocate General Van Gerven in the *Grogan* case, the European Court of Human Rights emphasised that "the protection afforded under Irish law to the right to life of the unborn is based on profound moral values concerning the nature of life". However, although the Court of Human Rights accepted that national authorities enjoy a wide margin of discretion with respect to moral issues and that they are generally in a better position to judge what the protection of morals at national level requires, it rejected the idea that this discretion was unlimited and emphasised its role as the body competent to determine whether restrictions of fundamental rights are compatible with the Convention. Essentially, the Court of Human Rights had to determine whether there was a pressing social need for the restriction and whether the restriction was proportionate to the legitimate aim being pursued by the Irish authorities.[28]

The Court first pointed to the "absolute" nature of the restriction and the fact that it imposed a perpetual restraint on the provision of information to pregnant women regardless of their age, state of health, or their reasons for seeking counselling on abortion.[29] It also rejected the link on which the Irish Courts had clearly based the injunction, between the provision of information and the destruction of life. The decision in each case remained with the women receiving the counselling and it was possible that many decided not to terminate their pregnancies after having received counselling. The counselling which was provided did not advocate or encourage any particular course of action.[30]

The Court also emphasised that the information which was the subject of the injunction was widely available from other sources and that the injunction did not appear to be effective, since large numbers of women continued to travel to the United Kingdom to terminate their pregnancies.[31]

Finally, the Court of Human Rights examined, and accepted, the evidence put forward by the applicants that the injunction had created a risk to the health of Irish women, since they were now seeking abortions at a later stage in pregnancy and they were not able to avail themselves of suitable aftercare as they had done previously.[32]

---

[27] [1987] ILRM 447, *supra* n 11.
[28] [1992] 15 EHRR 244 at para 70.
[29] *Ibid* para 73.
[30] *Ibid* para 75.
[31] *Ibid* para 76.
[32] *Ibid* para 77.

Given all these circumstances, the Court of Human Rights concluded that the injunction restraining the applicants from imparting information was disproportionate and, as such, was contrary to the freedom of expression as guaranteed in the Convention.

(d) A comparison of the two approaches

The Advocate General, Court of Justice and Court of Human Rights all recognised that the restrictions on the welfare clinics and the students' associations were an exercise of national discretion and were intended to protect the requirements of national morals. It goes without saying that national authorities are entitled to take action in order to protect ethical value-judgments enshrined in their Constitutions. However, the action they take must be compatible with the requirements of the fundamental rights enshrined in the Convention. These fundamental rights are part and parcel of the Community's *acquis communautaire.*

Unlike the other two bodies, however, the Court of Human Rights was clearly willing to scrutinise the effect of these measures on the welfare clinics, as well as on the women who actually or potentially availed of the services offered by the clinics. It pointed out what was perhaps an essential aspect of these cases: "Limitations on information concerning activities which, notwithstanding their moral implications, have been and continue to be tolerated by national authorities, call for careful scrutiny by the Convention institutions as to their conformity with the tenets of a democratic society".[33] The Court of Justice in *Grogan* had pointed out that it was not willing to substitute its view of the morality of abortion for the views of the legislatures in those Member States where it was legal. Of course, it was right not to do so, just as it was right not to interfere with a referendum in Ireland guaranteeing the right to life of the unborn. However, once the Court recognised that abortion is a service, it should have examined the effect of restrictions on the legal provision of such a service in another Member State and should have ensured that Member States, even when they derogate on the basis of public policy or imperative requirements, must still respect fundamental rights. The Opinion of the Advocate General laudably followed this line of reasoning, but his application of the principle of proportionality was unsatisfactory.

The Court of Human Rights, in contrast, emphasised how this prohibition might affect the women who availed of the clinics' services. The evidence available to it suggested that "the injunction had created a risk to the health of those women who are now seeking abortions at a later stage of pregnancy, due to lack of proper counselling, and who are not availing of customary medical supervision after the abortion has taken place".[34] Was this evidence available to the Court of Justice and if not, why not?[35]

---

[33] [1992] 15 EHRR 244 at para 72.
[34] *Ibid* para 77.
[35] See also De Búrca, (1993), *supra* n 7 at 312 and 315. As regards potential conflicts between the jurisprudence of the Court of Human Rights and the Court of Justice, the House of Lords Select

In addition, the Court of Human Rights held that information was widely available from other sources and that women continued to travel to the United Kingdom to terminate their pregnancies. The prohibition also paid no attention to the circumstances of individual cases (age, health, reasons for counselling and reasons for pregnancy) which might have led some women to seek assistance. Perhaps most importantly, the European Court of Human Rights was unprepared to accept the causal link between the counselling and termination of pregnancy which the Irish government had argued. The counselling was non-directive, women were not encouraged to terminate their pregnancies and "the decision as to whether or not to act on the information so provided was that of the woman concerned".

Why did the Court of Justice and Advocate General pay so little attention to the rights and the welfare of the recipients of the information and to the potential recipients of the service? Why did they not examine the causal link between the distribution of information and abortion and why did they not treat the women receiving this information as autonomous individuals capable of choice, as the European Court of Human Rights saw fit to do?

(iii) Further decisions of the Court of Justice which touch on family life

Diatta v *Land Berlin*[36] has been singled out before as an example of judicial weakness with respect to the rights of family members.[37] It involved the Senegalese wife of a French national resident in Germany. Soon after they arrived in Germany, Ms Diatta separated from her husband and went to live in separate accommodation. She was subsequently refused a renewal of her residence permit, since she was not regarded as a "family member" within the meaning of Community law. Given the separation, the German authorities considered that she no longer had a legal right to reside in Germany. The Court of Justice was asked whether a spouse in Ms Diatta's position (a third country national, married but separated from a Community worker) may be said to live "with the worker" within the meaning of Article 10(1) of Regulation (EEC) 1612/68. In addition, the national court wished to know whether spouses can enjoy an independent right

---

Committee for the European Communities has suggested that "It cannot, however, be assumed that the Luxembourg Court will always have full knowledge of [the European Convention] jurisprudence, whose quantity is steadily increasing". *Human Rights Re-examined,* 3rd report, 1993. If the European Convention is one the Court of Justice's sources in the field of human rights it would seem logical that the Court of Justice would be aware of the jurisprudence of the Strasbourg court and that it should deal with the same type of evidence available to the Court of Human Rights when confronted with similar cases.

[36] Case 267/83 [1985] ECR 567.

[37] See, in particular, Weiler, *supra* n 3. Case 12/86 *Demirel* [1987] ECR 3719, has also been criticised in the context of family reunion. It will not, however, be discussed in detail in this chapter.

of residence, regardless of the state of their relationship with the Community worker on the basis of Article 11 of Regulation (EEC) 1612/68.

Article 10(1) Regulation (EEC) 1612/68 confers a right to migrate and install themselves with the worker on a spouse, descendants who are under 21 or dependent and dependent relatives in the ascending line.[38] To its credit, the Court of Justice refused to interpret Article 10 restrictively and did not consider it necessary for the family defined in Article 10(1) to live under the same roof permanently. It also held, as regards the rights of spouses to install themselves, that "the marital relationship cannot be regarded as dissolved so long as it has not been terminated by the competent authority. It is not dissolved merely because the spouses live separately, even where they intend to divorce at a later date".[39]

However, the Court did not regard Article 11 of Regulation (EEC) 1612/68 as a source of an independent right of residence for Ms Diatta. Article 11 gave her a right to exercise an activity as an employed person within the territory, so long as the condition in Article 10 was fulfilled; or in other words, so long as she remained a family member or derived an independent right of residence from some other provision of Community law such as Regulation (EEC) 1251/70. The clear implication of the Court's decision is that spouses enjoy a derivative right to reside with their economically active spouse, even if they are separated and live under different roofs.[40] However, once the marriage is dissolved, the former spouse no longer enjoys this derivative right of residence and must rely, for the purposes of residence, on some other provision of Community law, if he or she is eligible under some other provision of Community law.

The decision of the Court of Justice in *Diatta* has been criticised for its failure to address the fundamental rights issues concerned. The Court of Justice did not, for example, address the Commission's claims that it would be contrary to fundamental rights if the Regulation did enable a worker to "remove, unilaterally and arbitrarily, the protection accorded by Community law to the members of his [or her] family".[41]

As Weiler points out, the Community legislature may indeed have intended and the Regulation may mean that, once divorced, a spouse no longer enjoys a derivative right of residence, but that does not imply that no fundamental rights

[38] Other secondary Community measures also refer to members of the worker's family and most reiterate or rely on the definition provided in Regulation (EEC) 1612/68. See, *inter alia*, Article 1 para 2 of Council Directive 64/221/EEC, JOCE, 4 April 1964, 850 or the special English edition 1963–64, at 117; Article 1 of Council Directive 68/360/EEC (OJ 1968 L 257/13); and Council Directive 73/148/EEC (OJ 1973 L 172/14). In contrast, Article 1(f) of Council Regulation (EEC) 1408/71, which concerns the application of social security schemes to employed persons, self-employed persons and members of their families, leaves the definition of "member of the family" to the legislation of the State under which the benefits are provided, or the Member State where the beneficiary is resident.
[39] Case 267/83 at para 20.
[40] In Case C-370/90 *The Queen* v *Immigration Appeals Tribunal and Surinder Singh, ex parte Secretary of State for the Home Department* [1992] ECR I-4265; [1992] 3 CMLR 358, the Court of Justice allowed the husband to use the protection of Community law even though the first stage of a divorce had been achieved and the parties had obtained a *decree nisi*.
[41] Case 267/83 at 585.

are at issue.[42] If a binding fundamental rights norm does exist, the Court of Justice may find that the Community legislation is not in violation. However, "if there is a norm and it does appear to be in conflict with the Community measure, the Court has two . . . options: either to construe the Community measure in such a way that it does not conflict with human rights norms (as the Commission) or to strike the Community measure down".[43]

National courts have also had to address the type of issues which arose in *Diatta*. Prior to *Diatta*, in *The Queen v Secretary of State, ex parte Sandhu*[44], the English High Court had to decide whether a male non-EEC national who enters the United Kingdom by virtue of being married to a non-British EEC national and has resided in the United Kingdom for a number of years can be deprived of all his immigration rights if there is a separation between them or a divorce, and/or if the wife no longer resides in the United Kingdom. According to Comyn J, Article 10 of Regulation (EEC) 1612/68 could not "be construed as meaning that there is a permanent cloak thrown around the non-EEC partner . . . But it gives him a status of which, in my judgment, the other party by a unilateral act [such as divorce or separation] cannot deprive him".[45] His decision was subsequently overturned by the Court of Appeal which considered that "the regulations and directions which establish rights for an EEC national . . . only create rights in the dependant himself when they are derivative rights depending on the exercise by the European national of his or her own rights, except where the legislation itself specifically confers independent rights."[46]

Weatherill and Beaumont maintain that the social integration rationale behind the free movement of persons suggests that even a person who is not a national of a Member State who is divorced by a Community worker does not inevitably and immediately lose derivative rights. They therefore regard the *Sandhu* decision as dubious in the light of *Diatta*.[47] However, it is difficult to see how this argument can stand up to the fact that the *Diatta* decision in fact emphasised the derivative nature of the rights of spouses and the fact that their rights only survive as long as the relationship between the two is not legally dissolved.

In a recent case in the United Kingdom, *The Queen v Secretary of State for the Home Department, ex parte Kulwinder Kaur Phull and ors*,[48] the Court of Appeal was asked to grant judicial review of a refusal to revoke a deportation order.

The applicant, a British national, was married to an Indian national who had been served a deportation order. Unlike Ms Diatta, the Indian spouse in *Phull* could not derive rights from Article 10 of Regulation (EEC) 1612/68, because her husband was not in a situation contemplated by the Regulation or the free movement provisions. He was British, resident in Britain and the case therefore

---

[42] See Weiler (1992), *supra* n 3 at 87.
[43] *Ibid.*
[44] [1982] CMLR 553.
[45] *Ibid* para 33.
[46] [1983] CMLR 131 at para 10. See also the decision of the House of Lords to the same effect, *The Times*, 5 October 1985.
[47] See Weatherill and Beaumont, *European Community Law* (1993) 490.
[48] See the draft judgment of 17 August 1995.

appears to be one internal to the United Kingdom and governed by British rules on family reunion.[49]

The applicants in *Phull*, however, were trying to base their rights of residence on Article 8(a) EC, which establishes a right of free movement and residence for Member State nationals, or Union citizens as they are now known. Essentially, the Phulls claimed that, as a Union citizen, Mr Phull not only had a right to reside on the basis of Community law, but also a right to have his spouse reside with him.

The Court of Appeal has held, however, that Article 8(a) does not really extend the rights of Community nationals and that it certainly does not create a right to family reunion for Community nationals such as Mr Phull, who have not moved to another Member State and resided there. Indeed, the Court held that even if such a right to family reunion could be said to flow from Article 8(a), subordinate legislation would still be required to give effect to it.[50]

The *Sandhu*, *Diatta* and *Phull* cases highlight what could be regarded as a fundamental weakness in the treatment of the rights of family members by the Community legislature and by the Court of Justice. Derivative and, as *Diatta* proves, limited rights, have been extended to family members on the basis of Articles 10 and 11 Regulation (EEC) 1612/68.

Since then, most developments with respect to the rights of family members have stemmed from the Court's interpretation of social advantages in Article 7(2) of the same Regulation.[51] Legislative attempts have been made to extend the definition of family members to include unmarried partners.[52]

However, the right of Community workers to be joined by their unmarried partners is treated as a "social advantage" by the Court of Justice which is afforded to workers as a means to facilitate their free movement.[53]

---

[49] Similarly, see the decision of the Court of Justice in Joined Cases 35 and 36/82 *Morson and Jhanjan* [1982] ECR 3723. In Case A/138 *Berrehab* v *The Netherlands* [1989] 11 EHRR 322, however, a Moroccan migrant in the Netherlands successfully argued before the European Court of Human Rights that deportation after the breakdown of his marriage would deny him the right to see his child and would, therefore, be an infringement of the right to respect family life contained in Article 8 of the European Convention of Human Rights.

The fact that the United Kingdom does not treat the European Convention of Human Rights as part of its internal law means that the applicants in *Phull* may have problems relying on the Convention outside the context of Community law.

[50] The 1990 Residence Directives adopted prior to the TEU, which establish a right of free movement and residence for economically inactive persons, retired persons and students, all provide for derivative rights of residence for family members. In the case of the students' residence Directive, however, the right to family reunion is limited to the spouse and dependent children.

[51] Article 7(2) provides that "[workers] shall enjoy the same social and tax advantages as national workers".

[52] See the Commission's modified proposal for a Regulation amending Regulation (EEC) 1612/68, which provides for a right of residence for "the spouse or any person with similar status under the system of the host country and their descendants (OJ 1990 C 119/10)". See also the European Parliament's broader proposal in OJ 1990 C 68/88, where it provided that "the right to install themselves shall also cover the person with whom the worker lives in a *de facto* union recognised as such for administrative and legal purposes whether in the Member State of origin or the host Member State, . . . 3. The death of the worker, dissolution of the marriage, or ending of the *de facto* union shall not prejudice the rights acquired under paras 1 and 2 of this article".

[53] See Case 59/85 *Netherlands* v *Reed* [1986] ECR 1283.

In *Reed* the Court refused to extend the definition of family members in Regulation (EEC) 1612/68 in the absence of a "general social development" to this effect in the Member States. Instead, the Court stuck to a "notional 'nuclear' family norm, a family form which is more of an ideological construct than a reality and which has been in steady decline across Europe for many years".[54] Why have subsections of a section of a piece of secondary legislation been used to do what the principle of non-discrimination in Article 6 EC could have done handsomely on its own?[55] The Court's use of Article 7(2) may have helped to develop the social dimension of free movement and European citizenship.[56] However, it has also arguably based the rights of family members on an inadequate legislative, rather than constitutional, basis and has meant that entitlement to social rights in Community law has remained firmly based on the "male breadwinner" concept of the family.

This brings us back to the second weakness which Weiler identified in the *Diatta* case, namely, that the free movement and residence of spouses is regulated in Community law with reference to the objectives of free movement and economic integration. Community law "views the spouse not as an individual and as an end in itself, the fundamental rights of whom must be protected because of his or her humaneness, but rather as an instrumentality, a means to ensure the economic goal of free movement of all the factors of production".[57] This is also evident in the fact that Member State nationals who have availed of the free movement provisions and been economically active in another Member State may rely on Community law rights when returning to their own Member State,[58] whereas Mr Phull appears to have no similar right to rely on Community law, despite the fundamental rights issues involved in his case and despite the creation of Union citizenship. Indeed it is arguable that the creation of Union citizenship has simply emphasised this division between economically active persons and persons who do not engage in an economic activity, since there is no equivalent of Regulation (EEC) 1612/68 for Union citizens relying on Article 8(a).

(iv) Conclusions

The object of this chapter is simply to demonstrate that the response of the Court of Justice to issues touching on family life has not always been satisfactory from the point of view of family members and the protection of fundamental rights. The difficulties encountered by the Court of Justice in the *Grogan* case are understandable. It was confronted with a highly sensitive and morally

---

[54] See Ackers (1994), *supra* n 5 at 398.
[55] I am grateful to Ms Elspeth Guild for a few insights in this respect. I bear full responsibility for the quality of the argument however.
[56] See Ackers (1994), *supra* n 5 at 392.
[57] See Weiler (1992), *supra* n 3 at 90.
[58] See Case 115/78 *Knoors* [1979] ECR 399; and Case C-370/90 *Singh*.

charged national issue, the prospect of a ruling by the European Court of Human Rights in a similar case in the near future and a belligerent Irish Supreme Court anxious to safeguard its interpretation of its national constitutional values. However, as the decision of the Court of Human Rights demonstrated, it is possible to respect national constitutional ethical values, while examining whether or not the means chosen to effect those values respect fundamental rights. The Court of Human Rights also proved that it was possible to carry out this examination with the health and welfare of women in mind.

The cases on family reunion also demonstrate the difficulties which the primarily economic objectives of the Community and the elusive "scope of application of the Treaty" create for the Court of Justice (and national courts when implementing Community law) when determining the level of protection which the Community affords family members. The traditional role of women as the primary home-carers has changed rapidly in recent years. Nevertheless, women who do not work outside the home, or women who do not qualify as Community workers because of the nature of their employment,[59] or the fact that they are third country nationals, are highly dependent on their spouses as regards the enjoyment of the protection of Community law. Unmarried partners are also in a vulnerable position and do not even qualify under the Community's definition of family members. It is, of course, easy to criticise and more difficult to suggest solutions. Two points of departure might be a more coherent and adventurous application of the principle of non-discrimination in Article 6 and a rigorous examination of the possible fundamental rights implications of the Court's rulings.

SIOFRA O'LEARY
Assistant Director of the
Centre for European Legal Studies,
University of Cambridge,
UK

---

[59] See Ackers (1994), *supra* n 5 at 391–393.

Chapter 17

USING EC LAW TO CHALLENGE SEXUAL ORIENTATION DISCRIMINATION AT WORK*

(i) Introduction

This chapter focuses on the arguments for, and against, the use of European Community law to challenge sexual orientation discrimination[1] at work.[2] Arguments in cases from jurisdictions outside the Community will be considered and an attempt will be made to assess the way in which the Court of Justice might deal with them.

(ii) The importance of sexual orientation discrimination at work

Most European case law on homosexuality, particularly before the European Court of Human Rights ("ECHR") relates to discrimination under criminal law.[3] However, the employment context will be more significant for most workers. Lesbians may be affected by workplace discrimination while, in the United Kingdom for example, only a male homosexual act can constitute a crime.[4] Even that will usually be punished by a relatively small fine, whereas discrimination at work may incur loss of earnings or even of livelihood.

---

*This chapter was written by Virginia Harrison. The views expressed are those of the author and do not necessarily represent those of the UK Government.
[1] Here, reference is made generally to sexual orientation, which is taken to include the sexual preference of those who do not limit themselves exclusively to same sex relationships.
[2] Legislative reform is considered in Waaldijk and Clapham, *Homosexuality: A European Community Issue. Essays on Lesbian and Gay Rights in European Law and Policy* (Dordrecht: Martinus Nijhoff, 1993) ("Waaldijk and Clapham").
[3] See *infra*, n 19.
[4] See, for example, Sexual Offences Act 1956 s 32.

The discrimination may include failure to engage or dismissal.[5] The motive will frequently be difficult to prove, although occasionally it may be given openly. An example currently before the United Kingdom courts concerns the United Kingdom policy that homosexuality is incompatible with military service.[6] This has led to the discharge of those discovered to be homosexual.[7]

Such discrimination could be tackled by law based upon a "neutral difference" strategy. Sexual orientation is arguably an irrelevant personal difference and so no worker should suffer discrimination because of it.

In contrast, a worker may complain that, while she is formally treated equally to her heterosexual colleagues, there is an absence of substantive equality. Accordingly compassionate leave may be available to attend the illness or funeral of an opposite sex cohabitee or spouse, but not where the partner is of the same sex. There may also be discrimination with regard to pay if the partner is excluded from pension benefits, medical insurance or travel concessions.

Defrenne v *Sabena No 2*[8] shows that sex equality legislation, particularly Article 119, has two aims: a "level playing field" for the regulation of traders across the Union (the economic reason) and the improvement of living conditions mentioned in Article 2 EC (the social reason).[9]

There is the additional economic benefit of maximising resources invested in training, for example, by easing the return of mothers to work. This is also relevant to sexual orientation discrimination where a highly trained worker is dismissed.[10] The social reason may be more controversial because of disagreement over the proper extent of social policy. It may be argued that a single market requires competitive differences.[11]

It is realistic to recognise that for sexual orientation discrimination none of these arguments will necessarily be accepted. Prohibiting discrimination may have perceived economic disadvantages, for example the risk to co-workers' jobs if business is lost because of customers' prejudice. Many religious organizations, including the Roman Catholic Church, oppose the practice of homosexuality. Some may feel that the economic costs of discrimination are outweighed by the impact of open same sex relationships on society. Much of the literature has taken the adverse effects of sexual orientation discrimination as self evident, but judges have often disagreed.

---

[5] Harassment at work is also recognised as a form of discrimination which affects gay men and lesbian women, see *infra* n 29.
[6] *R* v *Ministry of Defence ex parte Smith* (unpublished transcript of High Court judgment given on 7 June 1995). At the time of writing, the Court of Appeal's judgment on appeal is awaited.
[7] The Ministry of Defence has since announced that the policy is to be reviewed (reported in *The Times*, 5 September 1995).
[8] Case 43/75 [1976] ECR 455.
[9] See Barnard, in this volume.
[10] It was reported that a Lieutenant who admitted that she was a lesbian and was suspended, "would probably have been called upon – as a Serbo-Croat speaker – to negotiate the release of British hostages in Bosnia" (*Daily Telegraph*, 3 July 1995, 2).
[11] The extent of EC social policy is, of course, already highly controversial, particularly for the United Kingdom which has secured a Protocol rendering the Agreement on Social Policy and measures thereunder inapplicable in the UK.

(iii) Relevant EC and related provisions

It is assumed that the reader is familiar with Article 119 EC, together with the Equal Pay Directive (75/117/EEC) ("EPD") and the Equal Treatment Directive (76/207/EEC) ("ETD"). While this "hard" legislation forms the basis of the arguments considered, there is also relevant "soft" law which may be significant.

Firstly, there is the right to equality,[12] present in several specific Treaty provisions.[13] The Court of Justice has said that these merely express "the general principle of equality which is one of the fundamental principles of Community law", requiring that "similar situations shall not be treated differently unless the differentiation is objectively justified".[14] Therefore the Court may find unlawful discrimination which is not specifically prohibited under Community legislation. In *Prais* v *Council*,[15] for example, the principle was applied in addition to non-discrimination provisions in Staff Regulations and to the European Convention of Human Rights.[16]

This may provide a valuable model for those challenging sexual orientation discrimination, if it is accepted that the employment of a gay man or a lesbian woman is not materially different from the employment of a heterosexual.

Secondly, the European Convention of Human Rights is at least evidence of the constitutional traditions common to all Member States.[17] The Court of Justice, although not bound by the Convention, may look for guidelines in ECHR jurisprudence. Homosexuals have relied, in particular, on Articles 8 and 14.[18]

However, apart from the criminalisation of conduct,[19] most other interferences with gays' private life have been held justified under Article 8(2).

---

[12] This is a fundamental right which the Court will safeguard because it has to draw inspiration from constitutional traditions common to the Member States (Case 4/73 *Nold* v *Commission* [1974] ECR 491).

[13] For example, Articles 6 and 40(3) EC.

[14] Cases 103, 145/77 *Royal Scholten-Honig* v *IBAP* [1978] ECR 2037 at 2072; Case 300/86 *Van Landschoot* v *Mera* [1988] ECR 3443 at 3460.

[15] Case 130/75 [1976] ECR 1589.

[16] The Court held that the principle of equality required conditions for Commission entry tests to be the same for all candidates. This meant holding the tests on the same date although the principle was to be balanced in this case against the applicant's need to observe a religious holiday.

[17] ". . . *international Treaties for the protection of human rights* on which Member States have collaborated or of which they are signatories, can supply guidelines which should be followed *within the framework of Community law*" (Case 4/73 *Nold, supra* n 12).

[18] Article 8(1) provides that everyone has the right to respect for, *inter alia*, her private and family life. Article 8(2) permits interference with the exercise of this right by a public authority only where it is "in accordance with the law and is necessary in a democratic society in the interests of national security, public safety or the economic well-being of the country, for the prevention of disorder or crime, for the protection of health or morals or for the protection of the rights and freedoms of others". Article 14 provides that the rights and freedoms in the Convention are to be secured "without discrimination on any ground such as sex, . . . ". Sexual orientation is not specifically mentioned.

[19] On criminalisation of conduct see, for example, the judgment of the Court of 22 October 1981, *Dudgeon*, Series A, No 45, 18; and judgment of 26 October 1988, *Norris*, Series A, No 142, 21. For a detailed examination of this case law see Van Dijk, "The treatment of Homosexuals under the European Convention of Human Rights" in Waaldijk and Clapham, *supra* n 2.

There is an evident tension in the ECHR's judgments between the need to reflect prevailing attitudes and the importance of supporting the individual against the majority where his or her rights are threatened.[20]

Not only does the ECHR appear ready to find interference with the right justified, the European Commission of Human Rights has also held that interference with homosexual activity or orientation is interference not with family life, but, possibly, with private life.[21] No reason was given for this view, but it may impact upon the applicability of provisions protecting family rights in EC law.[22]

There are recent indications of a shift by the ECHR.[23] Moreover, Simon Brown LJ has now said in the United Kingdom High Court that he considers that defending the United Kingdom's Armed Services policy from Convention challenge is becoming more difficult.[24]

However, the Court of Justice need not wait for the ECHR's decisions to draw upon the principles in the Convention when interpreting Community law. Indeed it has been argued that, because the Community has to establish a legal order for the single market, it cannot and should not give the same margin of appreciation to States as the ECHR perhaps can in setting what could be seen as minimum standards.[25]

The Community's own institutions have undertaken some relevant non-binding measures.[26] The European Parliament has produced a number of reports and resolutions urging the application of the principle of equal treatment to sexual orientation discrimination.[27] The Commission, while ultimately acknowledging *competence* under the Treaties to address the issue,[28] has chosen to confine itself to non-binding measures.[29]

On one hand it might be argued that the absence of specific hard law in response to Parliament's reports indicates that the EC institutions do not wish to tackle the issue. On the other, the Court may not only rely on the "soft law"

---

[20] See, for example, *Cossey* v *United Kingdom* [1991] 13 EHRR 622, in which the ECHR considered whether denial to a transsexual of the opportunity to marry was a violation of her rights under Article 8. The majority decided that the policy was consistent with the necessary balance between the individual and the general interest. Judge Martens, dissenting, asserted that the Court's "mission" was "to protect the individual against the collectivity" (663).

[21] Application 9369/81 *X and Y* v *United Kingdom* (1983) DR 32, 220 at 221.

[22] For example, in the reference to "family status" in Article 2(1) of the ETD.

[23] See, for example, *B* v *France* (Judgment of 25 March 1992, Series A, No 232–C).

[24] *Ex parte Smith, supra* n 6. Curtis J took the opposing view that, even if Article 8(1) had been breached, Article 8(2) applied.

[25] See Hall, "The European Convention on Human Rights and Public Policy Exceptions to the Free Movement of Workers under the EEC Treaty" 16 ELRev (1991), 466.

[26] National courts are to take non-binding Community measures into account when interpreting Community legislation to see whether they are designed to supplement Community provisions (Case C-322/88 *Grimaldi* [1989] ECR 4407).

[27] For the names of the reports and their specific references see Russell "Sexual orientation discrimination and Europe" NLJ (1995), 374–5.

[28] In its formal response to the complaint by Peter Tatchell, referred to by Russell, *ibid.*

[29] It played a part in setting up the Clapham and Waaldijk survey, *supra* n 2. It also referred specifically to harassment of gay men and lesbian women in its Code of Practice, "Protecting the Dignity of Women and Men at Work", which accompanied its Recommendation of 27 November 1991 (OJ L 49/92). See text accompanying, *infra* n 55.

in interpreting the provisions, but gay workers may use it to show a general social development which should be reflected in a broad construction of the hard legislation[30] to include sexual orientation discrimination.

(iv) Arguments which challenge sexual orientation discrimination

(a) Direct sex discrimination

Occasionally, anti-gay discrimination may arise against a woman or a man simply because he/she is male/female. Therefore the United Kingdom Equal Opportunities Commission issued a non-discrimination notice[31] against Dan Air for limiting recruitment of cabin staff to females. The employer's "defence" was that most male applicants tended to be homosexual and that there might be a health risk in the event of an air accident.[32] In such a case an action could be brought under Article 119 EC, under the ETD or the EPD, depending on the nature of the discrimination.

(b) Indirect sex discrimination

Sexual orientation discrimination arguably applies a condition to all employees (that they be heterosexual). If it can be shown that the proportion of one gender (for example, males) who can comply is considerably smaller than the proportion of females, it could be shown to be indirect sex discrimination. This would depend on showing that the proportion of the male population which is gay is considerably higher than the proportion of the female population which is lesbian. The argument also assumes that homosexuality is not gender specific.

In *De Santis* v *Pacific Telephone and Telegraph Co. Inc.*,[33] it was argued, *inter alia*, that discrimination against homosexuals disproportionately affected men. This was, firstly, because of an alleged greater incidence in the male population and, secondly, because the employer was more likely to discover male homosexuality.[34] Circuit Judge Sneed, dissenting, favoured allowing the appellants to bring evidence on the point. He pointed out that to prove discrimination they would have to show a disproportionate impact upon males in general, not merely upon male homosexuals as against lesbian women.[35]

Indirect discrimination is clearly established in the Court of Justice's case law

---

[30] See Case 59/85 *Netherlands* v *Reed* [1986] ECR 1283.

[31] Under the Sex Discrimination Act 1975 s 67.

[32] Since this was direct discrimination, objective justification would not have been relevant. However, medical evidence was produced to show that there was no such health risk.

[33] 608 F 2d 327 (9th Circuit), a US case heard before the Court of Appeals on that Circuit.

[34] In the UK this might be because males face the possibility of criminal prosecution

[35] The majority of the Court would not allow evidence of disparate impact. Circuit Judge Choy described the argument as an attempt to "bootstrap" protection for homosexuals under the guise of protecting men generally.

and indeed in the ETD itself[36] so that where a disparate impact upon either sex can be shown without objective justification, Article 119 EC, the EPD or the ETD might be used as applicable. In practice, however, it is likely to be difficult to show the statistical evidence of the impact. Fear of discrimination and harassment leads many homosexuals to conceal their orientation.[37]

The evidence of disparate impact will have to be established at the level of the national court.[38] It is interesting to consider the success of a disparate impact argument before the United Kingdom Court of Appeal in *R* v *Secretary of State for Employment, ex parte Seymour-Smith*.[39] While showing that the Court of Appeal is prepared to rely upon statistical arguments, the case effectively demonstrates the uncertain nature of indirect discrimination claims. Their success may depend upon the time when the statistical comparison is made. The fact that the Divisional Court reached a different conclusion demonstrates the scope for disagreement.[40]

(c) Sexual orientation discrimination as discrimination "on grounds of sex"

Article 119, the EPD[41] and the ETD[42] all refer either to "discrimination based on sex"[43] or "discrimination on grounds of sex", so that this argument is potentially available in EC law.

One approach would be to argue that sexual orientation is predetermined just as gender usually is.[44] It appealed to one judge in the Supreme Court of Hawaii, who referred to the controversy over whether homosexuality is determined by genetics or environment.[45] He concluded that this would have to be decided as a matter of fact before the Court could determine whether the word "sex" in the Hawaii Constitution included orientation.

However, differences of expert opinion suggest we must be far from a final resolution of the question. Meanwhile, it is doubtful that judges are the best

---

[36] Article 2(1). Indirect discrimination in relation to pay has also been held contrary to Article 119 EC and the EPD, e.g. Case C-127/92 *Enderby* v *Frenchay Area Health Authority and Secretary of State for Health* [1993] ECR I-5535.

[37] Kitzinger explains the "pervasive heterosexual consensus" at work, where everyone is assumed to be heterosexual (Kitzinger, "Lesbians and Gay Men in the Workplace: Psychosocial Issues" in Davidson and Earnshaw, *Vulnerable Workers: Psychosocial and Legal Issues* (1991).

[38] See Case C-127/92 *Enderby*, supra n 36.

[39] *The Times*, 3 August 1995.

[40] Indirect discrimination may also be capable of objective justification. Justification advanced for anti-gay discrimination includes arguments relating to discipline, e.g. in the Armed Forces. The issue is not covered here, but there is clearly scope for further work.

[41] Article 1.

[42] Article 2.

[43] Article 119 EC refers in its concluding paragraph to "equal pay *without discrimination based on sex*".

[44] Transsexualism is, of course, an exception to the assertion that gender is pre-determined. See Flynn, in this volume.

[45] James S Burns, Intermediate Court of Appeals Judge, concurring for his own reasons with the majority decision of the Supreme Court of Hawaii in *Baehr* v *Lewin* (852 P 2d 44 (Hawaii 1993) at 69).

people to decide it. Nor does the argument take account of those who have same sex relationships through choice or circumstances.

The Court of Justice would be deciding upon a question which is highly controversial ethically as well as scientifically. Its case law indicates that it tends to avoid such controversies.[46] It may not need to confront them to prevent sexual orientation discrimination because of the other arguments available.

Another highly contentious argument was put to the Vancouver Trial Division by the applicant's advocate, in *Nielsen* v *Canada*.[47] She contended that, in heterosexual society, women are expected to be "socially submissive to, and sexually available to, men only". Homosexuals, particularly lesbians, in her view, challenge that submissive role and its heterosexual context. Because heterosexuality is a vehicle for sex inequality, sexual orientation discrimination is sex discrimination, reinforcing inequality between men and women. Muldoon J, giving judgment in the case, held that the very controversial nature of the argument made it unsuitable for endorsement by a court of law.

The argument seems equally unlikely to succeed before the Court of Justice. While the Court has been eager to address issues of female inequality, much of its case law could be seen as ensuring that women will be free to fulfil their traditional family responsibilities, for example by working part-time. Moreover, the Court is likely to avoid a decision which might be seen as undermining family life.[48]

It may be contended that "sex" in these and similar provisions includes "sexual orientation" as a matter of legislative interpretation. In *De Santis*,[49] this was unanimously rejected on the ground that the legislature would have made the inclusion express if it had been intended. It appeared that several Bills extending the relevant provision to include sexual orientation had been introduced into Congress but none had been enacted.

In *Re Board of Governors of University of Saskatchewan and Saskatchewan Human Rights Commission*,[50] Johnson J held that "on the basis of sex" had its ordinary meaning as on the basis of whether the person was male or female, not on "sexual orientation, . . . sexual proclivity or sexual activity". He recognised a relaxation in public attitudes and decided that, if the legislature had meant to cover sexual orientation discrimination, it would have said so expressly.

In *Ex parte Smith*[51], Counsel referred to two human rights cases in which "sex" was taken to include "sexual orientation".[52] It was argued that the ETD should

---

[46] *Cf.* Case C-159/90 *SPUC* v *Grogan* [1991] ECR I-4685, in which the Court "sidestepped" the need to decide whether the freedom to provide services included the right to distribute information in Ireland about UK abortion clinics. See O'Leary, in this volume.

[47] 1992 2 CF 561 at 573.

[48] *Cf.* Case 59/85 *Reed, supra* n 30. See O'Leary, in this volume.

[49] See *supra* n 33. The argument was made in relation to the Civil Rights Act 1964.

[50] [1976] 66 DLR (3d) 561 (Saskatchewan Queen's Bench).

[51] See *supra* n 6.

[52] *Toonan* v *Australia Communication* IHRR Vol 1 No 3 (1994), a decision of the Human Rights Committee on Articles 2(1) and 26 of the International Covenant on Civil and Political Rights; and *S* v *United Kingdom*, a decision of the European Commission of Human Rights, in which a lesbian partner was held unable to rely on a provision in favour of those who "live together as husband and wife", but where apparently it was accepted that "sex" in Article 14 of the Convention (*supra* n 18) included sexual orientation.

be read accordingly. Simon Brown LJ said that the argument "appeared to founder on the plain and unambiguous language of the [ETD], an instrument which says everything about gender discrimination, but ... nothing about orientation discrimination". He distinguished the cited human rights cases on the ground that the Conventions concerned were clearly designed to give protection across the board, whereas the ETD was intended, in his judgment, to meet "an altogether narrower concern". ECHR jurisprudence, as we have seen, not only allows comparison in the interpretation of analogous provisions. It should also demonstrate "guidelines which should be followed within the framework of Community law".[53] The difficulty then is that the ECHR's case law does not clearly prohibit anti-gay discrimination.[54]

Another of Counsel's arguments in *ex parte Smith* was based upon the reference to harassment of gay men and lesbians in its Code of Practice on sexual harassment.[55] The preamble to the accompanying Recommendation states that sexual harassment "may in certain circumstances, be contrary to the principle of equal treatment". Simon Brown LJ pointed out that the phrase "in certain circumstances" shows that not all sexual harassment will be contrary to the principle and so it is not necessarily true that harassment of gay people contravenes it. Logically, this must be correct, although the Court of Justice may choose to draw upon the Recommendation's general approach in interpreting "hard" law.

Looking more generally at legislative interpretation, the Court of Justice's teleological approach contrasts with that of common law courts. Ascertaining legislative intent, for example, is not a historic exercise to understand the intentions of Treaty makers. The Court is the guardian of the Treaties, interpreting them in a dynamic way.[56] Although Directives have reasons in their preambles, which can aid interpretation, Directives are also the result of negotiation.[57]

The reasons on which the EPD is stated to be based refer to "the implementation of the principle that men and women should receive equal pay contained in Article 119". They also recite that "it is desirable to reinforce the basic laws by standards aimed at facilitating the practical application of the principle of equality in such a way that all employees in the Community can be protected in these matters". The ETD's reasons refer to the "principle of equal treatment for men and women".

These reasons and the rest of the preambles to the Directives could either be used to limit each Directive's purpose or to show that a wider understanding of

---

[53] See Case 4/73 *Nold, supra* n 12.
[54] The decision in *S v United Kingdom* is, of course, only a decision of the Commission of Human Rights.
[55] See, *supra* n 29.
[56] Judge Kutscher wrote extra-judicially "Interpretations based on the original situation would in no way be in keeping with a Community law orientated towards the future".
[57] Judge Pescatore pointed out in a 1963 lecture that in negotiations, "divergent even conflicting intentions may perfectly well underlie a given text ... the art of treaty-making is in part the art of disguising irresolvable differences". This seems equally applicable to Council negotiations.

equality leads to protection from this form of discrimination. They certainly refer to "men and women" but it is arguable that the principle of equality allows a broader approach than that of mere comparison between males and females.

There is clear precedent for such a broad interpretation of the words "on grounds of sex" in the ETD. One example is the interpretation used in cases of sex discrimination on the ground of pregnancy.[58] Conceptual problems over the lack of a male comparator for the pregnant female have been met by a broad application of the principle of equal treatment. As pregnancy is exclusive to females, a woman would not suffer pregnancy discrimination but for her sex. It could be argued that homosexual or lesbian experiences respectively are gender specific too; only men can experience the physical aspects of male homosexual activity and only women can experience those aspects of lesbian activity. The *experiences* are entirely different.

If it is accepted that same sex relationships are gender specific, the focus is placed upon the worker suffering the discrimination and not upon his or her partner. So, arguably, discrimination against a person for having a partner of the same sex is discrimination on the ground of gender: a woman employee is treated unfavourably for having a relationship with a woman in contrast to a male employee having a relationship with a woman and vice versa. Thus sexual orientation discrimination becomes straightforward sex discrimination, differentiating between men and women, and the argument could be used in relation to Article 119 EC, the ETD or the EPD. The approach has been endorsed in one decided case, that of *Baehr* v *Lewin*.[59] Here the Supreme Court of Hawaii considered denial of marriage to same sex couples to be not sexual orientation discrimination but sexual discrimination.

The majority rejected the argument that only parties of opposite sexes could marry because that was the nature of marriage itself. They called that argument "circular and unpersuasive" and held that it was the State's regulation of access to the status of married persons, on the basis of the applicants' sex, that gave rise to the question whether the applicant couples had been denied the equal protection of the laws.

The same logic could be applied to discrimination against same sex partners because they are same sex partners. However, both United States and Canadian Courts[60] have said the discrimination is for choosing a partner of the same sex, not for being a man living with a man rather than a woman living with a man. In the Canadian *Knodel*[61] case, Rowles J expressed the firm view that "sexual orientation is not gender specific, nor is it a characteristic that affects one gender primarily".

It could be argued, however, that this is merely a question of terminology in choosing to refer to male homosexuality and lesbianism under the same terms

---

[58] See for example, Case 177/88 *Dekker* [1990] ECR I-3941. See Szyszcak, in this volume.
[59] *Supra* n 45 at 570.
[60] See *Vogel* v *Manitoba (AG)* ((1992) 90 DLR (4th) 84) (*"Vogel II"*) and *De Santis, supra* n 33.
[61] [1991] 6 WWR 728 at 743.

such as "sexual orientation" and "homosexuality". Wintermute[62] points out the analogy, that to prohibit "interracial marriage" is racial discrimination even though it could be said that all races are excluded from it. Male homosexuality and lesbianism have not always been identified together, for example the criminal law often singles out male homosexual activity for prohibition.

This leads to some attempt by those opposing protection to distinguish between same sex and opposite sex relationships so that it can be said that the discrimination is justified. For example it has often been said that the distinction is the impossibility of reproduction for same-sex couples.[63] This argument is used particularly to oppose same sex marriage. Even for marriage it is unconvincing, since marriage is permissible between opposite sex couples who are unable to have children, through age, disability or other circumstances. As a basis for distinction between same sex and opposite sex cohabitees, it is even less persuasive. Many opposite sex cohabitees will not have procreation as their goal or intention. In any case, same sex couples now often have the opportunity for assisted reproduction and of course for raising children by adoption or step-parenting. The only remaining biological difference is the potential of opposite sex couples for penile-vaginal intercourse. Some opposite sex couples will not have this either, however, and it seems dubious that such an intimate detail of private life should form the basis of differential treatment of an employee.

This "gender specific" argument could certainly be used in a Community context. It has the advantage that it does not directly threaten existing social institutions.

(d) Marital or family status

The ETD refers to "discrimination . . . on grounds of sex directly or indirectly by reference in particular to marital or family status" (Article 2.1).

It is not clear whether the reference to marital or family status just provides examples of forms of sex discrimination. If so, it may be argued that gay workers could not assert that they had suffered marital or family status discrimination, unless they could show sex discrimination itself.

(1) Marital status

If, however, an employer refused promotion to a newly married man because of his marriage, it would surely be no answer to an action under the ETD or implementing provisions that he would have treated a newly married woman in the same way. The married person who suffers such discrimination must be either male or female. However, the reason for the discrimination is not his/her gender but the marriage. If the newly married man does not have an action

---

[62] Wintermute, "Sexual Orientation Discrimination as Sex Discrimination: Same-Sex Couples and the Charter in *Mossop, Egan* and *Layland*" 39 McGill L J (1994), 429.
[63] See, for example, the discussion of *Vogel II, supra* n 60, later in this chapter under the heading "Family status".

under the ETD, it is hard to see what the phrase on marital status adds to discrimination on the grounds of sex.

If marital status is strictly defined as the state of being single, married, widowed, separated or divorced, this head of discrimination is unlikely to be relevant in relation to sexual orientation, at least as long as marriage is not available to homosexuals. The provision could only assist if marital status included cohabitation and if cohabitation, for this purpose, comprehended same sex couples.

The Court of Justice has considered the meaning of "spouse" in *Reed*.[64] Ms Reed sought to bring herself within the meaning of spouse in Article 10 of Regulation (EEC) 1612/68 so as to be allowed to take up residence and employment with her cohabitee with whom she had moved from the United Kingdom to Holland.

The Court decided that the meaning of spouse could not be extended to cover a cohabitee but that to allow her to move with her partner was to accord her partner the same "social advantages" as Dutch nationals who were allowed under Dutch law to bring their unmarried companions to live with them in Holland. The Court stated:

> In the absence of any indication of a general social development which would justify a broad construction and in the absence of any indication to the contrary in the regulation, it must be held that the term "spouse" in Article 10 of the Regulation refers to a marital relationship only.

As D'Oliveira[65] has suggested, once a general social development can be traced in favour of stable non-marital relationships, it seems there will be scope for a broader construction. It may be arguable even now that marital status in the ETD is to be broadly construed in view of the general growth of extramarital cohabitation.

To trace such a social development in relation to same sex cohabitation itself might be difficult. Canadian cases have dealt with alleged marital status discrimination in relation to the exclusion of a worker's same sex partner from benefits under a dental care plan. In *Nielsen* v *Canada*,[66] benefits were available under the plan to "common law spouses". Muldoon J, however, held that "that concept bespeaks disparity of gender in the relationship". The Court of Justice's disinclination to undermine established institutions suggests it might take a similar view.

Even if the argument were to succeed for the gay worker, however, its usefulness would be limited to the scope of the ETD. It could apply to discrimination in conditions covered by the ETD (such as dismissal, reduction in working conditions, lack of compassionate leave or denial of promotion) but not to questions of pay, including pensions covered by Article 119 EC or by the EPD. These are likely to be of central concern.

---

[64] Case 59/85 *Reed, supra* n 30.
[65] D'Oliveira, "Lesbians and Gays and the Freedom of Movement of Persons" in Waaldijk and Clapham, *supra* n 2.
[66] *Supra* n 47.
[67] 543 NE 2d 49 at 54 (NY 1989).

(2) Family status

As in the case of marital status, there are forms of family status discrimination which are definitely not gender-based, yet which one might anticipate that the Court of Justice would find prohibited by the ETD. A worker might suffer discrimination because of his/her family commitments, such as care of a child, parent or disabled spouse.

An employer who refuses to engage such a carer is not basing his decision on the applicant's sex at all but on the extent of his, or her, family responsibilities. If discrimination on such grounds is covered within the ETD then family status discrimination could be said to be a separate ground.

Whether a same-sex relationship falls within the meaning of "family status" will obviously depend upon the definition given to "family". In the United States, contradictory dicta have been expressed. In *Braschi* v *Stahl Associates Co*, it was said that "family includes two adult [same-sex] lifetime partners".[67] However in *Bowers* v *Hardwick* in contrast, the Court pronounced that "No connection between family . . . and homosexual activity has been demonstrated".[68]

In *Vogel II*, two sociologists gave conflicting expert testimony on the meaning of family status.[69] One pronounced the criteria of familial relationship as sharing a residence, co-operating economically, having an emotional relationship with one another and sharing a sexual relationship. If all were present, a couple could be said to be in a familial relationship. The other said that the basic characteristic of a family was the involvement of children, of a male and a female and the ability for procreation. Hirschfield J decided that a family unit without children was included if there was the potential to conceive them. It followed, he held, that same sex couples without children and without the potential for procreation might be familial in character but would not be families in the accepted sense.

If an infertile and childless heterosexual couple is a family there is a good argument for saying that a gay couple is one too. However, the argument has even more force when the couple are living with children of one or both of them (whether from the previous relationship of one, from adoption or from artificial insemination). In English, we speak of a "one parent family". It seems inevitable that if a same sex partner permanently joins that parent in the home and shares the financial and caring responsibilities for the children, we are still looking at a family.

It would be highly controversial for the Court of Justice to find that a gay or lesbian couple was a family. It is more likely that the Court would seek to avoid the substance of the issue as it did in *SPUC* v *Grogan*.[70] Even if the argument worked, it would only assist those in established households. It could not help those who suffer discrimination on the ground of casual relationships.

Even for those within the definition, there seem likely to be few rights depending on "family status". Canadian cases on the point have concerned for

---

[68] 478 US 186 at 191.
[69] *Supra* n 60.
[70] *Supra* n 46.

example the right to compassionate leave to attend a partner's funeral[71] or the partner's right to benefits under a dental services plan.[72] Pension rights in particular usually depend on being a spouse, or at least a cohabitee, and are often not available to a worker's family members.

It seems also possible that gay couples, particularly where they do not have children, see themselves as having an alternative lifestyle, which should be valued as such without the need to conform to a heterosexual stereotype.

(v) An overview

Should a case come before the Court of Justice on the issue, it will be a policy question whether the arguments discussed will succeed. The Court may well try to find a way of addressing the case before it without making a controversial finding of more general significance.[73] If a more general principle is to be established, it may be influenced by the cost implications of its ruling. So, for instance, there might be significant budgetary implications if same sex partners were to be entitled to pension provision and recent cases on pensions have shown clearly the Court's awareness of such a point.[74]

For this reason at least there may be a temptation to distinguish between discrimination which causes a detriment (for example, dismissal) from discrimination which incurs additional costs for the employer (for example, the payment of pension or insurance contributions to partners who would otherwise have had no entitlement). It might be said that gay workers are asking for privacy in seeking to have their home lives ignored and then seeking to have those home lives taken into account for their employee benefits. Such an argument was put by Robertson JA in his judgment in *Egan* v *Canada*.[75] It may be answered that the workers are not asking essentially for privacy but for equality.

(vi) Conclusion

Gay men and lesbian women are subject to a variety of forms of workplace discrimination. Some forms can simply be classified as direct or indirect sex discrimination because they are undoubtedly based on gender. Most will require some innovative interpretation by the Court if they are to be covered within existing Community law. Whether this happens will depend upon whether the Court sees the innovation as justified by the same social and economic argu-

---

[71] *Mossop* v *Canada* [1993] 1 SCR 554, 100 DLR (4th) 658.
[72] E.g. *Nielsen* v *Canada, supra* n 47.
[73] See Case C-159/90 *SPUC* v *Grogan, supra* n 46, and Case 59/85 *Reed, supra* n 30.
[74] Moore, for example, has argued that the Court appears to be restricting itself in applying the principle of equal pay to occupational pension schemes because of its awareness of the economic cost (Moore, "'Justice Doesn't Mean a Free Lunch' The Application of the Principle of Equal Pay to Occupational Pension Schemes" 20 ELRev (1995), 159–177).
[75] [1993] 3 FC 401, 103 DLR (4th) 336 (CA).

ments upon which female equality law has developed. It will also depend upon whether the existing treatment of homosexuals is seen as violating fundamental human rights and the principle of equality.

It would be naive for advocates of the gay cause not to accept that the Court will be influenced by attitudes to homosexuality within Member States, by the political climate in the other Community institutions and by national governments' attitudes to the development of Community social policy in general.

Community case law indicates that the Court will avoid making far-reaching decisions which challenge important institutions such as marriage and the family. If persuaded of the importance of granting redress in an individual case, it may find a less controversial basis for doing so. This would lead to sporadic and therefore slower progress. Nevertheless, it may give time for public opinion to grow more favourable, leading to specific legislation or to a more innovative response from the Court.

VIRGINIA HARRISON
*Lawyer with the Department
of the Environment,
UK*

Part VI

WOMEN AND THE INTERNAL MARKET

Chapter 18

LAW, GENDER AND THE INTERNAL MARKET*

(i) Introduction

It is characteristic of the *sui generis* nature of the European Union that it possesses both a legal order and a set of policies which are neither complete nor wholly coherent. There is no necessary logic to every provision contained in the EU Treaties.

It is well known, for example, that the inclusion of the free movement of labour was a trade off for Italy, and that the Common Agricultural Policy (most obviously benefiting France) balanced the benefits to be derived by Germany from access to French markets for her goods. Similarly, the inclusion of Article 119 EC can be traced back to the circumstances of one particular Member State, in this case once again France, which already had a similar domestic guarantee.[1] However, what cannot be doubted is that the decision to include Article 119 has decisively shaped the balance of EU social policy, in so far as it has created a legislative and judicial focus on questions of discrimination and equal treatment which has itself in turn generated a huge body of comment by academics and practitioners alike. It has also, as I shall argue, to a large extent structured and dominated the responses (such as they exist) of feminist legal writers to the European Union.

There are good practical and conceptual reasons for the development of an extended literature on sex equality law. For nearly 20 years, Article 119 remained dormant as a "paper" provision of the Treaty of Rome. However, what was significant was its very presence in the Treaty, capable of being exploited as so-called "second-wave feminism", generated a new interest within the feminist community regarding the availability or feasibility of legal remedies against discrimination in the workplace. It has been important to analyse the legislative

---

*This chapter was written by Jo Shaw.
[1] See Barnard, in this volume.

measures of the EU institutions and the judicial interpretations placed upon these
measures by the Court of Justice and national courts alike, both in order to clarify
the opportunities and limitations contained in the texts and in order to locate EU
sex equality law within a broader conceptual canvas of equality laws. Even outside
the arena of legal scholarship, there has been a tendency to articulate the interaction between women and the EU primarily in terms of employment and pay issues,
and questions of equality.[2]

The point to be made here is that, just as it is argued from time to time that
the energy devoted by feminist activists to the pursuit of struggles within the
legal process may distract from other non-legal aspects of the feminist project,[3]
so it can be argued that the focus on sex equality law has distracted from the
possibilities of analysis from a gender perspective of other aspects of the EU
legal order. To a certain extent, the one-sided nature of feminist concern with EC
law is gradually being addressed by a broadening of academic comment upon
the content and nature of equality law: by work going, as it were, beyond equality law formally defined. In particular, partly as a reaction to some of the inconsistencies and unhappy distinctions drawn in the field of EU sex equality law,
the attempt by the Court of Justice to draw a bright line between the public and
private spheres, and between the world of work and the world of the home, the
family and the domestic environment, has been vigorously challenged.[4] Secondly, there is now a willingness to problematise the operation of the free
movement provisions in terms of their gendered content, not only as socio-economic fact, but also as a matter of legal analysis which challenges the veneer or
mask of universality placed upon migration rights by the Court of Justice.[5]
Thirdly, within scholarship on EU sex equality legislation and case law, there is
now a body of work which adopts a more theoretical and comparative perspective.[6] Perhaps gradually legal scholarship on EU is beginning to take account of
the movement of feminist legal scholarship in general from "a critique of sexism in the law into an increasingly sophisticated jurisprudence".[7]

---

[2] See Pillinger, *Feminising the Market. Women's Pay and Employment in the European Community* (1992).
See also the emphasis placed in Cox, "Equal Opportunities" in Gold, *The Social Dimension. Employment Policy in the European Community* (1993) 41–63.

[3] Lacey, "Legislation against sex discrimination: questions from a feminist perspective" 14 *Journal of
Law and Society* (1987), 411–421.

[4] Cullen, "The Subsidiary Woman", *Journal of Social Welfare and Family Law* (1994), 407–422.

[5] Ackers, "Women, Citizenship and European Community Law: The Gender Implications of the
Free Movement Provisions" 16 *Journal of Social Welfare and Family Law* (1994) 391–406; Ackers,
"Research Report: Women, Citizenship and European Community Law: The Gender Implications
of the Free Movement Provisions", 17 *Journal of Social Welfare and Family Law* (1995) 498–502;
Hervey, "Migrant workers and their families in the European Union: the pervasive market ideology
of Community law" in Shaw and More, *New Legal Dynamics of European Union* (Oxford
University Press, 1995) Scheiwe, "EC Law's Unequal Treatment of the Family: The Case Law of the
European Court of Justice on Rules Prohibiting Discrimination on Grounds of Sex and Nationality"
3 *Social and Legal Studies* (1994), 243–265.

[6] See especially More, "'Equal Treatment' of the Sexes in European Community Law: What does
'Equal' mean?" 1 *Feminist Legal Studies* (1993), 45–74; Luckhaus, "Individualisation of Social Security
Benefits" in McCrudden, *Equality of Treatment between Women and Men in Social Security* (1994), 147–161.

[7] Sandland, "Between 'Truth' and 'Difference': Poststructuralism, law and the power of feminism" 3
Feminist Legal Studies (1995), 3–47 at 3; see, in particular, the contribution by Flynn, in this volume.

The area of concern to be addressed in this chapter is the law of the EU internal market. It begins by briefly reviewing the well documented fact that there is a serious dislocation between the economic situation of women in the European Union and the brave new world of the internal market as it was "sold" to the Member States and other dominant actors in the mid-1980s. This provides the basis for a critical appraisal of the law of the internal market from a gender perspective. The chapter then proceeds to the level of legal analysis by looking at a number of possible interactions between the category of gender and the normative framework of the internal market.

One way of looking at the gender/internal market interaction is to view the internal market as practically synonymous with the policy-making activities of the EU. A serious practical proposal in the context of policy making is to alter the balance of the legislative process by incorporating gender audit.[8] Closely linked to this would be the auditing of the institutions themselves, and the struggle to ensure the adequate representation of women in positions of power in those institutions. This argument will not be considered further in this chapter.[9]

A second position which can be taken is to explore the notion that the law of the internal market embodies a set of values and principles which are inimical to the interests of women. To support this argument, the proposition must be accepted that law is capable of having a gendered content or reflecting a gendered perspective. This argument will be examined in Section (iii) *infra* and will be used to examine some of the assumptions which underlie the political objective of integration, which lies at the heart of the project to create an internal market within the EU.

Finally, I shall endeavour in Section (iv) to assess the impact of the internal market and its legal framework upon the citizenship of women. So far little of the burgeoning body of politico-legal work on the foundations and structures of "European" citizenship (a notion closely linked to the so-called "market citizen" who is the vigorous, combative and competitive inhabitant of the internal market) has specifically considered the gender aspects of citizenship. Section (iv) considers the two related questions:

- can women be "market citizens"?; and
- does the impact of "market citizenship" make it impossible for women to be European Union citizens?

In this chapter the term "gender" is not taken as synonymous with "women". It adopts a generally accepted definition of gender as implying the social relations

---

[8] Beveridge and Nott, "Women, Wealth and the Single Market", Paper presented to the Conference on The Evolution of the Rules for a Single European Market, Exeter, September 8–11, 1994; see also the contribution by Beveridge and Nott, in this volume.

[9] See, with a particular focus on the role of women in development policy, EUROSTEP and WIDE, *Gender Mapping the European Union*, Report Prepared by Mandy Macdonald, Brussels, March 1995; *cf.* a similar exercise undertaken on a continuing basis in Scotland by ENGENDER, *Gender Audit 1995. Putting Scottish Women in the Picture.* For a general approach to these questions see Phillips, *Engendering Democracy* (1991). See also Flynn, in this volume.

between and among the sexes.[10] The focus on relationships encourages an awareness of differences of power, especially economic power, between men and women considered as groups. As Williams has argued, feminist analysis has gone beyond the argument that women should be given the same opportunities as men, thus allowing them to assimilate themselves to the situation of men.[11] The focus on differences helps to highlight, for example, the feminisation of poverty:

> which dramatises the chronic and increasing economic vulnerability of women. Feminists now realise that the assimilationists' traditional focus on gender-neutrality may have rendered women more vulnerable to certain gender-related disabilities that have important economic consequences.[12]

This is of particular relevance in an assessment of the EU internal market and its law. By definition, a self-consciously wealth-creating economic project is bound to have an impact upon the relative economic statuses of the sexes. It is therefore particularly important for the analysis in this chapter to tease out what Graycar and Morgan have termed the "hidden gender of law".[13] The impact of feminist work on law can be that of exposing the ways in which a body of knowledge (that is, legal doctrines and legal practices) is constructed so as to exclude the interests of the less powerful, in particular women.[14] A useful focus of analysis can be upon legal categories and the ways in which they are used by policy makers and adjudicators in a manner which reflects a particular vision of the world. This chapter begins the task of uncovering the "gender" of the law of the internal market. It is analytical rather than reformist in nature, in that it proposes a framework for analysis rather than putting forward a series of concrete proposals for change.[15]

(ii) Women and the internal market: the balance sheet

The controversy of "feminist method" has sustained many lengthy academic debates.[16] Whatever its precise nature, however, there does appear to be "general agreement that feminist method begins with the primacy of women's experience".[17]

---

[10] Jones and Jónasdóttir, "Introduction: Gender as an Analytic Category in Political Theory" in Jones and Jónasdóttir, *The Political Interests of Gender* (1988) 1–10 at 6.
[11] Williams, "Deconstructing Gender" in Bartlett and Kennedy, *Feminist Legal Theory* (1991) 95–123.
[12] *Ibid* 95.
[13] Graycar and Morgan, *The Hidden Gender of Law* (1990).
[14] See also Finley, "Breaking Women's Silence in Law: The Dilemma of the Gendered Nature of Legal Reasoning" 64 *Notre Dame Law Review* (1989), 886.
[15] Sandland (1995), *supra* n 7.
[16] For a concise review of the issues raised in relation to law see the section on "Feminist Epistemology" in Graycar and Morgan, *supra* n 13 at 56 *et seq.*
[17] Cain, "Feminist jurisprudence: Grounding the Theories" in Bartlett and Kennedy (1991) *supra* n 11, 263–280 at 263.

What is envisaged by this is "[listening] to women when they describe the harms they experience as women"; if we are careful to do this, we are "likely to get the legal theory right (that is, perceive the problem correctly and propose the right solutions)".[18] However, in the absence of a significant body of ethnographic research about the effect of the internal market upon women and of their perceptions of that market,[19] our starting point here has to be the available information concerning the actual and/or potential impact of integration processes upon the economic situation of women living and working within the geographical area of the internal market.

At one level, the creation and management of an internal market is the relatively straightforward core of the integrationist project conceived in Western Europe in the 1950s, and has developed since then in terms of scope and geographical spread. The terminology of the original Treaties might refer to a "common market", but the two concepts can be taken for most practical purposes as synonymous. The creation of a market without internal frontiers within the EU, in which goods, services, labour, enterprise and capital may flow freely, clearly goes to the very heart of the integration process and integration concept themselves.[20] At that level, enquiring into the impact of the internal market upon women requires medium range historical assessment of changes in the economic situation of women since the inception of the European Communities.

One difficulty might be in separating out the specific impact of integration processes on women's economic status, just as it is difficult for economists to assess the impact of integration as a whole upon patterns of trade and wealth creation.

A different level of analysis involves viewing the internal market more narrowly as a political opportunity seized in the 1980s for the relaunch of an ailing and stagnated EC integration project. The momentum created by the so-called "1992 project" still continues today, at a more attenuated level. It is this level of analysis which is used in this chapter, relating the question of gender more specifically to a particular political movement, and the body of legal regulation most immediately associated with it. For it is from that movement that moves towards matters such as EU citizenship (considered *infra*) are derived.

Much was, of course, made of the opportunities of "1992" in official and quasi-official propaganda.[21] Significant wealth creation was envisaged as a result of the removal of the barriers to free trade within the European Community.

---

[18] *Ibid.*

[19] See now, however, the work by Ackers (1994), *supra* n 5, and Ackers, in this volume; see also, on a different, but parallel, subject the work of Grüsser, White and Dorn, "Free Movement and Welfare Entitlement: EU Drug Users in Berlin" 5 *Journal of European Social Policy* (1995), 13–28.

[20] See Article 7A EC. See Gialdino, "Some Reflections on the *Acquis Communautaire*" 32 *Common Market Law Review* (1995), 1089–1121 at 1114.

[21] Cecchini, *The European Challenge 1992: The Benefits of a Single Market* (1988) summarised and discussed by El-Agraa in "The economics of the Single Market" in El-Agraa, *The Economics of the European Community*, 4th Edition (1994) 155–169. But see also the sustained critique provided by Cutler *et al, 1992 – The Struggle for Europe. A Critical Evaluation of the European Community* (1989).

That is not to say, however, that the anticipated impact of "1992" upon women was in any way ignored by the EU institutions.[22]

The Commission had a document drawn up on the impact of the completion of the internal market on women in the European Community, with conclusions that were far from sanguine.[23] It accepted that women's unemployment was higher and that they were more vulnerable to many aspects of restructuring, particularly in the service industries.

The European Parliament, in a similar vein, adopted a Resolution calling for the conditions to be put in place in which men and women could enter 1993 on equal terms.[24] The political conclusions reached by the institutions have been well backed up by a wealth of statistical evidence, particularly on women in the labour market.[25]

Moreover, a similar tone has been maintained since 1993, as the EU has entered a new period in which unemployment rather than growth has been the first preoccupation, and management and administration rather than regulation and policy initiation have been the leitmotifs of the Commission's work. There is nothing in the Green and White Papers on Social Policy,[26] in the material produced by the Commission on Social Europe, or in the general flow of "soft law" from both Council and Commission (action programmes, resolutions, and the like) to suggest that the specific concerns of women are not, at least at some general level, being taken into account in the policy making process.

There is much in the rhetoric to commend. Many noble statements about "real" equality of opportunity, combating secondary labour markets, protecting atypical work, developing enhanced training strategies, promoting proper and effective childcare, and such like, are to be found. It is perhaps unfortunate that the Delors White Paper on Growth and Competitiveness[27] appears to make little of sex differences in patterns of unemployment; a point recognised by the ECOSOC in its Opinion on that document.[28] That point is perhaps best redressed by a Resolution of the Council and of the Representatives of the Member States meeting within Council of December 1994 on equal participation by women in an employment-intensive economic growth strategy within the European Union.[29] The upbeat rhetoric is best captured by the very last

---

[22] See also from secondary literature: Whitting, "Women and 1992: opportunity or disaster?" *Social Policy Review* (1989–90), 214–228; Springe, "Women – Winners or Losers in the New Europe" in Templeton, *A Woman's Place?* (1993) 109–116; Schunter-Kleemann, *EG-Binnenmarkt – EuroPatriarchat oder Aufbruch der Frauen?* (1990); Hoskyns, "The European Community's Policy on Women in the Context of 1992" 15.1 *Women's Studies International Forum* (1992), 21–28.

[23] *The Impact of the Completion of the Internal Market on Women in the European Community,* Working Document prepared for DGV, CEC, Equal Opportunities Unit, Doc V/506/90–EN, 1990.

[24] Resolution on the 1992 Single Market and its implications for women in the EC (OJ 1991 C 48/222); see also Report drawn up on behalf of the Committee on Women's Rights on the 1992 Single Market and its implications for women in the EC (Rapporteur van Hemeldonck), EP Doc. 143.485/fin, December 6 1990.

[25] See for example EUROSTAT, *Women in the European Community,* 1992, Luxembourg: OOPEC.

[26] COM(93) 551; COM(94) 333.

[27] Bull, EC Supp, 6/93.

[28] OJ 1994 C 295/57; OJ 1994 C 295/62.

[29] OJ 1994 C 368/3.

paragraph of a Council Resolution adopted at the same time, which addresses the need for a European Union social policy which is to include:[30]

> by means of an ongoing process, specific matters relating to women and men and to equal opportunities for them, in the definition and implementation of all Community policies and, to this end, to strive towards developing methods for the ongoing integration of equal opportunities for women and men in economic and social policies.

(ii) The values of the internal market

Does it seem fair, in the light of the foregoing, to suggest that there is really a problematic relationship between the category of gender and the values of the internal market? At a simple practical level, there is a marked failure on the part of the EU institutions to live up to the principles established at a rhetorical level. A detailed examination of EU measures shows that the objective of ensuring that women's interests are incorporated is not achieved. For example, R and D measures on the training and mobility of researchers adopted as recently as 1994 failed to make specific reference to women, even though they explicitly addressed the "promotion of human resources", the interests of "less-favoured regions", and "young" and "distinguished" scientists.[31] Women are underrepresented in the field of science and R and D, and likely to remain so for as long as bodies like the EU ignore this question. However, these are first and foremost matters to be addressed by "audit", which falls outside the scope of this chapter.[32] Instead, this chapter will concentrate on the embedding of values within the legal system; in order to develop such an argument it is important to define and delimit briefly the law of the internal market.

(a) The law of the internal market

Simply put, the legal structure of the internal market composes three principal elements. In the first place, freedom of movement is guaranteed by primary principles contained in the Treaty (Articles 30, 48, 52, 58, and 73B EC), subject to certain exceptions and limitations, such as those contained in Articles 36, 48(3) and 56 (principally, but not exclusively, reasons of public policy, and public health or safety).

Secondly, there exists a very significant body of interpretative case law generated by the Court of Justice which in itself contains important principles giving a broad meaning to the rules of primary EC law. For example, the *Dassonville* case gave a wide definition of what may constitute a measure having equivalent effect to a quantitative restriction on trade in goods within the mean-

---

[30] Council Resolution OJ 1994 C 368/6.
[31] Council Decision 94/916/EEC (OJ 1994 L 361/90). *Cf.*, however, Council Decision 94/915/EEC (OJ 1994 L 361/77) on targeted socio-economic research which does contain measures specifically aimed at women.
[32] See, *supra* nn 8 and 9.

ing of Article 30.[33] Any measure actually or potentially restricting interstate trade will fall within the scope of that provision, and will require some form of justification to escape prohibition.

Similarly, in the context of freedom to provide services, recent Court of Justice case law appears to support a broad interpretation of Article 59 as covering, in principle, any form of restriction on freedom to provide services.[34]

On the other hand, however, these points do need to be viewed in the light of the Court's apparent retreat in respect of the impact of EC law principles on national measures which appear to have a relatively tenuous link to interstate trade and which do not actually discriminate against non-national goods. A good example is Sunday trading rules, deemed by the Court now to fall outside the scope of Article 30.[35] The point to be made here concerns the power of the Court to define the proper limits of the internal market and to identify what might be termed a reserved area of "local police powers" for Member States which permits them to regulate without restriction certain aspects of economic life.

The Court of Justice has also had a considerable impact upon the third source of internal market law – EU legislation. In the first place, it has defined the balance between measures of liberalisation (contained principally in the Treaty), and the necessary scope of measures of harmonisation, which will operate where liberalisation alone is insufficient to secure a single market. In particular, the *Cassis de Dijon* decision in which the Court both articulated and defined the limits of the so-called mutual recognition principle highlighted fairly precisely the extent of legislation needed to secure the possibility of freedom of movement in the light of the need to protect recognised values such as consumer safety and the protection of the environment.[36] To put it another way, the Court has secured the boundary between market or negative integration and positive integration. Secondly, the Court of Justice has intruded in a significant way into the legislative process through its case law on the legal basis of measures. It has attempted, for example, to define the difference between a measure concerned with the internal market which should be based principally on Article 100A EC and one concerned with the environment for which Article 130S is the appropriate legal basis.[37]

(b) Law, values and gender

In what respect might it be argued that the law of the internal market, as presented, reveals a problematic relationship with gender, used as a category of analysis?

To answer this question, it is useful to define the limits of the internal market.

---

[33] Case 8/74 *Procureur du Roi* v *Dassonville* [1974] ECR 837.
[34] Case C-275/92 *Customs and Excise* v *Schindler* [1994] ECR I-1039.
[35] Cases C-306/88 etc *Stoke-on-Trent City Council* v *B & Q plc* [1992] ECR I-6457; see also Cases C-267 and 268/91 *Criminal Proceedings against Keck and Mithouard* [1993] ECR I-6097.
[36] Case 120/78 *Rewe-Zentrale AG* v *Bundesmonopolverwaltung für Branntwein* [1979] ECR 649.
[37] Case C-399/89 *Commission* v *Council (Titanium Dioxide)* [1991] ECR I-2867; Case C-155/91 *Commission* v *Council (Waste Directive)* [1993] ECR I-939.

At one level, it seems difficult to argue that any EU legislation concerned with socio-economic behaviour or market regulation should not be regarded as "internal market legislation". However, there are constitutional, practical and ideological reasons why a core of that legislation is emerging as part of the so-called *acquis communautaire.*

The *acquis* (literally the Community "patrimony") has formally achieved a special status under the EU system. It is one of the objectives of *Union* under Article B TEU to maintain in full the *acquis communautaire.* This would seem to indicate that the *acquis* is a body of rules and principles which go to the essence of the integration project as it has been developed and refined since the 1950s. They are the principles and rules which cannot be changed as a matter of party political or ideological dogma, but define what it is to be a "Community" or a "Union".

For a piece of EU legislation, as opposed to provisions of the constitutive Treaties, being part of the *acquis* might be said to confer some form of entrenchment against repeal. However, there is no conclusive judicial definition of either the meaning or the scope of the *acquis* and Article B TEU is not a justiciable provision before the Court of Justice. Hence, the practical impact of this concept of entrenchment must remain a matter of conjecture.[38]

Practically, however, as the Union grows geographically, and as new methods for assimilating entrant countries are developed, the *acquis* is becoming a useful tool to define the irreducible minimum of internal market legislation which should be introduced by, for example, the countries of Central and Eastern Europe as they attempt to adjust their economies and legal systems to the discipline of EU membership during the pre-accession phase.[39] These processes are governed by the so-called "Europe Agreements" between those countries and the European Community, and are guided now by an important Communication from the Commission on preparation for accession.[40] This Communication adopts a pragmatic approach to the question "What is the *acquis?*" For the purposes of preparation for accession, which requires a major concentration of regulatory resources, it is defined as the "Treaty articles and secondary legislation . . . [which] directly affect the free movement of goods, services, persons or capital. It is legislation without which obstacles to free movement would continue to exist or would reappear". It excludes "other legislation which indirectly affects the operation of the single market, for example because it affects the competitive situation of firms . . .".[41]

The Commission then goes on to make certain specific points about the legislation of the social dimension:

> The social dimension is an essential element of internal market policy. This is explicit in the Treaty. Moreover, much social legislation has an internal market

---

[38] See Gialdino, *supra* n 20.
[39] On accession, of course, the full *acquis* must be accepted, subject to negotiated transitional periods: see Gialdino, *supra* n 20 at 1091 *et seq.*
[40] *Preparation of the Associated Countries of Central and Eastern Europe for Integration into the Internal Market of the Union,* COM(95) 163 of 3 May 1995.
[41] *Ibid* at para 3.5.

reasoning among its justifications. An uneven approach in national legislation concerning workers' rights or health and safety in the workplace could result in unequal costs for economic operators and threaten to distort competition . . .

At the same time, certain social legislation is not aimed exclusively at achieving a level playing field. High levels of social protection are a fundamental aim of the Union. They are served by, among other things, the economic benefits arising from the internal market . . . [Included are] those parts of social legislation which affect the functioning of the internal market or which are a necessary complement to other measures identified as key instruments . . . .

What this passage indicates is an ascription of priorities. It confirms the long-standing "Cinderella" status of social policy[42] within the pantheon of EU objectives. And yet this conclusion is by no means inevitable, in economic terms, as Pelkmans has argued. For is it right that the EU should be seeking to pursue the objective of economic interpenetration principally by applying:

rigorous scrutiny of the hindrances to the free movement of goods, services and capital, with a multitude of proposals about the minimum harmonisation needed to achieve such freedoms; complemented by a fairly strict competition policy applied to distortions in product and services markets; with, on the other hand, little or no scrutiny of the economic obstacles to the free movement of workers or massive distortions of competition in the labour markets?[43]

Can one, he concludes, "speak of a completed internal market if the national regulatory provisions with respect to the labour market are highly restrictive and diverse"? In similar terms, Beveridge and Nott speak critically of the economic/social divide in what they describe as the "geometry of Europe".[44] The argument that economic and social issues can logically be divided is easy to challenge.[45] On the other hand, there is a clear bifurcation of treatment in respect of the powers provided under the Treaty. Article 100A (strategically introduced by the Single European Act to facilitate the introduction of single market legislation) explicitly excludes from its scope, and therefore from qualified majority voting, measures relating to the free movement of persons and the rights and interests of employed persons (para 2). Even after the introduction of new qualified majority voting possibilities under the Social Policy Agreement for the Member States minus the United Kingdom, there are still explicit restrictions for some aspects of social policy, such as social security and social protection of workers.

---

[42] See, for example, Szyszczak, "Social Policy: a Happy Ending or a Reworking of the Fairy Tale?" in O'Keeffe and Twomey, *Legal Issues of the Maastricht Treaty* (1994) 313–327.
[43] "Towards Economic Union" in Ludlow, *Setting European Community Priorities 1991–1992* (1991) 63.
[44] *Supra* n 8.
[45] Two good examples of the tensions inherent in the divide are to be found in the case law of the Court of Justice: Case 31/87 *Gebroeders Beentjes v Netherlands State* [1988] ECR 4635 (tension between the principle of non-discrimination and local authority contracting policies aimed at alleviating long-term unemployment); and Case C-113/89 *Rush Portuguesa Lda v Office National d'Immigration* [1990] ECR I-1417 (tension between free movement of services and national employment legislation).

It is clear that many aspects of social policy are regarded as protected domains for the Member States.

While none of these points necessarily indicate any particular "take" by the EU on the gender question, what they actually do is indicate the ways in which the internal market concept can be manipulated to achieve specific political objectives. In fact, a number of authors have argued that there is an unhappy fit between categories of women, their lives, their work, their social reality, and the ideology and practice of the internal market. Hervey, for example, has argued that despite the universalist terminology of EC law, it is in fact dominant social groups (that is white men of EU origin) who benefit most greatly from the protections which it confers.[46] She demonstrates that one mechanism whereby this occurs is the "all-pervasive concept of the 'market'",[47] showing that the operation at a legal level of free movement rights is highly gendered. This point is echoed also by Ackers[48] who shows that while women do form almost 50% of intra-EU migrants (contrary to popular perceptions of women as somehow more immobile then men), there is a very strong link between migrant women having children and their ability to participate in the labour market.[49]

Of course, there has always been a problematic relationship between women and both the concept and the practice of competition.[50] For nineteenth century women, tradition and a dominant order said it was "unwomanly"; for twentieth century feminists, it might be thought "unsisterly"![51]

The point is made by Pateman that women were excluded from the original social contract which not only lies at the heart of political authority in modern society, but also constructs the ability of citizens to operate in the public sphere; including the marketplace.[52] If women are subjects of the social contract, rather than participants in it, what is their relationship to the market order which lies quite explicitly across that original contract?[53] The explicit refusal of the Court of Justice to consider the implications of market equality for the sexual division of labour[54] highlights the extent to which the treatment of sex equality in EC law is simply an overlay upon an existing unchanged system of gendered labour markets, not a genuinely reformist project.[55]

In view of these points it is important, however, to re-emphasise the practical significance for women of social policy, and of the welfare system; a point

---

[46] Hervey, *supra* n 5.
[47] *Ibid* 93.
[48] Ackers, *supra* n 5.
[49] See also the detailed study provided by Bhaba and Shutter, *Women's Movement. Women under Immigration, Nationality and Refugee Law* (1994).
[50] For thought-provoking discussions see Miner and Longino, *Competition. A Feminist Taboo?* (1987).
[51] See in particular Longino, "The Ideology of Competition" in Miner and Longino, *ibid.*
[52] Pateman, *The Sexual Contract* (1988); Pateman, "Fraternal Social Contract" in *The Disorder of Women* (1989).
[53] See Cornell, "The Philosophy of the Limit: Systems Theory and Feminist Legal Reform" in Cornell, Rosenfeld and Carlson, *Deconstruction and the Possibility of Justice* (1992) 73–74.
[54] Case 184/83 *Hofmann v Barmer Ersatzkasse* [1984] ECR 3047; see Scheiwe, *supra* n 5, and Cullen, *supra* n 4.
[55] Sandland, *supra* n 7.

reconsidered in the context of the discussion of citizenship *infra.* Just because
these matters are constructed as questions of *national* competence rather than
primarily EU concerns does not necessarily relegate them to lower status.
Nonetheless, the choice between a more or less limited concept of "what is the
European Union" is important in terms of gender. Moreover, because of the
canonical status of "market" law within the EU, it must carry some message
about priorities, embedded values and the allocation of resources. Above all, it
restates a fundamental tenet of modern welfare capitalism, namely the consistent undervaluing of the unpaid work done primarily within the home and the
family by women.[56]

(iv) Citizenship, gender and the internal market[57]

As with other so-called universal categories, personhood as a state of being has
proved to be particularly inaccessible to women.[58] The absence of women from
theories of political obligation or authority, whether based on personal consent or
on hierarchy, is not simply a product of the prejudice of the times in which they
might have been written, but also symptomatic of systems of thought in which
the term "person" is conditional rather than absolute. Consequently, citizenship,
as a refined form of personhood, as well as the definition of the entitlements
conventionally linked to citizenship, have posed a number of intractable problems when viewed through a perspective of gender.[59] As Phillips has argued:

> starting with 'humanity', moving on to 'equality', 'rights', 'freedom', and 'democracy',
> feminists have queried most of the basic concepts of political thinking, arguing that
> theorists have always built on assumptions about women and men, though they have
> not always admitted (even to themselves) what these are. One of the most common
> tricks of this trade is to smuggle real live men into the seemingly abstract and inno-
> cent universals that nourish political thought. The 'individual' or the 'citizen' are
> obvious candidates for this form of gendered substitution.[60]

---

[56] Siim, "Towards a Feminist Rethinking of the Welfare State" in Jones and Jónasdóttir (1988), *supra*
n 10 at 160–186; Lewis, "Gender and the development of welfare regimes" 2 *Journal of European
Social Policy* (1992), 159–173; Sainsbury, *Gendering Welfare States* (1994).
[57] See the contribution of Everson, in this volume.
[58] Spelman, *Inessential Woman* (1990) (Women's Press); Naffine, *Law and the Sexes* (1990); (Allen and
Unwin), esp 100–123 ("The man of law"); in the context of legal analysis, the point is made particularly clearly by Sachs and Wilson, *Sexism and the Law: A Study of Male Beliefs and Legal Bias in Britain
and the United States* (1978).
[59] See, for example, Hernes, "The Welfare State Citizenship of Scandinavian Women" in Jones and
Jónasdóttir (1988), *supra* n 10 at 187–213; Yuval-Davis, "The Citizenship Debate: Women, Ethnic
Processes and the State" 39 *Feminist Review* (1991), 58; Dietz, "Context is All: Feminism and Theories
of Citizenship" in Mouffe, *Dimensions of Radical Democracy* (1992) 63–85; Vogel, "Is Citizenship
Gender-Specific?" in Vogel and Moran, *The Frontiers of Citizenship* (1991) 58–85; Vogel, "Marriage
and the Boundaries of Citizenship" in van Steenbergen, *The Condition of Citizenship* (1994) 76–89.
[60] Phillips, "Citizenship and Feminist Theory" in Andrews, *Citizenship* (1991) 76–88 at 77.

There are two significant "moves" in the postwar history of citizenship which can best be recounted in order to locate the question of gender. The first is the reconceptualisation of citizenship into stages by the sociologist TH Marshall.[61] Marshall divided citizenship rights into civic, political and social rights. Civic rights are basic civil liberties, gained (if the stages of citizenship are matched against British political/constitutional history) in the eighteenth century. That is, at least for men. Political rights are rights of political participation gained, again at least for men, in the nineteenth century. The twentieth century history of citizenship is a history of increased social and economic rights established by the evolution of welfare capitalism. But as Pateman has noted, once more the development of new rights is gendered. While Marshall might have included a right to employment as part of the pantheon of social rights in the "final stage" of citizenship, he did so just as the architects of the welfare state were constructing the framework of welfare provision around the figure of the male bread-winner and dependent wife.[62] The conclusion to be drawn here is that the Marshallian vision of the citizen is one in which women are not fully in focus.

The second dimension of citizenship theory deserving of particular comment in this context is the recent revival of interest in "active citizenship"[63] and the increasing tendency to articulate all manner of social and political questions about power, democracy, freedom and so on, through a prism of citizenship and participation.[64] In the particular context of gender, the dilemma of active participation in a society has been problematised in the tension between the individual and the group, between difference and belonging. In that sense, it is part of the very large question about the possibility or impossibility of universal citizenship. Is this an unattainable ideal which should be abandoned in favour of special group rights of representation and self-government for oppressed categories such as women and ethnic minorities?[65] Young puts the argument thus:[66]

> In a society where some groups are privileged while others are oppressed, insisting that as citizens people should leave behind their particular affiliations and experiences to adopt a general point of view serves only to reinforce that privilege; for the perspectives and interests of the privileged will tend to dominate this unified public, marginalising or silencing those of other groups.

While this argument has been criticised for its impracticability at the level of implementation[67], what it does do is serve to remind us of the political nature of

---

[61] Marshall, "Citizenship and Social Class" in Marshall, *Class, Citizenship and Social Development* (1976) 65–122.
[62] Pateman, "The Patriarchal Welfare State" in Pateman, *The Disorder of Women* (1988).
[63] See in particular Kymlicka and Norman, "Return of the Citizen: A Survey of Recent Work on Citizenship Theory" 104 *Ethics* (1993–94), 352–381; Andrews, *supra* n 60.
[64] Van Steenbergen, "The Condition of Citizenship: An Introduction" in Van Steenbergen, *The Condition of Citizenship* (1994) 1–9.
[65] Young, "Polity and Group Difference: A Critique of the Ideal of Universal Citizenship" 99 *Ethics* (1989), 250–74.
[66] Young, *ibid* at 257.
[67] Kymlicka and Norman (1993–4), *supra* n 63 at 373 *et seq.*

citizenship. Being a good citizen is more, for example, than being a good mother.[68] In the feminist context, being a good citizen would involve challenging the gendered division of labour at a political level, rather than simply challenging it on an individual basis within the household.[69]

It will be apparent from this discussion that the tradition of critique is alive and flourishing in the broader field of citizenship scholarship, although as Vogel has noted, feminist theories of citizenship do not speak "with one voice", and there are a variety of different approaches to achieving either common citizenship, citizenship based on women's particular identity, women-centred citizenship or a new "active citizenship", based on women's involvement in new social movements today.[70] In contrast, where citizenship and Europe have intersected, the dimension of gender has received very little scrutiny.[71] This might be partly because the tradition of critique itself is only slowly emerging in relation to "European" citizenship. This provides at best, however, a partial explanation. An attempt to remedy this lacuna should start, it is argued, with the concept of "market" and in particular "market citizen", drawing then upon the feminist approaches to citizenship sketched out briefly *supra*.

(a) Can women be "market citizens"?

The market citizen is the inhabitant of the brave new world of the single European market – someone who has a positive role in the construction of the future society based around that market. The Court of Justice itself is widely credited with having generalised the protections and rights contained into the EC Treaty which are principally concerned with economic activities into an incipient form of European citizenship.[72]

---

[68] Phillips, *supra* n 60; Dietz, "Citizenship with a Feminist Face: The Problem with Maternal Thinking", 13 *Political Theory* (1985), 19–35; Dietz, *supra* n 59. This point is a refutation of so-called "maternalist" thinking which celebrates the virtue of mothering and of women's role in the private sphere. See in particular Elshtain, *Public Man, Private Woman* (1981); Ruddick, "Maternal Thinking" 6 *Feminist Studies* (1980), 342–67.

[69] These are examples given by Phillips (1991), *supra* n 60.

[70] Vogel, "Is Citizenship Gender-Specific?" in Phillips (1991), *supra* n 60 at 78 *et seq.*

[71] A good example is the otherwise excellent collection, Rosas and Antola, *A Citizen's Europe. In Search of a new Order* (1995). But see, however, Meehan, whose book *Citizenship and the European Community* (1993) includes a chapter "Sex and citizenship" (very largely focused on the EU's sex equality policies); Ackers, "Citizenship, Gender and Dependency in the European Union: The position of Migrant Women" *Social Politics* (1995) (does not consider the broader implications of EC law for women's citizenship); Close, *European supra-citizenship, consumption and gender: a contribution to sociological analysis* (Centre for European Social Research, University of Derby, Occasional Papers, European Citizenship Series, no 12, 1995); Ward, Gregory and Yuval-Davis, *Women and citizenship in Europe. Borders, rights and duties* (1992) (provides little direct critique of EU citizenship).

[72] See already in 1976 Plender, "An Incipient Form of European Citizenship" in Jacobs, *European Law and the Individual* (1976) 39–53. The key cases since then have been Case 186/87 *Cowan* v *Le Trésor Public* [1989] ECR 195 and Case 293/83 *Gravier* v *City of Liège* [1985] ECR 593, in which the Court extended the protection of the non-discrimination principle to cover tourists and students respectively; functionally they can be seen as the recipients of services, and therefore as representing the reverse side of the coin under which free movement of services is protected. The reality, it can be argued, is more than the sum of the parts. See Pollard and Ross, *European Community Law. Text and Materials* (1994) 592.

The idea of the market citizen, it will be argued here, is almost archetypically "male". He (*sic*) appears in two guises: as the *active* market citizen who takes advantage of free movement (as a trader, as a professional, as a worker), and as the *passive* market citizen who reaps the benefits of the enlarged choice which results from freedom of movement, generally as a consumer. In the latter context, he is confident and informed.[73] He is now recognised as an autonomous figure under EC law, in Article 129A EC which was introduced by the Treaty of Maastricht.

That figure is, however, a gendered figure, for the relationship between women and consumption continues to be problematic. The gendered division of labour has historically meant that women are more closely associated with consumption, and men with production. However, the division of power and access to wealth within the domestic sphere may equally mean that women have little autonomy and choice regarding what they purchase, where they purchase it, and for how much. The emergence of the consumer as a key figure (in both symbolic and practical terms) for the success of the single market project adds a new level of complexity to the role of consumer goods and consumption processes as a "crucial area for the construction of meanings, identities, gender roles, in post-modern capitalism".[74] In particular, it generates a focus on the distributional and acquisitional dimensions of consumption – or, to put it another way, the public aspects of consumption – once more hiding away the relational or interpersonal questions of human experience.[75] In that sense, the treatment of consumption mirrors the treatment of labour processes in the EC Treaty.

The active market citizen (for example the worker) is (in the image constructed by EC law) unconstrained by restrictions on mobility other than those swept away by the limited family reunion rights and non-discrimination rights contained in Article 6 EC and the relevant secondary legislation.[76] This vision has been the subject of extensive critique,[77] particularly for its false universalism. While recent research by Ackers is sweeping away the preconception that quantitatively women make less use of mobility rights, it nonetheless emphasises the qualitative difference, for example, in the impact upon fertility rates.[78]

What reveals perhaps most starkly, however, the gendered nature of the "market citizen" is the imbalance in developmental terms between the market and welfare aspects of the post-1992 European polity. As I argued in Section (iii),

---

[73] Weatherill, "The Role of the Informed Consumer in European Community Law and Policy" *Consum. L.J.* (1994) 49–69.

[74] Bocock, *Consumption* (1993) at 96.

[75] See further Close (1995), *supra* n 71; Costa, "The Periphery of Pleasure or Pain: Consumer Culture in the EC Mediterranean of 1992" in Wilson and Estellie-Smith, *Cultural Change and the New Europe. Perspective on the European Community* (1993) 81–98.

[76] Council Regulation (EEC) 1612/68 (OJ 1968 L 257/1 at 475); Council Directive 64/221/EEC (OJ 1964 850/64 at 117); Council Directive 68/360/EEC (OJ 1968 L257/13 at 485); Council Regulation (EEC) 1251/71 (OJ 1970 L 142/24 at 402); Council Directive 73/148/EEC (OJ 1973 L 172/14).

[77] Hervey, *supra* n 5; Ackers, *supra* n 5; Scheiwe, *supra* n 5.

[78] Ackers (1995), *supra* n 5; *Internal migration within the European Union: The Presence of women in migration flows and the characteristics of female migrants*, Report to the Equal Opportunities Unit of the European Commission, DGV.

questions of social policy, and in particular welfare provision, have been constructed primarily as questions of national competence and concern. While
aspects of women's citizenship in terms of labour market participation, or even in
terms of dependence upon a [mobile] male breadwinner, have been "unionised"
and consequently incorporated at least partially into the vision of the European
market citizen, questions of dependence upon the state remain strictly "national-
ised". The strictness of this division has been constructed above all by the Court
of Justice's interpretation of the Social Security Directive[79] and its refusal tocon-
sider in an integrated way both the caring roles taken by women within the family
and their desire or need for continued participation in the labour market.[80]

(b) Does the impact of "market citizenship" make it impossible for women to be European Union citizens?

It follows from the argument developed above that the position of women as
"European Union citizens" is likely to be highly problematic. This is because the
concept of market citizenship dominates the figure of the EU citizen, to the
extent that citizenship of the European Union cannot be described as a form of
citizenship in the sense in which it is conventionally understood.[81] Part of the
rhetorical and symbolic power of citizenship is its ability to provide a complete
system of membership, with comprehensive answers to all questions about civil,
political and social entitlements. By definition, EU citizenship does not, and
probably never could, offer that sense of completeness or wholeness. The centrality
of free movement and non-discrimination at the level of residence and market
participation are self-consciously the central pillars of the new provisions of the
EC Treaty constituting the European Union Citizen (Articles 8–8E EC).

At one level, great hopes and aspirations have been invested in the possibility
and potential of post-national citizenship or membership for "Europe". It represents the possibility of constructing a moral core for the European Union;[82] a
new form of constitutional patriotism which is beyond national identity;[83] a
"public space of fellow-citizenship" in which the ideals of "building Europe" can
be attained.[84] However, at another level what has been achieved so far has
proved to be a profound disappointment, in particular as it is functionally
grounded in freedom of movement, and not in a human rights pillar.[85] In that

---

[79] Council Directive 79/7 (EEC) (OJ 1979 L 6/24).

[80] Sohrab, "An Overview of the Equality Directive on Social Security and its implementation in four social security systems" 4 *Journal of European Social Policy* (1994), 263–276; McCrudden (1994), *supra* n 6.

[81] Everson, "The Legacy of the Market Citizen" in Shaw and More (1995), *supra* n 5.

[82] Weiler, "Does Europe need a Constitution? Reflections on Demos, Telos and the German Maastricht Decision", I *European Law Journal* 219–258.

[83] Habermas, "Citizenship and National Identity" in van Steenbergen (1994), *supra* n 64 at 20–35.

[84] Tassin, "Europe: A Political Community" in Mouffe (1992), *supra* n 59 at 169–192. See also Soysal, *Limits of Citizenship. Migrants and Postnational Membership in Europe* (1994).

[85] D'Oliveira, "European Citizenship: Its Meaning, Its Potential" in Dehousse, *Europe After Maastricht. An Ever Closer Union?* (1994) 126–148; Twomey, "The European Union: Three Pillars without a Human Rights Foundation" in O'Keeffe and Twomey (1994), *supra* n 42 at 121–132.

sense it carries not just a legacy, but also a gendered legacy, which is characterised by a reluctance to consider afresh what exactly it means to be a "member" of the European polity. For example, while EU law has so far had some marginal impact upon the profoundly controversial field of reproductive rights[86], the most distinctive feature of constitutional, legislative and judicial action whenever such questions have been raised has been timidity and a reluctance to face up fully to the issues of reconstruction thrown up by processes of European integration. Similarly, while the process of economic integration may have changed the formal contours of "public space" within the geographical boundaries of Europe, it has done nothing to confront the true meaning of public and private spaces for many women, namely the fear of and reality of [male] violence and the associated question of rights to physical and mental security.[87] The conclusion to be drawn, therefore, is that Citizenship of the Union comes little, if any, closer to the realities of women's lives than its progenitor, market citizenship.

(v) Conclusion

This chapter began by reflecting upon the question of the *status quo* in relation to feminist scholarship and the European Union, and highlighted a significant *lacuna* in relation to the study of the internal market. There is an urgent need for gender to be inserted as a category of analysis into areas of EC law outside the domain of sex equality and rights to non-discrimination.

This chapter has taken a closer look at a number of aspects of the internal market – its ideology, its values and its law – in order to tease out the interrelationship between the processes of European integration and the situation and status of women, as a gendered category. The task approach taken here has been to raise questions, as much as to provide answers, an endeavour which will undoubtedly require further research. Work is required which applies the insights and methods of feminist jurisprudence to EC law. It has been argued here that it is possible to reveal a gender dimension beneath the surface of EU constitutional and legal provisions. In particular, the project to create, through regulatory action, an internal market within the European Union can have a wholly different meaning when it is viewed through a lens of gender. Consequently, women are not yet – and perhaps may never be – full citizens of the European Union.

JO SHAW

Professor of European Law,
Centre for the Study of Law in Europe,
University of Leeds, UK

---

[86] Case C-159/90 *Society for the Protection of the Unborn Child* v *Grogan* [1991] ECR I-4685. See Flynn, and O'Leary, in this volume.

[87] See Close (1995), *supra* n 71. See also McGlynn, in this volume.

Chapter 19

THE BODY POLITIC(S) OF EC LAW*

(i) Introduction

EC law has attracted an enormous amount of scholarly discussion and comment, as befits a legal order that embraces 15 Member States and affects many aspects of social organization within those States. Critical commentary on the norms and provisions of EC law can be found in this mass of literature, but for the most part writing on EC law tends to accept the premises which that legal system itself proffers.

Writings on EC law informed by feminist perspectives have been amongst the most successful of these critically-oriented works. However, the principal focus of feminist analyses of EC law has, until recently, been in the field of social policy. A great deal of valuable work has been done in this area. However, this work can be seen as peripheral within the hierarchy of importance given by EC law to legal issues. Those fields perceived as most directly related to operation of the market economy, such as free movement of goods or competition law, are considered to be central in understanding the substantive law of the EC.[1] As a direct result, social policy remains relatively insecure within EC law because of the primacy that the Treaties confer on the market.[2] In addition, the essentially *ad hoc* origin of Article 119 EC[3] also serves to weaken the place of this element

---

*This chapter was written by Leo Flynn.

[1] This ranking can be seen in the lists of contents of almost any textbook on EC law. Thus Wyatt and Dashwood deal with social security for migrants, sex discrimination and vocational training, the only elements of social policy considered, in 76 pages out of a total text of 673 pages (Wyatt and Dashwood, *European Community Law* (1993)).

[2] Szyszczak speaks of social policy having started as "the Cinderella of the common market", only to become "an ugly sister of the internal market". See "Social Policy: A happy ending or a reworking of the fairy tale?" in O'Keeffe and Twomey, *Legal Issues of the Maastricht Treaty* (1994) 313–328. One might make similar observations about environmental policy, consumer protection, etc. See, generally, on the spillover the Community activity into areas outside the market, Wallace, *The dynamics of European integration* (1990).

[3] See Barnard, in this volume.

of social policy[4], notwithstanding its subsequent constitutionalisation by the Court of Justice.[5]

More recently, feminist writing has turned its attention to the rights of personal mobility in EC law[6] and to the new concept of citizenship introduced by the Treaty on European Union.[7] Such writers have noted that the promise offered by this latter concept is belied by its deeply gendered foundations.[8] However, Union citizenship does not possess a great deal of substance yet, certainly not when compared with other well developed areas of EC law.[9] This leaves large areas of EC law almost untouched by feminist insights, including the agricultural and fisheries policies, regional policy, competition law, external affairs, substantial parts of Union constitutional law, and many aspects of the EC internal market.[10] If a feminist perspective on EC law does not embrace those areas of law and policy, it may simply indicate that feminism does not share the premises that support this internal ordering of significance. However, if feminist legal analysis has nothing to say about these fields, then it runs the risk of being excluded in advance in any critical consideration of EC law as a whole because of its limited area of application.

This chapter hopes to meet that challenge. It seeks to outline a feminist critique that can be applied to some of those central aspects of EC law. It will first indicate in rather general terms the key features of three forms of feminist legal analysis, and will describe how these have been used regarding domestic law. The application of each of these analyses to EC law will be sketched out in the next three sections. It will commence by looking at the composition of the institutions and decision-making bodies in the EC and will examine the claim that EC law is sexist. This will be followed by an analysis of the dominant methods of legal reasoning that are applied by the Court of Justice in its judgments to evaluate a claim that EC law is masculine in nature. This study will culminate in examining how the female body is treated in EC law. If the juridical subject is, as many feminist legal scholars claim, male and if law is, at least in part, responsible for the inculcation of the traits that are identified as masculine and feminine,

---

[4] See Forman, "The equal pay principle under Community Law – A commentary on Article 119 EEC" LIEI (1982/1) 17–36 at 19.
[5] Case 43/75 *Defrenne* v *Sabena No 2* [1976] ECR 455.
[6] See Ackers, in this volume.
[7] See Everson, and McGlynn, in this volume.
[8] For feminist writings on citizenship in general, see Elshtain, *Public man, private woman: Women in social and political thought* (1981); Okin, "Women and the making of the sentimental family" 11 *Philosophy and Public Affairs* (1981), 65; Young, "Polity and group difference: A critique of the ideal of universal citizenship" 99 *Ethics* (1989), 250. For commentary on the figure of the Union Citizen, see Ward, Gregory and Yural-Davis, *Women and citizenship in Europe: Borders, rights and duties* (1992); Hervey, "Migrant workers and their families in the European Union: The pervasive market ideology of Community law" in More and Shaw, *New legal dynamics of European Union* (1995).
[9] See generally, O'Keeffe, "Union citizenship" in O'Keeffe and Twomey, *Legal issues of the Maastricht Treaty* (1994); Rosas and Antola, *A citizens' Europe: In search of a new order* (1995).
[10] Where the internal market has been examined it has been principally in connection with free movement of persons. See, e.g., Scheiwe, "EC Law's unequal treatment of the family: The case law of the European Court of Justice on rules prohibiting discrimination on grounds of sex and nationality" 3 *Social and Legal Studies* (1994), 243–265; Hervey, *supra* n 8.

then law may operate as a gendering mechanism. This claim will be tested against some of the case law where the Court of Justice has been faced by the female body or by representations of the female body, and by scrutinising the responses of the Court to those cases. That section will conclude by inquiring how the Court may respond to a request to define what makes a body female or male.

(ii) Critical feminist legal scholarship

Over the past 20 years, feminist legal scholarship has developed a diverse and powerful set of critiques to analyse legal systems and legal reasoning. Amongst the most important developments within this feminist jurisprudence has been the creation of a distinctive method, refuting liberal thought's distinction between theory and practice,[11] and establishing alternative approaches for legal analysis based on women's experiences.[12] Accordingly, this chapter attempts to refer to women's experiences as affected by the operation of EC law. This experiential approach carries the possibility of falling into a well known trap of essentialism. It is therefore necessary to state that this chapter does not seek to make claims about all of law, or about all women, or about all men; nor does it claim to have a single lens through which all of EC law is to be seen. Instead, it is proposed to develop "local" arguments here that will provide a more effective critique of EC law.[13]

This chapter will examine three theoretically distinct feminist perspectives on law that have been identified (though not all endorsed) by the British feminist, Carol Smart. As a preliminary matter, we might note that each of these analyses, or strategies, is not necessarily compatible with the others. Smart sets out three principal variants of feminist analysis of law, ranging from arguing that the law is sexist, through to claiming that the law is male, and finally asserting that the law is gendered.[14] The "law is sexist" set of claims focuses on the manner in which law allocates resources, opportunities and power. These arguments and studies demonstrate that the law perpetuates the disadvantage of women as a group in society through its operations. Work of this kind formed the basis for much of the critique offered on the legal system by "first-wave" feminism during the nineteenth and early twentieth centuries. Using this methodology, feminist writers focused their attention on the inability of women to vote, and to participate fully in education and in the market, because of various discriminatory prohibitions.[15] They

---

[11] See, e.g., MacKinnon, "From theory to practice, or what is a white woman anyway?" 4 *Yale Journal of Law and Feminism* (1991), 13.

[12] Bartlett, "Feminist legal methods" 103 *Harvard Law Review* (1990), 829–888.

[13] Jackson, "Contradictions and coherence in feminist responses to law" 20 *Journal of Law and Society* (1993), 398–411.

[14] Smart, "The Woman of legal discourse" 1 *Social and Legal Studies* (1992), 29, 30–34.

[15] Thus Millet wrote that, "our society, like all other historical civilizations, is a patriarchy. . . . [E]very avenue of power within the society, including the coercive force of the police, is entirely within male hands." (*Sexual Politics* (1971), 25).

claimed that women were as rational and capable of autonomy as men, and that the dominance of men who ignored this fact in decision-making bodies led to unjust and unequal rules.

The second group of arguments claim that the "law is male" and proceed on the basis that law incorporates values, attitudes and norms perceived as masculine in our culture. The "second-wave" feminism of the 1960s and '70s developed this approach in several areas, such as employment law, and the rules regarding self-defence and provocation in criminal law. This strategy shows why the application of seemingly gender-neutral rules, drafted in an objective fashion, often works to the systematic detriment of women. What counts as "objective" or "neutral" in our society, reflects a set of deeply embedded assumptions that are valued above competing considerations. Feminists have argued that those assumptions are "masculine" because of the implicit connections that exist between them and the concept of masculinity. For example, it emerges, when one looks more closely, that the apparently ungendered "rational individual" of liberal thought is actually assumed to be male.[16] This critique is also applicable to the juridical subject, the "reasonable person" of the common law, who remains in all important matters the reasonable man. The most important conclusion drawn from this argument is that women may have to adapt themselves and ignore their knowledge of the world to conform to this male standard if they wish to engage fully with the legal system.

The final approach Smart outlines is to treat the law as gendering and gendered entity. This analyses law as "a process of producing fixed gender identities rather than simply as the application of law to previously gendered subjects".[17] The "law is gendered" stream of analysis has produced accounts of how legal discourse helps to shape many of the social structures that we meet with, including that of gender.[18] It does not accept that law develops a pre-existing set of categories of thought and assumptions that possess a stable existence in their own right. Analysing law in this fashion does not pre-suppose the association of any set of traits or characteristics with individuals or groups, nor does it accept as already given the outline of those individual or group entities. Instead, it looks to the specific mechanisms of power that are employed by law in particular social settings. In addition, it also denies the utility of grand theorising that can be applied to all aspects of law.

There are significant distinctions between each of these modes of analysis, as Smart makes clear. This chapter will not seek to rank these methods because, notwithstanding the weaknesses that may affect individual models, each one has some insight to offer. In addition, each can be used in a way that complements

---

[16] See Lloyd, *The man of reason: "Male" and "Female" in Western philosophy* (1984).

[17] Smart, "The Woman of Legal discourse", *supra* n 14 at 34.

[18] For example, Sheldon, in her work on English abortion law, explores how the female legal subject placed under legislative scrutiny in the passage of the Abortion Act of 1967 relies on "certain assumptions about (a) women's maternal role and (b) the essential irresponsibility and (c) sexual immorality of the sort of Woman who would seek to terminate a pregnancy". See "Who is the mother to make the judgment?: The construction of Woman in English abortion law" 1 *Feminist Legal Studies* (1993), 3, 15.

the others, taking the analysis to a deeper level. Having outlined these variants of feminist legal analysis, this chapter will now apply them to EC law.

(iii) EC law as sexist

Given the pivotal role which EC law has assumed for progressive forces, including women's organizations, in many of the Member States,[19] it may seem to be churlish to speak of Community law as a sexist institution. However, if we regard a sexist institution as one that distributes life opportunities and resources unevenly between the sexes, then EC law may not be immune from scrutiny on this charge.

If the membership of the key institutions is considered, an overwhelming male dominance can be discerned. Starting with the judicial institutions, the Court of Justice of the European Community has had no female judges since its formation over 40 years ago.[20] As for the office of Advocate General, the situation is only slightly better. One set of commentators on the Court who use the masculine personal pronoun when referring to the Advocate General in their work state that this practice intends "no disrespect to the first woman Advocate General, Mme Simone Rozès, or the other Portias who will follow her on the Kirschberg".[21] This formulation coyly omits any mention of the fact that Advocate General Rozès is, to date, the only female member of the Court of Justice. As for the Court of First Instance (CFI), its composition does include some female members but it is only a slight and recent improvement on the record of the senior court. The CFI has two female judges in its current membership, both of whom were nominated by Member States which joined the Union in 1995.[22] This state of affairs is somewhat ironic given that the Council of Ministers, responsible for appointing the members of the European courts, urged the promotion of positive action for women over a decade ago.[23] That recommendation specifically called for positive action through the recruitment and promotion of women at levels where they are under-represented, particularly concerning positions of responsibility. While further resolutions have been

---

[19] This attraction is most evident in those Member States where domestic law is not particularly responsive to demands for gender equality. However, in those Member States where the internal political and legal order is more advanced in this regard, women's groups have been less enthusiastic about the Community. This is particularly the case for the Nordic Member States. See Karvonen and Selle, *Women in Nordic politics: Closing the gap* (1995).

[20] In their study of the Court Brown and Kennedy observe, before giving an outline of the judges' biographical details, that these will deal exclusively with men because, "a woman has still to be appointed to this office, although . . . the French, with true republican '*égalité*', chose a woman for appointment as Advocate General in 1981". Brown and Kennedy, *The Court of Justice of the European Communities* (1994), 55.

[21] Brown and Kennedy, *ibid* 61.

[22] Neville Brown, "The first five years of the Court of First Instance and appeal to the Court of Justice: Assessment and statistics" 32 CMLRev (1995), 743–761, 751.

[23] Recommendation of 13 December 1984 (OJ 1984 L 331/34).

passed on this matter, there is little sign of any change in the States' practices up to now.[24]

Moving from the judicial to the political institutions,[25] the situation is not much better. The extent to which there are female participants in the Council of Ministers obviously varies from Council to Council, and depends in turn on the vagaries of national political forces. To date Margaret Thatcher of the United Kingdom has been the sole female member of the European Council. The Court of Auditors has no female members at present. The Commission is a little better. Two female Commissioners were present in the second Delors Commission (1989–93),[26] only one remained in the third Delors Commission (1993–5),[27] and the present Commission, with five women amongst its 20 members, is the least male-dominated to date.[28] On the other hand, the Commission has developed an extensive institutional framework within which issues having a particular impact on women are discussed. However, this consultation and decision-making apparatus does not always extend to best practice within the Commission itself.[29]

The European Parliament is most representative of all the Community institutions. It also has the longest history of concern with the distribution of resources and life opportunities between the sexes. The extent of female representation in the European Parliament has grown steadily over the years. It has moved from a maximum of 11 out of 198 under the appointment system before 1979; to 66 out of 410 in the first direct election in 1979; to 75 out of 434 in 1984; and 96 out of 518 in 1989.[30] As of 1 January 1995, there were 147 women amongst the 626 MEPs; its highest proportion to date. The Parliament established a permanent Committee on Women's Rights in 1984 that has exerted significant pressure on DG V which has responsibility for social affairs.

The Parliament has issued reports and resolutions drawing attention to the situation of women, both in the Community and abroad.[31] However, although the Parliament has been a staunch advocate of women's rights and has been the

---

[24] In fact the Council has adopted another resolution on 27 March 1995 on balanced participation by men and women in decision-making which extends both Member States and the EC institutions and bodies (Bull. 3–1995, point 1.3.148).

[25] The phrase is Professor Hartley's. See Hartley, *Foundations of European Community Law* (1994).

[26] Vasso Papandreou (Social Affairs) and Christine Scrivener (Taxation). Ms Papandreou left the Commission in 1991.

[27] Christine Scrivener (Taxation).

[28] Emma Bonino (Fisheries); Édith Cresson (Science, research and development); Monika Wulf-Mathies (Regional policies); Ritt Bjerregaard (Environment); and Anita Gradin (Immigration, justice and home affairs).

[29] Case 111/86 *Delauche v Commission* [1987] ECR 5345, where the Commission resisted any role for preferential hiring of women in the Commission. Even though women occupied less that 2% of the top three grades of Commission officials, the Commission refused to adapt its hiring policies so that preference would be given to women where the shortlisted candidates for a post were equally well qualified.

[30] See Smyth with Roche, *Stratégies pour la promotion des femmes en politique. Sondage dans les Etats membres de la CE pour la Lobby Européen des Femmes* (1992).

[31] See, for example, Parliament resolution of 18 May 1995 on support for Algerian women, (OJ 1995 C 151/283); Parliament resolution of 16 March 1995 on equal treatment and equal opportunities for men and women (OJ 1995 C 89/143).

most representative of the institutions, it is still very much the junior partner in the legislative and policy-formation processes in the Community. As long as this remains the case, and as long as the other institutions fail to represent proportionately the majority of EU citizens who are female, it is correct to identify sex as the other "democratic deficit" in the Union.[32]

The result of this gender gap is that the institutions of the Community and the legislation and policies that they produce are open to the charge of being sexist. However, changing the number of women within the top ranks of the Community's legal and political order would not necessarily change the nature of the system without a major culture shift. To support that contention, we will use the two other strategies within feminist legal scholarship that are identified by Smart, the claim that law is male and that it operates as a gendering mechanism.

(iv) EC law as masculine

As mentioned earlier, there is a substantial collection of feminist literature dealing with EC law in the fields of citizenship, personal mobility and social rights. This literature has taken up and developed critiques used by feminist legal scholars elsewhere concerning the concepts deployed in EC law. This literature's principal claim is that the style of reasoning and the specific conceptions of values utilised in EC law can be characterised as male because they are identified as masculine in our society. Thus, without claiming that EC law's dominant goals, and its methods of achieving these, are inherently masculine or exclusively confined to members of the male sex, these critics demonstrate that the patriarchal nature of law, including EC law, is deeply entrenched.

These claims have been most extensively explored regarding Article 119 of the Treaty and the equality Directives. Feminist writers have challenged the conception of equality adopted concerning the principle of non-discrimination between men and women in EC law. For example, Gillian More has argued that the apparently gender neutral concept of equality that is used by the Court of Justice in many of its decisions on equal pay and equal treatment uses a hidden, male-based perspective to set a standard against which inequality must be measured.[33] She shows that this purportedly "neutral" test actively reinforces a market order organized around the needs and aspirations of male workers and employers.

Another instance of this type of analysis can be seen in writings where feminists have convincingly critiqued the division between the public and private worlds of the market and domestic life under the equality Directives and in the related case law.[34]

---

[32] See Mushaben, "The other 'democratic deficit': Women in the European Community before and after Maastricht" in Lützeler, *Europe after Maastricht: American and European Perspectives* (1994).

[33] More, " 'Equal treatment' of the sexes in European Community law: What does 'Equal' mean?" 1 *Feminist Legal Studies* (1993), 45–74. See also Sohrab, "Avoiding the 'Exquisite Trap': A Critical look at the equal treatment/special treatment debate in law" 1 *Feminist Legal Studies* (1993), 141–162.

[34] More, "Equality of treatment in European Community law: A critique" in Bottomley, *Feminist perspectives on the foundation subjects of law* (forthcoming, 1996).

The use of a feminist framework of this kind for analysis allows an understanding of Community law's limits in generating change. It enables us to predict where EC law will fail to remedy the adverse treatment of female workers because it identifies the gender based assumptions that animate the legal concepts employed within EC law.[35]

The claim that EC law is masculine or operates within a framework of male values and methods can also be demonstrated at a more general level of abstraction. Both the priority given by Community law to the market, and the particular concept of the market that is found in EC law, indicate a strongly masculine orientation.[36] It has been noted that the culture of the market and principles of market efficiency and competition are central to the creation of the internal market, and to the legitimacy of the EC legal order that rests on it.[37]

However, as Kirsten Scheiwe notes, "[i]t is not simply a 'market logic' that affects and fuels the dynamics of . . . developments [in EC law], but a selective logic (with a gender dimension) which excludes or includes certain policy areas according to criteria of relevance other than ill-defined 'market-connectedness'".[38]

To understand better how this process operates, one can draw on the work of Carol Gilligan regarding developmental psychology generally and, more specifically, the conception of justice that prevails in our society and our reliance on rights. She notes that our culture suppresses a "different voice" in matters of moral reasoning and problem solving[39] and that this style of reasoning is associated with women.[40] That different voice rests on the value of inter-connection with other individuals and the world. It operates from within a holistic world view. By contrast, conventional moral (and legal) reasoning applies a conflict-laden perspective to discrete, atomistic entities. This different voice stands opposed to a masculine, market logic that sees relationships with other humans and the natural world as a set of isolated calculations to be made in an *ad hoc* fashion about the balance of pre-allocated rights in situations of conflict.

The idea that the market is gendered in this fashion is not easily accepted by many within the legal academy.[41] However, using the feminist model of law as a sexist institution, we note that "[m]arket theory always takes attention away from the full range of human potential in its pursuit of a divinely willed, rationally inspired, invisibly handed economic actor";[42] and that, as we shall see, this market perspective is highly influential within EC law. In addition, the same

---

[35] See, for example, Fenwick and Hervey, "Sex equality in the single market: New directions for the European Court of Justice" 32 CMLRev (1995), 443–470.

[36] See Shaw, in this volume.

[37] Weiler, "Problems of legitimacy in post 1992 Europe" 46 *Aussenwirtschaft* (1991), 411, 428.

[38] Scheiwe, *supra* n 10 at 247.

[39] Gilligan, *In a different voice: Psychological theory and women's development* (1982).

[40] I do not intend to claim that any such different voice is essentially feminine, or that it is necessarily superior to other "voices". See, generally, Larrabee, *An ethic of care: Feminist and interdisciplinary perspectives* (1993).

[41] Williams speaks of her students being "paralysed by the notion that property might have a gender". See Williams, "The brass ring and the deep blue sea" in *The alchemy of race and rights* (1991) 13.

[42] Williams, "On being the object of property" in *The alchemy of race and rights* (1991) 220.

analytical framework shows that this market actor is not without a body or a context. In fact, when its traits are examined in more detail it appears that this figure is gendered as masculine.[43]

Robin West, a cultural feminist, has taken issue with the assertion that the market represents an adequate account of the conditions for human flourishing and offers a sound basis for the construction of social institutions, including law.[44] Her work is concerned with the US "Chicago School" of Law and Economics, but her critique of that movement is also applicable to EC law's market primacy. She rejects over-dependence on an uncritical conception of the market in establishing institutional structures and legal norms. She also rejects descriptions of behaviour and interaction that claim to be based on market norms (and so to be neutral) because they incorporate only a narrow set of attitudes and interests. West argues that this is closely bound up with a failure to discern or to acknowledge the motivational complexity of individuals, and suggests as an alternative that "we need to develop rich and true descriptions of the subjective experiences of our institutions [including legal norms]".[45] This approach abandons attempts to subordinate all experience to a framework constructed around the market, a way of seeing the world that is built on male experience. This critique of market centred perspectives as reductive and hierarchical, can be applied to EC law and is also closely linked to other feminist perspectives.[46] The deeply embedded place of these values within EC law grounds the claim made here that EC law can be described as male.[47] The role of the market in EC law will be examined in more detail in the following section.

(v) EC law as a gendering enterprise

The claim that EC law operates as a system for developing gender identities will be explored here with Community law's treatment of the body, and specifically the female body, as our main focus. If we accept the feminist claim that the legal subject is not the ungendered entity that law proclaims it to be, this opens out a series of difficulties for women regarding law. The most fundamental of these issues is how the female body itself is regulated and treated by law.

---

[43] West, "Jurisprudence and Gender" 55 *University of Chicago Law Review* (1988), 1.

[44] West, "Authority, autonomy, and choice: The role of consent in the moral and political visions of Franz Kafka and Richard Posner" 99 *Harvard Law Review* (1985), 384–428.

[45] West, *ibid* at 427.

[46] See Polan, "Toward a theory of law and patriarchy" in Kairys, *The politics of law* (1982) 294; Rifkin, "Toward a theory of law and patriarchy" 3 *Harvard Women's Law Journal* (1980), 83.

[47] See also Radin, "Market-Inalienability" 100 *Harvard Law Review* (1987), 1849–1937. Radin carefully analyses calls for universal commodification found in many strands of liberal legal thought. A similar dynamic of commodification can be discerned within EC law. See, e.g., Case 7/68 *Commission* v *Italy* [1968] ECR 423, 428–9; Case C-2/90 *Commission* v *Belgium* [1992] ECR I-4431. Radin also argues that this market centred vision distorts any attempt to account for our attachments and desires, and notes the particular damage that this perspective can inflict on women. See 1921–36 on prostitution, baby-selling and surrogacy.

In any consideration of this issue, we should start by noting the dominance of a market paradigm within Community law. This means that the legal framework used for analysing problems relating to the body will, for the most part, be centred on a set of market-related issues. The first issue that will be considered in this section is when, if at all, the treatment of the body cannot be contained within a legal perspective based on the market. Then, within that market paradigm, we will see how the Court of Justice has taken both the female body itself and representations of that body, and read a set of traits and values onto that figure. In doing so, it has contributed to the gendering of our social world.

In the final section we will look briefly at the challenge posed to the Court where it has been asked directly to consider what elements are necessary to be female as a matter of EC law.

(a) The boundaries of the market in EC law

The EC institutions have, for the most part, maintained that any activity and any object can be assimilated to the market. A wide definition of the objects and subjects incorporated into the internal market's legal order is evident in a Commission's statement that, "contrary to what is widely imagined, the EEC Treaty applies not only to economic activities but, as a rule, to all activities carried out for remuneration, regardless of whether they take place in the economic, social, cultural (including in particular information, creative or artistic endeavours and entertainment), sporting or any other sphere."[48]

The Court of Justice also has a broad view of the market, as seen in its jurisprudence on what constitute "goods" for the free movement rules contained in the Treaty.[49] This approach does not flow automatically from any internal rationale of EC law, found within the norms and the jurisprudence of EC law; rather it is a question of bringing transactions, administrative actions and individuals within the jurisdiction of the Commission and the Court. What emerges from a critical consideration of its case law is that the Court defines the market, it does not discover it. It gives pre-eminence to a market paradigm, disregarding critics who assert, regarding free movement of goods, that, "the central problem is that the EEC fails to differentiate between different kinds of goods. One should look to the nature of the good because all goods are *not* the same. After all, some commercial transactions have a negative environmental impact".[50] This critique of the Court's inability to differentiate products based on their effects on the environment treats this as a local anomaly. Once the masculine nature of EC law is identified, a systemic failure can be recognised. A basic feature of EC law is its powerful impulse towards market

---

[48] Commission of the European Communities, *Television without frontiers*, Green Paper on the Establishment of the Common Market for Broadcasting especially by Satellite and Cable, COM (84) 300 final, 6.
[49] See cases cited *supra* n 47.
[50] Demiray, "The movement of goods in a green market" *Legal Issues of European Integration* (1994) 73–110 at 109. Emphasis added by the author.

deference.[51] The primacy of market access as a value in EC law often subordi-
nates other core legal values such as consistency.[52] That failure cannot be
addressed until EC law adopts other values, of connection and solidarity, and a
different epistemology, embracing "masculine" assumptions of atomistic, de-
contextualised objects and individuals as well as a "feminine", holistic vision.
Until such a shift occurs then human bodies, including female bodies, will be
considered primarily as market objects in EC law, and there is no reason to suppose that the impact of this apparently neutral market order will have the same
impact or allocate similar burdens between the sexes.

However, the scope of the market is not wholly unlimited within EC law or
the institutions which frame and implement that law. For example, recent
debates on the draft Biotechnology Patent Directive involved a clash of
approaches to commodification of life. The Commission originally proposed a
Directive in October 1988[53] that sought to protect inventions developed
through biotechnology and genetic engineering. It maintained that such inventions should not be refused protection simply on the ground that they involved
living matter. The proposal then went to the European Parliament which proposed far-reaching amendments to the Draft Directive.[54] The Parliament took
the view that the original focus on economic and technical matters alone was
too narrow and in its proposals for amendment observed:

> Whereas it is desirable to include in the body of the Directive such a reference to
> public policy and morality to highlight that some applications of bio-technological
> inventions, by dint of their consequences or effects, are capable of offending against
> them . . .
>   Whereas, in the light of the general principle that the ownership of human
> beings is prohibited, the human body or parts of the human body *per se* must be
> excluded from patentability . . .[55]

The Council accepted these specific amendments when it adopted a common
position on the amended proposal, but it rejected certain other proposed amendments that were also concerned to limit the untrammelled operation of the market.[56] The dispute over the amendments went to a Conciliation Committee and
eventually back to the European Parliament which then vetoed the legislation.[57]

---

[51] See also Phelan, "Right to Life of the Unborn v Promotion of Trade in Services: The European
Court of Justice and the normative shaping of the European Union" 55 *Modern Law Review* (1992),
670–689; Ward, "In search of a European identity" 57 *Modern Law Review* (1994), 315–329 at 327.
[52] Contrast, for example, Case 27/76 *United Brands Company and United Brands Continentaal BV v Commission* [1978] ECR 207 and Case 185/84 *Commission v Italian Republic* [1987] ECR 2013: the "market for bananas" cases.
[53] Proposal for a Council Directive on the legal protection of biotechnological inventions (OJ 1989
C 13/3).
[54] Amended proposal for a Council Directive on the legal protection of bio-technological inventions
(OJ 1993 C 44/36). See also Commission's opinion on European Parliament's amendments, COM
(94) 245 final.
[55] *Ibid* at 37.
[56] Common position (EC) No 4/94 (OJ 1994 C 101/65).
[57] OJ 1995 C 68/26.

The basic objection to commodification of the human body in this way is that "it contributes towards a society in which the bodies of persons are regarded as resources. The action of selling one's own body contributes to the prevailing ethos of everything being for sale, everything having a price. It reinforces the ethic of the market".[58] Thus, as a result of the Parliament's intervention the market failed to trump all other values in EC law on this occasion. However, in most situations the market will be a framework within which the control of bodies will be assessed.

(b) Regulating the female body

The Court of Justice has had to consider the regulation of the female body on several occasions. Two of its decisions will be considered here, *Adoui and Cornuaille*[59] and *SPUC* v *Grogan*.[60] In both cases the legal issue before the Court was whether national measures regulating, directly or indirectly, activities carried out mainly by women conflicted with the free movement rules established under the Treaty. The cases thus involved the extent of Member States' freedom of manoeuvre under the Treaty. However, the subject matter of the cases (prostitution and abortion, respectively) directly relates to the control of the female body.

In *Adoui and Cornuaille*[61] the Court of Justice considered a series of questions referred to it from the Tribunal de Première Instance in Liège concerning the deportation of, and refusal of residence permits for, French nationals who allegedly were female prostitutes.[62] The main question before the Court was whether Belgium could justify its conduct as a derogation to the principle of free movement of persons under Article 48(3) of the Treaty. The Court held that the Member State could do so only if it took repressive measures or other genuine and effective measures intended to combat such conduct against its own nationals. In addition, unrelated circumstances could not be considered in specific cases, and the Court went on to elaborate a series of procedural safeguards that must accompany any use of the public policy derogation. In essence, therefore, the Court of Justice considered the extent to which Member States retain their discretion to order public space as they see fit. EC law does not, according to the Court, impose a normative system of its own.[63] It is, in a

---

[58] Chadwick, "The market for bodily parts" 6 *Journal of Applied Philosophy* (1989), 129–140, 137. See also Wells, "Patenting new life forms: An ecological perspective" 15 *European Intellectual Property Review* (1994), 111. For a sceptical response to these arguments, see Crespi, "Biotechnology patenting: The wicked animal must defend itself" 17 *European Intellectual Property Review* (1995), 431–436.

[59] Joined Cases 115 and 116/81 [1982] ECR 1665.

[60] Case C-159/90 [1991] ECR I-4685.

[61] Joined Cases 115 and 116/81 [1982] ECR 1665.

[62] In the observations of the Member States and the Commission, the Opinion of the Advocate General, and the judgment of the Court, the arguments advanced and the lines of reasoning developed all assumed that the women were prostitutes. They themselves made clear in their observations that they denied this claim, that they had never been charged as prostitutes and that while they had been working as waitresses in bars in Liège, they wished to obtain other employment. *Ibid* 1680.

[63] "Community law does not impose upon the Member States a uniform set of values". *Ibid* point 9 at 1708.

word, neutral. Its only demand is that the State act consistently and not turn a blind eye to those of its own nationals engaging in prostitution while acting against aliens who do so.

The Court did not directly address the issue of prostitution in its judgment. The decision of the Court focuses on the issue of constitutional significance raised in the case, the powers of Member States under Article 48(3), and ignores the fact that it also directly affects how sex workers' lives are regulated through a linked set of threats; the removal of their co-workers from the State, in the case of national sex workers; and deportation, in the case of sex workers, from other Member States. However, the issue of prostitution was discussed to some extent in the Opinion of Advocate General Capotorti and in the observations supplied by several Member States and the Commission.

The national court had asked the ECJ, *inter alia*, whether the exercise of a trade that is not prohibited (but on the contrary is protected from exploitation and is lawfully taxable), may constitute a serious threat to a fundamental interest of society. Advocate General Capotorti observes in his Opinion on this matter that Member States may legitimately take action against aliens of either sex who have entered into the territory to carry on prostitution.[64] None of the other parties or decision makers in the case make any such comment as to the sex of sex workers. This single remark of the Advocate General purports to underline the sex neutral nature of the prohibition in national law. However, placed as it is in parentheses in his Opinion, it highlights that prostitution is an activity that is predominantly, though not exclusively, carried out by women. This remark also returns our attention to the point where the impact of the Court's judgment will ultimately be most acutely felt – on women, and how they used (and are forced to use) their bodies.

The referring national court also asked whether Member States are entitled to take into account the private life of the persons concerned in deciding to refuse or withdraw residence permits. In its decision, the Court did not respond directly to this question, submerging it in the issue of the disparity between the measures taken against national, as opposed to foreign, sex workers. However, this question provoked widely differing responses from those Member States that submitted observations to the Court.[65] The Commission's observations are the most interesting and insightful in the case because it noted the malleability of this category of private life. It stated that "there are various types of conduct, of the sexual and other kinds, which are purely private, and which are viewed very differently as between one Member State and another and even, within a

---

[64] *Ibid* 1721.

[65] The Belgian government took the view that the women had acted in public (being visible in the windows of the bars where they worked), *ibid* 1685. The French government did not deal with the issue of whether their conduct was in public or was private. It maintained that criminal conduct occurring within the scope of private life may be a valid reason for expulsion (*ibid* 1690). On the other hand, the Italian government claimed that private morality is exclusively for each individual and that no Member State can intervene (*ibid* 1694). The Dutch government claimed that the criterion of whether conduct must be in public was an inadequate one because interests that the State regards as public may be seriously jeopardised by actions in private life (*ibid* 1697).

single Member State, from one period to another".[66] While the Court of Justice did not express any view on this point, it would not have had to compare the treatment of nationals and non-nationals from other Member States unless it concluded that public policy issues were raised in the case. Therefore, it must either have accepted that the acts (and/or the consequences of those acts) were in the public domain, or that the Member States are free to draw the scope of the public as they fit.

The latter conclusion is difficult to reconcile with other elements of the Court's jurisprudence on public policy that limit, without eliminating, the Member States' discretion to identify what is a fundamental interest of society and, as a consequence, a public matter.[67] As a result, it seems most likely that the Court accepted that sex workers' activities come within the public gaze and are therefore appropriate objects of regulation. This positioning of sex workers reinforces the gendering strategies of domestic laws which place women in transgressive roles in the public sphere and penalises them for their presence there.

The second case that we will consider concerning the regulation of the female body in EC law is *SPUC* v *Grogan*,[68] one of a series of high-profile cases dealing with a provision in the Irish constitution that recognises the "right to life of the unborn".[69] The Irish High Court referred a series of questions to the Court of Justice under Article 177 of the Treaty relating to abortion. The questions arose out of attempts by a "pro-life" pressure group to obtain an injunction preventing the distribution of information by Irish student organizations regarding termination of pregnancy services lawfully available in the United Kingdom. This was an extremely delicate issue and it was handled gingerly by the Court of Justice.

The Court held that the medical termination of pregnancy, performed in accordance with the law of the State in which it is carried out, constitutes a service within the meaning of Article 60 of the Treaty.[70] However, departing from the Opinion of Advocate General Van Gerven, it went on to hold that because the students' activities lacked any economic connection with the medical terminations of pregnancies carried out in clinics in other Member States, the link between the provision of information and the service was too tenuous to constitute a restriction under Article 59 of the Treaty.[71] This conclusion put the activities of the students outside the scope of the market and, according to the Court, beyond the scope of the Treaty.[72]

This judgment reinforces the conclusions drawn earlier about the primacy of

---

[66] *Ibid* 1702.
[67] See Case 41/74 *Van Duyn* v *Home Office* [1974] ECR 1337; Case 67/74 *Bonsignore* v *Stadt Köln* [1975] ECR 297.
[68] Case C-159/90 [1991] ECR I-4685. See O'Leary, in this volume.
[69] See Ailbhe Smyth, "The X case: Woman and abortion in the Republic of Ireland, 1992" 1 *Feminist Legal Studies* (1993), 163.
[70] Case C-159/90 [1991] ECR I-4739 point 21.
[71] *Ibid* I-4740 points 24 and 26.
[72] *Ibid* I-4741 point 31.

the market in EC law, and the dominance of the masculine logic that is associated with it. It is not necessarily undesirable to be placed *outside* the market. Patricia Williams points out that while the market's precise boundaries vary over time, it is, nonetheless, constant in one feature:

> whether something is inside or outside the marketplace . . . has always been a way of valuing it. Where a valued object is located outside the market, it is generally understood to be too "priceless" to be accommodated by ordinary exchange relationships; if the prize is located within the marketplace, then all objects placed outside become "valueless". Traditionally, the *Mona Lisa* and human life have been the sort of objects removed from the fungibility of commodification, as priceless. Thus when black people were bought and sold as slaves, they were placed beyond the bounds of humanity.[73]

In short, to be excluded from the market, as the Court of Justice did to the information providers in *SPUC* v *Grogan*, is not to share even the limited benefits that it offers. This reminds us that it is not the market itself that is problematic. Instead, our concern should be that the market could become the only source of valuing others and the world around us. However, it may be that we should press for EC law to abandon the market as its primary source of legitimacy because the concept cannot endure the transformational pressures this would entail and/or because the market cannot deliver what women require of it.

In the present case, by placing the students' information distribution activities outside the scope of the market, the Court marginalised and deprecated their efforts, finding that there was no basis on which EC law could consider the restrictive regulations imposed on them by Ireland.

The Court excluded voluntary action, organised through a loose network and based on collective effort, from the scope of activities valued and capable of receiving protection from EC law. This form of organisation was devalued and undermined, notwithstanding the strong integration element that is fostered by local, low-level co-ordination between voluntary groups in different Member States. Instead, the Court implicitly favoured more orthodox and formal processes of exchange between individuals and undertakings through contracts, agency agreements, and other forms of business interaction directly constituted by law. This business mode of organisation is one that ignores the many activities by women in informal economic sectors.[74]

The judgment therefore ignores the activities of many women, economically significant though their actions may be. It also ignores the under-representation of women amongst the ranks of autonomous decision-makers in that business world. In effect, the judgment forces women, the ultimate recipients of abortion services, to accept the overwhelming control over pregnancy termination ser-

---

[73] Williams, *supra* n 42 at 227. As Case 7/68 *Commission* v *Italy* [1968] ECR 423 indicates, EC law is not so deferential toward art treasures as Williams might expect.
[74] Leonard, "Women's paid and unpaid handiwork in a Belfast estate" 3 *Journal of Gender Studies* (1994), 187.

vices by men (through the medicalisation of these procedures and the commercialisation of support services). By denying a form of action that is often exploited by women and by encouraging a male-oriented mode of organization and interaction, *SPUC* v *Grogan* reinforces the qualities of passivity and acquiescence read onto the female body (especially when pregnant) by a patriarchal society.

(c) Regulating representations of the female body

The Court of Justice has been concerned with representations of the female body in a number of its cases arising out of Member States' control on the free movement of goods. In *R* v *Henn and Darby*[75] the Court of Justice had to consider the meaning of the public morality element of Article 36 of the Treaty (the derogation to the free movement of goods principle) following a preliminary reference from the House of Lords.

The case concerned an appeal by two individuals against their criminal convictions for importing indecent or obscene articles into the United Kingdom, and of being knowingly concerned in the fraudulent evasion of that prohibition on the importation of indecent or obscene articles. The materials were Danish in origin and consisted of films and magazines showing activities, including rape, abduction of a woman, buggery (involving humans and animals), indecent assault and acts of gross indecency towards children under 14 years of age, which were contrary to United Kingdom criminal law.

The appellants argued that the legislation under which they had been convicted was incompatible with Articles 9 and 30 of the Treaty.

The Court of Justice took the view that Article 36 allows a Member State lawfully to impose prohibitions on the import of articles that are indecent or obscene under its domestic laws. It also held that the Member State may apply such prohibitions throughout all of its territory, even if there are regional variations in its different constituent parts as to the laws in force about the matter in question.

Neither the Court of Justice, nor the Advocate General, nor the Member States who intervened in the case, considered the nature of the harm that is constituted by pornography. All the aforementioned accepted that pornography is legitimately regulated under standards which rest on obscenity and indecency, or as the Court accepted, in relation "to a single idea, that of offending against recognised standards of propriety".[76] The Court did not examine this concept in any detail. It may have agreed with the observations of the United Kingdom in the case that public morality, unlike public policy, is comparatively self-defining.[77] There is no indication in the case that the political economy of pornography was considered or that the application of the public policy derogation to free

---

[75] Case 34/79 [1979] ECR 3795.
[76] *Ibid* 3811 point 6.
[77] *Ibid* 3804.

movement of goods was considered a more appropriate basis for regulation of these goods.

The work done by feminists dealing with pornography has undermined the traditional liberal/conservative lines of debate on pornography that frame the Court's analysis.[78]

The harm of pornography, the reason that best justifies control of its production, distribution and consumption, relates to the damage that it does to women and not the offence it causes when exposed to the public gaze.[79] The complex debate on the appropriate legal regulation of pornography will not be reopened here. However, the Court does not indicate that there is any need to discuss such issues; the only questions that arise are whether materials are obscene or indecent and whether the Member State has developed a single standard for domestic and imported goods.

The test endorsed by the Court is based on pornography's disruption of public space, because of the offence it engenders when placed in the public gaze.

The result is that the Court compounds the adverse effect that pornography has on women. It does not hint that pornography has a role to play in the persistent political and economic inequalities of women. The gendering strategy evident in this case is one silencing women, rendering the female figure a silent and acquiescent one. The Court in *Henn and Darby* finds women as a set of two dimensional figures to be seen and not heard, and it leaves them in that position as well.[80]

(d) Defining the female body

The feminist claim that law (and other normative systems) operate as a group of gendering mechanisms often clashes with a traditional world view that champions the constancy of the body, and certain of its sex-related characteristics. The core of this outlook is that certain aspects of human experience, in particular the human body, do not change from one context to another.

Thus we can refer to the body as a touchstone to assess other, less constant features of our experience. This perspective allows people to acknowledge the variation in personal appearance that is possible and sanctioned from place to place, or in the same place over time[81], as well as the wide scope for body modification[82], without being forced to adopt the claim that gender and other key aspects of our existence are socially constructed.

---

[78] For an overview of the feminist disruption of this debate, see Brown, "Debating pornography: The symbolic dimensions" 1 *law & critique* (1990), 131; Jackson, "The problem with pornography: A critical survey of the current debate" 3 *Feminist Legal Studies* (1995), 49.

[79] The moral framework that is embedded in this public gaze, and the epistemology integral to that way of seeing reflect a set of male norms and assumptions. See Flynn, "Interpretation and disputed accounts in sexual harassment cases: *Steward* v *Cleveland Guest (Engineering) Ltd*" 4 *Feminist Legal Studies* (1996), 109–122.

[80] A similar analysis might be offered of Case 121/85 *Conegate* v *H.M. Customs & Excise* [1986] ECR 1007.

[81] Flynn, "Gender equality laws and employers' dress codes" 24 *Industrial Law Journal* (1995) 255–272.

[82] Bibbings, "Touch: Body play" in Bently and Flynn, *Sensational jurisprudence: law and the senses* (1996 forthcoming).

This idea, that the body is a stable entity, provides a solid foundation on which other elements of personal identity can be built, without placing our claim to subjectivity in jeopardy.

This approach to the body as the repository of a set of ascertainable, durable, and essential information about ourselves is challenged by the advent of medical procedures that allow for extensive modification of an individual's sex.[83] These procedures are not widely performed within the European Union except on transsexuals, individuals with Gender Identity Disorder (GID) whose gender allocation is ambiguous. GID occurs in certain forms of pre-natal development in which the brain develops with a female inclination while the body's physical attributes are male, or vice versa. In these cases the individual is born with the body of one sex and the brain of the other sex, and grows up as a male while being aware of her female identity in terms of personality, and emotional and psychological development. The possibility of realigning a transsexual's physical sex to her female gender through medical procedures, including surgery and hormonal treatment, undermines the apparent reliability of the body as a source of identity. It also reinforces the refusal of certain feminist legal scholars to accept the usual classification of two sexes as a natural and unassailable fact[84], and highlights the full scope of the gendering power of law.

Gender reassignment poses a challenge to the legal system because it is committed to the essentialist view of the human body outlined above. That stance creates difficulties where an individual has had a gender reassignment performed and wishes to be recognised by law in her "new" post-operative gender. For example, under the English common law a person born with the body of a male is treated as remaining a male whatever changes by way of surgical operations there may have been.[85]

The issue has been raised under the European Convention on Human Rights, and the jurisprudence on the matter is mixed.[86]

Although, it has not yet been the subject of judicial pronouncement by the Court of Justice, the Industrial Tribunal in Truro, Cornwall, has referred questions to the Court on the application of the Equal Treatment Directive[87] to the dismissal of a transsexual for a reason related to her gender re-assignment.

While the Court has not yet given its judgment in *P v S and Cornwall County Council*[88], nor received the Opinion of Advocate General Tesauro, it is obvious that this case will give an important insight into the conceptual assumptions made in EC law. The United Kingdom government asked the Court to refrain

---

[83] On the centrality of sex to identity, see Foucault, *History of Sexuality: The Care of the Self* (vol 1) (trans Robert Hurley) (1978).
[84] See Gibson, "Continental drift: Context in feminist jurisprudence" 1 *law & critique* (1990), 173 at 195 *supra* n 38.
[85] *Corbett* v *Corbett* [1971] P 83; *White* v *British Sugar Corporation* [1977] IRLR 121.
[86] *Rees* v *United Kingdom*, Series A, No 106, judgment of 17 October 1986, (1986) 9 ECHRR 56; *Cossey* v *United Kingdom* Series A, No 184, judgment of 27 September 1990, (1991) 13 ECHRR 622; *B* v *France*, Series A, No 232–C, judgment of 25 March 1992, (1992) 16 ECHRR 1.
[87] Directive 76/207/EEC.
[88] Case C-13/94, heard by plenary court on 21 March 1995.

from dealing with the status of *P*, arguing that whether she was a man or a woman, her dismissal was related to the choice she made to undergo surgery and not to her sex as such. The Commission has also indicated that it is unwilling to see the question of what is a man and what is a woman for the purpose of the Directive taken up in this case. Both the United Kingdom and the Commission would confine the Directive to discrimination against a man where a woman in a similar situation would not suffer adverse treatment. On the other hand, the Court is being asked by the applicant to hold that EC law is gender-blind, and that its protection applies to any person, whether male or female, who is discriminated against on the basis of sex.[89] This would mean that individuals would be protected without having to show how male or female they were, and side-step any necessity to define the civil status of being male or female.

It is too early to do more than note the possibilities that this case holds. When judgment is given, it will certainly mark an interesting development in EC law regulating the body. The Court will have to engage in some form of gendering of individuals with GID. The absence of any judgment as yet, however, and the divergent results that one might anticipate in the case, make it clear that there is nothing inherently wrong with law being a gendering instrument. It may be inevitable that some form of gendering procedure will occur in law (though it need not be the one that we are currently familiar with). What is required, therefore, is close attention to how that process of gendering operates, and the extent to which it reinforces or disrupts the allocation of power and opportunities in society.

(vi) Conclusion

When feminist legal scholars have tackled EC law they have concentrated on social policy. This is an understandable area on which to focus, given its immediate significance to many women and the possibilities for change it contains. However, there is also a danger that social policy will become the Community equivalent of "women's law"[90] with the dangers to which that line of analysis is subject.[91] In particular, that analysis fails to question deeply the criteria used by those who make, practice and study EC law. There is also a danger in any attempt to broaden the scope of feminist consideration of EC law, incorporating those areas defined as central by that system, that a new approach will simply reiterate premises and not challenge them. While trying to avoid those pitfalls, this chapter has claimed that more of EC law can be rigorously and constructively inspected from a feminist perspective.

The male dominance of decision-making and authority in the Community is most clearly evident in the absence of gender balance amongst EC institutions

---

[89] See also in a different context Harrison, in this volume.

[90] Stang-Dahl, *Women's Law: An Introduction to Feminist Jurisprudence* (1985).

[91] See Gibson, "The Structure of the Veil" 52 *Modern Law Review* (1989), 420–471. See Shaw, in this volume.

and bodies. This imbalance does not in itself call those groups' policies and decisions into question. However, it does place the onus on them to show that they are not ignoring or actively subordinating women's interests in the course of their activities. That gender deficit in the EC political and judicial bodies cannot be repaired merely by some form of gender auditing.[92]

As was shown in the case of the Court of Justice, its mode of operation and its constituting conceptual framework are riddled with a set of masculine values and outlooks. That inadequacy can be traced in specific areas but it is also a failing on the macro-level. There is no point in changing the gender balance in the Court if the same masculine patterns of thought, reductionist, hierarchical and market dominated, remain in place. It is also important, however, to continue to focus on the Court's activities and on EC law more generally. The Court's character as a gendering agent moves it from merely reinforcing a set of sex-based assumptions as to what men and women are and do, to a more active role, formulating some of the key indices of gender through its decisions.

The law is always a powerful institution, deploying both coercive power and discursive authority, in a manner that shapes many features of our existence, even when we are not conscious of this. In that sense, it is naive to look for EC law not to affect women and men. There is little point in calling for the withdrawal of law from that sphere or for the withdrawal of feminists from law.[93] If there is to be a serious engagement with EC law from a feminist perspective, however, it must be able to tackle the issues that are taken seriously by EC law itself. That, in turn, will tell us more about the gender politics of the body of EC law.

LEO FLYNN
Centre for European Law,
Kings College London,
UK

---

[92] The phrase is used in a different sense from that used by Beveridge and Nott, in this volume.
[93] But see Smart, *Feminism and the power of law* (1989).

Chapter 20

THE ECONOMIC OBJECTIVES OF ARTICLE 119*

Ever since Gabrielle Defrenne, the Belgian air hostess, relied upon Article 119 to claim equal pay with her male colleagues in 1976[1] the attention of labour lawyers has been focused on the potential offered by Article 119 to challenge a wide variety of discriminatory pay practices. Based on ILO Convention No 100 on equal remuneration for men and women workers for work of equal value[2], Article 119 on equal pay for equal work was one of the very few provisions creating a legal obligation to be included in the Title on Social Policy in the Treaty of Rome. However, as one commentator has observed, while the norms established by the ILO were primarily aimed at improving living and working conditions, the social provisions of the Treaty "respond above all to the fear that unless employment costs are harmonised, economic integration will lead to competition to the detriment of countries whose social legislation is more advanced".[3]

---

* This chapter was written by Catherine Barnard. She is extremely grateful to Silvana Sciarra and Franca Borgogelli for their help in obtaining the Italian materials, Marie-Therese Lanquetin for her advice about the situation in France and Tamara Hervey for her very helpful comments on an earlier draft of this text.

[1] Case 43/75 *Defrenne* v *Sabena No 2* [1976] ECR 455. See Barnard, "A European Litigation Strategy: the Case of the Equal Opportunities Commission" in Shaw and More, *New Dynamics of European Integration*, (Clarendon, Oxford, 1995).

[2] Article 119, as Advocate General Trabucchi pointed out in *Defrenne No 2, ibid*, is the extension, the "European translation", of ILO Convention No 100. The translation is not, however, perfect. For example, Article 119 talks only of "equal pay for equal work" while the Convention talks, in Article 2, of "equal remuneration . . . for work of equal value". The requirement for equal pay for work of equal value was included in Article 1 of the Equal Pay Directive 75/117/EEC which, as the Court made clear in Case 96/80 *Jenkins* v *Kingsgate* [1981] ECR 911, "is principally designed to facilitate the practical application of the principle of equal pay outlined in Article 119 of the Treaty [and] in no way alters the content or scope of that principle as defined in the Treaty". The definition of pay found in Article 119 is, however, a replication of the ILO Convention.

[3] Author's translation of Valticos, *Droit International du Travail*, para 80, cited in Budiner, *Le Droit de la Femme à l'égalite de salaire et La Convention No 100 de L'organisation international du travail*, Libraire Generale de Droit et de Jurisprudence, 1975, 3.

The European Court of Justice has recognised that Article 119 has a dual purpose. In its landmark judgment in *Defrenne (No 2)* the Court said:

> Article 119 pursues a double aim. First, . . . the aim of Article 119 is to avoid a situation in which undertakings established in States which have actually implemented the principle of equal pay suffer a competitive disadvantage in intra-Community competition as compared with undertakings established in States which have not yet eliminated discrimination against women workers as regards pay. Second, this provision forms part of the social objectives of the Community, which is not merely an economic union, but is at the same time intended, by common action to ensure social progress and seek the constant improvement of living and working conditions of their peoples . . . This double aim, which is at once economic and social, shows that the principle of equal pay forms part of the foundations of the Community.

This chapter will suggest that economic rather than social factors were the motivating force behind the inclusion of Article 119 in the Treaty, and that these economic factors have been highly influential in shaping the jurisprudence of the Court. It will also suggest that neither the economic nor the subsequent social objectives of Article 119 have been fully realised, and that Article 119, in its present form, confined as it is to equal pay, provides an inadequate legal basis to secure real equality of opportunity for men and women.

(i) The historical background to the inclusion of Article 119 in the Treaty of Rome

Those who favour the creation of transnational labour standards have argued their case in a variety of forums over many years. For example, the Ohlin report of ILO experts[4] argued for the transnational harmonisation of social policy in some areas, including equal pay, but not in others. It argued that differences in nominal wage costs between countries did not, in themselves, pose an obstacle to economic integration because what mattered was unit labour costs, taking into account the relationship between nominal costs and productivity. Because higher costs tended to accompany higher productivity, differences between countries were less than they seemed. In addition, Ohlin suggested that the system of national exchange rates, which might be expected to reflect general prices and productivity levels within States, would cancel out the apparent advantage of low-wage States, so avoiding social dumping – the phenomenon of standards of social protection either being depressed in States with higher standards, fearing that they might lose out competitively, or at least prevented from rising, by increased competition from States with substantially lower social

---

[4] Ohlin, "Social Aspects of European Economic Co-operation: Report by a Group of Experts" 102 *International Labour Review* (1956), 99–123.

standards. Consequently, Ohlin argued that the market itself would ensure that conditions of competition were not distorted.

However, Ohlin also recognised that if a country enjoyed an advantage which was not related to productivity but occurred due to social discrimination or by differences in regulation which had no clear economic rationale, then the industry in question was viewed as receiving a subsidy. This resulted in unfair competition, with workers and firms in other countries losing out to less efficient, artificially subsidised competitors. It concluded that equal pay was one such area ripe for harmonisation. As Ohlin explained:

> A certain distortion of international competition arises from differences in the extent to which the principle of equal pay for men and women applies in different countries. Countries in which there are large wage differentials will pay relatively low wages in industries employing a large proportion of female labour and these industries will enjoy what might be considered a special advantage over their competitors abroad where differentials according to sex are smaller or non-existent.

Harmonisation of working time regulations and of levels of social charges were also discussed, but the report concluded that in these areas distortions of competition would be limited in scope and difficult to identify.

The Spaak Report, delivered to the foreign ministries of the six founding States[5], relied heavily on Ohlin. Spaak envisaged a "gradual coalescence of social policies" as one of the key factors necessary to provide the common market with a firm foundation. The gradual assimilation of social and labour legislation was intended to achieve two purposes: the first was to facilitate the free movement of labour in order to allow workers to move to find available work; the second was to remove distortions of competition. In this context, the Report envisaged only limited, but deliberate and concerted, action necessary for the functioning of the common market. It rejected the idea of trying to harmonise the fundamental conditions of an economy – its natural resources, its level of productivity, the significance of public burdens – considering that any harmonisation might be the *result*, as opposed to a condition precedent, of the operation of the common market and the economic forces which it released.[6] In the social field this anticipated Article 117, which failed to provide any legal basis for the harmonisation of social policy, insisting that higher social standards would ensue from the functioning of the common market.

Instead, the Report suggested that action must "correct or eliminate the effect of specific distortions which advantage or disadvantage certain branches of activity".[7] Among the factors of distortion, the Report mentioned working

---

[5] Comité Intergouvernemental Crée par la Conférence de Messine, Rapport des Chefs de Délégations aux Ministères des Affaires Etrangères of 21 April 1956. The Committee, comprising of the heads of delegations, was established at the Messina conference in June 1955 under the chairmanship of M Paul Henri Spaak, then Belgian foreign minister.
[6] See further Barnard and Deakin, "Social Policy in Search of a Rôle: Integration, Cohesion and Citizenship" in Caiger and Floudas (eds.), *1996 Onwards: Lowering the Barriers Further* (Wiley, 1996).
[7] *Supra* n 5 at 61 (author's translation).

conditions of labour, such as the relation between the wages of men and women, the systems of working time, overtime and paid holidays.[8] The Report concluded that:

> Even if the existing disparities did not cause distortions, it would be necessary for the governments to make a special effort to harmonise progressively the existing systems with regard to:
> - the principle of equality of men and women's wages;
> - the length of the normal working week beyond which working time is payable and the rates of overtime pay; and
> - the length of paid vacations.[9]

These policies were incorporated in the Treaty in the form of Article 119 on equal pay for men and women; Article 120 on paid holiday schemes; and the third protocol on "Certain Provisions Relating to France" on working hours and overtime.[10]

Kahn-Freund has suggested that these policies were not as clearly reflected as might have been the case[11], perhaps because the relevant provisions were drafted only at the end of a crucial conversation between the French and German Prime Ministers.[12] At the time of the Treaty negotiations, there were important differences in the scope and content of social legislation in force in the States concerned.[13] France, in particular, had a number of rules which favoured workers, including legislation on equality for men and women, and rules permitting French workers longer paid holidays than in other States.[14] French workers were also entitled to overtime pay after fewer hours of work at basic rates than elsewhere. This raised concerns that the additional costs borne by French industry would make French goods uncompetitive in the Common Market. Consequently, the French argued that an elimination of gross distortions of competition was not enough, and that it would be necessary to assimilate the entire labour and social legislation of the Member States, so as to achieve a parity of wages and social costs.

The Germans, however, were strongly committed to a minimum level of

---

[8] *Ibid* 62–3 (author's translation).

[9] *Ibid* 65–6 (author's translation).

[10] This provided that the Commission was to authorise France to take protective measures where the establishment of the common market did not result, by the end of the first stage, in the basic number of hours beyond which overtime was paid for and the average rate of additional payment for overtime industry did not correspond to the average obtaining in France in 1956. It does not seem that France has called upon this safeguard clause – Budiner, *Le Droit de la femme à l'égalité de salaire et la Convention No 100 de l'organisation internationale du travail*, Librairie Generale de Droit et de Jurisprudence, 1975.

[11] Kahn-Freund, "Labour Law and Social Security" in Stein and Nicholson, *American Enterprise in the European Common Market: A Legal Profile*, 1960, 300.

[12] *Ibid* citing Katzenstein, "Der Arbeitnehmer in der europaischen Wirtschaftgemeinschaft" 31 *Betriebsberater* (1957), 1087.

[13] This draws on Ellis, *European Community Sex Equality Law* (1991) 38.

[14] *Ibid*. However, rules on equal pay were introduced by Loi No. 72/1143 of 22 December 1972. See Lanquetin, Pettiti and Sutter, *L'Égalité Juridique Entre Femmes et Hommes Dans La Communauté Européene* (OPEC, Brussels).

government interference in the area of wages and prices. The resulting compromise is reflected in the Treaty's social policy provisions. In the words of one commentator, Articles 117 and 118 on the need to improve working conditions and co-operation between States, even if textually broad, are legally shallow – at least when considered in isolation from Article 100.[15] Articles 119 and 120, by contrast, are specific provisions designed to protect French industry.[16]

It seems that the French were particularly concerned about equal pay, especially the discriminatory pay rates resulting from collective agreements in Italy. At that time France had one of the smallest differentials between the salaries of male and female employees (7% compared to 20–40% in the Netherlands and in Italy).[17] This risked placing parts of French industry which employed a very large female workforce, such as textiles and electrical construction, in a weaker competitive position than identical or similar industries in other Member States employing a largely female workforce at much lower salaries.[18] In addition, France had ratified ILO Convention No 100 by Law No 52–1309 of 10 December 1952.[19] By 1957 the Convention had also been ratified by Belgium, France, Germany and Italy, but not by Luxembourg and the Netherlands.[20]

Article 37 of the Italian Constitution on equality between men and women, introduced in 1948, was considered to give ILO Convention No 100 the force of law in Italy.[21] It provided that:

> The working woman has the same rights and, for equal work, the same remuneration as the man. Working conditions should permit the fulfilment of her essential family function and ensure the mother and her child a special, adequate protection.

Reflecting the views of its time, the Article focused on the domestic responsibilities of women, rather than on their full social involvement. Consequently, it seems that there was little contemporaneous discussion of the possible inconsistency between the protective measures envisaged by the Article and the principle of equal pay.[22]

---

[15] Forman, "The Equal Pay Principle under Community Law" 1 LIEI, (1982) 17–36.

[16] According to the French Advocate General Dutheillet de Lamothe in Case 80/70 *Defrenne v Sabena No 1* [1971] ECR 445: "It appears to be France which took the initiative, but the article necessitated quite long negotiations".

[17] Budiner, *Le Droit de la femme à l'égalité de salaire et la Convention No 100 de l'organisation internationale du travail*, Librairie Generale de Droit et de Jurisprudence, 1975, citing Sullerot, "L'emploi des femmes et ses problèmes dans les Etats Membres de la Communauté Européene", CEC, Luxembourg, 1972, 177.

[18] Budiner, *ibid*, citing Ribas, "L'égalité des salaires feminins et masculins dans la Communauté Economique Européene", 1966 *Droit Social*, para 1, and Clair, "L'article 119 du Traité de Rome. Le Principe de l'égalisation des salaires masculins et feminins dans la CEE", 1968 *Droit Social*, 150.

[19] *Journal Officiel*, 11 Decembre 1952.

[20] Luxembourg ratified the Convention in 1967 and the Netherlands in 1971. All 15 States of the European Union have now ratified the Convention.

[21] Camera dei Deputati, Senato della Repubblica, *Relazioni della Commissione parlamentare di inchiesta sulle condizioni dei lavoratori in Italia*, volume vii, indaini sul rapporto di lavoro, tomo III, relatori: Calvi and Tonietti, Rome MCMLXII, 276.

[22] Ballestrero, *Equality between Male and Female Workers in Italian Law*, Presses Universitaires de Louvain, 259.

During the decade that followed the enactment of Article 37, it seems that the provision of equality was not actually implemented and large disparities between the wages of men and women continued to exist. This was due in part to structural factors and in part to the job classifications adopted by collective agreements. A parliamentary inquiry at the time[23] found that a collective agreement of 6 December 1954 on pay in the industrial sector fixed the differences in pay between men and women at 16%.[24] However, interconfederal collective agreements of 6 December 1945 and 23 May 1946 provided that if women performed jobs on the same terms and with the same productivity as men they would then receive the same pay as men.[25] Nevertheless, the parliamentary inquiry found that in practice such terms were rarely applied. Indeed, in one large company specialising in metals the commission could not find a single case of a female worker who was considered to be carrying out work traditionally performed by men. Consequently, women were not paid the same remuneration as men. This approach was reinforced by judicial interpretation of Article 37. In the 1950s equal work was considered to be work having the same length, the same position in a job classification scheme, and the same intrinsic value and economic productivity as that performed by men. This allowed the courts to justify the practice of underpaying women performing equal work (in respect of the number of hours worked and the position held) on the ground that women's work was less productive than the corresponding work performed by men.[26]

The situation in Italy raised concerns in France about social dumping. Consequently, Article 119 was included in the Treaty to impose parity of costs on the Member States and to prevent such destructive competition. This point was noted, albeit somewhat obliquely, by the French Advocate General Dutheillet de Lamothe in *Defrenne No 1*,[27] the first case to consider the application of Article 119. He said that although Article 119 had a social objective it also had an economic objective "for in creating an obstacle to any attempt at 'social dumping' by means of the use of female labour less well paid than male labour, it helped to achieve one of the fundamental objectives of the common market, the establishment of a system ensuring that 'competition is not distorted'". He continued that "This explains why Article 119 of the Treaty is of a different character from the articles which precede it in the chapter of the Treaty devoted to social provisions".

Were the French engaged in a form of disguised protectionism? By removing Italy's comparative advantage (its low paid workforce) it removed one of the incentives for companies in need of low-skilled or unskilled labour to open up

---

[23] Camera dei Deputati, Senato della Repubblica, *Relazioni della Commissione parlamentare di inchiesta sulle condizioni dei lavoratori in Italia*, volume vii, indaini sul rapporto di lavoro, tomo III, relatori: Calvi and Tonietti, Rome MCMLXII.

[24] This shortened the gap between men and women's pay by 2–3 points.

[25] Similar terms were reproduced in various collective agreements including Art 21 (food); Art 20 (chemical industry); Art 24 (paper industry); Art 25 (metal industry).

[26] Ballestrero, *supra* n 22 at 262.

[27] Case 80/70 *Defrenne* v *Sabena No 1* [1971] ECR 445.

operations in Italy.[28] Consequently, it could be suggested that including Article 119 in the Treaty had the effect of undermining Italy's comparative advantage, thereby hindering its economic development, while at the same time reinforcing the position of strength enjoyed by France, a more developed and prosperous country. However, if the Ohlin analysis is accepted, and a market failure has occurred with Italy offering labour at wages which, due to discrimination, were below the productivity of the workers concerned, the Community was justified in intervening to offset a distortion of competition by enacting Article 119.

Similarly, in 1990 the Commission felt that the Community should intervene in respect of the harmonisation of rules governing part-time and temporary employment, albeit that such intervention would exceed what was originally envisaged by the Ohlin and Spaak reports. In its Explanatory Memorandum, the Commission said that "relative cost differences resulting from different kinds of rules on different types of employment relationships, . . . may provide comparative advantages which constitute veritable distortions of competition".[29] However, the Commission's arguments were weakened by its attempts to suggest that while harmonisation of indirect wage costs resulting from social security taxation and employment regulation should take place, harmonisation of direct costs (rules governing wages and salaries) was unnecessary because "differences in productivity levels attenuate these differences in unit labour costs to a considerable degree". Such a distinction has little merit from either an economic or legal standpoint and it had the effect of rejecting the very argument put forward in 1957 for the adoption of Article 119.[30]

(ii) Article 119 and the jurisprudence of the Court of Justice

It is clear from this historical survey that Article 119 was included in the Treaty for economic purposes; any social benefits were merely an advantageous consequence of the desire to avoid distortions of competition. In some of the earliest cases decided on Article 119, the arguments of the parties and the Advocate Generals referred back to the economic purpose of Article 119. For example, in *Macarthys* v *Smith*[31] the employer paid its female manager £10 less a week than the male manager who had previously done the job. Advocate General Capotorti cited with approval the Commission's arguments that if an undertaking could pay lower wages, solely by replacing its male employees with female employees, that would result in it having an unfair competitive advantage over undertakings

---

[28] See, for example, Kierman and Beim, "On the Economic realities of the European Social Charter and the Social Dimension of EC 1992" 2 *Duke Journal of Comparative and International Labour Law* (1992), 149, discussed in Barnard, *EC Employment Law* (1995) 83.
[29] COM(90) 228.
[30] Deakin and Wilkinson, "Rights vs Efficiency? The Economic case for Transnational Labour Standards", 23 (ILJ (1994) 289), 302–3.
[31] Case 129/79 [1980] ECR 1275.

which contemporaneously employ men and women to carry out the work in question.

In *Burton* v *British Railways Board*[32] Mr Burton argued that the double aim of Article 119 would be frustrated if the principle of equal pay was not applied to redundancy benefits. He continued "undertakings established in States which have applied the principle to redundancy benefits would suffer a competitive disadvantage as compared with undertakings established in States which have not". In *Worringham and Humphreys* v *Lloyd's Bank*[33] Advocate General Warner again referred back to Advocate General Dutheillet de Lamothe's statement in *Defrenne No 1* that the first purpose of Article 119 was to "avoid a situation in which undertakings established in Member States with advanced legislation on the equal treatment of men and women suffer a competitive disadvantage as compared with undertakings established in Member States that have not eliminated discrimination against female workers as regards pay". Nevertheless, as a result of these cases social justice was also achieved – Mrs Smith received the same rate of pay as her male predecessor; and Lloyd's Bank was required to pay contributions to a retirement benefits scheme for men and women on equal terms.[34]

In subsequent cases, references back to the earlier case law and the origins of Article 119 no longer take centre stage and the cases seem more explicable by reference to the social function of Article 119. For example, the Court has extended the obligation of equality, via the mechanism of indirect discrimination, to part-time workers in the context of the contract of employment[35], collective agreements[36] and statutes.[37] It has also extended the definition of "pay" to bring a wider range of discriminatory measures within the net of Article 119. For example, the Court has ruled that supplementary and contracted-out occupational pensions[38], survivor's benefits[39] and bridging pensions[40] all constitute "pay" within the meaning of Article 119.

However, it could be argued that a closer reading of these cases suggests that the motivating force behind these decisions is not merely social justice but concerns about distortions of competition. The part-time workers cases provide a

---

[32] Case 19/81 [1982] ECR 554.
[33] Case 69/80 [1981] ECR 767.
[34] In a much criticised decision in *Burton supra* n 33 the Court concluded that the difference in ages for payment of voluntary redundancy was caught by the derogation in Article 7(1) of Directive 79/7/EEC. For criticism of this decision, see Lester, "The Uncertain trumpet, References to the Court of Justice from the United Kingdom: Equal Pay and Equal Treatment without Sex Discrimination" in Schermers, Timmermans, Kellermann and Watson, *Article 177 EEC: Experiences and Problems* (1987).
[35] Case 96/80 *Jenkins* v *Kingsgate* [1981] ECR 911, Case 170/84 *Bilka-Kaufhaus Gmbh* v *Weber von Hartz* [1986] ECR 1607.
[36] Case C-33/89 *Kowalska* v *Freie und Hansestadt Hamburg* [1990] ECR I-2591; Case C-184/89 *Nimz* v *Freie und Hansestadt Hamburg* [1991] ECR I-297.
[37] Case 171/88 *Rinner-Kühn* v *FWW Spezialgebäudereinigung Gmbh* [1989] ECR 2743; Case C-360/90 *Bötel* v *Arbeiterwohlfahrt der Stadt Berlin* [1992] ECR I-3589.
[38] Case 170/84 *Bilka-Kaufhaus* [1986] ECR 1607; Case C-262/88 *Barber* v *Guardian Royal Exchange Assurance Group* [1990] ECR I-1889.
[39] Case C-109/91 *Ten Oever* v *Stichting Bedrijfpensioenfonds voor het Glazenwassers- en Schoonmaakbedrijf* [1993] ECR I-4879.
[40] Case C-132/92 *Bird's Eye Walls* v *Roberts* [1993] ECR I-5579.

good illustration of this: if a large part of the workforce of State A worked part-time and part-time workers could be paid less than full-time workers, that country might enjoy a competitive advantage unrelated to its productivity, in respect of the other Member States. Although the Court made no reference to any such analysis in either *Jenkins* v *Kingsgate* or *Bilka-Kaufhaus* v *Weber von Hartz*[41] it did rule that paying part-time workers less than full-time workers con-travened Article 119 if it was found that a much lower proportion of women than men worked part-time and the undertaking could not show that the pay practice was objectively justified.[42]

The Court has therefore employed the notions of direct and indirect discrimin-ation to eliminate many of the barriers towards securing equality between men and women in respect of pay. The Court's notion of equality is a fairly narrow one: it seems committed to formal equality, ensuring that men and women should be viewed as the same and treated alike. It takes no account of the fact that men and women may be differently situated and have different needs. This approach is consistent with that adopted in the context of other fundamental economic provisions of the Treaty concerning discrimination on the grounds of nationality. Articles 48, 52 and 59 on the free movement of persons in essence require equal treatment of Community nationals with the nationals of the host State, without taking into account the difficulties that non-nationals may experi-ence in coming to the host State to find work.[43] The Court firmly placed Article 119 in the broader context of the Treaty when, in *Birds Eye Walls* v *Roberts*[44], it talked of Article 119 embodying in a "specific form the general principle of non-discrimination".

As Fenwick and Hervey point out[45], formal equality affects the market by inducing it not to act in an arbitrary and ultimately inefficient fashion. Formal equality, if fully established, disallows the individual biases of employers (or pur-chasers) to feed the market, and may therefore promote genuine competition based on individual merit, thereby preventing the unwarranted under – or over – advantaging of certain groups. However, while this insistence on formal equality helps assuage concerns about social dumping and goes a long way towards cre-ating a level playing field of competition, it does not necessarily help improve the position of women. It does not recognise the fact that due to the domestic

---

[41] Case 170/84 *Bilka-Kaufhaus* [1986] ECR 1607.

[42] However, in the Draft Atypical Workers Directive (COM) (90) 228 the Commission said that dif-ferences in direct costs did not need harmonisation yet as a result of *Bilka-Kaufhaus* they could be challenged under Article 119.

[43] For example, the Court does not look at the difficulties that, for example, a foreign teacher has in obtaining the necessary skills to find a job abroad (Case 379/87 *Groener* v *Minister for Education* [1989] ECR 3967) nor the difficulties a foreign language assistant experiences in looking for work abroad. Instead it insists only on equal treatment in respect of the terms and conditions of employ-ment itself (Case C-272/92 *Maria Chiara Spotti* v *Freistaat Bayern*, judgment of 20 October 1992). Leg-islation, in the form of Regulation (EEC)/1612/68, in the context of workers, and Directive 73/148/EEC on establishment and services, goes some way towards addressing these problems.

[44] *Supra* n 40.

[45] Fenwick and Hervey, "Sex equality in the Single Market: New Directions for the European Court of Justice", 32 CMLRev (1995), 443–470.

role played by many women, they are not necessarily in a position to compete equally with men by, for example, moving to find jobs or gain promotion or working long hours. Notions of substantive equality, by contrast, require that the real situation of many women which may place them in a weaker position in the market, should be addressed.[46]

The Court has, however, refused to allow Article 119 to be used as an instrument of social engineering to achieve substantive equality. For example, in *Bilka-Kaufhaus*, it said:

> the scope of Article 119 is restricted to the question of pay discrimination between men and women workers. Problems related to other conditions of work and employment, on the other hand, are covered generally by other provisions of Community Law, in particular Articles 117 and 118 of the Treaty with a view to the harmonisation of the social systems of the Member States and the approximation of the legislation in that area.[47]

Consequently, the Court ruled that Article 119 does not have the effect of requiring an employer to organize its occupational pension scheme in such a manner as to take into account the particular difficulties faced by people with family responsibilities in meeting the conditions for entitlement to such a pension; a view reiterated by the Advocate General in *Stadt Lengerich v Helmig*.[48] This more restrictive approach could be explained by reference to the economic, rather than social, origins of Article 119 and a recognition by the Court that legislation "to harmonise the social systems of the Member States" would be more appropriate than judicial intervention on an uncertain legal basis.

In the meantime, the Court has shown itself so determined to achieve formal equality in the workplace that the situation of women has actually suffered. In *Smith v Avdel Systems*,[49] for example, the employer, in order to ensure equality in its own occupational pension scheme, decided that with effect from 1 July 1991 both men and women would receive their occupational pensions at 65. This represented a levelling down of the women's conditions of employment to the inferior terms offered to the men. The Court said that as regards periods of service completed after the entry into force of rules designed to eliminate discrimination (1 July 1991) Article 119 did not preclude measures which achieved equal treatment by reducing the advantages of persons previously favoured (levelling down), since Article 119 merely required that men and women should receive the same pay for the same work without imposing any specific level of pay.[50]

---

[46] *Ibid* 444–445.

[47] Citing Case 149/77 *Defrenne v Sabena No 3* [1978] ECR 1365.

[48] Cases C-399/92, 409/92, 425/92, 34/93, 50/93, 78/93 *Helmig et al* [1994] ECR I-5727.

[49] Case C-408/92 [1994] ECR I-4435. The Court reached similar conclusions in Case C-28/93 *Van den Akker v Stitching Shell Pensioenfonds* [1994] ECR I-4527.

[50] This ruling compares unfavourably with its judgment in Case 43/75 *Defrenne No 2, supra* n 1, nearly 20 years earlier when the Court ruled against the argument that compliance with Article 119 could be achieved in other ways than by raising the lowest salaries, in view of the connection between Article 119 and the harmonisation of working conditions while the improvement is being maintained. See Article 117 and Case 126/86 *Zaera* [1987] ECR 3697.

(iii) Conclusions

The decision in *Smith* v *Avdel Systems* highlights the tensions caused by a Treaty provision drafted to achieve an economic purpose but considered by many to have social objectives. The historical origins of Article 119 define its inherent limitations: since it was intended only to avoid distortions of competition it requires equal treatment without an obligation that the inferior standards be raised to the superior level.

When the Court in *Defrenne No 2* talked of the dual purpose of Article 119, it was trying to reflect the changing social and political environment at the time, including the advent of the Draft Directive on equal pay and equal treatment.[51] Nevertheless it had set itself the task of trying to reconcile the irreconcilable: the conflicting aims of protecting economic and social interests. This has raised expectations in the minds of litigants which may be frustrated and has been exacerbated by the fact that the Court has seemed very conscious of the need to accommodate the objectives of Article 119 to a management hostile to the idea that principles of equality should take precedence over both freedom of contract and over any economic benefits which might be derived from operating a discriminatory pay policy. Consequently, the Court has steered a difficult course between ensuring equality and taking account of the needs of the market. As a result, it has allowed indirect discrimination to be justified by objective factors, which have included market forces arguments[52] and it has imposed temporal limitations on the retrospectivity of judgments.[53]

Yet even the economic purpose of Article 119 has not been achieved – large wage differentials by sex continue to exist in some Member States, giving them a comparative advantage over their competitors abroad where differentials according to sex are smaller or non-existent. For example, recent statistics (which the Court has never considered) suggest that for non-manual workers in the manufacturing industry, women's average earnings are, at European level, between 30 and 40% lower than men's (see the following table 1). For manual workers in the same industry, the pay differential is 15–35%, exceeding 30% only in Luxembourg and the United Kingdom.[54] The fact that pay differentials are greater among non-manual workers than manual workers is explained by the range of possible jobs and the tendency for men to be managers and

---

[51] In the UK there had also been recent legislation addressing the problems of sex discrimination – the Equal Pay Act 1970 and the Sex Discrimination Act 1975.

[52] Case C-127/92 *Enderby* v *Frenchay Health Authority and Secretary of State for Health* [1993] ECR I-5535.

[53] See, for example, Case C-262/88 *Barber, supra* n 39, Case C-109/91 *Ten Oever, supra* n 39.

[54] *Women and men in the European Union: A Statistical Portrait*, Eurostat, OPEC, 1995. The authors note that all the data presented are drawn from harmonised statistics on earnings. These statistics provide averages that mask any differentials between men and women as regards the structure of occupations, skills, occupational experience, length of working life, length of service and age. This means that the data should be considered with caution. Also the figures showing pay differentials between women and men are based on average gross hourly earnings for manual workers and average gross monthly earnings for non-manual workers.

Table 1: Gross monthly earnings of non-manual workers, 1993 (in national currency). NB: for the retail trade – Spain 1992, Luxembourg, 1990

	B	Dk	D	GR	E	F	IRL	I	L	NIL	P	UK
Manufacturing												
Women	73,368	-	4,355	206,071	180,679	11,175	-	-	88,607	3,653	112,782	1,1131
Men	109,968	-	6,379	301,292	275,209	16,257	-	-	146,876	5,435	163,972	1,882
Total	100,223	19,468	5,833	277,784	251,886	14,720	1,659	-	136,802	5,116	145,273	1,663
Retail trade												
Women	52,881	-	3,172	125,300	121,094	8,310	-	-	48,791	2,615	76,620	871
Men	72,164	-	4,520	155,656	161,706	11,692	-	-	78,681	3,734	105,644	1,329
Total	59,459	-	3,705	138,250	137,456	9,851	-	-	56,056	3,211	90,654	1,084

Source: Eurostat: Basic statistics of the European Union (1995).

Table 2: Average gross hourly earnings (excluding overtime) 1994

	Manual	Non-manual	All
Full-time men	614p	1093p	865p
Full-time women	445p	742p	688p
Differential:m/f	169p	351p	177p
Women's earnings as % of men's	72.5%	67.9%	79.5%

Source: New Earnings Survey 1994 Central Statistical Office. Crown Copyright 1994. Reproduced by the permission of the Controller of HMSO and the Central Statistical Office.

Table 3: Average gross weekly earnings (including overtime) 1994

	Manual	Non-manual	All
Full-time men	280.7	428.2	362.1
Full-time women	181.9	278.4	261.5
Differential:m/f	98.8	149.8	100.6
Women's earnings as % of men's	64.8%	65.0%	72.2%

Source: New Earnings Survey 1994 Central Statistical Office. Crown Copyright 1994. Reproduced by the permission of the Controller of HMSO and the Central Statistical Office.

women to be secretaries. In the cases of manual workers the range of jobs and therefore the pay levels is more restricted.[55]

In the United Kingdom the New Earnings Survey reveals that while the pay gap between women's and men's earnings has continued to narrow – 79.5% in 1994 compared to 78.9% in 1993 – women still earn at least 20% less than men (see table 2). In the higher level of earnings, the gender pay gap is wider with non-manual female workers earning only 67.9% of male earnings. Women also tend to be grouped at the lower end of the earnings distribution. For example, 21.4% of men earned less than £220 per week compared with 46.6% of women. At the top end of the earnings distribution, 19.5% of men earned more than £470 per week compared with 5.6% of women.[56]

In its memorandum on equal pay for work of equal value, the Commission has tried to explain that "the segregation effect, exacerbated by the undervaluing of feminine occupations, is one of the main reasons why significant disparities persist between levels of pay".[57] While, as the case of *Enderby*[58] has demonstrated, Article 119 can be used to help break down these barriers, on its own it is clearly insufficient to achieve this task. Indeed, it could be argued that the Court's jurisprudence on Article 119 bears some responsibility for creating the problem. The Court has created the perception that it has been taking steps to address the problem of sex discrimination, and it has therefore given the legisla-

---

[55] Eurostat, *ibid* 156.

[56] EOR No 58, November/December 1994.

[57] COM(94) 6 final.

[58] In Case C-127/92 *Enderby*, *supra* n 52, speech therapists (predominantly female) were paid less than pharmacists and psychologists (predominantly male). When Enderby brought a claim for indirect discrimination the Court accepted that different rates of pay, arrived at as a result of separate collective bargaining in two professional groups, was not sufficient objective justification, even though the collective bargaining was carried out by the same parties and, taken separately, the individual collective agreements had in themselves no discriminatory effect.

ture the excuse to take no further action,[59] in particular by not providing an adequate legal basis for ensuring equality between the sexes.[60]

Further intervention, by the legislature and through labour market policies, may provide part of the answer. However, to date the emphasis of Community initiatives seems to focus on means of encouraging women's access to and participation in employment on an equal basis with men. Concrete assistance was given to women through the creation of the NOW (New Opportunities for Women) programme which aims to promote opportunities for women in the field of education and vocational training. The scheme provides financial assistance in creating small enterprises and co-operatives by women and supports vocational training and other measures, including financing childcare schemes designed to help women find employment.

As long as attention is focused on trying to place women in employment, the economic purpose of Article 119 will not be realised and so long as the economic purpose of Article 119 remains its principal focus, its social dimension as part of a programme of measures to attain "real equality of opportunity",[61] will remain illusory.

One possible solution would be for a revised version of Article 119 to be included as part of a broader catalogue of fundamental social rights introduced into the Treaty. Such rights might include a more general provision prohibiting discrimination on the grounds of colour, race, disability, sexual orientation, age, opinions and beliefs.[62] This would place the principle of equal pay in the more natural environment of a social fundamental right rather than continuing to allow it to sit rather uneasily, as we have seen, with the other fundamental economic provisions of the Treaty. This approach would mark a significant change of emphasis and would necessitate an amendment to the Treaty. There is widespread support for such a move: the European Parliament, ECOSOC and the ETUC, in their responses to the Green Paper on Social Policy, called for "the establishment of fundamental social rights of citizens as a constitutional element of the European Union[63]", and a similar approach was recommended by the Molitor Report on legislative and administrative simplification (with the British representative dissenting). It is unlikely that this will happen in the short term, particularly while the present British government remains so implacably opposed to the creation of transnational social rights, but it may eventually become an important prerequisite towards the successful creation of a Political Union.

CATHERINE BARNARD

Lecturer in Law, Trinity College, University of Cambridge, UK

---

[59] Article 6 of the Social Policy Agreement repeated Article 119 verbatim. In addition, it did allow Member States to provide for "specific advantages in order to make it easier for women to pursue a vocational activity or to prevent or to compensate for disadvantages in their professional careers".

[60] This can be contrasted with the situation in respect of the environment where, when it became apparent that the existing legal bases were inadequate, the Single European Act 1986 filled the lacuna.

[61] Case 14/83 *Von Colson* [1984] ECR 1891; Case C-271/91 *Marshall No 2* [1993] ECR I-4367.

[62] See Hervey, in this volume. See also Blanpain, Hepple, Sciarra and Weiss, *Fundamental Social Rights: Proposal for the European Union* (Peeters, 1996).

[63] COM(94) 333, 69.

Part VII

PERSPECTIVES ON SEX EQUALITY LAW: PROPOSALS FOR REFORM

Chapter 21

THE SWEDISH CASE – THE PROMISED LAND OF SEX EQUALITY?*

In August 1995, a United Nations Development Programme Report, in using two indices (the gender-related development index (GDI) and the gender empowerment measure (GEM)) found that: "The four top-ranking countries in the GDI are from the Nordic belt – Sweden, Finland, Norway and Denmark, in that order. It is hardly surprising. These countries have adopted gender equality and women's empowerment as a conscious national policy".[1] The GDI is based upon factors such as life expectancy, educational attainment and adjusted real income. As regards the GEM, Sweden and Norway ranked at the top, followed at a distance by Finland and Denmark. The GEM examines whether women and men are able to participate actively in economic and political life and take part in decision-making. Equally striking is the finding showing that some developing countries outperform much richer industrial countries in gender equality. Belgium, Hungary, the United Kingdom, Switzerland are lagging behind nations like Barbados, the Bahamas, Trinidad and Tobago and Cuba; Spain and Japan are behind China, Costa Rica and Guyana, whereas France is behind the Philippines and Colombia.[2] It is no wonder that sex equality has met with such great interest in the European Community.

It is not my aim to paint a rosy picture of Swedish sex equality in such broad terms as has been done in the United Nations Report. My aim is to highlight some of those aspects of the Swedish legislation regarding sex discrimination, since its stumbling start in the late 1970s, and also occasionally to compare new developments in Swedish law with those in European Community equality law.

---

* This chapter was written by Ronnie Eklund.
[1] United Nations Development Programme (UNDP), *Human Development Report 1995* (Oxford University Press 1995), 73–86 at 75.
[2] *Ibid* 83.

(i) A quick look at the sex discrimination law in Sweden

It is imperative to outline certain aspects of the background to the development of laws on sex discrimination in Sweden, before bringing up a few important issues of the Sex Discrimination Act as seen against EC equality law.

First of all it must be said that there is a sex discrimination ban to be found in the *1975 Swedish Constitution*, Chapter 1 Section 2(3) second sentence, which reads: "The community shall guarantee equal rights to men and women . . .".

Furthermore, Chapter 2 Section 16 provides: "No law or other decree may imply the discrimination of any citizen on account of sex, unless the relevant provision forms part of efforts to bring about equality between men and women . . .". It must be noted, however, that this provision is no springboard for any affirmative action in recruitment cases.[3]

As regards *State employees*, Chapter 11 Section 9(2) also applies. The provision reads: "When making appointments to posts within the State administration attention shall be paid only to objective factors such as service merits and competence". Here the term "service merits" implies the taking into account of the length of the time of employment. "Competence" refers to skills and education. Even such aspects as sex equality or labour market considerations, however, are to be taken as objective factors.[4]

For *municipal employees* (in local government), another provision in the Constitution (which is addressed to the community as such), Chapter 1 Section 9 applies: "Courts and public authorities as well as others who carry out functions within the public administration, shall in their activities observe the equality of all persons under the law and shall maintain objectivity and impartiality". This is what is generally called the *objectivity principle* in Swedish administrative law.

The above-mentioned constitutional guarantees apply, however, solely to the public sector. The Constitution does not formally apply to private employers. It is also at this point that the Sex Discrimination Act enters into the picture. The Act applies to all employers, whether public or private.[5] In fact, disputes concerning the applicability of the 1979 Act to the public sector form an interesting part of legislative history. One of the members of the Swedish Law Council questioned the view that the Act should apply to the public sector on constitutional grounds.[6] He suggested that it would be almost preposterous to assume

---

[3] See Petrén and Ragnemalm, *Sveriges grundlagar (The Swedish Constitution)* (1980) 288.

[4] When a State employer appoints a civil servant, such a decision may be appealed against in the administrative order by the job applicant who was refused the job. This is not always the case in the Nordic countries. In Norway, e.g., there is no right of appeal.

[5] It follows from Case 248/83 *Commission v Germany* [1985] ECR 1459 para 16 that Article 119 of the Treaty and the two core Directives on Equal Pay and Equal Treatment are of general application and apply to employment in the public service.

[6] The Law Council is a body composed of three high judges from the Supreme Court and the Administrative Supreme Court. The Council's main duty is to scrutinise the legal-technical aspects on any important legislation before such legislation is put before the Parliament.

that the State or municipal authorities acted unconstitutionally.[7] It is therefore ironical that the first cases to be tried before the Swedish Labour Court after the enactment of the 1979 Act dealt with just such cases. It is equally ironical that 29 out of the total of 41 sex discrimination cases tried before the Labour Court between the years of 1980–95 concerned public employers.[8]

In fact, the 1979 Sex Discrimination Act met with a somewhat reluctant start. During the 1970s only the MPs of the Liberal Party advocated the introduction of sex discrimination legislation in Sweden. The United States' Civil Rights Act had inspired the proponents. In fact, the first 1979 Act was a halfway-house and never obtained legal force.[9] After the 1979 national elections, the earlier, partly rejected, Government Bill was again submitted before the Parliament and this time it was accepted.[10] The statute was officially called the Act concerning equality between men and women in working life and entered into force on 1 July 1980. I will call this piece of legislation the *Sex Discrimination Act*, to shorten the official, long-winded name.

Two background features of the 1979 Act must be highlighted here.

First of all, the equality principle had gained political acceptance by that time in Sweden.[11] Equality in working life between men and women, however, is only a minor piece of the pie. Equality also extends to other areas of social and political life, such as education, tax and social insurance systems, family and social policy issues, access to daycare, etc.[12] It is pertinent here to remind the reader of the United Nations Report on gender inequalities mentioned earlier. *In the 1979 Act the legislator tried to pave the way for a timely sex equality legislation applied to working life in order to make justice to the equality principle.* Legislation on sex equality was deemed to form a part of a relentless campaign seeking to change the social mores, the natural inertia and the old patterns exhibited by people in general in order to promote equality.[13]

The second matter that met with a good deal of concern in the 1979 legislation and that preoccupied the legislator very strongly was the interaction between sex discrimination bans and the equivalent affirmative actions taken on the part of the social partners. It is true that consensus had been reached among the political parties, promulgating that the main responsibility for the implementation of the proposed sex

---

[7] Prop 1978/79:175 at 167.

[8] The Labour Court is the court with proper authority to deal with labour disputes in Sweden. Some cases are first tried in the District Court, but they may be appealed against to the Labour Court. The Swedish Labour Court is a tri-partite body, but it is a court of justice in the strict sense. It is composed of three neutral members, two employer members, and two employee members. All members are appointed by the Government. The lay judges swear the judge's oath.

[9] See the first report, SOU 1978:83. *Jämställdhet i arbetslivet (Equality in Working life)*, prop (Bill) 1978/79:175 and SFS (Official Gazette) 1979:503.

[10] Prop 1979:56, SFS 1979:1118.

[11] See SOU 1978:83 at 59, prop 1978/79:175 at 17.

[12] See extensively in prop 1978/79:175 at 11–18.

[13] Prop 1978/79:175 at 17, 24, 28, 70; see also SOU 1978:83 at 61. "State intervention in the market may be necessary to perfect competition; anti-discrimination legislation is justified by this", according to Hervey, *Justifications for Sex Discrimination in Employment* (1993), 35. Such a sophisticated argument was not used when the first stumbling steps were taken in the late 1970s to introduce sex discrimination legislation in Sweden.

discrimination legislation had to be laid in the hands of the social partners.[14] Strong criticism was launched, however, by both the trade unions and the organized employers against the proposals of the 1978 Report on Equality in Working Life. What had upset the social partners so much was the fact that the 1978 Report suggested that the content of the social partners' collective agreements on sex equality should be at least equivalent to the affirmative action provisions of the Act, and that the Equal Opportunities Ombudsman should be given powers to supervise the agreements.[15] The social partners raised strong doubts against the proposal to set up the Equal Opportunities Ombudsman, whose tasks (they claimed) definitely implied uncalled-for intervention that would lead to an unnecessary bureaucratisation. The Government yielded to the criticism. The social partners were given broad powers concerning the affirmative actions, as laid down in section 6 of the 1979 Act.[16] Section 6 was made *quasi-mandatory*, which enabled the social partners to derogate from the Act, thus evading society's control. The Minister of Labour said that she "relied upon the fact that the social partners will make use of the Act's option to conduct efficient work to promote equality".[17] It was a false hope. None of the social partners took any affirmative action of the kind envisaged by the legislator in 1979.

The former critique levelled against the 1979 sex discrimination legislation was soon no longer heard.[18] Other aspects relating to the application of the Act were brought up instead. In 1985, a provision relating to disclosure of information in sex discrimination disputes was inserted into the Act.[19] The criticism was also directed at the efficiency of the Act, and the possibilities of promoting equality in working life. Sexual harassment was also seen as a problem.

As a result of the critique, the Government appointed an investigator in 1988. A Report was handed down in 1990.[20] After public comment, the Government was able to submit a new bill on sex equality legislation before the Parliament. As a result, the 1991 Sex Discrimination Act came into being.[21] The 1991 Act left the basic structure of the 1979 Act quite untouched. Certain characteristics were, however, new, as compared to the 1979 Act. First, the 1991 Act extended the area of application to include, for instance, sexual harassment on the part

---

[14] SOU 1978:83 at 69.

[15] SOU 1978:83 at 130, 172, prop 1978/79:175 at 24–25.

[16] In fact, the major social partners, LO (Confederation of Trade Unions in Sweden), SAF (Confederation of Swedish Employers) and PTK (Cartel for Salaried Employees in Private Industry) entered into two equality collective agreements in 1977, and wanted to assess the effects of those agreements before any legislative actions were taken by the Parliament. In 1983, the two agreements were consolidated into one, with all three social partners active as parties to the agreement. In the Labour Court judgment 1990 No 34 such a collective agreement on equality was tried as applied to the building industry when a female building worker applied for jobs, but was refused. Her complaint was dismissed.

[17] Prop 1978/79:175 at 31.

[18] It comes to mind here that the enactment of the first Collective Agreements Act and the setting up of the Swedish Labour Court in 1928 met with a similar reaction. These proposals were ardently opposed in the Parliament by the Social Democrats and the LO. After a couple of years, however, the opposition had dissolved.

[19] SFS 1985:34.

[20] SOU 1990:41. *Tio år med jämställdhetslagen (Ten Years With the Sex Discrimination Act)*.

[21] Prop 1990/91:113, SFS 1991:433, repealing the 1979 Act.

of the employer. Secondly, some provisions were reformulated and extended, in particular, those relating to affirmative action programmes. Thirdly, a few provisions were amended in the light of the equivalent EC sex equality law as regards, for example, work of equal value and indirect sex discrimination.[22]

The 1991 Act was amended in 1994 inasmuch as a provision related to the making of detailed equality plans including stated wage differentials between men and women was inserted into the Act (Section 9a). Since the earlier expectations that were laid upon the social partners to take decisive affirmative action had not been met, the Act was amended to reduce the legal impact of the social partners' collective agreements (Section 12). As a consequence the Equal Opportunities Ombudsman's power of action was reinforced.[23] However, the Ombudsman must seek in the first instance to persuade employers voluntarily to follow the provisions of the Act (Section 31).

(ii) The sex discrimination prohibitions vs affirmative action in the 1991 Sex Discrimination Act

The particular sex discrimination prohibitions (Sections 16–20) have been listed in the Act and apply to: *Engagement; Promotion; Training; Terms of employment such as wages; Direction of work; Termination of employment; Transfers; Lay offs; Dismissals and Other related matters.* The prohibitions cannot be derogated from by contract.[24] The prohibitions only take heed of individual cases and – time and time again this has been emphasised in the legislative history – *the aim is to guarantee justice to an individual.*[25] This implies that the sex discrimination prohibitions are not meant to apply to the under-represented sex as a group.[26] There

---

[22] It might be added here that in the subsequent Bill on the EEA-Agreement, prop 1991/92:170. App 10 at 5 a question is raised as regards the Swedish sex equality legislation in the light of Case C-177/88 *Dekker* v *Stichting Vormingscentrum voor Volwassenen Plus* [1990] ECR I-3941. It is evident from the wording of the Swedish statute that it does not protect a woman (or man) who is discriminated against on grounds of sex if there is no comparator involved. In the EEA-Bill it was held that *Dekker* needed to be analysed more closely and that the matter would be brought up again if it was found that the Swedish sex equality law did not comply with the EC standard. However, the issue was not commented upon in prop 1994/95:19 related to the Swedish Entry into the European Union. I would say that there are strong doubts as regards the compatibility of the Swedish Sex Discrimination Act with EC law in a case like *Dekker*, see also Sigeman, "Consequences for Swedish Labour Law of the Treaty on the European Economic Area" *The International Journal of Comparative Labour Law and Industrial relations* (1994), 109.
[23] Prop 1993/94:147, SFS 1994:292. A proposal to let the Equal Opportunities Ombudsman's control be extended to employers bound by equality collective agreements had been raised in fact already in SOU 1978:83 at 130.
[24] In the Labour Court judgment 1986 No 67 the Court held that recruitment norms laid down in a collective agreement could not be legally binding inasmuch as the Act was mandatory. On the other hand, the Court said that such norms may shed light on the employer's procedure in connection with recruitment of personnel.
[25] Prop 1978/79:175 at 40, 55, 73.
[26] Prop 1978/79:175 at 54–55. In the Labour Court judgment 1988 No 50 the Court reminded of this fact in a case that concerned a female repairer applying for a post in a metal shop where male employees dominated.

is also a separate ban on sexual harassment in the Act (Section 22). The prohibitions can be enforced in court by the person who is discriminated against. Violation of the prohibitions may be declared null and void, or damages may be awarded (Sections 23–27).[27]

The Act's affirmative action provisions (Sections 3–12) are designed differently. The employer is generally "obliged" to promote equality between the sexes, but the "obligation" is of quite a different character than what is usually implied by law. It means that the employer shall initiate affirmative (positive) actions, often by means of collective agreements, including equality plans.

The affirmative action's goal is to support and promote the under-represented sex as a group.[28] In this regard, the Act lays down guidelines concerning the employer's personnel policy in the following matters: *purposeful work for equality, working conditions, recruitment and related matters, questions concerning pay and a plan of action.* The provisions are promotional and "goal-oriented". Section 2, for example, lays down the important principle that the employer and the employees shall co-operate to "level out and prevent differences in pay and other terms of engagement between men and women who perform work that is rated as equal or of equal value".[29] It is also said that the employer "shall promote . . . an even distribution of men and women in various types of work and within different categories of employees" (Section 7). The legislative history shows that the breakeven line is often set at 40%.[30] It is further held that "when at a workplace there is not, in the main, an even distribution of men and women in a certain type of work or within a certain category of employees, an employer shall make special efforts to obtain applicants of the under-represented sex and endeavour to see that the proportion of employees of that sex gradually increases" (Section 9). An individual employee cannot raise a legal claim on the grounds of these provisions – the case must be presented by the Equal Opportunities Ombudsman. The "obligations" are not sanctioned by damages, but a penalty of a fine (Section 35) may be served in cases of recalcitrant employers who do not lift a finger to promote equality.

(iii) Sex discrimination in connection with engagement of employees

It is stated in Section 16(1) of the 1991 Act that: "Unlawful sex discrimination shall be considered to exist when an employer . . . engages someone in prefer-

---

[27] Both sanctions must be said to be both "effective" and "deterrent", see Case 14/83 *Von Colson* v *Land Nordrhein-Westfalen* [1984] ECR 1891. In the Labour Court judgment 1989 No 122, general damages of 40,000 SEK were granted to the applicant-employee who was discriminated against.
[28] The distinction made in the legislative history between "creating justice in the single case" and "the promotion of equality by means of positive action" is made a legal watershed of the Act. However, this distinction may be difficult to uphold in wage discrimination cases, see *infra*, Section (v).
[29] Section 2 is a reflection of the paramount interest on the part of the legislator to lay stress on the equal pay principle, see Laurén, "Lönediskriminering av kvinnor", *Studier i arbetsrätt (Studies in Labour Law)* (1993) 209.
[30] SOU 1978:83 at 127, prop 1978/79:175 at 85.

ence to someone else of the opposite sex although the person passed over is objectively better qualified for the work".[31] Section 16(1) lays down a very important prerequisite stating that a comparator (of the opposite sex) must be found if the ban is to apply.[32] If the employer chooses not to employ anybody, no legal claim can be raised by a job applicant even if one may suspect that he/she may have been discriminated against on grounds of sex.[33] The general justification for this is held to be that it is always up to the employer to decide whether to employ personnel or not, as the employer is the sole decision-maker as regards redundancies.[34] Congruity governs both situations. This is logical in the light of the Swedish employment protection legislation. From the point of view of sex discrimination, it is more probable, however, that the argument is in violation of EC sex equality law.[35]

The Swedish Act is based upon a rather "advanced" model as far as the burden of proof in sex discrimination cases is concerned. The burden of proof has been reversed. If it can be shown that the person discriminated against is deemed to be have been "*better qualified*" than the comparator, a *presumption* for sex discrimination exists.[36] The essence of this is that once the presumption has been fulfilled, discrimination will have been fully proved, irrespective of whether the intentions of the employer were discriminatory or not.[37] The plaintiff does not have to prove that the employer intended to discriminate against her/him, which is usually considered to be rather difficult, unless the burden of proof can be modified in some way.[38]

---

[31] The derogations to Section 16(1) are dealt with specifically, *infra* Section (iv).

[32] The issue is extensively dealt with in prop 1978/79:175 at 60–63. However, Section 20 of the Act, which applies to cases of termination of employment, transfers, layoffs, dismissals or other related matters, does not presuppose a comparator to apply. This mode of action is more in conformity to EC sex equality law. Dismissal of a female worker on account of pregnancy constitutes direct discrimination on grounds of sex, Case C-179/88 *Hertz* v *Dansk Arbejdsgiverforening acting for Aldi Marked KS* [1990] ECR I-3941 and Case C-32/93 *Webb* v *EMO Air Cargo (UK) Ltd* [1994] ECR I-3567. Termination of an employment contract on account of the employee's pregnancy, whether by annulment or avoidance, also constitutes direct discrimination on grounds of sex, Case C-421/92 *Habermann-Beltermann* v *Arbeiterwohlfahrt, Bezirksverband Ndb./Obf. ev* [1994] ECR I-1657.

[33] Prop 1978/79:175 at 62.

[34] Prop 1978/79:175 at 61. The Swedish courts are not assumed to second-guess the employer's decision in such cases.

[35] In *Dekker* the Court of Justice did not require a male comparator in the light of Art. 3(1) of the Equal Treatment Directive, Case C-177/88, *Dekker, supra* n 22.

[36] It has been held that the Swedish burden of proof satisfies the Community standard, see SOU 1990:41 at 285. The way in which the burden of proof should be designed was a much debated issue in the legislative history of the Swedish Act, see SOU 1978:83 at 161–162, prop 1978/79:185 at 45–49, 59. The burden of proof in sex discrimination cases has also been a matter of great concern in the EC: see, e.g., Case 109/88 *Handels- og Kontorfunktionærernes Forbund* v *Dansk Arbejdsgiverforening (Danfoss)* [1989] ECR 3199, where the Court of Justice concluded that "the Equal Pay Directive must be interpreted as meaning that where an undertaking applies a system of pay which is totally lacking in transparency, it is for the employer to prove that his practice in the matter of wages is not discriminatory" (para 16).

[37] Prop 1978/79:175 at 48 and the Labour Court judgment 1982 No 139. It may seem harsh to the employer to accept such a view, since the primary purpose of the Act must have been to stigmatise those employers who showed intention to discriminate on grounds of sex, see SOU 1990:41 at 232.

[38] *Cf.* cases where the right to organize is violated in the Swedish labour law. The burden of proof is modified in those cases. The plaintiff employee has fulfilled the burden of proof if "probable grounds" for the violation have been shown. Such burden of proof was in fact advocated in sex discrimination cases in the 1978 Report, SOU 1978:83 at 161–162.

In 1991, however, a partial retreat from the blunt presumption rule was made. Section 17 of the Act provides that the employer violates the law if the employer "engages someone in preference to someone else of the opposite sex who objectively has equivalent prerequisites for the work . . . if it is probable that the employer . . . aimed to discriminate against someone on grounds of sex". The primary target of the additional provision is to come to grips with cases where women are unwanted in male-dominated workplaces. It is also to be noted in this case that it is sufficient for the female job applicant to have equal qualifications for the job, and not objectively better, as stated in Section 16.[39] In this case the job applicant must show *probable grounds* that the employer had discriminatory intentions.[40] If the burden of proof is satisfied, the onus is on the employer to justify his decision on grounds similar to those stated in Section 16(2).[41] Section 17 does not apply when there is only one job-applicant seeking the job. The employer is the only judge of the question whether supplementary manpower is needed.[42]

Now, judging from the way in which Section 16 is designed, the Court has to apply a test in two stages. Firstly, the Court has to undertake an assessment of the applicants' merits – which is often a tedious and time-consuming task. The affected individual's personal merits and objective qualifications for the work are closely scrutinised.[43] The outcome of such an analysis may be that it is shown that the plaintiff-applicant has better qualifications. In this case, the plaintiff is judged to have been discriminated against prima facie on grounds of sex. In such a situation, the Court must, secondly, consider the employer's counter-evidence based upon Section 16(2).[44] The merits' issue may not once again be discussed within the framework of Section 16(2).

The best penetrated area of the Labour Court's case law concerns the issue of the applicant's merits.[45] Generally speaking, such aspects as the applicant's *previous education, working life, professional experience and personal suitability* are usually dealt with.[46] The Court's meticulous procedure is similar to that undertaken in

---

[39] SOU 1990:41 at 238, prop 1990/91:113 at 82, 108.

[40] Prop 1990/91:113 at 81. It would seem that this standard is approximately the same as applied in the proposed EC Directive on the burden of proof with regard to sex discrimination: see COM(88) 269 final.

[41] *Infra* Section (iv).

[42] Prop 1990/91:113 at 82. This is in line with the general principles of the Swedish employment protection law. Neither is Section 17 assumed to apply to cases where a pregnant woman applies for a post when the employment is of short duration and the woman in question cannot reasonably be found to perform any work.

[43] Prop 1978/79:175 at 51, 119.

[44] However, this was not done in the Labour Court judgment 1987 No 51, where the Court instead tried the case in the light of Section 16(2) at once; similarly in 1987 No 83.

[45] Twenty-nine of the total of 41 cases have dealt with cases involving Section 16 of the Act (formerly Section 3 of the 1979 Act). See the Labour Court judgments 1981 Nos 169, 171; 1982 Nos 102, 139; 1983 Nos 50, 78, 83, 102, 104; 1984 Nos 1, 12, 22, 100; 1986 Nos 67, 84, 103; 1987 Nos 1, 8, 35, 51, 67, 83, 140, 152; 1988 No 50; 1989 Nos 40, 122; and 1993 No 49.

[46] It would bring me too far out into the deep waters to even deal with such an aspect as the applicants' *personal suitability* for a job. This aspect is often dealt with in the Labour Court case law with regard to references, interviews, gossips, hearsay etc. See the Labour Court judgments 1981 Nos 169, 171; 1983 Nos 50, 78; 1984 No 1; 1986 Nos 67, 84; 1987 No 67; 1989 No 40.

cases where a dismissal is questioned under Section 7 of the 1982 Swedish Employment Protection Act.[47] In assessing the merits, the Court must be able to conclude, however, on the basis of its findings that there is "*a clearly discernible difference*", or "*a relatively clear difference*" between the plaintiff applicant and the person given preference to.[48] The test does not apply if the applicants' merits are equal on the whole; the employer is then free to employ any of the applicants.[49]

A fundamental starting-point to the Court's analysis of the merits is the view that the employer may make use of the norms which are usually applied by him in connection with the recruitment of personnel, irrespective of whether these norms are found in statutes, collective agreements, or ensue from accepted practice.[50] In private industry, one may find that there are no such generally applicable norms, especially with respect to work which does not require specialised knowledge. In such cases, the affected job-applicants may often be deemed equal as far as their merits are concerned. The employer is then at will to employ any of the applicants.[51]

A few concrete examples and guidelines taken from the legislative history and case law should suffice to facilitate the understanding of the width and complexity of the merits' issue.

It is obvious that the employer may always engage a person whom he/she believes will perform the most efficient work. *Thus, the employer may make a rational choice among the job-applicants.*[52] The courts are not supposed to second-guess the applicable norms used by the employer.[53] The norms must not, however, be directly or indirectly sex discriminatory; that is, the employer's assessment of the applicants must not be based upon "real or perceived differences between men and women".[54] This shows that there is no room for arbitrariness or

---

[47] The employer is then under a strain to justify an "objective cause" for the dismissal: see prop 1978/79:175 at 52.

[48] Prop 1978/79:175 at 55. See also the Labour Court judgments 1981 No 169, 1983 No 1, 1984 No 12, and 1986 Nos 84, 103. In the Labour Court judgment 1987 No 152 the Court satisfied itself, in a case of the appointment to a research assistant where scientific skills were at stake, that no expert report was sex-biased. The Court refrained from reassessing the expert reports with reference to the fact that "it is not a question for the Court in a sex discrimination case to analyse more closely the different nuances between various ways of apprehending the applicants' scientific skilfullness".

[49] Prop. 1978/79:175 at 53.

[50] This statement is found in prop 1978/79:175 at 51, 119.

[51] See the Labour Court judgment 1987 No 35. See also SOU 1990:41 at 150: "Those cases that have dealt with recruitments in the private sector have shown, not unexpectedly, that private employers have not laid down firm norms of merits to the same extent as in the public sector".

[52] Prop 1978/79:175 at 52. See also the Labour Court judgments 1987 Nos 1, 8 (the employer may always give the contract of employment a content which suits the needs of his business).

[53] Prop 1978/79:175 at 50 and the Labour Court judgment 1983 No 102. In the Labour Court judgment 1987 No 35 the Court found that a female applicant had a longer time of employment at the workplace than a male employee, who got the job, but since the employer normally did not pay any major attention to such facts, the Court could not rule to the contrary. In the Labour Court judgment 1988 No 50, the Court found that the employer was justified when he paid regard to the fact that the male applicant's *continuous* period of time of employment with another employer was far longer than the female applicant's. Likewise, it was justified for the employer, in the Labour Court judgment 1989 No 40, to pay regard to the efforts made to reduce the length of the leaves of absence due to sickness at the workplace.

[54] Prop 1978/79:175 at 119. See also the Labour Court judgment 1987 No 35 (average differences between men and women as regards physical strength or endurance must not be decisive, but such

subjective value judgments when employees are recruited.[55] The employer cannot justify the choice of an applicant by stating that customers or fellow-workers show preference of one of the sexes.[56] It is an important principle in the Act that an individual has a right to be assessed according to his or her individual prerequisites for the work. The norms applied must be *"explainable"* and *"appear in the main to be rational to an outsider"*.[57]

Vacancies' advertisements have also been dealt with by the Labour Court. The crucial question has been here to judge whether the content of the advertisement should be binding upon the employer when the merits and qualifications of the affected applicants are to be assessed by the Court. The Court has stated that such advertisements are not "absolutely binding", but if the employer alleges that some other criterion than the ones stated in connection with the actual recruitment is decisive, the employer must stand a closer scrutiny to avoid "concealed" sex discrimination.[58] This approach is probably a decent compromise even in the light of the Court of Justice case law.[59]

(iv) Justifications for sex discrimination in engagement cases

The employer may allege other reasons than those relating to the merits' issue to justify his decision not to employ a specific person. Section 16(2) of the Act

---

aspects may be taken heed of if they are objectively justified). It is pertinent here to add that cases of indirect discrimination have played an insignificant role in the Swedish Labour Court's case law. Cases of indirect discrimination are, no doubt, embraced by the Act: see prop 1978/79:175 at 43–44, 121–122 and prop 1990/91:113 at 80; see also SOU 1990:41 at 369. According to the statistics, (see 1995 Statistical Yearbook of Sweden (Table 193)) 41 % of all the working women are part-timers, while only 9 % of the males are. Only twice has the Labour Court, to my knowledge, dealt with the issue of indirect discrimination; see the Labour Court judgments 1984 No 100 (a male applicant was appointed to be a reindeer consultant in spite of the fact that on the whole only males could acquire such experience) and 1987 No 8 (males were appointed to positions of tele-electricians in spite of the fact that very few females had gained such education). The outcome of the latter case, in the light of EC sex equality law, is highly questioned in a Swedish report, Ds 1993:77. *EG-domstolen och jämställdheten (The European Court of Justice and the Sex Equality Issue)* at 120.
[55] Prop 1978/79:175 at 51. It is held in the Labour Court judgment 1981 No 169 that this implies that the employer must justify and substantiate his decision with objectively acceptable reasons.
[56] Prop 1978/79:175 at 58.
[57] Prop 1978/79:175 at 51. See also the Labour Court judgments 1986 No 67, 1989 No 40, and 1993 No 49.
[58] The test was set forth in the Labour Court judgment 1984 No 12. The test was later applied to the recruitment of a chief of personnel in a smaller municipality in southern Sweden. In the Labour Court judgment 1984 No 22 the employer preferred to appoint a former trade union male representative as chief of personnel with reference to his experience as a negotiator and his knowledge of the labour law legislation. Those aspects were not taken up in the employment advertisement. Based upon the other qualification requirements set out in the advertisement, the female job applicant was held to have supreme qualifications in comparison with the male comparator. She was found to have been discriminated against.
[59] In Case 248/83 *Commission* v *Germany, supra* n 5, the issue of "impartial" advertisements was discussed. The Court of Justice said that the Directive imposes no obligation on the Member States to enact general legislation concerning offers of employment, but "it must be observed . . . that offers of employment cannot be excluded a priori from the scope of Directive No 76/207, inasmuch as they are closely connected with access to employment and can have a restrictive effect thereon" (para 43).

states, albeit in rather vague terms, the grounds on which the employer may justify his decision. Those grounds are:

1. that the decision has no direct or indirect connection with the sex of the person discriminated against; 2. that the decision is part of the endeavours to promote equality in working life; or 3. it is warranted out of consideration for an idealistic interest[60] or some other special interest which is of such a kind that it should manifestly not be subordinate to the interest of equality in working life.

Those grounds may be referred to as "*bona fide (or genuine) occupational qualifications*."[61] The evidence in defence of the derogation must be strong.[62]

It is not easy to assess whether the grounds for the Swedish sex justifications are equivalent to the ones found in EC sex equality law. This is basically due to the fact that Article 2 of the Equal Treatment Directive is drafted differently from the Swedish Act. A few examples may suffice to substantiate the difficulties. Article 2(3) of the Directive, which refers to the "protection of women, particularly as regards pregnancy and maternity", does not correspond to any similar provision in the Swedish Act. However, women's rights to protection are found elsewhere in the Swedish labour legislation.[63] On the other hand, the Directive lacks the broadly phrased derogation as found in Section 16(2) p 1 of the Swedish Act.

It is noteworthy in this context that the Court of Justice in *Dekker* found that Article 2(2), (3) and (4) of the Directive do provide for the exceptions to the principle of equal treatment set out in Article 2(1). Thus, the Directive does not

---

[60] The word "idealistic" is probably not the appropriate word in English. In Swedish, the words "ideellt intresse" are used in the Act. It is difficult to find another English term which corresponds to the Swedish expression. I have followed the semi-official translation of the Act issued by the Equal Opportunities Ombudsman.

[61] It is highly doubtful whether this rather vague enumeration corresponds to the "complete and verifiable list, in whatever form, of the occupations and activities excluded from the application of the principle of equal treatment", provided for in Art 9(2) and which may justify a derogation from Art 2(2) of the 1976 Equal Treatment Directive: see Case 248/83 *Commission* v *Germany, supra* n 5, para 38. See also a report, Ds 1993:77 at 84–85, where the view is submitted as to whether Sweden has implemented the Directive in a correct way in this regard. The Court of Justice said in Case 318/86 *Commission* v *France* [1988] ECR 3559, para 25 that the assessment in Art 9(2) of the said Directive "may relate only to specific activities, [and] that they must be sufficiently transparent so as to permit effective supervision by the Commission".

[62] Prop 1978/79:175 at 57. The evidence must be stronger in cases where the person discriminated against has far better merits than the comparator who has been given preference by the employer; see also the Labour Court judgment 1982 No 102.

[63] The EC Pregnancy and Maternity Directive 92/85 is implemented into Swedish law by means of the 1995 Act on Leave for Parents, replacing the former 1978 Act; see prop 1994/95:207. The implementation represents – paradoxically – a paternalistic approach which deviates from the previous Swedish standard. Protective measures of the kind which the Directive and the Court of Justice uphold were actually done away with in Swedish social labour law a long time ago. The view propounded, e.g., by the Court of Justice according to Art 2(3) in Case 184/83 *Hofmann* v *Barmer Ersatzkasse* [1984] ECR 3047 (upholding the German provisions on the exclusive right for mothers to enjoy special benefits in relation to maternity leave) represents a rather outdated view in the light of the Swedish sex-neutral parental legislation. See also Case 163/82 *Commission* v *Italian Republic* [1983] ECR 3273 (the adoptive father was refused the same rights as the mother as regards the right to maternity leave in the light of Art 6 of the Equal Treatment Directive). The corresponding Swedish provisions are strictly sex-neutral.

make liability on the part of the person guilty of discrimination conditional in any way on proof of fault or on the absence of any ground discharging such liability under national law.[64] The considerations in *Dekker* were set out in the light of the penumbra of Article 6 of the Equal Treatment Directive and the possibility of recourse to any specific form of sanction due to unlawful discrimination. It is also worthwhile mentioning that the Swedish burden of proof in relation to sex discrimination is reversed and sets a pattern for the analysis concerning the counter-evidence brought about by the employer. It is not easy to assess the Swedish reversed burden of proof rule in a *Dekker* context. What is more is that the justifiable grounds referred to in Section 16(2) p 1, as well as those aspects which the employer may adduce concerning the merits issue according to Section 16(1), also seem to be relatively easy to substantiate. The justifications may come very close to the standard of "reasonableness".[65]

On the other hand, it follows from *Johnston* that derogations according to Article 2(2) from the equal treatment principle "must be interpreted strictly". The principle of proportionality applies, and "that principle requires that derogations remain within the limits of what is appropriate and necessary for achieving the aim in view".[66]

I now intend to discuss the Swedish justifications as set out in Section 16(2) of the Act.

As far as the first justification is concerned, the legislative history suggests that, in apprehending the applicants' merits, *the employer may have made an "inexcusable mistake"*.[67] The employer, however, may also refer to "*some other substantial reason which has nothing to do with the applicant's sex*".[68] For example, the employer may be able to justify his decision with reference to the fact that another law must be applied, such as the provisions found in the Employment Protection Act.[69]

---

[64] Case C-177/88, *Dekker*, *supra* n 22, paras 22, 24–25.

[65] Such considerations seem to prevail in the law of the United Kingdom, see Hervey, *supra* n 13 at 91–92. See also, *ibid* at 107: "The ruling of the European Court in *Bilka* is accepted in the United Kingdom, but is understood and applied in a different way to that of the European Court. The UK courts . . . focus on the standard of 'reasonableness', rather than 'proportionality'".

[66] Case 222/84 *Johnston* v *Chief Constable of the Royal Ulster Constabulary* [1986] ECR 1651, paras 36, 38. In *Johnston* a derogation from Art 2(2) of the Directive was allowed with reference to "public safety". See also Case 318/86 *Commission* v *France*, *supra* n 61, where the Court of Justice, in the light of Art 2(2) annulled the French recruitment procedure as applied to the national police force, which was based upon quotas for male and female applicants. The quotas did not "actually correspond to specific activities" (para 27).

[67] Prop 1978/79:175 at 49. Such a mistake may, however, be the result of the laxity of procedure which is not excusable, see the Labour Court judgment 1982 No 139.

[68] Prop 1978/79:175 at 56. It was not until 1987, that this passage played a rather unimportant role in the exposition of the reasons which the employer could allege for defence of his action; see the Labour Court judgment 1987 No 51. On the other hand, if the employer deviates from the usual norms to be applied in connection with recruitment, the Labour Court is apt to be more reluctant to accept such a procedure, see, e.g., the Labour Court judgments 1982 No 139 and 1989 No 122. The Court has adopted a strict approach in such cases because the Court is fully aware of the possibility that the employer's action might well conceal discrimination on grounds of sex.

[69] Prop 1978/79:175 at 123. In the Labour Court judgment 1983 No 83 the Court did not have to rule on the issue as to whether the statutory re-employment right according to Section 25 of the Employment Protection Act applied inasmuch it was not shown that the male comparator who did not receive the job as cook had better qualifications than the female applicant.

The employer may also have had strict personal reasons for employing the selected person (a relative, spouse or friend), or for avoiding the engagement of someone.[70] The Labour Court has made clear that the employer's justification must be *"well-founded from an objective point of view"*.[71] In the Labour Court's judgment 1987 No 83, the Court states that it:

> is not prepared to accept such reasons forwarded by the employer which are deemed to be non-objective in the sense that they are strictly subjective, or else of a kind which makes it impossible in hindsight to assess the reasons with sufficient certainty. If, on the other hand, it can be shown in a convincing manner that the employer's decision is based upon reasons which have nothing to do with the applicant's sex, the required burden of proof has been satisfied.

The Court's statement makes it clear that the employer must make his reasons transparent.

The second justification in Section 16(2) is based on *affirmative action programmes instituted at the workplace*. The best way for the employer to show that a decision is based upon an affirmative programme is to refer to rules or guidelines set up after consultations with the trade unions, irrespective of whether a collective agreement concerning equality between the sexes is in force.[72] Such a plan must apply to the affected category of employees at the employer's workplace, and must not be extended to other workplaces in the country.[73] The plan must be the result of a systematic activity.[74]

Since 1 July 1995, various provisions have entered into force, aiming to promote the employment of female professors and research-assistants at Swedish universities.[75] The Bill submitted to Parliament propounded a rather gloomy view, showing that the past findings were discouraging; only 7% of all professors were females.[76] The new scheme therefore implies that female applicants are to be given priority as long as they have sufficient qualifications from the scientific and pedagogical point of view, albeit another male comparator is deemed to be better qualified for the post. In the light of Chapter 11 Section 9 of the Swedish Constitution, however, it is said that the difference between the two applicants of the opposite sex may not be too large; if this is the case, the priority given to a female applicant may be incompatible with the Constitution.[77]

---

[70] Prop 1978/79:175 at 123.

[71] Labour Court judgment 1983 No 104 (female applicant was given preference for labour market reasons). See also the Labour Court judgments 1987 No 1 (male applicant was given preference for "efficiency reasons"); 1987 No 51 (male applicant rejected because he opposed the employer's business concept); and 1981 No 169 (internal labour markets must be conducted systematically to be given a decisive importance).

[72] The Labour Court has not yet ruled on the status of such affirmative programmes. One may wonder, e.g., if a derogation is permitted in cases when the employer has unilaterally instituted such a plan and applies it systematically.

[73] Labour Court judgment 1981 No 171.

[74] Prop 1978/79:175 at 84, 124. The equality work must imply that it is carried out in an active and effective way; see the Labour Court judgment 1981 No 171. See also the Labour Court judgments 1982 No 102 and 1987 No 1 (active equality work justified the employer's decision).

[75] SFS 1995:936, 944.

[76] Prop 1994/95:164.

[77] Prop 1994/95:164 at 36.

Article 2(4) of the Equal Treatment Directive provides that equal opportunities may be promoted. Quite recently, the Court of Justice in *Kalanke* disapproved of the Bremen City legislation promulgating that, in the case of appointment or promotion, women who have the same qualifications as men and apply for the same post, are to be given priority when their sex is under-represented.[78] Under-representation of women was deemed to exist when they made up less than half of the staff. The Court of Justice said that in the light of the principle of equal treatment, as laid down in Article 2(1) of the Directive:

> A national rule that, where men and women who are candidates for the same pro-motion are equally qualified, women are automatically to be given priority in sectors where they are under-represented, involves discrimination on grounds of sex – it must, however, be considered whether such a national rule is permissible under Article 2(4) . . . That provision is specifically and exclusively designed to allow mea-sures which, although discriminatory in appearance, are in fact intended to eliminate or reduce actual instances of inequality which may exist in the reality of social life.

Article 2(4) was not, however, meant to be an open-ended exception to the rule and the Court pointed out that:

> As a derogation from an individual right laid down in the Directive, Article 2(4) must be interpreted strictly . . . National rules which guarantee women absolute and unconditional priority for appointment or promotion go beyond promoting equal opportunities and overstep the limits of the exception in Article 2(4) of the Directive.[79]

Quotas are thus not acceptable rectification measures of the historical inequalities between men and women. Accordingly, if implemented, the Swedish provisions as regards university professors and research assistants, although limited by nature, will apparently directly violate EC sex equality law, as can be seen from the ruling of the Court of Justice in *Kalanke*. It is tempting to say that: "Laws can become an important ally of women. . . . But even when legal discrimination is removed, it can take generations for practice to catch up with the revised law".[80]

The third justification in Section 16(2) may apply to *specific situations of special interest*; for instance, when actors, singers, models or tourist guides are employed in countries where women are not allowed to work, or in the case of employers with a small number of employees.[81] The employer may not justify

---

[78] Case C-450/93 *Kalanke* v *Freie und Hansestadt Bremen*, 17 October 1995, nyr, paras 16–18, 21–22.

[79] In Case 312/86 *Commission* v *France* [1988] ECR 6315, para 15, the Court of Justice concluded that Art 2(4) of the Equal Treatment Directive did not justify "that a generalised preservation of special rights for women in collective agreements may correspond to the situation envisaged in that provision".

[80] *Human Development Report* (1995), *supra* n 1 at 42–43.

[81] See further prop 1978/79:175 at 43, 120, 124–126; SOU 1978:83 at 88, 101–103, 134. Other ex-amples are: when respect must be paid to decency or privacy (such as the employment of both sexes on board a small fishing vessel), or an elderly person's unwillingness to accept male workers in the social home-service, or the hospital patients' wishes to be treated by women, or the exclusion of female priests in other congregations than the Swedish Church. It would seem to be an open ques-

his action if only slightly less costly measures would have been sufficient to uphold the equality principle.[82] In the Labour Court judgment 1986 No 103 it was held to be of "special interest" to let the employer engage a male therapist whose tasks, alongside those of a female colleague, were to conduct co-therapy in a church parish. The Court said that an opt-out with reference to Section 16(2) p 3 may be accepted, only if the employer's need cannot be met in any other way.[83]

(v) Wage discrimination between sexes

When the preparatory work started before the entry into force of the 1979 Act, it was held (and that was a bit of an understatement) that the wage differences between men and women were "at least less obvious than they were some decades ago".[84] The wage gap had been narrowed as the result of the solidarity wage policy heralded by the LO during the '60s and '70s in the blue-collar field, as well as in other sectors of the labour market. So-called "women wage pots" were also inserted into the national wage agreements.[85] It was not until the 1980s that the structural wage gap was approached more directly.[86] The most recent reports regarding wage discrimination and sex-segregation on the labour market in Sweden show, on the basis of the accumulated statistics from 1991, that the average wage of a full-time female employee is some 75–90% of a full-time male employee's wage.[87] If the figures are broken down into various sectors of the labour market, and factors such as profession, degree of difficulty of the work, education, age and qualifications are taken into consideration, the gap is narrowed finally to some 1–8%. It cannot be stated with any certainty that

---

tion as to whether the Swedish justifications, as here summarised, are more narrowly described than the equivalent examples taken from many other European Member States, see Case 248/83 *Commission* v *Germany*, *supra* n 5 para 34. The Court struck off in Case 165/82 *Commission* v *United Kingdom* [1983] ECR 3431, para 16, the British 1975 Sex Discrimination Act's exclusion of all employments in private households and in small undertakings with no more than five employees with reference to "its generality", but accepted that the occupation of midwife could be reserved to female workers with reference to "personal sensitivities . . . in relations between midwife and patient" (para 20). See also Case 318/86 *Commission* v *France*, *supra* n 61, in which the Court of Justice accepted that sex segregation was permitted at various posts (head warden) in French prisons with reference to the interests of decency and privacy of the inmates.

[82] Prop 1978/79:175 at 51.

[83] In the Labour Court judgment 1989 No 122 the Court disapproved the preference given to a male applicant, who had been recruited as a nurse for retarded people under hospitalisation, with reference to the already established relationship of the male with one of the patients for two years. This was not held to satisfy the condition of "special interest" in the Act.

[84] SOU 1978:83 at 114.

[85] Such clauses may be found even today. Such "wage pots" may be counterproductive. This is due to the fact that the centrally decided "woman wage pot" may be counteracted by a wage drift on the local level to the benefit of men only, see Wadstein, "Arbetsvärdering som instrument för ökad jämställdhet", *Att arbeta i Europa (To Work In Europe)* (1990) 164.

[86] See, e.g., Ericsson, *Systematisk arbetsvärdering. Ett lönesättningsinstrument i närbild (Systematic Job Evaluation. A Review of the Wage-Discrimination Instrument)* (1991) 105, 211–214.

[87] SOU 1993:7. *Löneskillnader och lönediskriminering (Wage Differences and Wage Discrimination)*, 131–132, 153–54. Various explanations of the Swedish sex-segregated labour market are found in Ericsson, *ibid* 42–49.

the gap is to be perceived as unjustified wage discrimination. The 1993 Report holds that:

> The experience shows that women profit if clear-cut norms are used when their work and personal competence and abilities are assessed. It is a fundamental pre-requisite that the wages and the factors . . . in the wage setting are made transparent and that the employers and the trade unions adopt a clear and straightforward wage policy.[88]

To redress wage discrimination Section 18(1) of the 1991 Act states that "unlawful sex discrimination shall be considered to exist when an employee has recourse to lower pay or otherwise poorer terms of employment . . . than those for an employee of the opposite sex when they both carry out work that is rated as equal or of equal value". A wage discrimination on face value may, however, be justified according to Section 18(2), "if the employer can show that the difference in terms of employment is due to similarities in the employees' objective prerequisites for the work or that the difference has, at any rate, no direct or indirect connection with the sex of the employee".

A few comments relating to the starting-points of the analyses are necessary. Section 18 presupposes that a reference to a comparator must contain a *concrete reference* to a person/persons who is/are in the employ of the employer; to extend the comparison to entire groups of employees is to stretch the law too far.[89] Furthermore, Section 18 presupposes that the affected employees must be employed by the *same employer*.[90] Any comparison between jobs in other enterprises falls outside the scope of the Act.[91] The concept of *equal work* in Section

---

[88] SOU 1993:7 at 276.

[89] Prop 1990/91:113 at 88. It is an open question whether such an approach is altogether tenable in the light of EC sex equality law. See, e.g., Case C-400/93 *Specialarbejderforbundet* v *Dansk Industri (Royal Copenhagen)*, Judgment of 31 May 1995. The case involved some 26 male automatic-machine operators who were better paid on average than some 156 "blue-pattern painters", all of whom except one were females. The Court of Justice said that the assessment of the national court "will necessarily have to be a global assessment in the light of all the factors set out" (para 18). The burden of proof is also shifted, if the employer applies a pay system "wholly lacking in transparency . . . if a female worker establishes, *in relation to a relatively large number of employees*, that the average pay for women is less than that for men" (para 24) (italics added). As regards the specific issue of the composition of the groups to be compared, the Court concluded that the national court must satisfy itself that "the two groups of workers . . . can be considered to be in a comparable situation and that they *cover a relatively large number of workers* ensuring that the differences are not due to purely fortuitous or short-term factors or to differences in the individual output of the workers concerned" (para 38) (italics added).

[90] In Case 129/79 *Macarthys* v *Smith* [1980] ECR 1275, a woman was entitled to compare her wage with that of the male predecessor in the post. The Court held that Art 119 of the Treaty was "not confined to situations in which men and women are contemporaneously doing equal work for the same employer," (para 13). On the other hand, no reference could be made to any "hypothetical male worker"; any such point of departure would imply "comparative studies of entire branches of industry" (paras 14–15). In Case 143/83 *Commission* v *Denmark* [1985] ECR 427, the Court did not rule upon the issue as to whether the Danish 1976 Act on Equal Pay, which applied "to work at the same place of work" (intended to permit geographical differences in pay within Denmark) satisfied EC law. See also Case 43/75 *Defrenne* v *Société Anonyme Belge de Navigation Aérienne Sabena No 2* [1978] ECR 1365 (comparator must be employed in the same establishment or service).

[91] Any such far-reaching proposals were rejected in prop 1978/79:175 at 75.

18 means approximately the "same" or "similar" work with respect to easily observed facts relating to the work tasks.[92] The concept *work of equal value* implies that the work tasks in question need not be comparable on face value.[93] The legislative history also tells us that the wage discrimination claim may be quite easily refuted, since a presumption of wage discrimination is not held to be very strong.[94] *Structural wage discrimination* is not covered by Section 18.[95] Structural discrimination is a concept often used to describe various phenomena existing on the labour market, for example, that women are often found in low wage industries, in poorly paid jobs, or in industries in which employers offer lower wages than in other industries where most of the manpower is male.[96] In such cases, affirmative action, taken by the social partners, is assumed to be able to rectify the disparities.

The rather narrow approach taken in Section 18 implies a limited area of application of the wage discrimination ban. This is intentional. In order fully to understand the ramifications, it is necessary to clarify the background to the provisions of the former Section 4 of the 1979 Act (corresponding to Section 18 of the 1991 Act). Section 4 stipulated that sex discrimination occurred when two employees of the opposite sexes were paid differently when "the work in question, according to the collective agreement or the established practice within the area of the business activity is deemed to be equal or is of equal value according to the job evaluation agreed upon". The wage discrimination scheme had been drafted in order to let the social partners continue setting wages on their own, without any major intervention from the courts.[97] Section 4 was therefore susceptible to the same kind of criticism as the corresponding provisions in the English 1970 Equal Pay Act. Section 4 was once fashioned along the lines of the British model. The British Act's job evaluation standard was later disapproved of by the Court of Justice under Article 1 of the Equal Pay Directive in 1982.[98]

---

[92] Prop 1978/79:175 at 75, similarly in prop 1990/91:113 at 86, 110. Insignificant differences in the work tasks should be discarded.

[93] Prop 1978/79:175 at 75–76.

[94] Prop 1978/79:175 at 76.

[95] From this point of view, "class actions" as a means of achieving wage equality between men and women have been discussed in the Swedish legislative history, see SOU 1990:41 at 347–354, SOU 1993:7 at 275–276, prop 1993/94:147 at 58–59 and, more extensively, in SOU 1994:151. *Grupprättegång (Class Actions)* Pt A at 268–271 and Pt B at 495–512.

[96] SOU 1993:7 at 32–33.

[97] Prop 1978/79:175 at 71–76. Section 4 of the former Act was construed narrowly by the Labour Court in 1984 No 140. On the whole, the Labour Court is unwilling to intervene in the wages area, see, e.g., the Labour Court judgment 1984 No 79. Two other sex discrimination cases, the Labour Court judgments 1985 No 134 and 1987 No 132, have dealt with clauses where males have attacked maternal benefits laid down by means of collective agreements. In the first case, the clause was struck off as sex discriminatory; in the second case, the clause was upheld. In the first case, the Swedish Sex Discrimination Act filled in the gap and the male person that had been discriminated against was entitled to receive the benefit. This is which was in compliance with EC sex equality law; see Case C-33/89 *Kowalska* v *Freie und Hansestadt Hamburg* [1990] ECR I-2591. The collective agreement is, hence, partially set aside, which also is in accordance with EC sex equality law; see Case C-184/89 *Nimz* v *Freie und Hansestadt Hamburg* [1991] ECR I-297.

[98] Case 61/81 *Commission* v *United Kingdom* [1982] ECR 2601.

Only one of the two cases decided by the Labour Court on the basis of the 1979 Act has survived. The Labour Court's judgment 1991 No 62 deals with the issue of equal pay for equal work. In this case the employer had engaged a female journalist at a lower pay rate (10,800 SEK) than a male journalist, who was engaged nine months later (11,500 SEK). The employer alleged that he could not pay less because the male applicant demanded such a high salary. In the local wages' round one year after, the female journalist was given a slightly higher salary (13,452 SEK) than the male journalist (13,373 SEK). *The critical question was whether the employer could prove that the initial salary of the male journalist that was higher than that of the female journalist did not depend on grounds of sex according to the formerly Section 4 p. 1 in the 1979 Act (equivalent to Section 18(2) in the 1991 Act).* The Court came to the conclusion that the fact that the male applicant demanded a higher salary than the employer wanted to give him originally but finally had to yield to, was "a consideration which all serious employers do in fact pay regard to according to established practice in relation to the principle of individual wage-setting on the labour market".[99] The complaint was dismissed, but the Court said in an obiter dictum that if the two employees had been engaged at the same time, the conclusion would probably have been the opposite.

In the 1991 Act, the 1979 Act's restrictions were struck off with reference to the EC sex equality law.[100] In the future, as in the United Kingdom, one has to foresee cases where a cook's job is compared to a carpenter's, a painter's, a repairer's, and so on.[101] The legislator presupposes, however, that any accepted/recognised job evaluation system will "evidently" still be applied by the courts, provided that they are not sex-discriminatory.[102] It is an open question as to whether there are any such generally recognised systems of job evaluation to be found on the Swedish labour market.[103] Local job evaluation systems exist, even though they may not be formally recognised by the social partners.[104]

---

[99] On face value, such a consideration does not seem to violate the principle, as set forth in Case 129/79 *Macarthys* v *Smith, supra* n 90 para 12 the meaning of which is that "a difference in pay between two workers occupying the same post but at different periods in time may be explained by the operation of factors which are unconnected with any discrimination on grounds of sex".

[100] Prop 1990/91:113 at 87.

[101] Such as in *Hayward* v *Cammell Laird Shipbuilders Limited* [1988] IRLR 257 (HL).

[102] Prop 1990/91:113 at 110. This is quite similar to the approach adopted in a case concerning collectively agreed upon piece-work rates which were set under fire in Case C-400/93 *Specialarbejderforbundet* v *Dansk Industri (Royal Copenhagen), supra* n 89 para 46. The Court of Justice said: "[T]he fact that the rates of pay have been determined by collective bargaining or by negotiation at local level may be taken into account by the national court as a factor in its assessment of whether differences between the average pay of two groups of workers are due to objective factors unrelated to any discrimination on grounds of sex".

[103] See SOU 1993:7 at 201–205.

[104] The first job evaluation system in Sweden was set up in a glassworks factory in 1947, see Ericsson, *supra* n 86 at 64. Job evaluation was introduced by the employers in order to increase the wage differences between workers in the private industry, see Ericsson, *ibid* 72–75. Such systems in the Swedish industry were more systematically made use of in the late 1950s; see an early pamphlet from the LO, *Arbetsvärdering under debatt (Job Evaluation Under Debate)* (1962) 29. It is said at that the art of job evaluation is no science: "Those who believe that a systematic job evaluation is a science and involves objectivity ought to reduce their view to reasonable proportions in view of the fact that job evaluation is made by a human being, with all his shortcomings and merits".

If, however, no job classification system is found, job evaluation must be based upon other evidence, such as hearings of witnesses or experts in court.[105]

Some aspects of a job evaluation system were highlighted in connection with the 1994 amendments of the Sex Discrimination Act.[106] It is held that if no job evaluation system is found at the workplace, aspects such as *skill, effort, responsibility and working conditions* are to be taken account of by the courts. Such factors are strictly related to the work in question.[107] On the other hand, factors, such as *merits and competence*, are related to the employee's *ability to perform* the specific working tasks. Those aspects are not deemed to enter into an objectively defined job evaluation system. The legislator could not see that a job evaluation system was incompatible with individual wage-setting.[108] External conditions, such as the market forces and the market's effects upon wages, were, however, not commented upon in the 1994 Bill.[109]

In fact, two cases of this kind were recently brought before the Swedish Labour Court in 1995. In one of the cases, the Equal Opportunities Ombudsman argued that a female midwife's work was of equal value as compared to that of two male clinical engineers employed at a county council. It was argued that the difference in wages (midwife's: 14,600 SEK a month, clinical engineers': 19,200 and 18,800 SEK a month respectively) was in violation of Article 119 of the Treaty, the Equal Pay Directive and of Section 18 of the Swedish Act. The wages had been set by means of local collective agreements. The 80-page report on job evaluation submitted by the Ombudsman before the Labour Court implied that a midwife's work was even of higher value than that of the two

---

[105] Prop 1990/91:113 at 110.

[106] Prop 1993/94:147 at 51–55. The discussion should be viewed against the background that the 1993 report on wage discrimination had extensively discussed the same issues, SOU 1993:7 at 199–253. Job evaluation aspects were only a skimpily discussed issue in prop 1990/91:113 at 88–89.

[107] See Case 237/85 *Rummler* v *Firma Dato-Druck* [1986] ECR 2101. The Court of Justice concluded that the job classification criteria must be "*objectively required by a specific job*" (para 22, italics added). *Cf.* also Case 109/88 *Handels og Kontorsfunktionærernes Forbund i Danmark* v *Dansk Arbeidsgiverforening (Danfoss), supra* n 36. In this case, the employer made part use of individual pay supplements in addition to the basic wage. The individual increments were calculated, *inter alia*, on the basis of "mobility", "training" and "seniority". The Court found that criteria such as mobility and training could be justified only if they were "*of importance for the performance of specific tasks entrusted to the employee*" (para 23, italics added). On the other hand, seniority did not have to be justified, since it "goes hand in hand with experience and since experience generally enables the employee to perform his duties better, the employer is free to reward it without having to establish the importance it has in the performance of specific tasks entrusted to the employee" (para 24). The seniority aspect is also discussed in Case C-184/89 *Nimz* v *Freie und Hansestadt Hamburg, supra* n 97 para 14, where it is held that "the objectivity of such a criterion depends on all the circumstances in a particular case", thus seemingly circumscribing the slightly broader approach in *Danfoss.*

[108] Prop 1993/94:147 at 55, in rejecting the employers' view.

[109] See SOU 1993:7 at 63–66. It is held in this report that when wages are set on an individual and differentiated basis the parameters are: the characteristics of the post, individual aspects and the market forces. See also Ericsson, *supra* n 86 at 160–63 on the manifold of devices which the employers may make use of to correct the job evaluation in order to cope with the market forces when setting wages. The European Court of Justice has recognised that "the state of the employment market, which may lead to an employer to increase the pay of a particular job in order to attract candidates, may constitute an objectively justified economic ground" (para 26), Case C-127/92 *Enderby* v *Frenchay Health Authority* [1993] ECR I-5535.

male engineers'.[110] The county council employer rejected the claims, and held, *inter alia*, that the jobs in question were not of equal value, or, if so, that the wages were set with regard to factors which were not based on grounds of sex. The employer explained that wages are set on an individual and differentiated basis, and are usually based on the situation of the market, the character of the post and individual aspects. The employer argued that the clinical engineers had a relatively large alternative job market. The wages were thus set in the light of the market forces. The midwives as a group did not have such an alternative market, but the lower wages had nothing to do with the midwife's sex.[111]

To conclude, there is no doubt that Section 18 of the Swedish Sex Discrimination Act has reinforced the legal basis of a wage discrimination claim. It has opened up a new landscape. The legalistic approach may as well destroy the inherent values of systems based upon collective agreements in wage-setting and may marginalise the role of the social partners in the future.

RONNIE EKLUND
Professor of Private Law,
School of Law,
Stockholm University,
Sweden

---

[110] The Swedish legislative history does not discuss ways in which to cope with a case of that kind. In Case 157/86 *Murphy and Others* v *An Board Telecom Eireann* [1988] ECR 673, it was held that a person may rely upon Art 119 of the Treaty to obtain at least equal pay in such cases, the basis being that a "contrary interpretation would be tantamount to rendering the principle of equal pay ineffective and nugatory", leaving the equal pay principle open for circumvention (para 10). In a report, Ds 1993:77 at 42 it is said that *Murphy* is relevant under Section 18 of the Swedish 1991 Act.

[111] The judgment in the "Midwife Case" (Case nr A 153/95) is expected in late April 1996. A similar case (Case nr A 235/94) brought before the Labour Court by the Equal Opportunities Ombudsman concerns a post as an economist in various administrations of a smaller municipality in Sweden. The Ombudsman is arguing that the woman economist has lower wages than two male comparators who perform equal work or work of equal value. The employer has rejected the claims. The Labour Court found in its judgment 1995 No 158 that the employer could not show that the wage discrimination was based upon considerations not grounded on sex. The female economist was awarded both economic and general damages (40,000 SEK).

Chapter 22

THE NORDIC MODEL OF GENDER EQUALITY LAW*

(i) Introduction

The Nordic countries have strong cultural, historical and linguistic ties, as well as firmly rooted democratic traditions. This has enabled those countries to succeed in developing a pattern of close, constructive co-operation in various areas. A body has been established to ensure continuous co-operation and discussion between the Nordic countries, namely the Nordic Council of Ministers.

As a result of the homogeneity of the countries and co-operation between them, the Nordic countries have reached a more or less uniform state of law in some legal areas. One of these areas is gender equality, where the countries have agreed to certain standards and adopted goals. Although there are some differences between the systems of the different countries, the similarities are such as to create a discernable "Nordic model" of gender equality law. The Nordic model is based upon the assumption that women and men must have the same rights, obligations and opportunities in all essential areas of life. This broad concept of equality in turn imposes demands on the fundamental structure of society and on its various functions.

Although the main principles and the goals are the same, the Nordic countries have chosen somewhat different ways of establishing gender equality by law. Also, the systems of law enforcement and organizational structures differ to some extent. In the following analysis, the Norwegian model will be described, with reference to some of the main differences of the systems of the other Nordic countries.

---

*This chapter was written by Gender Equality Ombudsman Anne Lise Ryel, Norway.

(ii) The system of law enforcement and organizational structure

One of the main apparent differences between gender equality law in other European countries and that in Nordic countries is that the Nordic countries have established separate bodies to ensure the implementation and drafting of the relevant legislation. The five Nordic countries have adopted somewhat different approaches when devising the appropriate organizational structures to promote gender equality. In Norway, Sweden and Finland, a Gender Equality Ombudsman ensures that the relevant Act on Gender Equality is duly complied with, while other bodies (for instance, councils) draft policy on this issue and related matters. In Denmark and in Iceland, a Gender Equality Council is responsible for both drafting and implementation of the relevant legislation. The details of the structures vary; despite apparent identity, obviously no two systems are completely alike. All Nordic countries, however, share the defining feature that work on gender equality is overseen by public offices connected to and established by the central authorities: principally, the office of Ombudsman. The Ombudsman is a parliamentary Commissioner, and a public official appointed to hear and investigate complaints.

(a) The Norwegian model

Norway is not a member of the European Union. However, due to international agreements[1], Norwegian gender equality law is nevertheless required to be in accordance with that of the EC. It must also be observed that Norway has been working to improve gender equality for a long period of time.[2] Norway may therefore have established law which in fact goes further than EC law.

(b) The Gender Equality Ombudsman

The Gender Equality Act (the Act)[3] established the Gender Equality Ombudsman and the Gender Equality Board of Appeals. The first Ombudsman was appointed in 1979. The Ombudsman is appointed by the King (that is, by the Government) for a period of six years and has a staff of lawyers.

The primary task of the Gender Equality Ombudsman is to ensure that the provisions of the Act are followed. The Ombudsman receives complaints on alleged breaches of the provisions and may also consider cases on the initiative of the office. Individuals, groups of people and organizations (for instance, trade unions and employers' federations) may bring cases before the Ombudsman. The Ombudsman normally has no power to make binding decisions, but

---

[1] Article 69 European Economic Agreement.
[2] By independent official bodies since 1959, when Norway ratified ILO Convention No 100, and established an Equal Pay Council; and by the Ombudsman since 1979.
[3] Lov av 9 juni 1978 om likestilling mellom kjønnene (Likestillingsloven).

should try to achieve voluntary settlements in cases where a breach of the Act is found. However, it is inherent in a system of ombudsmen that the decisions and opinions of the Ombudsman are to be complied with. If this is not the case, there is a right of appeal to the Board of Appeals. For public or state offices it may be considered a breach of rules of conduct within administrative authorities to ignore a decision given by the Ombudsman in the absence of an appeal.

A second function of the Ombudsman is to provide the public with information about the Act, in particular concerning interpretation of its provisions. The Ombudsman is also to ensure that the institution of the Gender Equality Ombudsman is well known, and to ensure that public authorities, employers and employees, organizations and others are familiar with the provisions and the practice of the Ombudsman and the Board of Appeals.

(c) The Gender Equality Board of Appeals

The Gender Equality Board of Appeals consists of seven members with deputies. The members and deputies are appointed for a four-year period. The Norwegian Federation of Trade Unions and the Confederation of Norwegian Business and Industry each recommend the appointment of two members with deputies. The King (the Government) appoints the chairperson and the deputy chairperson, one of whom must possess the qualifications specified for a judge. The Board is summoned to hear and decide upon complaints from the parties to the work of the Ombudsman or cases the Ombudsman has submitted for consideration.

(d) The Gender Equality Council

The Gender Equality Council was established in 1972 and replaced the Equal Pay Council which had been operative since 1959. The function of the Gender Equality Council is to put forward measures to promote gender equality in various areas of family life, education, general business conditions and community life. The Council is to be the liaison body for organizations and the public in matters concerning gender equality, and is also to take the initiative in providing study reports and research in this respect. The Council itself is politically appointed and is summoned at regular intervals. However, a Secretariat conducts the daily work, thereby ensuring continuity in the work of the Council. The Secretariat and the Ombudsman are located in the same offices and are able to co-operate closely.

(e) The Ministry on Children and Family Affairs

The Ministry on Children and Family Affairs is the relevant responsible body in the Governmental system. The Ministry controls the extent of the budget and thereby sets the framework for the activities of the Ombudsman and the Council.

However, the Ministry has no authority to give instructions concerning the discharge of their tasks as described by law.

(iii) The legislation

The Nordic countries have also chosen slightly different approaches to the legislative regulation of gender equality. While the Swedish Act on Gender Equality is concerned with gender equality in working or economic life only, the Norwegian Act covers gender equality in working and economic life, and additionally, equality in private life, public administration and the functioning of the State in general. Both Norway and Sweden, however, have one Act comprising the rules on gender equality. Denmark, in contrast, has five different acts concerning gender equality, for instance the Act on Equal Pay.

(a) The Norwegian Gender Equality Act

The Gender Equality Act was adopted in 1978. The Government proposal assumed that a special gender equality act would wield great influence on increasing the awareness of the injustices which occurred. A general act would also increase the possibilities of establishing a suitable enforcement apparatus. The Bill had pointed out that an Act which ensures equal treatment of men and women was only one of many different instruments to be used. The Act might prevent discriminatory difference in treatment. It could not, however, prearrange all the conditions necessary for substantive gender equality, including the necessary changes in societal attitudes.

The Act was given a two-fold aim. On one hand, it is to ensure substantive gender equality in most areas. On the other hand, the Act is intended to influence attitudes to roles of women and men, committing the authorities to work actively for gender equality through instruments which are not explicitly encompassed by the Act itself, for instance by plans or programmes on how to achieve gender equality in the respective areas.

Conscious that women in working life (and otherwise) had a somewhat weaker position than men, it was found necessary to give women certain advantages for a period of time in an attempt to equalise opportunities for women and men. This provision on "positive action" led to a divided objective of the Act. As expressed in Article 1, the objective is to promote gender equality, but at the same time the Act is aimed particularly at improving the position of women.

In principle the Act applies to all sectors. Wherever it occurs, discriminatory treatment of men and women on account of gender will be in conflict with the law. However, an exception is made for internal conditions in religious communities. The reason for this exception is Article 2 of the Constitution which gives every individual the right to the free practice of religion and it includes both dissenting communities and the Church of Norway (the state church).

The term "internal conditions" comprises questions the religious communities themselves reasonably consider to be theological questions, for instance, the question of appointing female priests is still considered a theological question. In this respect the Ombudsman cannot consider complaints or specific cases, but only give comments or opinions about the question in general. The appointment of staff whose tasks are not connected to the practice of the religion is not regarded as an "internal condition" and must therefore be in conformity with the Act.

The Gender Equality Act also applies to family life and purely personal matters, but the Act shall not be enforced by the Ombudsman or the Board in these matters. The inclusion of family life and purely personal matters was intended merely to exercise a reforming influence on attitudes and to provide a clear statement of the opinion of the Government regarding discrimination on the basis of gender within private life.

An important feature of the Act is its imposition of a special duty on public authorities, including those acting as employer, that they are to facilitate gender equality in all sectors of society. This has been interpreted to mean that public authorities, both governmental and municipal, are obliged to work actively to promote gender equality by means other than those expressly encompassed by the Act; for example, gender equality programmes for the public sector may be drawn up. This duty to facilitate gender equality has proved to be of considerable value. In many cases concerning recruitment or promotion it may be difficult for the Ombudsman, for example to conclude that the rejection of a qualified female applicant was an act of sex discrimination. However, if the employer is a public authority, it may be said that the employer as a public authority should have done more to improve the position of women, and could have done so by appointing a woman to the position.[4] This may especially apply to cases where the vacancy is a position of power or leadership within the sector of the public authority.

(b) The general clause

The general clause, which operates to supplement and complement the other provisions of the Act, is the most important provision of the Gender Equality Act. The principal provision establishes that any form of discriminatory treatment of men and women on the grounds of their gender is prohibited. The term "discriminatory treatment" means any act which places men and women on an unequal footing because they are of different sexes.

Acknowledging the principle of freedom of speech, and as such statements cannot be considered to be "discriminatory treatment", the provision does not include expressions (that is, oral or written statements). However, teaching aids used in schools and other educational institutions must be based upon the principle of gender equality as teaching aids are a major influence on children's view of roles of men and women.

---

[4] See Eklund, in this volume.

In addition to obvious discriminatory treatment, the general clause also prohibits treatment which indirectly discriminates against men or women on the grounds of gender (*de facto* discrimination). For instance, differential treatment of full-time and part-time employees may constitute a breach of the law on the grounds that part-time work is much more widespread among women than among men. Such differential treatment may in effect place women at an unreasonable disadvantage.[5]

The majority (but not all) of the complainants under the provisions of the Act are women. Many of the complaints the Ombudsman receives from male complainants concern their rights as fathers. During the last few years the Government has strengthened the right to parental leave and parents are now entitled to paid leave of up to one year (or longer with a time-account plan).[6] Traditionally it is the mother who stays home for most of this period. In an attempt to increase fathers' participation in caring for infants and small children, a quota of four weeks of parental leave is now reserved for the father. However, many of the rights given in connection with becoming parents remain directly connected to the mother. Fathers enjoy derived rights, not independent rights, for example to paid leave. The Ombudsman is constantly working on these subjects.[7] Complaints on differential treatment concerning parental leave along with complaints on differential treatment concerning social security and national insurance constitute the main group of cases which do not concern professional or working life.

(c) Positive action

The third provision in the general clause states that differential treatment of men and women may be in accordance with the law if the treatment can promote gender equality in accordance with the objective of the Act. Conscious that it would not be possible to achieve gender equality merely by prohibiting discriminatory treatment, measures which provide the one sex with certain advantages in some areas for the short or the long term were necessary.[8] In the current context, a Gender Equality Act which prohibited measures to improve the position of women would have defeated its own purpose. In accordance with the objective of the Act, positive action has mainly been accepted for the benefit of women.

In practice, positive action is currently based mainly upon provisions in collective agreements with the Act as legal authority.[9] The provisions are to be enforced by the parties to the agreements, and not the Ombudsman. The

---

[5] Compare Case C-170/84 *Bilka-Kaufhaus Gmbh* v *Weber von Hartz* [1986] ECR 1607.
[6] Compare Case 184/83 *Hofmann* v *Barmer Ersatzkasse* [1984] ECR 3047.
[7] Compare EC Commission's work on the Reconciliation of Working and Family Life.
[8] Compare Article 119 EC, which has no equivalent provision. But see Equal Treatment Directive 76/207/EEC, Article 2 (4), and the recent ruling of the European Court of Justice in Case 450/93 *Kalanke* v *Freie und Hansestadt Hamburg*, Bremen, 17 October 1995, nyr.
[9] See Bercusson, in this volume, for the importance of collective labour law in the promotion of sex equality.

Ombudsman may, however, decide upon questions on whether or not a provision of this kind in an agreement is in accordance with the Gender Equality Act. Due to this system, the Ombudsman itself does not initiate positive action but may encourage systems which are introduced in schools, universities or commercial enterprises.

A review of the relevant provisions has recently led to the conclusion that a modest form of positive action now may be used for the benefit of men. However, this is only in regard to certain professions connected with the tuition of and care for small children. Otherwise positive action in favour of men will still normally be viewed as in conflict with the Act and its purpose. The provision on positive action in favour of men is to be enforced by the Ombudsman; as opposed to positive action provisions for the benefit of women which are based on collective agreements. Finally, women may still acquire certain special rights in connection for instance with pregnancy, child birth and breast-feeding.[10] This right is specifically expressed in Article 3 and is to be seen as independent of the provision on positive action.

(d) Recruitment, promotion and dismissal

Article 4 of the Act provides that announcements of job vacancies must be neutral as regards gender. Exceptions may be made if the employer has obvious reasons for announcing a vacant position for one sex only, or for indicating in the announcement that applicants of a certain sex are preferred. The Ombudsman and the Board have interpreted this provision strictly and have accepted exceptions only in clear cases, such as cases concerning actors and models.[11] Cases where the reason is a well-founded need for an employee of a certain sex, for instance, to be able to give complete and successful treatment to certain patients, are also accepted. This may be the case within psychiatric wards or child custody institutions. The main principle is, however, that applicants must be assessed on the basis of qualifications regardless of gender. The aspiration is that neutral announcements will act as an encouragement to both sexes to apply for jobs regardless of traditional roles.

In connection with this, the provision states that no distinction must be made between women and men in connection with appointments, promotion, notice to leave or temporary lay-offs. This applies both to full-time employment, part-time employment and temporary jobs. Employers may consider a particular job unsuitable for women. This clearly constitutes an act of illegal discrimination. Men and women may also be evaluated differently during the selectional process; they may be asked different questions during job interviews, or the qualification, qualities and other background factors may be assessed differently of men and women, often to men's advantage. Differential treatment of this kind would normally be in contravention to the Act.

---

[10] Compare the situation in EC law; see Fenwick, and Kilpatrick, in this volume.
[11] Compare Directive 76/207/EEC, Article 2 (2).

Many of the cases brought before the Ombudsman regarding Article 4 (recruitment) concern pregnant women or women who are about to take parental leave.[12] In principle it is a breach of the Act to reject an application from a woman on the ground that she is pregnant, especially if the vacancy is a permanent job.[13] It may also be considered a breach of the Act, however, to reject a pregnant applicant for a temporary position depending on the length of the vacancy and the leave, the possibility of getting a substitute and so on.[14] Rejecting women on grounds of pregnancy or child care may also be in contravention with the provision on *de facto* discrimination.[15] These cases differ from others in the sense that it is not necessary to compare the woman with a male counterpart.[16] The issue is considered to be a typical field where women may be discriminated against, and considering that giving birth is not to be considered a disadvantage for society as such,[17] the Act is interpreted to include cases where the employer has rejected a pregnant woman to the advantage of another woman (as opposed to a man) and the reason for doing so is pregnancy and child care.

As far as promotion is concerned, the employer is required to treat men and women equally. This also counts for courses and tasks which give competence for promotion and are distributed by the employer. Equally, the employer cannot discriminate between men and women in the event of dismissals or temporary lay-offs. This also applies to cases where the employer offers the employees other positions within the enterprise. Dismissal of part-time employees before full-time employees may constitute a breach of the Act. Since most part-time workers are women, such a policy would place them at an unreasonable disadvantage compared to men and consequently be considered a *de facto* discrimination.

There is a reversed burden of proof in cases concerning recruitment, promotion, notice to leave or temporary lay-offs.[18] If differential treatment of women and men can be established in these cases, the employer bears the burden of demonstrating that this is not due to the gender of the applicants or the employees. The reversed burden of proof also applies in cases concerning equal pay for work of equal value.[19]

---

[12] Compare Case C-177/88 *Dekker* v *Stichting Vormingscentrum voor Jong Volwassenen Plus* [1990] ECR I-3941.

[13] Compare Case C-32/93 *Webb* v *EMO Air Cargo (UK) Ltd* [1994] ECR I-3567.

[14] Compare Case C-32/93 *Webb, ibid*, in which there appear to be no equivalent qualifications to these.

[15] In European Community law, discrimination on grounds of pregnancy is not usually characterised as indirect sex discrimination, but as direct sex discrimination. See Case C-177/88, *Dekker, supra* n 12.

[16] As is the case in EC law; see Case C-177/88, *Dekker, supra* n 12.

[17] See Syzszczak, in this volume.

[18] See, for an example in the Swedish context, Eklund, in this volume.

[19] The European Commission's proposed directive on reversal of the burden of proof in sex discrimination (proposal COM(88) 269 final) met with opposition in Council, and appears to have been more or less permanently shelved. It is now the subject of consultation between the social partners – see "Europe" No 6516, Thursday 6 July 1994.

(e) Equal pay for work of equal value

Ever since the work of the first council (the Equal Pay Council) began in 1959, the question of equal pay for work of equal value has been one of the main issues at large in the promotion of gender equality. This issue is still subject to discussions and disagreements and is a considerable issue on the Ombudsman's agenda, as men still seem to be considerably better paid than women.[20]

Article 5 reads:

> Women and men employed by the same employer shall have equal pay for work of equal value.
>
> The term "pay" shall mean ordinary remuneration for work together with other supplements or cash bonuses, or other benefits given by the employer.
>
> The term "equal pay" shall mean that pay shall be determined in the same manner for women and men regardless of sex.

In the *travaux préparatoires* of the Act, it was presupposed that certain criteria were to be used as a basis for comparing payment, but these were not specified in the Act itself. The Ombudsman may undertake comparisons and job evaluations regardless of the employer's explanation of the difference in pay.

The provision has its limitations. Comparisons must be limited to the same enterprise and, in practice, the same employer. In the *travaux préparatoires* it was also presupposed that unless the tasks to be compared had strong external similarities, in order to be susceptible to comparison, the comparators were required to belong to the same profession.

One case[21] brought before the Ombudsman concerned a comparison of the pay of charge nurses and engineers in charge of divisions in Oslo Municipality (regarded as an individual employer in terms of the Act). The Gender Equality Board of Appeals[22] ruled that the occupations involved were too different to permit comparison. The opinion of the Board was that the positions were related to the respective occupations in such a way as to make an exchange (and therefore comparison) of positions inconceivable.

In another case[23] brought before the Ombudsman, the salaries of biomedical engineers who were men were compared to those of medical laboratory technologists who were women. The Ombudsman concluded that the two groups did execute work of equal value and consequently should be paid equally. The case was also brought before the Labour Disputes Court[24] which reached the same conclusion that the tasks of both groups were so similar that they could rightly be said to perform work of equal value. The two groups of employees co-operated on a number of tasks and their functions were seen as components of an integrated process.

---

[20] See Ellis, and Barnard, in this volume.
[21] Case No 83/441 and 90/52.
[22] Case No 6/1990.
[23] Case No 86/166.
[24] Case No 36/1989 lnr 18/1990.

The question of whether to allow comparison between different professions within the same enterprise or not had previously been under debate and is now back on the agenda. The Gender Equality Act, including the provision on equal pay in Article 5, is at present undergoing revision. After the revision the provision may make available comparison between different professions within the same enterprise, and require that criteria (that is, tasks, working conditions, responsibilities, and so on) should be specified when comparing work. The revision of Article 5 is expected to be finalised during 1996.

In connection with the revision of Article 5, consideration of the adoption of a provision which states that every employer with a certain minimum number of employees must have a gender equality agreement is also on the agenda. Such an agreement must include specific plans on how to improve the situation concerning gender equality with respect to pay, promotion, career advancement, and so on. Sweden and Finland have already adopted such a provision.

(f) Representation of both sexes on official bodies

In 1981 the Parliament (the Storting) adopted a new Article 21 which aimed at increasing the number of women on all publicly appointed and elected committees, boards, councils and other bodies. The provision has recently been amended (in 1995). The main principle is that both men and women shall be represented on all official bodies, councils and committees. When a public body appoints or elects a committee with four members or more, each sex shall be represented with at least 40% of the members.[25] Both sexes shall be represented in committees with two or three members. The provision also applies to deputy members. This provision sets a minimum standard and exceptions may be granted only where special circumstances render the requirements evidently unreasonable. In practice, this means that it must have proved to be impossible to find any women (or men) at all qualified for the committee. Committees, which pursuant to statutory law, may only consist of members from directly elected bodies are also excepted from these provisions.

Article 21 should to be seen in coherence with the provision in the Act on local and county authorities.[26] The Act on local and county authorities applies to all committees established on the basis of local and county government elections and sets the same minimum standards as the Gender Equality Act. The standards, however, are intended to be automatically fulfilled through provisions concerning the electoral system. The Ombudsman is not charged with enforcement of this Act.

---

[25] Compare Case 450/93 *Kalanke, supra* n 8.
[26] Lov av 25 september 1992 nr 107 om kommuner og fylkeskommuner (Kommunenloven).

(iv) Conclusion

It is the Ombudsman's opinion that equal pay, the situation for pregnant women in relation to the labour market and questions concerning how to promote more women into leading positions in various parts of society, are among the most important issues in today's society, and are issues on which the State apparatus on gender equality must work to improve in the future.

The Nordic Council of Ministers has recently published the "Programme for Nordic co-operation on Gender Equality 1995–2000". The programme states *inter alia* that the Nordic co-operation measures will be concentrated on activities which promote equal access for women and men to the political and economic decision making processes; promote equality in economic status and influence (including equal pay); promote gender equality on the labour market; improve the possibilities for both sexes to combine parenthood with a job and influence European and broader international development in the field of gender equality.

The Gender Equality Ombudsman trusts that the Nordic countries will continue the co-operation in the field of gender equality, and in this respect the law of the EC will be considered. The co-operation is carried out both in meetings and exchange of information and proposals for improvements between the Ombudsmen and the Councils in the five Nordic countries, as well as at governmental level through the Nordic Council of Ministers. As three of the five Nordic countries are members of the European Union, further co-operation will naturally include the politics and the law on gender equality as expressed by the European Union. The co-operation may thus, in turn, influence the further development of gender equality law within the European Union as well as within the Nordic countries.

ANNE LISE RYEL
The Gender Equality
Ombudsman in Norway

Chapter 23

BEYOND SEX EQUALITY: THE LIMITS OF SEX EQUALITY LAW IN THE NEW EUROPE*

(i) Introduction

It has become almost commonplace now to establish sex equality as an un-arguable good, and then to decry the failings of European law adequately to effect this good in the European Community. In this chapter I want to subvert these preconceptions, because, like all preconceptions, they are infinitely deconstructible, and their deconstruction, rather than threatening their veracity, can only serve to strengthen them. In the first part of the chapter, I want to introduce some of the basic tenets in contemporary feminist jurisprudence which have tended to enjoy dominion in current debate surrounding the nature of sex equality in the Community. I then want to introduce an alternative, explicitly postmodern feminist approach which, I will suggest, takes feminism well "beyond" the now rather stale "limits" of the sex equality debate. In the second part, I will place this jurisprudence within the specific context of European Community law, and suggest why the postmodern alternative might offer something more in the new Europe.

(ii) Beyond the sex equality debate

I do not intend here to dwell too long on the standard arguments surrounding what sex equality should mean, or how substantive problems of inequality should be addressed. Indeed one of the problems in current feminist jurisprudence is that the arguments are only too familiar. Like all discourses, the sex equality debate has been captured and objectified, the alternatives set in jurisprudential stone. This is not an error, because it was not something which could be avoided. The wisdom lies in knowing that all discourses are ultimately

---

*This chapter was written by Ian Ward.

objectified, and can only progress if their (pre)conceptions are subverted. How-ever, at the risk of momentarily entrenching further the sanctification of this discourse, I will briefly examine the arguments that need to be subverted, so that we can be better aware of what we are going to go "beyond".

It must first be emphasised that there is no uniform feminist theory, on sex equality or for that matter any other issue. It is the perception that there might be which must be addressed. The pervasive argument in sex equality, until recent years at least, has been that of sameness and difference. The dominion that this debate enjoys, and the dangers which it poses, have been uncompro-misingly articulated by Catherine MacKinnon. The sameness/difference debate, as MacKinnon suggests, gives women just two choices; they can either aspire to be the same as men, and to enjoy the same rights, or they can cam-paign to have their difference from men recognised in law. Either way, women are compared with a male norm, and by presenting women with these two choices, and these two choices only, the debate immediately establishes parameters.

Any such rights-based approach tends to be founded on "a claim to similarity". A collateral argument here is that the formal enactment of rights for women, aside from being made in a comparative sense, will not address in reality the myriad of substantive inequalities which women face. In other words, a liberal rights-based approach – and it is no suprise that MacKinnon cites Ronald Dworkin as the arch-exponent of such an approach in contemporary juris-prudence – actually serves to entrench the real inequalities which women encounter, and does more harm in practice, than good. Thus, as MacKinnon concludes, the phrase "sex equality law" contains three particular preconcep-tions. First it assumes a particular determination of "sex" as denoting differ-ence. Second, it then presumes that any "inequalities" must be the result of "mistakes" in addressing difference. Third, "law" explicitly assumes that the problem is something which can somehow be resolved by law.[1]

What we are really talking about, rather than sameness or difference, are questions of power, and MacKinnon has developed her critique along these lines in her more recent writings, suggesting that, in place of sameness/difference, a more critical legal approach should be adopted, concentrating on confronting more immediate inequalities in practical terms.[2] What can be seen most clearly during the 1990s is an intensification of concern in the politics of law. It can almost be termed an anti-philosophical backlash. The enthusiasm for "critical" legal feminism is a testimony to this impulse.

One who has allied this pragmatic impulse to an identifiable critical legal feminism is Deborah Rhode. Rhode urges the replacement of sameness/difference with a focus on "disadvantage".[3] Like MacKinnon, Rhode rejects what she calls "liberal legalism" as represented in contemporary legal and political structures. Classical liberalism, she rightly suggests, is a predominantly economic ideology

---

[1] For a concise summary of MacKinnon's original position, see *Toward a Feminist Theory of State* (1989) chapter 12. MacKinnon's ideas have developed from this statement, as we shall shortly see.
[2] MacKinnon, "Reflections on Sex Equality Law" 100 *Yale Law Journal* (1991), 1281–1328.
[3] Rhode, *Justice and Gender* (1989) 318.

which sanctifies the role of the contract, both in public and private law guise, as the norm of "affiliative" relationships. In place of such an abstract and mythological liberal ideology, she advocates the idea of "social" relationships. In line with received Critical Legal Studies (CLS) wisdom, she suggests that all "choices" are ideologically charged, and made in pervasively social settings.[4]

Where Rhode, interestingly, distinguishes critical legal feminism from CLS in general, and perhaps to a certain extent from MacKinnon, is in her approach to rights. Whilst challenging the nature of liberal, autonomous, rights, she clings to an alternative theory, of socially constructed rights, which are better capable of reflecting the common "lived experience" of women. Rights, she suggests, have a "special resonance" and their presence, or indeed potential, as tools for improving the situation of women, cannot be denied.[5]

Perhaps the most eloquent defence of such an approach is Patricia Williams's. Williams clings to rights because, quite simply, it is the only game in town, and writing not just as a woman, but as a black woman, she can testify to the benefits which were accessed by black people in the United States by litigating rights under the Constitution. She does not wish to "idealise" rights, but neither does she wish to deconstruct them, for the sheer joy of deconstruction. Such an exercise can only serve the interest of women if it presents a viable and more effective alternative. The more deconstructive edge of CLS and feminist critical legal theory, she suggests, does not offer any such alternative. Rather like Rhode then, Williams suggests that rights must be reconstructed or "reconfigured" in a more "civil" or "societal", as opposed to individual, form, rather than simply abandoned.[6] This is not a reactionary or even liberal approach. Such an assignation would be to miss the point of Williams's critique entirely. What it is, is a supremely pragmatic critique, and a supremely political one in its primarily strategic sense.

A similarly "strategic" position has been taken by Diane Majury. The "equality" debate, she acknowledges, is the dominant one, and so cannot be ignored. However, the welter of alternative equality "models" presented by various feminist scholars militates against any objective determination of "equality", either in theory or in practice. Moreover, echoing MacKinnon, she suggests that the "equality" debate distracts us from appreciating the power(lessness) and (dis)advantage debates which more accurately reflect the deeper structures which underpin the real situation of women in contemporary society. The debate, she thus argues, must then be redirected towards "inequality". An "inequality based strategy" does not establish goals, but is rather directed towards addressing substantive and particular inequalities. (In)equality is thus a symbol of a strategy. Ultimately, this strategy must concentrate on enhancing the female discourse in a general sense, by encouraging dialogue and conversation between women[7], which can then contribute to the crystallising of women's

---

[4] Rhode, "Feminist Critical Studies" 42 *Stanford Law Review* (1990), 617–638.
[5] *Ibid.*
[6] Williams, "Alchemical Notes: Reconstructing Ideals from Deconstructed Rights" 22 *Harvard Civil Rights-Civil Liberties Review* (1987), 401–433.
[7] See Everson, in this volume.

"interests". What is implicit in this conclusion is the fact that equality is, in any situation, an intellectual fiction. There can be no single meaning of sex equality, because there is no single determination of women, as of course there is not of men.[8] Different women must fight to establish their different particular determinations of equality.[9] The first duty of the feminist legal thinker is not to pronounce on sex equality, or perceived inadequate approximations to it, but radically to destabilise any pretended determination of the idea, in practice or reality.[10]

With Majury certainly, and to a lesser extent with Rhode and Williams also, we are witnessing the approaching influence of postmodernist thinking. CLS fell prey to the tempting of postmodernism by the late 1980s, and over the last few years an identifiable postmodern feminism has emerged from within critical legal feminism.[11] As Joan Williams has suggested, postmodernism offers a recourse "beyond" any of the sameness/difference debates which pervade, not only feminism, but also related theories of exclusion, most obviously, perhaps, race theory. Indeed, reflecting on the absence of a distinctive critical legal feminist "narrative", Williams suggests that postmodernism offers itself as the only source for an identifiably feminist legal voice, because it is the only narrative which triumphs difference and particularity.[12]

The essence of the postmodern feminist critique is the dismissal of these "metanarratives" and a determination to concentrate solely on the particular. Gender questions, as Mary Joe Frug stressed, cannot be considered simply as gender questions. They are, at once, questions of politics, economics, art, culture, text and so on. Thus, sex equality laws and any complementary sex equality debate cannot simply concentrate on the nature of law *per se*, or indeed the operation of those laws in a predetermined political setting. To pursue such a debate is to concede to its preordained and objectified limits. In other words, the sex equality debate cannot presume any given meaning of what sex equality law can possibly mean. There is no one definition of sex, or of woman, of equality, or of law.[13]

Undoubtedly the most substantive account of postmodern legal feminism is Drucilla Cornell's. Cornell concentrates on developing a postmodern "ethics" from the deconstruction of law, which can then furnish a viable feminist political agenda. Founded upon the Derridean deconstruction of "identities", Cornell seeks to go "beyond" what she terms the "premature objectivism" of CLS writers, and most particularly Roberto Unger. More specifically she advocates the capacity

---

[8] See Hervey, in this volume.
[9] See Williams, "Dissolving the Sameness/Difference Debate: A Post-Modern Path Beyond Essentialism in Feminist and Critical Race Theory" *Duke Law Journal* (1991), 322–23.
[10] Majury, "Strategising In Equality" in Fineman and Thomadsen, *At the Boundaries of Law: Feminism and Legal Theory* (1991) 320–337.
[11] As witnessed by Rhode herself. See "Studies", 617–638. See also Frug, *Postmodern Legal Feminism* (1992), for a general discussion of the origins of postmodern legal feminism. For the relationship between CLS and postmodernism, see Goodrich, "Critical Legal Studies in England: Prospective Histories" 12 *Oxford Journal of Legal Studies* (1992), 195–236.
[12] Williams (1991), *supra* n 9 at 296–323.
[13] See Frug (1992), *supra* n 11, particularly chapters 2, 7 and 8.

of Richard Rorty's "conversationalism" to effect a fluid theory of communicative or dialogic ethics, as an "ethic of citizenship":

> Dialogism involves a commitment to universality: we are all to be recognised as participants in our collective conversation, and we are to hold it out as a possibility that generalisable interests will emerge in the course of that conversation.[14]

Cornell's community is a fractured community which inheres multiple interests, and wherein political power is dispersed in a radically plural and (echoing certain CLS scholarship), participatory democracy.[15] The overarching characteristic of the jurisprudence of such a community is its "transformative potential". It is a radically destabilised community, fiercely resistant to any objectification of rights. There are no unarguable goods, sex equality included. The concentration on "transformative potential" is, of course, resonant of Unger's "transformative rights", but Cornell seeks to go "beyond" the perceived objectification immanent in Unger's rights-thesis, and instead concentrates on the preservation of a "fluid" ethics.[16] In her most recent work, Cornell has characterised this as the "philosophy of the limit", and has intensified its radically plural ethical component:

> I . . . suggest that the entire project of the philosophy of the limit is driven by an ethical desire to enact the ethical relation. Again, by the ethical relation I mean to indicate the aspiration to a non-violent relationship to the Other, and to otherness more generally, that assumes responsibility to guard the Other against the appropriation that would deny her difference and singularity.[17]

The preservation of particularity of the individual is thus the key component of the philosophy of the limit.

The effect of this philosophy of the limit on feminist legal theory is considerable, because it denies the phenomenology of critics such as MacKinnon, which, Cornell suggests, positivises a determination of women and, to use the Heideggerian terminology, women's situation in-the-world.[18] There is no fixed

---

[14] Cornell, "Toward a Modern/Postmodern Reconstruction of Ethics" 133 *University of Pennsylvania Law Review* (1985), 291–380, particularly 327–355 and 375–378, quotation at 378. For a discussion of Derrida and deconstruction in legal studies, see Balkin, "Deconstructive Practice and Legal Theory" 96 *Yale Law Journal* (1987), 743–786. By the term "premature objectivism", Cornell means the mistake of determining alternative political and legal identities. For an example of precisely such a determination, see Unger, *Politics: a Work in Constructive Social Theory* (1987) 3 vols. For Rorty's "conversationalism", see his *Contingency, Irony, and Solidarity* (1989).

[15] As opposed to more orthodox representative democracy, as traditionally espoused in liberal political theory. For an example of CLS discussions of pluralism and participatory democracy, see Hutchinson, *Dwelling on the Threshold: Critical Essays on Modern Legal Thought* (1988).

[16] Cornell, "Institutionalisation of Meaning, Recollective Imagination and the Potential for Transformative Legal Interpretation" 136 *University of Pennsylvania Law Review* (1988), 1135–1229, and *The Philosophy of the Limit* (1992) 59–60. For Unger's use of "transformative rights", see *The Critical Legal Studies Movement* (1983).

[17] Cornell, *Philosophy of the Limit*, ibid 62.

[18] For the particular critique of MacKinnon in this sense, see Cornell, *Beyond Accommodation: Ethical Feminism, Deconstruction and the Law* (1991), 119–164. The Heideggerian "situation-in-the-world" construction emphasises the temporality and spaciality of the female situation. It serves to crystallise the politics of the situation.

female reality. Any feminist "truth" must be written as feminist "truths", in the plural. This is an essential analogue of the Derridean conception of justice, as justice in the plural, not the singular, and is the "responsibility" of feminist legal theory.[19] Rather than the programmes of writers such as Unger or MacKinnon, the politics of which has served only to objectify, Cornell suggests a "full program" of transformative rights across society, which will effect a collateral "equivalence" in the condition of women. Such a programme will inhere both the ethic of "respect" and the ethic of "right":

> We need a full program of rights which will provide women with the conditions for equality of well-being and capability . . . A program of equivalent rights is the legal expression of the affirmation and valuation of sexual difference. "Equivalence" means of equal value, but not of equal value because of likeness. Equivalence does not demand that the basis of equality be likeness to men. Such a view would be to deny that we are sexuate beings. Ethical feminism denies the "truth" of the gender hierarchy by affirming the feminine within sexual difference as other to its current identifications.[20]

The programme of legal and political rights must be part of a far wider re-orientation of political and social culture. What Cornell terms the "dream of a new choreography of sexual difference",

> also has to do with the possibility of democracy itself, once we include participatory, dialogic structures in democracy. The psychical fantasy of Women . . . blocks the dialogue we associate with participatory democracy. Indeed, it blocks the recognition of women as citizens. Therefore it is not enough to just socialise the so-called realm of necessity in order for participatory democracy to exist, although this is clearly an important step in battling against the repudiation of the feminine and the devalorisation of feminine virtues. The realm of the political must also be feminised, but in a more radical way than has been suggested.[21]

To identify "women" is to deny the particularity of women, and to deny the possibility of emancipation in society. The concentration on the particular situation, as opposed to some metaphysical determination of women in general, clearly subverts any uniform or comprehensive theory of sex equality. Such is the fate of any theory which tries to place such an ephemeral concept as equality at its heart. There is no definition of (sex) equality, or rather there are too many, none of them right, as such, and none of them wrong. The philosophy of the limit, the postmodern alternative, is to identify (sex) equality as just one destabilised component in a series of such free-standing, non-determinative, dialogic encounters, which are themselves constitutive of a radically plural, participatory and community-determined "ethic of citizenship".

---

[19] Cornell, *Beyond Accommodation*, 115–116. For a discussion of the Derridean conception of justice, see Balkin (1987), *supra* n 14.
[20] Cornell, *Transformations* (1993) 123 and 141–142.
[21] Cornell (1993), *supra* n 20 at 168–169.

(iii) Identifying the new European woman

What is the philosophy behind sex equality law in the European Community, and more importantly perhaps, what is the philosophy which lies behind the critique of these laws? The first question is perhaps the easier to answer, although the two are very obviously related. The European Community, and its principal jurisprudential organs, most obviously the European Court of Justice, have loudly proclaimed their affiliation with rights and a rights-discourse. Not that this appears to have been the intention of the Treaty framers, for there is no reference to anything approaching substantive rights in the Rome Treaty.[22] However, encouraged by the Court, there is now much talk about rights to this and rights to that, and sex equality is very much part of this rights-talk.[23] Once again this is not the avowed intention of the Community's legislators. There is no express recourse to rights as such in the handful of statutory instruments which are directed towards sex equality. Statutory rhetoric is more suggestive of a principle of equal treatment, than a right to equal treatment. It is, however, explicit in the pervasive Community ideology, and has been more confidently assumed by the Court.

This ideology is, of course, a neo-classical free market one, based primarily on the integrity of the contract. Any rights are predetermined, to some degree, by this ideology. This is why commentators such as Koen Lenaerts can categorise social and aspirational rights, as distinct from fundamental rights.[24] Sex equality is a categorised right, defined and determined by the "limits" of the free market ideology. This is the potential fate of any rights-based theory of law, and the particular fate of a liberal one. Aside from the reality of cultural discrimination in western Europe, the Community actually enhances sex discrimination, by allowing the free market to run, and to make its own determination of rights.[25] Thus, as Stuart Holland has recently reminded us, gender discrimination in the Community is deeply structural.[26] Sonia Mazey has emphasised how the Community labour market actually promotes forms of job segregation which flourish upon gender discrimination.[27] Capitalism thrives on inequality. It needs inequality by definition. It needs to exploit, and it seizes upon those disadvantaged or already marginalised. The very ideology of capitalism is discriminatory. Sex discrimination represents the triumph of capitalism. It is a testimony to its

---

[22] For a discussion of rights in EC law in general, see Weiler, "Eurocracy and Distrust: Some Questions Concerning the Role of the European Court of Justice in Protection of Fundamental Rights within the Legal Order of the European Communities" 61 *Washington Law Review* (1986), 1103–1142, and Lenaerts, "Fundamental Rights to be Included in a Community Catalogue" 16 *European Law Review* (1991), 367–389. For the Court's use of a "rights-discourse", see, for example, Case 29/69 *Stauder* [1969] ECR 419; Case 4/73 *Nold No 2* [1974] ECR 491; and Case 44/79 *Hauer* [1979] ECR 3727.

[23] See, for example, Case 149/77 *Defrenne No 3* [1978] ECR 1365.

[24] Lenaerts (1991) *supra* n 22 at 367–389.

[25] See Fenwick and Hervey, "Sex Equality in the Single Market: New Directions for the European Court of Justice" 32 *Common Market Law Review* (1995), 443–470 at 443 and 449.

[26] Holland, *The European Imperative* (1993), 156–157.

[27] Mazey, "European Community Action on Behalf of Women: The Limits of Legislation" 27 *Journal of Common Market Studies* (1988), 63–84 at 64–67.

success.[28] Thus any strategy, based upon "inequalities" or even upon rights, must be directed against the entire metanarrative of the Community and its ideology.

The fallacy of concentrating on purely legal strategies relating to "formal" sex equality is plain for all to see.[29] Tinkering around with Article 119, or the handful of equal treatment Directives is not going to make much difference to the situation of the overwhelming number of women in Europe today.[30] Such a strategy is "limited" for a number of reasons. Firstly it ignores the vast majority of women who are excluded by the ideology of the right, because they are marginalised from the free market. Women who are outside the workplace are powerless. By way of example, this is particularly apparent in the area of Community social security law.[31] This exclusion is even more rigorous for those women who are outside the family nexus, and cannot therefore piggy-back the rights of spouses.[32] Indeed, women inside the family nexus are equally powerless, in that the Community has consistently refused to regulate the family.[33] Housework is not real work in Europe, at least not in jurisprudential terms.[34] Yet, as Kirsten Scheiwe has emphasised, the Community and its common market depend upon the integral operation of "unpaid servicing work", determined by a specious distinction between a private family and a public market.[35]

Secondly, for those who are actively participant in the free market, there is the problem that, as a liberal right, any sex equality or equal treatment "right" is a negative right. This means that the rights are formal, they "aspire" to an ideal of abstract right, and do not address the substantive inequalities which women face in the real Community. A classic example here is Article 5 of the Equal Treatment in Employment Directive, which was supposed to address the problem of harassment in the workplace.[36] As the Rubenstein Report emphasised, it is one thing to write a directive, it is quite another to effect a substantive change in the actual situation of women in the workplace. The fate of the Rubenstein Report, and its recommendations regarding harassment, and those subsequently articulated in the Vogel-Polsky Report, are a testimony to the Community's unwillingness to look "beyond" liberal legalism.[37] There is also the

---

[28] For a similar critique, see Fredman, "European Community Discrimination Law: A Critique" 21 *Industrial Law Journal* (1992), 119–134 at 130–32.

[29] For a critique of the "formal" sex equality approach see, Fenwick and Hervey (1995), *supra* n 25 at 443–471.

[30] The main Directives being the Equal Pay Directive 75/117/EEC (OJ 1975 L 45/19), the Equal Treatment Directives 76/207/EEC (OJ 1976 L 39/40) and 86/613/EEC (OJ 1986 L 359/56), and the Social Security Directives 79/7/EEC (OJ 1979 L 6/24) and 86/378/EEC (OJ 1986 L 225/40).

[31] See Steiner, in this volume.

[32] See Sohrab, "Women and Social Security: the Limits of EEC Equality Law" *Journal of Social Welfare and Family Law* (1994), 5–17.

[33] See O'Leary, in this volume.

[34] See Cullen, "The Subsidiary Woman" *Journal of Social Welfare and Family Law* (1994), 413–417.

[35] Scheiwe, "EC Law's Unequal Treatment of the Family: The Case Law of the European Court of Justice on Rules Prohibiting Discrimination on Grounds of Sex and Nationality" 3 *Social and Legal Studies* (1994), 243–265 at 255 and 261.

[36] OJ 1976 L 39/40. See Article 5(1) for measures relating to sexual harassment in the workplace.

[37] The Rubenstein report was entitled *The Dignity of Women at Work* (Commission of the European Communities, 1988). For the Vogel-Polsky report, see CREW Reports (1983), vol 3, nos 3, 4. For a discussion of the reports, see Ellis, *European Sex Equality Law* (1991) 149–151 and 174–178.

related and continuing problem of the consistent recourse, by both legislators
and lawyers, to the male comparator, which is again the result of a determination to approximate to some fictional notion of equality, and bound up with the
collateral and perennial problem of sameness and difference. A related example
of this cultural malaise is the continued acceptance in EC law of the family unit
as the norm, wherein welfare benefits are directed towards the heads of households. The law constructively determines these heads of households as male. A
similar example is the fact that any woman dependant upon a man is powerless
in EC law unless she can establish herself as a "spouse".[38]

Thirdly, as a related observation, the history of the European Court's interpretation of Article 119 and the equal treatment Directives consistently betrays
a willingness to determine the principle of equality in the light of the ideology
of a free market. Chris Docksey has referred to the Court's apparent reflexive
"deference to economic conditions".[39] In landmark cases, such as *Defrenne,*
although the Court was prepared to effect the principle of equal pay, it was
clear that it did so primarily because such a principle was in line with the wider
ambitions of a liberal free market.[40] As one commentator has noted, Article 119
is no more than a "by-product" of market regulation.[41] As Philippa Watson has
recently suggested, the case law makes it quite clear that the "principle" of sex
equality is a "variable" one, subject to the wider ambitions of the Community's
political economy.[42] A notorious example here is the Court's ruling in *Bilka-
Kaufhaus,* which permitted indirect discrimination if it could be "objectively justified", which, of course, meant economically justified.[43] It is all too clear that
the social ideal of sex equality has never alone been sufficient for either the
politicians or the judges of the new Europe.[44] Any form of social justice is
rationalised as desirable only because it will make the market more productive.
It is regrettable that this rationale remains at the heart of even the most radical
of contemporary programmes for social reform in the Community.[45]

What is perhaps most instructive is the fact that the new Europe clearly
intends to do little or nothing about sex equality. Sure, it may tinker a little
more with Article 119, and even throw in a few more equal treatment Directives. But it will certainly not look to address the substantive problems which lie
behind a liberal rights thesis based on the fiction of abstract equality. This is all

---

[38] The most obvious example of the family construct as the norm in EC law lies in Articles 48–51
relating to the free movement of migrant workers. For a discussion of this tendency, see Scheiwe
(1994), *supra* n 35 at 248–251.
[39] Docksey, "The Principle of Equality Between Women and Men as a Fundamental Right Under
Community Law", 20 *Industrial Law Journal* (1991), 258–280 at 274–76.
[40] Case 43/75 *Defrenne No 2* [1976] ECR 455. See Barnard, in this volume.
[41] Scheiwe (1994), *supra* n 35 at 245.
[42] Watson, "Equality of Treatment: A Variable Concept?" 24 *Industrial Law Journal* (1995), 33–48.
For a wide-ranging discussion of the Community's "political economy" and the concessions which it
demands of any such principles as equality or fairness, see Tsoukalis, *The New European Economy: The
Politics and Economics of Integration* (1991).
[43] Case 170/84 [1986] ECR 1607. See Townshend-Smith, in this volume.
[44] See Meehan, "Sex Equality Policies in the European Community" 13 *Journal of European Integration*
(1990), 185.
[45] See Holland (1993), *supra* n 26 at 157–159.

too apparent from the Maastricht Treaty. The principle of subsidiarity actually militates against any uniform approach to the problem of sex discrimination in the workplace.[46] This is not a problem *per se*, but it is within the particular context of a liberal rights-based ideology, with its concomitant pretence to universality. Similarly, Article 6 of the Social Policy Agreement repeats a commitment to equal pay, but in doing so merely reaffirms a commitment to formal equality alone.[47]

Perhaps even more unfortunate, is the reluctance of sex equality commentators to perceive the limitations, not merely of Community sex equality law, but of the European Community as a whole. It is the very ideology of the Community which must be reformed, not merely the text of its sex equality laws or judgments. There is much talk about the need to effect substantive, as opposed to merely formal, equality. There is certainly no doubting the inadequacy of formal equality, but how will substantive equality be effected, never mind defined? Feminist critiques of Community sex equality law still cling to an illusion of equality. Thus Evelyn Ellis rightly condemns an idea of formal equality which encourages women to "strive for male patterns of work and to conform to existing male values". But, in its place, she wants "genuine equality" to be effected by a wider legal and political strategy.[48] I would not disagree with the need for a wider strategy, providing it is one which is at once aware of the reality of particular situations, and the desirability of defining woman in the particular. But is there really a need to try to define a vision of genuine equality? Whose definition is this going to be? Any such definition can only assume some constituent definitions, not just of equality, but of women.

A more promising critic is Gillian More, who acknowledges that:

> The Community's formula for sex equality is . . . abstract, narrow and rigid: it is conceptually incapable of eradicating all but the most superficial inequalities faced by women. It helps only those women workers who are already well-assimilated to men; it reinforces inequalities based on gender differences; it restricts the use of positive action; and it masks the fact that many of women's inequalities at work are intimately related to their role in the family.[49]

More recognises that "equality", aside from being a rather ephemeral concept, is one which is all too easily determined in relation to dominant male comparators. Following MacKinnon's thesis, More rejects "equality" and the related notion of sameness and difference, and instead supports the idea of "disadvantage" as a guiding concept by which to adjudge alleged gender discrimination. The overriding quality of such an approach, as she acknowledges, is that it does not assume any metanarrative of the female condition in the EC, but rather concentrates on the particular situation of each disadvantaged woman.[50]

---

[46] Cullen (1994), *supra* n 34 at 408–409.
[47] Scheiwe (1994), *supra* n 35 at 244.
[48] See Ellis (1991), *supra* n 37 at 206–208.
[49] More, " 'Equal Treatment' of the Sexes in European Community Law: What Does 'Equal' Mean?'" 1 *Feminist Legal Studies* (1993), 45–74 at 64.
[50] *Ibid* 65–74.

It is here that a postmodern feminist approach can offer a means of going "beyond" sex equality. Most immediately, rather than attempting to define equality, and then concentrate strategies around this definition in relation to some sort of determined right, postmodern feminism demands that the position of women in law and in society, must be addressed from outside the "limits" of the law. In other words, there must be a wider critique of society and culture, with the legal critique as merely a constituent part. There is evidence that feminist critiques of Community sex equality law are moving in this direction.[51] Louise Ackers has recently emphasised that too much reliance on the law actually serves to distract attention from patent political inadequacies.[52] Sandra Fredman has similarly appealed for "legal strategies" to be accompanied by a "much more radical focus on structural disadvantage and the causes thereof".[53] Sonia Mazey has stressed the need to address the deeper structural problems of gender inequality. Only a concerted political initiative can attack the residual strength of both direct and indirect discrimination, and hope to make a real impact. Law and legal initiatives, she suggests, have "to date made no discernible impact on the problem of sex discrimination in the labour market".[54] As Rhode emphasises, classical liberalism is an ideology geared to the exploitation of the marginalised and disempowered. The European Community aspires to be the apogee of a classical liberal "state", founded upon a free and common market. A postmodern feminist critique of sex discrimination in the Community must identify precisely what it is writing against, and appreciate the strength of its ideological oppressor. The problem with the jurisprudentially determined "economic women" in the Community, is not with the determination of woman, but with the determination of "economic".[55] This is the deconstructive role for postmodern feminism.

The reconstructive role is just as important. Tantalisingly, it is here that the new post-Maastricht Europe might have something to offer. There are two particular ideas which we have already identified as central to postmodern feminist legal thinking, both of which have recently been redefined by the new Europe. The first of these is citizenship. Rhode, Majury and Cornell all suggest that there must be an alternative idea of citizenship as social citizenship.[56] At the same time, by redefining a social citizenship it is possible to redefine rights as social, as opposed to liberal individual rights.[57] Of course, the much triumphed conception of rights in the Maastricht Treaty is a decidedly political conception, where, most notoriously, citizenship of the Union is still to be determined via

---

[51] Fenwick and Hervey (1995), *supra* n 25 at 470–471.
[52] Ackers, "Women, Citizenship and European Community Law: The Gender Implications of the Free Movement of Persons", *Journal of Social Welfare and Family Law* (1994), 391–406 at 392.
[53] Fredman (1992), *supra* n 28 at 134.
[54] Mazey (1988), *supra* n 27 at 63, 70 and 82.
[55] As Tsoukalis has emphasised, the determination of "economy" in the EC is a peculiarly political one. See his *The New European Economy: The Politics and Economics of Integration* (1991). The alternative would, of course, be to describe a more socio-political determination.
[56] See Everson, and Shaw, in this volume.
[57] See Barnard, Hervey, and McGlynn, in this volume.

citizenship of a nation-state.[58] The exclusionary nature of such a definition, and particularly its role in constructing the effective exclusion of women, has already been noted by a number of commentators.[59] The only justiciable "rights" which flow from Article 8 citizenship are those pertaining to the Community laws of free movement and related legislation. As Louise Ackers has thus concluded, Article 8 citizenship does more to condemn women to an inferior constitutional status, than emancipate them from an already real status of economic inferiority. Only a conception of social citizenship, in which legal and welfare protection is extended to all persons, regardless of their role in the market, can hope to address the abuses of gender discrimination.[60]

However, despite these immediately discouraging prognoses, critics such as Paul Close have already detected a movement in Community rhetoric towards what he defines as a "new social citizenship". Social citizenship is the logical supplement to any socially, as opposed to purely economically, determined Union. It might, he predicts, be the determination favoured by any Union which evolves along these lines.[61] Such a conception is a postmodern one, simply because it is a post-political one, and the modern has always defined itself as the political. The emphasis on conversationalism and the dialogic "ethic of citizenship", as presented by Cornell, thus becomes a very real and viable model for an evolving Union conception of citizenship. Such a communicatively constructed citizenship will be effected only through the re-empowerment of marginalised, or "silenced" voices, of which women are just one. In other words there must be a radical transformation in the forms of governance in the new Europe. As Close emphasises, the reality of social citizenship in the new Europe is conditional upon such a transformation. Power must be pluralised, fragmented between various interests – individual and corporate.[62]

This introduces the second and related idea central to postmodern feminist thinking; that of alternative conceptions of democracy. Once again, the new Europe has gestured in this direction, in deciding to be more democratic, or at least appearing to be more democratic. Unfortunately, once again, it assumes that the most immediate form of democracy is representative democracy. But there are alternatives. Most obviously, there is the idea of pluralism and participatory democracy, as espoused by countless CLS writers in various forms, and taken on by a number of the more critical feminist legal theorists.[63] As we have already noted, for critics such as Rhode or Cornell, the fragmentation of power in a more plural polity, along with the enhanced potential to exercise

---

[58] The construction of Articles B TEU and 8 EC. For a commentary, see Closa, "The Concept of Citizenship in the Treaty on European Union", 29 *Common Market Law Review* (1992), 1137–1169.

[59] See, for example, Ackers (1994), *supra* n 52.

[60] *Ibid* 391–403. For a general critique of the political determination of citizenship in Article 8, see Closa, "Citizenship of the Union and Nationality of Member States" in O'Keeffe and Twomey, *Legal Issues of the Maastricht Treaty* (1994), 109–119.

[61] See Close, *Citizenship, Europe and Change* (1995), 45–81 and 198–222.

[62] *Ibid* 242–268.

[63] See Hutchinson (1988), *supra* n 15; Rhode (1990), *supra* n 4; Frug (1992), *supra* n 11; and Cornell (1988), *supra* n 16.

power in a participatory democracy, are central tenets of an alternative post-modern feminist political agenda. Only this fragmentation will give women the voice by which to "write" the feminine in a participatory democracy.[64] At first glance, the new Europe, like the old one, held in the thrall of the nation-states, might not seem to enjoy a particularly fertile potential.[65] This suspicion is enhanced by the pervasive assumption that democracy can only really mean representative democracy.

However, the tantalising exception is the much maligned concept of subsidiarity. The obfuscation surrounding the precise meaning of subsidiarity, as we know, is already the stuff of legend.

As John Peterson has stressed, its political survival in the negotiations surrounding the Maastricht Treaty depended upon this obfuscation. Subsidiarity had to mean everything and anything to everybody and anybody.[66]

There is a "fatal confusion" with regard to the extent to which the operation of subsidiarity will centralise or decentralise power.[67] If the principle only enjoys meaning within a recognisably centralised federal state, then subsidiarity will not be a principle which will help the empowerment of any disempowered voices. Neither will the decentralisation of power back to the nation-states (the interpretation loudly articulated by such as John Major) do more to help.

However, a radical interpretation of subsidiarity, stripping power away from both Brussels and Westminster, could do much to empower both interests and individuals, and not only on a classically functional-pluralist basis.

Certain legal commentators have favoured a decentralising, even pluralist, definition of subsidiarity. Nicholas Emiliou, for example, has championed subsidiarity as a mechanism for "diversification", but has done so within the idea of a hierarchical European state.[68] More recently, Ian Harden has perceptively noted that subsidiarity is more a "recognition" of a need than a "specific principle", and suggests that it encapsulates the spirit of a plural, participatory democracy. Subsidiarity, he says, is "not just about the relationship between States and the Union, but also about the search for a richer variety of collectivities, political and otherwise, which individuals can use as a meaningful context for their actions".[69] This chimes with the view taken by David Coombes, who has seen in subsidiarity the potential to realise just such a radically plural and participatory democratic polity. Subsidiarity as pluralism, he suggests, in the European context,

---

[64] See Everson, in this volume.

[65] For the continuing hold of the nation-states, see Milward, *The European Rescue of the Nation-State* (1992). I have discussed Milward's thesis from a legal perspective in "The European Constitution and the Nation-State" *Oxford Journal of Legal Studies*, forthcoming.

[66] Peterson, "Subsidiarity: A Definition to Suit Any Vision?" 47 *Parliamentary Affairs* (1994), 116–132 at 120–121.

[67] See Teasdale, "Subsidiarity in Post-Maastricht Europe" 64 *Political Quarterly* (1993), 187–197.

[68] Emiliou, "Subsidiarity: An Effective Barrier Against 'the Enterprises of Ambition'?" 17 *European Law Review* (1992), 383–407.

[69] Harden, "The Constitution of the European Union" *Public Law* (1994), 609–624 at 613, 620 and 624.

can represent "social" as opposed to "political" integration, which can then supplement a meaningful concept of social citizenship and even rights:

> If Europeans could successfully develop an alternative approach to the government of political communities and the relations between them, they would not only be responding to their own needs but also providing the kind of influence, by example, that is the only truly effective way of both defending one's own enjoyment of pluralist values pertaining to a civil society and ensuring their ultimate availability to others.[70]

Subsidiarity can provide the radically destabilised, plural and participatory model of governance which postmodern feminism advocates as the only viable means by which women can gain a "voice" in society, and thus contribute to the constitution of "ethical citizenship".

It may not be as whimsical as at first glance it seems to be. It can certainly be argued that it is likely to benefit women in concrete individual situations more effectively than the continual, and flawed, attempts to reach an understanding about what a jurisprudence of equality might mean.

As a concluding, and related, point, the feminist voice in European studies is not silenced. This book is testimony to this truth. In fact it is a louder voice than that of many marginalised interests in the new Europe. There is therefore a responsibility incumbent upon the feminist voice in Europe, and that is to speak for all the many marginalised and disempowered interests. The white working middle class European woman is still in an infinitely more empowered position that the black migrant unemployed male. Feminism, and particularly postmodern feminism, should have the confidence to present itself as a flagship for the many "silenced" in Europe; the political and economic ideology of which is founded upon the exploitation of the weak and the economically impoverished.

IAN WARD
Professor of Law,
University of Dundee,
UK

---

[70] Coombes, "Problems of Governance in the Union" in Duff, Pinder and Pryce, *Maastricht and Beyond: Building the European Union* (1994) 157–178, quotation at 177–178.

Chapter 24

GENDER AUDITING – MAKING THE COMMUNITY WORK FOR WOMEN*

Much has been said elsewhere in this volume about what the European Community has, or has not, done for women. The Single European Market was supposed to herald a period of economic growth and enhanced prosperity in Europe, yet this can hardly be said to have been maximised if half the population is systematically excluded from the opportunities which arise as part of this process. Thus, full participation by women in the economic life of the European Community can be regarded as vital to the success of the Single European Market.

This chapter presents an assessment of the record of the Community and concludes that European action to date has done little to address structural gender imbalances in the Member States. It is argued that greater attention should be paid to the potential gender impact of Community action through the instigation of a system of gender auditing. This would involve rigorous examination of proposed law and/or policy measures for their likely gender impact. Finally some potential models for such a process are identified, and questions raised about the form that such a process should take.

(i) Promoting equality: the record

Since its inception the European Community has been the source of numerous legal initiatives which have promoted sex equality in Member States and which have served as focal points for feminist action and campaigns. Article 119 EC pledges that men and women shall receive equal pay for equal work and four major Directives have been agreed by Member States in the cause of equal opportunities.[1] The Equal Treatment and the Equal Pay Directives, for example,

---

* This chapter was written by Fiona Beveridge and Sue Nott.
[1] Directive 75/117/EEC Equal Pay Directive (OJ 1975 L 45/19); Directive 76/207/EEC Equal Treatment Directive (OJ 1976 L 39/40); Directive 79/7/EEC Social Security Directive (OJ 1979 L 6/24) and Directive 86/378/EEC Occupational Social Security Directive (OJ 1986 L 225/40). See also Ellis, *EC Sex Discrimination Law* (1991).

introduced in order to give the Community a more "human" face, have achieved a great deal in improving the position of female, including pregnant, workers.[2]

Alongside these "hard law" initiatives the Community has also resorted to "soft law" to further the position of women.

Three Community Action Programmes on equal opportunities have been concluded and a fourth will be launched in 1996 with the objective of enhancing women's participation in the labour market and maximising their contribution to economic and social life. In recent months the Commission has accepted the need to ensure that equality of opportunity is addressed in all areas of Union policy.[3]

In its programme for 1995 the Commission announced the establishment of an open group of Commissioners, chaired by the President, to oversee this new "horizontal" approach to gender issues.[4] It has also announced plans for an annual report on equality between the sexes. In recent years the Community has addressed the question of equal opportunities within the European institutions.

Both the European Parliament and the Council of Ministers have called for greater participation by women in the institutions and in the decision-making process of the Community.[5]

The European Court of Justice has also been perceived as a supporter of equal opportunities. In its interpretation of Community law the Court has acknowledged that the elimination of discrimination, and discrimination on the grounds of sex in particular, forms part of the respect for human rights which is one of the basic principles of Community law.[6] The Court's application of the concepts of direct and indirect discrimination in relation to pay and working conditions have been praised as acknowledging the "constraints on women's full participation in the market, because of family responsibilities".[7] Undeniably the Court has shown itself willing on a variety of occasions to interpret Community law in a manner that is helpful to women.[8]

---

[2] In relation to pregnant workers see Case C-177/88 *Dekker* v *Stichting Vormingscentrum voor Jong Volwassenen Plus* [1990] ECR I-3941; Case C-32/93 *Webb* v *Emo Air Cargo (UK) Ltd* [1994] ECR I-3567. In relation to workers in general see the analysis of the Equal Pay and Equal Treatment Directives given in Ellis, *supra* n 1 Chapters 3 and 4. For an analysis of the Social Security Directives see Pennings, *Introduction to European Social Security Law* (1994) 263–292. See also Steiner, in this volume.

[3] See address by Jacques Santer, President of the Commission to the European Parliament on the occasion of the investiture debate of the new Commission, *Bulletin of the EU, Supp 1/95* 5, at 10. President Santer: "Particular attention will be given to equality between men and women. It is a democratic imperative . . . equality between men and women must run all the way through the Commission's activities: it is not just an employment issue".

[4] Commission programme for 1995 COM (95) 26 final at 3.2.

[5] See for example Parliament Resolution of 16 March 1995 on Equal Treatment and Equal Opportunities for men and women which *inter alia* calls on the EC institutions and the Member States as employers to set targets for the recruitment of women to positions of responsibility; Council Resolution of 27 March 1995 on Balanced Participation in Decision-Making (OJ 1995 C 168).

[6] Case 149/77 *Defrenne* v *Sabena No 3* [1978] ECR 1365 at 1385.

[7] Cullen, "The Subsidiary Woman" 16 JSWFL (1994), 407–421 at 409.

[8] See for example Case C-262/88 *Barber* v *Guardian Royal Exchange Assurance Group* [1990] ECR 1889. This is particularly so when compared with the rulings of national courts on such matters; compare, for example, the approach of the Court of Appeal in *Webb* v *EMO Cargo (UK) Ltd* [1992] 2 All ER 43 with that of the ECJ, *supra* n 2. The ECJ's interpretation of Article 119 has also been helpful with its flexible interpretation of what constitutes "pay"; Case 12/81 *Garland* v *British Rail Engineering Ltd* [1982] ECR 359; Case 170/84 *Bilka-Kaufhaus GmbH* v *Weber von Hartz* [1986] ECR 1607.

However the assumption that the Court is wholehearted in its commitment to equal opportunities should be "viewed with caution" in the view of some commentators.[9] The Court has consistently demonstrated a tendency to interpret the equality legislation in a conservative manner where a more radical ruling would throw an industry into confusion or impose considerable financial burdens.[10] It has also been keen to maintain the division between the market and the family and has emphasised that the equality Directives were not intended to achieve some degree of social engineering.

> A rigid separating line between two spheres, the market and the family, has been erected in case law and used by the Court to justify a narrow interpretation of the intended purpose of the equal treatment Directives. The ECJ argues that the equal treatment Directives are not designed to alter the division of labour of couples in private households or to take into account family obligations of employees.[11]

Much EC legislation in the social field is meant to benefit workers and hence it emphasises the divide between paid and unpaid work. The ECJ has been unwilling to bridge that divide and interpret a measure, such as Social Security Directive 79/7/EEC, as extending to circumstances where a woman has interrupted her employment in order to care for her family; ruling instead that this decision removes her from the working population and so places her beyond the scope of the Directive.[12]

Although in certain respects therefore the Community would appear to support the cause of equal opportunities,[13] its actions have had little impact on the actual situation of women. It is clear that women continue to lag behind men when rates of pay are compared across the Community,[14] and that women are disproportionately represented amongst the low-paid. Fundamental gender divisions

---

[9] Fenwick and Hervey, "Sex Equality in the Single Market: New Directions for the European Court of Justice" 32 CMLRev (1995), 443–470 at 469.

[10] See, for example, Case 179/88 Hertz v Dansk Arbejdsgiverforening acting for Aldi Marked KS [1990] ECR I-3979, where the ECJ declined to extend the protection from dismissal accorded pregnant workers beyond the period of maternity leave. It has been suggested that part of the explanation for this may have been the costs which employers might have incurred as a consequence; Barber, supra n 8.

[11] Scheiwe, "EC Law's Unequal Treatment of the Family" 3 Social and Legal Studies (1994), 243–265 at 261. See also Barnard, in this volume.

[12] Case C-31/90 Johnson v Chief Adjudication Officer [1991] ECR I-3723. Cf. Case 150/85 Drake v Chief Adjudication Officer [1986] ECR 1995, and Ellis, supra n 1 at 183.

[13] Rubenstein, "Beyond the Whinge" 11 Oxford Journal of Legal Studies (1991), 254–263.

[14] Indeed, research commissioned by the Equal Opportunities Commission concludes that in Britain four million women – one third of all female workers – are low-paid. The 1994 New Earnings Survey demonstrates that in the United Kingdom women earn substantially less than men. Women's average hourly earnings were 79.5% of men's in April 1995. When average weekly earnings are compared, and items such as overtime taken into account, women are found to earn only 72.25% of men's earnings. This is because, compared with men, women work little overtime and their overall working week is shorter. Women's earnings are at the lower end of the earnings scale with 46.6% of women earning less than £200 per week as compared with 21.4% of men. These trends in the United Kingdom are not unique and are repeated across Europe. Indeed in some Member States there is even greater disparity between the earnings of men and women. In Luxembourg, for example, women manual workers earn only 65% of men's pay whilst in Ireland this increases slightly to 68%. There is not a single Member State where parity exists between male and female manual workers. The narrowest gap is to be found in Italy at 83%.

in the labour market remain largely unchallenged and women are severely affected by social exclusion throughout the Member States.

A variety of factors contribute toward the economic imbalance between the sexes. The disproportionate number of female part-time workers is one. In 1989 one in eight workers in the Community worked part-time but few of these workers were men.[15] In the United Kingdom, for example, women constitute 84% of the part-time workforce and research has shown that their hourly earnings are significantly lower than the hourly rates of full-time male and female employees.[16]

Indeed additional payments which boost the earnings of full-time employees, such as overtime and premia payments, may not be readily available to part-time employees and attempts to demonstrate that this is contrary to Community law have failed.

In *Stadt Lengerich* v *Helmig*[17] the Court rejected the claim that it was discrimination contrary to Article 119 to pay overtime rates to part-timers only where normal working hours for full-time workers are exceeded.

Apart from part-time work, occupational segregation can also have far-reaching effects on the level of earnings. It is a frequently observed fact that women tend to be employed in certain occupations and "women's work" is on the whole less well-paid than men's. Research conducted on the behalf of the Equal Opportunities Commission concluded that gender segregation was associated with low pay.[18] Surveys conducted in the United Kingdom show that women are more likely to be employed in service industries such as education, health and hotel work than construction, manufacturing or transport. The same pattern is repeated throughout Europe.[19]

Unemployment is another phenomenon which affects men and women differently. Whilst unemployment rates vary from one Member State to another, women constituted over half the total of unemployed in all but two Member States.[20] This trend is repeated in the figures for the long-term unemployed.

> In 1988, 51% of the Community's long-term unemployed were women. Since the female workforce is smaller than the male one it is clear that women are badly affected by long-term unemployment.[21]

Finally, although unemployment and low pay adversely affect female workers it should be recalled that for all the increases in the number of women who are economically active, a substantial proportion of women do not work for some period in their lives and are then forced to depend on either a partner or the State for support.[22] The activity rate for men reaches a peak when they are 25

---

[15] Eurostat, *Europe in Figures*, 117.
[16] *New Earnings Survey, supra* n 14 Part F.
[17] Case C-399/92 [1994] ECR I-5727.
[18] Millward, *Targeting Potential Discrimination* (1995).
[19] Blau and Ferber, "Women's Work, Women's Lives: A Comparative Economic Perspective", in Kahne and Giele (eds), *Women's Work and Women's Lives* (1992) at 32–35.
[20] These were Ireland and the UK. See Eurostat, *Europe in Figures*, 122.
[21] *Ibid* 123.
[22] See Everson, in this volume.

and remains high until 50. In contrast the activity rate for women peaks between 20 and 24. After that age it drops because of marriage and family commitments.[23]

The reasons for the continuing disparity between the economic situation of men and women, despite the introduction of legal provisions designed to secure positive gains for women, are undoubtedly complex and deeply-rooted in the structures and institutions of society and culture. Women's work patterns, their role in childcare and elder care and the segregated nature of the labour market are implicated.[24] Women are more likely than men to take career breaks or work part-time with adverse consequences for earnings, for occupational benefits and for State benefits. Women work part-time because they are often in the position when they have to combine paid work with unpaid work in the home caring for children, elderly relatives or family members with disabilities. Women with caring responsibilities are also more likely to engage in atypical work such as home working, often very poorly paid and often structured as self-employment so that the burden of social insurance arrangements falls on the workers. Women tend still to be segregated in employment into sectors of the labour market which are low paid by comparison to those where men predominate[25] and, even where men and women are employed in equal numbers or women predominate, men still tend to occupy the top posts and hence enjoy superior earning power.[26] Women experience higher rates of unemployment. It seems that these factors are compounded by women's low expectations in relation to education, training and promotion.

It is against this picture of structural inequality that the Community's record must surely be assessed. Quite clearly the positive contributions made by the Community to the cause of equality identified at the beginning of this chapter are being outweighed by other more negative influences. Existing equal opportunities legislation would appear to be inadequate to tackle the structural causes of inequality in the labour market.[27] Few positive moves have been made to re-define work and the workplace in order to allow women to combine paid work more easily with their domestic responsibilities or indeed to shift some of the caring burden from them to men. Indeed the Court made it plain in the *Hofmann* case[28] that the Equal Treatment Directive was "not designed to settle questions concerned with the organization of the family, or to alter the division of responsibility between parents".[29] The Recommendation on Childcare[30],

---

[23] Eurostat, *supra* n 20 at 108.

[24] For an account of the relationship between women and wealth see Morris and Nott, *All My Worldly Goods* (1995).

[25] Blau and Ferber, *supra* n 19 at 32–35.

[26] Equal Opportunities Commission, *Women and Men in Britain* 1993, 29. In 1993, for example, 80% of primary school teachers were women but less than half of primary school headteachers were women.

[27] As Ellis states, it embodies a notion of equality that allows women to aspire to male patterns of work and to seek male jobs and opportunities. Ellis, *supra* n 1 at 207.

[28] Case 184/83 *Hofmann* v *Barmer Ersatzkasse* [1984] ECR 3047.

[29] *Ibid* 3075.

[30] OJ 1991 C 129.

though full of worthy sentiments, carries little legal weight. Directives on
parental leave and atypical work are still not in place due to opposition on the
part of some Member States.

More generally it might be said that so long as questions such as caring for
children and the elderly are categorised as "social" rather than "economic"
activities, they will be seen as secondary to the main business of the Community
which is the furtherance of the Single Market.[31] Yet if improving the standard of
living is one of the goals of the Community and wealth creation is the principal
objective of the Single European Market, little of that prosperity has found its
way into the hands of women. 1992 may well have marked the opening up of
new opportunities, but these have not, on the whole, been opportunities for
women.

(ii) Women in the Community institutions

Indeed it is not only the law's content that may prove inimical to equal opportunities but the Community institutions themselves. Despite a commitment to
openness, the law-making/decision-taking process within the Community
revolves round a system of negotiation, compromise and lobbying which is
far from transparent and which can be assumed to operate in the interests of
powerful organized interest groups rather than being "woman-friendly".

The central role played by the Council of Ministers in the adoption of legislation provides a direct conduit from the male-dominated state apparatus of the
Member States to the heart of the European power structure.

Well-organized, strong interest groups (business associations, economic interest groups, the professions) already in a position of power and with access to
resources are best placed to utilise the European institutions to further their
existing advantage.[32]

Against this background it may be very difficult for women's voices to be
heard in the appropriate place and at the right times; for women's groups and
organizations to make a significant contribution to policy formulation. Moreover, any measure which starts off with the potential to benefit women may be
progressively "watered down" in the course of the lengthy and complex process
by which legislation is adopted.[33]

It can be argued that, as a result of such processes, measures which are implemented represent the Community's conception of what is in the best interests
of women rather than women's own views on this topic. A view has prevailed
that some, indeed any, law is better than no law and, as a result, compromise
"solutions" have been accepted even when the resultant legislation works

---

[31] Shaw, "Twintrack Social Europe – the Inside Track" in O'Keeffe and Twomey, *Legal Issues of the
Maastricht Treaty* (1994) 295. See Barnard, Flynn, and Hervey, in this volume.
[32] See Flynn, in this volume.
[33] Pedlar, "ETUC and the Pregnant Women" in Pedlar and Van Schendelen, *Lobbying the European
Union* (1994) 241.

against women's interests. The Pregnant Workers Directive, for example, was passed as a health and safety measure since this was the only way in which the relevant majorities might be secured. The negative perception this gives of pregnancy, with its emphasis on safeguarding the well-being of the mother-to-be and the foetus, may work against those who advocate a woman's right to choose how she conducts herself in the course of her pregnancy.[34]

If women achieve a place at the heart of the decision-making process they may still face dilemmas not experienced by their male counterparts. The European Parliament, from the time when it was directly elected, has always had a substantial female membership as compared with national legislatures though there is no parity between male and female members.[35] Female MEPs must, however, in order to be elected, appeal to both male and female voters and hence their commitment to advancing women's interests must be tempered by political expediency. Once elected, female MEPs will become members of one or more of the specialised standing committees. Here a tendency has been identified for women MEPs to be selected as members of those committees which match what are seen as women's traditional concerns – for example education, health and welfare.[36] Committees dealing with more technical issues such as transport and economic and monetary affairs have a lower female membership. Indeed to take an interest in women's issues has been seen as running the risk of being marginalised within the European Parliament. Female MEPs are, therefore, faced with a dilemma. If they wish to succeed politically they should perhaps not choose to concentrate on women's issues. If, however, they follow this advice, the likelihood is that matters which are of particular importance to women will be ignored since male MEPs show little inclination to take up such causes.

The Women's Rights Committee is one of the specialised standing committees of the European Parliament.[37] This particular Committee came into being in 1979 as an *ad hoc* committee to consider matters concerning the situation of women in Europe. Although it eventually became a permanent Committee, there was a difference of opinion at the time over the wisdom of such a development. Some female MEPs felt that the Committee's existence would marginalise women's issues and allow others to ignore them. The contrary view and the one which prevailed was that the Committee represented a way of keeping women's issues to the fore of the European Parliament's agenda.[38]

Currently the Women's Rights Committee has a membership of 30 MEPs

---

[34] See Fenwick, in this volume.

[35] After the 1994 European elections female MEPs constitute over 25% of the total membership (145 of the 567 MEPs) as compared with 18% for the Parliament elected in 1989. See Flynn, in this volume.

[36] Vallance, "Do Women Make a Difference? The Impact of Women MEPs on Community Equality Policy" in Buckley and Anderson, *Women, Equality and Europe* (1988) 126 at 130. See also *Women of Europe Newsletter* No 43 April 1994.

[37] For an account of the role of the specialised committees of the European Parliament see Jacobs, Corbett and Shackleton, *The European Parliament* (1992) chapter 7.

[38] Vallance, *supra* n 36.

most, but not all, of whom are women and, in common with other specialised committees, it has a number of tasks to perform; giving reports and opinions on formal legislative proposals from the Commission or Council; responding to resolutions from individual MEPs; and drawing up reports on its own initiative on a subject of its own choosing (though permission must be sought).

In practice since the Women's Rights Committee does not carry a heavy legislative load, it spends a sizeable proportion of its time on own initiative reports.

The question then arises of whether this Committee can effectively represent women's interests in the Community. There are some drawbacks. First the Committee may comment only on those legislative proposals allocated to it in the organization of Parliamentary business. A measure that has obvious repercussions for women will not necessarily be referred to the Women's Committee. When the Pregnant Workers Directive was in preparation, for example, that was considered by the Social Affairs Committee and the Women's Rights Committee was simply asked for an opinion.[39] The Women's Rights Committee is therefore commenting on only a fraction of what is relevant to women.

Second there is no guarantee that this Committee's responses to legislative proposals will be acted upon and incorporated into any legislative measure and this indeed was the case with the Pregnant Workers Directive.[40]

Third the politics of the European Parliament, and of the Community in general, hamstring the Committee. Political compromise dictates what can be achieved and hence the policies that emerge will not always be in women's best interests. In any case, by the time that proposals fall to be considered by parliamentary committees in the European law-making process the shape or tenor of the measure may already be determined. It would be unrealistic then to expect too much of the Women's Rights Committee.

What emerges from this review of the policies, legislation and institutions of the Community is an organization that is still the source of many negative measures that adversely affect women and ignore their experiences. There are always limits to what the law can achieve by adopting pro-women laws which always run the danger of reinforcing the stereotypes that many women wish to challenge. To adopt measures on equal pay and equal treatment is helpful but it is a piecemeal approach to what is a systematic vice – namely discrimination against women. Legislation has the additional disadvantage of being an insecure remedy to a perceived problem since it is always capable of repeal. What is required is a much broader-based approach.

---

[39] This is unsatisfactory because the committee with primary responsibility for considering a proposal can ignore the recommendations of any committee that is simply asked to give an opinion. See Jacobs, Corbett and Shackleton, *supra* n 37 at 113.

[40] See Pedlar (1994), *supra* n 33; and Beveridge and Nott, "Women, Wealth and the Single Market"; Paper presented to ESRC/COST A7 Conference "The Evolution of Rules for a Single European Market", September 1994, reproduced in "Making Ourselves Heard", Working Paper No 3, Feminist Legal Research Unit, Faculty of Law, University of Liverpool. The Parliament had little impact overall on the final version of this Directive.

(iii) Gender auditing

It is very apparent that the decisions in cases such as *Barber*[41] or *Habermann-Beltermann*[42] or the contents of the Equality Directives are of importance to women. It is also possible to appreciate and predict the positive and the adverse consequences that those policies may produce for women. Yet specifically gender-friendly legislation represents only a fraction of the law-making/decision-taking that occurs in the Community.

It is certainly possible, and perhaps very likely, that what on the surface appears as gender-neutral decision-making may have as many adverse consequences for women as those decisions that specifically concern them. Transportation policy, for example, may place a great deal of emphasis on the use of the motor car as opposed to public transport. At first sight a policy of this nature works neither to the advantage of men nor women. In practice this is not so. Since women have less disposable income than men they are more likely to depend on public transport and, therefore, any policy which reduces the availability of public transport affects them disproportionately. If they own a car then measures that make it more expensive to run will also affect them disproportionately, claiming a larger proportion of their (typically smaller) disposable income.

Feminist theory insists on the importance of questioning *all* laws and asking the "woman question" of all of them. The "woman question" seeks to discover the degree to which legal rules and the legal system of which they are part take account of women's experiences.[43] If the law fails to address those experiences or does so in a negative manner then women, either some or all, will suffer and those whose interests the law does address (that is men, though not necessarily all men) will gain. The assumption behind the "woman question" and feminist jurisprudence in general is that the law serves male interests and, until this fundamental issue is tackled, women will have little to gain from the law and the pressure to abandon law altogether as an agent for change may increase.[44] The problem is whether it is possible to devise a method of expanding the law's perspective beyond its essentially male stance. Moreover is it possible, and indeed justifiable, to devise a procedure for predicting the adverse consequences that all decision-taking and policy-making may have on women?

A process of gender auditing, since this is what such a procedure would involve, is intended to demonstrate whether women would benefit to the same degree as men from a particular policy and if not whether steps could be taken to address this. This is not to say that *if* a particular policy can be shown to prejudice women, but not men, it cannot be acted upon. Rather if it were vital that a particular policy be pursued and little could be done to protect women

---

[41] C-262/88 *Barber, supra* n 8.
[42] Case C-421/92 *Habermann-Beltermann v Arbeiterwohlfahrt* [1994] ECR I-1657.
[43] See, for example, Bartlett, "Feminist Legal Methods" 103 *Harvard Law Review* (1990), 829. On the "maleness" of laws and legal systems see MacKinnon, *Toward a Feminist Theory of the State* (1989).
[44] Smart, *Feminism and the Power of Law* (1989).

from its adverse consequences then it might proceed but with the clear understanding that it was prejudicing women. Compensatory measures might in such circumstances be viewed as appropriate.

The term "gender auditing" may have an alarming ring to those who have not encountered the expression. It may be perceived as political correctness carried to the extreme with only those policies or decisions which work to women's advantage being allowed to stand. Further reflection will make it plain that, far from representing an innovation, gender auditing is simply a way of measuring social impact and this is already an accepted practice in other contexts. Policies and decisions are already reviewed in certain circumstances in order to determine their impact on the environment, on small and medium-sized enterprises or on women. The objective is to examine how such a process might become a systematic and effective part of law-making in the Community.

Examples of social auditing exist both at a Community and at a national level. Many of the procedures which do exist (for example environment impact assessment (EIA)) concentrate on a single issue and how policy-making and decision-taking will affect that specific issue. If women are to be the target of an analogous auditing procedure then some justification has to be given for singling women out, since they are not the sole "victims" of social exclusion. The disabled, the elderly and ethnic minorities are only some of the groups that could claim that their concerns are neglected. One justification for focusing on gender, at least to begin with, arises from the central role played by gender in social exclusion generally. Studies of groups such as the elderly and the disabled show that the women in these groups suffer disproportionately; that they are doubly disadvantaged. Tackling gender discrimination is therefore a vital part of tackling many other forms of discrimination.

However in proposing a system of gender auditing the intention is not to suggest that this is the only "social exclusion" factor worthy of attention. A multi-factored "social audit" might be justified. The focus on gender in this chapter should therefore be understood as a means to give clear direction to a question which may be asked generally of the European Community: who benefits from Community action?

(iv) The search for models

Both the proposal to adopt gender auditing and the precise form such a process might take require further exploration. Whilst it is relatively easy to describe the essential reasoning behind adopting gender auditing as a stage in the policy-making and decision-taking process it is clear that such a process raises questions about the accountability, openness and democratic arrangements of the Community and national institutions, since law-making is fundamental to the constitutional arrangements of nation States and supra-national organizations. An attempt must be made to find a theoretical justification for the process of gender auditing as well as practical precedents. Consideration must be given to the enforcement of such a procedure (would a measure be regarded as a nullity if a full gender audit had not been carried out?) and to the comparability of such a process with the notion of "shared" competences[45] and subsidiarity.

Questions arise regarding the form that such a process might take – who will be consulted; at what stage in the process; by whom; what information will be generated; to whom will this information be available and to what uses will it be put? Perhaps the most important question of all is what types of measures will be regarded as "candidates" for gender auditing?

Potential problems already emerge. Can such a process be designed so that it will remain reflective of, and responsive to, the real position of women rather than some sort of institutionalised "state feminism"? Finally what is it that such a process might be expected to achieve and would it work? If laws and institutions are "inherently" male as sometimes suggested, can the inclusion of a "gender audit" process alter this? In examining the precedents for social auditing which already exist, answers must be sought to these questions. Three existing examples of social auditing processes are examined below: environmental impact assessment in the EC, small and medium enterprises in the EC and Policy Action and Fair Treatment (PAFT) in Northern Ireland.

(a) Environmental impact assessment

Environmental impact assessment (EIA) originated in the United States and then spread to Europe where, as a consequence of Directive 85/337/EEC[46], Member States of the European Community are now required to employ the procedure. Its introduction via the Community met with some resistance since it was regarded as yet more bureaucracy requiring answers to questions which were already being addressed in the development control process. EIA is not required in relation to all proposed developments, merely those projects "likely to have significant effects on the environment by virtue, *inter alia*, of their nature, size or location".[47] Its purpose is to measure the potential impact a major development may have on the environment; that is on flora, fauna, human beings, water quality, air quality, landscape and heritage. EIA is a stage in the decision-making process that allows damage to be identified and, if possible, avoiding action to be taken. It is both an information-gathering exercise and a basis for negotiation between the developer and the decision maker. An "adverse" EIA does not automatically mean that a development will be halted, though it might be. Instead it allows problems to be identified ahead of work commencing on a project and alternatives considered and possible compromises reached.

As currently utilised EIA is a very focused process since it deals with specific

---

[45] That is, competences shared between the Community institutions and the Member States.
[46] Directive 85/337/EEC on the assessment of the effects of certain public and private projects on the environment.
[47] *Ibid* Article 2.

projects. Within the European Community new legislation was proposed in November 1992 to complement EIA with strategic environmental assessment (SEA).[48] SEA has been defined as:

> the formalised, systematic and comprehensive process of evaluating the environmental impacts of a policy, plan or programme and its alternatives, including the preparation of a written report on the findings of that evaluation, and using the findings in publicly accountable decision-making.[49]

The draft Directive proposed that policies, programmes and plans concerned with issues such as land use, agriculture, transport or waste would be assessed for their impact on the environment, for instance, on flora, fauna or landscape. This SEA would be carried out by the body instigating the policy, programme or plan and an environmental authority would be established to advise on the adequacy of the assessment. In other words, SEA extends the procedure of evaluating environmental impact beyond specific projects to strategic issues.[50] Government would determine its *policy* on a question such as transport or waste management and specific *plans* would then be agreed for achieving these policy objectives, culminating eventually in a *programme* of projects for building specific roads or establishing waste disposal sites. Whereas EIA affects only the particular project, SEA allows an evaluation to be made of the policy, planning and programme stages for their impact on the environment.

The wholesale introduction of SEA into the EC has met with opposition. There were arguments over the stage at which SEA should be carried out, since it is not always easy to determine when something becomes policy; in addition, policies, plans and programmes are modified over time. Policy-making is also seen as a matter of political judgment. Hence the policies of a political party that favours deregulation, privatisation and a mixed economy may be very different from those of a party which favours public ownership and State intervention in the economy. The interaction between the agencies which carry out SEAs and the political party in power is, therefore, seen as fraught with potential disagreements.

(b) Small and medium enterprises in the EC

The Small and Medium Enterprise Task Force was established in 1986 and is charged *inter alia* with monitoring the Fiche de "Impact" system by which all Commission proposals in the EC must be accompanied by an assessment of their likely impact on Community businesses, especially small and medium enterprises.

Article 130 EC provides that the Community and the Member States "shall

---

[48] Proposal for a directive on the environmental assessment of actions approved during the planning process (Document XI/745/92).

[49] Glasson, Therivel and Chadwick, *Introduction to Environmental Impact Assessment* (1994) 300.

[50] SEA is employed in the USA, most notably in California, and in Europe in countries such as the Netherlands and even, to a very limited extent, the United Kingdom: *ibid* 305.

ensure that the conditions necessary for the competitiveness of the Community's industry exist" and shall aim their action at *inter alia* "encouraging an environment favourable to initiative and to the development of undertakings throughout the Community, particularly small and medium-sized undertakings".

Article 130F, dealing with Research and Technological Development, provides that to strengthen the scientific and technological basis of European industry the Community will encourage undertakings, including small and medium-sized undertakings (SMEs), in their research and technological development activity; support their efforts to co-operate with one another, especially where these aim to enable undertakings to develop the potential of the internal market. Specifically mentioned are the opening up of public contracts, the definition of common standards and the removal of legal and fiscal barriers.

In 1992 the Council adopted a Resolution on administrative simplification for enterprises, especially small and medium-sized enterprises[51] which built on a number of previous resolutions, decisions and recommendations and which strengthened the "consultation" process in relation to the impact of measures on small and medium enterprises. The Commission was invited to prepare impact assessments on all proposals which might give rise to substantial impacts on SMEs[52] while the Council undertook to take full account of the Commission's impact assessments (and avoid the imposition of unjustified burdens on enterprises) and to discuss regularly the effectiveness of this impact assessment system.[53]

---

[51] 92/C 331/02 (OJ (1992 C 331/3).

[52] *Ibid* para 4 reads: 4. Invites the Commission:

(a) to ensure that full account is taken of the costs and benefits to enterprises by preparing an impact assessment on all Commission proposals which may give rise to a substantial burden for enterprises;

(b) to ensure:

- the appropriate publication in the Official Journal of the European Communities of a list of those proposals on which an impact assessment is to be completed and for a reference to be made to the assessment when the proposal is published in the Official Journal:
- that the impact assessments will be made available to interested parties upon request;
- that impact assessments are revised when substantial amendments to proposals are accepted by the Commission, in the context of the inter-institutional legislative process;

(c) to indicate at the earliest possible time, before any measure which was not included in the Commission's work programme is proposed, whether that proposal will be the subject of an impact assessment;

(d) to collect information on the impact on enterprises of existing Community legislation in the light of experience gained from implementation, and to formulate proposals to reduce the burden to a minimum consistent with achieving the legislative objectives;

(e) to produce a report every three years on administrative simplification in the Commission and in Member States; and

(f) to ensure that an impact assessment is available whenever the Council acts on Commission proposals which may give rise to a substantial burden for enterprises.

[53] *Ibid* para 5 reads: Undertakes:

(a) to continue to take full account of the Commission's impact assessments in discussions of legislative proposals in the Council;

(b) to indicate to the Commission any other legislative proposals on which it thinks there should be an impact assessment, as soon as possible after the publication of the information outlined in 3(c);

(c) to discuss the effectiveness of the impact assessment system regularly;

(d) to avoid all unjustified burden on enterprises in its decisions on the Commission's proposals . . . .

Para 6 invites the Member States to co-operate in this process, to encourage the participation of business organizations in the assessments of potential costs and to take the impact on enterprises into account when implementing and enforcing Community law.

DGXXIII for Enterprise Policy, Distributive Trades, Tourism and Co-operatives is principally concerned with the promotion of SME development. The Commission sees its role in this area as being two-fold: both to create a favourable administrative, legal, cultural and social environment within Europe and to provide practical assistance to small and medium enterprises wishing to develop new products/markets.[54]

One consequence of the focus in Community policy on the prospects of small and medium enterprises was the emergence of increasing quantities of information, both from EC and private sources. In 1993 the Commission attempted to deal with this by creating a research organization – the European Observatory for Small and Medium-Sized Enterprises. Its membership consists of research organizations with expertise in studying SMEs drawn from individual Member States. The task assigned to the Observatory is in part a quantitative one since it analyses statistics relating to SMEs which are provided by organizations such as Eurostat. The purpose behind this is to measure the economic well-being and financial future of SMEs, since they constitute the majority of business enterprises within the Community. If enterprises such as these are not prospering, then this threatens economic growth within the Union. Therefore the second aspect of the Observatory's business is to recommend policy changes to the Commission.

The initiatives taken in relation to SMEs are clearly very different from EIA or SEA. Instead of having an additional stage in the decision-making process, agencies have been charged with promoting the economic well-being of SMEs. Those agencies assess any policies which are likely to produce substantial burdens for SMEs, rather than concentrating on measures that specifically apply to them. The fact that the Community is willing to treat SMEs in so favourable a fashion is perhaps yet another example of the emphasis the Community places on the market and the economic sphere. In theory there seems to be no reason why women could not be treated in a similar fashion with policies being examined for their adverse impact on women's ability to compete in the market and attain a greater degree of financial equality with men. Perhaps this would too closely resemble "social engineering" and meet with the Community's often repeated claim that it is not part of its business to interfere in the private sphere of the family and relations between men and women?[55]

(c) Policy action and fair treatment

A precedent does exist for the review of policies in order to ensure that they observe certain values/rights and that is Policy Appraisal and Fair Treatment (PAFT). PAFT is an initiative launched in Northern Ireland by the Northern

---

[54] An example of the latter is that financial assistance is available for projects in which groups of SMEs pool their resources to develop internationally competitive products. European Information Centres aim to provide advice to SMEs, matching organizations seeking and offering specialist financial, commercial or technical resources.

[55] See Barnard, and O'Leary, in this volume.

Ireland Office. It requires government departments and agencies in the Province to consider how any new policy or revision of existing policy affects certain groups in society.[56] These groups include people of different religious beliefs or political opinions, men and women, people of different ethnic groups and people of differing sexual orientation. In particular the question must be asked whether the policy under consideration leads to direct or indirect discrimination or differential impact directed against one of these groups. If this is the case and the policy would be unlawful, unjustifiable or undesirable then alternatives can be considered if this should prove appropriate.

PAFT appears to be a social audit looking at the potential impact of policies and actively attempting to promote equal opportunities. It is, however, a process which is in its infancy and little evidence exists as to its effectiveness. In principle it demonstrates that an audit can be built into the policy-making/decision-taking process with the capacity to predict differential impact. However there are dangers. Because it is a process conceived of by government and implemented by civil servants, there is a risk that it may prove no more than a paper exercise. One proposal referred to in the first annual report on PAFT[57] – the White Paper "Security, Equality, Choice: the Future for Pensions"[58] would appear to have obvious gender consequences but was deemed to have "[n]o differential impact, within the PAFT principles".[59] This may be attributable to the second weakness with PAFT. If only examples of direct and indirect discrimination or disproportionate impact are sought, then PAFT may fail to have any impact on structural inequalities that disadvantage vulnerable groups such as women. Long experience of the Sex Discrimination Act 1975 has shown that direct and indirect discrimination promote not substantive equal opportunities but formal equality. Hence, although PAFT does provide a model for social auditing worthy of further investigation, the early signs are that considerable attention must be paid to the questions for which answers are sought in any such audit.

(v) A scheme for a gender audit

The examination of these precedents for social impact assessment has clearly demonstrated a number of options for a prospective gender audit. They range from a full-blown policy audit to the more politically acceptable option of a fact-finding exercise.

Whilst the precise form that a gender audit might take is contentious, the case for such a procedure is strong. If women are to achieve substantive, as

---

[56] PAFT aims "to ensure that, in practice, issues of equality and equity condition policy-making and action in all spheres and at all levels of Government activity, whether in regulatory and administrative functions or in the delivery of services to the public" (Central Community Relations Unit, *Policy Appraisal and Fair Treatment Annual Report 1994*, 6).
[57] *Ibid.*
[58] HMSO 1994.
[59] *Supra* n 56 at 74–75.

opposed to purely formal, equality there has to be some way of predicting the potential impact of policy-making and decision-taking on women.

As this chapter has pointed out, powerful market forces are at work which can rob even the most "women-friendly" policies of their full impact. Indeed the Community and the laws which are part of it with their emphasis on rights and their promotion of economic initiatives at the expense of social policies have an overwhelmingly male ethos. To dilute that maleness and to allow women to share equally in the financial benefits of the single market requires an impartial assessment of how women will be affected by particular policies whilst they are in the planning stage.

FIONA BEVERIDGE
Lecturer in Law,
Feminist Legal Research Unit,
University of Liverpool,
UK

SUE NOTT
Senior Lecturer in Law,
Feminist Legal Research Unit,
University of Liverpool.
UK

Chapter 25

THE FUTURE FOR SEX EQUALITY LAW IN THE EUROPEAN UNION*

(i) Introduction

This final chapter of the book aims to explore some future prospects for sex equality law in the European Community and Union. The aim of the chapter is to show that it would be possible to reconceptualise the concept of sex equality in the context of EC law, and to redraw its scope, even within its current framework. I contend that the reconceptualisation I propose (essentially from a unified to a differentiated approach) is also *desirable*, as it would allow the concept of sex equality in the EC context to become less fixed and confined, in particular by the market ideology of EC law, and therefore more beneficial to women.[1]

EC sex equality law is defined and confined by a particular ideology. This ideology has been variously expressed[2]: I use as a shorthand the phrase "market ideology". The entire system of the EC (and the EU[3]) is historically founded upon the economic goal of the creation and expansion of the single internal

---

* This chapter was written by Tamara K. Hervey. She is extremely grateful to Jo Shaw, Catherine Barnard, Helen Fenwick, Neil Duxbury and David O'Keeffe for their comments on earlier drafts of this chapter.

[1] It is not the purpose of this chapter to ask whether EC law (or indeed any legal system) is an appropriate mechanism for promoting sex equality. The chapter begins from the position, at least implicit in EC law, and in particular in the jurisprudence of the European Court of Justice, (see, for instance Case 43/75 *Defrenne No 2* [1976] ECR 455 para 15) that the function of (sex) equality provisions is to improve the position of those in the under-privileged or excluded group, that is, women.

[2] See Treaty of Rome, preamble, and Articles 1–3. See also Fenwick and Hervey, "Sex Equality in the Single Market: New Directions for the European Court of Justice" 32 CMLRev (1995), 443–470 at 448; Nielsen and Szyszczak, *The Social Dimension of the European Community* (1993), 15–18; Hoskyns, "Women, European Law and Transnational Politics" 14 IntJSocLaw (1986), 299–315. See also, in a different context, Szyszczak, "Race Discrimination: the Limits of Market Equality" in Hepple and Szyszczak, *Discrimination: The Limits of Law* (1992) 125–147.

[3] Although it would perhaps be arguable that the move towards European union is based on political, rather than economic, goals of European integration.

market, by virtue of the free play of market forces unfettered by discrimination on grounds of nationality, as a means to European economic (and perhaps ultimately political) union. The economic basis of the Community legal system tends to lead to the conceptualisation of social goals as adjuncts to, or byproducts of, market goals and economic integration.[4] Such a conceptualisation is as applicable to sex equality provisions as to other measures of Community social policy. The result is an apparently inherent limitation of the sex equality provisions.[5] The limitation is undesirable, because it tends to give a privileged position to "market interests" (however these are formulated), at the expense of other interests, for instance "social interests" (in this context, the interests of women).

The aim of this chapter is to suggest that, with some reconceptualisation of the function of the EC sex equality provisions, it would be possible profitably to redraw the boundaries of sex equality law in the EC (and EU) context. This reconceptualisation might find expression in legislative measures.[6] However, given the current institutional balance of the EC, and in particular the almost total paralysis of the social affairs Council[7], I am assuming that redefining EC sex equality law would be a task for the Court of Justice.

A reconceptualisation along the lines I suggest would definitely entail a certain destabilising of the dominant ideology of market forces mentioned above. On the other hand, the move from European community towards European union[8] might be considered as providing the perfect opportunity to put that ideology into question.[9] In this respect, this chapter resonates with those of Everson, McGlynn, Shaw and Ward in this volume, in that it suggests that the new European Union concepts, in particular that of citizenship, might form the foundation-stones of a new socio-political identity (and ideology) for the European Union. However, the scope of this chapter is rather limited: its focus is the possible refinement or development of the *law* on sex equality in the EU, with a view to expanding its social (as opposed to economic) foundations, thereby

---

[4] See Fenwick and Hervey, *supra* n 2; Nielsen and Szyszczak, *supra* n 2; Hoskyns, *supra* n 2; Szyszczak, *supra* n 2; Shaw, "Twin Track Europe – The Inside Track" in O'Keeffe and Twomey, *Legal Issues of the Maastricht Treaty* (1994) 295–311 at 296–297.

[5] I have explored this limitation, and in particular its effect upon the jurisprudence of the Court of Justice in interpreting and applying EC sex equality provisions, elsewhere. See Fenwick and Hervey, *supra* n 2.

[6] For instance, the Commission proposal on the Reconciliation of Professional and Family Life, which is now the subject of negotiation by the social partners; Council Recommendation on Child Care (OJ 1992 L 123/16).

[7] See Gold, "Overview of the social dimension" in Gold, *The Social Dimension: Employment Policy in the European Community* (1993) 16; Grahl and Teague, *1992 – The Big Market* (1990) 206–210; Nielsen and Szyszczak, *supra* n 2 at 44; Wise and Gibb, *Single Market to Social Europe* (1993) 145–146. The reluctance of the Commission to pursue an innovative legislative programme is also relevant. See White Paper on Social Policy COM(94) 333 13; Commission's Programme for 1994 Bull Supp 1/94 20; see for example *Europe* No 6472 2/3 May 1995; FT 12/13 April 1995; *Agence Europe*, 17 November 1994.

[8] Terms for stages in European integration, see Article A TEU ". . . a new stage in the process of creating an ever closer union among the peoples of Europe".

[9] But see Weiler, "Fin-de-Siècle Europe" in Dehousse, *Europe After Maastricht: An Ever Closer Union?* (1994) 203–216 at 213.

destabilising the economic assumptions which at present still underpin that law, so as to benefit women in the EU.[10]

(ii) Redrawing the scope of EC law on sex equality

Sex equality in EC law is at present limited to the areas of employment and some aspects of social security.[11] The Court has already done a great deal to expand that limited scope. The most well-known example of this is probably the extension of "pay" in the sense of Article 119 into the area of occupational pension entitlements. The Court's ruling concerning the scope of Article 119 in the *Beune* case[12] is only the most recent in a long line of case law.

However, the limits which the Court has drawn on the scope of EC sex equality law are open to criticism. For example, the ruling in *Jackson and Cresswell*[13] excluding income support from the scope of Directive 79/7/EEC is difficult to justify from a perspective of disadvantage. The "directly and effectively linked" test which the Court has developed in construing the scope of the Directive seems surprisingly narrow and legalistic.[14] The application of the test resulted in discrimination against women in the provision of social security benefits essentially on the grounds that the benefits in question are not sufficiently closely linked to "unemployment". Other examples of the Court's narrow approach may be found in *Smithson* and *Graham*.[15] The narrowing of the scope of the Directive by the Court in these cases had the effect of perpetuating women's disadvantage in the structure of social security provision.[16]

Even in the social security field[17], and far more so in the employment field,

---

[10] It should be made clear that that focus upon the existing EC sex equality measures is not intended to imply that these measures are sufficient in terms of the broader political move towards genuine or substantive equality for women in the EC. Legal strategies alone are insufficient to effect adequate equality for women with men in the European Union. Legal strategies (and litigation in particular) can only be seen as part of a broader political strategy for equality. See, for example, Fredman, "European Community Discrimination Law: a critique" 21 ILJ (1992), 119–134; Lacey, "From Individual to Group" in Hepple and Szyszczak, *supra* n 2 at 99–124; Lacey, "Legislation Against Sex Discrimination: Questions from a Feminist Perspective" 14 JLS (1987), 411–421.

[11] See Article 119 EC; Protocol No 2 on Article 119 annexed by the Treaty on European Union; Directive 75/117/EEC (OJ 1975 L 45/19); Directive 76/207/EEC (OJ 1976 L 39/40); Directive 79/7/EEC (OJ 1979 L 6/24); Directive 86/378/EEC (OJ 1986 L 225/40); Directive 86/613/EEC (OJ 1986 L 359/56); Directive 92/85/EEC (OJ 1992 L 348/1).

[12] Case C-7/93 *ABP* v *Beune* [1994] ECR I-4471 para 16. See Moore, "Justice Doesn't Mean a Free Lunch: The Application of the Principle of Equal Pay to Occupational Pension Schemes" 20 ELRev (1995), 159–177; Whiteford, "Lost in the Mists of Time. The ECJ and Occupational Pensions" 32 CMLRev (1995), 801–840.

[13] Cases C-63 and 64/91 *Jackson and Cresswell* v *Chief Adjudication Officer* [1992] ECR I-4737.

[14] See Steiner, in this volume.

[15] Case C-243/90 *Smithson* [1992] I-ECR 467; Case C-92/94 *Graham* Judgment of 11 August 1995.

[16] See Sohrab, "Women and Social Security: the Limits of EEC Equality Law" 16 JSocWFL (1994), 5–17; Luckhaus, "Changing Rules, Enduring Structures" 53 MLR (1990), 655–668.

[17] Directive 79/7/EEC Article 2.

the scope of EC sex equality law is constrained by the concepts of "employment", "work" and "worker". The assumption is that the social institution of
work is gender-neutral, and that consequently women and men need only be
treated the same in respect of work-related entitlements.

As Christine Littleton[18] shows, this "same treatment" definition of the scope
of the equality principle is open to criticism not least on the grounds that it fails
to cope with differences in women's and men's relationships to work. The
apparent gender-neutrality of the concept of worker in a patriarchal or "phallo-
centric"[19] society turns out to be a male worker.[20]

This kind of reasoning may be found in the Court's definitions of "work"
which have tended in effect to privilege a male model of work, and to ignore
the interface between public work and private family responsibilities.[21] Thus, for
instance, the Court asserted in *Hofmann* that the scope of EC sex equality law
could not extend to the division of labour within the family, even where that
had a direct consequence for the ability of a woman to (re)enter the public
workplace.

In *Helmig*, the Court excluded from its calculation of work, for the purposes
of determining equal pay of part-timers with full-timers, domestic or care work
undertaken outside the public workplace. In *Grau-Hupka* the Court did not
include time spent on the work of child-rearing in its calculation of equal pay.
This male model of work, with its assumptions concerning the propriety of legal
intervention in the private domain, and what constitutes the public domain, has
long been the focus of criticism of sex equality law, not only in the EC.[22]

The Court has adopted a functional approach to the definition of work and
worker in the context of the free movement provisions.[23] I want to suggest that a
functional approach could be adopted to the concept of work in the context of
sex equality; the function of sex equality provisions being to improve women's
position where women are disadvantaged. This would allow a much broader
stance to be taken on the question of whether equality between men and
women is present in a particular situation. Unpaid work (care work, domestic

---

[18] Littleton, "Reconstructing Sex Equality" in Bartlett and Kennedy, *Feminist Legal Theory* (1991)
35–56.
[19] Littleton, *ibid* 43.
[20] See also Conaghan, "The Invisibility of Women in Labour Law: Gender-neutrality in model building" 14 IntJSocL (1986), 377–392; Phillips, "Citizenship and Feminism Theory" in Andrews, *Citizenship* (1991) 76–88 at 77. See also Shaw, in this volume.
[21] For example, see Cases C-63 and 64/90 *Jackson and Cresswell, supra* n 13; Case 184/83 *Hofmann v
Barmer Ersatzkasse* [1984] ECR 3047 para 24; Case C-399/92 *Stadt Lengerich v Helmig* [1994] ECR I-
5727; Case C-297/93 *Grau Hupka v Stadtgemeinde Bremen* [1994] ECR I-5535. See Ackers, O'Leary,
and Shaw, in this volume.
[22] For the limitation of sex equality to the "public sphere", see J S Mill, *On the Subjection of Women*
(1929). For critical comment, see, for example, MacKinnon "Feminism, Marxism, Method and the
State: Toward Feminist Jurisprudence" in Bartlett and Kennedy, *supra* n 18; O'Donovan, *Sexual Divisions in Law* (1985).
[23] The Court views the function or aim of these provisions to be to ensure that legal, administrative
or practical barriers to free movement of workers are removed, or at least minimalised in their
impact. See, for example, Case 66/85 *Lawrie Blum v Land Baden-Württemburg* [1986] ECR 2121; Case
53/81 *Levin v Staatssecretaris van Justitie* [1982] ECR 1035; Case 139/85 *Kempf v Staatssecretaris van
Justitie* [1986] ECR 1741.

work) could be included in the calculation of whether there is equal pay or equal treatment. So, for instance, the Court faced with a similar situation to that in *Helmig* could find that part-time overtime was not equally compensated if paid at the same rate as full-timers' normal hours, as the unpaid work of the part-timers had not been taken into account. Similarly, in a situation analogous to that in *Hofmann,* the Court could see that the entitlement to be treated equally with respect to the work of caring for one's child should be extended to men and women alike.[24]

This extension of the scope of EC regulation of equality in employment and social security could, I think, be coupled with the Court extending and developing its *general principle* of (sex) equality into other areas within the scope of EC law. Several chapters in this book have been concerned with analysis of such disparate areas of EC law as free movement of persons,[25] citizenship,[26] human rights[27] and free movement of goods[28] in the light of sex equality. The gendered elements of those parts of EC law traditionally seen as nothing to do with sex equality should be exposed.[29] The two concepts of *EC law in general,* and *sex equality in EC law* (which at present is conceived as concerned with employment and social security) are not separate. Sex equality should be conceptualised as permeating the whole of the Community legal order.

(iii) Redefining sex discrimination

Sex discrimination is defined in EC law as failure to grant, in certain situations (in particular employment and social security provision) equal treatment (or pay) on grounds of sex.[30] The definitions of "equal" and "on grounds of sex" are often considered to be broad and generous.[31] For instance, equal pay includes equal pay for work of equal value.[32]

Discrimination may be either direct, based upon the sex of the person disadvantaged; or indirect, where a condition or requirement which appears to be sex-neutral conceals an unjustified disproportionate adverse impact on women (or on men).[33] However, the Community definition of discrimination is in some respects a limited concept. In this section, I aim to show some of the ways in

---

[24] For obvious reasons, men cannot be entitled to equal treatment in respect of the "work" of child-bearing.

[25] See Ackers, in this volume.

[26] See Everson, in this volume.

[27] See McGlynn and O'Leary, in this volume.

[28] See Flynn, in this volume.

[29] See Beveridge and Nott, in this volume.

[30] See Ellis, "The Definition of Discrimination in European Community Sex Equality Law" 19 ELRev (1994), 563–580, and the case law cited therein.

[31] Barnard, *EC Employment Law* (1995) 190; Craig and de Búrca, *EC Law: Text, cases and materials* (1995) 814; Nielsen and Szyszczak, *supra* n 2 at 116–129; Steiner, *Textbook on EC Law* (1994) 280; Weatherill and Beaumont, *EC Law* (1995) 617; Ellis, *EC Sex Discrimination Law* (1991).

[32] Directive 75/117/EEC, *supra* n 11.

[33] Case 96/80 *Jenkins* v *Kingsgate Ltd* [1981] ECR 911; Case 170/84 *Bilka-Kaufhaus* v *Weber von Hartz* [1986] ECR 1607.

which this is the case. I also propose to explain how discrimination might be reconceptualised within the Community context.

The concept of discrimination in EC law is constrained in various ways. One of these is its focus upon the formal equality (treating like as like) approach and the necessity, under that approach, for a comparator. The limits of this definition of discrimination are most notoriously exposed in cases concerning discrimination on grounds of pregnancy.[34] Here (at least for permanent employees[35], with uncomplicated pregnancies[36]) the Court appears to have been sensitive to the limitations of the need to find a comparator, and the comparative model's implicit acceptance of the male as the norm.[37] In the area of pregnancy, according to EC law, discrimination on grounds of sex may be established without the need for a comparator.[38] The woman is regarded as discriminated against because of her pregnancy, that is, a sex-specific condition, therefore discrimination on grounds of sex is established.[39]

There are other areas in which the Court could reconceptualise the concept of discrimination by redrawing the comparative element in discrimination claims. For instance, in the *Helmig* decision,[40] the Court compared "overall pay" of full-time and part-time workers, holding that there was no difference in pay between the two groups for the same hours worked. This particular comparative approach, which is narrow and formalistic, obscured the different experience of part-timers who worked extra hours, from that of full-timers who would have worked those hours anyway. The different position of part-timers (predominantly women, as women tend to undertake more (unpaid) domestic and care work than men) was not taken into account by the Court. The comparative definition of discrimination adopted resulted in the conclusion that the different pay did not breach Article 119. Had the Court adopted a less narrowly formulated comparison, essentially treating as comparable the work done in the workplace with that done at home, part-timers would have been entitled to over-time pay for hours extra to *their* workplace hours, rather than the "normal" full-time hours. This construction of equal pay would have benefitted a greater proportion of women than men, as women are over-represented among part-time workers.

A narrow comparative approach to defining discrimination may be even more problematic in equal value claims. Here the need to find a suitable comparator or comparators may preclude any litigation at all, or may render litigation exceedingly expensive and time-consuming.[41]

---

[34] See, for example, in the UK context, *Hayes* v *Malleable Working Men's Club* [1985] ICR 703; *Turley* v *Allders Department Stores* [1980] ICR 66; *Berrisford* v *Woodard Schools (Midland Division) Ltd* [1991] IRLR 247.

[35] Case C-32/93 *Webb* v *EMO Air Cargo (UK) Ltd* [1994] ECR I-3567. See Szyszczak, in this volume.

[36] Case C-179/88 *Hertz* v *Dansk Arbejdsgiverforening, acting for Aldi Markt KS* [1990] I-ECR 3979. See Kilpatrick, and Szyszczak, in this volume.

[37] Case C-177/88 *Dekker* v *Stichting Vormingscentrum voor Jong Volwassenen Plus* [1990] ECR I-3941.

[38] Case C-177/88 *Dekker, ibid*; Case C-179/88 *Hertz, supra* n 36; Case C-421/92 *Habermann-Beltermann* v *Arbeiterwohlfahrt, Bezirksverband Ndb/Opf eV* [1994] ECR I-1657; Case C-32/93 *Webb, supra* n 35.

[39] Case C-177/88 *Dekker, supra* n 37 para 12.

[40] Cases C-399/92; C-409/92, C-425/92, C-34/93, C-50/93, C-78/93 *Stadt Lengerich* v *Helmig, supra* n 21.

[41] See Ellis, and Townshend-Smith, in this volume.

A formalistic approach to what constitutes an appropriate comparator might effectively prevent claims in all but the most blatant situations of unequal pay for work of equal value.

The Court seems to have adopted a rather unsympathetic approach to the matter of comparison in, for example, the *Royal Copenhagen* case.[42] The Court held that in a piece-rate system of pay, non-discrimination on grounds of sex requires that pay of comparator groups "is to be calculated on the basis of the same unit of measurement".[43] This unit of measurement must ensure that, where the work of two workers is of equal value, their "total individual pay" is the same.[44] Thus, the Court required a complex notional comparison to be carried out, in order to establish discrimination. The Court expressly excluded the possibility that differences in average hourly pay of two groups of workers, where those coincide with the sex of those in each of the groups, would constitute prima facie sex discrimination. Average hourly pay of two groups would be a much simpler matter to show and therefore to compare. Allowing comparisons of average hourly pay would enable the use of the equal value provisions to challenge sex-segregation and the consequent lower pay of groups of workers in which women predominate.[45]

A second limitation on the Community concept of discrimination may be found in the concept of "justification" for discrimination. The Court has held that indirect discrimination may be justified on a number of grounds.[46] Recently, the Court has hinted that justification for direct sex discrimination may also be available.[47] The difficulty with the concept of justification within a formal equality model,[48] in particular in the context of EC law, is that it places those differently situated beyond the reach of sex equality law. If women's domestic and parental roles tend to differ from those of men, and those roles

---

[42] Case C-400/93 *Specialarbejderforbundet i Danmark* v *Dansk Industri, acting for Royal Copenhagen*, Judgment of 31 May 1995.

[43] *Ibid* para 20.

[44] See Hervey "Note on *Royal Copenhagen*" forthcoming *Journal of Social Welfare and Family Law.*

[45] See Women and Men in the European Union: A Statistical Portrait, Eurostat, OPEC, 1995. See Barnard, in this volume.

[46] See, for example, Case 170/84 *Bilka-Kaufhaus Gmbh* v *Weber von Hartz* [1986] ECR 1607; Case 171/88 *Rinner-Kühn* v *FWW Spezial-Gebäudereinigung Gmbh* [1989] ECR 2743; Case 109/88 *Handels-og Kontorfunktionaernes Forbund* v *Danfoss* [1989] ECR 3199; Case C-184/89 *Nimz* v *Freie und Hansestadt Hamburg* [1991] ECR I-297; Case C-33/89 *Kowalska* v *Freie und Hansestadt Hamburg* [1990] ECR I-2591; Case C-360/90 *Arbeiterwohlfahrt Stadt Berlin* v *Bötel* [1992] ECR I-3589; Case 30/85 *Teulings-Worms* v *Bestuur van de Bedrijfsvereniging voor de Chemische Industrie* [1987] ECR 2497; Case C-229/89 *EC Commission* v *Belgium* [1991] ECR I-2205. See Hervey, *Justifications for Sex Discrimination in Employment* (1993) 47–79.

[47] Case C-132/92 *Birds Eye Walls* [1993] ECR I-5579; Case C-32/93 *Webb, supra* n 35. See Szyszczak, in this volume.

[48] Several feminist writers have pointed out that the principal limitation of the formal equality principle is that it assumes that the male is the norm. MacKinnon puts it particularly aptly, "Why should you have to be the same as a man to get what a man gets simply because he is one?" See MacKinnon, "Difference and Dominance: On Sex Discrimination" in Bartlett and Kennedy, *supra* n 18 at 85; see also Conaghan, *supra* n 20 at 377; Fredman, *supra* n 10 at 120–121; Lacey, *supra* n 10 at 417; Lacey, *supra* n 10 at 103–104, Littleton, *supra* n 20 at 35–41, MacKinnon, "Reflections on Sex Equality Under Law" 100 *Yale Law Journal* (1991), 1281–1328 at 1286–1293. The application of this idea in the context of EC law in particular is explored further in Fenwick and Hervey, *supra* n 2.

interfere with women's role as (cost efficient) workers, where the male is taken as the norm and a women is assumed to be like a man, a woman may justifiably (and lawfully) be treated differently. I am not suggesting here that different treatment of women should *never* be justified.[49] The point is that, within the current EC ideology, market forces justifications are likely to find favour, thus restricting the concept of discrimination to an unacceptable extent.

Probably the best example of this may be found in the *Enderby* decision.[50] Here the Court accepted "the state of the employment market"[51] as a possible justification for indirect discrimination. The Court took into account the market forces in question, which were the shortage of candidates for the more highly paid jobs of clinical psychologist and pharmacist, and the consequent need to offer higher pay in those jobs in order to attract candidates. This justification may have potentially obscured discriminatory market assumptions in terms of valuing the different professions compared. Where two jobs are of equal value, but that held by the woman attracts lower pay, the reason for the differentiation cannot be said to be the "accidental" or "innocent" operation of the sex-neutral mechanism of the market. On the contrary, the market tends to function on the traditional expectation that a woman will not be the breadwinner and will therefore be willing to work for less.[52]

In order to obtain equal pay, according to this model, a woman would have to "choose" to work in a traditionally male, rather than a traditionally female, occupation. Some women will be able to do so; however, the requirement impacts disproportionately upon women. *Enderby* demonstrates how an approach based on excluding (or at least questioning) market justifications for discrimination might significantly improve the definition of unlawful discrimination in the Community sphere from the point of view of women's interests. A market justification would no longer be presumptively neutral on grounds of sex, but might be specifically required to be shown to be neutral.[53] The difference in women's average pay could no longer be accepted as inherent in the value of women's work (and even of women), but seen as arising from women's relationship with the social institution of the labour market.[54]

A third aspect of the current EC conceptualisation or definition of discrimination is its formal equality "symmetrical" approach. Women are to be treated the same as men, men the same as women. It cannot be denied that the apparent "even-handedness" of this symmetrical approach has been very useful in terms of its political and popular impact. That men such as Douglas Barber should have their Community sex equality rights protected as much as women such as Helen Marshall has done a great deal for the "image" of EC sex equality law,

---

[49] See Townshend-Smith, in this volume.
[50] Case C-127/92 *Enderby* v *Frenchay Health Authority and Secretary of State for Health* [1993] ECR I-5535.
[51] *Ibid* para 26.
[52] See for example, Fredman, "Equal Pay and Justification" 23 ILJ (1994), 37–41 at 41, who notes that in 1980 shortages of qualified speech therapists had *not* resulted in raising of speech therapists' pay, suggesting that the market is not a sex-neutral indicator of job value.
[53] See Townshend-Smith, in this volume.
[54] See Littleton, *supra* n 18.

especially in the media.[55] Perhaps controversially,[56] what I am suggesting is that this approach may not always be appropriate. The reason for this is that a symmetrical approach is blind to issues of power imbalance and disadvantage. The EC definition of sex discrimination (with the possible exception of discrimination on grounds of pregnancy) is discrimination *on grounds of sex*. The deeper function of sex equality legislation might be said to be to ensure non-discrimination *against women* – the disadvantaged group. In some circumstances, this deeper function would mandate (temporary) preferential treatment of women.

I am aware that adopting a preferential treatment or positive action approach to sex equality has its own difficulties. Wendy Williams has espoused this position particularly strongly in her rejection of asymmetrical approaches: "we can't have it both ways, we need to think carefully about which way we want to have it".[57]A unified definition of equality based on asymmetry would indeed be open to the criticism that it is only a small step away from a return to the inimical "separate spheres" ideology.[58] However, this potentially serious disadvantage can, I think, be alleviated in a number of ways. One way might be to disaggregate different types of asymmetrical approaches. Special protection for women is arguably the most "dangerous"[59] version of asymmetry, because of its close link with the further reifying of women as victims and the oppressed or weak group, in need of protection.

Therefore, in the kind of differentiated approach to equality which I am suggesting, special protections for women could, and should, be limited to situations where women's biological difference from men mandates differential treatment.[60] Where differences are socially and culturally determined, the need for asymmetry might need to be established by reference to women's comparative social disadvantage. From the perspective of a formal equality model, it might be objected that I am suggesting that women ought to be treated the same where they are the same, but differently where they are different. Of course, from that perspective, this is a circular definition. But it is not the case that it gets us no further forward in defining "equality". It espouses a view of women which resolutely refuses to adopt an essentialist position, either in the

---

[55] See, for example, *Financial Times*, 26 January 1993.

[56] But see, for example, Lacey, "From Individual to Group", *supra* n 10; Lacey, "Legislation Against Sex Discrimination: Questions from a Feminist Perspective" *supra* n 10; More, "'Equal Treatment' of the Sexes in European Community Law: What does 'Equal' mean?" 1 *Feminist Legal Studies* (1993), 45–74.

[57] Williams, "The Equality Crisis" in Bartlett and Kennedy, *supra* n 18 15–34 at 26.

[58] The separate spheres ideology is probably best known in the context of race discrimination, and found judicial expression in early case law in the United States of America, such as *Plessy* v *Ferguson* 163 US 567 [1896] where it was held that people of colour were "separate but equal" to whites where statute provided for separate railway carriages for whites and people of colour. In the context of sex equality, the ideology has tended to find expression in the idea that men and women "naturally" belong to separate spheres (men belong to public life, women to home and family life) and should be treated as such.

[59] Williams, *supra* n 18 at 26.

[60] That is, the cases of pregnancy and childbirth. Even here special protection should be kept to the minimum mandated by the biological differences between women and men, and not extend into socially constructed differences concerning, for instance, childcare. See Fenwick, in this volume.

sense that women are essentially the same as men, or in the sense that women are essentially different. It therefore constitutes a method of exploring women's difference (and sameness) as created by a complex web of social structures – in other words difference as relational, dependent upon circumstance and particularity; rather than inherent, as part of the essense of womanhood. If we recognise difference (and sameness) as relational, and dependent upon circumstance, then we also need a relational and dependent definition of sex equality.

A recent example of the Court's symmetrical approach to the concept of discrimination may be found in the Court's ruling in *Kalanke*[61] on quotas for women. The Court held that, in principle, the application of an affirmative action provision constitutes discrimination on grounds of sex.[62] The Court's assessment of the affirmative action provision at issue as inconsistent with EC law[63] limits the use by the Member States of measures of public policy which seek to remove historical disadvantage of women, in order to ensure equal opportunities in the present and future. Where the disadvantage to women consists in their exclusion from policy-making and decision-taking bodies, the equal participation of men and women in public life might be a situation which mandates a stronger asymmetrical approach.[64]

There are already some situations in which the Community institutions are prepared to take an asymmetrical approach to the definition of discrimination. One of these is discrimination on the grounds of pregnancy. The Court reasons that discrimination on grounds of pregnancy is always direct sex discrimination.[65] EC sex equality law prohibits the unfair disadvantage suffered by the woman because of her pregnancy. It is not a question of her being treated like or unlike a male comparator, but a question of her being treated fairly or being disadvantaged by her pregnancy.[66]

Another example of a situation where EC law may be viewed as countenancing an asymmetrical approach is that of workplace harassment.[67] Compensating women for sexual harassment does not lend itself to an entitlement to being treated like a man. The protection is not against being treated differently from a man, but against being sexually harassed. The same treatment might not be harassment of a man, but may well be harassment of a woman.[68] For example,

---

[61] Case C-450/93 *Kalanke* v *Freie Hansestadt Bremen* Judgment of 17 October 1995, nyr.

[62] *Ibid* para 16.

[63] The specific ruling was that the provisions concerned failed to meet the stringent test of proportionality required by Directive 76/207/EEC, Article 2 (4); Case C-450/93 *Kalanke, supra* n 62 para 24.

[64] Compare the situation in Norway: see Ryel, in this volume.

[65] Case C-177/88 *Dekker, supra* n 38.

[66] Otherwise, if the entitlement were applied symmetrically, there would be an equivalent protection for men who suffer male-specific medical conditions. See Szyszczak, in this volume.

[67] Or harassment in other relationships in the public domain, see Case No MA4 05788 *Heald* v *Thomson Tour Operators Ltd* (*Guardian*, 2 August 1995) in which two women relied on the Package Holiday Directive 90/314/EEC (OJ 1990 L 158/59) in their claim concerning sexual harassment by hotel staff.

[68] For instance, the physical contact of a hand placed upon the shoulder.

faced with sexually explicit pin-ups at work, male employees are unlikely to suffer *the same* experience of objectification and consequent feelings of inadequacy, dehumanisation and powerlessness that a woman experiences. The Commission Recommendation on the Protection of the Dignity of Women and Men at Work[69] with its victim-centred definition of harassment may allow for such a woman-centred definition of sexual harassment. This asymmetrical approach could be translated into construction of the Equal Treatment Directive (and implementing provisions of national law) in harassment cases.[70]

I am not arguing here for any one particular unified definition of sex equality in the Community context. I do not propose, for instance, that positive action in favour of women (the asymmetrical approach) should always be adopted. Such a position, although it may seem appealing, has several drawbacks. Not least among these is its essentialist perspective of women as victims and the oppressed or disadvantaged. Treating women preferentially may undermine the very equality it seeks to achieve.[71] Substituting that unified definition for the current (formal market equality) definition of sex equality, will only replace the current problems with a new set of problems.

What I *am* arguing for is a differentiated approach to sex equality in EC law. I am suggesting that women's position in EC law, as in any other (legal) context, should be conceptualised as not fixed, but contingent. What exactly would constitute equality for a woman (or women) in a situation which falls within the scope of EC law may only be determined by the position of that woman (or those women) in relation to various social structures. What substantive equality requires may depend, for instance, on whether she is in paid employment, works full-time, undertakes domestic or care work, works in a "traditionally female" occupation, is pregnant, is being sexually harassed, or is represented on or participating in a policy-making body. The current fixed definition of sex equality is not always able to take appropriate cognisance of that particular and fluctuating construct of equality for the woman. Within the current definition we can only ask (with a few exceptions) whether the woman is being treated the same as a man, within the constraints of what may be compared, within the market ideology.

Reconceptualising sex equality so as to undermine market explanations for different treatment, and, where appropriate, to permit different treatment to account for women's biological differences, and (temporary) privileged treatment to account for women's past or present social or cultural disadvantage would, it is suggested, greatly improve the position of women's protection under EC law. I submit that it would be open to the Court, even within the current framework of EC law, to redefine the Community concept of sex discrimination.

---

[69] OJ 1992 L 49/3.

[70] Unfortunately this does not appear to be the case at present, at least not in the United Kingdom. See *Stewart* v *Cleveland Guest Engineering Ltd* [1994] IRLR 440 in which the EAT held that, as a man might be equally offended by pin-ups of naked women at work, Ms Stewart had not been differently treated on grounds of sex.

[71] See Fenwick, in this volume.

Faced with similar situations to the exemplary cases outlined above, the Court could adopt new definitions of discrimination. This is particularly so given the refocused aims and spirit of the Treaty of Rome since Maastricht.[72] Sex discrimination could then be seen in Community law as an expression of social and political power structures. Once that is revealed, the social and political foundations of sex equality law can be expanded. EC sex equality law would no longer be seen as underpinned by an essentially economic ideology.

(iv) Moving from market to social equality

One of the dangers of the approach I suggest is the discretion which it necessarily gives to the Court. In response to this it might first be pointed out that the Court already exercises a great deal of discretion in interpreting and applying the concept of sex equality in EC law, and therefore even if we are no better off with a differentiated approach to sex equality, we may well be no worse off.

Secondly, I suggest that the discretion given to the Court needs to be underpinned by a new understanding of the function of sex equality provisions in EC law, to which I alluded earlier.[73] The touchstone for a differentiated approach to sex equality is the function of improving the position of women. This is an unapologetically social (and even political) function, and as such has little to do with the economic rationale[74] for Article 119, which has thus far underpinned its construction. A specific Treaty amendment to this effect might not have any apparent legal significance. But it might curtail the Court's discretion in constructing sex equality in particular situations.

Thirdly, I suggest that the "open texture" of a differentiated definition of sex equality might be seen as a strength, rather than a weakness. An overtly differentiated definition of equality recognises explicitly that questions of gender difference are not readily solvable by application of one "right answer". Rather, it implies that equality will need to be constantly reconstructed in the light of new understandings of men's and women's relationships to each other and to social and political institutions. A differentiated approach assumes a role for constant critique of the law. Where new insights or new interpretations lead to uncertainties and potential injustices (for instance to employers, or providers of social security) the Court already has in place principles of legitimate expectations[75] to provide a remedy. Indeed these principles themselves might be open to further critique, for example on the grounds that they over-privilege market actors at the expense of women, or that their application fails to accord appropriate status to the social function of sex equality provisions.

---

[72] Articles 2 and 3 EC; Article B TEU. The Court has always interpreted provisions of EC law in the light of the aims and spirit of the Treaties.

[73] *Supra*, p 402.

[74] See Barnard, in this volume.

[75] Case 43/75 *Defrenne No 2* [1976] ECR 455; Case C-262/88 *Barber v Guardian Royal Exchange Assurance Group* [1990] ECR I-1889; Case C-338/91 *Steenhorst-Neerings* [1993] ECR I-5475; Case C-410/92 *Johnston No 2* [1994] ECR I-5483.

I therefore suggest that the development of EC sex equality law should now be concerned with moving from equality for men and women as market actors to equality for men and women as social, and even political, actors. This would necessarily entail a development of equality policy as part of the social sphere of the Community and Union endeavour. As the Union begins to acquire some of the "badges of statehood", and increasingly resembles a "quasi-state", so the Union acquires obligations and duties towards its citizens and those living within its boundaries. One of the duties of a State is generally accepted to be the protection of disadvantaged or minority groups within its territory from unlawful discrimination. Women have traditionally been considered to be such a disadvantaged group.

The "human face" of the EC has been present in Community provisions for at least ten years, since Delors' "Espace Sociale Européenne" introduced as a counterbalance to the 1992 programme for creating the single European market,[76] and arguably much longer. The preambles for existing legislative texts include social purposes for sex equality provision.[77] Perhaps these purposes take on a new meaning in the context of European union with its increased social functions.[78] The new European concepts of citizenship,[79] and even "social cohesion",[80] may now begin to spill over into the Court's construction of EC provisions on sex equality and free movement. This may even extend to other provisions of EC law which affect human beings in a social, as well as economic capacity.[81]

(v) Equality in the European Union

The aim of this chapter has been to explore possibilities for the future development of sex equality law in the the European Union. I have attempted to be constructive in this exploration, rather than undertaking an exercise in pure deconstruction of existing norms. One of the themes in the analysis is that there is scope for change in the current dominant ideology of EC law. Modifying our understanding of specific provisions of EC law (in this context, sex equality provisions) might eventually lead to a discernible modification of the framework, function and ideology within which the EC institutions (in particular the Court) construe EC law in general. At the same time, a shift in the general dominant ideology of the EC could translate into modifications in the interpre-

---

[76] "The creation of a vast economic area, based on the market and business co-operation, is inconceivable – I would say unattainable – without some harmonisation of social legislation. Our ultimate aim must be the creation of a European social area." Delors, President of the EC Commission, *Bulletin of the EC* 1986, 12.

[77] Preamble to the Treaty of Rome, recitals 2 and 3; preamble to Directive 75/117/EEC, recital 3; preamble to Directive 76/207/EEC, recital 3.

[78] Articles A and B TEU.

[79] Articles 8–8e EC.

[80] Articles 130A–E EC.

[81] For example, provisions on education and training, immigration and asylum policy.

tation and application of specific provisions of EC law, for instance the sex equality provisions. In other words, the provisions of EC sex equality law, their interpretation, and the dominant ideology within which they are understood, and which defines and confines them, are not separate items. Together they form part of the structure of Community law and policy.

Of course, these are not new ideas. It may be the case, however, that the way in which the EU institutions approach equality provisions (and so far, these have tended to mean sex equality provisions[82]) is particularly significant in developing ideas of the Community or Union endeavour and focus, and the ideological constraints on that endeavour. The reason for this may be found in two interrelated ideas. First, the EC, as a legal order based on the liberal-democratic notions of equality and fairness, derives legitimacy from protecting notions of equality within its legal system. Second, the notion of "belonging" to the EC, which the TEU seeks to promote by its concept of citizenship of the EU[83], and is a notion dear to the promoters of European integration, is bolstered by granting equal rights and entitlements to all those who belong. A reconceptualisation of who "belongs" within the scope and protection of EC law (put broadly, from economic actors only to the inclusion of social actors) might have an impact upon the conceptualisation of sex equality provisions in the areas of work and social security. Conversely, a reconceptualisation of the scope and impact of EC sex equality laws in those areas might, along with other changes, translate into a modification of our (or perhaps more importantly, the EU institutions') understanding of the nature and limits of the EC and EU endeavour.

Such a modification might lead to reconceptualisation of EU equality law in general, and a broadening of its scope. One of the amendments being called for in the 1996 IGC is the inclusion in the Treaty of an equality article of broader remit than sex equality, based on Article 119.[84] It does seem increasingly incongruous that the EU prohibits discrimination on grounds of sex and nationality[85] but leaves more or less unregulated[86] other grounds of discrimination such as race and religion, which are internationally recognised as forbidden.[87]

I therefore suggest that one possible future for EC sex equality law might find its place in a Treaty amendment to the effect that there shall be no unjustified discrimination in the European Union within the scope of the Treaty on various grounds. Such an entitlement should inhere in all individuals within the

---

[82] Although the Court has also developed a "general principle" of equality. See, for example, Case 50/86 *Grand Moulins de Paris* [1987] ECR 4857 para 10; Case 117/76 *Ruckdeschel* [1977] ECR 1769 para 7; Case 281/82 *Unifrex* [1984] ECR 2745 para 30; Case 20/71 *Sabbatini* [1972] ECR 351 para 12.

[83] Articles 8–8E EC.

[84] *Financial Times*, 22 May 1995; *Agence Europe* 20 January 1995.

[85] Article 6 EC.

[86] With the exception of the relatively few circumstances where a general principle of equality may apply, for example Case 130/75 *Prais* v *Council* [1976] ECR 1589.

[87] See, for example, European Convention for the Protection of Human Rights and Fundamental Freedoms 1950, Article 14; International Convention on the Elimination of all forms of Racial Discrimination 1966.

territory of the European Union, not only citizens of the European Union. The "forbidden grounds" might be enumerated in a non-exhaustive list: I suggest sex (in its broad sense, including gender, and sexuality), race, religion, physical and mental ability, and age, as a "wish list". Further grounds could be added in the future by Treaty amendment or by purposive interpretation by the Court of Justice. The provision itself would need to be the subject of the type of critical analysis I suggest above for the sex equality provisions. The political significance of such a general provision, as an expression of the EU's view on its own "outsiders", might turn out to be more important than its legal significance. Coupled with a refocussed Social Europe, the presence of such a provision would establish the basis for the development of a jurisprudence based upon empowerment[88] by the Court of Justice. Members of other disadvantaged groups within the European Union could then begin to profit from the benefits so far enjoyed by women through the promotion of sex equality in the European Union.

TAMARA K. HERVEY
Lecturer in Law,
University of Manchester,
UK

---

[88] By this I mean an approach to law which seeks to include, empower or enable those excluded by state structures or hegemonies. The approach is termed "outsider jurisprudence" by Harris: see, Harris, "The Jurisprudence of Reconstruction" 82 Calif L Rev (1994), 741–785.

INDEX

Social Chapter and, 98
social policy and, 97–98
Stoeckel case and, 101–105
women and, 71–72, 97–108
Nordic countries
Gender Equality Ombudsman in, 358
sex discrimination in, 357–367
Northern Ireland, 396–397
Norway
dismissal in, 363–364
equal pay in, 365–366
equal value in, 365–366
Gender Equality Act in, 360–366
Gender Equality Board of Appeals and,
359
Gender Equality Council and, 359
Gender Equality Ombudsman in,
359–360, 362–365
job evaluations in , 365–366
Ministry on Children and Family Affairs
in, 359–360
parental leave in, 362, 364
part-time workers in, 362, 364
positive action in, 362–363
pregnancy discrimination in, 364
Programme for Nordic Cooperation on
Gender Equality 1995–2000 and,
367
promotion in, 363–364
recruitment in, 363–364
sex discrimination ion, 358–367

Occupational pensions, 21–33
ABP case and, 31–33
access to schemes and, 22, 33
age conditions and, 28–32
Article 119 and, 21, 22–27, 29, 32–33,
94
exclusions from, 144
Barber case and, 24, 26, 29, 31
benefits and, 21, 23–24, 26, 27, 33
Birds Eye Wallis case and, 28–33, 57
Burton case and, 28–30
contributions and, 21, 22–23, 27, 169
Equal Opportunities Commission and,
175, 177
equal pay and, 32
homosexuals and, 279

part-time workers and, 22, 153
retirement ages and, 126–129, 330
sex equality law and, 401
statutory schemes and, 27–33
temporal limitations and, 24–27,
144
Treaty on European Union and, 25
Overtime, 324

Parental leave, 51–52, 76, 89, 96 *See also*
Maternity leave,
Paternity leave
Equal Treatment Directive and, 52
length of, 61
Norway in, 362, 364
pay and, 243
Part-time workers
article 119 and, 328–329, 386
Equal Opportunities Commission and,
174
gender auditing and, 386
Germany in, 194
migrant women and, 233, 234
Norway in, 362, 364
occupational pensions and, 22, 153
sex discrimination and, 404
social security and, 119, 121, 123–124
small firms and, 125
time limits and, 154–155
women as, 239, 387
Paternity leave, 93
Pensions *See* **Occupational pensions**
**Policy Appraisal and Fair Treatment
(PAFT)**, 396–397
Pornography, 316–317
Positive discrimination, 341–342, 362–363
Pregnancy discrimination *See also*
Maternity
armed forces and, 144, 151
badge of protection model and, 82–84
Brown v *Rentokil Ltd* and, 84–85
comparators and, 404
damages and, 149
Dekker case and, 52, 55, 57–58, 72,
77–78, 82
illness and, 92
direct, 57–59, 78, 82, 84, 408
Directive on, 74–79, 80, 81–97

Index compiled by Kim Harris

Titles of Related Interest

Bright/The EU: Understanding the Brussels Process
0-471-95608-2 230 Pages

Daintith/Implementing EC Law in the United Kingdom
0-471-95225-7 400 Pages

Greaves/EC Block Exemption Regulations
0-471-93653-7 300 Pages

Handoll/Free Movement of Persons in the European Union
0-471-95230-3 750 Pages

Hancher/EC State Aids
0-471-93652-9 550 Pages

Cameron Markby Hewitt/Business Guide to Competition Law
0-471-95704-6 330 Pages

Kendall/EC Consumer Law
0-471-94253-7 520 Pages

O'Keeffe/Legal Issues of the Maastricht Treaty
0-471-95567-1 370 Pages

Stanbrook and Hooper/A Business Guide to European
Community Legislation, Second Edition
0-471-95341-5 1090 Pages

Cockfield/The European Union: Creating the Single Market
0-471-95207-9 180 Pages